STRE

G000255174

East Sussex

Brighton and Hove

First published in 1994 by

Philip's, a division of
Octopus Publishing Group Ltd
2-4 Heron Quays, London E14 4JP

Third colour edition 2004
Second impression 2006
ESUCA

ISBN-10   0-540-08650-9 (pocket)
ISBN-13   978-0-540-08650-4 (pocket)

© Philip's 2004

Ordnance Survey®

This product includes mapping data licensed from
Ordnance Survey® with the permission of the
Controller of Her Majesty's Stationery Office.
© Crown copyright 2004. All rights reserved.
Licence number 100011710.

Printed by Toppan, China

Contents

III **Key to map symbols**

IV **Key to map pages**

VI **Route planning**

VIII **Administrative and Postcode boundaries**

1 **Street maps** at 2⅔ inches to 1 mile

189 **Street maps of centres of Brighton and Lewes** at 5⅓ inches to 1 mile

191 **Index** of towns and villages

193 **Index** of streets, hospitals, industrial estates, railway stations, schools, shopping centres, universities and places of interest

Digital Data

The exceptionally high-quality mapping found in this atlas is available as digital data in TIFF format, which is easily convertible to other bitmapped (raster) image formats.

The index is also available in digital form as a standard database table. It contains all the details found in the printed index together with the National Grid reference for the map square in which each entry is named.

For further information and to discuss your requirements, please contact Philip's on 020 7644 6932 or james.mann@philips-maps.co.uk

Symbol	Description
	Motorway with junction number
	Primary route – dual/single carriageway
	A road – dual/single carriageway
	B road – dual/single carriageway
	Minor road – dual/single carriageway
	Other minor road – dual/single carriageway
	Road under construction
	Tunnel, covered road
	Rural track, private road or narrow road in urban area
	Gate or obstruction to traffic (restrictions may not apply at all times or to all vehicles)
	Path, bridleway, byway open to all traffic, road used as a public path
	Pedestrianised area
DY7	**Postcode boundaries**
	County and unitary authority boundaries
	Railway, tunnel, railway under construction
	Tramway, tramway under construction
	Miniature railway
Walsall	**Railway station**
	Private railway station
South Shields	**Metro station**
	Tram stop, tram stop under construction
	Bus, coach station

Symbol	Description
	Ambulance station
	Coastguard station
	Fire station
	Police station
	Accident and Emergency entrance to hospital
H	**Hospital**
+	**Place of worship**
i	**Information Centre** (open all year)
P P&R	**Parking, Park and Ride**
PO	**Post Office**
	Camping site, caravan site
	Golf course
	Picnic site
Prim Sch	**Important buildings, schools, colleges, universities and hospitals**
	Built up area
	Woods
River Medway	**Water name**
	River, weir, stream
	Canal, lock, tunnel
	Water
	Tidal water
Church	**Non-Roman antiquity**
ROMAN FORT	**Roman antiquity**
87 228	**Adjoining page indicators and overlap bands** The colour of the arrow and the band indicates the scale of the adjoining or overlapping page (see scales below)

Enlarged mapping only

Symbol	Description
	Railway or bus station building
	Place of interest
	Parkland

Acad	**Academy**	Inst	**Institute**	Recn Gd	**Recreation Ground**
Allot Gdns	**Allotments**	Ct	**Law Court**		
Cemy	**Cemetery**	L Ctr	**Leisure Centre**	Resr	**Reservoir**
C Ctr	**Civic Centre**	LC	**Level Crossing**	Ret Pk	**Retail Park**
CH	**Club House**	Liby	**Library**	Sch	**School**
Coll	**College**	Mkt	**Market**	Sh Ctr	**Shopping Centre**
Crem	**Crematorium**	Meml	**Memorial**	TH	**Town Hall/House**
Ent	**Enterprise**	Mon	**Monument**	Trad Est	**Trading Estate**
Ex H	**Exhibition Hall**	Mus	**Museum**	Univ	**University**
Ind Est	**Industrial Estate**	Obsy	**Observatory**	W Twr	**Water Tower**
IRB Sta	**Inshore Rescue Boat Station**	Pal	**Royal Palace**	Wks	**Works**
		PH	**Public House**	YH	**Youth Hostel**

■ The small numbers around the edges of the maps identify the 1 kilometre National Grid lines
■ The dark grey border on the inside edge of some pages indicates that the mapping does not continue onto the adjacent page

The scale of the maps on the pages numbered in blue is 4.2 cm to 1 km • 2⅔ inches to 1 mile • 1: 23810	0 — ¼ — ½ — ¾ — 1 mile 0 — 250m — 500m — 750m — 1 kilometre
The scale of the maps on pages numbered in red is 8.4 cm to 1 km • 5⅓ inches to 1 mile • 1: 11900	0 — 220 yards — 440 yards — 660 yards — ½ mile 0 — 125m — 250m — 375m — ½ kilometre

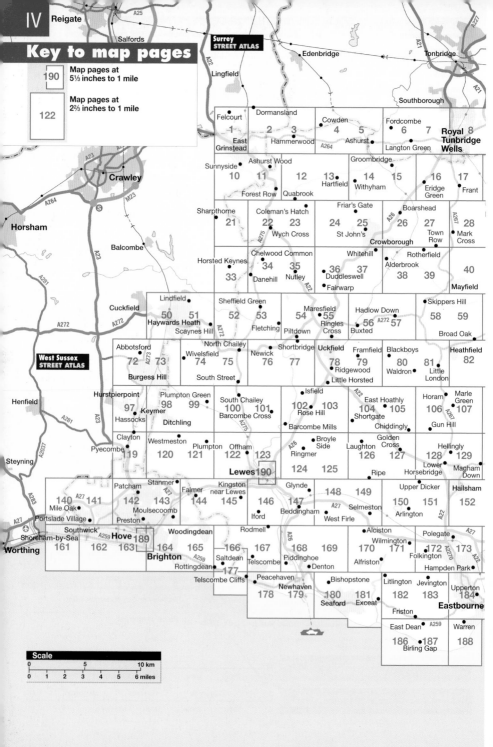

IV Reigate

Key to map pages

| 190 | Map pages at 5⅓ inches to 1 mile |
| 122 | Map pages at 2⅔ inches to 1 mile |

Surrey STREET ATLAS

West Sussex STREET ATLAS

Scale

0 ——— 5 ——— 10 km

0 — 1 — 2 — 3 — 4 — 5 — 6 miles

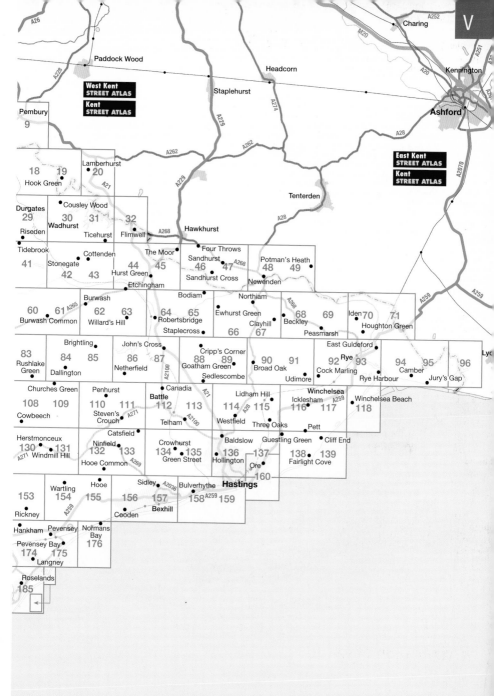

V

Charing
Kennington
Ashford

A252
M20
A20
A251
A2070
A28

A26
A228
Paddock Wood
Headcorn
Staplehurst

Pembury
9

A262
A229
A274
A262

Lamberhurst
18 **19** **20**
Hook Green
A21

Durgates
29 **30** **31** **32**
Cousley Wood
Wadhurst
Riseden
Ticehurst Flimwell Hawkhurst
Tidebrook
The Moor Four Throws
41 Cottenden **44** **45** Sandhurst Potman's Heath
Stonegate **46** **47** **48** **49**
42 **43** Hurst Green Sandhurst Cross
Etchingham Newenden

A29
A268
A268
A28
A259

Bodiam Northiam
Burwash **64** **65** Ewhurst Green **68** **69** Iden **70** **71**
60 **61** **62** **63** Robertsbridge Clayhill Beckley Houghton Green
Burwash Common Willard's Hill Staplecross **66** **67** Peasmarsh
A265
A268
A259
Lyc

Brightling John's Cross East Guldeford
83 **84** **85** **86** **87** Cripp's Corner **89** **90** **91** **92** Rye **93** **94** **95** **96**
Rushlake Netherfield Goatham Green Broad Oak Cock Marling Camber
Green Dallington Sedlescombe Udimore Rye Harbour Jury's Gap
A2100

Churches Green Penhurst Canadia Winchelsea
108 **109** **110** **111** Battle **112** **113** Lidham Hill **114** **115** Icklesham **116** **117** Winchelsea Beach
Cowbeech Steven's **118**
Crouch Telham Westfield Three Oaks Pett
A271
A2100
A28
A259

Catsfield Baldslow Guestling Green Cliff End
Herstmonceux Ninfield Crowhurst **138** **139**
130 **131** **132** **133** **134** **135** **136** **137** Fairlight Cove
Windmill Hill Hooe Common Green Street Hollington Ore
A271
A269
160

Sidley Bulverhythe
Hooe **156** **157** **158** **159**
Wartling Cooden Bexhill Hastings
153 **154** **155** A2036 A259
Rickney
A259

Hankham Pevensey Norfmans
Pevensey Bay **175** Bay
174 **176**
Langney

Roselands
185

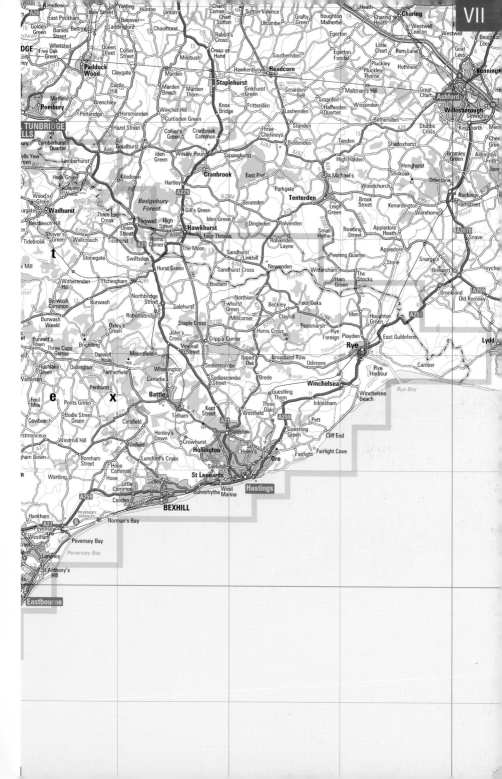

Major administrative and Postcode boundaries

Scale

County and unitary authority boundaries
District boundaries
Postcode boundaries
Area covered by this atlas

0   5   10   15 km
0   5   10 miles

Surrey

West Sussex

Kent

East Sussex

Rother

Hastings

Wealden

Eastbourne

Lewes

City of Brighton & Hove

TQ   TR
TV

TQ
TV

TN29
TN30
TN31
TN32
TN33
TN34
TN35
TN36
TN37
TN38
TN39
TN40
TN17
TN18
TN19
TN20
TN21
TN22
TN1
TN2
TN3
TN4
TN5
TN6
TN7
TN8
TN11

RH7
RH16
RH17
RH18
RH19

BN1
BN2
BN3
BN6
BN7
BN8
BN9
BN10
BN20
BN21
BN22
BN23
BN24
BN25
BN26
BN27
BN41
BN42
BN43
BN45

Camber
Rye
Iden
Peasmarsh
Winchelsea
Northiam
Broad Oak
Pett
Westfield
Baldslow
Hastings
St Leonards
Bexhill
Battle
Salehurst
Robertsbridge
Crowhurst
Pebsham
Hurst Green
Ticehurst
Burwash
Heathfield
Rushlake Green
Herstmonceux
Hailsham
Pevensey
Langney Bay
Eastbourne
Lamberhurst
Wadhurst
Stonegate
Mayfield
Frant
Royal Tunbridge Wells
Groombridge
Langton Green
Crowborough
Buxted
Framfield
Hartfield
Cowden
Nutley
Maresfield
Uckfield
Berwick
Polegate
Alfriston
East Dean
Seaford
East Hoathly
Laughton
Glynde
Ringmer
Lewes
Newhaven
Barcombe Cross
Newick
Peacehaven
Saltdean
Horsted Keynes
Haywards Heath
Keymer
Burgess Hill
Pyecombe
Patcham
Woodingdean
Brighton
Hove
Portslade-by-Sea
Southwick
Shoreham-by-Sea
East Grinstead
Forest Row
Sandhurst
Newenden

Surrey STREET ATLAS

C1
1 THE BROWNINGS
2 BYRON GR
3 CHAUCER AVE
4 TENNYSON RISE
5 THE SAYERS
6 WORDSWORTH RISE

D2
1 YEW CT
2 BIRCH HO
3 BEECH CL
4 ELM CT
5 FERNSIDE
6 SOUTHWICK HO

7 BEECH CT
8 ST CATHERINE'S CT

E1
1 GLENSIDE
2 GREGORY CT
3 WHITEHALL PAR
4 INSTITUTE WLK
5 CANTELUPE MEWS
6 NORMANS GDNS

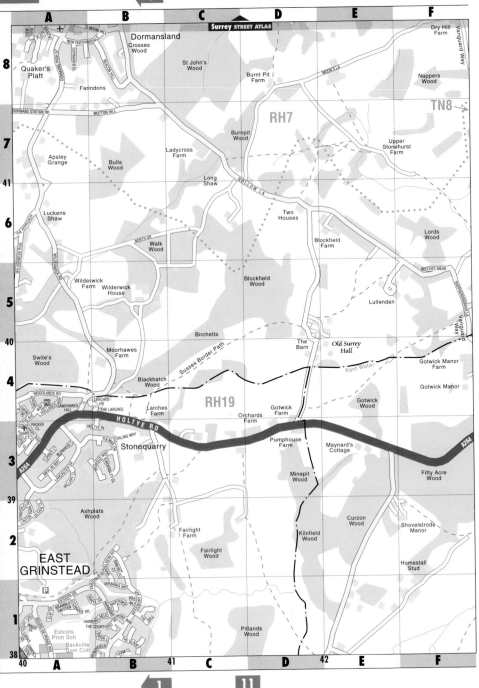

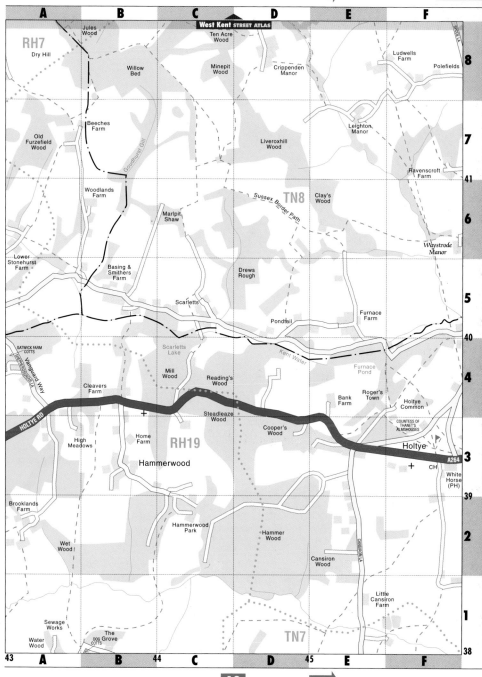

West Kent STREET ATLAS

RH7
Dry Hill
Jules Wood
Ten Acre Wood
Willow Bed
Minepit Wood
Crippenden Manor
Ludwells Farm
Polefields

Beeches Farm
Old Furzefield Wood
Liveroxhill Wood
Leighton Manor
Ravenscroft Farm

Woodlands Farm
TN8
Clay's Wood
Waystrode Manor

Marlpit Shaw
Sussex Border Path

Lower Stonehurst Farm
Basing & Smithers Farm
Drews Rough

Scarletts
Pondtail
Furnace Farm

GATWICK FARM COTTS
Scarletts Lake
Kent Water
Furnace Pond

Vanguard Way
Mill Wood
Reading's Wood
Bank Farm
Roger's Town
Holtye Common

Cleavers Farm
COUNTESS OF THANET'S ALMSHOUSES

HOLTYE RD
High Meadows
Home Farm
Steadleaze Wood
Cooper's Wood
Holtye
A264

RH19
Hammerwood
CH
White Horse (PH)

Brooklands Farm
Hammerwood Park
Hammer Wood
CANSIRON LA
Cansiron Wood

Wet Wood

Sewage Works
The Grove COTTS
Little Cansiron Farm

Water Wood
TN7

43 44 45

8 7 41 6 5 40 4 3 39 2 1 38

4
12
4

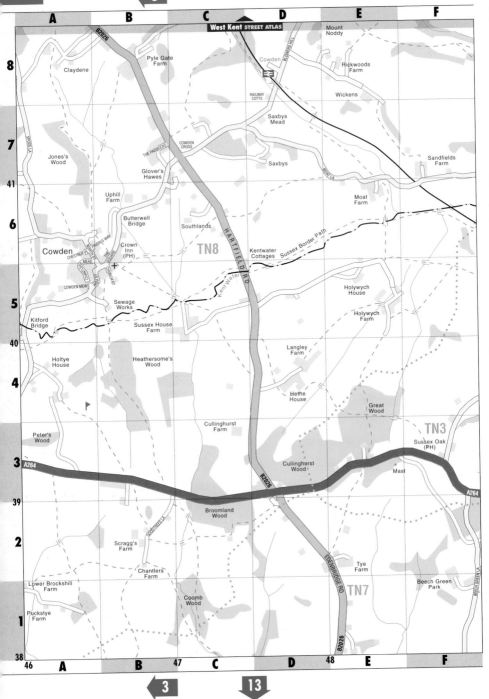

3

West Kent STREET ATLAS

8

7

41

6

5

40

4

3

39

2

1

38

A B C D E F

46 47 48

3

13

Claydene

Pyle Gate Farm

Cowden

Mount Noddy

Rickwoods Farm

Wickens

RAILWAY COTTS

Saxbys Mead

Jones's Wood

THE PADDOCKS

COWDEN CROSS

Glover's Hawes

Saxbys

Sandfields Farm

Uphill Farm

Butterwell Bridge

Southlands

TN8

Moat Farm

Crown Inn (PH)

Cowden

Kentwater Cottages

Sussex Border Path

HARTFIELD RD

Kentwater Rd

Holywych House

COWDEN MEWS

Sewage Works

Holywych Farm

Kitford Bridge

Sussex House Farm

Holtye House

Heathersome's Wood

Langley Farm

Hethe House

Great Wood

Peter's Wood

Cullinghurst Farm

TN3

Sussex Oak (PH)

A264

Cullinghurst Wood

Mast

A264

Broomland Wood

Scragg's Farm

SCOTSFIELD LA

B2026

Chantlers Farm

Tye Farm

EDENBRIDGE RD

TN7

Beech Green Park

Lower Brockshill Farm

Coomb Wood

Puckstye Farm

B2026

BEECH GREEN LA

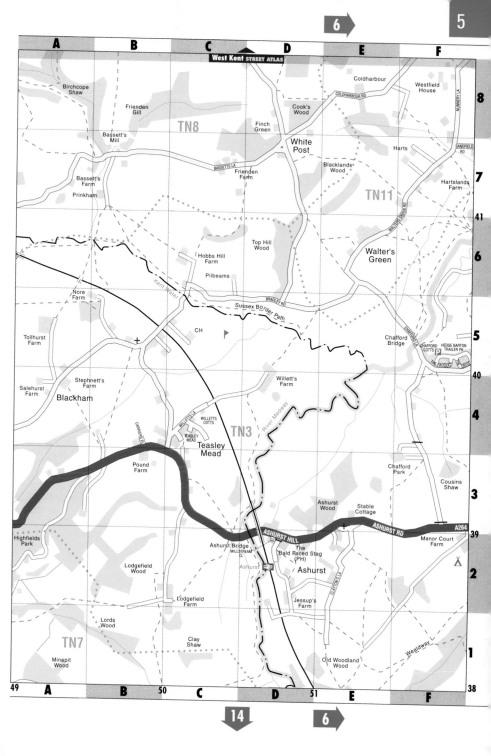

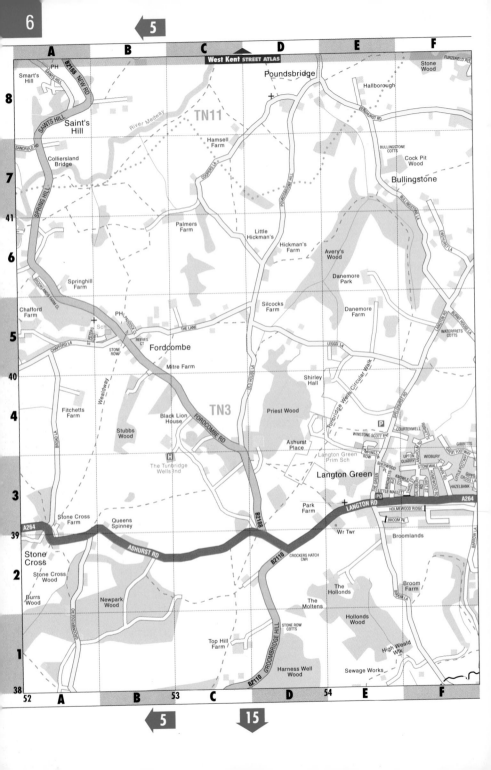

West Kent STREET ATLAS

A   B   C   D   E   F

PH
Smart's
Hill
B2188 NEW RD
SANTS HILL

Poundsbridge

Stone
Wood
FURZEFIELD AVE

Halborough

8

SAINT'S HILL
Saint's
Hill

River Medway

TN11

RENSHURST RD

SANDFIELD RD

Hamsell
Farm

BULLINGSTONE
COTTS

Cock Pit
Wood

SPRING HILL

Colliersland
Bridge

COOPERS LA

POUNDSBRIDGE HILL

BULLINGSTONE LA

Bullingstone

7

41

Palmers
Farm

Little
Hickman's

Hickman's
Farm

Avery's
Wood

WATERFRETS LA

6

CHAFFORD FARM CL

Springhill
Farm

Danemore
Park

Chafford
Farm

PH

ST PETER'S COURT

Sch

MAIDSTONE

THE LANE

Silcocks
Farm

Danemore
Farm

FINCH GREEN RD

WATERFRETS
COTTS

5

CHAFFORD LA

REEVES
CT

STONE
ROW

Fordcombe

LEGGS LA

SPELDHURST RD

TUNBRIDGE WELLS CIRCULAR WALK

40

Wealdway

Mitre Farm

OLD HOUSE LA

TN3

Shirley
Hall

4

FITCHETTS LA

Fitchetts
Farm

Black Lion
House

FORDCOMBE RD

Priest Wood

Ashurst
Place

WINSTONE SCOTT AVE

P
COURTENWELL

RUSSETS

GIBBETTS

FAT FOOTWAY

Stubbs
Wood

H
The Tunbridge
Wells Ind

Langton Green
Prim Sch

CAMPING CL
SHERWOOD
PL
THE GREEN

UPTON
QUARRY

WIDBURY

STONEWALL

LITTLE MALLETT

HAZELBANK

3

Stone Cross
Farm

Queens
Spinney

Park
Farm

LANGTON RD

HOLMEWOOD RIDGE

BROOM PK

Langton Green

KNOWLE
PL

THE GREEN
LITTLE MALLETT

A264

GUMPS
CROSS LA

CROSS WOOD RD

A264

Stone
Cross

Wr Twr

Broomlands

39

ASHURST RD

B2110

CROCKERS HATCH
CNR

BROOM LA

Broom
Farm

2

Stone Cross
Wood

OLD ROUNDWELL

The
Hollonds

Burrs
Wood

Newpark
Wood

The
Moltens

Hollonds
Wood

High Weald
Wlk

1

GROOMBRIDGE HILL

Top Hill
Farm

STONE ROW
COTTS

Harness Well
Wood

Sewage Works

38

B2110

52   A   B   53   C   D   54   E   F

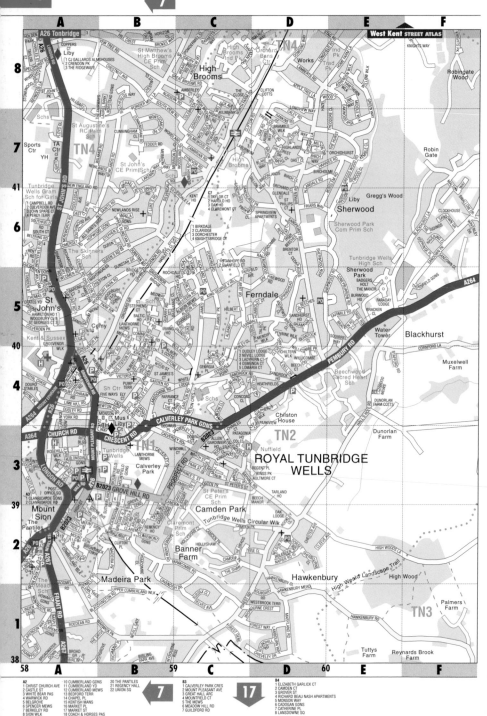

West Kent STREET ATLAS

A2
1 CHRIST CHURCH AVE
2 CASTLE ST
3 WHITE BEAR PAS
4 WARWICK RD
5 BELGROVE
6 SPENCER MEWS
7 BERKELEY RD
8 SION WLK
9 EDEN WLK

10 CUMBERLAND GDNS
11 CUMBERLAND YD
12 CUMBERLAND MEWS
13 BEDFORD TERR
14 CHAPEL PL
15 KENTISH MANS
16 MARKET ST
17 MARKET ST
18 COACH & HORSES PAS
19 SUSSEX MEWS

20 THE PANTILES
21 REGENCY HALL
22 UNION SQ

B3
1 CALVERLEY PARK CRES
2 MOUNT PLEASANT AVE
3 GREAT HALL ARC
4 MOUNTFIELD CT
5 THE MEWS
6 MEADOW HILL RD
7 GUILDFORD RD

B4
1 ELIZABETH GARLICK CT
2 CAMDEN CT
3 GROVER ST
4 RICHARD BEAU NASH APARTMENTS
5 MONSON WAY
6 CADOGAN GDNS
7 CATHERINE PL
8 LANSDOWNE SQ

A21 Sevenoaks(A225). M25
A228 Paddock Wood

TN11

Sandhill Farm

Newbars Wood

Lower Green

Pembury Sch

Snipe Wood

Marshleyharbour Wood

Forest Wood

Liby

Pembury

Romford

Pembury Grange

Superstore

Woodhill Pk
Greenleas
Woodgate Way

Priory Farm

Henwood Green

Pembury

The Coach House

Cornford Cl
Cornford Cotts
Sycamore Cotts

Pembury

Camden Ct

Stabledene Way

Playing Field

Salvadori Ct

Hubble's Farm

PEMBURY RD A264

Oakley Sch

Larkfield Hall

Chalket Farm

TN2

High Weald Landscape Trail
Tunbridge Wells Circular Walk

HASTINGS RD A21 Hastings

Pastheap Farm

Fletchers

Fletchers Farm

Mouseden

Little Bayhall Farm

Great Bayhall

Brickhurst Wood

TN12

Great Bayhall Farm

Gull Rough Wood

Little Bayhall

Old Dundle

TN3

Dodhurst

River Teise

Dundale Farm

Dundale Wood

Brown's Lodge

61   A   B   62   C   D   63   E   F   38

18

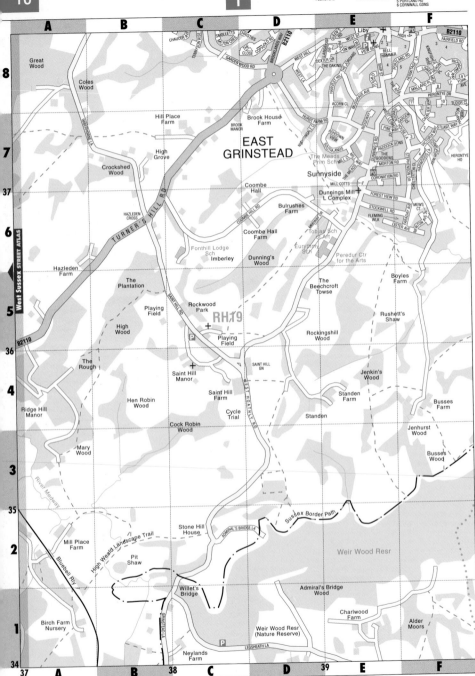

1

E8
1 JUDGE'S TERR
2 OLD STONE LINK
3 JUDGES CL
4 ELMSTEAD

F7
1 CROMWELL PL
2 CLARENCE DR
3 HARWOODS CL
4 COLLINGWOOD CL

F8
1 MIDDLE ROW
2 FOREST LODGE
3 SACKVILLE CT
4 GREAT HOUSE CT
5 PORTLAND HO
6 CORNWALL GDNS

7 NORMANDY CL
8 WILLOW MEAD
9 KINGS COPSE
10 REGAL DR
11 BECKETT WAY

EAST GRINSTEAD

West Sussex STREET ATLAS

Great Wood

Coles Wood

Hill Place Farm

High Grove

Crockshed Wood

Hazleden Farm

The Plantation

Playing Field

High Wood

The Rough

Ridge Hill Manor

Mary Wood

Hen Robin Wood

Cock Robin Wood

Saint Hill Manor

Saint Hill Farm

Cycle Trial

Rockwood Park

Playing Field

Saint Hill GN

Fonthill Lodge Sch
Imberley

Coombe Hall Farm

Dunning's Wood

Bulrushes Farm

Coombe Hall

Brook House Farm

BROOK MANOR

Sunnyside

Dunnings Mill L Complex

Tobias Sch of Art

Eurythmy Sch

Peredur Ctr for the Arts

The Beechcroft Towse

Boyles Farm

Rushett's Shaw

Rockingshill Wood

Jenkin's Wood

Standen Farm

Standen

Jenhurst Wood

Busses Farm

Busses Wood

Mill Place Farm

Pit Shaw

Willet's Bridge

Stone Hill House

Neylands Farm

Birch Farm Nursery

River Medway

Bluebell Rly

High Weald Landscape Trail

Admiral's Bridge La

Sussex Border Path

Weir Wood Resr

Admiral's Bridge Wood

Charlwood Farm

Alder Moors

Weir Wood Resr (Nature Reserve)

Legsheath La

Liby

Fairfield Rd

B2110

RH19

Turner's Hill Rd

Saint Hill Rd

West Hoathly Rd

Grinstead La

Coombe Hill Rd

B2110

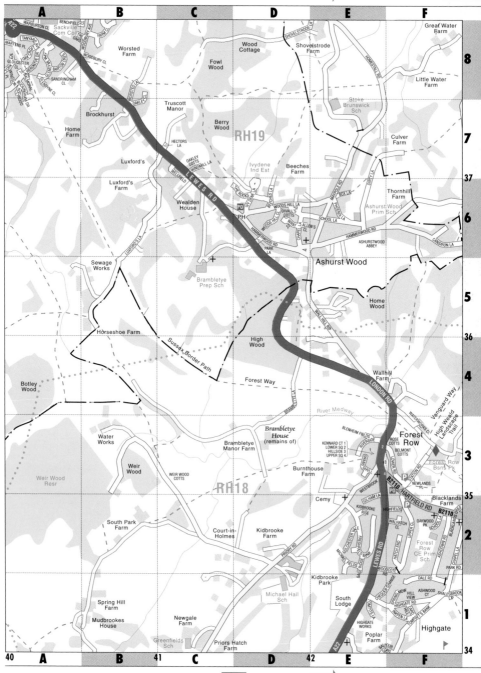

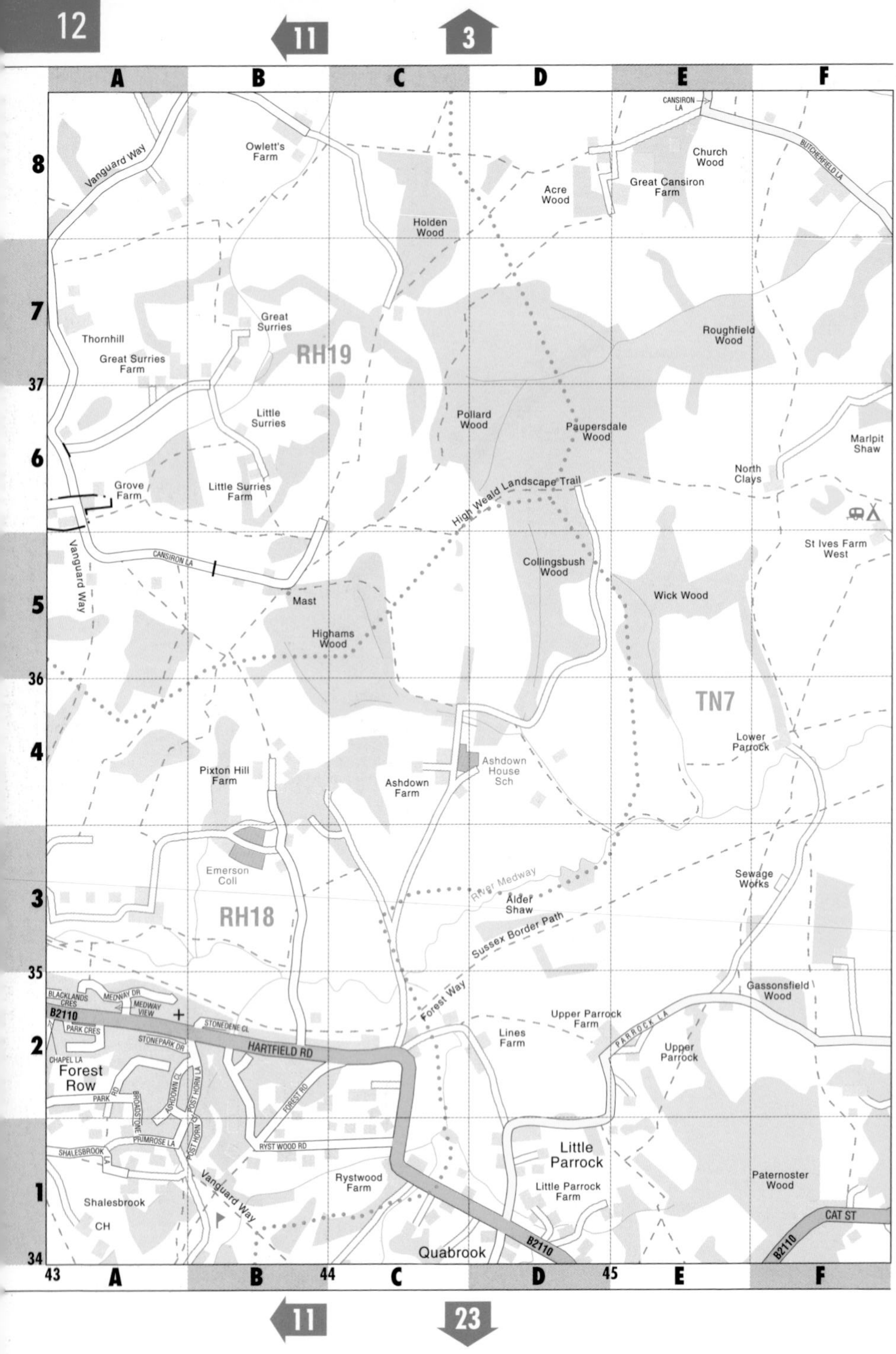
11
3
A
B
C
D
E
F
8
7
37
6
5
36
4
3
35
2
1
34
43
44
45
23
Vanguard Way
Owlett's Farm
Holden Wood
Acre Wood
Great Cansiron Farm
Church Wood
CANSIRON LA
BUTCHERFIELD LA
Thornhill
Great Surries Farm
Great Surries
RH19
Roughfield Wood
Little Surries
Pollard Wood
Paupersdale Wood
Marlpit Shaw
North Clays
Grove Farm
Little Surries Farm
High Weald Landscape Trail
St Ives Farm West
CANSIRON LA
Collingsbush Wood
Wick Wood
Mast
Highams Wood
TN7
Lower Parrock
Ashdown House Sch
Pixton Hill Farm
Ashdown Farm
Emerson Coll
River Medway
Sewage Works
Alder Shaw
RH18
Sussex Border Path
Forest Way
Gassonsfield Wood
Upper Parrock Farm
PARROCK LA
Lines Farm
Upper Parrock
BLACKLANDS CRES
MEDWAY DR
MEDWAY VIEW
B2110
PARK CRES
STONEDENE CL
STONEPARK DR
HARTFIELD RD
CHAPEL LA
Forest Row
PARK RD
BROADSTONE
ASHDOWN CL
POST HORN LA
FOREST RD
PRIMROSE LA
RYST WOOD RD
SHALESBROOK LA
Little Parrock
Rystwood Farm
Little Parrock Farm
Paternoster Wood
CAT ST
Shalesbrook
CH
Quabrook
B2110

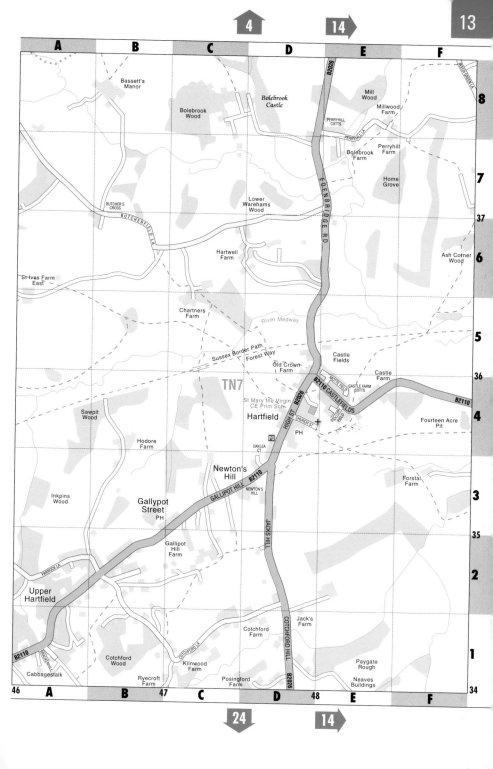

| A | B | C | D | E | F |

Minepit Shaw

Blackham Court

Pond Wood

Burrswood Home Farm

8

Hale Court Farm

River Grom

7

Lyewood Common

Lyewood House

Ham Farm

BEECH GREEN LA

Top Hill Farm

Sussex Border Path

Withyham

37

B2110 WITHYHAM RD

Ham Bridge

Sussex Border Path

6

Wealdway

River Medway

Forest Way

Stoneland's Farm

Summerford Farm

Hendal Farm

Balls Green

Jackass Shaw

Hendal Wood

5

BALL ST GN

St Michael's Prim Sch

SHOB RD

TN7

Hunt's Farm

36

TN3

B2188

4

B2110

Hewkins Bridge

Duckings

The Dorset Arms (PH)

DORSET COTTS

The Warren

LADIES MILE

Cherry Gardens Farm

Withyham

The Plain

3

High Weald Landscape Trail

Bullen's Wood

Motts Down

CORSELEY RD

PLUMEY FEATHER COTTS

35

Buckhurst Park

Plumyfeather Farm

Thatchers

Jockey's Wood

2

Millpond Rough

Coppice Wood

TN6

High Weald Landscape Trail

Park Grove Farm

Badbrook Wood

1

Lye Green House

Lye Green

FISHER'S GATE COTTS

Millpond Wood

B2188

Bingles

34

| 49 | A | | B | 50 | C | | D | 51 | E | | F |

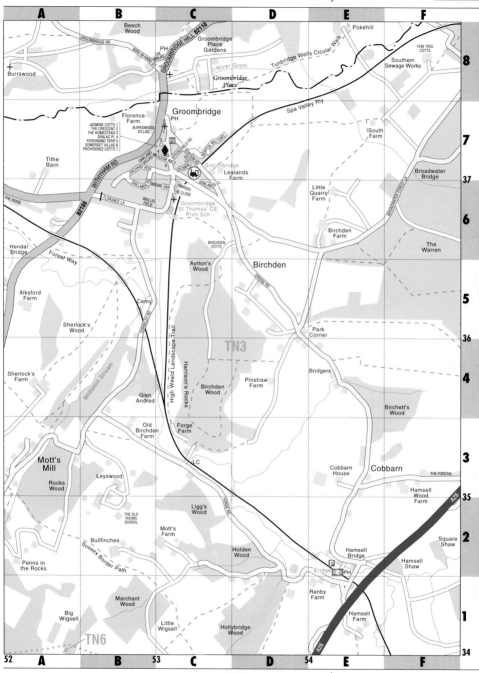

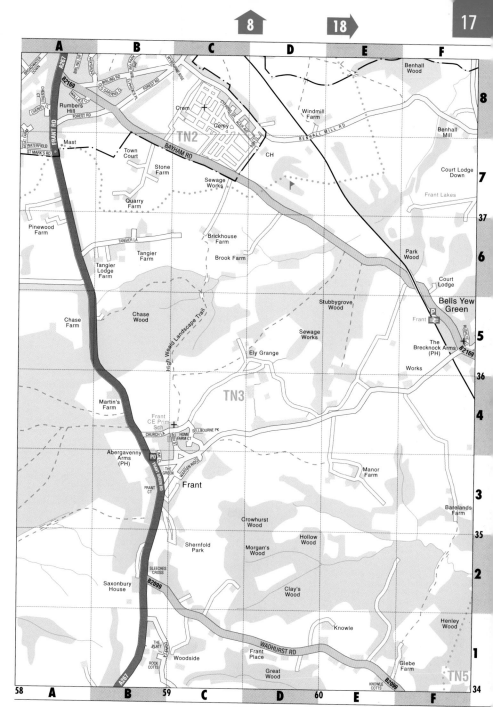

17 9

A   B   C   D   E   F

8 Coker's Down
Brown's Wood
Sunninglye Farmhouse

Rushlye Down

7 Coneyburrow Wood
Furnace Wood
River Teise
Tollslye
The Bothy

Oxpasture Wood

37

6 Hollow Wood
Jews Wood
Great Coppice Wood
Bayham Lake

Rushlye Farmhouse

Highfield
CROCKERS CL
MIDDLE RD
LY LA

Abbots Down
Diamonds

5 TN3
Forest Lodge

B2169
Burnt Wood
Upper Sluice Wood
LITTLE BAYHAM COTTS

36 BAYHAM RD
B2169
Little Bayham

4 Higham Wood
Higham Farm
Bartley Mill Wood
BARTLEY MILL LA
Bartley Mill

Verridge Wood
Wickhurst Farmhouse

Churchfield Wood
Little Shoesmiths
Bartley House

3 Sewers Bridge
BARTLEY MILL RD

35 Brookland Wood

Grigg's Wood
Shoesmith's Wood
Brick Kiln Wood

2 Camden Wood
Great Shoesmith Farm
Hewley Wood

TN5
Sussex Border Path

1 Henley Wood

DEWHURST LA
WHITEGATE LA
Sewage Works

34
61 A   B 62 C   D 63 E   F

17 29

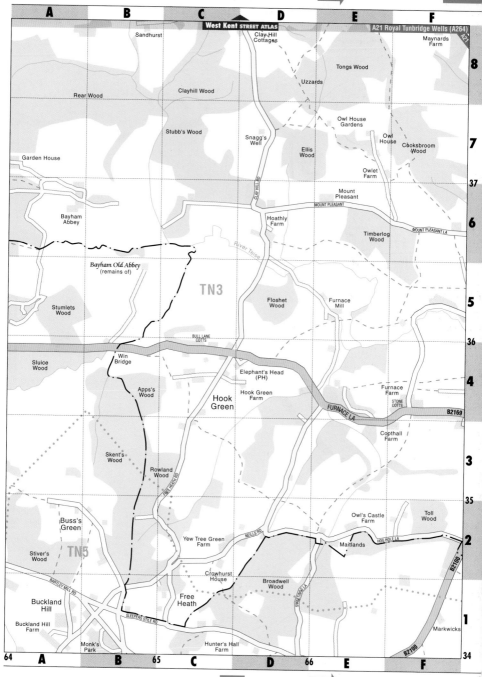

West Kent STREET ATLAS

A21 Royal Tunbridge Wells (A264)

Sandhurst

Clay Hill Cottages

Maynards Farm

Tongs Wood

Uzzards

Clayhill Wood

Rear Wood

Owl House Gardens

Stubb's Wood

Snagg's Well

Owl House

Cooksbroom Wood

Ellis Wood

Garden House

Owlet Farm

Mount Pleasant

Bayham Abbey

Hoathly Farm

MOUNT PLEASANT

MOUNT PLEASANT LA

Timberlog Wood

River Teise

Bayham Old Abbey
(remains of)

TN3

Floshet Wood

Furnace Mill

Stumlets Wood

BULL LANE COTTS

Sluice Wood

Win Bridge

Elephant's Head (PH)

Furnace Farm

STONE COTTS

FURNACE LA

B2169

Apps's Wood

Hook Green Farm

Hook Green

Copthall Farm

Skent's Wood

Rowland Wood

Buss's Green

Owl's Castle Farm

Toll Wood

Stiver's Wood

TN5

Yew Tree Green Farm

NEILLS RD

Maitlands

HOG HOLE LA

B2100

Buckland Hill

Crowhurst House

Broadwell Wood

Free Heath

SMALL HYTHE LA

Buckland Hill Farm

BARTLEY MILL RD

SLEEPERS STILE RD

Monk's Park

Hunter's Hall Farm

Markwicks

B2100

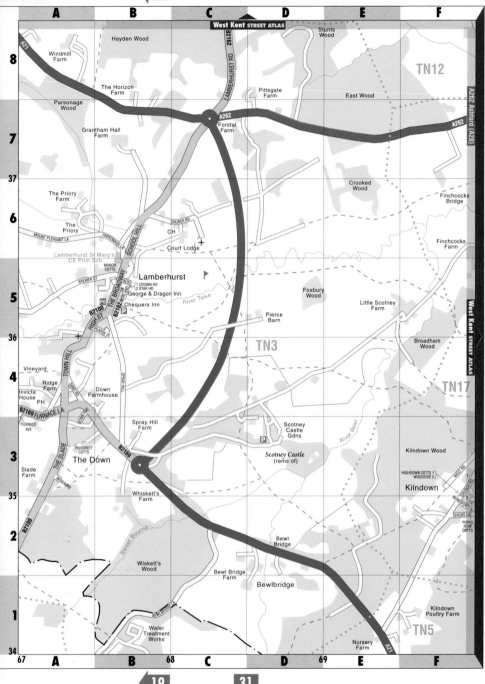

West Kent STREET ATLAS

West Kent STREET ATLAS

TN12

TN3

TN17

TN5

19

31

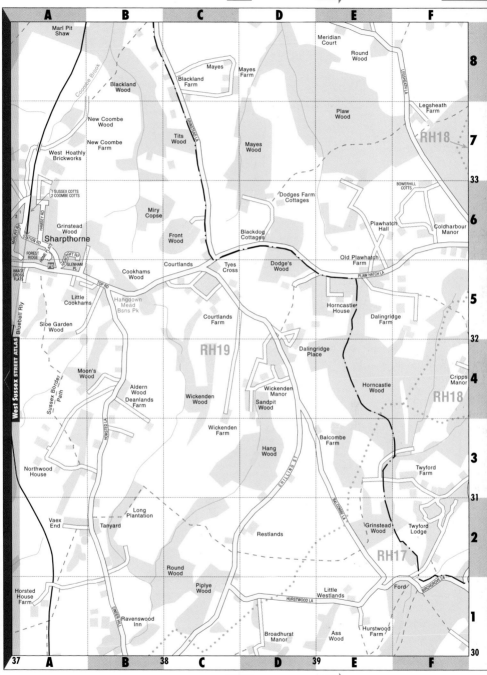

8

7

33

6

5

32

4

3

31

2

1

30

A   B   C   D   E   F

RH19

Fernhill

Kidbrooke
Wood

Balfour Gdns

Greenhall
Cottage

Tompset's
Bank

Ashdown
Pl

Wych
Warren

Meml

Lavender
Platt

Old Cherry
Orchard

RH19

Hindleap
Warren

RH18

Broadstone Warren
Scout Camp

Broadstone
Warren

Pixie La
Plaw Hatch
La

Hindleap Farm

Hindleap Warren
Outdoor Education Ctr

Colemans Hatch Rd

Eighteen Acre
Wood

Wych
Cross

Smockfarthing

Roebuck
Hotel

Wych Cross
Fruit Farm

Half Moon
Copse

Wych Cross
Place

Ashdown Forest
Llama Farm

Hillsdown
Farm

Press Ridge
Warren

Garde

Suttons Farm

RH17

Stumblewood
Common

Mill Brook

Broadhoole La

Birch Grove
House

Isle of Thorns

Chapel Brook

Red Lion
(PH)

The White
House

TN22

Gosses
Farm

Beaconsfield
Rd

Langrish La

A275 Lewes Rd

40   A   B   41   C   D   42   E   F

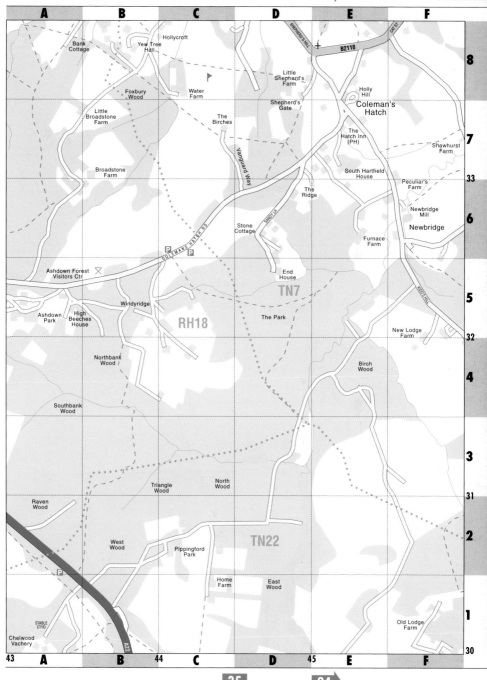

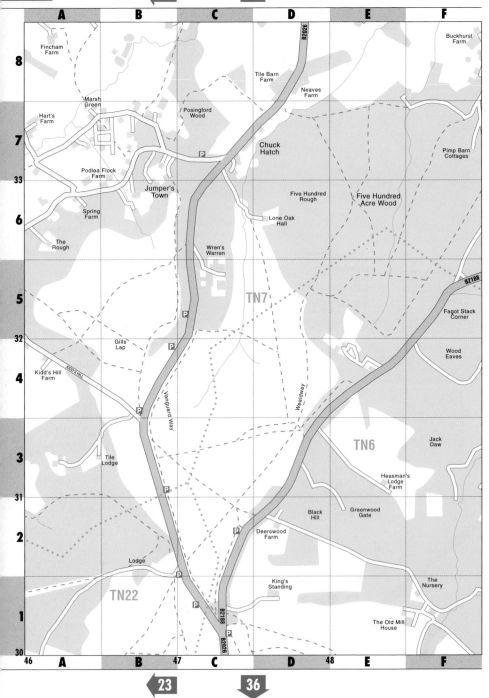

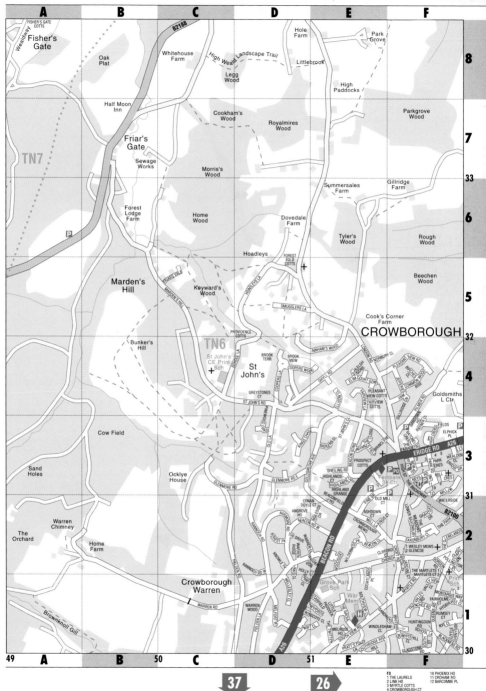

F3
1 THE LAURELS
2 LINK HO
3 MYRTLE COTTS
4 CROWBOROUGH CT
5 MAYVERN CT
6 PARK LA
7 NEVILL TERR
8 CROYDON COTTS
9 WARREN CT
10 PHOENIX HO
11 CROHAM RD
12 BARCOMBE PL

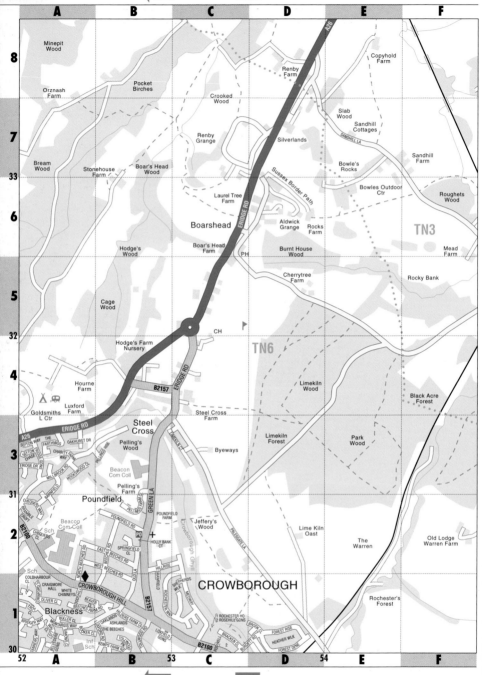

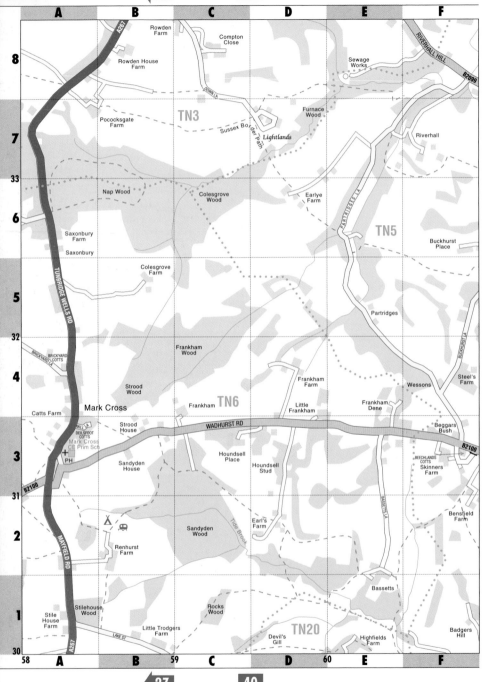

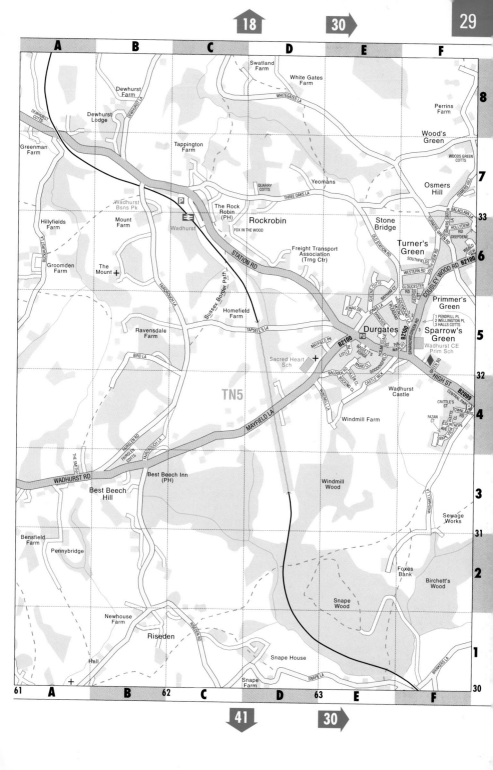

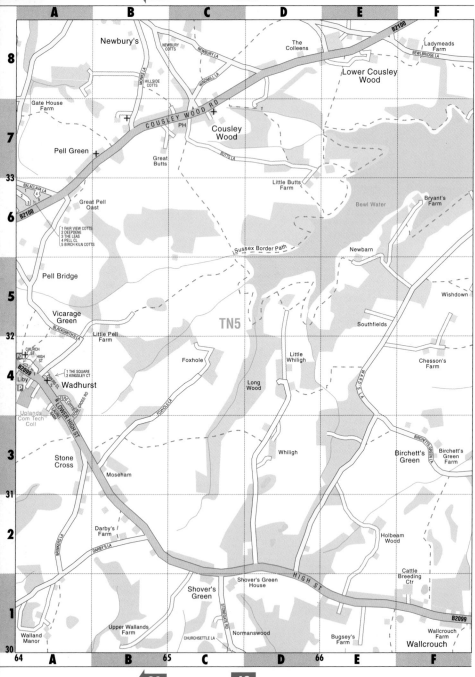

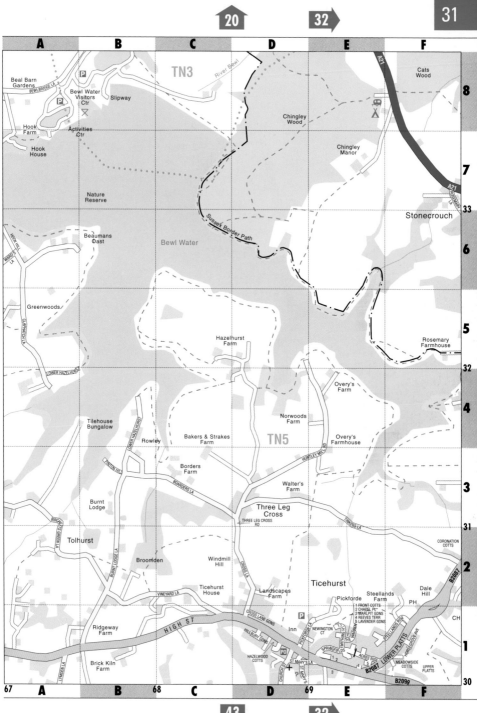

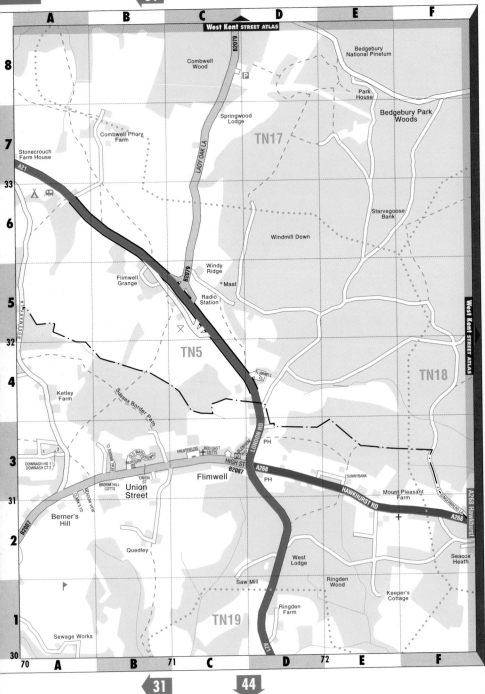

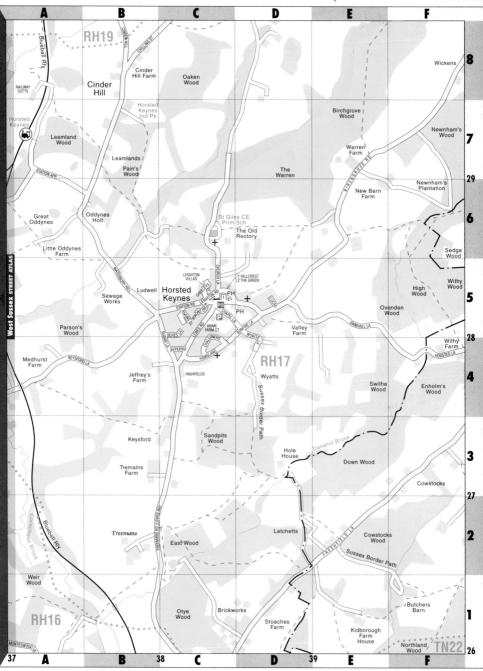

West Sussex STREET ATLAS

A **B** **C** **D** **E** **F**

RH19

Wickens **8**

Cinder Hill Farm

Oaken Wood

RAILWAY COTTS

Cinder Hill

Horsted Keynes Ind Pk

Birchgrove Wood

Newnham's Wood **7**

Horsted Keynes

Leamland Wood

Leamlands

Pain's Wood

Warren Farm

The Warren

Newnham's Plantation **29**

STATION APP

Great Oddynes

Oddynes Holt

New Barn Farm **6**

St Giles CE Prim Sch

The Old Rectory

Sedge Wood

Little Oddynes Farm

Leighton Villas

Ludwell

Horsted Keynes

STATION RD

1 HILLCREST 2 THE GREEN

High Wood

Withy Wood **5**

Sewage Works

PH

PH

Ovenden Wood

Valley Farm

DANEHILL LA

Parson's Wood

HOME FARM CT

Withy Farm **28**

Medhurst Farm

KEYSFORD LA

HIGHFIELDS

Wyatts

RH17

Sussex Border Path

Swithe Wood

Enholm's Wood **4**

HORSTED LA

Jeffrey's Farm

Keysford

Sandpits Wood

Hole House

Danehill Brook

Down Wood

Cowstocks **27**

Tremains Farm

Treemans

Latchetts

Cowstocks Wood

Sussex Border Path **2**

FRESHFIELD LA

Weir Wood

Bluebell Rly

Cockhaise Brook

East Wood

Otye Wood

Brickworks

Stoaches Farm

Kidborough Farm House

Butchers Barn

Northland Wood **1**

RH16

MONTESWOOD LA

TN22 **26**

37　**A**　**B**　38　**C**　39　**D**　**E**　**F**

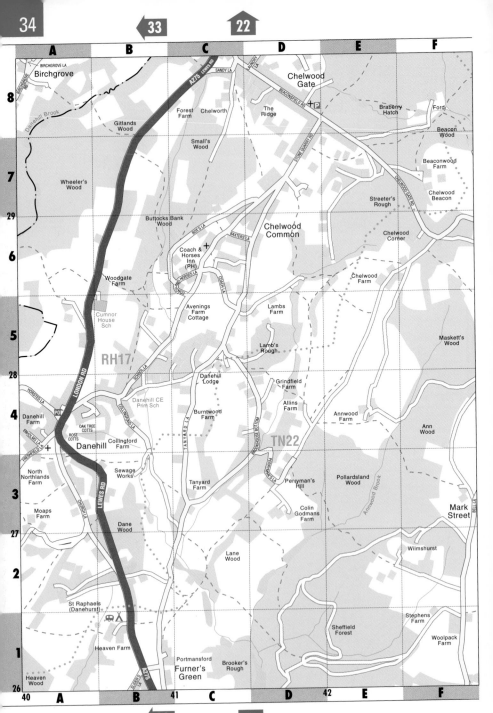

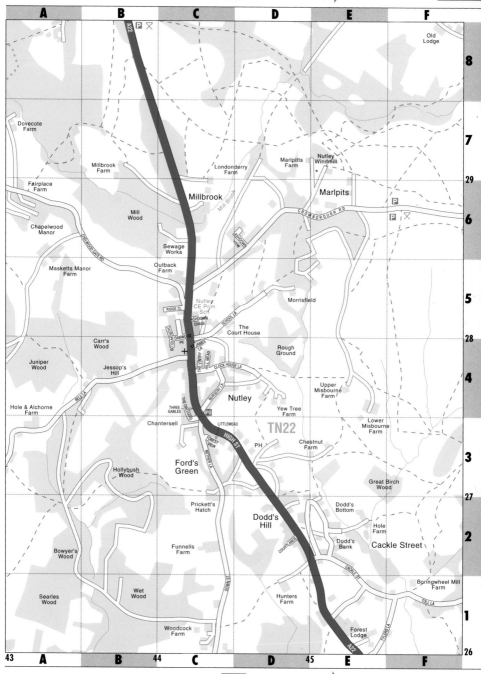

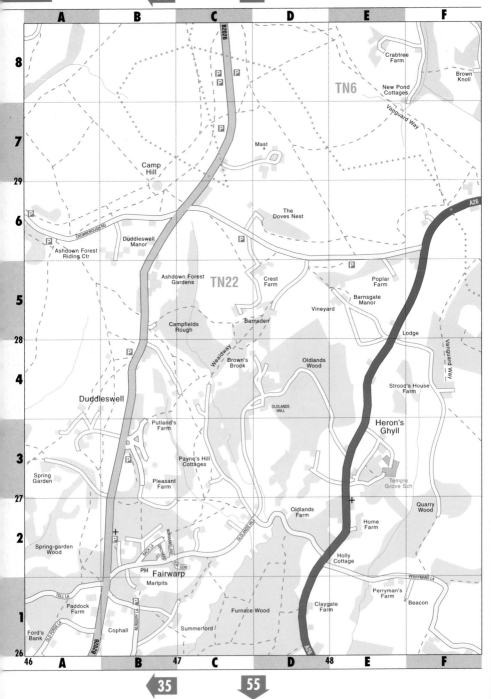

B2026

8

7

29

6

5

28

4

3

27

2

1

26

A B C D E F

46 47 48

Crabtree Farm

Brown Knoll

New Pond Cottages

TN6

Vanguard Way

A26

Mast

Camp Hill

The Doves Nest

Duddleswell Manor

Ashdown Forest Riding Ctr

CROWBOROUGH RD

Ashdown Forest Gardens

TN22

Crest Farm

Poplar Farm

Barnsgate Manor

Vineyard

Lodge

Campfields Rough

Barnsden

Vanguard Way

Wealdway

Brown's Brook

Oldlands Wood

Strood's House Farm

Duddleswell

OLDLANDS HALL

Heron's Ghyll

Putland's Farm

Payne's Hill Cottages

Temple Grove Sch

Spring Garden

Pleasant Farm

Oldlands Farm

Quarry Wood

Home Farm

Spring-garden Wood

OLDLANDS LA

Holly Cottage

NURSERY LA

PH Fairwarp

Marlpits

Perryman's Farm

Beacon

PERRYMANS LA

TOLL LA

Paddock Farm

Cophall

Summerford

Furnace Wood

Claygate Farm

OLD FORGE LA

Ford's Bank

B2026

A26

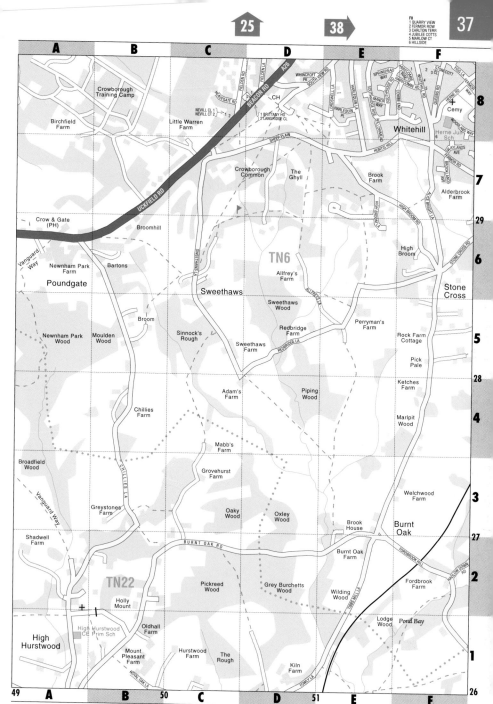

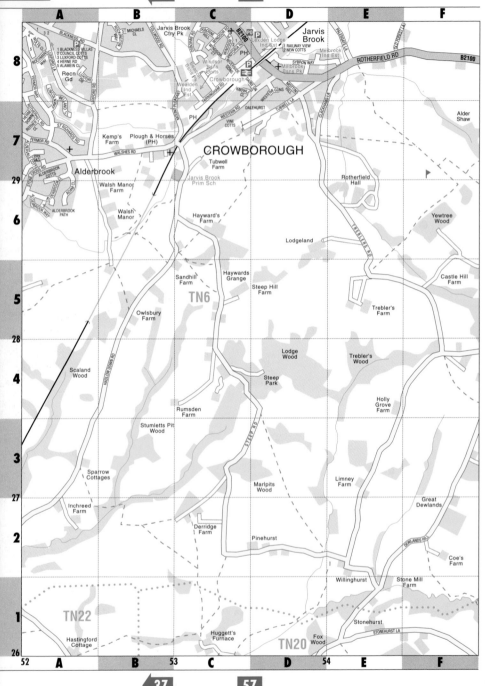

A   B   C   D   E   F

8

1 BLACKNESS VILLAS
2 COUNCIL COTTS
3 LUXFORD COTTS
4 HERNE RD
5 ALAMEIN CL

BLACKNESS RD

ST MICHAELS CL

Jarvis Brook
Ctry Pk

B2100

Lexden Lodge
Ind Est

Jarvis
Brook

1 RAILWAY VIEW
2 NEW COTTS

PH

Recn
Gd

Windsor
Bsns
Units

Crowborough

Wealden
Ind Est

PH

SYBRON WAY

Millbrook
Bsns Pk

Millbrook
Ind Est

ROTHERFIELD RD

B2100

Alder
Shaw

7

Kemp's
Farm

Plough & Horses
(PH)

WALSHES RD

PH

WESTERN RD

DALEHURST

TIDWELL LA

Rotherfield
Hall

29

Alderbrook

ALDERBROOK
COTTS

Walsh Manor
Farm

CROWBOROUGH

Jarvis Brook
Prim Sch

Tubwell
Farm

VINE
COTTS

6

ALDERBROOK
PATH

Walsh
Manor

Hayward's
Farm

Lodgeland

TREBLERS RD

Yewtree
Wood

5

Sandhill
Farm

TN6

Haywards
Grange

Steep Hill
Farm

Trebler's
Farm

Castle Hill
Farm

28

Owlsbury
Farm

Lodge
Wood

Trebler's
Wood

4

Scaland
Wood

HADLOW DOWN RD

Steep
Park

Holly
Grove
Farm

Rumsden
Farm

Stumletts Pit
Wood

STEEP RD

3

Sparrow
Cottages

Marlpits
Wood

Limney
Farm

Great
Dewlands

27

Inchreed
Farm

Derridge
Farm

Pinehurst

DEWLANDS RD

Coe's
Farm

2

Willinghurst

Stone Mill
Farm

1

TN22

Stonehurst

STONEHURST LA

26

Hastingford
Cottage

Huggett's
Furnace

TN20

Fox
Wood

52   A   B   53   C   D   54   E   F

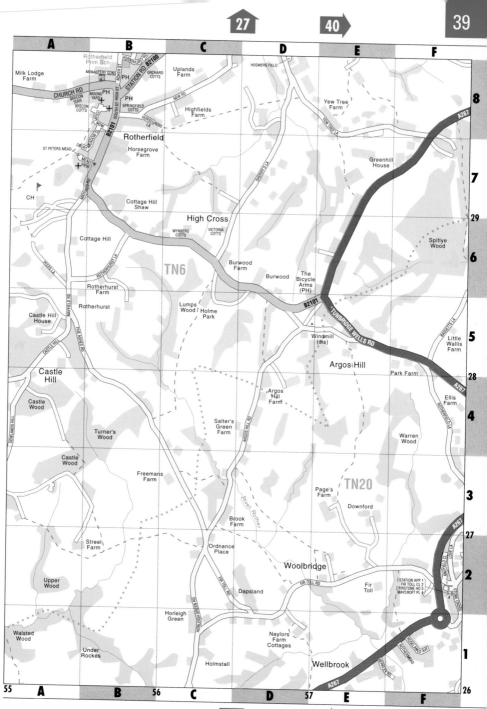

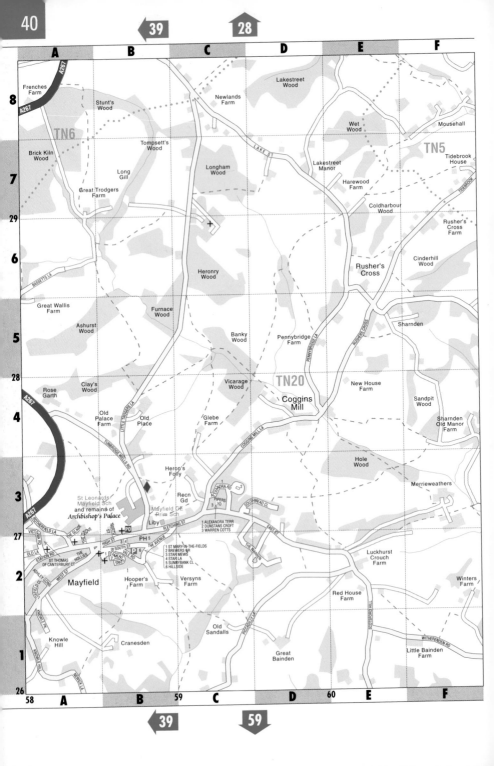

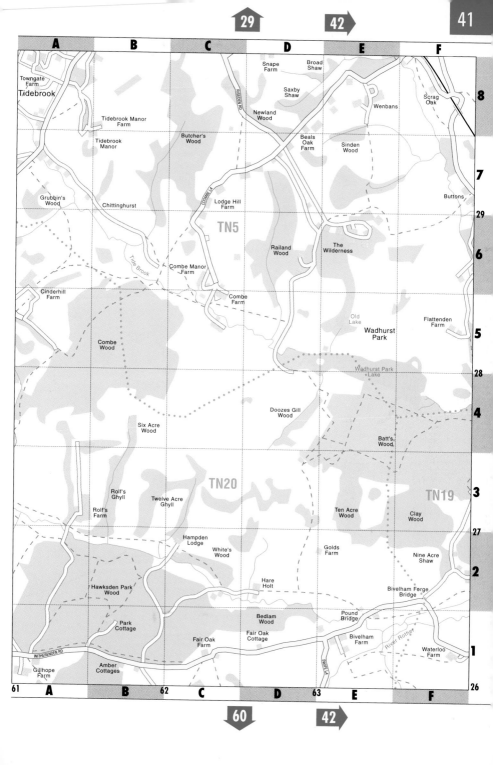

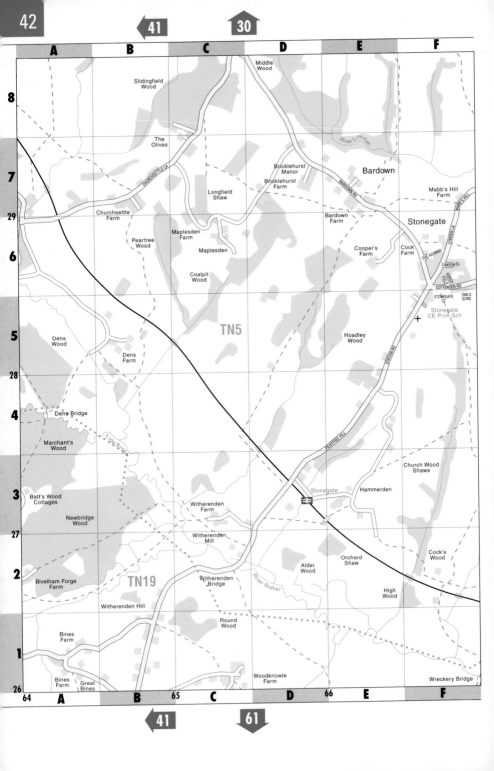

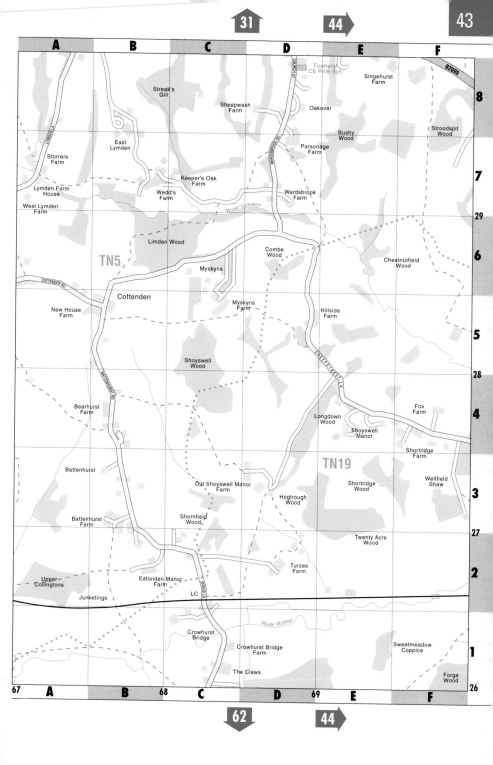

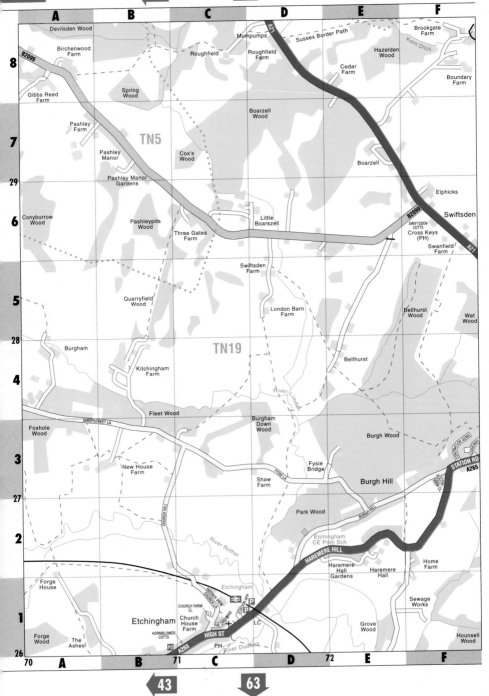

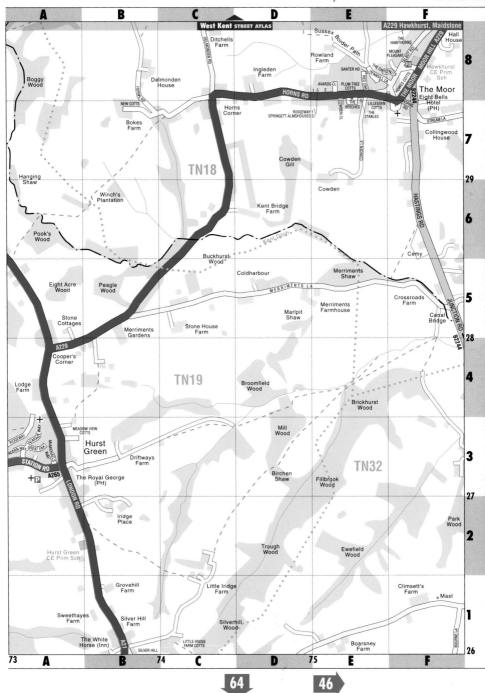

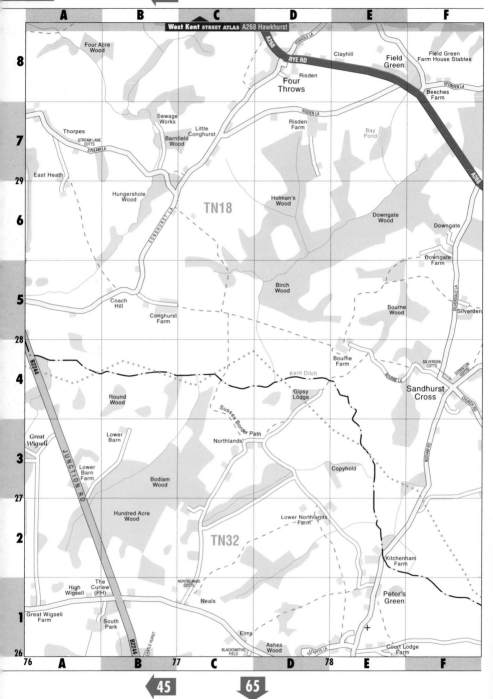

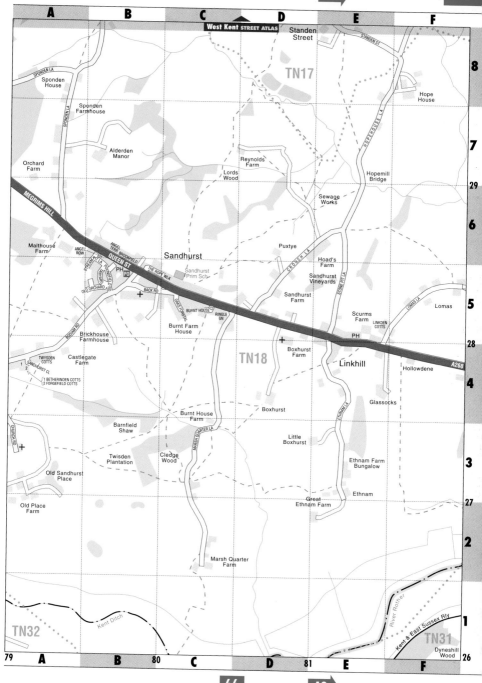

West Kent STREET ATLAS

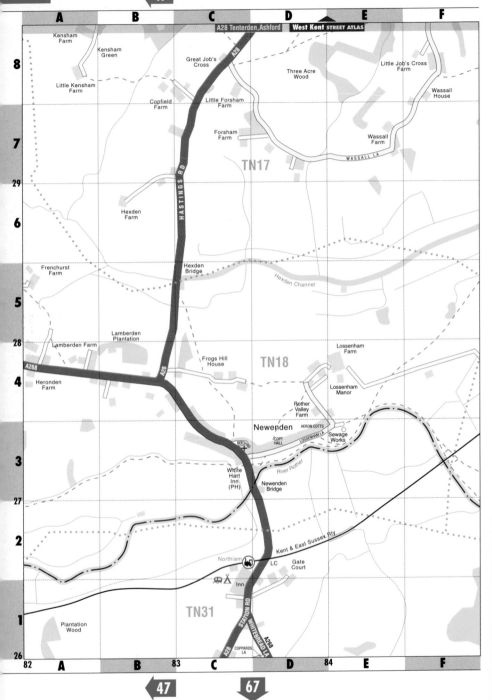

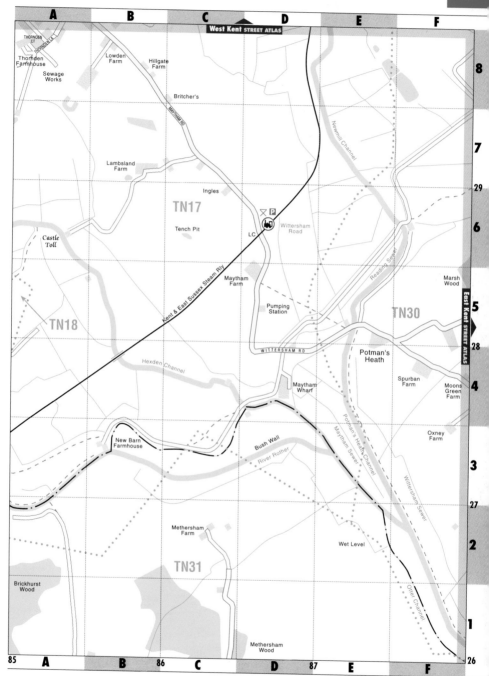

East Kent STREET ATLAS

THORNDEN CT

THORNDEN CL

Thornden
Farmhouse

Sewage
Works

Lowden
Farm

Hillgate
Farm

Britcher's

Lambsland
Farm

Ingles

TN17

Tench Pit

Castle
Toll

TN18

Kent & East Sussex Steam Rly

Maytham
Farm

Pumping
Station

Hexden Channel

Newmill Channel

Wittersham
Road

LC

Reading Sewer

Marsh
Wood

TN30

Potman's
Heath

WITTERSHAM RD

Spurban
Farm

Moons
Green
Farm

New Barn
Farmhouse

Maytham
Wharf

Bush Wall

River Rother

Potman's Heath Channel

Maytham Sewer

Oxney
Farm

Wittersham Sewer

Methersham
Farm

TN31

Wet Level

Brickhurst
Wood

Methersham
Wood

Otter Channel

8

7

29

6

5

28

4

3

27

2

1

26

85   A   B   86   C   D   87   E   F

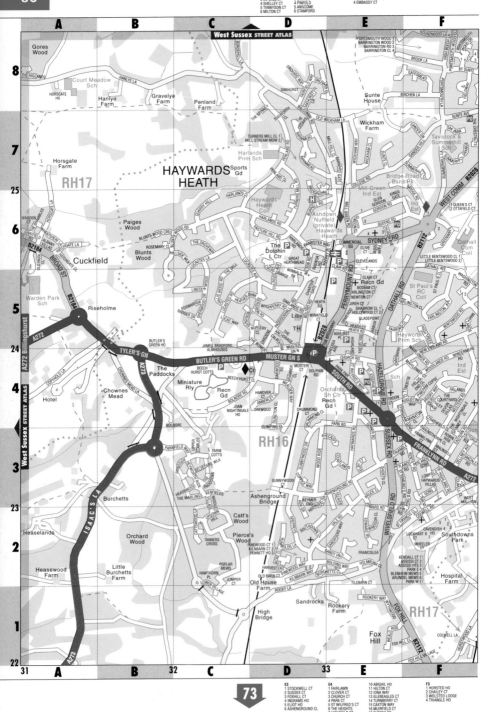

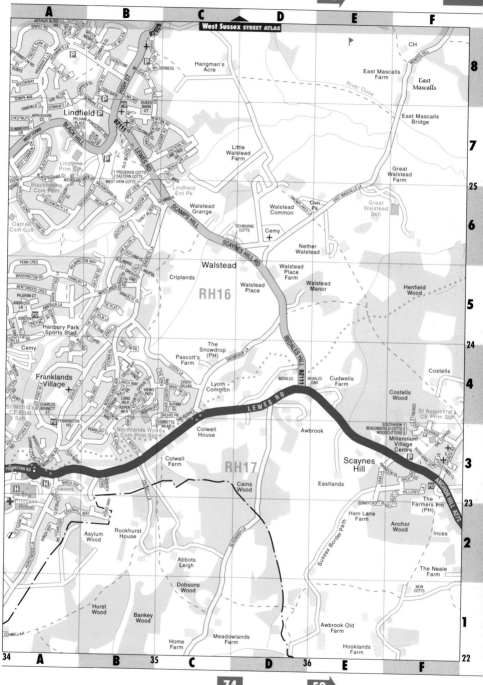

West Sussex STREET ATLAS

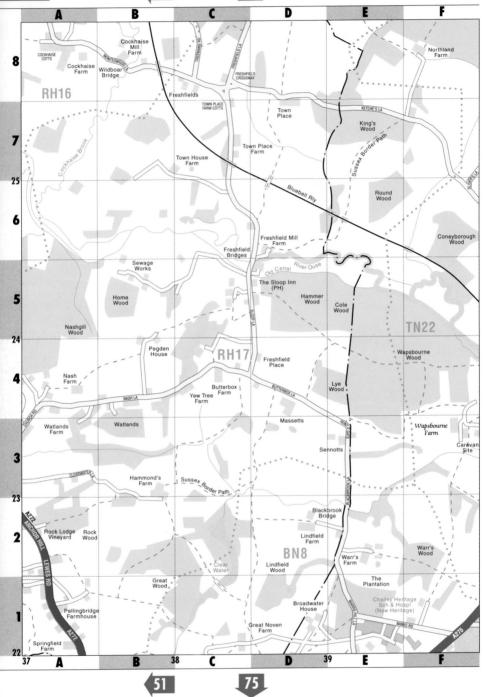

51
33

COCKHAISE
COTTS

Cockhaise
Mill
Farm

Cockhaise
Farm

Wildboar
Bridge

MONTESWOOD LA

FRESHFIELD LA

FRESHFIELD LA

Northland
Farm

SLUGWELL LA

RH16

Freshfields

TOWN PLACE
FARM COTTS

Freshfield
Crossway

Town
Place

KETCHE'S LA

King's
Wood

Cockhaise Brook

Town House
Farm

Town Place
Farm

Sussex Border Path

Bluebell Rly

Round
Wood

Freshfield Mill
Farm

Coneyborough
Wood

Sewage
Works

Freshfield
Bridges

River Ouse

Old Canal

The Sloop Inn
(PH)

Home
Wood

Hammer
Wood

Cole
Wood

TN22

Nashgill
Wood

SLOOP LA

Pegden
House

RH17

Freshfield
Place

Wapsbourne
Wood

Nash
Farm

NASH LA

Butterbox
Farm

Yew Tree
Farm

BUTTERBOX LA

Lye
Wood

Wapsbourne
Farm

CHURCH RD

Watlands
Farm

Watlands

Massetts

TURKEYSTO RD

Caravan
Site

CLEARWATER

Hammond's
Farm

Sussex Border Path

Sennotts

Blackbrook
Bridge

A272

ANCHOR HILL

Rock Lodge
Vineyard

Rock
Wood

Clear
Water

Lindfield
Farm

BN8

Warr's
Farm

Warr's
Wood

LEWES RD

Great
Wood

Lindfield
Wood

The
Plantation

Chailey Heritage
Sch & Hospl
(New Heritage)

A272

Pellingbridge
Farmhouse

Broadwater
House

WAPSES HILL LA

BANKS RD

A275

Springfield
Farm

Great Noven
Farm

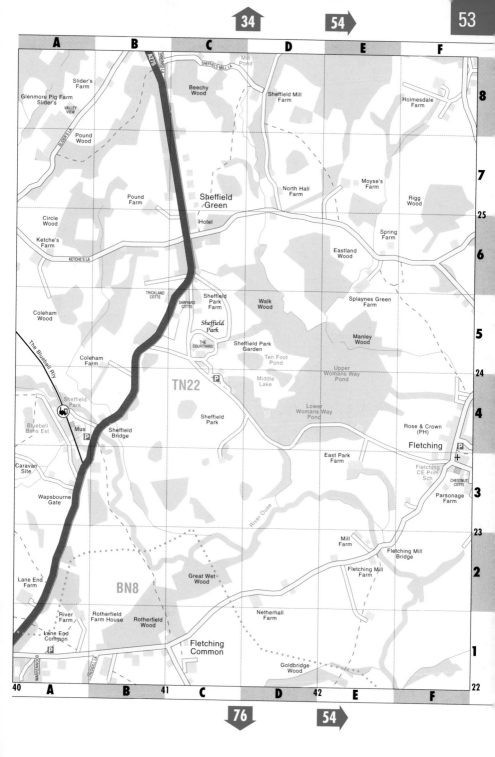

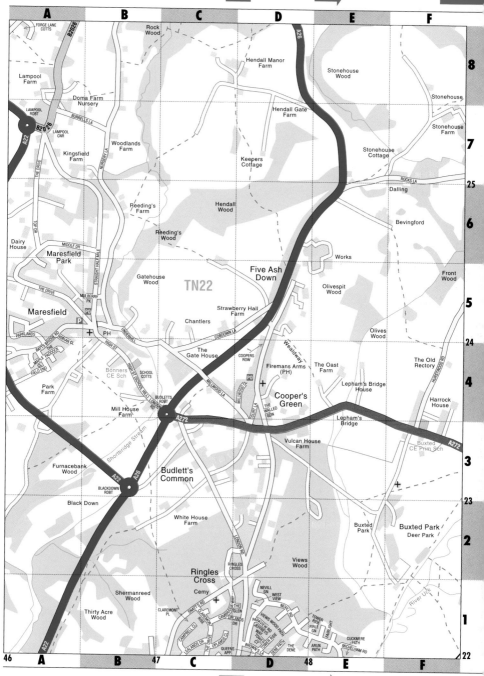

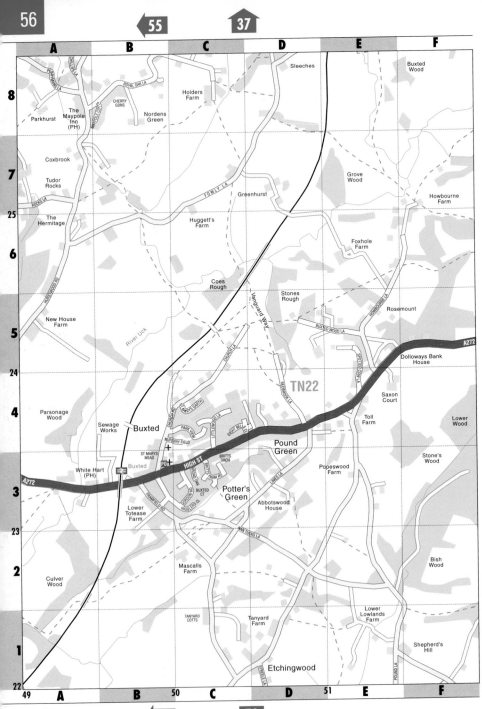

A **B** **C** **D** **E** **F**

8

Buxted
Wood

Sleeches

Holders
Farm

The
Maypole
Inn
(PH)

Parkhurst

CHILLIES LA
PARKHURST LA
MAYPOLE LANE
ROYAL OAK LA
CHERRY GDNS

Nordens
Green

7

Coxbrook

Grove
Wood

Tudor
Rocks

Howbourne
Farm

ROCKS LA
FOWLY LA

25

Greenhurst

The
Hermitage

Huggett's
Farm

Foxhole
Farm

6

Coes
Rough

Stones
Rough

Rosemount

New House
Farm

HURSTWOOD RD

River Uck

Vanguard Way

BUXTED WOOD LA
HOWBOURNE LA

5

A272

Dolloways Bank
House

24

TN22

Saxon
Court

4

Parsonage
Wood

Buxted

CHURCH LA
REDBROLS LA
SPOTTED LA

Toll
Farm

Lower
Wood

Sewage
Works

PARK RD
LIMS RO
LITTLE RD

Pound
Green

Stone's
Wood

ST MARYS
MEAD

NURSERY FIELD

Buxted

HIGH ST

EIGHT BELL
BRITTS
ORCH

Popeswood
Farm

White Hart
(PH)

A272

FRAMFIELD RD
HIGGLERS CL
BUXTED
CT
BROOK
BROAD OAK

Potter's
Green

Abbotswood
House

LIMES LA

3

Lower
Totease
Farm

23

MAX TUCKS LA

2

Culver
Wood

Mascalls
Farm

Bish
Wood

Lower
Lowlands
Farm

1

TANYARD
COTTS

Tanyard
Farm

POUND LA
STREELE LA

Shepherd's
Hill

22

Etchingwood

A **B** **C** **D** **E** **F**
49 50 51

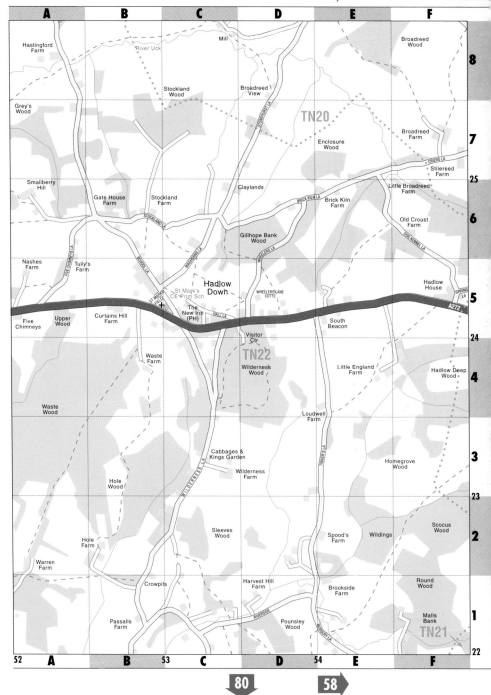

A B C D E F

8

Hastingford
Farm

River Uck

Mill

Broadreed
Wood

Stockland
Wood

Broadreed
View

TN20

7

Grey's
Wood

Enclosure
Wood

Broadreed
Farm

CRIERS LA

Stilereed
Farm

25

Smallberry
Hill

Gate House
Farm

Stockland
Farm

Claylands

BRICK KILN LA

Brick Kiln
Farm

Little Broadreed
Farm

STOCKLAND LA

Old Croust
Farm

6

Gillhope Bank
Wood

DOG KENNEL LA

WHEELERS LA

VIRGINSMS LA

Nashes
Farm

Tully's
Farm

FIVE CHIMNEYS LA

SCHOOL LA

Hadlow
Down

St Mark's
CE Prim Sch

WHEELERS LANE
COTTS

Hadlow
House

SPRING LA

5

Five
Chimneys

Upper
Wood

Curtains Hill
Farm

ST MARKS
FIELDS

The
New Inn
(PH)

HALL LA

South
Beacon

A272

24

Visitor
Ctr

TN22

Waste
Farm

Wilderness
Wood

Little England
Farm

Hadlow Deep
Wood

4

Waste
Wood

Loudwell
Farm

Cabbages &
Kings Garden

WILDERNESS LA

Wilderness
Farm

Homegrove
Wood

TINKERS LA

3

Hole
Wood

23

Hole
Farm

Sleeves
Wood

Spood's
Farm

Wildings

Scocus
Wood

2

Warren
Farm

Crowpits

Harvest Hill
Farm

Brookside
Farm

Round
Wood

Malls
Bank

Passalls
Farm

RIVERSIDE

Pounsley
Wood

HORSEY LA

TN21

1

22

52 A B 53 C D 54 E F

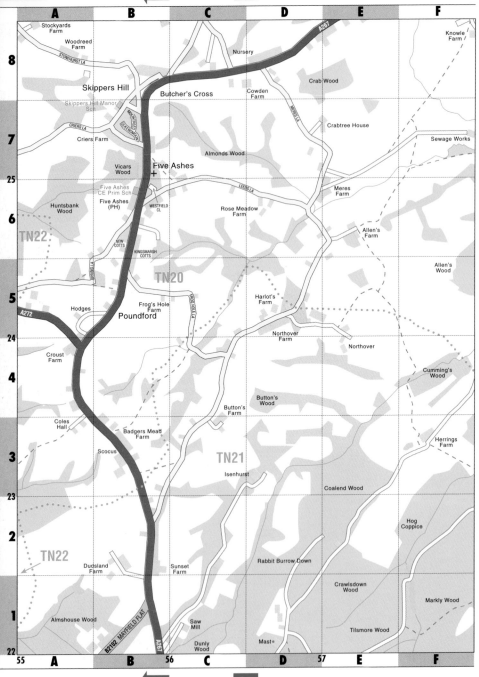

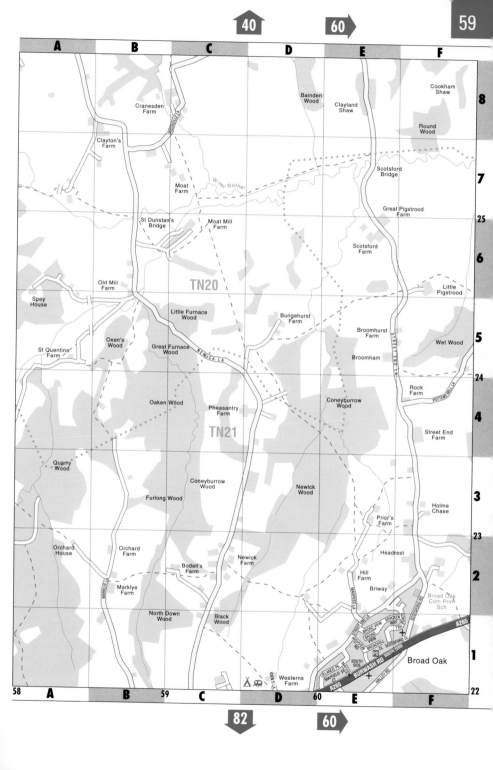

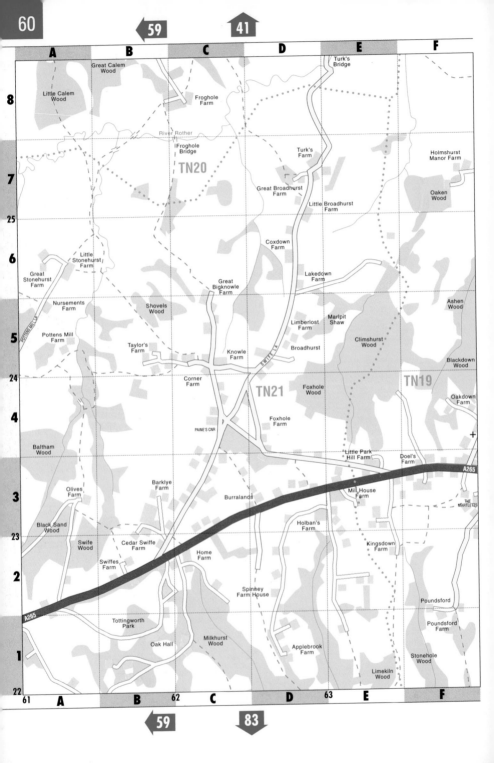

Map labels

Great Calem Wood

Little Calem Wood

Froghole Farm

River Rother

Froghole Bridge

TN20

Turk's Bridge

Turk's Farm

Holmshurst Manor Farm

Great Broadhurst Farm

Little Broadhurst Farm

Oaken Wood

Coxdown Farm

Little Stonehurst Farm

Great Stonehurst Farm

Lakedown Farm

Nursements Farm

Shovels Wood

Great Bigknowle Farm

Limberlost Farm

Marlpit Shaw

Ashen Wood

Pottens Mill Farm

Taylor's Farm

Knowle Farm

Broadhurst

Climshurst Wood

Blackdown Wood

Corner Farm

TN21

Foxhole Wood

TN19

Oakdown Farm

PAINE'S CNR

Foxhole Farm

Baltham Wood

Little Park Hill Farm

Doel's Farm

A265

Olives Farm

Barklye Farm

Burralands

Mill House Farm

THE MARTLETS

Black Sand Wood

Swife Wood

Cedar Swiffe Farm

Holban's Farm

Kingsdown Farm

Swiffes Farm

Home Farm

A265

Spinney Farm House

Poundsford

Tottingworth Park

Oak Hall

Milkhurst Wood

Applebrook Farm

Poundsford Farm

Limekiln Wood

Stonehole Wood

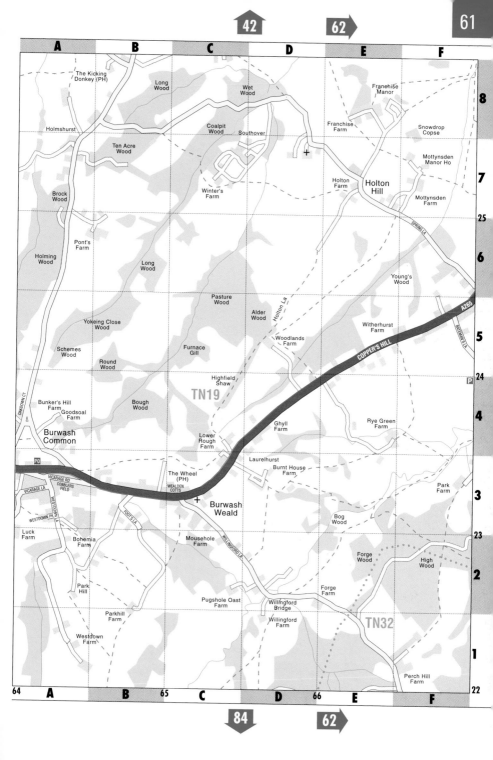

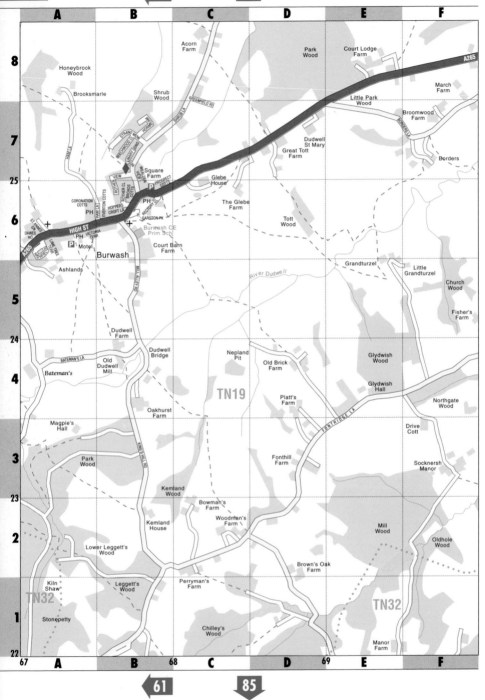

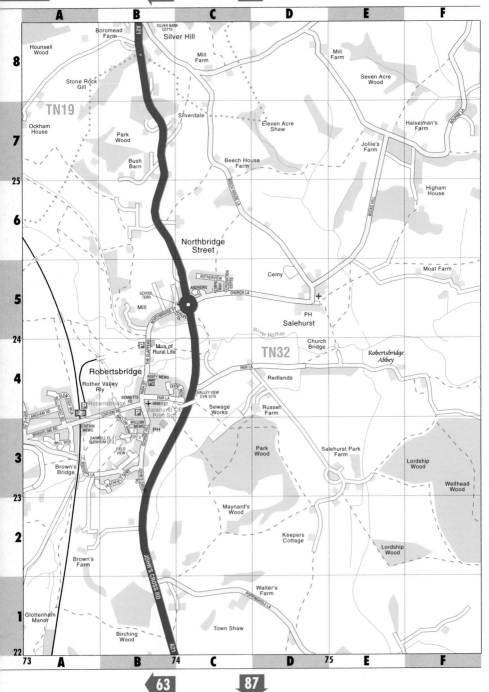

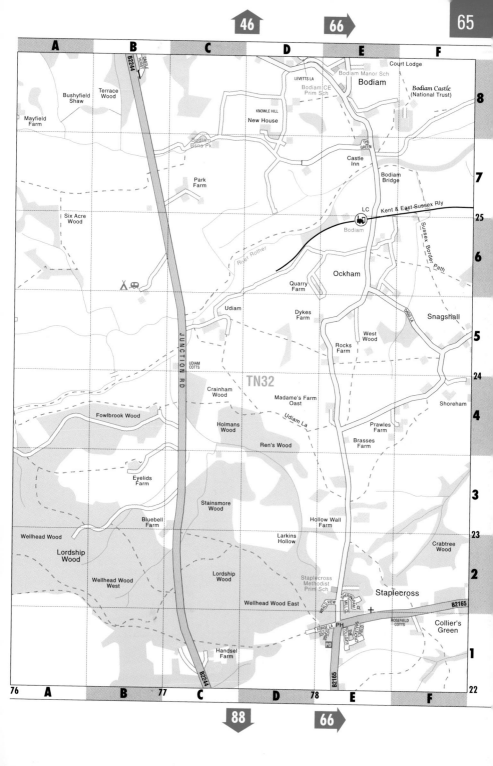

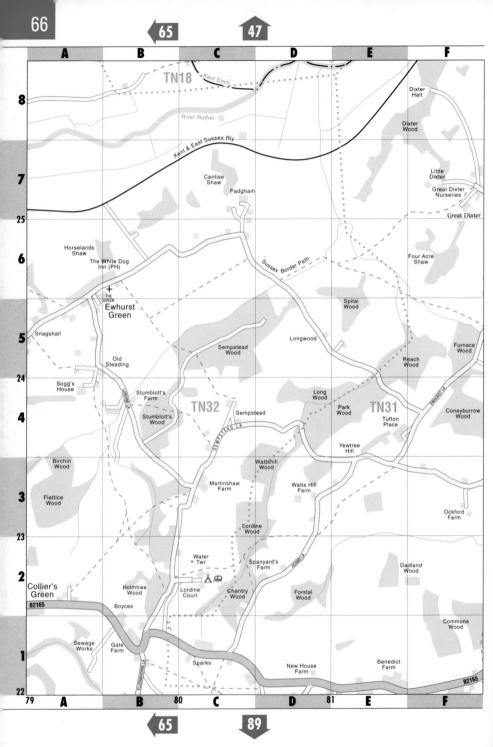

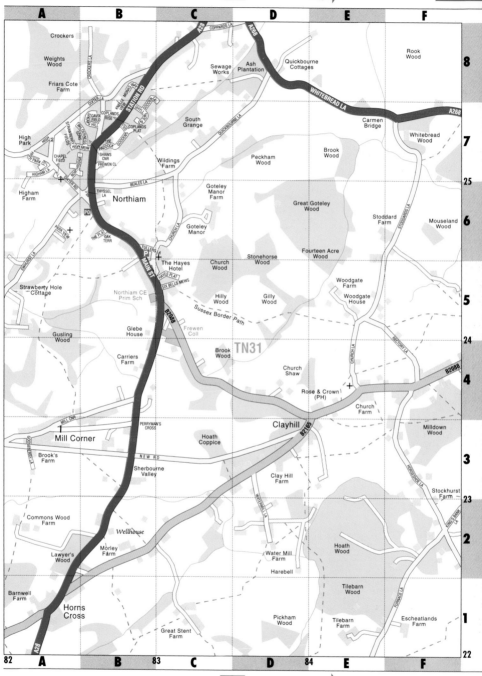

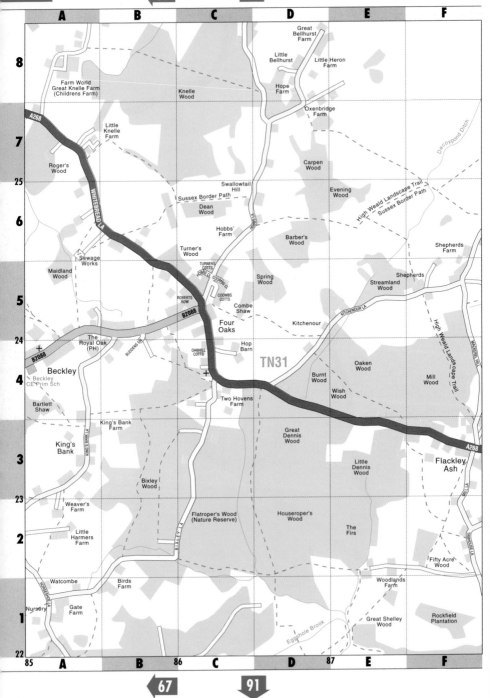

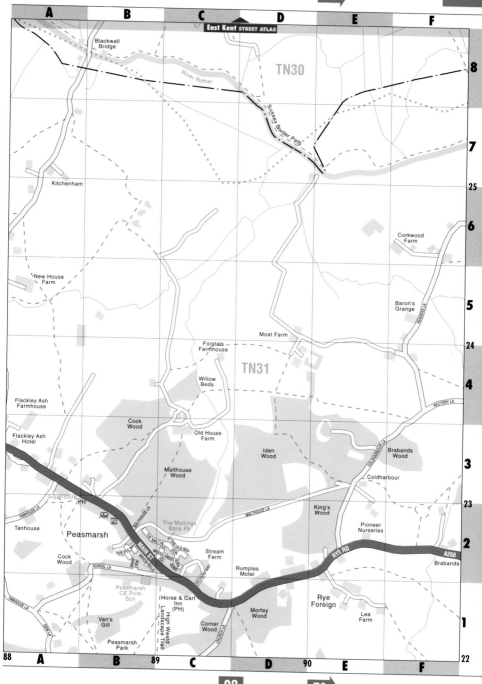

East Kent STREET ATLAS

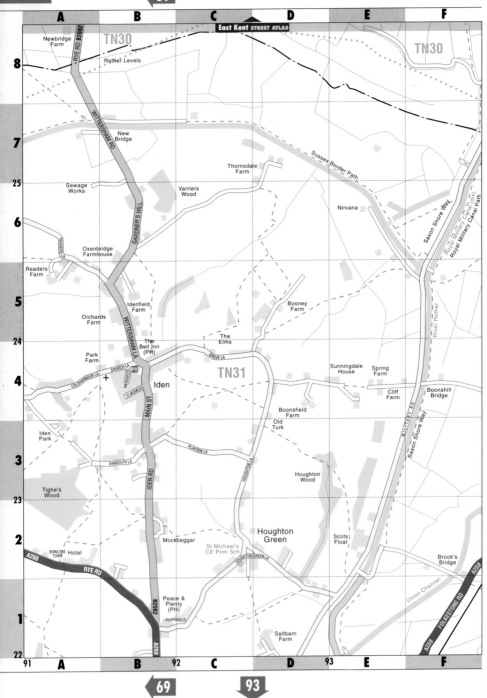

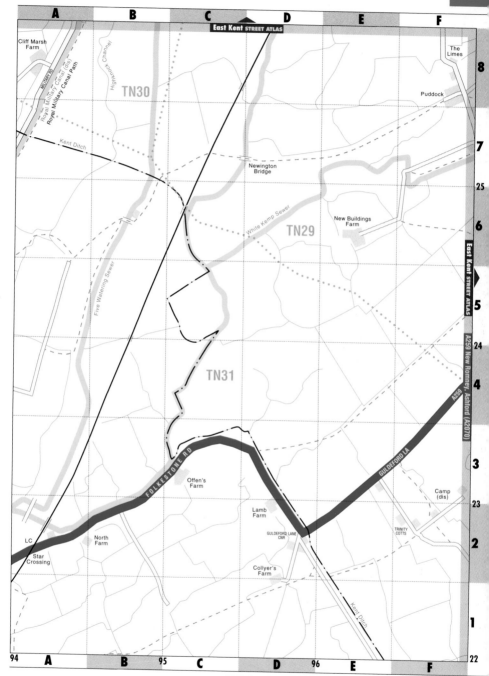

TN30

Cliff Marsh Farm

The Limes

Puddock

Highknock Channel

Royal Military Canal (dis)
Royal Military Canal Path
MILITARY RD

Kent Ditch

Newington Bridge

White Kemp Sewer

TN29

New Buildings Farm

Five Watering Sewer

TN31

A259

GULDEFORD LA

FOLKESTONE RD

Offen's Farm

Lamb Farm

Camp (dis)

GULDEFORD LANE CNR

TRINITY COTTS

North Farm

LC

Star Crossing

Collyer's Farm

Kent Ditch

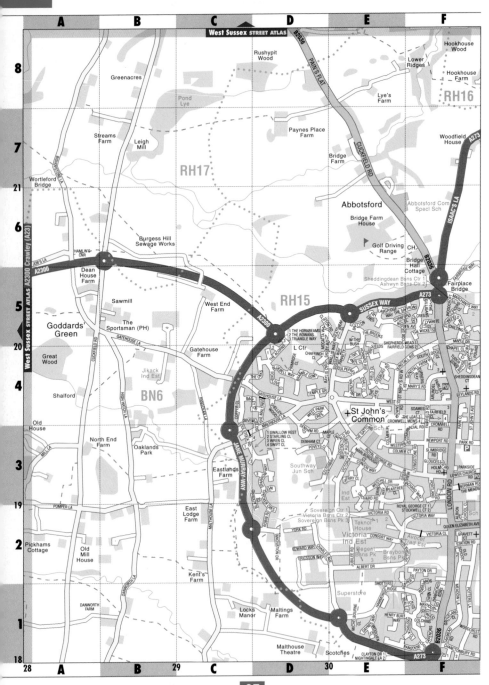

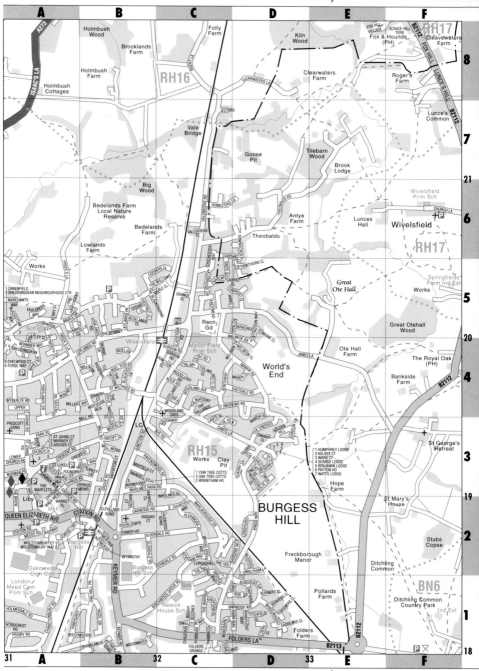

73
51

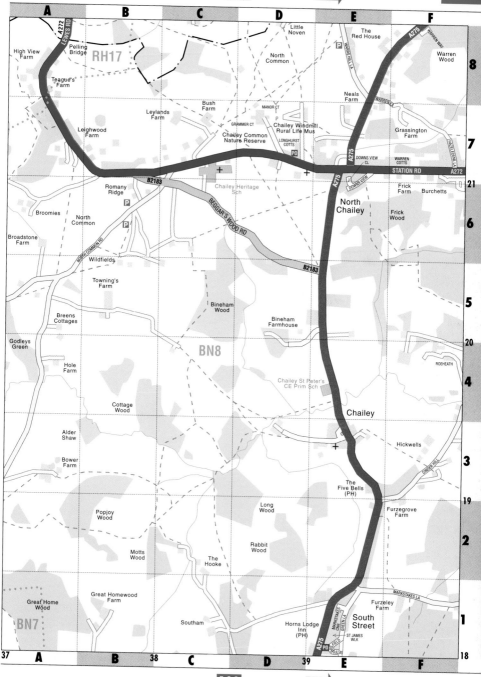

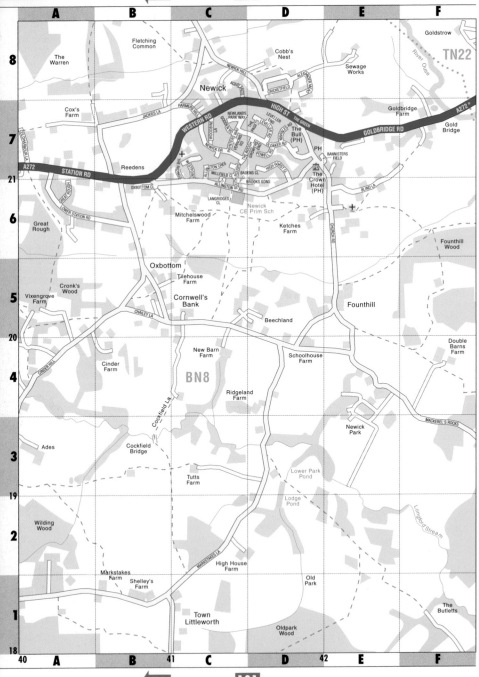

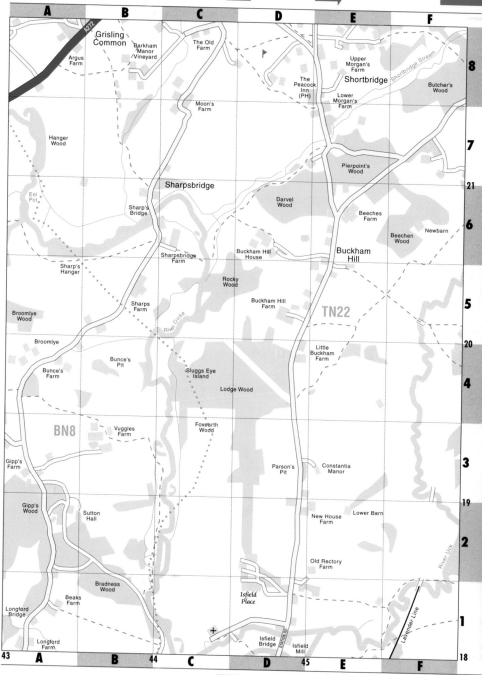

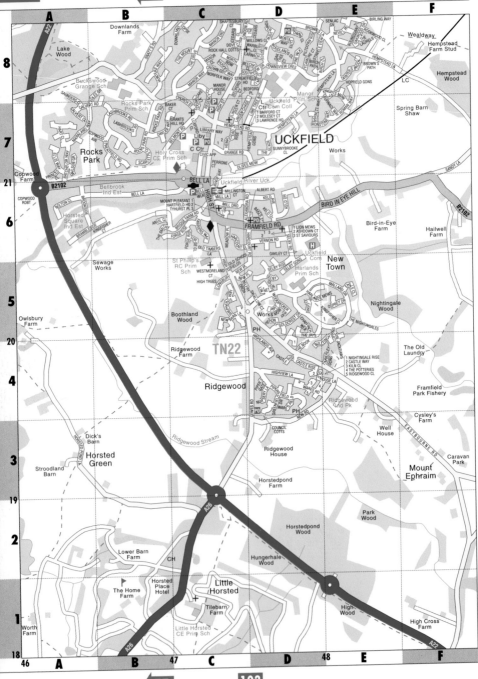

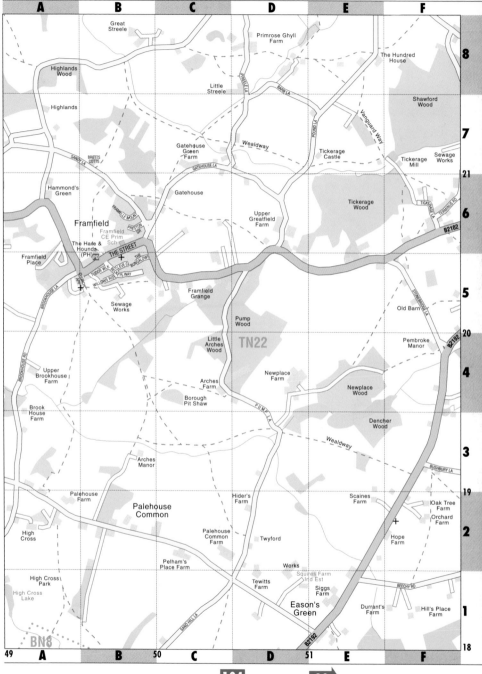

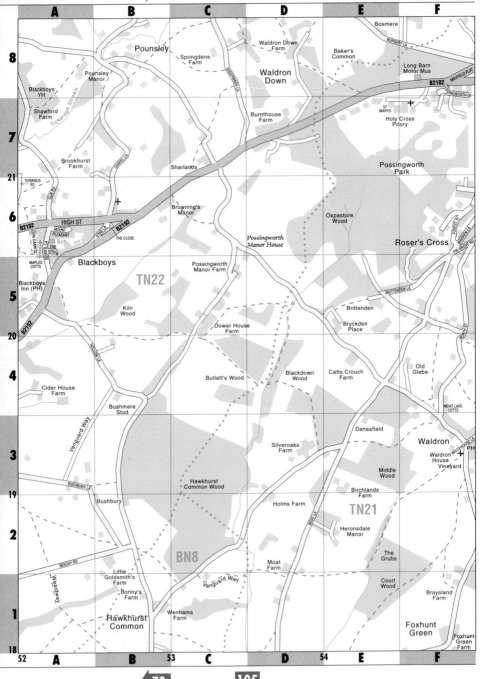

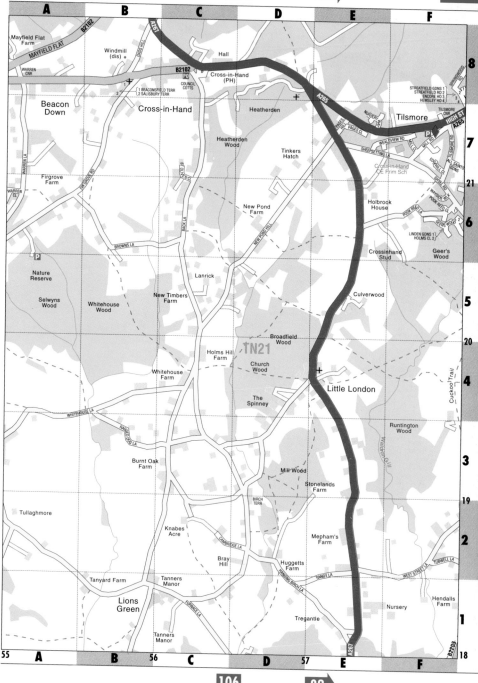

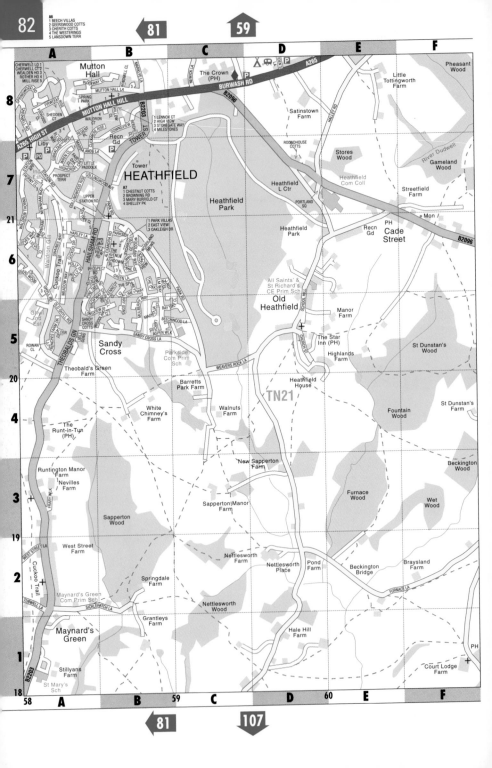

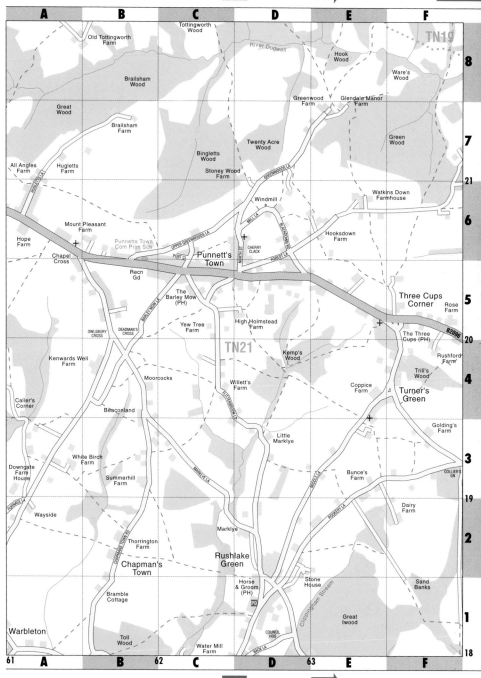

TN19

A · B · C · D · E · F

Old Tottingworth Farm

Tottingworth Wood

River Dudwell

Hook Wood

Ware's Wood

Brailsham Wood

Greenwood Farm

Glendale Manor Farm

Great Wood

Green Wood

Brailsham Farm

Twenty Acre Wood

Bingletts Wood

All Angles Farm

Hugletts Farm

Stoney Wood Farm

Greenwoods La

21

Windmill

Watkins Down Farmhouse

Mount Pleasant Farm

Upper Greenwoods La

Mill La

B'Jondown Rd

Hooksdown Farm

Hope Farm

Punnetts Town Com Prim Sch

Cherry Clack

Chapel Cross

Pont Cl

Punnett's Town

Forest La

Three Cups Corner

Rose Farm

Recn Gd

The Barley Mow (PH)

High Holmstead Farm

The Three Cups (PH)

B2096

20

Owlsbury Cross

Deadman's Cross

Yew Tree Farm

TN21

Kemp's Wood

Rushford Farm

Kenwards Well Farm

Moorcocks

Willett's Farm

Coppice Farm

Trill's Wood

Turner's Green

Caller's Corner

Beaconland

Little Marklye

Golding's Farm

Downgate Farm House

White Birch Farm

Marklye La

Bunce's Farm

Collier's Gn

19

Summerhill Farm

Rocrett La

Wood La

Dairy Farm

Wayside

Furnace La

Chapmans Town Rd

Thorrington Farm

Marklye

Chapman's Town

Rushlake Green

Stone House

Sand Banks

Bramble Cottage

Horse & Groom (PH)

Clippingham Stream

Great Iwood

Warbleton

Toll Wood

Water Mill Farm

Council Hos

Back La

18

61 · A · B · 62 · C · D · 63 · E · F

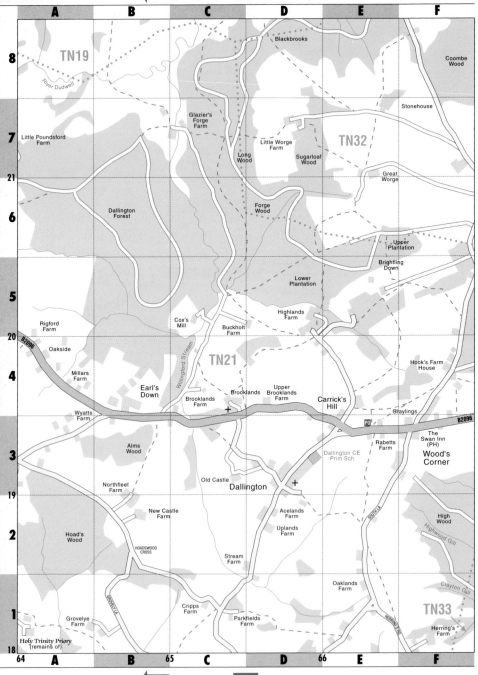

8 TN19

River Dudwell

Blackbrooks

Coombe
Wood

Stonehouse

7 Little Poundsford
Farm

Glazier's
Forge
Farm

Little Worge
Farm

TN32

21

Long
Wood

Sugarloaf
Wood

Great
Worge

6 Dallington
Forest

Forge
Wood

Upper
Plantation

Brightling
Down

Lower
Plantation

5

Highlands
Farm

Rigford
Farm

Cox's
Mill

Buckholt
Farm

Hook's Farm
House

20 B2096

Oakside

Willingford Stream

TN21

4 Millars
Farm

Earl's
Down

Brooklands

Upper
Brooklands
Farm

Carrick's
Hill

Graylings

B2096

Brooklands
Farm

Wyatts
Farm

PO

The
Swan Inn
(PH)

Rabetts
Farm

Wood's
Corner

3 Alms
Wood

Dallington CE
Prim Sch

19 Northfleet
Farm

Old Castle

Dallington

High
Wood

Highwood Gill

New Castle
Farm

Acelands
Farm

2 Hoad's
Wood

HOADSWOOD
CROSS

Uplands
Farm

Stream
Farm

Oaklands
Farm

Clayton Gill

TN33

1 Grovelye
Farm

Cripps
Farm

Parkfields
Farm

Herring's
Farm

Holy Trinity Priory
(remains of)

18

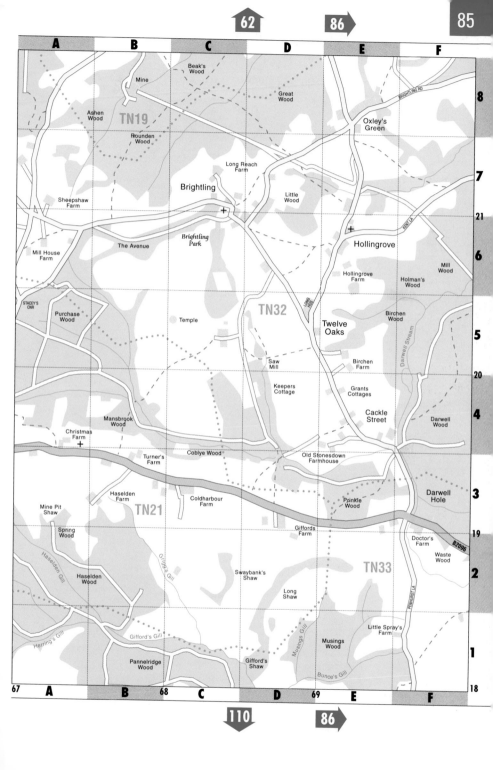

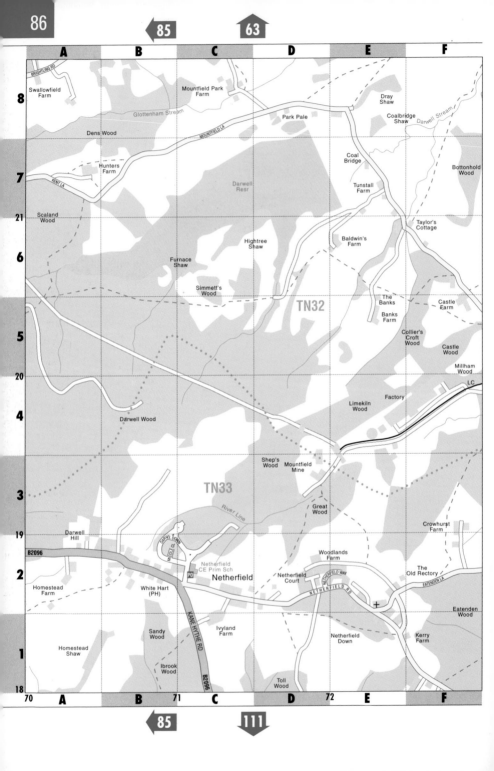

85
63

A B C D E F

8 Swallowfield Farm
Mountfield Park Farm
Dray Shaw
Coalbridge Shaw
Darwell Stream

BRIGHTLING RD
Glottenham Stream
Park Pale
Dens Wood
MOUNTFIELD LA

7 Hunters Farm
Coal Bridge
Bottonhold Wood
KENT LA
Tunstall Farm
Darwell Resr

21 Scaland Wood
Taylor's Cottage

6 Hightree Shaw
Baldwin's Farm
Furnace Shaw
Simmett's Wood
TN32
The Banks
Banks Farm
Castle Farm
Collier's Croft Wood

5 Castle Wood
Millam Wood

20 LC
Limekiln Wood
Factory
4 Darwell Wood
Shep's Wood
Mountfield Mine

3 TN33
Great Wood
River Line
Crowhurst Farm

19 Darwell Hill
Woodlands Farm
B2096
CARWELL DOWN
Netherfield CE Prim Sch
Netherfield Court
The Old Rectory
EATENDEN LA
2 Homestead Farm
White Hart (PH)
Netherfield
NETHERFIELD WAY
NETHERFIELD RD
Eatenden Wood
KANE HYTHE RD
Sandy Wood
Ivyland Farm
Kerry Farm
1 Homestead Shaw
Netherfield Down
Ibrook Wood
B2096
Toll Wood

18
70 A 71 B C 72 D E F

85
111

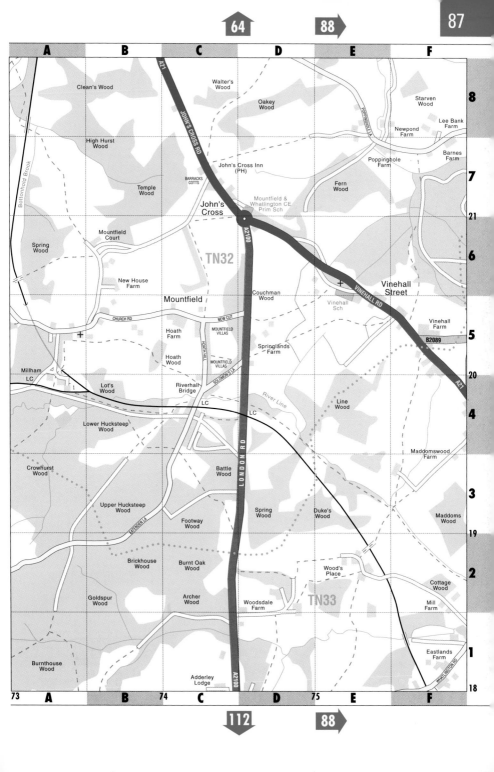

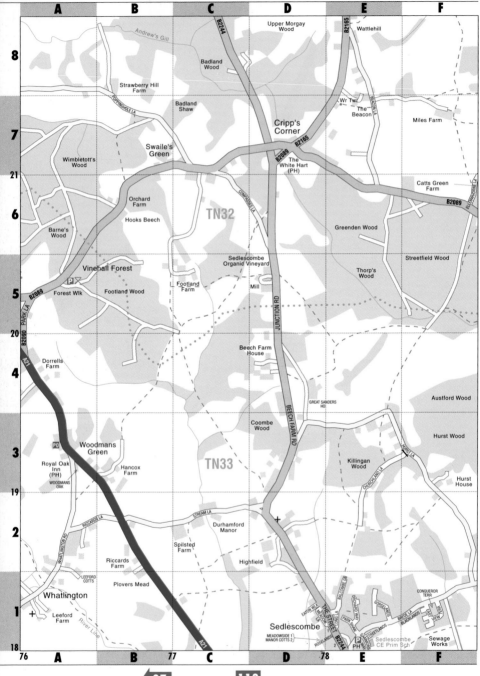

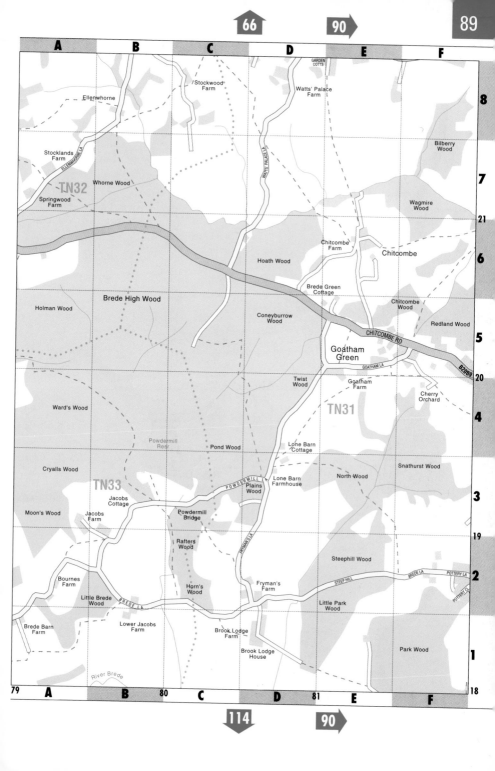

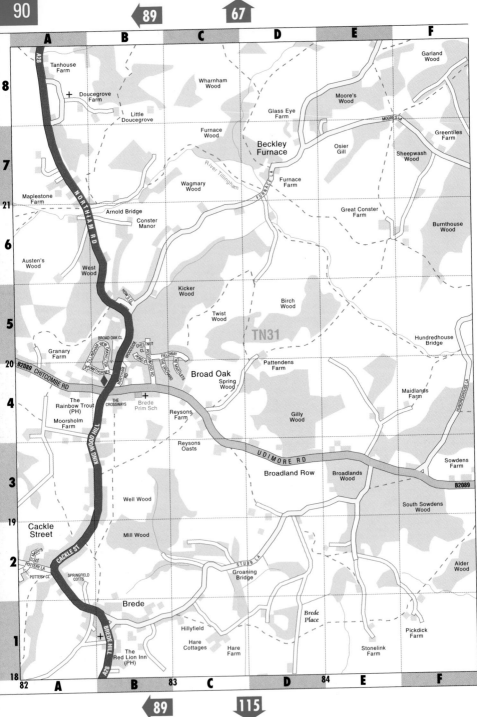

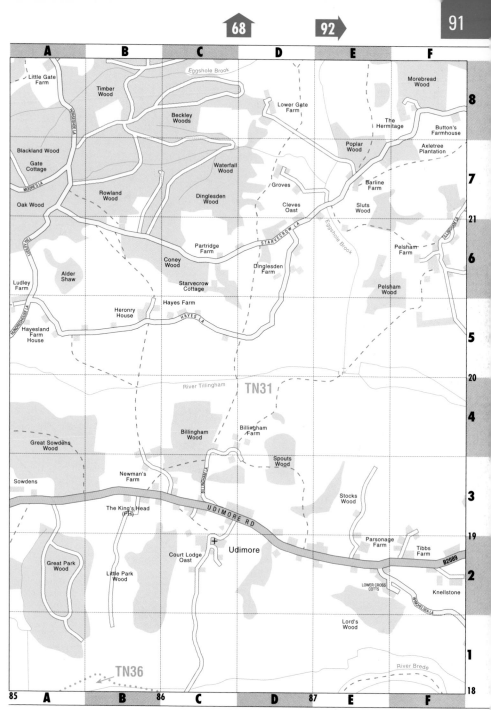

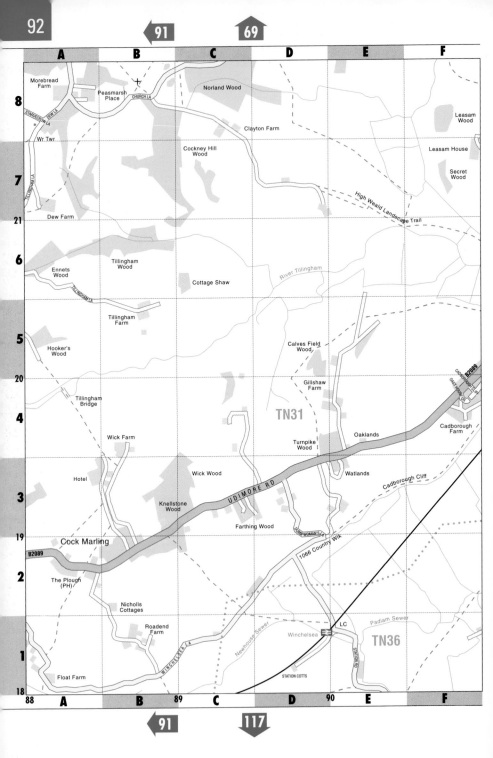

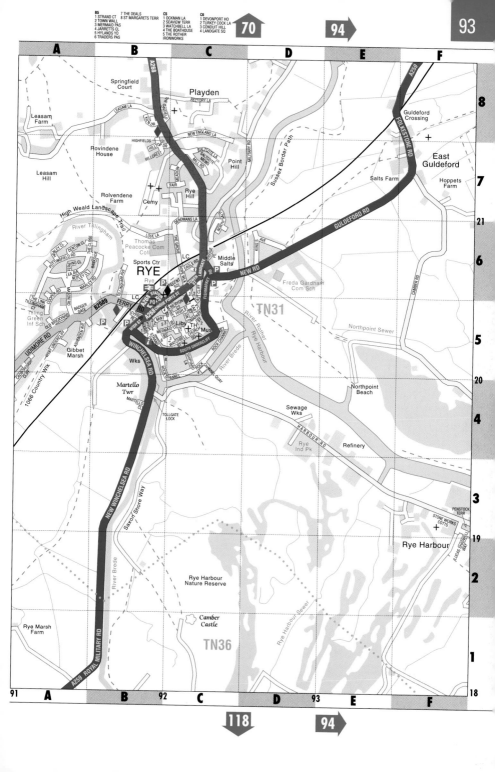

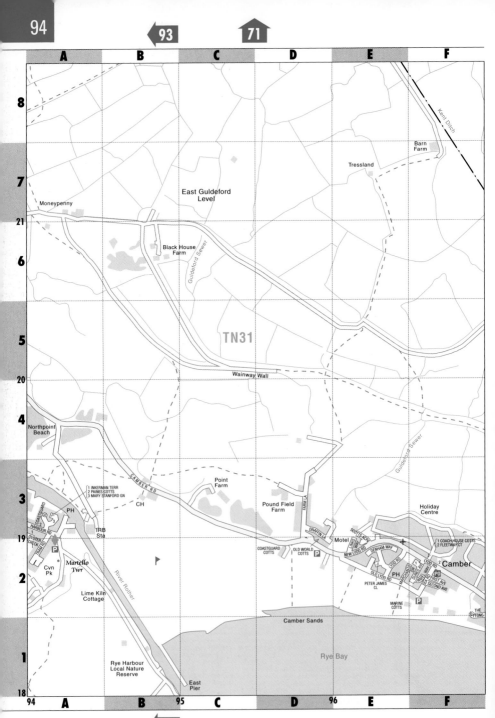

A　B　C　D　E　F

8

7

East Guldeford
Level

Barn
Farm

Tressland

Moneypenny

21

Black House
Farm

Guldeford Sewer

6

TN31

5

20

Wainway Wall

Guldeford Sewer

4

Northpoint
Beach

CAMBER RD

Point
Farm

Pound Field
Farm

FARM LA

Holiday
Centre

3

1 INKERMAN TERR
2 PAINES COTTS
3 MARY STANFORD GN

CH

DRAFFIN LA

Motel

1 COACH HOUSE COTTS
2 FLEETWAY CT

COASTGUARD
COTTS

PH

IRB
Sta

19

OYSTER
CREEK RD

MARY RD

HARBOUR RD

COASTGUARD
COTTS

P

COASTGUARD
COTTS

OLD WORLD
COTTS

P

SCOTTS ACRE

NEW LYDD RD

SENHAM WAY

LYDD RD

Camber

PO

P

Cvn
Pk

Martello
Twr

River Rother

OLD LYDD RD

PH

FIRST AVE

SECOND AVE

P

THE
SUTTONS

2

PETER JAMES
CL

MARINE
COTTS

Lime Kiln
Cottage

1

Rye Harbour
Local Nature
Reserve

Camber Sands

Rye Bay

East
Pier

18

94　A　B　95　C　D　96　E　F

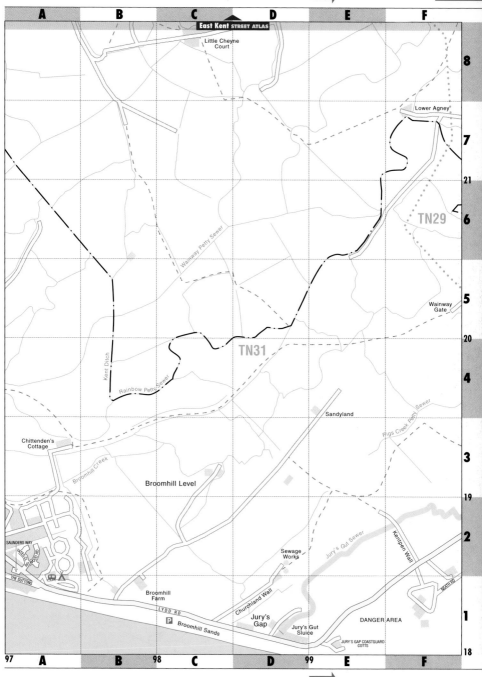

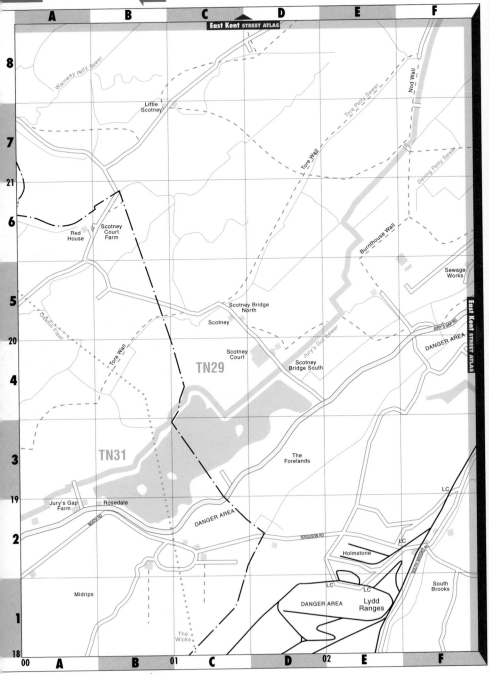

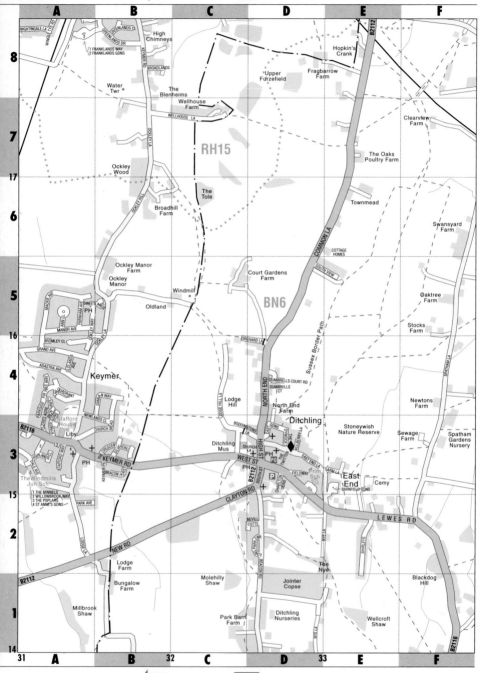

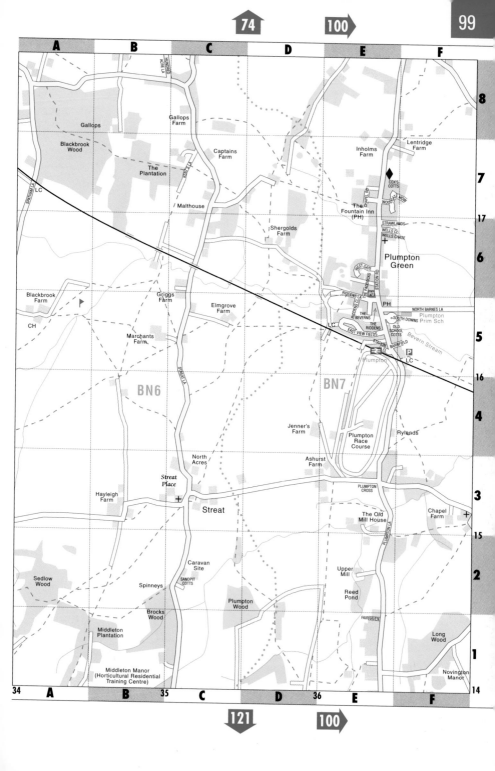

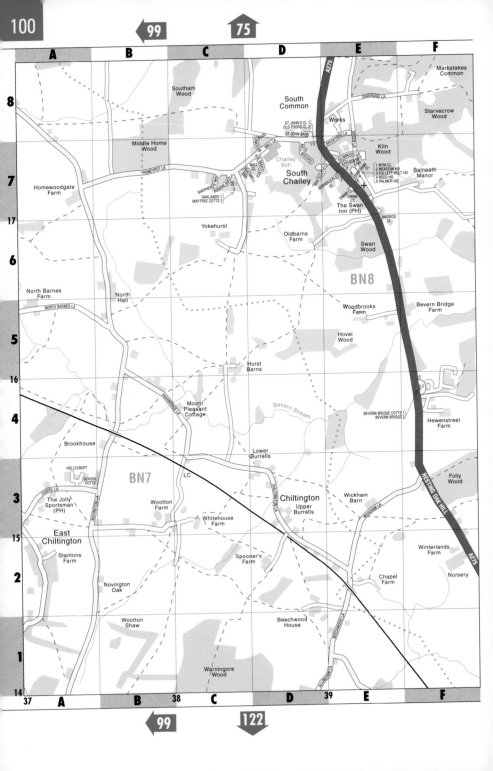

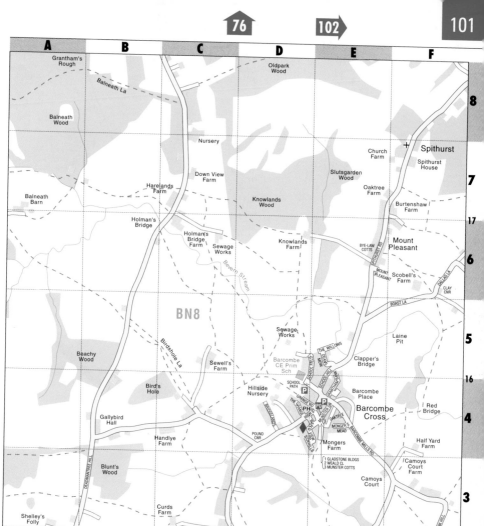

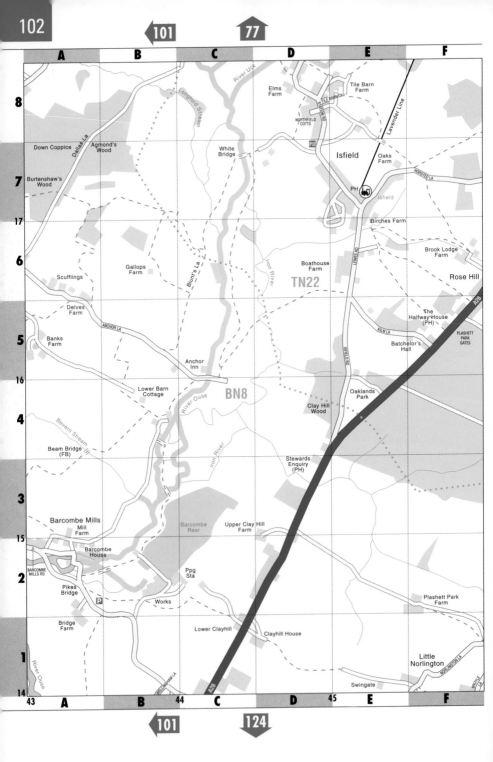

101

77

A B C D E F

8

River Uck

Elms Farm

Tile Barn Farm

NORTHFIELD COTTS

PO

Isfield

Oaks Farm

HORSTED LA

Down Coppice

Agmond's Wood

White Bridge

Dallas La

7

Burtenshaw's Wood

PH

Isfield

Birches Farm

17

Brook Lodge Farm

Rose Hill

6

Scufflings

Gallops Farm

Blunt's La

Iron River

Boathouse Farm

TN22

LEWES RD

Longford Stream

Delves Farm

ANCHOR LA

KILN LA

The Halfway House (PH)

PLASHETT PARK GATES

5

Banks Farm

Batchelor's Hall

M26

16

Lower Barn Cottage

Anchor Inn

River Ouse

BN8

ISFIELD RD

Oaklands Park

4

Bevern Stream

Clay Hill Wood

Beam Bridge (FB)

Iron River

Stewards Enquiry (PH)

3

Barcombe Mills

Barcombe Resr

Upper Clay Hill Farm

15

Mill Farm

Barcombe House

BARCOMBE MILLS RD

2

Pikes Bridge

Ppg Sta

Plashett Park Farm

P

Works

Little Norlington

1

Bridge Farm

Lower Clayhill

Clayhill House

NORLINGTON LA

BRICKLE LA

River Ouse

M26

Swingate

14

43 A 44 B C 45 D E F

101

124

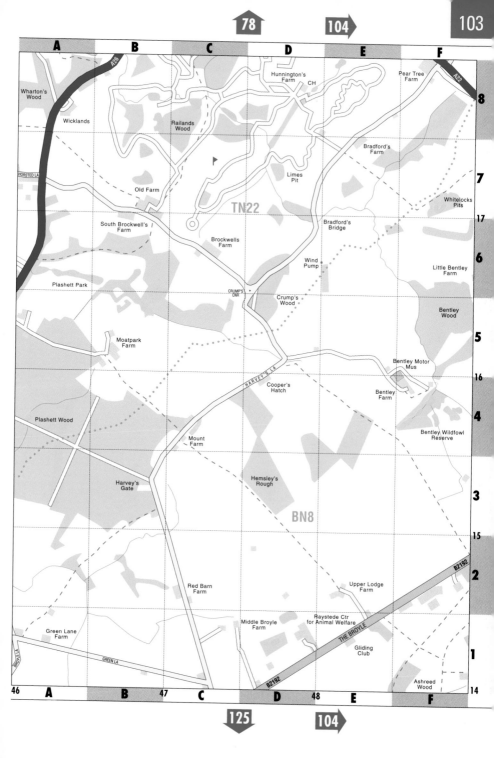

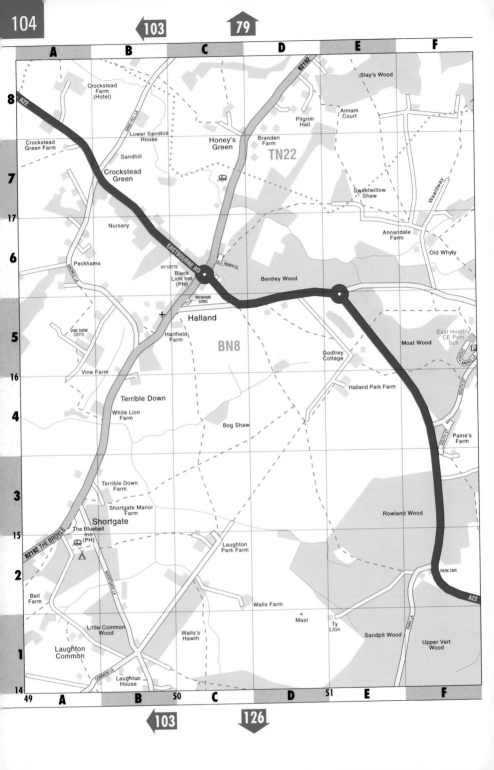

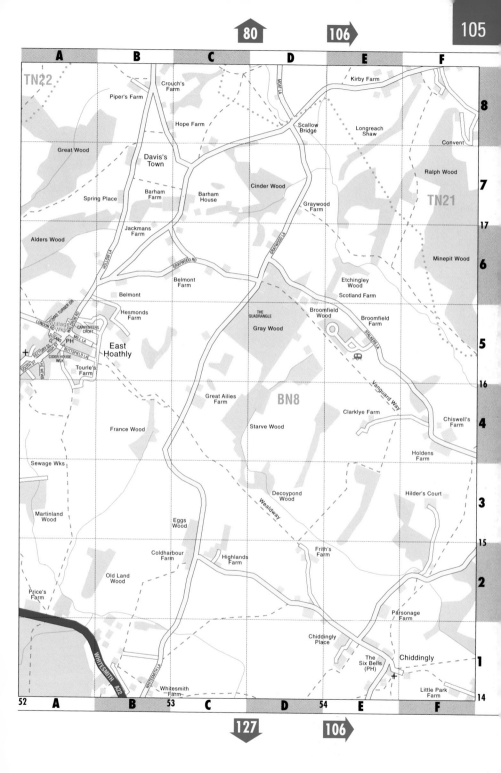

105
81

A **B** **C** **D** **E** **F**

8

Dernlea Farm
Roughland Wood
FURNACE LA
Bridge Farm
Stream Farm
Cuckoo Trail
SHARP'S CNR
LITTLE LONDON RD
A267
B2203
HIGH ST

Visitation Convent
Hook's Farm
Horam
Home Farm
MEADOW RISE 1
HIGHFIELD RD 2
THE RISE 3
Sussex Farm Mus & Nature Trails
MANOR RD
B2203
P

7

Summersbrook Farm
Coneyburrow Wood
Factory
BEAUFORD RD
WOOD RD
HORAM

Summersbrook Wood
DERN LA
Copford Farm

17

TN21

Coxlow House

6

Clearhedge Wood
Coxlow Farm

Longshaw Farm
Great Dern Wood
May Garland (PH)

MYPE VILLAS

CH
Oakhurst Farm

5

Coneyburrow Wood
East Knowle Wood
KINGSTON VILLAS
Burlow

Little Easterfields Farm
Horeham Flat Farm

16

Stream Farm
East Knowle
Cinderghyll

4

Forge Wood
Stonehill Farm
Highlands Farm

STONEHILL
Stone Hill
Gamelands Farm

PICK HILL
Pick Hill
Rose Bank Farm
COGGER'S LA
A267

SAPPLANDS LA
Stream Mill
Mill Wood
Charity Farm
COGGER'S CROSS
NORTH ST

3

BN8
Beard's Farm
Swansbrook Wood

15

Smithlands Wood
GUN HILL
Gunhill Wood
Swansbrook Farm
BN27

Bull Bridge
Strood Farm
SWANSBROOK LA

2

HALE GN
Hale Farm
Pickly Wood
Wellshurst
CH

Hale Green
Gatehouse Wood
Gatehouse Farm
Gun Hill (PH)
North Street Wood

Gun Hill

1

Wealdway
West Street Farm

14

Carter's Farm
Rock Harbour Farm

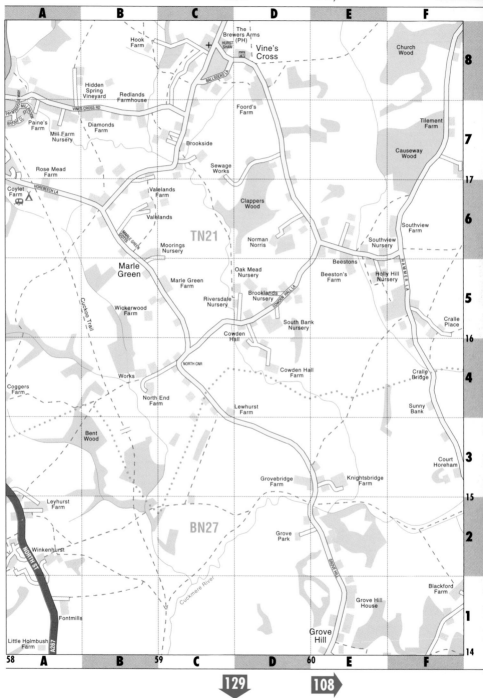

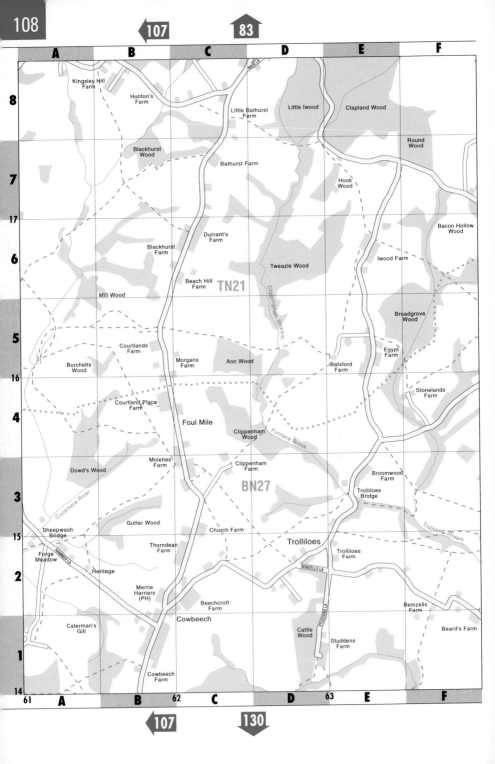

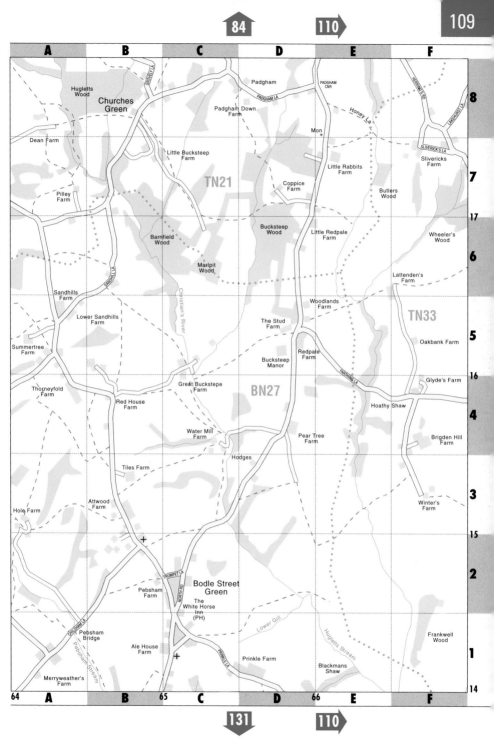

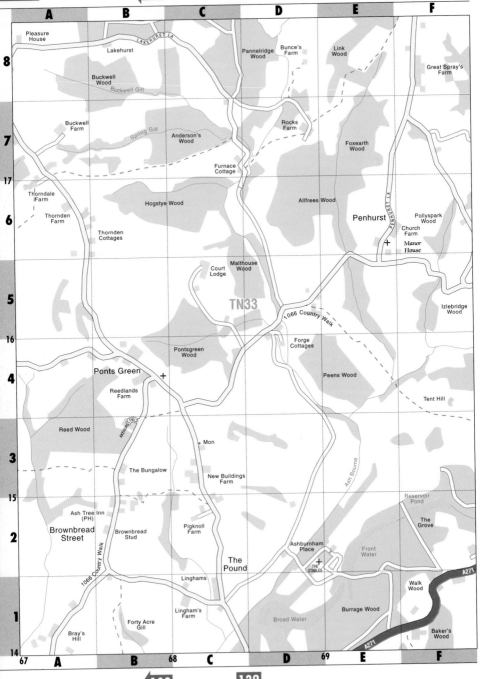

109
85

A   B   C   D   E   F

8
Pleasure House
Lakehurst
LAKEHURST LA
Buckwell Wood
Buckwell Gill
Pannelridge Wood
Bunce's Farm
Link Wood
Great Spray's Farm

7
Buckwell Farm
Spring Gill
Anderson's Wood
Rocks Farm
Foxearth Wood

17
Furnace Cottage

Thorndale Farm
Thorden Farm
Hogstye Wood
Allfrees Wood
Penhurst
Pollyspark Wood

6
Thorden Cottages
Church Farm
Manor House

5
Court Lodge
Malthouse Wood
TN33
1066 Country Walk
Izlebridge Wood

16
Pontsgreen Wood
Forge Cottages

4
Ponts Green
Reedlands Farm
Peens Wood
Tent Hill

Reed Wood
MORRIS LANE FIELD
Mon

3
The Bungalow
New Buildings Farm
Ash Bourne

15
Ash Tree Inn (PH)
Reservoir Pond
The Grove

2
Brownbread Street
Brownbread Stud
Pigknoll Farm
Ashburnham Place
THE STABLES
Front Water
Walk Wood
A271

The Pound
Linghams

1
Lingham's Farm
Broad Water
Burrage Wood
Baker's Wood

Bray's Hill
Forty Acre Gill
1066 Country Walk
A271

14
67   A   B   68   C   D   69   E   F

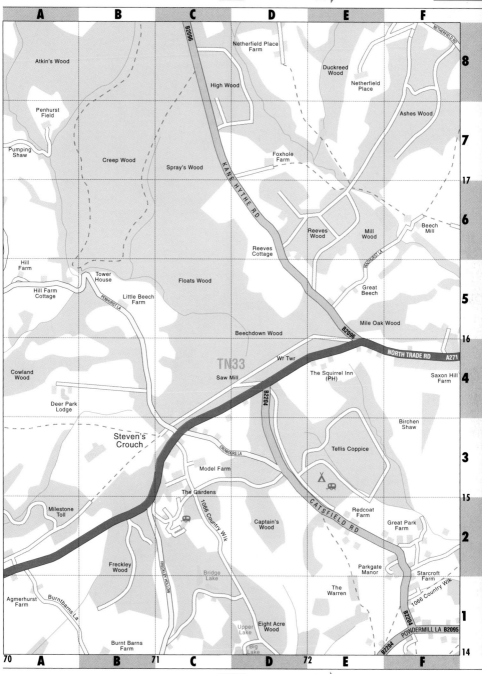

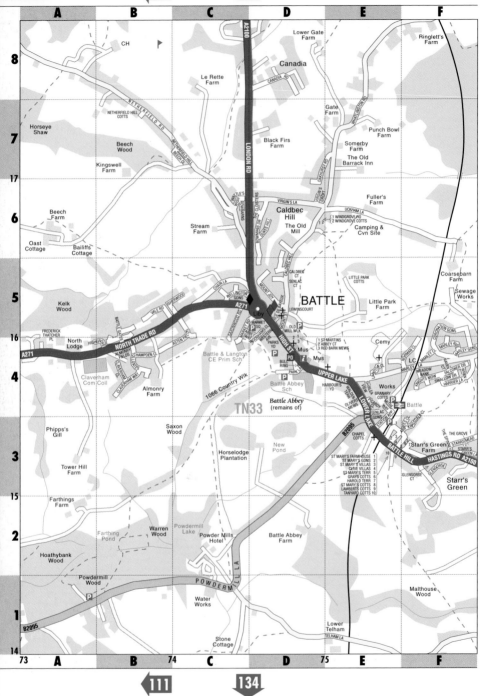

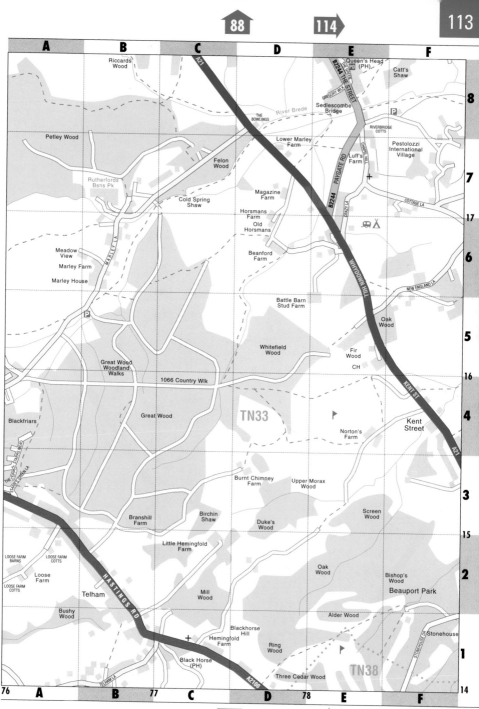

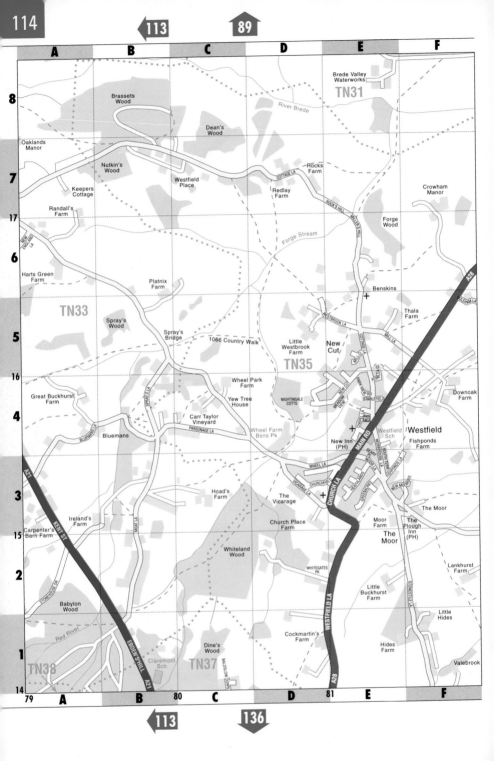

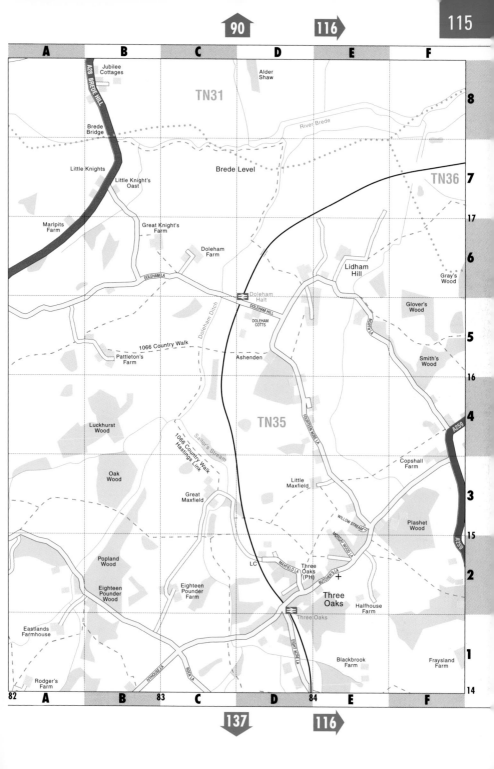

A   B   C   D   E   F

Jubilee
Cottages

A28
BREDE HILL

TN31

Alder
Shaw

8

Brede
Bridge

River Brede

Little Knights

Brede Level

7

TN36

Little Knight's
Oast

17

Marlpits
Farm

Great Knight's
Farm

Doleham
Farm

Lidham
Hill

6

Gray's
Wood

DOLEHAM LA

Doleham
Halt

Doleham
Ditch

Doleham
COTTS

DOLEHAM HILL

NORTH LA

Glover's
Wood

1066 Country Walk

Pattleton's
Farm

Ashenden

Smith's
Wood

5

16

Luckhurst
Wood

Sailor's Stream

1066 Country Walk
Hastings Link

TN35

FOURTEEN ACRE LA

Copshall
Farm

A259

4

Oak
Wood

Great
Maxfield

Little
Maxfield

Plashet
Wood

A259

3

15

Popland
Wood

LC

MAXFIELD LA

WILLOW STREAM LA

MARSH WOOD LA

Three
Oaks
(PH)

BUTCHER'S LA

2

Eighteen
Pounder
Wood

Eighteen
Pounder
Farm

Three
Oaks

Halfhouse
Farm

Eastlands
Farmhouse

Three Oaks

Blackbrook
Farm

Fraysland
Farm

1

Rodger's
Farm

IVYHOUSE LA

ROCK LA

EIGHT ACRE LA

14

82   A   B   83   C   D   84   E   F

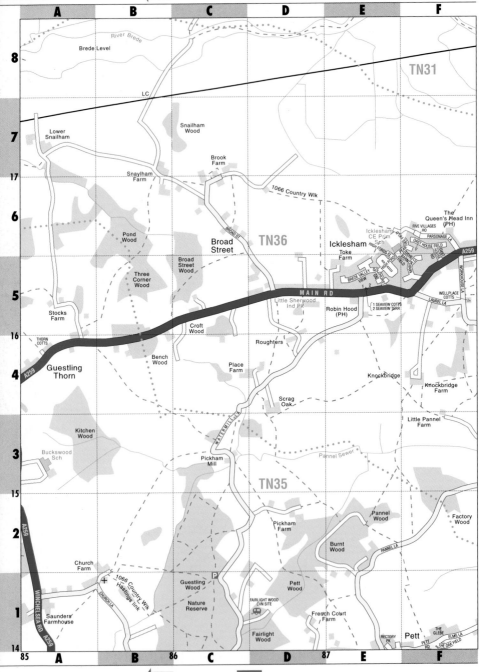

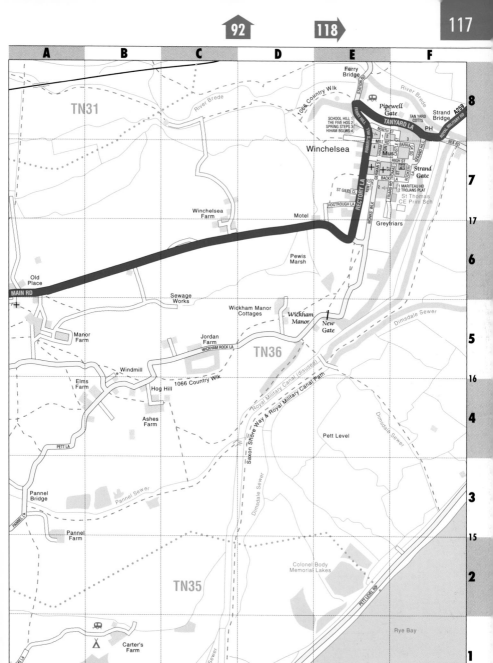

TN31

River Brede

1066 Country Wlk

Ferry
Bridge

River Brede

Pipewell
Gate

Strand
Bridge

SCHOOL HILL 1
THE FIVE HOS 2
SPRING STEPS 3
HIHAM BGLWS 4

TAN YARD
COTTS

TANYARD LA

PH

Winchelsea

Mus

ST GILES CL

HOGTROUGH LA

Motel

Strand
Gate

1 MARITEAU HO
2 TROJANS PLAT

Greytriars

St Thomas
CE Prim Sch

17

Pewis
Marsh

Old
Place

MAIN RD

Sewage
Works

Wickham Manor
Cottages

Wickham
Manor

New
Gate

Dimsdale Sewer

Manor
Farm

Jordan
Farm

WICKHAM ROCK LA

TN36

Windmill

Elms
Farm

Hog Hill

1066 Country Wlk

Royal Military Canal (disused)

Saxon Shore Way & Royal Military Canal Path

Ashes
Farm

Dimsdale Sewer

PETT LA

Pett Level

Dimsdale Sewer

16

Pannel
Bridge

Pannel Sewer

Dimsdale Sewer

Pannel
Farm

PANNEL LA

15

Colonel Body
Memorial Lakes

TN35

PETT LEVEL RD

Rye Bay

Carter's
Farm

Marsham Sewer

FULL LA

Eastlands
Shaw

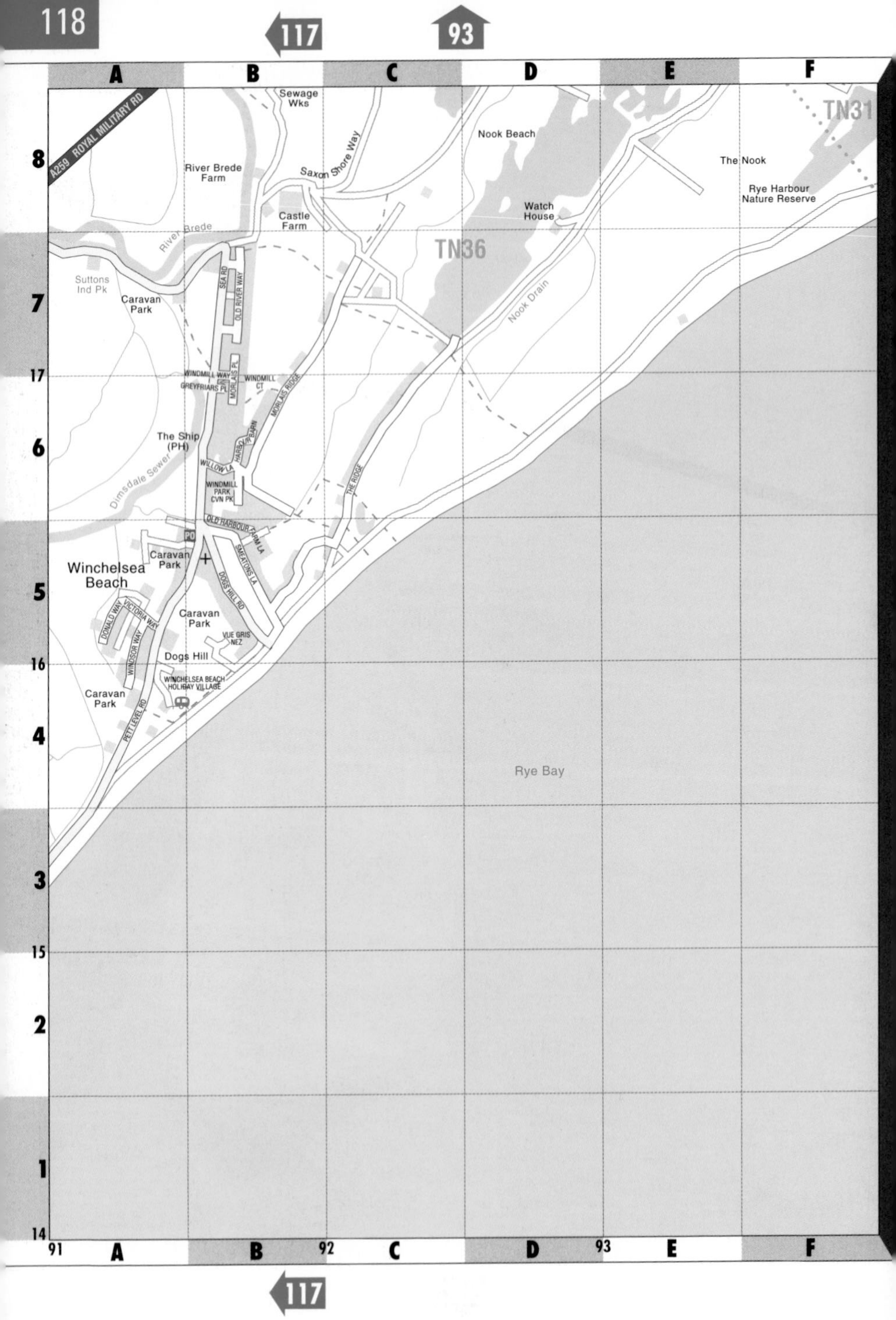

117
93

A259 ROYAL MILITARY RD

TN31

Sewage Wks

River Brede Farm

Saxon Shore Way

Nook Beach

The Nook

River Brede

Castle Farm

Watch House

Rye Harbour Nature Reserve

Suttons Ind Pk

Caravan Park

TN36

SEA RD

OLD RIVER WAY

Nook Drain

WINDMILL WAY

MARLAS PL

WINDMILL CT

GREYFRIARS PL

MAIN ST ROAD

THE RIDGE

The Ship (PH)

Olmsdale Sewer

WILLOW LA

MARINE PL

WINDMILL PARK CVN PK

OLD HARBOUR CVN LA

Caravan Park

Winchelsea Beach

PH

SEAS WAY

NOOK DING LA

Caravan Park

DOGS HILL RD

COVAL WAY

VICTORIA WAY

VUE GRIS NEZ

WINDSOR WAY

Dogs Hill

WINCHELSEA BEACH HOLIDAY VILLAGE

PETTLESS RD

Caravan Park

Rye Bay

91 A 92 B C D 93 E F
14

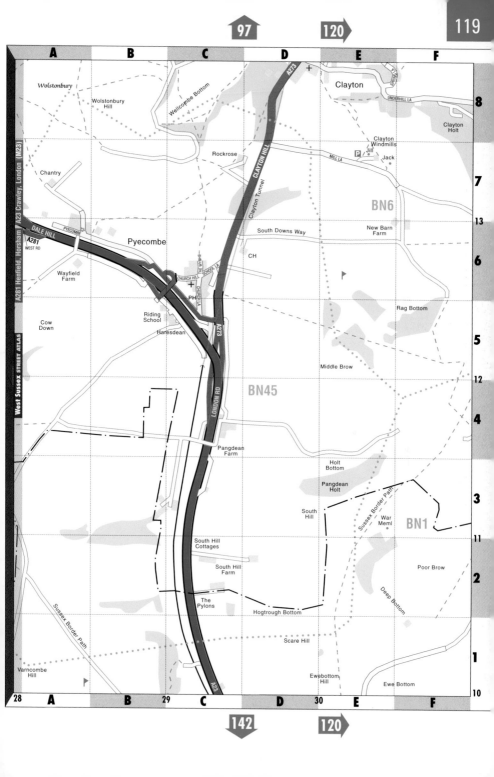

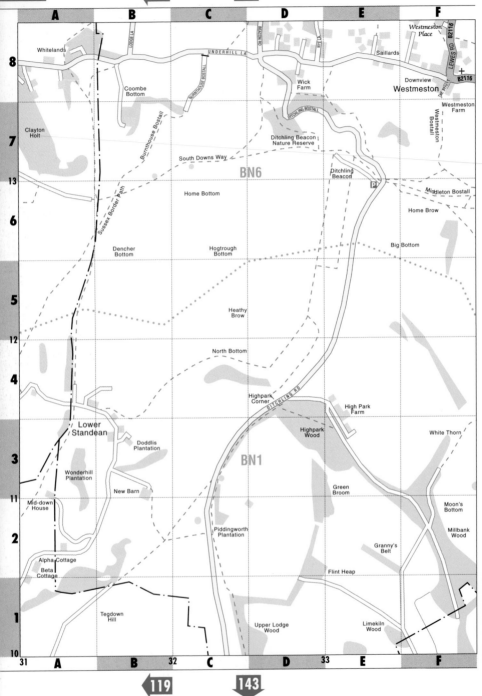

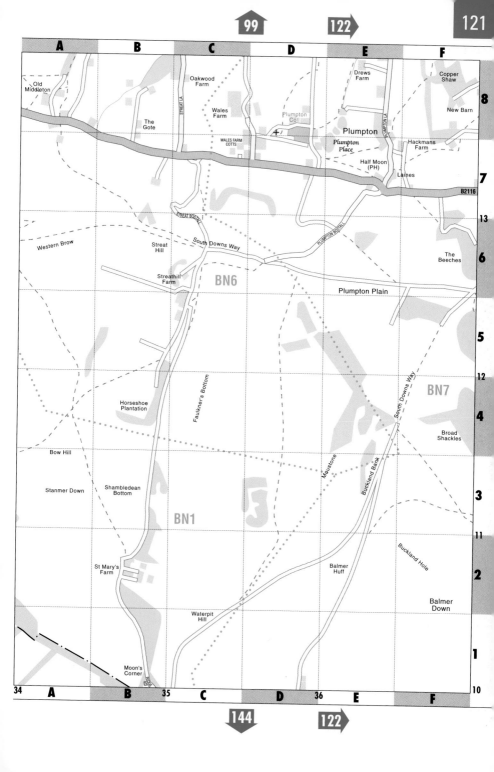

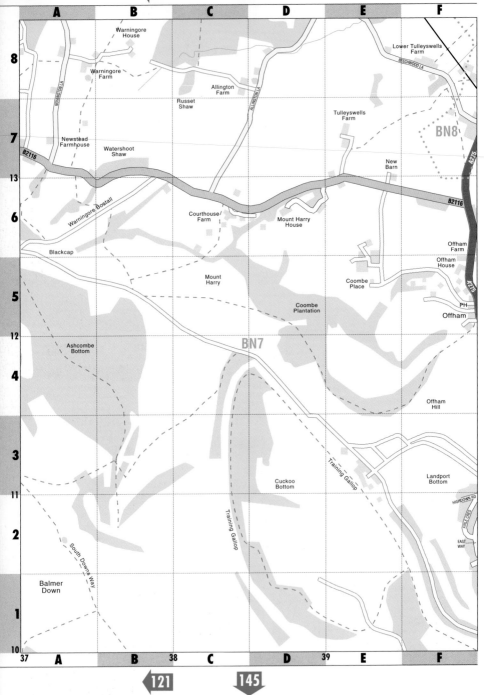

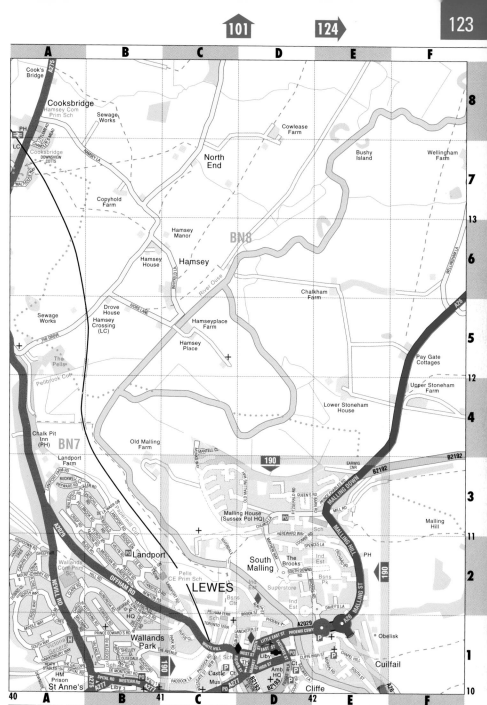

101
124

Cook's Bridge
A275
Cooksbridge
Hamsey Com Prim Sch
Sewage Works
LITTLEWOOD
PH
LC
DOWNSVIEW COTTS
HAMSEY LA
North End
Cowlease Farm
Bushy Island
Wellingham Farm
Copyhold Farm
Hamsey Manor
BN8
WHITFELD
Hamsey House
Hamsey
River Ouse
Chalkham Farm
A26
Drove House
Hamsey Crossing (LC)
IVORS LANE
Hamseyplace Farm
Sewage Works
THE DROVE
Hamsey Place
Pay Gate Cottages
Upper Stoneham Farm
The Pells
Pellbrook Cut
Lower Stoneham House
WELLINGHAM LA
Chalk Pit Inn (PH)
BN7
Old Malling Farm
MANTELL CL
EARWIG CNR
B2192
B2192
Landport Farm
Landport Farm Rd
BUCKWELL CL
HAYWARD RD
190
OLD MALLING WAY
QUEEN'S RD
FITZGERALD RD
BARN RD
PRIDE CHARLES RD
MILL RD
MALLING DOWN
Malling Hill
DE LA WARR RD
Prrmill CL
Malling House (Sussex Pol HQ)
CHURCH
HEREWARD WAY
SPENCES LA
ORCHARD
PH
MALLING HILL
Landport
South Malling
The Brooks
Ind Est
Bsns Pk
190
Wallands Com Prim Sch
OFFHAM RD
Superstore
SOUTH DOWNS
Ind Est
A26
MALLING ST
NEVILL RD
HILL RD
LEWES
RIVERDALE
Bsns Ctr
Bsns Ctr
Ind Est
DAVEY'S LA
Obelisk
A2029
PELHAM TERR
BROOK ST
PHOENIX PL
PHOENIX CSWY
Cuilfail
A26
A277
Victoria
H
PRINCE EDWARD'S RD
WHITE HILL
SCH
LANCASTER ST
LITTLE EAST ST
EAST ST
P
P
Wallands Park
THE AVENUE
190
Castle Mus
PADDOCK
WEST ST
Liby
HIGH ST
CLIFFE HIGH ST
CHAPEL HILL
P
HM Prison
St Anne's
A275
A277
A277
SPITAL RD
WESTERN RD
Liby
TH
Amb HQ
B2193
B2193
Cliffe
A277

1 NEVILL TERR
2 BARN STABLES
3 ST ANNE'S CRES
4 DE MONTFORT TERR
5 NUNNERY STABLE
6 ST ANNE'S TERR
7 IRELANDS LA

For full street detail of the highlighted area see page 190.

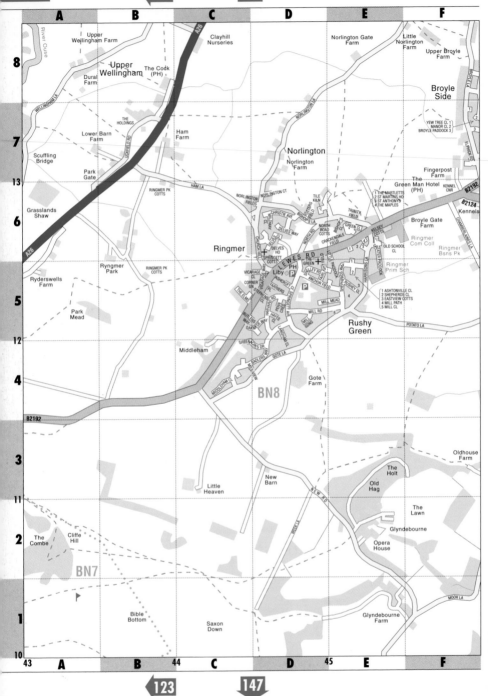

123

102

A B C D E F

8

Upper Wellingham Farm
Clayhill Nurseries
Norlington Gate Farm
Little Norlington Farm
Upper Broyle Farm

Upper Wellingham
The Cock (PH)
Broyle Side

Dural Farm

YEW TREE CL 1
MANOR CL 2
BROYLE PADDOCK 3

THE HOLDINGS

7

Lower Barn Farm
Ham Farm
Norlington

Scuffling Bridge
Park Gate
Norlington Farm

Fingerpost Farm

13

RINGMER PK COTTS
The Green Man Hotel (PH)

NORLINGTON FIELDS
NORLINGTON CT
TILE KILN
1 THE MARTLETTS
2 ST MARTINS HO
3 ST ANTHONYS
4 THE MAPLES

Grasslands Shaw
KENNEL CNR
Kennels
B2192
B2124

6

CHRISTIE AVE
NORTH ROAD COTTS
TRINITY FIELD
GREEN CL
Broyle Gate Farm

DELVES WAY
CRACKENDALE FIELD
KELSEY HEIGHTS
Ringmer Com Coll
Ringmer Bsns Pk

Ringmer
DELVES HO
SPRINGETT COTTS
Ringmer Prim Sch

Ryngmer Park
RINGMER PK COTTS
VICARAGE
LEWES RD
GREEN
Old School Cl

Ryderswells Farm
CORNER MEAD
THE CI MI
ASHCROFT
ASHMERS
VALLEY RD
ANCHOR FIELD

5

Park Mead
SHEPHERDS WAY
OAKMEAD
SPRINGETT AVE
MILL MEAD
MILL RD
1 ASHTONVILLE CL
2 SHEPHERDS CL
3 EASTVIEW COTTS
4 MILL PATH
5 MILL CL

12

Middleham
GREEN ACRES DR
SALT FIELD
GOTE LA
Rushy Green
POTATO LA

4

MIDDLEHAM
MILL DROVE
Gote Farm

B2192
BN8

3

Oldhouse Farm

Little Heaven
New Barn
NEW RD
The Holt
Old Hag

11

The Lawn

2

The Combe
Cliffe Hill
Glyndebourne

BN7
Opera House

1

Bible Bottom
Saxon Down
Glyndebourne Farm
MOOR LA

10

43 A B 44 C D 45 E F

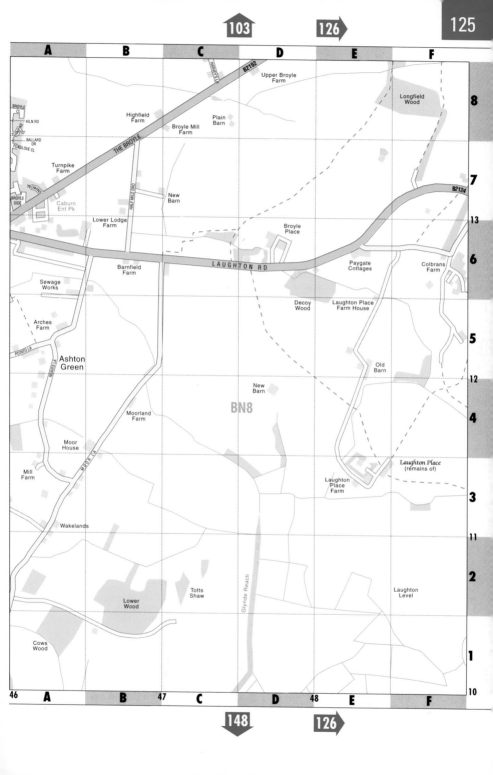

A B C D E F

8

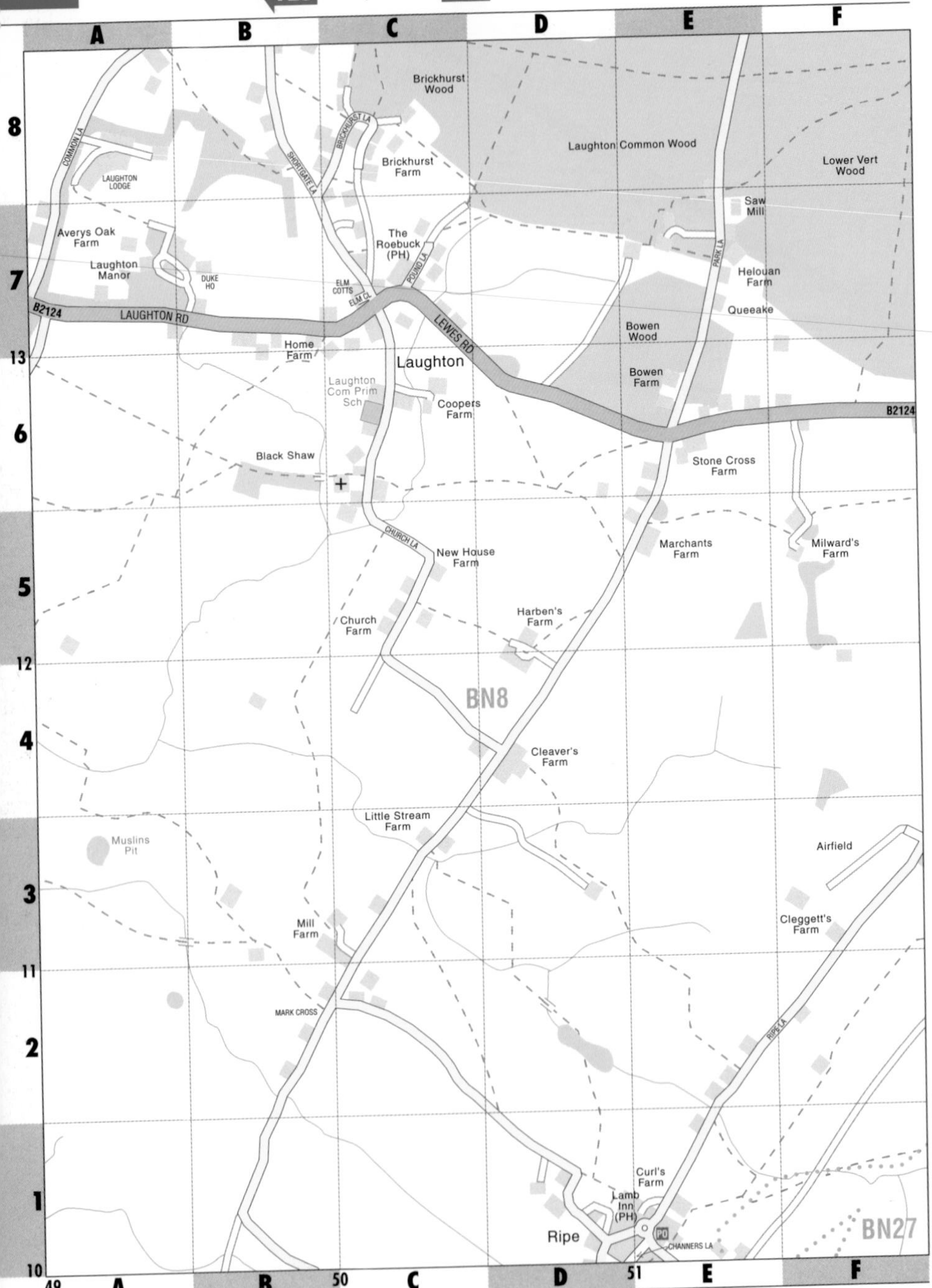

Brickhurst
Wood

Laughton Common Wood

Lower Vert
Wood

BRICKHURST LA

SOUTHDOWN LA

Brickhurst
Farm

Saw
Mill

7

COMMON LA

Laughton
Lodge

Averys Oak
Farm

Laughton
Manor

DUKE
HO

The
Roebuck
(PH)

ELM
COTTS

ELM LA

FARM LA

Helouan
Farm

Queeake

B2124

LAUGHTON RD

LEWES RD

Home
Farm

Laughton

Bowen
Wood

13

Laughton
Com Prim
Sch

Coopers
Farm

Bowen
Farm

B2124

6

Black Shaw

Stone Cross
Farm

CHURCH LA

New House
Farm

Marchants
Farm

Milward's
Farm

5

Church
Farm

Harben's
Farm

12

BN8

4

Cleaver's
Farm

Little Stream
Farm

Airfield

3

Muslins
Pit

Cleggett's
Farm

11

Mill
Farm

MARK CROSS

RIPE LA

2

Curl's
Farm

1

Lamb
Inn
(PH)

PO

CHANNERS LA

BN27

Ripe

10

49 A B 50 C D 51 E F

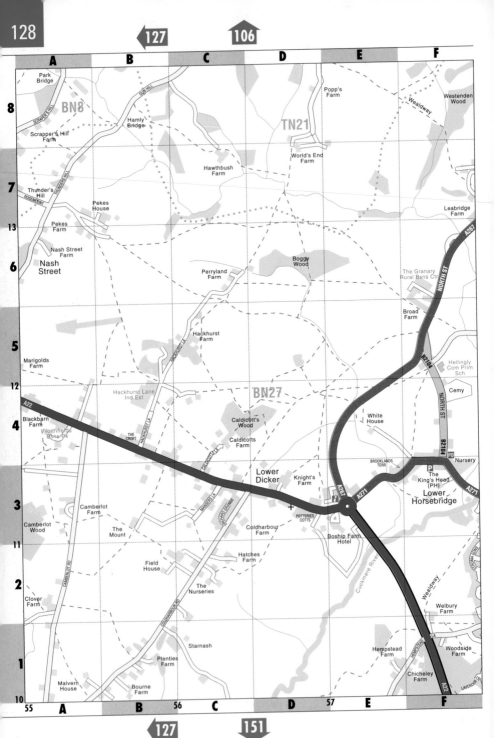

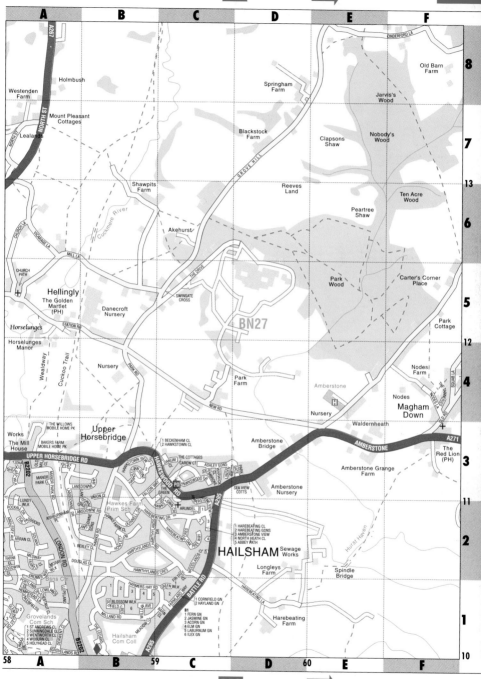

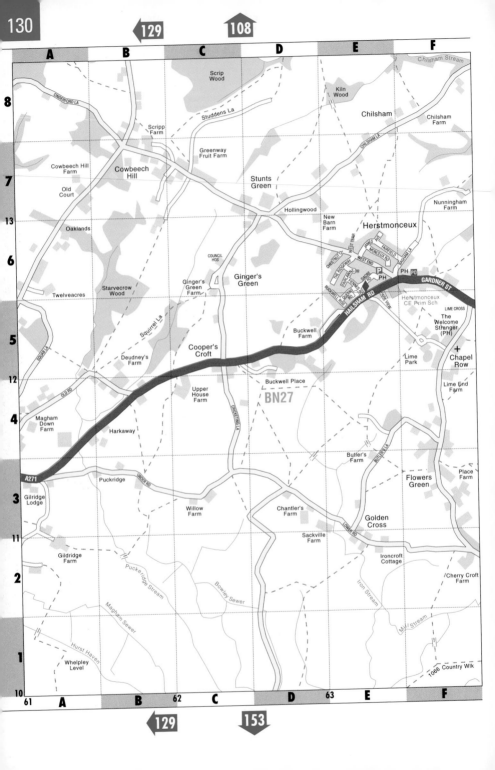

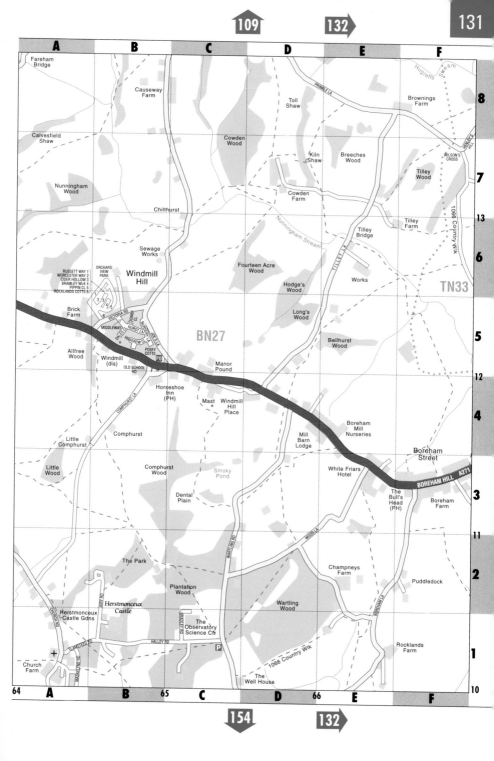

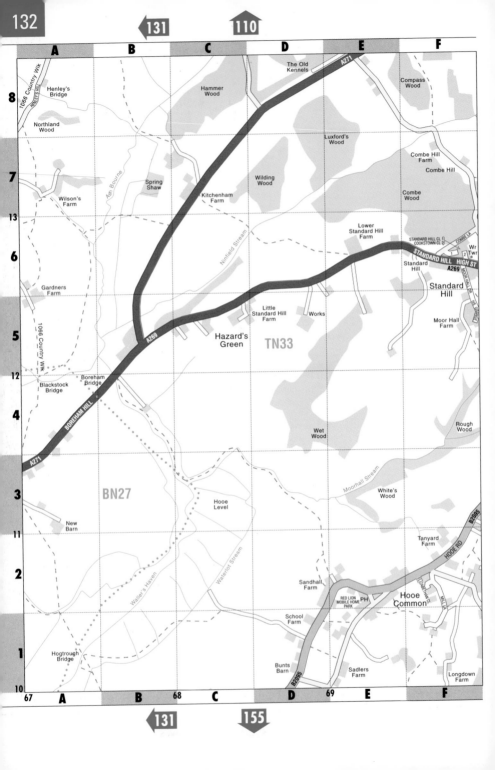

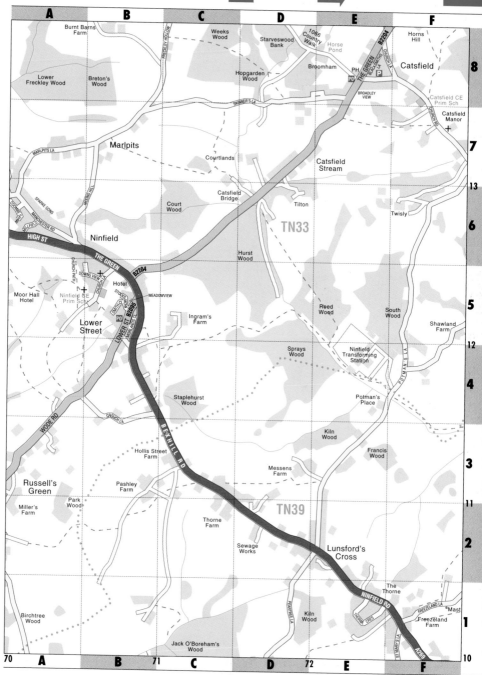

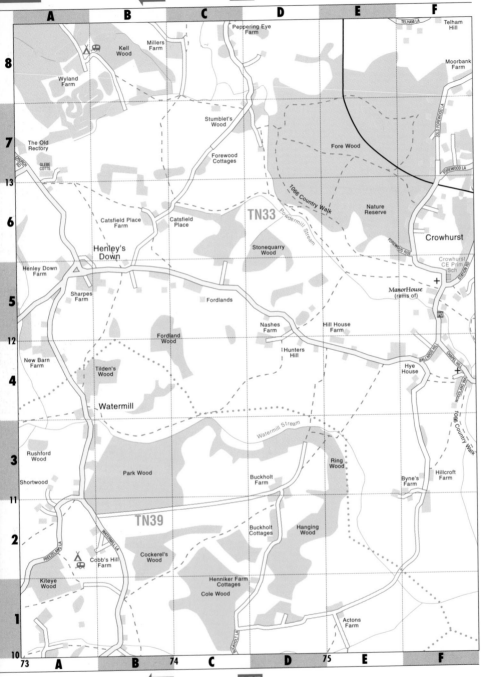

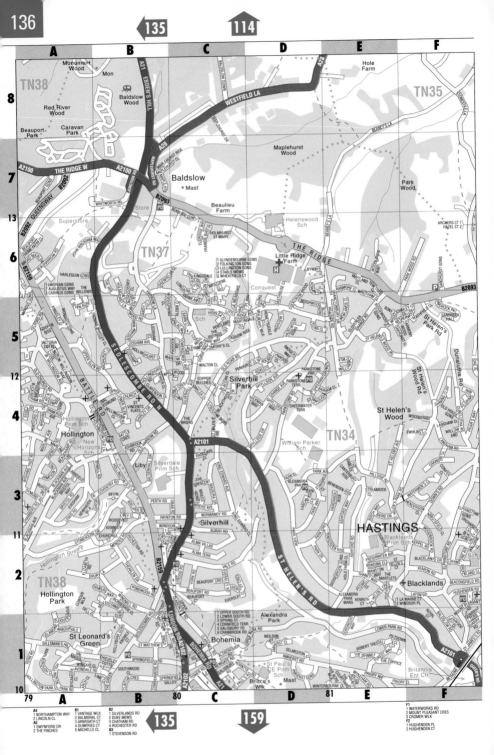

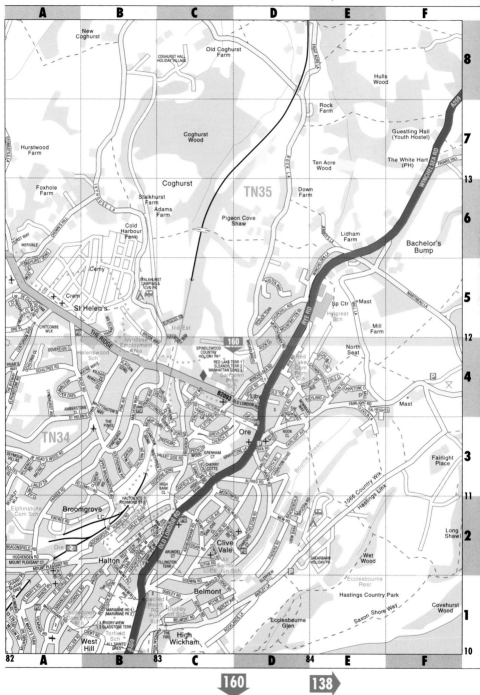

137
116

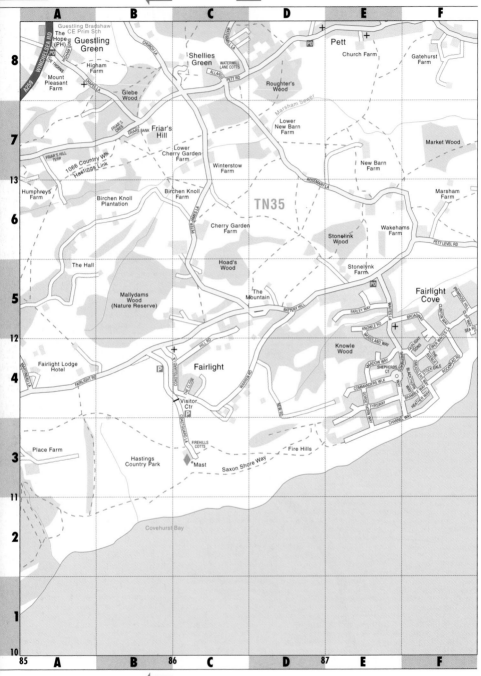

Lunsford

Pett
Level

COASTGUARDS

PETT RD

CHICK HILL

CANAL BANK

Marsham Sewer

OLD
COASTGUARDS

IRB Sta

PETT LEVEL RD

The
Smuggler
(PH)

Old
Marsham
Farm

Cvn
Pk

Cliff End

CLIFF END LA

TN35

Sewage
Wks

Stumblet
Wood

Fairlight

Saxon Shore Way

STREAM LA

BRIDGE CL

LOWER WAITES LA

SEA RD

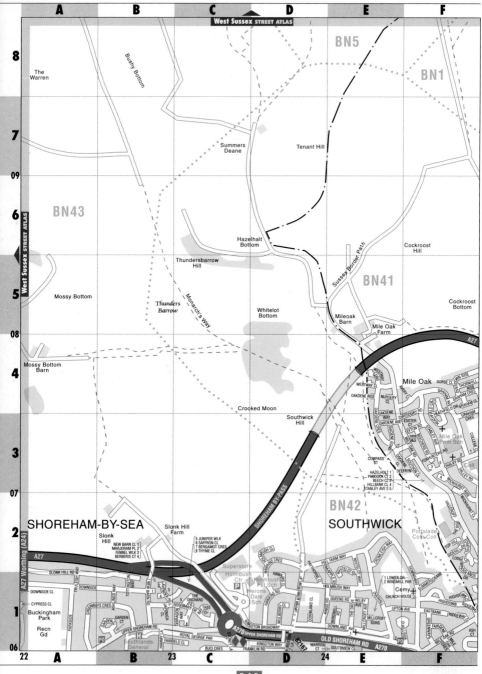

BN5

BN1

The Warren

Bushy Bottom

Summers Deane

Tenant Hill

BN43

Hazelhalt Bottom

Cockroost Hill

Thundersbarrow Hill

Sussex Border Path

BN41

Mossy Bottom

Thunders Barrow

Monarch's Way

Whitelot Bottom

Mileoak Barn

Cockroost Bottom

Mile Oak Farm

A27

Mossy Bottom Barn

Crooked Moon

Southwick Hill

Mile Oak

GORSE RISE

JOHN RISE

WESTWAY CL

WESTWAY CL

OAKDENE RISE

NURSERY CL

OAKENE WAY

OAKDENE AVE

Mile Oak Prim Sch

COMPASS ST

CHALKY RD

HAZELHOLT 1
PADDOCK CT 2
BEECH CL 3
HILLBANK CL 4
STANLEY AVE S 5

BN42

SHOREHAM-BY-SEA

Slonk Hill Farm

SOUTHWICK

Portslade Com Coll

Slonk Hill

A27 Worthing (A24)

A27

Slonk Hill

NEW BARN CL 1
MARJORAM PL 2
FENNEL WLK 3
BERBERIS CT 4

5 JUNIPER WLK
6 SAFFRON CL
7 BERGAMOT CRES
8 THYME CL

SHOREHAM BY-PASS

SLONK HILL RD WAY

DOWNSIDE CL

CYPRESS CL

Buckingham Park Recn Gd

Southlands General

Superstore
Holmbush Ctr

Herons Dale Sch

THE ORCHARD

UPPER SHOREHAM RD

ROYAL GEORGE PAR

FAIRFIELD CL

BUCI CRES

HOLMBUSH WAY

QUEENS RD

Kingston Broadway

KINGSTON WAY

FRANKLIN RD

WARREN CT

1 LOWER DR
2 WINDMILL PAR

Cemy
CHURCH HOUSE CL

UPTON AVE

MILLCROFT GDNS

OLD SHOREHAM RD

A270

SOUTHVIEW CL

EASTBANK

RIDGEWAY

ASH CT

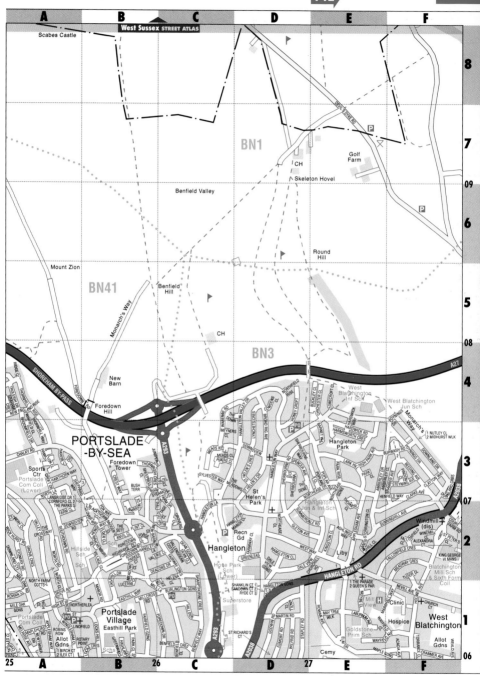

West Sussex STREET ATLAS

Scabes Castle

8

BN1

7

CH

Golf
Farm

09

Skeleton Hovel

Benfield Valley

6

Mount Zion

Round
Hill

BN41

Benfield
Hill

Monarch's Way

5

CH

08

BN3

A27

SHOREHAM BY-PASS

4

New
Barn

West
Blatchington
Inf Sch

West Blatchington
Jun Sch

FOREDOWN RD

Monarch's Way

Foredown
Hill

1 NUTLEY CL
2 MIDHURST WLK

PORTSLADE
-BY-SEA

A293

Foredown
Tower

Hangleton
Park

3

Sports
Ctr

BUSH
TERR

07

Portslade
Com Coll
(Lower)

SYCAMORE

St Helen's
Park

Windmill
(dis)

WINDMILL

ALEXANDRA

Hangleton
Jun & Int Sch

KING GEORGE
VI MANS

Hillside
Sch

HANGLETON LA

Recn
Gd

Liby

HANGLETON RD

Blatchington
Mill Sch
& Sixth Form
Coll

2

Hangleton

WEST WAY

A2038

NORTH FARM
COTTS

Hope Park
Sch
(Lower)

SHANKLIN CT 1
SANDOWN CT 2
RYDE CT 3

1 THE PARADE
2 QUEEN'S PAR

Clinic

MILE OAK RD

Mill
View

West
Blatchington

Hospice

Portslade
Com Coll

Portslade
Village
Easthill Park

Superstore

MAY TREE
WLK

ST RICHARD'S
CT

Goldstone
Prim Sch

Allot
Gdns

ROBINS
ROW

LINDFIELD

Allot
Gdns

1 BIRCH CT
2 ILEX CT

A293

Cemy

A2038

CHAMMER AVE

1

25

A

B

26

C

D

27

E

F

06

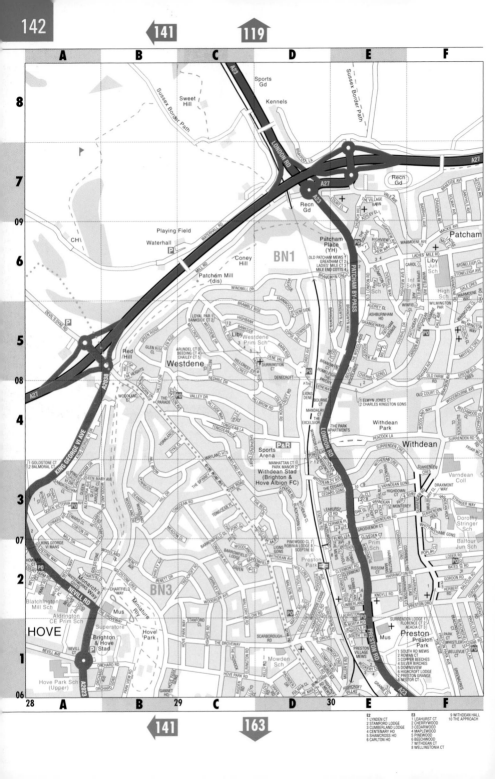

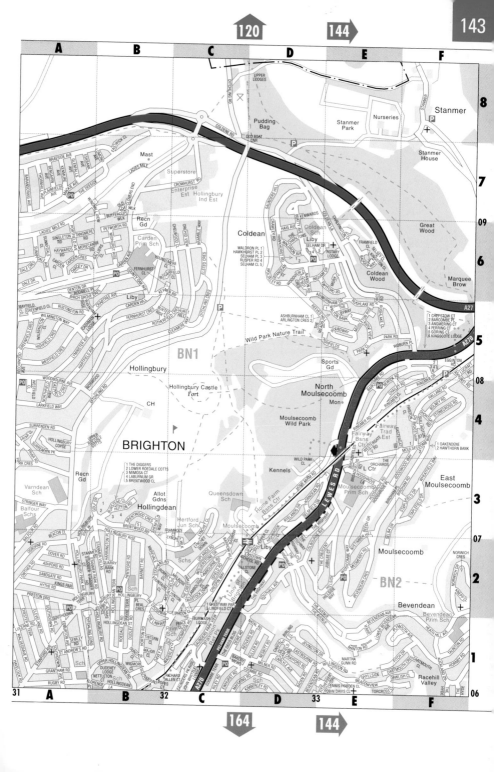

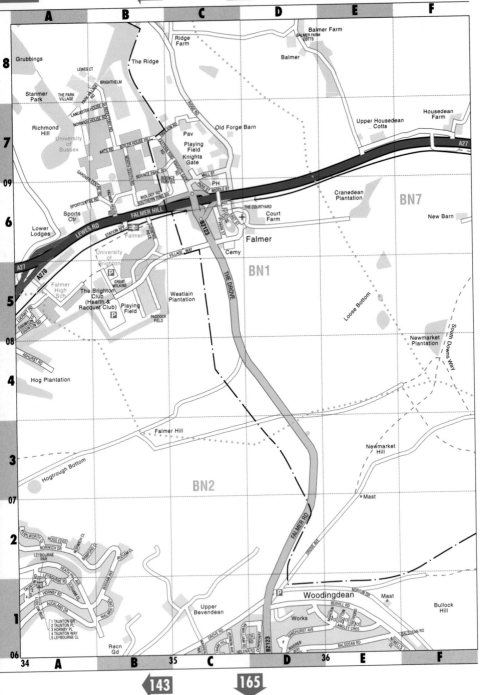

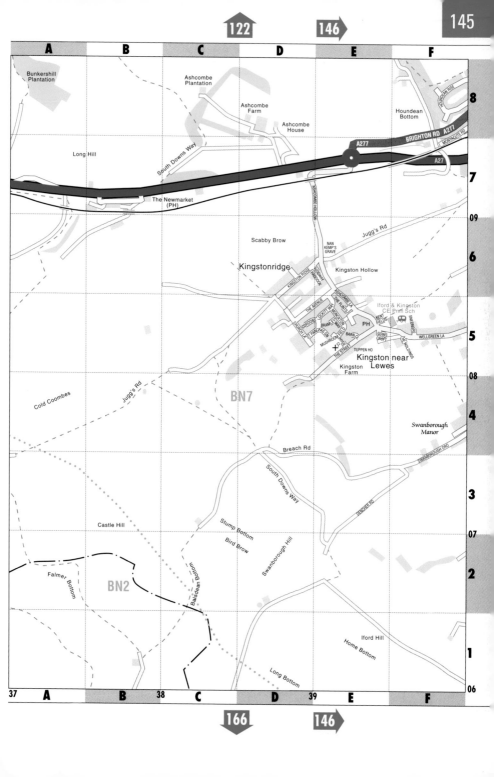

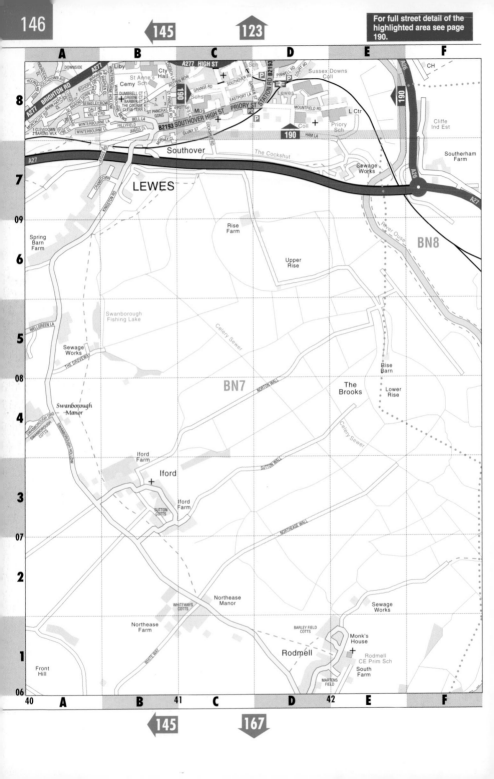

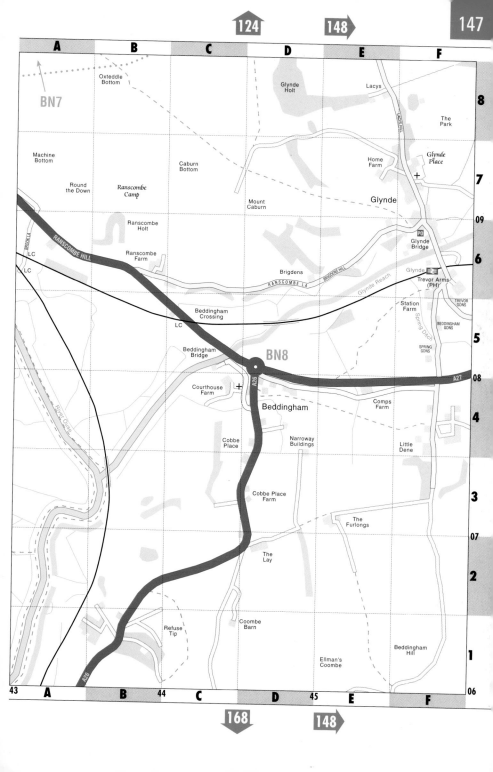

147
125

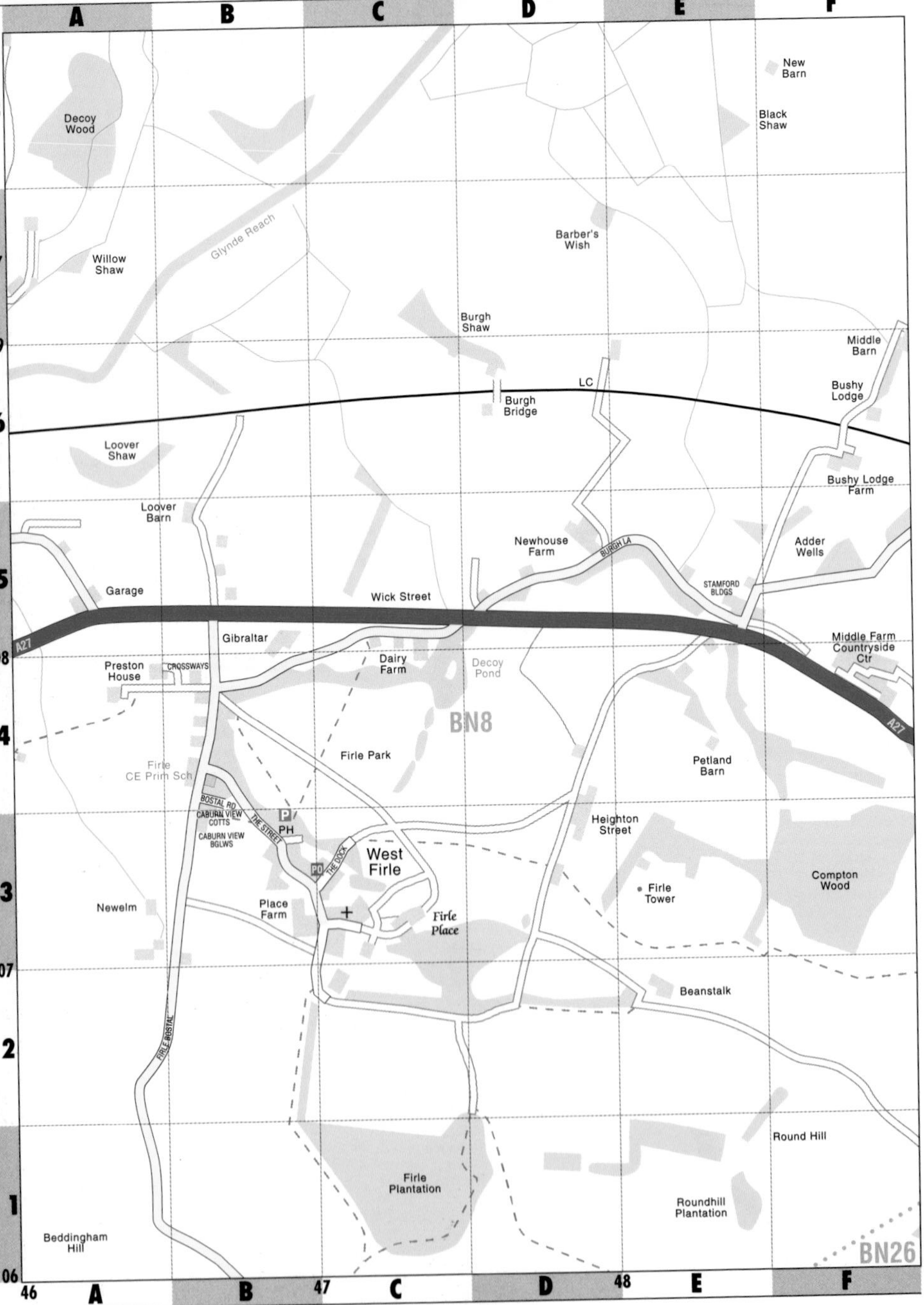

A **B** **C** **D** **E** **F**

8

New Barn

Decoy Wood

Black Shaw

7

Willow Shaw

Glynde Reach

Barber's Wish

09

Burgh Shaw

Middle Barn

Bushy Lodge

6

Loover Shaw

Burgh Bridge

LC

Loover Barn

Bushy Lodge Farm

5

Garage

Wick Street

Newhouse Farm

BURGH LA

Adder Wells

STAMFORD BLDGS

08

A27

Gibraltar

Dairy Farm

Decoy Pond

Middle Farm Countryside Ctr

Preston House

CROSSWAYS

A27

4

Firle CE Prim Sch

Firle Park

BN8

Petland Barn

BOSTAL RD

CABURN VIEW COTTS

CABURN VIEW BGLWS

P

THE STREET

PH

Heighton Street

Compton Wood

3

Newelm

PO

THE DOCK

West Firle

Firle Tower

Place Farm

+

Firle Place

07

THE BOSTAL

Beanstalk

2

Round Hill

1

Firle Plantation

Beddingham Hill

Roundhill Plantation

BN26

06

46 **A** **B** 47 **C** **D** 48 **E** **F**

147
169

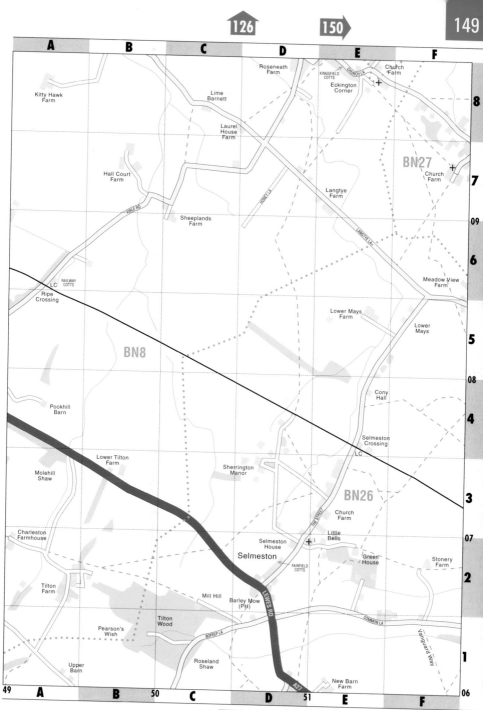

A B C D E F

Roseneath
Farm

Church
Farm

KINGSFIELD
COTTS

Eckington
Corner

CHURCH LA

Kitty Hawk
Farm

Lime
Barnett

8

Laurel
House
Farm

BN27

Church
Farm

7

Hall Court
Farm

Langtye
Farm

KIRLE RD

DONKEY LA

09

Sheeplands
Farm

LANGTYE LA

6

RAILWAY
COTTS

LC

Meadow View
Farm

Ripe
Crossing

Lower Mays
Farm

Lower
Mays

5

BN8

08

Pookhill
Barn

Cony
Hall

4

Selmeston
Crossing

LC

Molehill
Shaw

Lower Tilton
Farm

Sherrington
Manor

BN26

3

Charleston
Farmhouse

Church
Farm

THE STREET

Little
Bells

07

Selmeston
House

Green
House

Stonery
Farm

Tilton
Farm

Selmeston

FAIRFIELD
COTTS

2

Mill Hill

LEWES RD

Barley Mow
(PH)

COMMON LA

Pearson's
Wish

Tilton
Wood

BOPEEP LA

Vanguard Way

1

Upper
Barn

Roseland
Shaw

A27

New Barn
Farm

49 A B 50 C D 51 E F 06

	A	B	C	D	E	F

8

Yew Farm

Yew Tree (PH)

Diplocks Farm

BN27

Selmeston Croft

Clifton Farm

The Plough (PH)

High Barn

7

Chalvington

Vanguard Way

Lower Claverham Farm

Claverham Manor

Park Wood

09

Bungalow Farm

Wickstreet Farm

Parkwood Farm

6

Lower Claverham House

Wickstreet

Batbrooks Farm House

5

Batbrook Cottages

Sessingham Farm

Cobb Court

08

Ludlay Coppice

BN26

Raylands Farm

TYE HILL RD

4

Vanguard Way

Cuckmere River

Wealdway

Arlington

3

Ludlay

Ludlay Farm

P

Arlington Resr

The Yew Tree Inn (PH)

Wilbees Farm

07

PRINCES FIELD

DOWNSWAY

Polhill's Farm

Copyhold Cottages

Stapley's

2

Berwick

LC

Berwick Inn (PH)

STATION RD

Chilverbridge House

Works

Endlewick / Cottages

Chilver Bridge Farm

1

COMMON LA

Endlewick Farm

Moors Hill

06

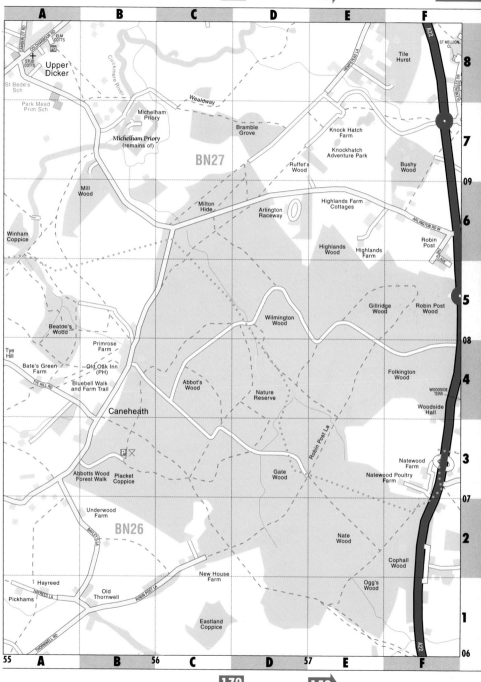

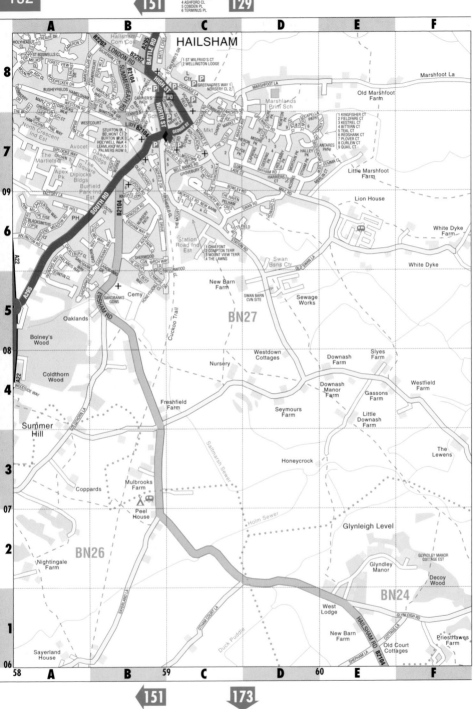

151
129

C7
1 MARKET SQ
2 ELIZABETH CT
3 SOUTHDOWN CT
4 ASHFORD CL
5 COBDEN PL
6 TERMINUS PL

C7
7 DEER PADDOCK LA

HAILSHAM

1 ST WILFRID'S CT
2 WELLINGTON LODGE

GREENACRES WAY 1
NORSERY CL 2

1 KINGFISHER CT
2 FIELDFARE CT
3 KESTREL CT
4 BITTERN CT
5 TEAL CT
6 REDSHANK CT
7 PLOVER CT
8 CURLEW CT
9 QUAIL CT

1 CHAFFONT
2 COMPTON TERR
3 MOUNT VIEW TERR
4 THE LAWNS

Old Marshfoot Farm

Marshlands Prim Sch

Little Marshfoot Farm

Lion House

White Dyke Farm

White Dyke

Marshfoot La

New Barn Farm

Swan Bsns Ctr

Swan Barn CVN SITE

Sewage Works

BN27

Westdown Cottages

Nursery

Downash Farm

Slyes Farm

Westfield Farm

Downash Manor Farm

Gassons Farm

Freshfield Farm

Seymours Farm

Little Downash Farm

The Lewens

Summer Hill

Coppards

Mulbrooks Farm

Peel House

Honeycrock

Glynleigh Level

BN26

Nightingale Farm

Glynleigh Manor

Glynoley Manor Cottage Est

Decoy Wood

BN24

West Lodge

New Barn Farm

Old Court Cottages

Priestthawes Farm

Sayerland House

Oaklands

Bolney's Wood

Coldthorn Wood

151
173

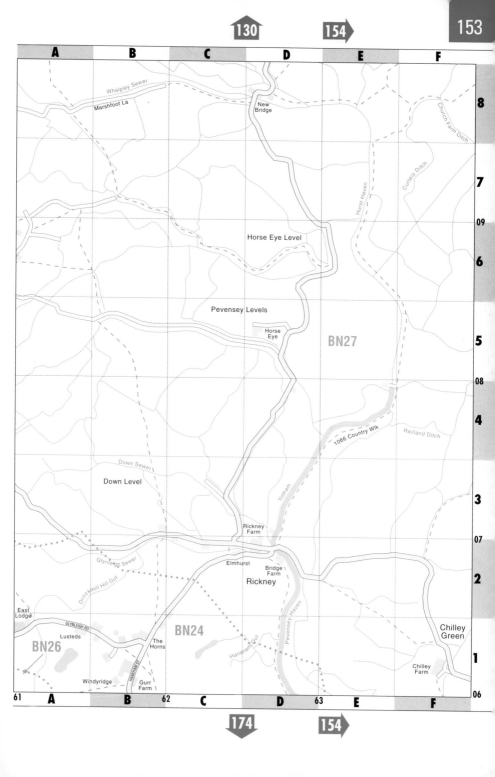

130
154
174
154

Whelpley Sewer
Marshfoot La
New Bridge
Church Farm Ditch

8

7

Hurst Haven
Curteis Ditch

09

Horse Eye Level

6

Pevensey Levels

Horse Eye

BN27

5

08

1066 Country Wlk
Railland Ditch

4

Yotham

Down Sewer

Down Level

3

07

Rickney Farm

Glynleigh Sewer

Elmhurst
Bridge Farm

Rickney

2

Brockmill Hill Gut

Chilley Green

East Lodge
GLYNLEIGH RD
Lusteds
The Horns

BN24

BN26

Hankham Gut
Pevensey Haven

Chilley Farm

1

HANKHAM ST

Windyridge
Gurr Farm

61   A   B   62   C   D   63   E   F   06

153
131

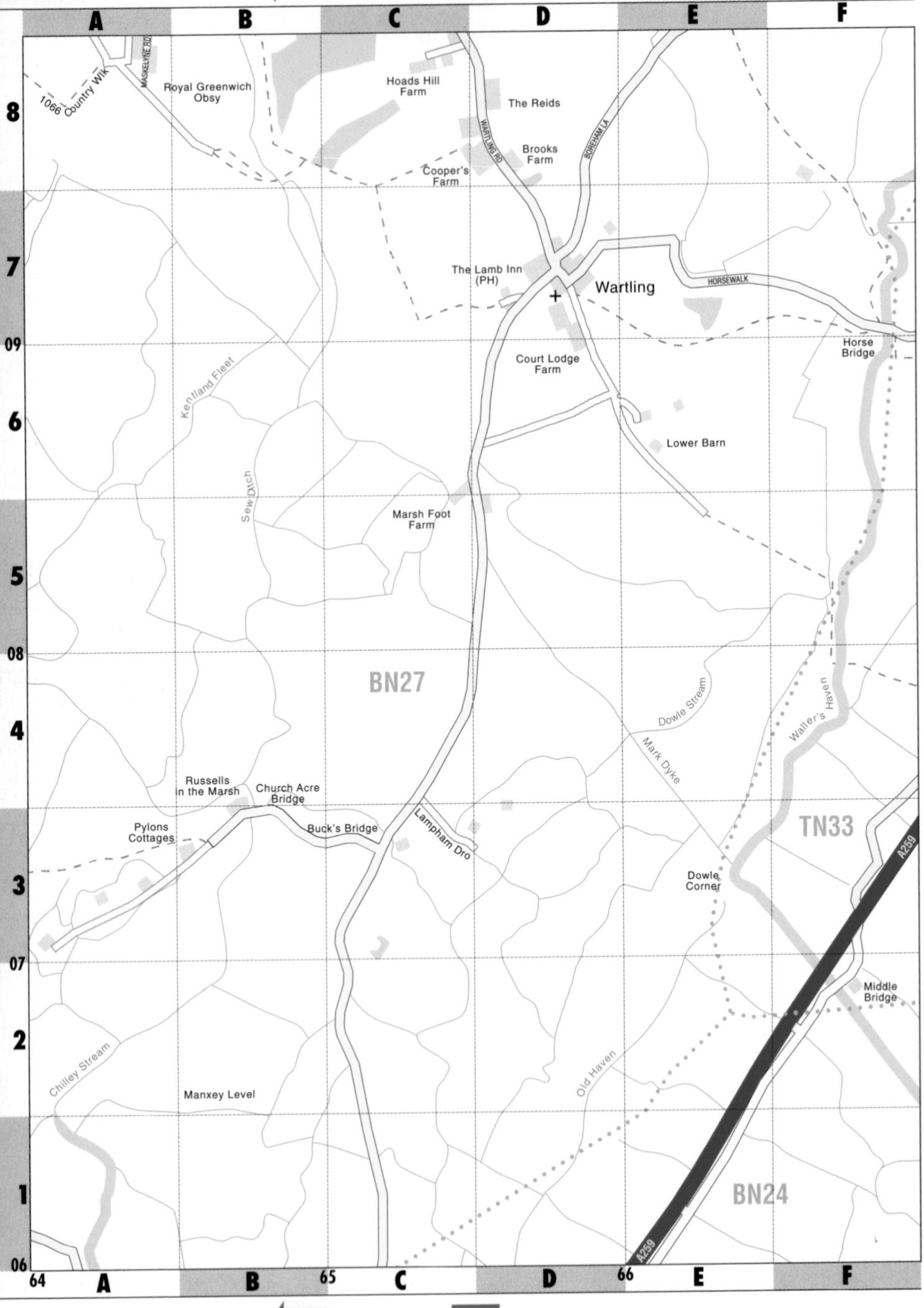

8

A B C D E F

MACKERELYE RD

1066 Country Wlk

Royal Greenwich Obsy

Hoads Hill Farm

The Reids

WARTLING RD

Cooper's Farm

Brooks Farm

7

The Lamb Inn (PH)

+ Wartling

HORSEWALK

ROSSENA LA

Horse Bridge

09

Kentland Fleet

Court Lodge Farm

6

Sew Dyke

Lower Barn

Marsh Foot Farm

5

Dowle Stream

08

BN27

Walter's Haven

4

Mark Dyke

TN33

Russells in the Marsh

Church Acre Bridge

Pylons Cottages

Buck's Bridge

Lampham Dro

Dowle Corner

A259

3

07

Middle Bridge

2

Chilley Stream

Manxey Level

Old Haven

A259

1

BN24

06

64 **A** B 65 **C** D 66 **E** F

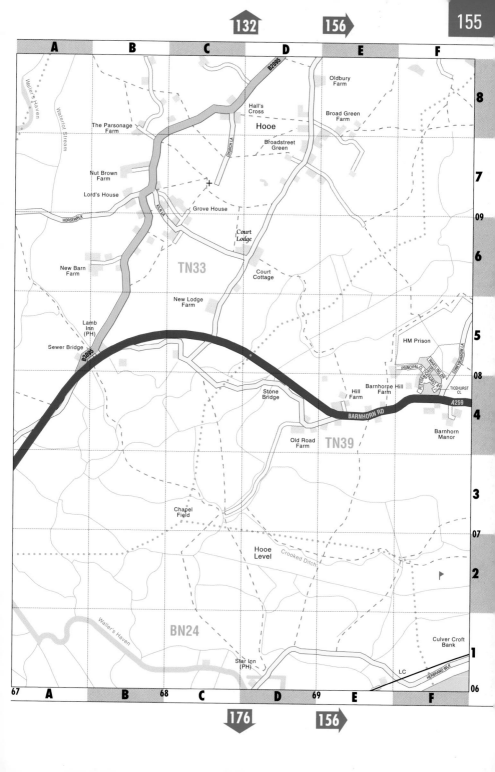

155
133

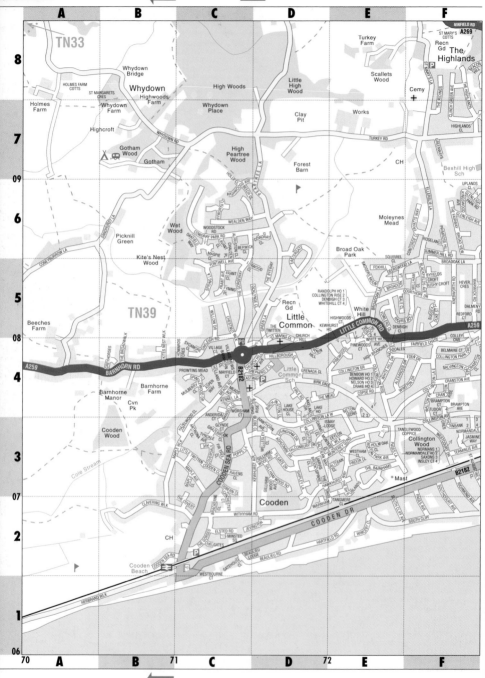

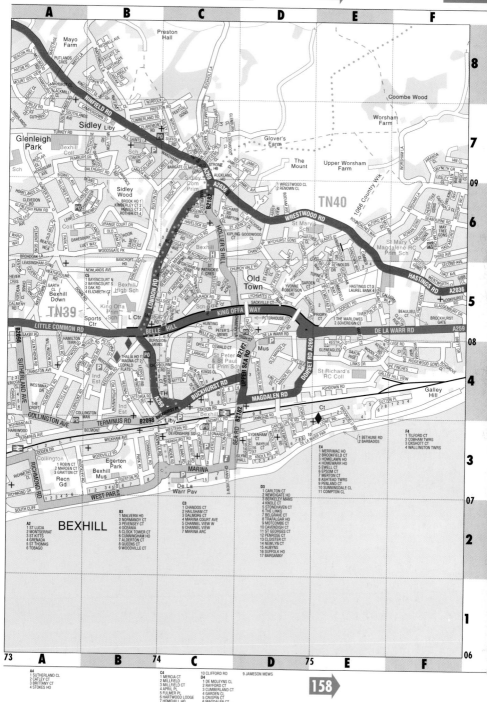

8

Mayo Farm

Preston Hall

Coombe Wood

Worsham Farm

Sidley Liby

7

Glenleigh Park

Bexhill Coll

Glover's Farm

The Mount

Upper Worsham Farm

09

Sidley Wood

Sidley Com Prim

TN40

1 WRESTWOOD CL
2 RENOWN CL

6

WRESTWOOD RD

St Mary's Sch

St Mary Magdalene RC Prim Sch

PO

Bexhill High Sch

C5
1 BAYENCOURT N
2 BAYENCOURT 3
3 OAK RD
4 ELIZABETH CT

Old Town

Bexhill Down

TN39

King Offa Prim Sch

Sports Ctr

L Ctr

Hastings Rd

A2036

5

Little Common Rd

KING OFFA WAY

1 THE MARLOWES
2 SOVEREIGN CT

De La Warr Rd

A259

08

B2098

BELLE HILL

Mus

DORSET RD A269

St Richard's RC Coll

Galley Hill View

Galley Hill

4

BUCKHURST RD

UPPER SEA RD

MAGDALEN RD

F4
1 TILFORD CT
2 COBHAM TWRS
3 OXSHOTT CT
4 WALLINGTON TWRS

Collington Ave

TERMINUS RD B2098

Bexhill Liby

1 BETHUNE RD
2 BARBADOS

3

Collington

1 ROBIN CT
2 MARDEN CT
3 GRATTON CT

Egerton Park

Bexhill Mus

E4
1 MERRIMAC HO
2 BROOKFIELD CT
3 HOMELAWN HO
4 HOMEWARR HO
5 EWELL CT
6 EPSOM CT
7 MERTON CT
8 ASHTEAD TWRS
9 PENLAND CT
10 SUNNINGDALE CL
11 COMPTON CL

Recn Gd

WEST PAR

De La Warr Pav

D3
1 CARLTON CT
2 NEWDIGATE HO
3 BERKELEY MANS
4 KNOLE CT
5 STONEHAVEN CT
6 THE LINKS
7 BELGRAVE CT
8 TRAFALGAR HO
9 MOTCOMBE CT
10 CAVENDISH CT
11 ST GEORGES CT
12 PEMBROKE CT
13 CLOISTER CT
14 NEWLYN CT
15 ALBYNS
16 SUFFOLK HO
17 BARGANNY

07

BEXHILL

A2
1 ST LUCIA
2 MONTSERRAT
3 ST KITTS
4 GRENADA
5 ST THOMAS
6 TOBAGO

B3
1 MALVERN HO
2 NORMANDY CT
3 PEVENSEY CT
4 OCEANIA
5 CLOCK TOWER CT
6 CUNNINGHAM HO
7 ALDERTON CT
8 QUEENS CT
9 WOODVILLE CT

C3
1 CHANDOS CT
2 HAILSHAM CT
3 DALMORE CT
4 MARINA COURT AVE
5 CHANNEL VIEW W
6 CHANNEL VIEW
7 MARINA ARC

2

1

06

A4
1 SUTHERLAND CL
2 CATLEY CT
3 BRITTANY CT
4 STOKES HO

C4
1 MERCIA CT
2 MILLFIELD
3 MILLFIELD CT
4 APRIL PL
5 FULMER PL
6 HARTWOOD LODGE
7 HOMEHILL HO
8 GRINLEY CT
9 CLIFFORD CT

10 CLIFFORD RD

D4
1 DE MOLEYNS CL
2 RAYFORD CL
3 CUMBERLAND CT
4 GARDEN CL
5 CRISPIN CT
6 MAGDALEN CT
7 CHICHESTER HO
8 ROMNEY CT

9 JAMESON MEWS

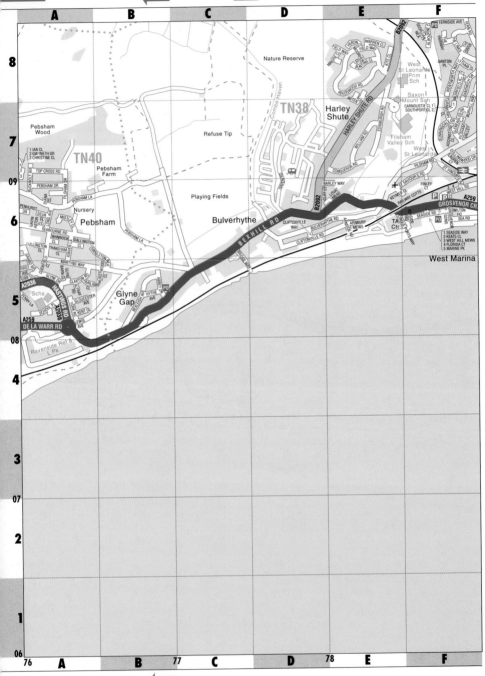

C7
1 STAINSBY ST
2 NORFOLK HO
3 ST RICHARDS CT
4 ROYAL TERR
5 EVERSFIELD MEWS N
6 ALAN CT

7 ASHLEY CT
8 ST MARY'S CT
9 CAVENDISH HO
10 DECIMUS BURTON WAY
11 UNION ST
12 MARLBOROUGH HO
13 BEAUFORT HO

14 ST GEORGES MOUNT
15 STOCKLEIGH CT
16 EVERSFIELD MEWS S
17 CHELSEA MEWS
18 ST MARYS COTTS

136

F8
1 WATERWORKS COTTS
2 STONEFIELD PL
3 ELFORD ST
4 WALDEGRAVE ST
5 CORNWALLIS ST
6 ST ANDREW'S SQ

160

F9 Robert Tressell Wkshps
8 QUEENS PAR
9 MIDDLE ST
10 KINGS WLK
11 PORTLAND COTTS
12 STONE ST

13 PORTLAND PL
14 WELLINGTON TERR
15 PORTLAND TERR
16 PORTLAND VILLAS
17 WELLINGTON RD
18 STATION RD

159

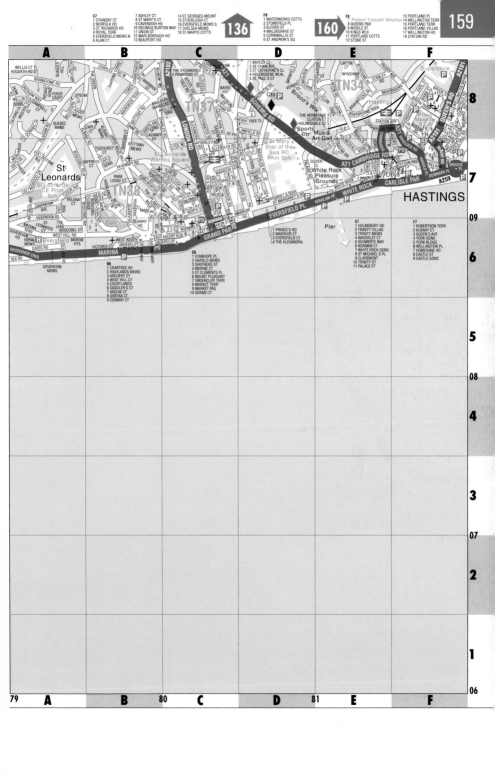

Key reference areas:

B6
1 CRABTREE HO
2 HIGHLANDS MEWS
3 ARCHERY CT
4 WEST HILL CT
5 COURTLANDS
6 SADDLER'S CT
7 ARCHIE CT
8 GREEBA CT
9 CONWAY CT

C6
1 STANHOPE PL
2 HAROLD MEWS
3 SHEPHERD ST
4 MARINE CT
5 ST CLEMENTS PL
6 MOUNT PLEASANT
7 UNDERCLIFF TERR
8 MARKET TERR
9 MARKET PAS
10 GRAND CT

D6
1 PRINCE'S RD
2 WARRIOR CT
3 EVERSFIELD CT
4 THE ALEXANDRA

E7
1 HOLMEBURY HO
2 TRINITY VILLAS
3 TRINITY MEWS
4 WAVERLEY CT
5 SCHWERTE WAY
6 NORMAN CT
7 WHITE ROCK GDNS
8 ST MICHAEL'S PL
9 CLAREMONT
10 TRINITY ST
11 PALACE CT

F7
1 ROBERTSON TERR
2 ALBANY CT
3 QUEEN'S AVE
4 YORK GDNS
5 YORK BLDGS
6 WELLINGTON PL
7 HOMEDANE HO
8 CASTLE ST
9 CASTLE GDNS

HASTINGS

Pier

79 A   B   80   C   D   81   E   F

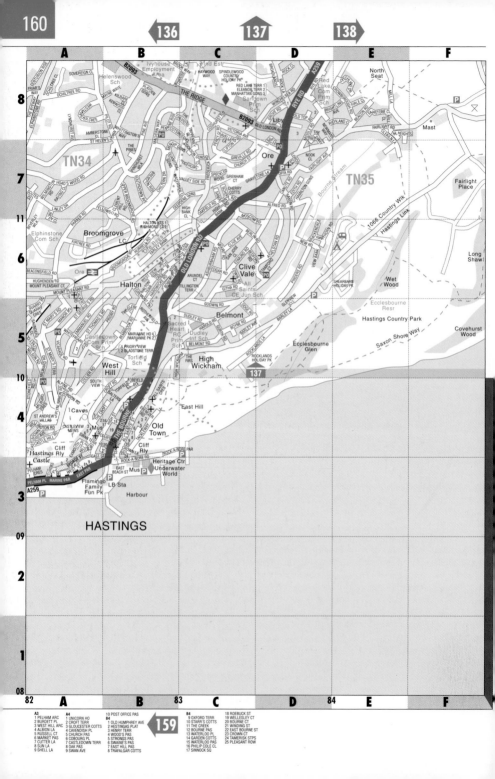

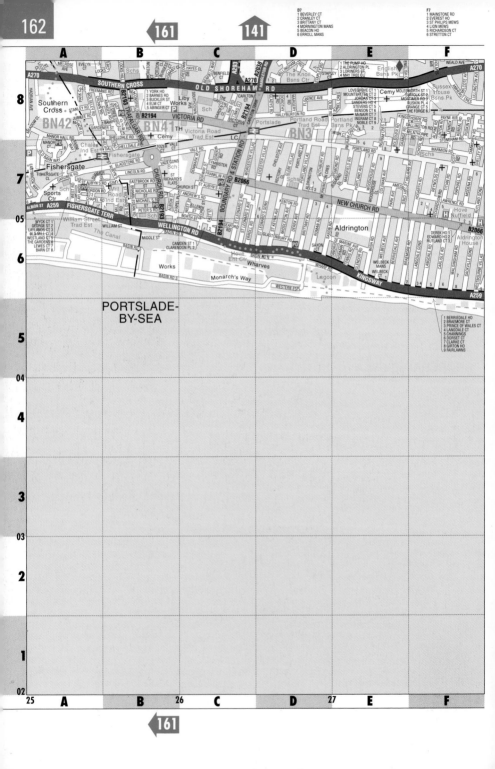

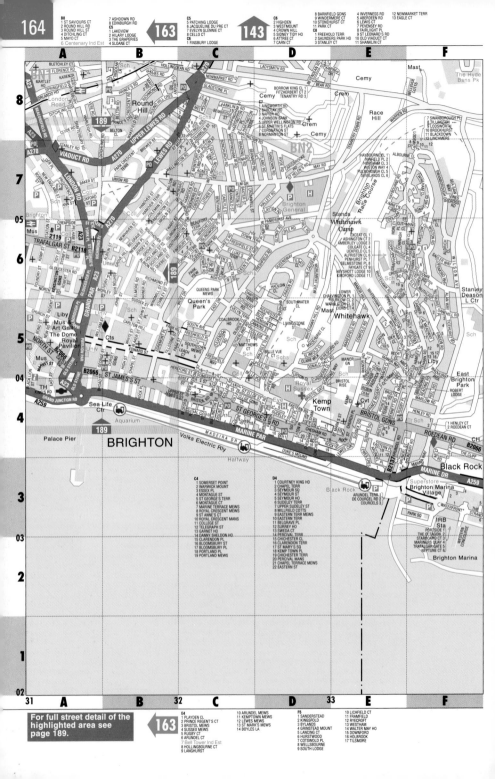

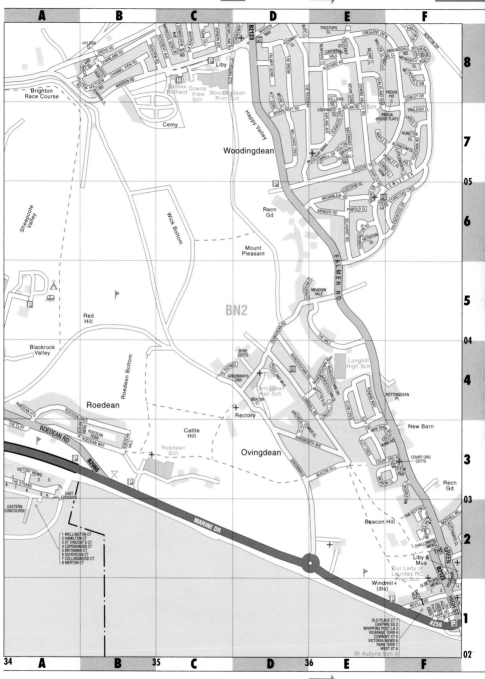

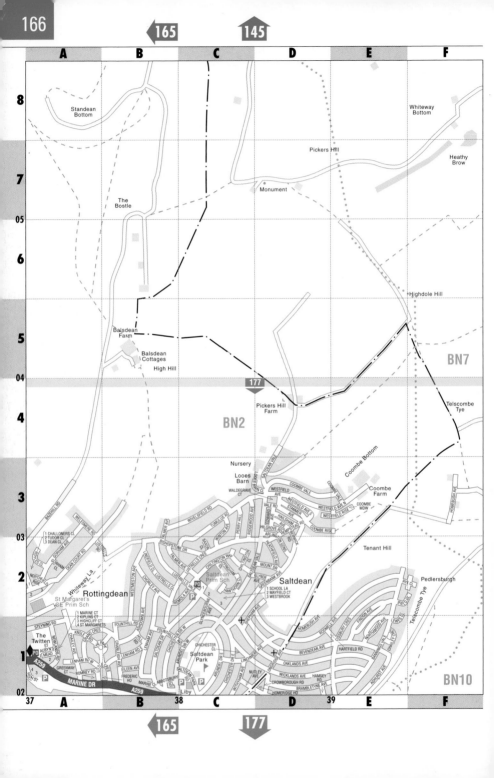

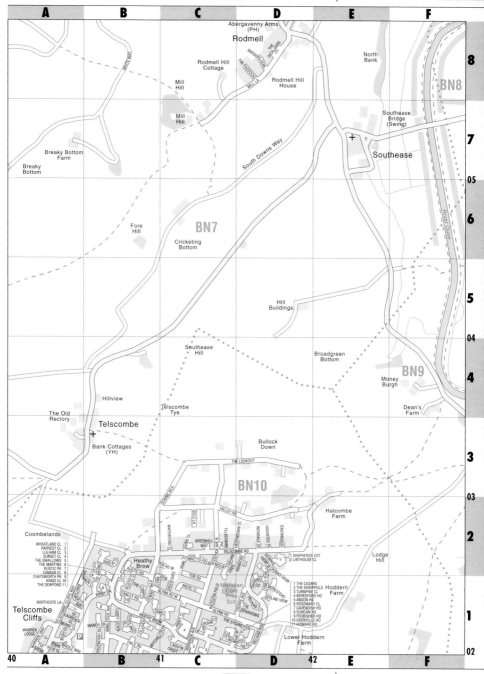

167
147

A B C D E F

8

BN8

White Lion Pond

Mast
Radio Sta

Red Lion Pond

LC
Southease

Itford Farm

Itford Hill

America Farm

South Downs Way

7

Well Bottom

05

Baydean

Baydean Bottom

Cow Wish Bottom

6

Itford Bottom

Muggery Pope

5

Stock Cottages

Durham Farm

04

Manor Farm

BN9

Court Farm

Tarring Neville

Page's New Barn

4

LC

New Barn

Works

DOWNS VILLAS
South Heighton Farm

South Heighton

3

River Ouse

Royal Oak (PH)

BROOKS

Piddinghoe

COURT FARM CL

The Wish

1 CEDARWELL CL
2 SHEPHERDS CL

PORTLAND TERR 1
FIRLE TERR 2
WEST VIEW TERR 3
MARTELLO CT 4
COTTAGE CL 5

1 SOUTH VIEW
2 ORCHARD MEWS
3 GUINNESS TRUST BGLWS

HEIGHTON RD

Denton

03

2

BN9

Nore Down

Brookside Farm

PIDDINGHOE MEAD

DENTON RD

Denton Comm Prim Sch

DENTON DR

THE CRESCENT

Mount Pleasant

KING'S AVE

1

Mus

Paradise Family Leisure Park

AVIS RD

GUINNESS CL

HOLMDALE RD

Cemy

Rich Ind Est

02

43 A 44 B C D 45 E F

167
179

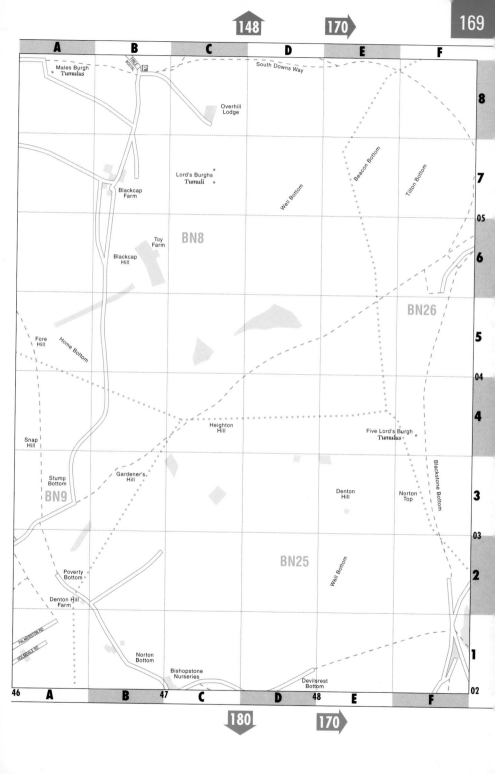

148 170

A B C D E F

South Downs Way

Males Burgh
Tumulus

P

Overhill
Lodge

8

Lord's Burghs
Tumuli

Beacon Bottom

Tilton Bottom

7

Blackcap
Farm

Well Bottom

05

Toy
Farm

BN8

Blackcap
Hill

6

BN26

Fore
Hill

Home Bottom

5

04

Heighton
Hill

4

Snap
Hill

Five Lord's Burgh
Tumulus

Blackstone Bottom

Gardener's
Hill

Stump
Bottom

Denton
Hill

Norton
Top

BN9

3

03

Poverty
Bottom

BN25

Well Bottom

2

Denton Hill
Farm

PALMERSTON RD

HOLMDALE RD

Norton
Bottom

1

Bishopstone
Nurseries

Devilsrest
Bottom

02

46 A B 47 C D 48 E F

180 170

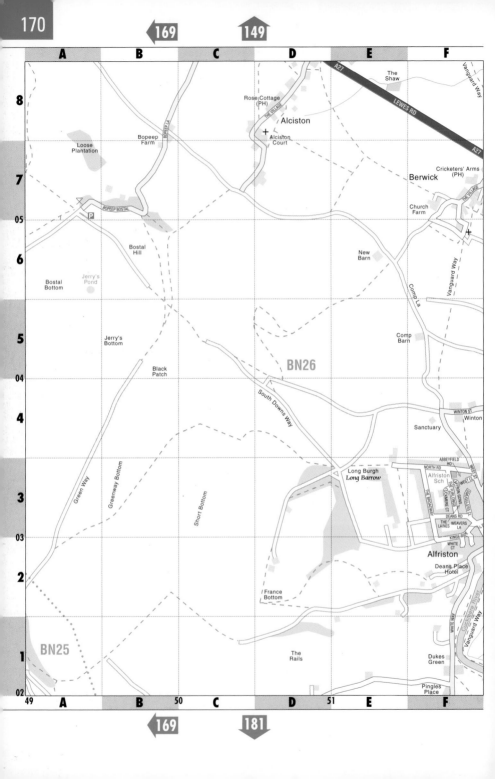

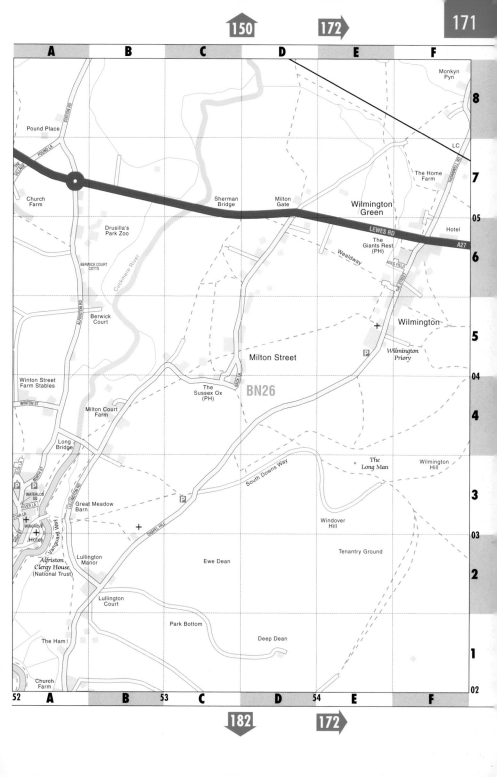

171
151

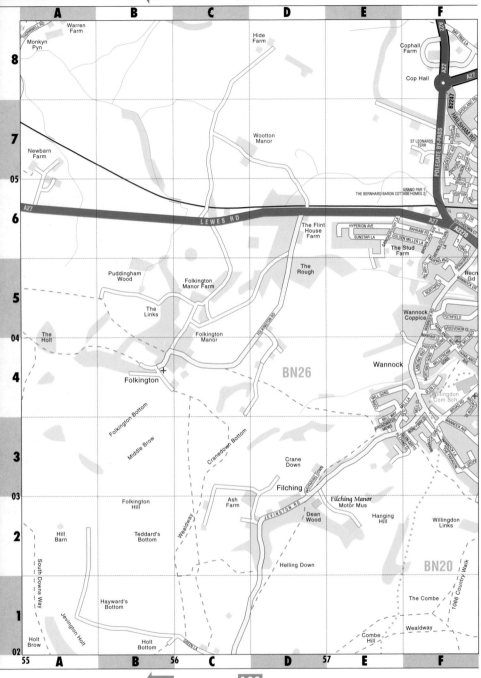

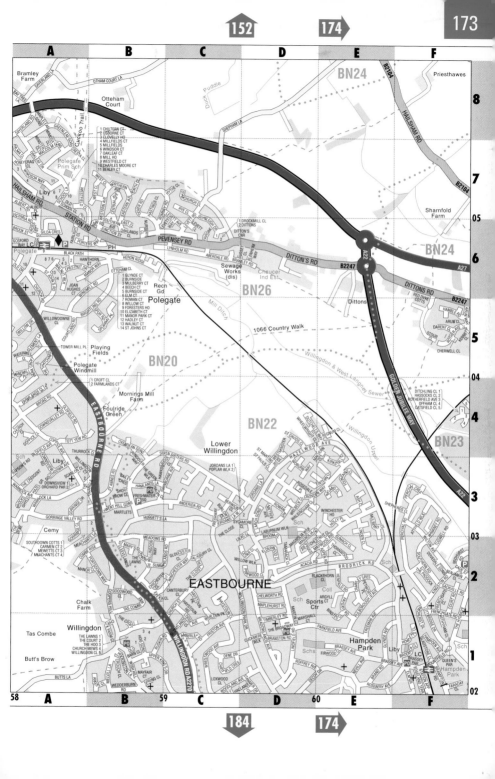

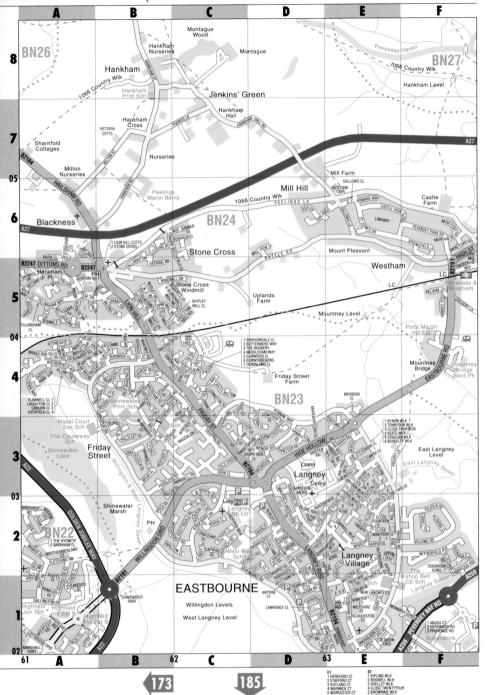

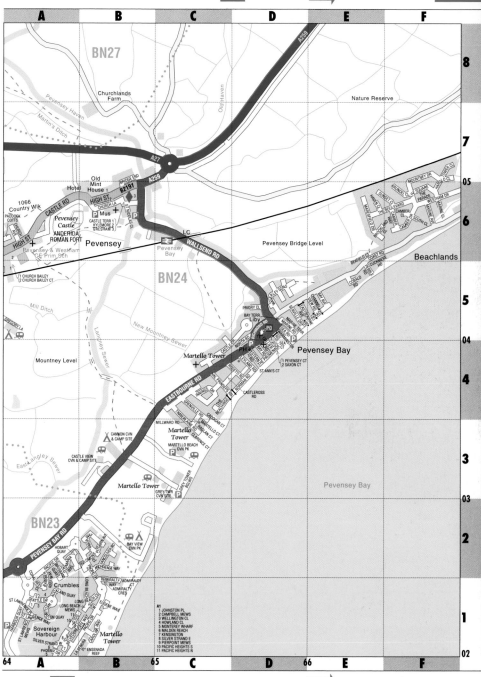

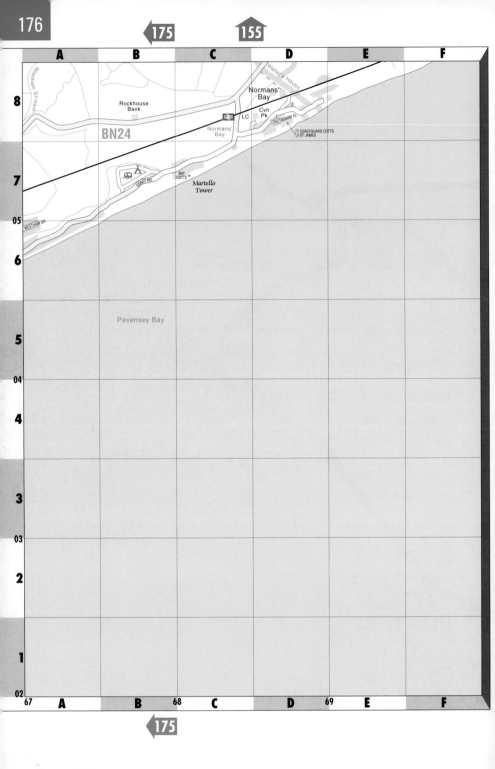

175
155
175

A B C D E F

8

BN10

Telscombe
Cliffs

GRASSMERE CT

WARREN WAY
PARK PARK AVE

LEA RD

BALCOMBE RD

St David's Ct
Hoddern
Jun Sch

Sch

ROSEMARY RD
FIRLE RD
THE GREEN

CAVELL AVE N
EDITH AVE N
DORSMAN AVE N
VIEW RD
FIRLE RD
TREE RD

SOUTH VIEW RD
BRAMBER CL

1 BALCOMBE CT
2 MERIDIAN DR
3 RODERICK CT
The Meridian
Ind Est

Peacehaven

Friar's
Bay

7

A259
GOLBY
THE ESPLANADE
PROMENADE

1 GREENACRES
2 DANA LODGE
3 CHANNEL GRANGE
4 AMBLESIDE CT
5 MARSDEN CT
6 FINCH CT

Libry
Ctr

HOWARD RD
GREENWICH WAY
ARUNDEL ROAD CENTRAL
JASON CL
HOYLE RD
WINTON RD
RAZMOND RD

ARUNDEL RD
PIDDINGHOE

CLIFF PARK AVE
DORCHESTER
CASSINGHAM AVE

THIRD RD
SECOND RD

01

SOUTH COAST RD

A259

OUTLOOK AVE

6

MARGARET CT 1
FAIRFIELD 2
HOMECOAST HO 3
PARK CT 4
JUBILEE CT 5
CAVELL CT 6
FITZALAN CT 7

CRESTA CT 1
DORITA CT 2
LURELAND CT 3

NEVILLE RD
PROMENADE

JAY RD
WELLINGTON
Motel

TUDOR ROSE
PK
THE HIGHWAY

Cvn Site

Peacehaven
Heights

Chene
Gap

5

Friars' Bay

00

4

3

99

2

1

98

40 A B 41 C D 42 E F

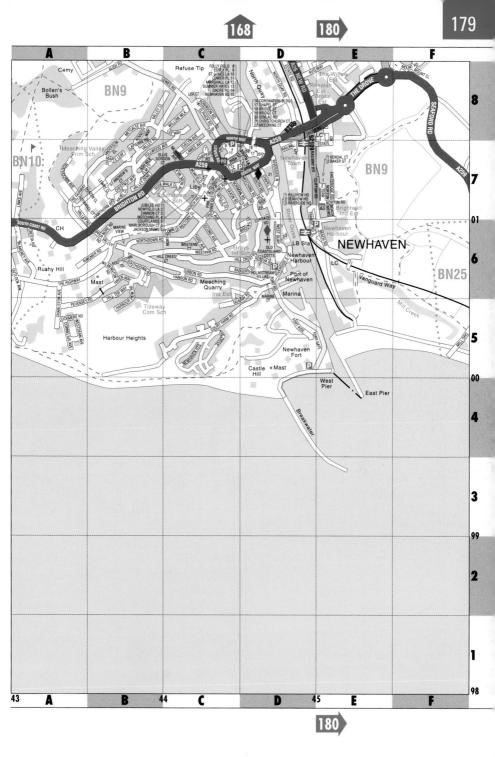

NEWHAVEN

BN9

BN10

BN9

BN25

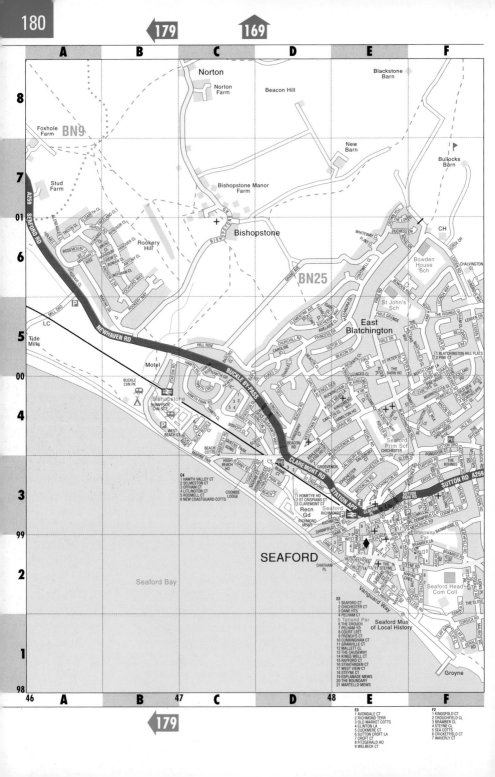

Norton

Norton
Farm

Beacon Hill

Blackstone
Barn

Foxhole
Farm

BN9

New
Barn

Bullocks
Barn

Stud
Farm

A259

SEAFORD RD

Bishopstone Manor
Farm

Bishopstone

Rookery
Hill

BN25

Whiteway Cl

Flint Cl

Duchess Dr

CH

Bowden
House
Sch

Chalvington
Cl

St John's
Sch

Firle Grange

East
Blatchington

1 BLATCHINGTON HILL FLATS
2 PINE CT

The
Ridings

Mill Dro

LC

Tide
Mills

Newhaven Rd

Hill Rise

Buckle By-Pass

St Peter's

1 HOMETYE HO
2 ST CRISPIANS CT
3 CLAREMONT CT

The
Barn Ho

North Camp La

Motel

Buckle
Cvn Pk

Bishopstone
Sunnyside
Cvn Site

Hawth Park Rd

Town Cl

Bishops Cl

West
Beach Ct

Beach
Cotts

Marine Par

High
Beach
Ho

Seaford
Prim Sch

Chichester

C4
1 HAWTH VALLEY CT
2 SELMESTON CT
3 OFFHAM CT
4 LITLINGTON CT
5 RODMELL CT
6 NEW COASTGUARD COTTS

Coombe
Lodge

Claremont Rd

Station App

Sutton Rd A259

Recn
Gd

Seaford
Richmond

Richmond
Mews

1 HOMETYE HO
2 ST CRISPIANS CT
3 CLAREMONT CT

Dannfields Ct

Seaford
Mus
of Local History

SEAFORD

Chatham
Pl

The
Steyne

Seaford Bay

Vanguard Way

Seaford Head
Com Coll

The
Close

E2
1 SEAFORD CT
2 CHICHESTER CT
3 DANE HTS
4 PECHAM CT
5 TALLAND PAR
6 THE CROUGH
7 PELHAM YD
8 COURT LEET
9 FRENCH'S CT
10 CUNNINGHAM CT
11 GRANVILLE CT
12 MALLETT CL
13 THE CAUSEWAY
14 KINGS WELL CT
15 RAYFORD CT
16 STRATHNDEN CT
17 WEST VIEW CT
18 STEYNE CT
19 ESPLANADE MEWS
20 THE BOUNDARY
21 MARTELLO MEWS

Groyne

E3
1 AVONDALE CT
2 RICHMOND TERR
3 OLD MARKET COTTS
4 CLINTON LA
5 CUCKMERE CT
6 SUTTON CROFT LA
7 CROFT CT
8 FITZGERALD HO
9 WELBECK CT

F2
1 KINGSFOLD CT
2 CROUCHFIELD CL
3 BRAMBER CL
4 STEYNE CL
5 SEA COTTS
6 CRICKETFIELD CT
7 WAVERLY CT

A3
1 WELLINGTON PK
2 BARN COTTS
3 SHEEP PEN LA
4 EASTBOURNE TERR

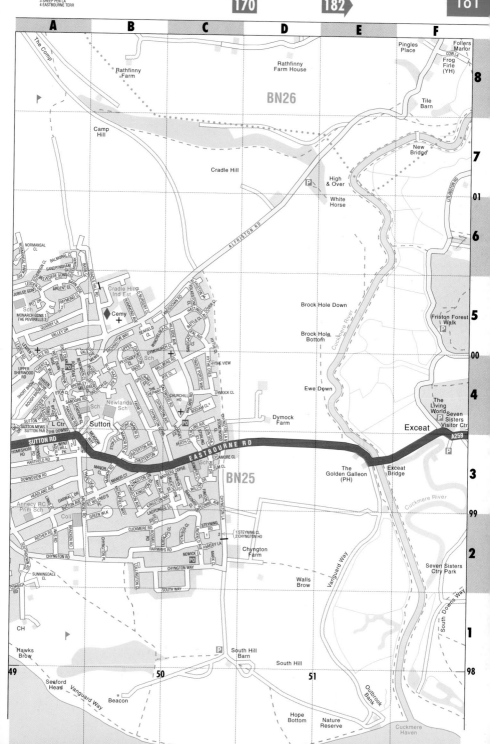

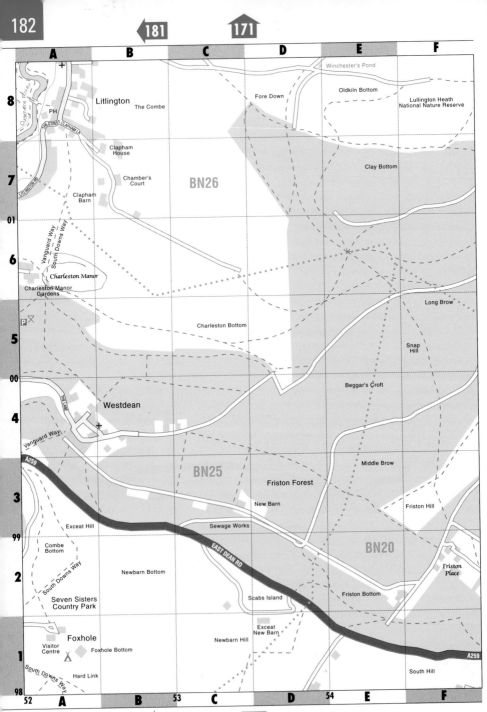

A   B   C   D   E   F

8
7
01
6
5
00
4
3
99
2
1
98

52   53   54

A   B   C   D   E   F

Winchester's Pond
Fore Down
Oldkiln Bottom
Lullington Heath
National Nature Reserve
Litlington
The Combe
PH
Clapham House
Clay Bottom
BN26
Chamber's Court
Clapham Barn
Vanguard Way
South Downs Way
Charleston Manor
Long Brow
Charleston Manor Gardens
P
Charleston Bottom
Snap Hill
Beggar's Croft
Westdean
Vanguard Way
A259
BN25
Middle Brow
Friston Forest
New Barn
Friston Hill
Exceat Hill
Sewage Works
BN20
Combe Bottom
99
EAST DEAN RD
South Downs Way
Newbarn Bottom
Friston Place
Seven Sisters Country Park
Scabs Island
Friston Bottom
Foxhole
Exceat New Barn
Visitor Centre
Newbarn Hill
Foxhole Bottom
A259
South Downs Way
Hard Link
South Hill

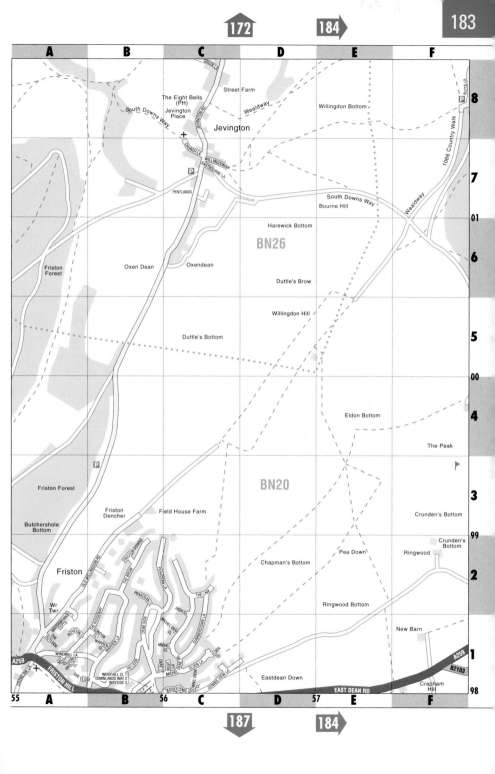

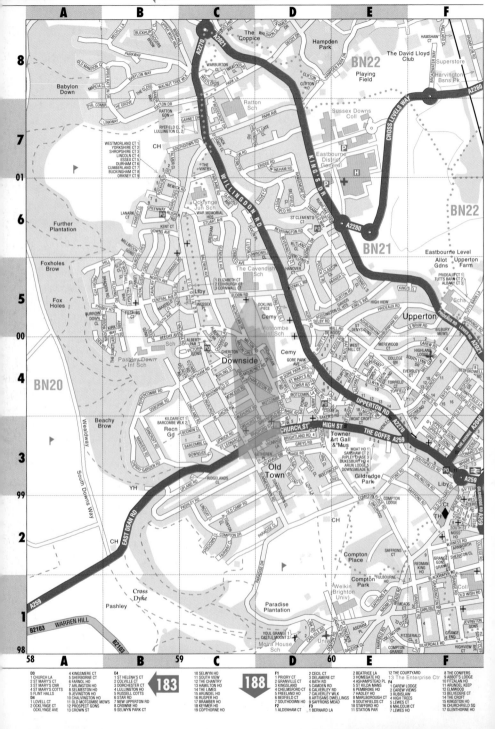

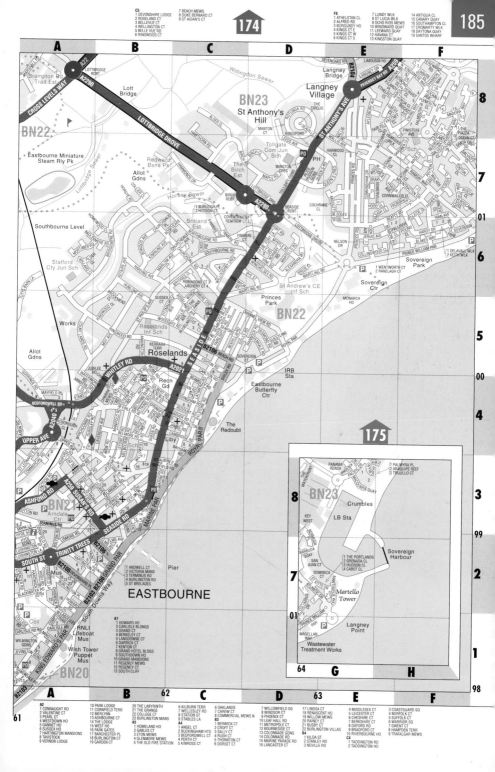

182

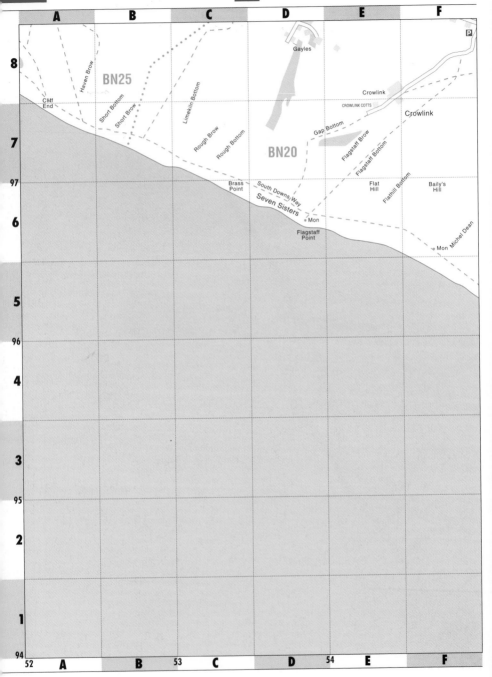

8

7

97

6

5

96

4

3

95

2

94

A B C D E F

Cliff End

Haven Brow

BN25

Short Bottom

Short Brow

Limekiln Bottom

Rough Brow

Rough Bottom

BN20

Gayles

Crowlink

CROWLINK COTTS

Crowlink

Gap Bottom

Flagstaff Brow

Flagstaff Bottom

Brass Point

South Downs Way

Seven Sisters

Flat Hill

Flathill Bottom

Baily's Hill

Mon

Flagstaff Point

Mon Michel Dean

52 A B 53 C D 54 E F

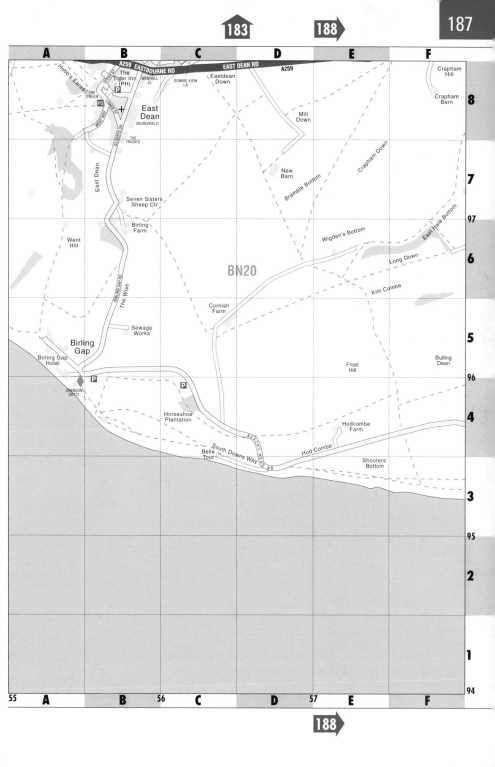

A | B | C | D | E | F

← 183
188 →

A259 EASTBOURNE RD   EAST DEAN RD   A259

Crapham
Hill

The Tiger Inn
(PH)

WENTHILL
CL

DOWNS VIEW
LA

Eastdean
Down

Crapham
Barn

8

THE
GREEN

East
Dean

CHURCHFIELD

Mill
Down

THE
FRIDAYS

New
Barn

Crapham Down

7

East Dean

Bramble Bottom

Seven Sisters
Sheep Ctr

East Hale Bottom

97

Birling
Farm

Wigden's Bottom

Went
Hill

Long Down

6

BN20

The Wish

BIRLING GAP RD

Kiln Combe

Cornish
Farm

5

Sewage
Works

Frost
Hill

Bulling
Dean

Birling
Gap

Birling Gap
Hotel

96

CRANGON
COTTS

Horseshoe
Plantation

Hodcombe
Farm

4

BEACHY HEAD RD

South Downs Way

Belle
Tout

Hod Combe

Shooters'
Bottom

3

95

2

1

94

55 | 56 | 57

A | B | C | D | E | F

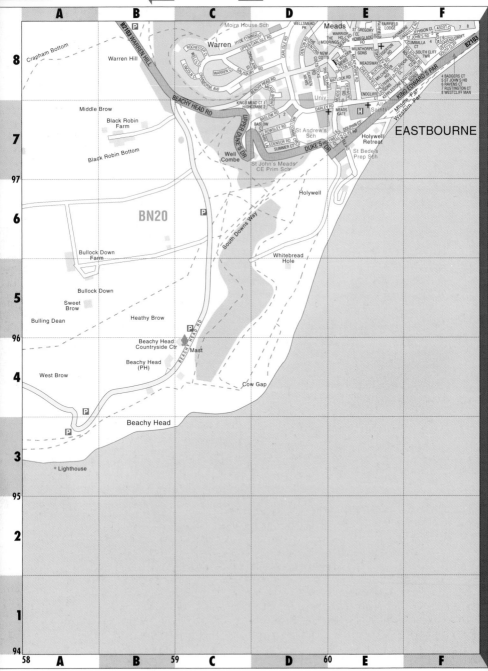

EASTBOURNE

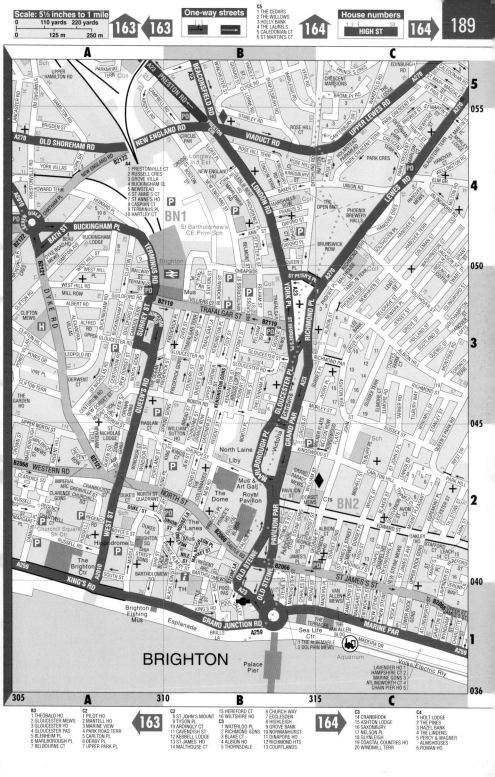

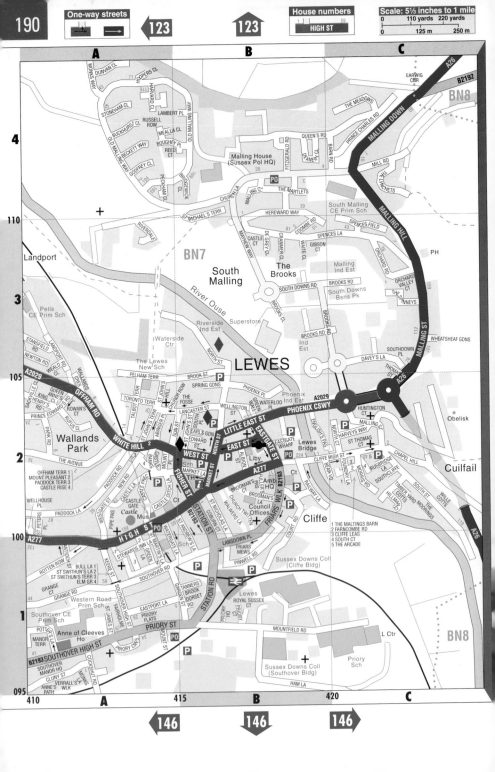

Index

Church Rd **6** Beckenham BR2.......... **53** C6

Place name	
May be abbreviated on the map	
Location number	
Present when a number indicates the place's position in a crowded area of mapping	
Locality, town or village	
Shown when more than one place has the same name	
Postcode district	
District for the indexed place	
Page and grid square	
Page number and grid reference for the standard mapping	

Public and commercial buildings are highlighted in magenta   **Places of interest** are highlighted in blue with a star★

Abbreviations used in the index

Acad	Academy	Comm	Common	Gd	Ground	L	Leisure	Prom	Promenade
App	Approach	Cott	Cottage	Gdn	Garden	La	Lane	Rd	Road
Arc	Arcade	Cres	Crescent	Gn	Green	Liby	Library	Recn	Recreation
Ave	Avenue	Cswy	Causeway	Gr	Grove	Mdw	Meadow	Ret	Retail
Bglw	Bungalow	Ct	Court	H	Hall	Meml	Memorial	Sh	Shopping
Bldg	Building	Ctr	Centre	Ho	House	Mkt	Market	Sq	Square
Bsns, Bus	Business	Ctry	Country	Hospl	Hospital	Mus	Museum	St	Street
Bvd	Boulevard	Cty	County	HQ	Headquarters	Orch	Orchard	Sta	Station
Cath	Cathedral	Dr	Drive	Hts	Heights	Pal	Palace	Terr	Terrace
Cir	Circus	Dro	Drove	Ind	Industrial	Par	Parade	TH	Town Hall
Cl	Close	Ed	Education	Inst	Institute	Pas	Passage	Univ	University
Cnr	Corner	Emb	Embankment	Int	International	Pk	Park	Wk, Wlk	Walk
Coll	College	Est	Estate	Intc	Interchange	Pl	Place	Wr	Water
Com	Community	Ex	Exhibition	Junc	Junction	Prec	Precinct	Yd	Yard

Index of localities, towns and villages

A

Abbotsford	72 E6
Alciston	170 D8
Alderbrook	38 A7
Aldrington	162 E6
Alfriston	170 F7
Argos Hill	39 E5
Arlington	150 F4
Ashurst	5 D2
Ashurst Wood	11 E5

B

Baldslow	136 C7
Baldwin's Hill	1 D4
Balls Green	14 C5
Banner Farm	8 C2
Barcombe	101 E2
Barcombe Cross	101 E4
Barcombe Mills	102 A3
Bardown	42 E2
Battle	112 D5
Beachlands	175 F6
Beacon Down	81 A7
Beckley	68 A4
Beckley Furnace	90 D7
Beddingham	147 D4
Bells Yew Green	17 F5
Belmont	137 C1
Berwick	170 F7
Best Beech Hill	29 B3
Bevendean	143 F2
Bexhill	157 A2
Birchden	15 D5

Birchett's Green	30 F3
Birchgrove	34 A8
Birling Gap	187 A5
Bishopstone	180 C6
Blackboys	80 A5
Blackham	5 A4
Blackhurst	8 F5
Blacklands	136 F2
Blackness Crowborough	26 A1
Blackness Eastbourne	174 A6
Black Rock	164 F3
Blackwell	1 E3
Boarshead	26 C6
Bodiam	65 E8
Bodle Street Green	109 C2
Bohemia	136 C1
Boreham Street	131 F4
Brede	90 B1
Brightling	85 C7
Brighton	164 B4
Brighton	189 B1
Broadland Row	90 D3
Broad Oak Hastings	90 C4
Broad Oak Heathfield	59 F1
Broad Street	116 C6
Broadwater Down	16 E7
Broomsgrove	137 A2
Brownbread Street	110 A2
Broyle Side	124 F8
Buckham Hill	77 E6
Budlett's Common	55 C3
Bullingstone	6 F7
Bulverhythe	158 C6
Burgess Hill	73 D2
Burgh Hill	44 E3
Burlow	106 F5
Burnt Oak	37 F3

Burwash	62 B6
Burwash Common	61 A4
Burwash Weald	61 C3
Butcher's Cross	58 B8
Buxted	56 B4

C

Cackle Street Battle	85 E4
Cackle Street Hastings	90 A2
Cackle Street Uckfield	35 E2
Cade Street	82 E6
Caldbec Hill	112 D6
Camber	94 F2
Camden Park	8 C2
Canadia	112 D8
Caneheath	151 B4
Castle Hill	39 A4
Catsfield	133 F8
Catsfield Stream	133 E7
Chailey	75 E4
Chalvington	150 A7
Chapel Row	130 F5
Chapman's Town	83 B2
Chelwood Common	34 D6
Chelwood Gate	34 D8
Chiddingly	105 F1
Chiltington	100 D3
Chitcombe	89 E6
Chuck Hatch	24 D7
Churches Green	109 B8
Cinder Hill	33 B8
Clayhill	67 D3
Clayton	119 E8
Cliffe	190 B2
Cliff End	139 B7

Clive Vale	137 C2
Cobbarn	15 E3
Cock Marling	92 A2
Coggins Mill	40 D4
Coldean	143 D6
Coleman's Hatch	23 E7
Collier's Green	66 A2
Cooden	156 D2
Cooksbridge	123 A8
Cooper's Green	55 D4
Cornwall's Bank	76 C5
Cottenden	43 B5
Cousley Wood	30 C7
Cowbeech	108 C1
Cowbeech Hill	130 B7
Cowden	4 A6
Cripp's Corner	88 D7
Cross-in-Hand	81 B7
Crowborough	26 C1
Crowborough Warren	25 C1
Crowhurst	134 F6
Crowlink	186 F7
Cuckfield	50 A6
Cuilfail	190 C2

D

Dallington	84 D3
Danehill	34 A4
Darwell Hole	85 F3
Deanland Village	127 B4
Denny Bottom	7 E4
Denton	168 F2
Ditchling	98 D3
Dodd's Hill	35 D2
Dormansland	2 B8

Dormans Park	1 E6
Downside	184 C4
Down Street	54 C5
Duddleswell	36 B4
Durgates	29 E5

E

Earl's Down	84 B4
East Blatchington	180 E5
Eastbourne	185 B4
East Chiltington	100 A3
East Dean	187 B8
East End	98 E3
East Grinstead	1 E2
East Guldeford	93 C7
East Hoathly	105 B5
East Moulsecoomb	143 F3
Eridge Green	16 B3
Etchingham	44 B1
Etchingwood	56 D1
Ewhurst Green	66 B3
Exceat	181 F4

F

Fairlight	138 C4
Fairlight Cove	138 F5
Fairwarp	36 B2
Falmer	144 D6
Felbridge	1 A6
Felcourt	1 C8
Ferndale	8 C5
Filching	172 D3
Fishergate	162 A7

Five Ash Down 55 D5
Five Ashes 58 B7
Flackley Ash 68 F3
Fletching 53 F4
Fletching Common 53 C1
Flimwell 32 C3
Flowers Green 130 F3
Folkington 172 B4
Fordcombe 6 B5
Ford's Green 35 C3
Forest Row 11 F3
Four Oaks 68 C5
Four Throws 46 D8
Foxhole 182 A1
Framfield 79 B6
Franklands Village 51 A4
Frant 17 C3
Friar's Gate 25 B7
Friar's Hill 138 B7
Friday Street 174 A3
Friston 183 A2
Furner's Green 34 C1

G
Gallypot Street 13 B3
Ginger's Green 130 C6
Glenleigh Park 157 A7
Glynde 147 E7
Glyne Gap 158 B5
Goatham Green 89 E5
Goddards' Green 72 A5
Golden Cross Hailsham 127 D6
Golden Cross
  Herstmonceux 130 E3
Green Street 135 B4
Grisling Common 77 B8
Groombridge 15 C7
Grove Hill 107 E1
Guestling Green 138 A8
Gun Hill 106 C2

H
Hadlow Down 57 C5
Hailsham 152 C8
Hale Green 106 A2
Halland 104 C5
Halton 137 B2
Hammerwood 3 B3
Hampden Park 173 E1
Hamsey 123 C6
Hangleton 141 C2
Hankham 174 B8
Harley Shute 158 E7
Hartfield 13 D4
Hassocks 97 E4
Hastings 159 F7
Hawkenbury 8 D2
Haywards Heath 50 C7
Hazard's Green 132 C5
Heathfield 82 B7
Hellingly 129 A5
Henley's Down 134 B6
Henwood Green 9 E6
Heron's Ghyll 36 E3
Herstmonceux 130 E6
High Brooms 8 C8
High Cross 39 C6
Highgate 11 F1
High Hurstwood 37 A1
High Wickham 137 C1
Holligdean 143 B3
Hollingbury 143 B5
Hollingrove 85 E6
Hollington 136 A4
Holton Hill 61 E7
Holtye 3 F3
Hooe 155 D8
Hooe Common 132 F2
Hook Green 19 C4
Horam 106 E7
Horney Common 54 E8
Horns Cross 67 A1
Horsted Green 78 A3
Horsted Keynes 33 C5
Houghton Green 70 D2
Hove 163 B5
Hungershall Park 7 E2
Hurst Green 45 B3
Hurstpierpoint 97 B6
Hurst Wickham 97 C6

I
Icklesham 116 E6

Iden 70 B4
Iford 146 B3
Isfield 102 E7

J
Jarvis Brook 38 D8
Jenkins' Green 174 C8
Jevington 183 C8
John's Cross 87 C7
Jury's Gap 95 D1

K
Kemp Town 164 D4
Keymer 98 B4
Kildown 20 F3
Kings Bank 68 A3
Kingston by Sea 161 C7
Kingston near Lewes 145 E5
Kingstonridge 145 D6

L
Lamberhurst 20 B5
Landport 123 B2
Langney 174 D3
Langney Village 174 E2
Langton Green 6 E3
Laughton 126 C6
Lewes 123 C2
Lewes 190 B3
Lidham Hill 115 E6
Lindfield 51 A7
Linkhill 47 E4
Litlington 182 B8
Little Bayham 18 F4
Little Common 156 D5
Little Horsted 78 C1
Little London 81 E4
Little Norlington 102 F1
Little Parrock 12 D1
Lower Cousley Wood 30 E8
Lower Dicker 128 D3
Lower Green Pembury 9 D8
Lower Green
  Royal Tunbridge Wells 7 C5
Lower Horsebridge 128 F3
Lower Standean 120 A3
Lower Street 133 B5
Lower Willingdon 173 C4
Lunsford's Cross 133 E2
Lye Green 14 D1

M
Madeira Park 8 B2
Magham Down 129 F4
Marden's Hill 25 B5
Maresfield 55 A5
Maresfield Park 55 A6
Mark Cross 28 A4
Mark Street 34 F3
Marle Green 107 B5
Marlpits Bexhill 133 B7
Marlpits Crowborough 35 E6
Mayfield 40 A2
Maynard's Green 82 A1
Meads 188 E8
Mile Oak 140 F4
Millbrook 35 C6
Mill Corner 67 A3
Mill Hill 174 D6
Milton Street 171 D5
Mott's Mill 15 A3
Moulsecoomb 143 E2
Mount Ephraim
  Royal Tunbridge Wells 7 F4
Mount Ephraim Uckfield 78 F3
Mountfield 87 C5
Mount Pleasant Lewes 101 F6
Mount Pleasant
  Newhaven 168 F1
Mount Sion 8 A2
Muddles Green 127 F8
Mutton Hall 82 A8

N
Nash Street 128 A6
Netherfield 86 C2
Nevill Park 7 D2
Newbridge 23 F6
Newbury's 30 B8

New Cut 114 E5
Newenden 48 D3
Newhaven 179 E6
Newick 76 C8
Newton's Hill 13 C3
New Town 78 E5
Ninfield 133 B6
Norlington 124 D7
Normans' Bay 176 D8
Northbridge Street 64 C6
North Chailey 75 E6
North End 1 B3
Northiam 67 B6
North Moulsecoomb 143 D4
Norton 180 C8
Nutley 35 C4

O
Offham 122 F5
Old Heathfield 82 D5
Old Town Bexhill 157 D5
Old Town Eastbourne 184 D3
Old Town Hastings 160 B4
Ore 137 D3
Ovingdean 165 D3
Oxbottom 76 B5
Oxley's Green 85 E8

P
Patcham 142 F6
Peacehaven 178 D7
Peasmarsh 69 B2
Pebsham 158 A6
Pell Green 30 A7
Pembury 9 C6
Penhurst 110 E6
Pett 116 F1
Pett Level 139 B8
Pevensey 175 B6
Pevensey Bay 175 D4
Pick Hill 106 D4
Piddinghoe 168 A2
Piltdown 54 B1
Playden 93 C8
Plumpton 121 E8
Plumpton Green 99 E6
Polegate 173 B5
Ponts Green 110 B4
Portslade-by-Sea 162 B5
Portslade Village 141 B1
Potman's Heath 49 E4
Potter's Green 56 C3
Poundfield 26 A2
Poundford 58 B5
Poundgate 37 A6
Pound Green 56 D4
Poundsbridge 6 D8
Pounsley 80 B8
Preston 142 E1
Punnett's Town 83 C5
Pyecombe 119 B6

Q
Quabrook 12 C1

R
Ramslye 7 D1
Rickney 153 D2
Ridgewood 78 C4
Ringles Cross 55 C2
Ringmer 124 C6
Ripe 126 D1
Riseden 29 B1
Robertsbridge 64 B4
Rockrobin 29 D6
Rocks Park 78 A7
Rodmell 167 D8
Roedean 165 B4
Romford 9 F7
Rose Hill 102 F6
Roselands 185 B5
Roser's Cross 80 F6
Rotherfield 39 B7
Rottingdean 177 A6
Round Hill 164 B8
Royal Tunbridge Wells 8 D3
Rusher's Cross 40 E6
Rushlake Green 83 D2
Rushy Green 124 E5
Russell's Green 133 A3
Rusthall 7 C4

Rye 93 B6
Rye Foreign 69 E1
Rye Harbour 93 F2

S
St Annes 123 A1
St Anthony's Hill 185 C8
St Helen's 137 A5
St John's Crowborough 25 D4
St John's
  Royal Tunbridge Wells 8 A5
St John's Common 72 E4
St Leonards 159 A7
St Leonard's Green 136 A1
Saint's Hill 6 A8
Salehurst 64 D5
Saltdean 177 D6
Sandhurst 47 C6
Sandhurst Cross 46 F4
Sandy Cross 82 B5
Scaynes Hill 51 E3
Seaford 180 D2
Sedlescombe 88 D1
Selmeston 149 D2
Sharpsbridge 77 C6
Sharpthorne 21 A6
Sheffield Green 53 C7
Shellies Green 138 C8
Sherwood 8 E6
Shoreham Beach 161 B6
Shoreham-by-Sea 161 A5
Shortbridge 77 E8
Shortgate 104 B3
Shover's Green 30 C1
Sidley 157 A7
Silverhill 136 C3
Silver Hill 64 B8
Silverhill Park 136 C4
Skippers Hill 58 B8
South Chailey 100 D7
Southease 167 E7
Southern Cross 162 A8
South Heighton 168 E2
South Malling 190 B3
Southover 146 B7
South Street 75 E1
Southwick 161 F7
Sparrow's Green 29 F5
Speldhurst 7 B7
Spithurst 101 F7
Splayne's Green 54 A5
Standard Hill 132 F6
Standen Street 47 D8
Stanmer 143 F8
Staplecross 65 E2
Starr's Green 112 F3
Steel Cross 26 B3
Steven's Crouch 111 B3
Stone Bridge 29 E6
Stone Cross Crowborough 37 F6
Stone Cross Eastbourne 174 C6
Stone Cross
  Royal Tunbridge Wells 6 A2
Stonecrouch 31 F6
Stonegate 42 F6
Stonequarry 2 B3
Streat 99 C3
Stunts Green 130 D7
Summer Hill 152 A4
Sunnyside 10 D7
Sutton 181 B4
Sweethaws 37 C6
Swiftsden 44 F6

T
Tarring Neville 168 D4
Teasley Mead 5 C4
Telscombe 167 B3
Telscombe Cliffs 177 F4
The Brooks 190 B3
The Down 20 A3
The Highlands 156 F8
The Moor 45 F8
Three Cups Corner 83 F5
Three Leg Cross 31 D3
Three Oaks 115 E2
Ticehurst 31 E2
Tidebrook 41 A8
Tilsmore 81 F7
Tompset's Bank 22 F8
Town Littleworth 76 C1
Town Row 27 C2
Trolliloes 108 D2
Turner's Green 83 F4
Turner's Green 29 F6

Twelve Oaks 85 E5

U
Uckfield 78 D7
Udimore 91 D2
Union Street 32 B3
Upper Dicker 151 A8
Upper Hartfield 13 A2
Upper Horsebridge 129 B3
Upperton 184 F5
Upper Wellingham 124 B8

V
Vinehall Street 87 E6
Vine's Cross 107 D8

W
Wadhurst 30 A4
Waldron 80 F3
Waldron Down 80 D8
Wallands Park 123 B1
Walstead 51 C5
Walter's Green 5 E6
Wannock 172 E4
Warbleton 83 A1
Warren 188 C8
Wartling 154 D7
Wellbrook 39 E1
West Blatchington 141 F1
Westdean 182 B4
Westdene 142 B5
Westfield 114 F4
West Firle 148 C3
Westham 174 E5
West Hill 137 B1
West Marina 158 F5
Westmeston 120 F8
Whatlington 88 A1
Whitehawk 164 E5
Whitehill 37 F8
White Post 5 D7
Whitesmith 127 B8
Whydown 156 B8
Wickstreet 150 D6
Willard's Hill 63 C5
Willingdon 173 A1
Wilmington 171 F5
Wilmington Green 171 E7
Winchelsea 117 E7
Winchelsea Beach 118 A5
Windmill Hill 131 B6
Withdean 142 E4
Withyham 14 A3
Wivelsfield 74 B5
Wivelsfield Green 74 C4
Woodingdean 165 D7
Woodmans Green 88 A3
Wood's Corner 84 F3
Wood's Green 29 F8
Woolbridge 39 E2
World's End 73 D4
Wych Cross 22 E5

A

Abberton Field BN6 ......97 B5
Abbey Cl BN10 ......167 C1
Abbey Ct Battle TN33 ......112 D4
  Robertsbridge TN32 ......64 B4
Abbey Dr TN38 ......158 B5
Abbey Mews TN32 ......64 B4
Abbey Path BN27 ......129 C2
Abbey Rd Brighton BN2 ......164 D4
  Eastbourne BN20 ......184 B5
Abbey View TN40 ......157 D6
Abbey Way TN33 ......112 D5
Abbeyfield Ho BN26 ......170 F7
Abbot's Lodge BN21 ......184 F4
Abbots Cl Battle TN33 ......112 E7
  Hassocks BN6 ......97 E4
Abbotsbury Cl BN2 ......177 B5
Abbotsfield Cl TN34 ......136 F3
Abbotsford Com Specl Sch
  RH15 ......72 E6
Abbotts 11 BN1 ......163 E5
Abbotts Cl BN22 ......185 A4
Abbotts Wood Forest Wlk*
  BN26 ......151 B3
Aberdale Rd BN2 ......165 F6
Aberdeen Rd 6 BN2 ......164 C8
Abergavenny Rd BN7 ......123 B1
Abigail Ho 10 RH16 ......50 E4
Abinger Ct BN41 ......162 B8
Abinger Pl BN7 ......190 A2
Abinger Rd
  Portslade-by-S BN41 ......162 B8
  Woodingdean BN2 ......165 E6
Acacia Ave BN3 ......141 F1
Acacia Ct BN1 ......142 F2
Acacia Rd
  Eastbourne BN22 ......173 D2
  Newhaven BN9 ......168 C2
Acer Ave TN2 ......17 C8
Acerlands BN6 ......76 C8
Acorn Cl
  East Grinstead RH19 ......10 E8
  St Leonards TN37 ......136 C4
Acorn Gn 3 BN27 ......129 B1
Acorn Way TN19 ......45 A3
Acorns The
  Burgess Hill RH15 ......72 D4
  Hailsham BN27 ......152 D7
  Stonegate TN5 ......42 F6
Acre Cl RH16 ......50 D7
Acres Rise TN5 ......31 E1
Adam Cl Crowborough TN6 ......38 A6
  St Leonards TN38 ......135 F4
Adams Cl BN1 ......143 B2
Adams La TN31 ......66 D2
Addingham Rd BN22 ......185 C4
Addington Ct TN38 ......158 F7
Addison Rd BN3 ......163 E7
Adelaide Cl BN25 ......180 E5
Adelaide Cres BN3 ......163 C5
Adelaide Rd TN38 ......136 B3
Adelaide Sq BN43 ......161 B7
Ades Field BN26 ......171 E6
Admiral's Bridge La
  RH19 ......10 C2
Admiralty Cres BN23 ......175 B1
Admiralty Ct BN23 ......175 B1
Admiralty Way BN23 ......175 B1
Adur Ct 10 BN41 ......161 C8
Adur Dr
  Shoreham-by-S BN43 ......161 A2
  Stone Cross BN24 ......174 A5
Adur Rd RH15 ......73 C4
Agincourt Cl TN37 ......135 F7
Agnes St BN1 ......164 C7
Ainsworth Ave BN2 ......165 D3
Ainsworth Cl BN2 ......165 D3
Ainsworth Ho 1 BN2 ......164 C7
Air St BN1 ......189 A2
Airlie Ho BN3 ......163 C6
Airy Rd BN27 ......131 B2
Akehurst Field TN33 ......110 B3
Alamein Cl TN6 ......38 A8
Alan Ct 6 TN37 ......159 C7
Alan Way BN2 ......164 F5
Albany Ct
  Eastbourne BN21 ......184 F5
  2 Hastings TN34 ......159 F7
Albany Hill TN2 ......8 C5
Albany Mans TN38 ......159 B8
Albany Rd Bexhill TN40 ......157 C3
  Seaford BN25 ......180 C3
  St Leonards TN38 ......159 B7
Albany Villas
  Cuckfield RH17 ......50 A6
  Hove BN3 ......163 B6
Albemarle Mans 9 BN3 ......163 B5
Albemarle The BN2 ......189 B1
Albert Cl RH16 ......51 A4
Albert Cotts TN1 ......8 B4
Albert Dr RH15 ......72 E2
Albert Mews BN3 ......163 A6
Albert Par BN21 ......184 C4
Albert Rd BN26 ......173 A7
Albert Rd Bexhill TN40 ......157 C3
  Brighton BN2 ......189 A3
  Hastings TN34 ......159 F7
  Polegate BN26 ......173 A7
  Southwick BN42 ......161 D7
  Uckfield TN22 ......78 D6
Albert St TN1 ......8 B4
Albion Cl Brighton BN2 ......189 C2
  Burgess Hill RH15 ......72 F2

Albion Hill BN2 ......189 C3
Albion Ho
  4 Brighton BN2 ......189 C3
  Southwick BN42 ......161 E7
Albion La 4 TN34 ......160 A3
Albion Mews TN1 ......8 C5
Albion Rd
  Eastbourne BN22 ......185 B4
  Royal Tunbridge Wells TN1 ......8 C5
Albion St Brighton BN2 ......189 C3
  Lewes BN7 ......190 B2
  Portslade-by-S BN41 ......162 B7
  Southwick BN42 ......161 E7
Albourne Cl
  Brighton BN2 ......164 F7
  St Leonards TN38 ......158 F8
Alces Pl BN25 ......180 E5
Aldborough Rd TN37 ......136 C1
Aldenham Ct 1 BN21 ......184 F4
Alder Cl Eastbourne BN23 ......185 C8
  Heathfield TN21 ......82 A5
  St Leonards TN38 ......158 F7
Alder Lodge TN4 ......7 E4
Alderbrook Cl TN6 ......38 A6
Alderbrook Cotts TN6 ......38 A7
Alderbrook Path TN6 ......38 A6
Alderbrook Way TN6 ......38 A6
Alders Ave RH19 ......1 E3
Alders View Dr RH19 ......137 A7
Alderton Ct 7 TN39 ......157 B3
Aldervale Cotts TN6 ......38 A7
Aldrich Cl BN2 ......164 F6
Aldrington Ave BN3 ......163 A8
Aldrington CE Prim Sch
  BN3 ......142 A2
Aldrington Cl BN3 ......162 D7
Aldrington House Hospl
  BN3 ......162 F6
Aldrington Pl BN3 ......162 D8
Aldrington Sta BN3 ......163 A8
Alexander Dr TN39 ......156 E4
Alexander Mead BN7 ......76 D8
Alexandra Cl BN25 ......180 E5
Alexandra Par TN34 ......136 D3
Alexandra Park Mans
  TN34 ......136 E2
Alexandra Rd
  Burgess Hill RH15 ......73 C2
  Eastbourne BN22 ......185 D6
  Heathfield TN21 ......82 B6
  Mayfield TN20 ......40 C3
  St Leonards TN37 ......159 C8
  Uckfield TN22 ......78 D6
Alexandra Terr TN20 ......40 C3
Alexandra Villas BN1 ......189 A3
Alford Way TN40 ......157 E6
Alfray Rd TN40 ......158 A5
Alfred St BN1 ......189 A3
Alfriston Cl Bexhill TN39 ......156 C6
  Brighton BN2 ......164 F6
  Eastbourne BN20 ......184 C2
Alfriston Clergy Ho*
  BN26 ......171 A2
Alfriston Pk BN25 ......181 C5
Alfriston Rd
  Alfriston BN26 ......170 F3
  Seaford BN25,BN26 ......181 D6
Alfriston Sch BN26 ......170 F3
Alice Bright La TN6 ......37 F7
Alice Cl 2 BN22 ......163 D5
Alice Hudson Gdns
  BN23 ......185 D7
Alice St BN23 ......185 C7
All Saints CE Jun Sch
  TN35 ......160 C6
All Saints CE Prim Sch
  TN39 ......157 B7
All Saints Gdns TN21 ......81 F7
All Saints La TN39 ......157 B7
All Saints Rd TN4 ......7 B6
All Saints Rise TN4 ......8 A6
All Saints' & St Richard's CE
  Prim Sch TN35 ......82 D6
All Saints' Cres TN35 ......160 B4
All Saints' Hospl BN20 ......188 E7
All Saints' St TN34 ......160 B4
Allan Cl TN4 ......7 D4
Allandale Rd TN2 ......8 D7
Allards TN35 ......138 C8
Allegria Ct TN38 ......159 B7
Allen Gardinier Ho TN2 ......8 C3
Allen Rd RH15 ......51 A4
Allen Way TN40 ......157 F7
Allix's Cl RH19 ......11 D6
Allfrey Rd BN22 ......185 D6
Allfreys La TN6 ......37 D6
Allington Cres BN8 ......76 C7
Allington Rd BN7 ......122 D7
Allington Rd BN8 ......76 C6
Allwood Cres RH17 ......74 C4
Alma Rd RH15 ......51 B8
Alma Terr TN37 ......136 C2
Alma Villas TN37 ......136 C2
Almonry Fields TN32 ......112 B4
Alpine Rd Hastings TN34 ......160 A4
  Hove BN3 ......163 B6
Alverstone Cl BN23 ......174 B4
Amanda Cl TN40 ......157 F7
Ambassadors The 10
  ......163 C6
Amber Ct 18 Hove BN3 ......163 C6
  8 Hove BN3 ......163 C6
Amberleaze Dr TN2 ......9 D7

Amberley Cl
  Burgess Hill RH15 ......73 A4
  Haywards Heath RH16 ......50 D4
  Hove BN3 ......141 E3
Amberley Ct TN34 ......8 C8
Amberley Dr BN3 ......141 E3
Amberley Lodge
  Brighton BN2 ......189 B4
  Brighton,Whitehawk BN2 ......164 F6
Amberley Rd BN22 ......173 C1
Amberstone BN27 ......129 E3
Amberstone Cl TN34 ......160 A8
Amberstone Hospl
  BN27 ......129 E4
Amberstone View BN27 ......129 C2
Ambleside Ave BN10 ......178 A8
Ambleside Cl BN10 ......178 A7
America La RH16 ......51 A5
Amesbury Cres BN3 ......162 E7
Amherst Cl TN34 ......136 D1
Amherst Cres BN3 ......162 F8
Amherst Gdns TN34 ......136 D1
Amherst Rd Bexhill TN40 ......157 C4
  Hastings TN34 ......136 D1
  Royal Tunbridge Wells TN4 ......8 A5
Amhurst Rd BN10 ......177 F3
Anchor Cl BN43 ......161 A6
Anchor Field BN26 ......124 D5
Anchor Hill RH17 ......52 A2
Anchor La BN8 ......102 B5
Anchorage The RH16 ......50 D4
Anchorage Way BN23 ......175 B2
Anderida Ct TN34 ......156 C4
Anderida Rd BN22 ......173 C3
Anderson Cl BN9 ......179 B7
Andrew Rd TN4 ......8 C8
Andrews Cl
  Northbridge Street TN32 ......64 C5
  Royal Tunbridge Wells TN2 ......8 D5
Andros Cl BN1 ......100 E6
Andwell Ct BN21 ......185 B2
Angel Cl 1 BN21 ......185 A4
Angel Row TN18 ......47 B5
Angel Terr TN18 ......47 B6
Angela Cl TN40 ......157 F7
Anglesea Mans TN38 ......159 B8
Anglesea Terr TN37,
  TN38 ......159 C8
Anglesey Ave BN27 ......129 A2
Angmering Ct BN1 ......143 F5
Angrove Ho TN1 ......8 C5
Angus Cl BN20 ......173 B5
Anjou Ct BN23 ......174 F1
Ann Cl BN6 ......98 A5
Ann St Brighton BN1 ......189 B4
  Hastings TN34 ......160 C6
Anne of Cleves House Mus*
  BN7 ......190 A1
Anne's Path BN7 ......190 A1
Annecy RC Prim Sch
  BN25 ......181 A2
Annington Rd BN22 ......185 B5
Anscombe 5 RH16 ......50 D6
Anson Cl BN23 ......174 F1
Anson Ho BN10 ......167 C1
Ansty Ct BN2 ......164 E5
Antares Path BN27 ......152 E7
Antigua Ct 11 BN23 ......185 F8
Antioch St BN7 ......190 A1
Antony Cl BN25 ......180 B6
Antrim Ct BN23 ......174 F1
Antrona Ct TN39 ......156 C3
Anvil Cl
  Portslade-by-S BN41 ......141 B2
  Uckfield TN22 ......78 B6
Anvil Ct TN37 ......136 C1
Anzac Cl BN10 ......167 C1
Apex Pk BN27 ......152 A7
Apple Tree La TN2 ......9 D8
Appledore Cnr BN8 ......100 E7
Appledore Cl BN23 ......174 F2
Appledore Ct RH16 ......51 A7
Appledore Gdns RH16 ......51 A6
Appledore Rd BN23 ......143 F4
Applesham Ave BN41 ......162 E2
Applesham Way BN41 ......141 A2
Applewood Ct TN37 ......136 B5
Approach The
  10 Brighton BN1 ......142 E3
  Dormans Park RH19 ......1 F6
April Pl 4 TN40 ......157 C4
Apsley St TN4 ......7 D4
Aqua Ho BN1 ......177 F3
Aquarium Sta* BN2 ......189 C1
Aquarius Ct BN10 ......178 C6
Aquila Pk BN25 ......181 A3
Araquipe Reef BN23 ......185 G8
Arbor Ct RH16 ......50 E5
Arbourvale TN38 ......158 A3
Arbroath Ct 3 TN38 ......136 B1
Arcade The BN7 ......190 C2
Archer Cl RH15 ......73 A3
Archers Ct TN34 ......8 C8
Archery Ct
  Eastbourne BN22 ......185 C6
  3 St Leonards TN37 ......159 B7
Archery Rd TN38 ......159 B8
Archery Wlk BN27 ......152 D8
Ardingly Ct 12 BN2 ......164 E4
Ardingly Rd BN2 ......177 D4
Ardingly St BN2 ......189 C2
Argent Cl BN25 ......181 A5
Argos Hill Rd TN20,TN6 ......39 C4
Argus Lofts BN1 ......189 B3
Argyle Rd BN1 ......189 A5
Argyll Ct 3 Bexhill TN39 ......157 A4
  Eastbourne BN22 ......173 E2

Arkendale RH19 ......1 A4
Arkwright Rd BN23 ......174 A1
Arlington Cres BN1 ......143 E5
Arlington Ct RH16 ......50 E5
Arlington Gdns BN2 ......177 D6
Arlington Ho 7 BN21 ......184 D4
Arlington Rd BN21 ......184 D4
Arlington Rd E BN27 ......152 A6
Arlington Rd W BN27 ......151 F6
Arlington Resr* BN26 ......150 C3
Armstrong Ct TN38 ......135 E4
Arnbury Mews TN38 ......159 A8
Arndale Ctr BN21 ......185 A3
Arnold St BN2 ......164 C7
Arnside Rd TN38 ......158 C6
Arnworth Ct BN21 ......185 A3
Arran Cl BN27 ......129 A2
Arthur Bliss Ho RH16 ......51 A8
Arthur Rd TN39 ......157 B4
Arthur St BN3 ......163 A8
Artisans Dwellings 8
  BN21 ......184 F2
Arts Rd BN1 ......144 B7
Arun Cl BN24 ......173 F5
Arun Ct 15 BN43 ......161 C8
Arun Lodge BN11 ......184 E3
Arun Path TN22 ......55 E1
Arun Way BN24 ......173 F5
Arundel Cl
  Beachlands BN24 ......175 C6
  Hailsham BN27 ......129 C2
Arundel Ct
  6 Brighton BN2 ......164 E4
  Brighton,Westdene BN1 ......142 C5
  Burgess Hill RH15 ......72 F4
  Hastings TN35 ......160 C6
  14 Shoreham-by-S BN43 ......161 C8
Arundel Dr E BN2 ......177 C5
Arundel Dr W BN2 ......177 C5
Arundel Gn BN2 ......123 B2
Arundel Ho 4 BN21 ......184 E4
Arundel Keep 11 BN21 ......184 F4
Arundel Mews
  10 Brighton BN2 ......164 E4
  Haywards Heath RH16 ......50 F2
Arundel Pl BN2 ......164 E4
Arundel Rd Brighton BN2 ......164 E4
  Eastbourne BN21 ......184 F4
  Newhaven BN9 ......168 F1
  Peacehaven BN10 ......178 D7
  Royal Tunbridge Wells TN1 ......8 B2
  Seaford BN25 ......181 A3
Arundel Rd W BN10 ......178 B7
Arundel Road Central
  BN10 ......178 C7
Arundel St BN2 ......164 E3
Arundel Terr BN2 ......164 E3
Ascham Ct BN20 ......184 E1
Ascot Cl BN20 ......188 F8
Ascot Mews TN38 ......159 A8
Ash Cl Eastbourne BN22 ......173 D7
  Hove BN3 ......142 C3
Ash Ct East Grinstead RH19 ......1 E3
  Hailsham BN27 ......152 A7
  Southwick BN42 ......140 F1
Ash Dr BN25 ......181 C3
Ash Gn
  Haywards Heath RH16 ......50 D2
  Westham BN24 ......174 D6
Ash Tree Cl TN21 ......82 A7
Ash Wlk BN9 ......179 B7
Ashampstead Pl 4
  BN21 ......184 F3
Ashbourne Ct
  18 Eastbourne BN21 ......185 A2
  Rusthall TN4 ......7 A4
Ashbrook Rd TN37 ......136 B4
Ashburnham Ct BN1 ......143 E5
Ashburnham Dr BN1 ......143 E5
Ashburnham Gdns
  BN21 ......184 F2
Ashburnham Ho BN1 ......142 E5
Ashburnham Pl BN27 ......129 A2
Ashburnham Rd
  Eastbourne BN21 ......184 F2
  Hastings TN35 ......160 C6
Ashby Cl TN39 ......157 A8
Ashcombe Dr TN39 ......156 D3
Ashcombe Hollow BN7 ......145 D7
Ashcombe La BN7 ......145 C5
Ashcroft 1 BN43 ......161 D7
Ashcroft Cl Ringmer BN8 ......124 D5
  Shoreham-by-S BN43 ......161 D8
Ashdown 16 BN3 ......163 C6
Ashdown Ave BN2 ......177 B5
Ashdown Chase TN22 ......35 C5
Ashdown Cl
  Forest Row RH18 ......12 A2
  Haywards Heath RH16 ......50 F2
  Royal Tunbridge Wells TN4 ......7 A4
Ashdown Ct TN38 ......135 E2
Ashdown Forest Llama
  Farm* RH18 ......26 B6
Ashdown Forest Visitors
  Ctr* RH18 ......23 A5
Ashdown House Sch
  RH18 ......12 D4
Ashdown Nuffield Hospl
  RH16 ......50 D5

Ashdown Pl
  Forest Row RH18 ......22 E8
  Heathfield TN21 ......82 B6
Ashdown Rd
  Bexhill TN40 ......157 E4
  7 Brighton BN2 ......164 B8
  Eastbourne BN20 ......11 F2
Ashdown View
  East Grinstead RH19 ......10 E7
  Marlpits TN31 ......35 D6
Ashenden Ave TN31 ......93 A5
Ashenden Wlk TN2 ......8 E8
Ashenground Cl 6 RH16 ......50 E3
Ashenground Rd RH16 ......50 E3
Asher Reeds TN3 ......7 A4
Ashford Cl 4 BN21 ......152 C7
Ashford Rd Brighton BN1 ......143 A2
  Eastbourne BN21 ......185 A3
  Hastings TN34 ......136 E3
Ashford Sq BN21 ......185 A3
Ashford Way TN34 ......136 E3
Ashgate Rd BN23 ......174 E2
Ashington Cl BN2 ......164 F6
Ashington Gdns BN10 ......178 F6
Ashington Rd BN22 ......174 A1
Ashlands TN6 ......26 B1
Ashleigh Gdns TN6 ......25 E4
Ashleigh Glegg Ho
  BN25 ......180 D4
Ashley Cl BN21 ......142 E7
Ashley Dr Bexhill BN3 ......163 C5
  7 St Leonards TN37 ......159 C7
Ashley Gdns
  Hailsham BN27 ......129 C3
  Mayfield TN20 ......40 A3
  Rusthall TN4 ......7 C5
Ashley Park Cl TN4 ......7 C5
Ashley Pk TN4 ......7 C5
Ashley Rd TN6 ......27 D1
Ashlings Way Hove BN3 ......141 E2
  Shoreham-by-S BN43 ......140 B1
Ashmore Cl BN10 ......167 D2
Ashtead Twrs 8 TN40 ......157 E4
Ashton Lodge 15 BN2 ......189 C3
Ashton Rise BN2 ......189 C3
Ashtonville Cl BN8 ......124 E5
Ashurst Ave BN2 ......177 E5
Ashurst Hill TN3 ......5 D2
Ashurst Pl RH16 ......50 E5
Ashurst Rd Brighton BN2 ......164 F5
  Seaford BN25 ......180 F2
Stone Cross TN3 ......6 B2
Ashurst Sta TN3 ......5 D2
Ashurst Wood Prim Sch
  RH19 ......11 E6
Ashway RH15 ......73 A2
Ashwood Ct RH14 ......72 F1
Ashwyn Bsns Ctr RH15 ......72 F5
Aspen Cl RH16 ......51 A4
Aspen Gdns BN22 ......173 E2
Aspen Way TN39 ......156 C4
Aspen Wlk
  Haywards Heath RH16 ......51 A4
  Heathfield TN21 ......82 A5
Assisi Ct RH16 ......50 F2
Assisi Hts TN37 ......50 F2
Astaire Ave BN22 ......185 B6
Asten Cl TN38 ......158 E7
Astra Ho BN1 ......163 E5
Athelstan Cl 1 BN21 ......185 F8
Athelstan Rd TN35 ......160 D6
Athenaeum The 16 BN3 ......163 C6
Atlantic Dr BN23 ......185 F7
Atlingworth Ct BN21 ......189 C1
Atlingworth St BN2 ......189 C1
Attfield Wlk BN22 ......173 E3
Attree Ct 6 BN2 ......164 C6
Attree Dr BN2 ......164 C6
Aubyns 15 TN40 ......157 D3
Auckland Dr BN2 ......143 F1
Auckland Ho TN40 ......157 C2
Auckland Quay BN23 ......175 A1
Auckland Rd TN1 ......8 C5
Audrey Cl Brighton BN1 ......143 A5
  Seaford BN25 ......180 D5
Audrey Sturley Ct TN4 ......7 D4
Augustines Way RH16 ......50 F4
Augustus Way TN35 ......135 F6
Aultmore Ct TN2 ......8 D3
Austen Cl RH19 ......1 E1
Austen Way TN35 ......137 D5
Austen Wlk BN23 ......174 C2
Avard Cres BN20 ......184 B6
Avards Cl TN18 ......45 E8
Avenue Ct 20 BN3 ......163 C6
Avenue La BN21 ......184 F3
Avenue The
  Brighton BN2 ......143 E1
  Eastbourne BN20 ......184 F3
  Fairlight Cove TN35 ......138 F5
  Hailsham BN27 ......152 B6
  Heathfield TN21 ......82 B6
  Horam TN21 ......106 F8
  Kingston near Lewes BN7 ......145 D5
  Lewes BN7 ......190 A2
  Mayfield TN20 ......40 B2
Avery Cl BN41 ......140 F4
Aviemore Rd TN6 ......25 D2
Avis Cl BN9 ......168 E1
Avis Par BN9 ......168 E1
Avis Rd BN9 ......168 E1
Avis Way BN9 ......168 E1

Avocet BN27 ....152 A7
Avocet Trad Est RH15 ...72 F2
Avon Ct BN22 ....189 C2
Avon St TN1 ....4 C3
Avondale Ct █ BN25 ...180 E3
Avondale Rd
  Eastbourne BN22 ....185 B4
  Hove BN3 ....163 D7
  Seaford BN25 ....180 F3
  St Leonards TN38 ....136 A1
Avonhurst RH15 ....73 B3
Avonmore BN20 ....188 E8
Awbrook Cl RH17 ....51 F3
Aylesbury BN3 ....163 E6
Aylesbury Ave BN23 .....185 E8
Aymer Ho █ BN3 ....163 A6
Aymer Rd BN3 ....163 A6
Aynsley Ct BN3 ....163 C8
Ayscue Cl BN23 ....185 F7

B

Babylon Way BN20 ....184 B8
Back La Alfriston BN26 ...171 C4
  Cross-in-H TN21 ....81 C6
  Fairwarp TN22 ....36 B2
  Rushlake Green TN21 .....83 D1
  Winchelsea TN36 ....117 E7
Back Rd TN18 ....47 B5
Backwoods Cl RH16 ......51 B6
Backwoods La RH16 ......51 B6
Baden Rd BN2 ....143 D1
Badens Cl BN8 ....76 C6
Badger Cl BN41 ....141 B2
Badger Dr RH16 ....50 C5
Badger Gate TN31 ....93 A5
Badger Way BN1 ....143 E6
Badgers Brow BN20 ......184 B8
Badgers Cl
  Crowborough TN6 ....25 E3
  Newhaven BN9 ....179 D6
Badgers Copse BN25 .....181 C3
Badgers Ct BN20 ....188 F8
Badgers Dene BN7 ....167 D8
Badgers Field BN10 ......167 C1
Badgers Holt TN2 ....8 C5
Badgers Mount TN39 ....156 E5
Badgers Way
  East Grinstead RH19 ....1 F2
  Hastings TN34 ....136 D5
Badgers Wlk
  Burgess Hill RH15 ....73 D2
  Golden Cross BN27 ......127 C3
Badlesmere Rd BN22 ....185 B6
Bagham La BN27 ....130 F6
Bahama Rd TN36 ....172 F6
Bailey Cres BN22 ....173 E3
Baillie Ave BN2 ....185 C5
Bainbridge Cl BN25 ......180 F3
Bainden Cl TN6 ....27 D1
Baird Dr TN34 ....136 E3
Baird Ho TN37 ....159 C8
Baker Ct TN22 ....78 C7
Baker St Brighton BN1 ...189 B4
  Newhaven BN9 ....179 E7
  Uckfield TN22 ....78 D6
Baker's Rd BN21 ....184 D3
Bakers Farm Mobile Home
  Pk BN27 ....129 A3
Bakery Mews BN1 ....143 C1
Bakewell Rd BN21 ....184 D4
Bal Edmund TN37 ....156 A3
Balaclava La TN5 ....30 A6
Balcombe Ct BN10 ....178 C8
Balcombe Gn TN33 ....88 E1
Balcombe La RH17,RH19 ..21 C4
Balcombe Rd
  Haywards Heath RH16 .....50 D7
  Peacehaven BN10 ....178 B8
Baldings Cotts RH17 ......74 B5
Baldock Rd TN5 ....29 E4
Baldslow Down TN37 ....136 C8
Baldslow Rd TN34 ....136 A1
Baldwin Ave BN21 ....184 C5
Baldwins Field RH19 ....1 C4
Baldwins Hill Prim Sch
  RH19 ....1 D3
Bale Cl TN39 ....156 E5
Balfour Gdns RH18 ....11 E1
Balfour Inf Sch BN1 ....143 A3
Balfour Jun Sch BN1 .....143 A3
Balfour Rd BN1 ....143 A2
Ball's Gn TN7 ....14 B5
Ballard Dr BN8 ....125 A7
Ballards Hill TN33 ....134 F4
Ballsocks La TN21 ....107 C8
Balmer Farm Cotts BN7 144 D8
Balmoral BN1 ....11 A8
Balmoral Ct Hove BN3 ...142 A3
  ❷ St Leonards TN38 .....136 B1
Balsdean Rd BN2 ....144 F1
Baltic Ho TN1 ....8 A3
Baltimore Ct █ BN3 ......163 C7
Bamford Cl BN2 ....144 A2
Bampfield St BN41 ....162 B8
Bancroft Ho TN39 ....157 B5
Bancroft Rd TN39 ....157 B5
Bank Rd TN39 ....157 C2
Banks Rd BN8 ....52 F1
Bankside Brighton BN1 ..142 C5
  Durgates TN5 ....29 E5
  Hassocks BN6 ....97 F5
  Rye TN31 ....93 B6

Bankside Ct BN1 ....142 C5
Banner Cl BN24 ....174 C6
Banner Farm Rd TN2 ......8 B2
Banner Way BN24 ....174 C6
Bannings Vale BN2 ....177 E5
Bannister Way RH16 ......50 D6
Bannisters Field BN8 .....76 D7
Baranscraig Ave BN1 ...143 A7
Barbados TN40 ....157 E3
Barber Ct BN7 ....146 B8
Barbican House Mus★
  BN7 ....190 A2
Barbuda Quay BN23 .....185 G7
Barchester Pl █ BN21 ...185 A2
Barclay Ho ❷ BN2 ....164 C7
Barcombe Ave BN25 .....181 C3
Barcombe CE Prim Sch
  BN8 ....101 D5
Barcombe Cl
  Eastbourne BN20 ....184 C3
  Seaford BN25 ....181 C3
Barcombe Mills Rd BN8 101 E4
Barcombe Pl
  Brighton BN1 ....143 F5
  █ Crowborough TN6 ......25 F3
Barcombe Rd BN1 ....143 E4
Barcombe Wlk BN20 ....184 C3
Barden Rd
  Eastbourne BN22 ....185 C4
  Speldhurst TN3 ....7 A8
Bardown Rd TN5 ....42 E7
Barford Ct TN22 ....78 C7
Barganny █ TN40 ....157 D3
Bargate Cl TN39 ....157 C7
Barham Cl TN34 ....136 A1
Barkdale RH15 ....73 D5
Barley Ave TN35 ....160 C5
Barley Cl BN10 ....167 B2
Barley Dr RH15 ....72 D4
Barley Field Cotts TN7 ..146 D1
Barley La TN35 ....160 D5
Barley Mow La TN21 ......83 B5
Barming Cl BN21 ....174 D2
Barn Cl Hailsham BN27 .129 C1
  Kingston near Lewes BN7 145 E5
  Seaford BN25 ....181 A6
  Stone Cross BN24 ....174 A6
Barn Cottage La RH16 ...51 A5
Barn Cotts ❷ BN25 ......181 A3
Barn Ct Southwick BN42 162 A7
  St Leonards TN37 ....136 C5
Barn Hatch Cl BN7 ....146 A8
Barn Ho The BN25 ....180 E5
Barn La TN22 ....79 D8
Barn Rd BN1 ....190 C4
Barn Rise Brighton BN1 142 D5
  Seaford BN25 ....181 A5
Barn Stables ❷ BN7 ....123 B1
Barnard Gate RH16 ......50 C7
Barnes Rd BN41 ....162 B8
Barnet Way BN3 ....141 E3
Barnett Rd BN1 ....143 B2
Barnetts Way TN4 ....8 C8
Barnfield
  Crowborough TN6 ....26 A3
  Plumpton Green BN7 ......99 E5
  Royal Tunbridge Wells TN2 ..7 B2
Barnfield Ct TN34 ....159 D8
Barnfield Gdns
  █ Brighton BN2 ....164 C6
  Ditchling BN6 ....98 E3
Barnham Cl BN22 ....174 A2
Barnhams The TN39 .....156 E3
Barnhorn Rd TN39 ....156 C4
Barnhorn Rd TN39 ....156 B4
Barnmead RH16 ....50 D7
Barnsgate Manor Vineyard★
  TN22 ....36 E5
Barnside Ave RH15 ....73 D1
Barons Cl BN25 ....180 C5
Barons Ct
  Burgess Hill RH15 ....73 B2
  Royal Tunbridge Wells TN4 ..8 B3
Barons Down Rd BN7 ...146 A8
Barons Way BN26 ....172 F5
Barons Wlk BN7 ....146 A8
Barrack Rd TN40 ....157 C5
Barrack Sq TN36 ....117 F7
Barracks Cotts TN32 ......87 C7
Barrhill Ave BN1 ....142 E4
Barrie Cl BN23 ....174 E2
Barrier Reef Way BN23 ..175 A1
Barrington Cl RH16 ....50 F8
Barrington Rd RH16 ......51 A8
Barrington Wood RH16 ..50 F8
Barrow Cl BN1 ....143 C2
Barrow La TN1 ....8 A2
Barrow Rise TN37 ....136 C5
Barrowfield Cl BN3 ......142 C3
Barrowfield Dr BN3 ......142 D2
Barrowfield Lodge BN3 142 C2
Barry Wlk BN2 ....164 C6
Bartholomew Sq BN1 ..189 B2
Bartholomews BN1 ......189 B2
Bartley Mill La TN3 ....18 B3
Bartley Mill La TN3 ....18 F4
Bartley Mill Rd TN3 ......18 F3
Barton Cres RH17 ....11 A8
Basin Rd N BN41 ....162 B6
Basin Rd S BN3,BN41 ...162 B6
Baslow Rd BN20 ....188 D7
Baslow Rd BN20 ....188 D7
Bassett's Forge TN5 ......29 E5
Bassetts La
  Argos Hill TN20 ....39 F5
  Mark Cross TN6 ....28 E2

Bassetts La continued
  White Post TN8,TN11 ......5 C7
Batcheler Cres TN6 ....25 F3
Batchelor Way TN22 .....78 A7
Batchelors TN2 ....9 E8
Bateman's★ TN19 ....62 A4
Bateman's La TN19 ....62 A4
Batemans Rd BN2 ....165 E7
Bates Rd BN1 ....142 F2
Bath Cl BN3 ....163 A5
Bath Rd █ BN21 ....184 F7
Bath St BN1 ....189 A4
Bathford Cl BN23 ....174 D2
Battenhurst Rd TN5 ....43 B4
Battery Hill TN35 ....138 D5
Battle & Langton CE Prim
  Sch TN33 ....112 C4
Battle Abbey★ TN33 ....112 C4
Battle Abbey Sch TN33 112 C4
Battle Cl BN25 ....181 C5
Battle Cres
  Hailsham BN27 ....152 B8
  St Leonards TN37 ....136 B4
Battle Gates TN33 ....112 B5
Battle Hill TN33 ....112 E3
Battle Rd Hailsham BN27 129 C1
  Battle TN33 ....112 B4
  Battle Sta TN33 ....112 B4
Batts Bridge Rd TN22 ....55 A4
Bavant Rd BN1 ....142 E2
Baxter Rd BN7 ....123 B2
Baxter St BN2 ....164 C7
Baxters La RH17 ....34 C6
Bay Ave BN24 ....175 E6
Bay Cl BN25 ....176 C2
Bay Pond Rd BN21 ......184 D4
Bay Rd BN24 ....175 A4
Bay Terr BN24 ....175 D5
Bay Tree Cl
  Heathfield TN21 ....82 C5
  Shoreham-by-S BN43 ...140 C1
Bay Tree La TN39 ....172 F8
Bay View Cvn Pk BN24 ..175 D5
Bay Vue Rd BN9 ....179 D7
Bayencourt N █ TN40 ...157 C5
Bayencourt S ❷ TN40 ...157 C5
Bayeux Ct Bexhill TN40 ..157 D3
  St Leonards TN37 ....159 D8
Bayhall Rd TN2 ....8 C3
Bayham Ct TN5 ....29 E6
Bayham Old Abbey★
  TN3 ....19 B5
Bayham Rd
  Bells Yew Green TN3 ......18 B4
  Eastbourne BN22 ....185 C4
  Hailsham BN27 ....152 D7
  Royal Tunbridge Wells TN2,
  TN3 ....17 C7
Baylis Cl RH15 ....151 B2
Baylis Cres RH15 ....72 D4
Bayview Rd BN10 ....178 E5
Baywood Gdns BN2 ......165 C8
Bazehill Rd BN2 ....165 F2
Beach Cl BN25 ....180 D3
Beach Cl ❷ BN43 ....161 A6
Beach Mews
  ❼ Eastbourne BN22 .....185 C5
  Newhaven BN9 ....179 E7
Beach Rd
  Eastbourne BN22 ....185 C5
  Newhaven BN9 ....179 E6
Beachings The BN24 ....175 C4
Beachy Head Countryside
  Ctr★ BN20 ....188 B4
Beachy Head Rd
  Eastbourne BN20 ....188 C3
  Eastbourne BN20 ....188 D8
Beachy Head View
  TN37 ....135 F7
Beacon Bsns Pk TN6 ....38 C8
Beacon Cl Brighton BN1 143 A2
  Crowborough TN6 ....25 E2
  Seaford BN25 ....180 D5
Beacon Com Coll
  Crowborough TN6 ....26 A2
  Crowborough TN6 ....26 B3
Beacon Dr BN25 ....180 E5
Beacon Gdns TN6 ....25 E3
Beacon Hill BN7 ....146 A6
Beacon Hurst BN6 ....98 B3
Beacon La TN32 ....88 E7
Beacon Rd
  Crowborough TN6 ....25 E2
  Ditchling BN6 ....98 D2
  Hastings TN35 ....160 E8
  Seaford BN25 ....180 D4
  Beacon Rd W TN6 ....25 E2
Beaconsfield Ho TN6 ....25 E2
Beaconsfield Rd 159 A4
Beaconsfield Terr TN1 ...81 B8
Beaconsfield Villas BN1 142 F1
Beaconsville Ct BN1 ....142 F1
Beagles Wood Rd TN2 ...7 B2
Beal Cres BN1 ....143 B2
Beale Rd RH15 ....72 F1
Beales La TN31 ....67 B6
Beame Ct BN25 ....180 D3

Beamsley Rd BN22 ......185 C4
Beaney's La TN34,TN35 136 E6
Bear Rd BN2 ....164 D8
Bear Yd BN7 ....190 B2
Beatrice La ❷ BN21 .....184 F3
Beatrice Wlk TN39 ....157 A6
Beatty Ave BN1 ....143 D6
Beatty Rd BN23 ....185 E7
Beau Ho TN1 ....8 A3
Beauchamp Rd TN38 .....136 A4
Beauford Rd TN21 ....106 F7
Beaufort Cres TN37 .....136 C2
Beaufort Ct TN37 ....136 C2
Beaufort Ho █ TN37 ....159 C7
Beaufort Rd TN34 ....136 C6
Beaufort Terr BN2 ....164 C6
Beauharrow Rd TN37 ...136 A6
Beaulieu Cl TN40 ....157 F5
Beaulieu Ct BN20 ....174 A5
Beaulieu Gdns TN37 ....136 C2
Beaulieu Lodge TN39 ...156 D2
Beaulieu Rd TN39 ....156 D2
Beauport Gdns TN37 ....136 A6
Beauport Home Farm Cl
  TN37 ....136 A6
Beaver Cl TN6 ....26 A1
Beckenham Cl BN27 ....129 B3
Becket Cl TN34 ....160 A5
Beckets Way TN22 ....79 B5
Beckett Way
  █ East Grinstead RH19 ..10 F8
  Lewes BN7 ....190 A4
Beckley CE Prim Sch
  TN31 ....68 A4
Beckley Cl Brighton BN2 164 E5
  St Leonards TN38 ....135 D2
Beckworth Cl RH16 ....51 A6
Beckworth La RH16 ......51 A6
Bedales RH17 ....51 D4
Bedales Cnr RH17 ....51 D4
Bedales Hill RH16,RH17 51 D4
Beddingham Gdns BN8 147 F5
Bedelands Cl RH15 ....73 B5
Bedford Ave TN40 ....157 D3
Bedford Cl TN22 ....78 C8
Bedford Gr BN21 ....184 E4
Bedford Pl Brighton BN1 163 E5
  Uckfield TN22 ....78 C8
Bedford Rd TN35 ....160 C6
Bedford Sq BN1 ....163 E5
Bedford St BN2 ....164 C4
Bedford Terr █ TN1 ....8 A2
Bedford Twrs ❷ BN1 ...163 E5
Bedfordwell Ct ❸ BN22 185 A4
Bedfordwell Rd BN22 ...185 A4
Bedgebury National
  Pinetum★ TN17 ....32 E8
Beech Ave BN10 ....178 C8
Beech Ave BN27 ....127 C3
  ❸ East Grinstead RH19 ...1 D2
  Portslade-by-S BN41 ....140 F3
Beech Cl
  ❼ East Grinstead RH19 ...1 D2
  Polegate BN26 ....173 A6
  Royal Tunbridge Wells TN2 ..8 D4
Beech Farm Rd TN33 ....88 D3
Beech Gr BN2 ....143 E3
Beech Green La TN7 ......14 B7
Beech Hill RH16 ....51 B4
Beech House La TN19,
  TN32 ....64 C6
Beech Hurst TN2 ....9 D7
Beech Hurst Cl RH16 ....50 C4
Beech Hurst Cotts RH16 50 C4
Beech Manor TN2 ....8 D3
Beech Rd TN18 ....48 C3
Beech St TN1 ....8 B1
Beech Villas █ TN21 .....82 A6
Beecham Pl TN38 ....135 F4
Beeches Rd BN41 ....140 F3
Beeches Cl
  Heathfield TN21 ....82 B8
  Uckfield TN22 ....78 D8
Beeches Farm Rd TN6 ..26 A1
Beeches La RH19 ....11 D6
Beeches Mead RH19 ....26 B2
Beeches Rd TN6 ....26 B2
Beeches The
  Brighton BN1 ....142 D3
  Crowborough TN6 ....26 B1
  Royal Tunbridge Wells TN2 ..8 D4
  St Leonards TN37 ....135 F6
  The Moor TN18 ....45 E7
Beechfield Cl BN24 ....174 B6
Beechfields RH19 ....1 F3
Beeching Rd TN39 ....157 B4
Beeching Park Ind Est
  TN39 ....157 B4
Beeching Way RH19 ......1 F1
Beechlands Cotts TN5 ...28 F3
Beechwood █ BN2 ......164 D8
Beechwood Ave
  Brighton BN1 ....142 F4
  Burwash TN19 ....62 B7
  Hailsham BN27 ....152 C8
Beechwood Cres BN20 184 D3
Beechwood Gdns TN35 160 C6
Beechwood La
  Cooksbridge BN7,BN8 ...122 F8
  Heathfield TN21 ....82 B5
Beechwood Mews TN2 ...8 E4
Beechwood Sacred Heart Sch
  TN2 ....8 E4

Beechwoods RH15 ....73 A1
Beechy Ave BN20 ....184 B5
Beechy Gdns BN20 ......184 B5
Beechy Rd TN22 ....80 A2
Beeding Ave BN3 ....141 F3
Beeding Ct Brighton BN1 142 C5
  ❹ Shoreham-by-S BN43 161 B8
Beggar's La BN24 ....174 B5
Beggar's Wood Rd BN8 75 C6
Beggarsbourne Cl ❼ BN1 189 B3
Belfast St BN3 ....163 B7
Belfield Rd TN7 ....9 D6
Belfry Orch TN22 ....78 D5
Belfry The BN27 ....152 A8
Belgrave Cres BN25 .....180 F5
Belgrave Ct █ TN40 .....157 D3
Belgrave Pl █ BN2 ......164 C4
Belgrave Rd
  Royal Tunbridge Wells TN1 ..8 B4
  Seaford BN25 ....180 E4
Belgrave St BN2 ....8 A3
Belgrove █ TN1 ....8 A2
Bell Alley Rd TN19 ....62 B5
Bell Banks Rd BN27 ....152 C7
Bell Hammer RH19 ....10 E8
Bell La Lewes BN7 ....146 A8
  Hastings TN38 ....35 A4
  Uckfield TN22 ....78 B6
  Uckfield TN22 ....78 C6
Bell Tower Ind Est ❼
  BN2 ....164 C4
Bell Wlk TN22 ....78 C6
Bellbrook Ind Est TN22 ..78 B6
Belle Hill Bexhill TN40 ...157 C5
  Bexhill TN40 ....157 C5
Belle Vue Ct BN2 ....164 D5
Belle Vue Gdns BN2 .....164 C6
Belle Vue Rd █ BN25 ...185 C5
Bellevue Cotts BN2 ......164 F8
Bellevue Ct Brighton BN1 142 F1
  ❸ Eastbourne BN22 .....185 C5
Bellhurst Rd TN37 ....64 A4
Bellingham ❼ BN3 ....163 D7
Bellingham Cres TN39 ..162 D8
Bellmead ❼ BN3 ....163 D7
Belmaine Ct TN39 ....156 F4
Belmont Bexhill TN39 ...157 B3
  Brighton BN1,BN3 ....163 E7
Belmont Cl BN6 ....97 E5
Belmont Ct RH18 ....11 F3
Belmont Ct
  ❹ Brighton BN1 ....163 E7
  Hastings TN35 ....152 B7
Belmont La BN6 ....97 C5
Belmont Rd
  Hastings TN35 ....160 C5
  Uckfield TN22 ....78 C7
Belmont St BN1 ....189 B3
Belmore Rd BN22 ....185 B4
Belton Cl BN2 ....164 B8
Belton Rd BN2 ....164 B8
Beltring Rd
  Eastbourne BN22 ....185 B4
  Royal Tunbridge Wells TN4 ..8 A6
Beltring Terr BN22 ....185 B4
Belvedere Brighton BN1 163 E8
  Eastbourne BN23 ....175 A1
Belvedere Ct █ BN2 .....164 B8
Belvedere Gdns
  Crowborough TN6 ....26 A1
  Seaford BN25 ....181 A5
Belvedere Pk TN38 ......159 A8
Belvedere Terr ❺ BN1 ..163 E6
Belvedere Wlk RH16 .....50 C2
Bembridge Rd BN23 ....174 B3
Bembridge St BN2 ....164 D8
Bembrook Rd TN34 ......160 B5
Bemzells La BN27 ....88 E4
Benbow Ave BN23 ....185 E6
Benbow Ho TN39 ....156 E4
Benchfield Cl RH19 ....2 B1
Benchfield La TN6 ....157 C5
Benenden Cl BN25 ......181 A4
Benenden Rise TN34 ....136 E3
Benett Ave BN3 ....142 B2
Benett Dr BN3 ....142 B2
Benfield Cl BN41 ....141 C1
Benfield Cres BN41 ......141 C1
Benfield Jun Sch BN41 141 C2
Benfield Way BN41 ....141 C1
Bengairn Ave TN3 ....143 A7
Benhall Mill Rd TN2,TN3 17 D8
Benham Ct ❸ BN41 .....141 B5
Benjamin Cl BN22 ....173 F2
Benjamin Lodge RH15 ..73 D3
Bennett Meml Diocesan Sch
  TN2 ....7 E6
Bennett Rd BN2 ....164 E4
Bennetts Yd TN32 ....64 B4
Benson Ct BN3 ....162 F2
Bentham Hill TN3 ....7 C4
Bentham Rd BN2 ....164 F8
Bentley Motor Mus★
  BN8 ....103 F5
Bentley Wildfowl Reserve★
  BN8 ....103 H4
Bentswood Cres RH16 ...51 A4
Bentswood Rd RH16 .....50 F5
Berberis Ct BN43 ....140 C1
Beresford Cl TN17 ....20 F2
Beresford Ct █ BN3 .....163 A7
Beresford Ho BN10 ......167 C1
Beresford Rd
  Brighton BN2 ....164 D5
  Newhaven BN9 ....168 A1
Bergamot Cres BN43 ...140 C1
Beristede Cl BN20 ....184 E1

Berkeley Cl TN2 .....9 E7
Berkeley Ct
  4 Eastbourne BN21 ...185 A1
  6 Hove BN3 ....163 E7
Berkeley Mans 3 TN40 .157 D3
Berkeley Rd 7 TN1 ......8 A2
Berkeley Row BN7 ....146 A8
Berkeley Wlk BN23 ....174 E3
Berkley Rd TN20 ....39 E1
Berkshire Ct 7 BN22 ..185 B4
Berlin Rd TN35 ....160 C6
Bermuda Pl BN23 ......185 G8
Bernard La 1 BN21 ....184 F3
Bernard Pl BN2 ....164 C2
Bernard Rd BN2 ....164 C7
Bernhard Baron Cottage
  Homes The BN26 .....172 F6
Bernhard Gdns BN26 ..172 F5
Berriedale Ave BN1 ....162 E6
Berriedale Ho BN3 .....162 E6
Berry Cl Burgess Hill RH15 .73 A5
  Telscombe Cliffs BN10 ..167 A1
Berwick Cl Bexhill TN39 .156 C6
  Eastbourne BN22 ....173 C3
  Seaford BN25 ....180 D4
Berwick Court Cotts
  BN26 ....171 A6
Berwick Ct 1 BN21 ....185 B3
Berwick Rd BN2 ....177 D7
Berwick Sta BN26 ......150 B2
Betchley Cl RH19 ....1 E3
Betherinden Cotts TN18 .47 A4
Bethune Rd TN40 ......157 E3
Bethune Way TN34 ....136 F1
Beulah Rd TN1 ....8 C4
Beuzeville Ave BN27 ..152 B8
Bevendean Ave BN2 ..177 D5
Bevendean Cres BN2 ..143 E2
Bevendean Prim Sch
  BN2 ....143 F1
Bevendean Rd BN2 ....143 D1
Beverington Cl BN21 ..184 D6
Beverington Rd BN21 ..184 D6
Beverley Ct 1 BN3 ....162 D7
Beverley Wlk TN34 ....160 A6
Bevern Bridge BN8 ....100 F4
Bevern Bridge Cotts
  BN8 ....100 F4
Beverns The BN7 ....99 E5
Bevin Ct TN38 ....136 B3
Bewl Bridge Cl TN5 ....32 B3
Bewl Water* TN5 ....31 C6
Bewl Water Visitors Ctr*
  TN3 ....31 B8
Bewlbridge La
  Lamberhurst TN3,TN5 ..20 B1
  Lower Cousley Wood TN5 .30 F8
Bexfield Ct
  Beachlands BN24 ......175 E6
  6 Eastbourne BN20 ....184 F1
Bexhill Coll TN39 ......157 A7
Bexhill High Sch TN39 .157 B5
Bexhill High Sch (Lower)
  TN39 ....157 A7
Bexhill Hospl TN40 ....157 C5
Bexhill Mus* TN39 ....157 C3
Bexhill Rd
  Eastbourne BN22 ......185 C5
  Lower Street TN33,TN39 .133 C3
  St Leonards TN38,TN40 .158 D6
  Woodingdean BN2 ......144 E1
Bexhill Sta TN40 ....157 C4
Bexleigh Ave TN38 ....158 B5
Bexley Cl BN27 ....129 B2
Bexley Ct BN26 ....173 A7
Bicton Gdns TN39 .....156 E4
Biddenden Cl BN23 ....174 C2
Bidwell Ave TN39 .....157 A7
Bigwood Ave BN3 .....163 D8
Bilbury Mews BN21 ...184 E5
Billingham La TN31 ....91 C3
Binsted Cl BN22 ....173 E1
Biology Rd BN1 ....144 B6
Birch Ave RH17 ....51 A3
Birch Cl Eastbourne BN23 .185 D7
  Haywards Heath RH17 ..51 B3
  Royal Tunbridge Wells TN2 ..7 B8
  Uckfield TN22 ....78 E3
Birch Ct BN42 ....141 A1
Birch Est The BN3 .....185 C7
Birch Grove Cres BN1 .143 A5
Birch Ho 2 BN2 ....1 D2
Birch Kiln Cotts TN5 ...30 A6
Birch Path TN22 ....78 D8
Birch Rd BN23 ....185 C7
Birch Rdbt BN23 ....185 C7
Birch Terr TN21 ....81 D2
Birch View TN35 ......160 C6
Birch Way
  Hailsham BN27 ....152 B6
  Hastings TN34 ....136 E3
  Haywards Heath RH17 ..51 A2
  Royal Tunbridge Wells TN2 ..8 B7
Birchden Cotts TN3 ....15 C6
Birchen La RH16 ....50 E8
Birches Cl TN6 ....25 F4
Birches Ind Est RH19 ....1 A3
Birchetts Ave TN3 ....6 E3
Birchetts Green La TN5 .31 A2
Birchgrove La RH17 ....22 A1
Birchgrove Rd RH17 ....22 A2
Birchington Cl TN39 ...156 D4
Bircholme TN2 ....8 D7
Birchwood Grove Com Prim
  Sch RH15 ....73 C1
Birchwood Grove Rd
  RH15 ....73 C1

Bird In Eye Hill TN22 ...78 E6
Bird in Hand St TN3 .....15 B8
Bird La TN5 ....29 B5
Birdham Pl BN2 ....143 E3
Birdham Rd BN2 ....143 F3
Birk Dale TN39 ....156 D4
Birkdale TN1 ....8 B6
Birken Rd TN2 ....8 D6
Birling Cl Brighton BN2 .143 D1
  Seaford BN25 ....180 D4
Birling Dr BN2 ....8 A1
Birling Gap Rd BN20 ...187 B6
Birling Park Ave TN2 ...17 B8
Birling Rd TN2 ....17 B8
Birling St BN21 ....184 C4
Birling Way TN2 ....78 E8
Birley Ave BN23 ....185 F8
Bishop Bell CE Sch The
  BN23 ....174 E1
Bishop's Cl
  Hurstpierpoint BN6 .....97 A7
  Ringmer BN8 ....124 E6
Bishop's Down TN1 ......7 F3
Bishop's Down Park Rd
  TN4 ....7 F4
Bishop's Down Prim Sch
  TN4 ....7 E5
Bishop's Down Rd TN4 ..7 F3
Bishop's La Ringmer BN8 .124 D6
  Robertsbridge TN32 ....64 A3
Bishop's Wlk TN40 ....157 F6
Bishops Cl BN25 ....180 C4
Bishops Ct TN4 ....7 F3
Bishops Dr BN7 ....146 A8
Bishops Rd BN3 ....142 C1
Bishopstone Dr BN2 ...177 B6
Bishopstone La BN6,RH17 .72 A7
Bishopstone Rd BN25 ..180 C6
Bishopstone Sta BN25 .180 B4
Bittern Ct BN27 ....152 D7
Bixley La TN31 ....68 B2
Black Hill RH16 ....51 A7
Black Lion La BN1 .....189 A2
Black Lion St BN1 .....189 B1
Black Path BN26 ......173 A6
Black Rock (for Marina)
  Sta* BN2 ....164 E3
Blackberry La RH7 ......1 E8
Blackberry Rd RH19,RH7 .1 D8
Blackbird Cl RH15 ......72 D3
Blackboys CE Prim Sch
  TN22 ....80 A6
Blackboys YH* TN22 ....80 A8
Blackbrook La BN8,RH17 .52 E2
Blackdon Hill TN3 ......27 B6
Blackdown BN2 ....164 F7
Blackdown Rd TN21 ....83 D6
Blackdown Rdbt TN22 ..55 B3
Blackfields Ave TN39 ..156 F5
Blackhorse Mews TN2 ...9 C6
Blackhouse La RH15 ....73 B4
Blackhurst La TN2 ....8 F6
Blacklands TN33 ....88 F1
Blacklands Cres RH18 ..11 F2
Blacklands Dr TN34 ...136 F2
Blacklands Prim Sch
  TN34 ....136 E2
Blackman Ave TN38 ...136 A4
Blackman St BN1 ......189 B3
Blackmill Cl TN39 .....157 A8
Blackmores RH17 ......74 A5
Blackness Rd TN6 ......38 A8
Blackness Villas TN6 ...38 A8
Blacksmith's Field TN33 .135 A4
Blacksmith's La TN5 ...30 A5
Blacksmiths Copse
  BN27 ....152 A6
Blacksmiths Field TN33 .46 C1
Blacksmiths La TN33 ..133 E8
Blackstone Way RH15 ..73 A5
Blackthorn Cl
  Brighton BN1 ....142 D3
  Eastbourne BN23 ......173 E2
  St Leonards TN38 .....141 B2
Blackthorn Way TN35 ..138 C4
Blackthorns RH16 ......51 A7
Blackthorns RH16 ......51 A7
Blackthorns Com Prim Sch
  RH16 ....51 A6
Blackthorns TN35 ......73 B5
Blackwater Rd
  BN21 ....184 F1
Blackwell Farm Rd RH19 ..1 F3
Blackwell Hollow RH19 ...1 F2
Blackwell Prim Sch RH19 .1 E3
Blackwell Rd RH19 ......1 F2
Blade Ct 8 BN2 ....189 C3
Blake Way TN2 ....8 D7
Blakeney Ave BN10,BN9 .179 A6
Blaker St BN2 ....189 C2
Blakes Way BN23 ......185 F6
Blatchington Cl BN25 ..180 F4
Blatchington Hill BN25 .180 E4
Blatchington Hill Flats
  BN25 ....180 F5
Blatchington Mill Dr
  BN24 ....172 E4
Blatchington Mill Sch & Sixth
  Form Coll BN3 ....141 F2
Blatchington Rd
  Hove BN3 ....163 B7
  Royal Tunbridge Wells TN1 ..8 B1
  Seaford BN25 ....180 E5
Blenheim Cl RH19 ....2 A3
Blenheim Ct
  1 Hove BN3 ....163 A6
  Robertsbridge TN32 ....64 B3

Blenheim Fields RH18 ...11 E3
Blenheim Mews RH16 ...50 F2
Blenheim Pl 5 BN1 ....189 B3
Blenheim Way
  Flimwell TN5 ....32 C3
  Polegate BN26 ....173 D6
Bletchinglye La TN6 ....27 E1
Bletchley Ct BN1 ......164 A8
Blind La BN8 ....76 E6
Blois Rd BN7 ....123 B2
Blomfield Rd TN37 ....159 D8
Bloomsbury Pl 7 BN2 ..164 C4
Bloomsbury St 18 BN2 .164 C4
Blossom Wlk BN27 ....129 B1
Blount Ave RH19 ....1 C1
Blowers Hill Cowden TN8 ..4 D8
  Speldhurst TN3 ....7 B8
Blue Haze Ave BN25 ...181 B4
Bluebell Cl
  East Grinstead RH19 ....1 B1
  Haywards Heath RH16 ...50 F4
Bluebell Glade BN27 ...24 C4
Bluebell Rly* RH17,RH19,
  TN22 ....21 A5
Bluebell Rly Mus* TN2 .53 A4
Bluebell Rly The* TN22 .53 A5
Bluebell Walk & Farm Trail*
  BN26 ....151 B4
Bluebell Way RH15 .....72 D4
Bluebird Ct 11 BN3 ...163 A6
Bluemans La TN33 .....114 A4
Bluestone Ct TN38 ....135 F2
Blunts Wood Cres RH16 .50 B6
Blunts Wood Rd RH16 ..50 C6
Blytons The RH19 ....1 B1
Boarders La TN5 ....31 C3
Boast La BN8 ....101 F5
Boathouse The 4 TN31 .93 C5
Bocking Ct TN5 ....29 E4
Bocks Hill TN32 ....64 F6
Boddingtons La BN6 ....98 D3
Bodiam Ave Bexhill TN40 .157 D6
  Brighton BN2 ....143 E4
Bodiam Bsns Pk TN32 ..65 C7
Bodiam Castle (NT)*
  TN32 ....65 F8
Bodiam CE Prim Sch
  TN32 ....65 E8
Bodiam Cl Brighton BN2 .144 B2
  Seaford BN25 ....181 C4
Bodiam Cres BN22 ....174 A2
Bodiam Ct BN25 ....181 C4
Bodiam Dr TN38 ....135 D2
Bodiam Manor Sch TN32 .46 F3
Bodiam Rd TN18,TN32 ...46 F3
Bodiam Sta* TN32 .....65 A6
Bodiam Ho 6 BN3 .....163 A6
Bodle Cres TN39 ......157 B7
Bodmin Cl BN20 ....184 C3
Bohemia Rd TN34,TN37 .159 D8
Boiler House Hill BN1 .144 B7
Bolding Way RH16 ......50 E2
Bolebrooke Rd TN40 ..157 D3
Bolney Ave BN10 ......178 C6
Bolney Rd BN2 ....143 F4
Bolnore Rd RH16 ....50 B4
Bolnore Rd RH16 ....50 C4
Bolsover Ct BN20 .....188 F8
Bolsover Rd
  Eastbourne BN20 ......188 F8
  Hove BN3 ....162 E8
Bolton Cl TN22 ....78 A6
Bolton Rd BN21 ....185 A2
Boltro Rd RH16 ....50 D5
Bonchurch Rd BN2 ....164 C7
Bond St BN1 ....189 B2
Bonfire La TN19 ....33 D5
Boniface Cl BN24 .....174 C6
Bonners CE Sch TN22 ..55 B4
Bonny Wood Rd BN6 ...97 E3
Booker Ct TN6 ....26 A1
Booth Mus of Natural
  History* BN1 ....163 E8
Bopeep Bostal BN26 ...170 B7
Bopeep La BN26 ......170 B8
Bordehill La RH16 ......50 A8
Border Ct RH19 ....1 F4
Boreham Hill BN27,TN33 .132 A4
Boreham La BN27 .....131 E2
Boredales TN30 ....156 E4
Borough La BN20 .....184 D3
Borough St BN1 ....189 A3
Borrow King Cl BN1 ...164 D8
Borrowdale Cl BN23 ...174 C4
Boscawen Ct BN23 ....185 F7
Boscobel Ct TN38 .....159 A6
Boscobel Lodge TN38 .159 A7
Boscobel Rd TN38 .....159 A7
Boscobel Rd N TN38 ..159 A7
Boship Cl BN23 ....174 A4
Bostal Rd BN8 ....148 B4
Boston Cl BN23 ....185 F7
Boston Rd RH16 ....51 A5
Boston St BN1 ....189 B4
Boswell Wlk 2 BN23 ..174 E2
Bough Beeches TN5 ....73 C1
Boughey Pl BN27 ......190 A4
Boulevard The BN24 ..175 D4
Boundary Pas 10 BN1 .163 E6
Boundary Rd
  Brighton BN2 ....164 F4
  Portslade-by-S BN41 ...162 C7
  Royal Tunbridge Wells TN2 ..8 D1
Boundary The
  Langton Green TN3 .....7 B3

Boundary The continued
  20 Seaford BN25 ......180 E2
Boundsway TN22 ....78 E8
Bourne-de-Peage Ave
  RH19 ....2 A1
Bourne Ct Brighton BN1 .142 D4
  20 Hastings TN34 ....160 B4
Bourne La
  Northbridge Street TN32 ..64 F7
  Sandhurst Cross TN18 ..46 C4
Bourne Pas 15 TN34 ...160 B4
Bourne Prim Sch BN22 .185 B3
Bourne St BN21 ....185 B3
Bourne The Hassocks BN6 .97 E5
  Hastings TN34 ....160 B4
Bourneside Ct 12 BN22 .185 B3
Bowden House Sch
  BN25 ....180 C6
Bowden Rise BN25 ....180 E6
Bowden Ct 11 BN3 ....163 C6
Bower Rd TN4 ....7 B4
Bower Cl TN37 ....136 B4
Bower The RH16 ....50 D5
Bowerhill Cotts RH19 ...21 C6
Bowlers Town TN31 ....70 A2
Bowles Outdoor Ctr TN6 .26 E6
Bowley Rd BN27 ....152 B8
Bowling The TN30 ....113 D8
Bowmans Dr TN33 ....112 D6
Bowood Ave BN2 .....185 B6
Bowrey Pl TN40 ....157 C5
Bowring Way BN2 .....164 D4
Bowsprit Mews TN38 ..135 E4
Box La RH19 ....11 C6
Box's La RH17 ....34 C6
Boxes La RH17 ....33 C5
Boxgrove Cl TN40 .....157 F4
Boyce's St BN1 ....189 A2
Boyles La 14 BN2 .....164 E4
Boyne Pk TN4 ....7 F4
Boyne Rd TN35 ....160 C5
Bracken Cl
  Crowborough TN6 ......26 C1
  Royal Tunbridge Wells TN2 ..8 E5
Bracken Rd
  Eastbourne BN20 ......184 B5
  Royal Tunbridge Wells TN2 ..8 E5
  Seaford BN25 ....181 A2
Bracken Way TN21 .....59 E1
Brackenbury Cl BN41 ..141 B2
Brackendale TN35 ....160 D6
Brackenhill TN7 ....13 A1
Brackerne Ct TN39 ...156 C2
Bradford Cl 9 BN25 ..185 B4
Bradford Rd BN7 ......123 B1
Bradford St BN21 .....184 D3
Brading Cl
  Eastbourne BN23 ......174 B4
  Hastings TN34 ....136 E2
Brading Rd BN2 ......164 C7
Bradley Rd
  Wartling BN27 ....131 C1
  White Post TN3 ....5 D5
Braemar Ct 3 TN34 ...157 A4
Braemar Ho 11 BN1 ...163 C6
Braemore Ct BN3 .....162 E6
Braemore Rd BN3 .....162 E6
Braeside Ave BN1 .....143 A7
Bramber Ave Hove BN3 .141 F3
  Peacehaven BN10 ......178 C2
Bramber Ave N BN10 ..178 C8
Bramber Cl
  Haywards Heath RH16 ...50 D4
  Eastbourne BN23 ......178 C8
  3 Seaford BN25 ......180 F2
Bramber Ct BN3 ......163 B7
  2 Shoreham-by-S BN43 .161 B8
Bramber Ho 17 BN21 ..184 E4
Bramber La BN25 .....180 F2
Bramber Rd BN25 .....180 F2
Bramber Way RH15 ....73 A4
Bramble Cr BN23 ......152 D3
Bramble Croft TN6 .....26 A2
Bramble Dr BN27 .....152 A7
Bramble Gdns RH15 ...72 D4
Bramble Rise BN1 .....142 C5
Bramble Twitten RH19 ...2 A1
Bramble Way
  Brighton BN1 ....143 C6
  Fairlight Cove TN35 ...138 F4
Bramble Wlk TN2 ......50 F2
Brambledean Rd BN41 .162 B7
Brambles The RH17 ....50 A6
Brambleside TN6 ....78 A6
Brambletye La RH19 ....1 B1
Brambletye Prep Sch
  RH19 ....11 C5
Brambletyne Ave BN2 .177 D5
Bramley Rd BN26 .....173 D6
Bramley Wlk BN27 ....131 B5
Bramleys RH17 ....145 E5
Brampton Ave TN39 ..156 F4
Brampton Ct TN39 ....156 F4
Brampton Rd BN23 ...174 A1
Brampton Road Trad Est
  BN22 ....185 A8
Brand Rd BN2 ....173 E1
Brands Cl BN9 ....168 E2
Brangwyn Ave BN1 ...142 E5
Brangwyn Cres BN1 ...142 E5
Brangwyn Dr BN1 ....142 E5
Brangwyn Way BN1 ...142 E5
Branksome Rd TN38 ..159 A8
Branston Rd BN22 ....173 D1
Brassey Ave BN22 ....173 E1
Brassey Par BN22 ....173 F1

Brassey Rd TN40 ......157 D3
Brasslands Dr BN41 ...140 F1
Braybon Ave BN1 .....142 F4
Braybon Bsns Pk RH15 ..72 E2
Braybrooke Cl TN34 ..159 B4
Braybrooke Rd TN34 ..159 B8
Braybrooke Terr TN34 .159 B8
Braypool La BN1 ......142 D7
Brazen Cl BN9 ....179 B7
Bread St BN1 ....189 B3
Breadsell La TN38 ....135 D6
Brecon Cotts TN6 ......39 A8
Brecon Ct 6 BN3 .....163 C7
Brecon Terr TN6 ....39 A8
Brede Cl Brighton BN2 .164 F5
  St Leonards TN37 .....135 F7
Brede Hill TN1 ....115 B8
Brede La Brede TN31 ...89 F7
  Sedlescombe TN31,TN33 .89 B2
Brede Prim Sch TN31 ..90 B4
Brede Valley View TN36 .116 E5
Breeds Pl TN34 ....159 F7
Brendon Cl
  Eastbourne BN23 ......174 E4
  Royal Tunbridge Wells TN2 ..8 D5
Brendon Rise TN34 ...160 B7
Brentor Ct TN2 ....8 D6
Brentwood Cl BN1 ....143 B3
Brentwood Cres BN1 ..143 B3
Brentwood Rd BN1 ...143 B3
Bretland Ct TN4 ....7 D4
Bretland Rd TN4 ....7 D4
Brett Dr TN40 ....157 F4
Bretton RH15 ....72 E5
Bretts Cotts TN22 ......79 B7
Bretts Field TN10 .....167 C2
Brewer St Brighton BN2 .189 C4
  Lamberhurst TN3 ......20 A5
Brewers Gr TN20 ....40 B2
Brian Cres TN4 ....8 B8
Briar Cl
  Fairlight Cove TN35 ...139 A5
  Woodingdean BN2 .....165 D7
Briar Pl BN23 ....174 B3
Briarcroft Rd BN2 .....165 D7
Briary The TN40 ......157 D5
Brick Kiln La TN20,TN22 .57 E6
Brickfield TN4 ....9 E8
Brickhurst La BN8 ....126 C8
Bricky The BN10 ......178 D8
Brickyard Cotts TN6 ...28 A4
Brickyard La
  Mark Cross TN6 ....27 E5
  South Chailey BN8 .....100 E7
Bridge Cl
  Burgess Hill RH15 .....72 F4
  Horam TN21 ....107 A7
Bridge Ct BN9 ....179 D2
Bridge End Rd TN34 ..175 B7
Bridge Farm Rd TN22 ..78 C6
Bridge Ho TN4 ....8 B5
Bridge Pl TN31 ....93 C6
Bridge Rd RH16 ....50 F6
Bridge Road Bsns Pk
  RH16 ....50 F7
Bridge St TN38 ....179 D7
Bridge Way TN38 .....158 C6
Bridgelands BN8 .....101 D4
Bridgemere Rd BN22 .185 B6
Bridger Way TN6 ....38 A6
Bridgersmill RH16 .....50 D6
Bridgewick Cl BN7 ....190 B4
Bridle Way BN10 ......167 A1
Briers Ave TN34 ....136 C3
Briers Gdns TN34 ....136 C3
Briers The TN37 ......136 C3
Brigden St BN1 ....189 A4
Briggs Hill BN8 ....149 C4
Bright Ridge TN4 ....7 E8
Brightelm BN1 ....144 B8
Brightland Rd BN20 ..184 D3
Brightling Rd TN35 ...160 E8
Brightling Rd
  Polegate BN26 ....173 B5
  Robertsbridge TN32 ....63 D2
Brighton & Hove High Sch
  BN1 ....163 E6
Brighton & Hove Stad
  BN3 ....142 B1
Brighton Bsns Ctr 5 BN2 .164 C5
Brighton College Pre-Prep
  Sch BN2 ....164 C5
Brighton Fishing Mus*
  BN1 ....189 A1
Brighton General Hospl
  BN2 ....164 C6
Brighton Marina BN2 ..164 F2
Brighton Marina Village
  BN2 ....164 F3
Brighton Mus & Art Gall*
  BN1 ....189 B2
Brighton Mus of Childhood*
  BN1 ....189 B2
Brighton Pl BN1 ......189 B2
Brighton Race Course
  BN2 ....165 A8
Brighton Rd
  Hassocks BN6 ....97 D2
  Newhaven BN9 ....179 A6
  Newhaven BN9 ....146 A8
  Shoreham-by-S BN43 ..161 B7
Brighton Sea Life Ctr*
  BN1 ....189 B1

Brighton Sq BN1 ....189 B2
Brighton Sta BN1 ....189 B3
Brighton Steiner Sch Ltd (John Howard Ho) BN2 ....164 F4
Brighton Toy & Model Mus The* BN1 ....189 B3
Brighton, Hove & Sussex Sixth Form Coll BN3 ...163 E8
Brightwell Ind Est BN9 ..179 E7
Brills La BN1 ....189 B1
Brincliffe TN6 ....25 E3
Brinkers La TN5 ....30 A2
Brisbane Quay BN23 ....175 A2
Bristol Gate BN2 ....164 D4
Bristol Gdns BN2 ....164 E4
Bristol Mews 3 BN2 ....164 E4
Bristol Pl BN2 ....164 E4
Bristol Rd Brighton BN2 ..164 C4
St Leonards TN38 ....136 A3
Bristol Rise BN2 ....164 D4
Bristol St BN2 ....164 E4
Bristol Way TN38 ....136 A3
Britannia Ct BN2 ....165 A3
Britannia Ent Ctr TN34 ..136 F1
British Engineerium Mus* BN3 ....142 B2
Britland Est BN22 ....185 C6
Brittany Ct
5 Bexhill TN39 ....157 A4
3 Hove BN3 ....162 D7
Brittany Ho TN6 ....37 D8
Brittany Mews TN38 ....159 B7
Brittany Rd Hove BN3 ....162 D6
St Leonards TN37,TN38 ...159 B8
Britten Cl BN23 ....174 D3
Brittenden La TN21 ......80 E5
Britts Farm Rd TN22 .....56 C3
Britts Orch TN22 ....56 C3
Broad Buckler TN37 ....136 A6
Broad Gn BN2 ....165 E6
Broad Gr TN2 ....8 A1
Broad Green Ave RH15 ...73 C2
Broad La TN3 ....6 A4
Broad Oak Buxted TN22 ....56 C3
Groombridge TN3 ....15 C6
Broad Oak Cl
Broad Oak TN31 ....90 B5
Eastbourne BN23 ....174 A4
Royal Tunbridge Wells TN2 ....7 F1
Broad Oak Com Prim Sch TN21 ....59 F2
Broad Rd BN20 ....173 A4
Broad Rig Ave BN3 .....141 D3
Broad St Brighton BN2 ....189 B1
Cuckfield RH17 ....50 A6
Icklesham TN36 ....116 C6
Seaford BN25 ....180 E3
Broad View Bexhill TN39 ..156 F6
Broad Oak TN21 ....59 E1
Broadcroft TN2 ....16 F8
Broadfields BN2 ....143 E3
Broadfields Rd BN2 .....143 E3
Broadhill Cl TN21 ....59 E1
Broadlands
Burgess Hill RH15 ....98 B8
Hastings TN35 ....160 D8
Broadley View TN33 .....133 E8
Broadmead TN2 ....16 F8
Broadmead Ave TN2 .....16 F8
Broadoak La
Bexhill TN39 ....156 E5
Bexhill TN39 ....156 F5
Broads Cotts TN19 ....62 B6
Broadstone RH18 ....12 A2
Broadview Cl BN20 ......172 F4
Broadwalk The TN39 ....156 B4
Broadwater Ct TN2 ....16 E8
Broadwater Down TN2 ...16 F8
Broadwater Down Prim Sch TN2 ....7 F1
Broadwater Forest La TN3 ....16 B7
Broadwater La
Royal Tunbridge Wells TN2 ...16 F8
Royal Tunbridge Wells TN2, TN4 ....7 F1
Broadwater Mews BN26 .172 E3
Broadwater Rise TN2 ......7 F1
Broadwater Way BN22 ..184 F8
Broadway
Fairlight Cove TN35 ....138 F5
Southwick BN42 ....161 F8
Broadway Ct 11 BN43 ...161 C8
Broadway The
Alfriston BN26 ....170 F3
Brighton BN2 ....164 F4
Crowborough TN6 ....25 F3
Eastbourne BN22 ....173 D1
Hastings TN35 ....160 D8
Haywards Heath RH16 .....50 E5
Lamberhurst TN3 ....20 B5
Brockhurst BN2 ....164 F7
Brockhurst Gate TN40 ...157 F5
Brockley Rd TN39 ....157 A3
Brocks Ghyll BN20 ......173 A3
Brodie Pl BN21 ....184 D4
Brodrick Cl BN22 ....173 F1
Brodrick Rd BN22 ....173 E2
Brokes Way TN4 ....8 B8
Bromley Cl
Eastbourne BN23 ....174 C2
Keymer BN6 ....98 A4
Bromley Rd
Brighton BN2 ....189 C5
Bromley Rd *continued*
Seaford BN25 ....181 A4
Brompton Cl BN1 ....142 E6
Brontes The RH19 ....1 D1
Brook Ave BN6 ....97 F3
Brook Cl Crowborough TN6 .26 D1
East Grinstead RH19 ....2 B1
Brook Ho TN39 ....157 C6
Brook La
Beddingham BN8 ....147 A6
Haywards Heath RH16 .....50 F8
Brook Manor RH19 ....10 C7
Brook Rd TN2 ....8 D7
Brook St Hastings TN34 ...159 F8
Lewes BN7 ....190 B2
Polegate BN26 ....172 F6
Brook Terr TN6 ....25 D4
Brook View TN6 ....25 D4
Brook Way TN35 ....160 B8
Brooker Pl BN3 ....163 A7
Brooker St BN3 ....163 A7
Brookfield TN18 ....47 B5
Brookfield Ct 2 TN40 ...157 E4
Brookfield Rd TN40 .....157 E4
Brookhouse Bottom TN22 ....34 D4
Brookhouse La TN22 .....79 A5
Brookhouse Rd TN22 .....79 A4
Brookland Cl
Beachlands BN24 ....175 E6
Hastings TN34 ....136 F2
Brookland Ho RH19 ....1 E1
Brooklands TN2 ....8 D7
Brooklands Ave TN6 ......37 F7
Brooklands Farm Cl TN3 ..6 A6
Brooklands Terr BN27 ...128 E3
Brooklands Way RH19 ....10 D8
Brooklyn Rd BN25 ....180 E3
Brookmead Cl BN22 .....185 B5
Brooks Cl Lewes BN7 ....190 B3
Newhaven BN9 ....179 D6
Brooks Gdns BN8 ....76 D6
Brooks Rd BN7 ....190 B3
Brooks The RH15 ....72 E5
Brookside
Piddinghoe BN9 ....168 B2
Uckfield TN22 ....78 A6
Brookside Ave BN26 ....172 F7
Brookside Cotts TN19 ....63 B8
Brookway
Burgess Hill RH15 ....73 C3
Lindfield RH16 ....51 A8
Broom Cl BN22 ....173 D2
Broom Hill Cotts TN5 ....32 B3
Broom La TN3 ....6 E2
Broom Pk TN3 ....6 E3
Brooman's Ct BN7 ......190 B2
Broomans La BN7 ....190 B2
Broomfield Ave BN10 ...177 F4
Broomfield Dr BN41 .....141 A3
Broomfield St BN20, BN21 ....184 C4
Broomfields BN8 ....100 D7
Broomgrove Rd TN34 ...160 B6
Broomham La BN8 ....127 B7
Broomhill Bank Sch TN3 ..7 C6
Broomhill Park Rd TN4 ....7 F8
Broomhill Rd TN3 ....7 D7
Bross Est BN9 ....179 D8
Brow The
Burgess Hill RH15 ....73 A2
Friston BN20 ....183 B2
Woodingdean BN2 ....165 D8
Brown Jack Ave BN26 ...172 F6
Brown Twins Rd BN6 .....97 B5
Brown's La TN22 ....78 D8
Brown's Path TN22 ....78 E8
Browning Rd 2 TN21 .....82 A7
Browning Wlk 5 BN23 ..174 E2
Brownings The 1 RH19 ....1 C1
Brownleaf Rd BN2 ....165 E6
Browns Cl TN22 ....78 D8
Browns La TN21 ....81 B6
Browns Wood RH19 ....1 E4
Broyle Cl BN8 ....125 A8
Broyle La BN8 ....124 F8
Broyle Paddock BN8 ....124 F7
Broyle The BN8 ....125 B7
Broyleside BN8 ....125 A7
Bruce Cl RH16 ....50 E3
Brunel Rd TN38 ....135 E4
Brunswick Mews 3 BN3 ....163 D5
Brunswick Pl BN3 ....163 D6
Brunswick Rd BN3 ......163 D6
Brunswick Row BN1 .....189 B4
Brunswick Sq BN3 ......163 D5
Brunswick St E BN3 ....163 D5
Brunswick St W BN3 ....163 D5
Brunswick Terr
Hove BN1,BN3 ....163 D5
Royal Tunbridge Wells TN1 ....8 A2
Brushes La RH16 ....51 B8
Bryants Field TN6 ....25 E3
Brydges Cl BN22 ....185 C6
Buci Cres BN43 ....140 C1
Buckholt Ave TN40 .....158 A7
Buckholt La TN39 ....157 C8
Buckhurst Cl
East Grinstead RH19 ....1 C3
Eastbourne BN20 ....184 B8
Lewes BN7 ....190 A4
Buckhurst La TN5 ....29 A6
Buckhurst Mead RH19 .....1 C4
Buckhurst Pl TN39 ......157 C4
Buckhurst Rd
Bexhill TN40 ....157 C4
Telscombe Cliffs BN10 ...177 F3
Buckhurst Way RH19 ......1 C3
Buckingham Cl
4 Brighton BN1 ....189 A4
Seaford BN25 ....180 E4
Shoreham-by-S BN43 .....161 A8
Buckingham Ct BN20 ...184 B6
Buckingham Dr RH19 ....11 A8
Buckingham Hts 2 BN22 ....185 A4
Buckingham Lodge BN1 ....189 A4
Buckingham Pl BN1 ....189 A4
Buckingham Rd
Brighton BN1 ....189 A3
Royal Tunbridge Wells TN1 ....8 B2
St Leonards TN38 ....136 A4
Buckingham St BN1 ....189 A3
Buckland Rd BN25 ......180 F5
Buckle By-Pass BN25 ...180 C4
Buckle Cl BN25 ....180 C4
Buckle Cvn Pk BN25 ....180 B4
Buckle Dr BN25 ....180 C4
Buckle Rise BN25 ....180 C4
Buckler St BN41 ....162 B8
Bucklers Cl TN2 ....8 C3
Buckley Cl BN3 ....141 E4
Buckswood Grange Sch TN22 ....78 B8
Buckswood Sch TN35 ....116 A3
Buckthorn Cl BN25 .....181 C3
Buckwell Ct BN7 ....123 A3
Buckwell Rise BN27 .....130 E5
Buddens Gn TN31 ....68 B5
Budletts Rdbt TN22 ....55 C4
Bugsell La TN32 ....63 F4
Bull La BN7 ....190 A1
Bull Lane Cotts TN3 ......19 C4
Bull Ring TN33 ....112 D4
Buller Cl TN6 ....26 A1
Buller Rd BN2 ....143 D1
Bullfinch Gdns TN22 .....78 E4
Bullingstone Cotts TN3 ....6 E7
Bullingstone La TN3 ....6 F7
Bulls Pl TN2 ....9 D6
Bulrush Pl TN38 ....135 E1
Bulverhythe Rd TN38 ...158 D6
Bungalows The TN22 .....79 B5
Bunny La TN3 ....16 E5
Bunting Cl TN38 ....158 E8
Burchetts Cl RH16 ....50 E2
Burden Pl TN38 ....136 A3
Burdett Pl 2 TN34 ....160 A3
Burdett Rd
Crowborough TN6 ....26 C1
Rusthall TN4 ....7 B4
Burdocks Dr RH15 ....73 D1
Burfield Park Ind Est BN27 ....152 B6
Burfield Rd BN22 ....185 B3
Burgess Ct BN41 ....162 B8
Burgess Hill Sch RH15 ....73 B2
Burgess Hill Sta RH15 ....73 B2
Burgess Rd TN35 ....137 C5
Burgh Hill TN19 ....44 E2
Burgh Hill Rd BN8 ....127 E6
Burgh La BN8 ....148 E5
Burgundy Ho 3 BN23 ...185 F8
Burhill Way TN38 ....158 F7
Burleigh Pl BN22 ....185 C6
Burlington Ct 18 BN21 ..185 A2
Burlington Gdns BN41 ..141 C1
Burlington Mans 23 BN21 ....185 A2
Burlington Pl BN21 .....185 A2
Burlington Rd BN21 .....185 B2
Burlington St BN2 ....164 C4
Burlington Villas 22 BN21 ....185 B3
Burlow Cl Brighton BN2 ..164 E5
Eastbourne BN22 ....173 C3
Burma Cl RH16 ....51 C4
Burners Cl RH15 ....73 D1
Burnes Vale BN2 ....165 F2
Burnham Cl BN2 ....165 F7
Burns Way RH19 ....1 C1
Burnside BN26 ....173 A6
Burnside Ct BN26 ....173 A6
Burnside Mews TN39 ...157 B4
Burnt House Cl TN18 .....47 C5
Burnt House La TN3 ......7 A5
Burnt Lodge La TN5 ......31 B2
Burnt Oak Rd TN22,TN6 ...37 C2
Burnthouse Bostall BN6 ....120 C8
Burrell Rd RH16 ....50 D6
Burrells La TN22 ....55 A7
Burrells The BN43 ....161 B6
Burrow Down BN20 ......184 B5
Burrow Down Cl BN20 ..184 A5
Burrswood Villas TN3 ....15 B7
Burry Rd TN37 ....136 C3
Burslem Rd TN2 ....8 E7
Burstead Cl BN1 ....143 B3
Burston Gdns RH19 ....1 D4
Burton Rd BN21 ....184 E5
Burton Villas BN3 ....163 D8
Burton Way TN38 ....159 B6
Burton Wlk BN27 ....152 B7
Burwash CE Prim Sch TN19 ....62 B6
Burwash Cl
Eastbourne BN23 ....174 B4
Hastings TN34 ....137 A5
Burwash Lodge BN1 .....143 C1
Burwash Rd
Broad Oak TN21 ....82 C8
Hove BN3 ....141 F3
Burwood Ho TN2 ....8 E5
Busby Ct 21 BN21 ....185 B3
Bush Cl
Telscombe Cliffs BN10 ....167 A1
Woodingdean BN2 ....165 D8
Bush Cottage Cl BN41 ...141 C2
Bush Farm Dr BN41 .....141 C3
Bush Rd BN9 ....179 B8
Bush Terr BN41 ....141 B3
Bushbury La TN22 ....80 A3
Busheyfields BN27 ......152 A8
Bushy Croft TN39 ....156 F5
Bushy Gill TN3 ....7 A3
Butcher's Cross TN7 .....13 B7
Butcher's La TN35 ....115 E2
Butcherfield La TN7 .....13 B6
Bute St BN2 ....164 D5
Butler's Green Ho RH16 ..50 B5
Butler's Green Rd RH16 ..50 C4
Butler's La BN27 ....130 E3
Butlers Way BN8 ....124 C5
Butterbox La RH17 ....52 D4
Buttercup Wlk BN1 .....143 B7
Butterfield RH19 ....1 B3
Buttermere Way BN23 ..174 C4
Button Ct BN2 ....189 C4
Butts Field BN27 ....152 C6
Butts La Cousley Wood TN5 .30 C7
Eastbourne BN20 ....173 A1
Butts Rd BN42 ....161 E7
Buttsfield La BN8 ....105 A5
Buxted CE Prim Sch TN22 ....55 F3
Buxted Ct TN22 ....56 C3
Buxted Rise BN1 ....143 B5
Buxted Sta TN22 ....56 B3
Buxted Wood La TN22 ....56 E5
Buxton Dr TN39 ....157 B6
Buxton Rd Brighton BN1 ..163 E7
Eastbourne BN20 ....188 E8
By Sunte RH16 ....50 F8
Bydown BN25 ....181 A4
Bye-Law Cotts BN8 .....101 E6
Byeway The Bexhill TN39 .156 D5
Hastings TN34 ....160 A8
Byeways The BN25 ......180 F4
Byfields Croft TN39 ....156 F5
Byland Cl BN22 ....173 E3
Bylands 3 BN2 ....164 F5
Byng Rd TN4 ....7 F5
Byre Cotts BN2 ....165 D4
Byron Ct 1 RH16 ....50 D5
Byron Gr 2 RH19 ....1 C1
Byron St BN3 ....163 A7
Byron Terr 1 BN3 ......163 A7
Byron Wlk BN23 ....174 E3
Byway The BN1 ....143 E5
Byways TN34 ....136 D6
Byworth Cl Bexhill TN39 ..156 C6
Brighton BN2 ....164 F6

C

Cabbage Stalk La TN4 .....7 E2
Cabbages & Kings Gdn* TN22 ....57 C3
Cabot Cl BN23 ....185 G7
Caburn Cl BN23 ....174 A4
Caburn Cres BN7 ....123 A2
Caburn Ent Pk BN8 ......125 A7
Caburn Rd BN3 ....163 E7
Caburn View Bglws BN8 ....148 B3
Caburn View Cotts BN8 ..148 B3
Caburn Way BN27 ......152 B6
Cackle St
Cackle Street TN31 ....90 A2
Dodd's Hill TN22 ....35 E2
Cacklebury Cl BN27 .....152 A6
Cadborough Cliff TN31 ...93 A4
Cade St BN22 ....173 F2
Cadogan Ct
Pevensey Bay BN24 ......175 C4
3 Brighton BN1 ....163 E7
Cadogan Gdns 6 TN1 .....8 B4
Cairngorm Cl BN23 .....174 D3
Cairo Ave BN10 ....178 A8
Cairo Ave S BN10 ....178 A7
Caister's Cl BN3 ....163 C8
Caius Ct 16 BN43 ....161 C8
Calbourne RH16 ....50 D5
Caldbec Ct TN33 ....112 D5
Caldbec Hill TN33 ......112 D5
Caldicotts La BN27 .....128 C4
Caledonian Ct 5 BN2 ...189 C5
Caledonian Rd BN2 .....189 C5
Caley Rd TN2 ....8 D7
Calgary Rd TN39 ....157 B7
Callao Quay BN23 ......185 G8
Callums Wlk TN40 ......157 E5
Calverley Ct TN1 ....8 C3
Calverley Park Cres 1 TN1 ....8 B3
Calverley Park Gdns TN1 ..8 C4
Calverley Pk TN1 ....8 B3
Calverley Rd
6 Eastbourne BN21 ......184 F2
Royal Tunbridge Wells TN1 ....8 B3
Royal Tunbridge Wells TN1 ....8 B4
Calverley St TN1 ....8 B4
Calverley Wlk 7 BN21 ...184 F2
Calvert Cl TN22 ....78 A7
Calvert Rd Hastings TN34 .160 A6
Uckfield TN22 ....78 A7
Camber Castle* TN36 ....93 C1
Camber Cl
Beachlands BN24 ....175 F6
Bexhill TN40 ....157 E6
Camber Cl *continued*
Brighton BN2 ....164 F5
Camber Dr BN24 ....175 F6
Camber Rd TN31 ....94 B3
Camber Way BN24 ......175 F6
Camberlot Rd BN27 .....128 A2
Cambrian Rd TN4 ....8 C7
Cambridge Gdns
Hastings TN34 ....159 E7
Royal Tunbridge Wells TN2 ....8 B2
Cambridge Gr BN3 ......163 C7
Cambridge La TN21 ......81 C2
Cambridge Mews BN3 ...163 C7
Cambridge Rd
Bexhill TN40 ....157 C6
Eastbourne BN22 ....185 C4
Hastings TN34 ....159 E7
Hove BN3 ....163 D6
Cambridge St TN2 ....8 C3
Cambridge Way TN22 ....55 C1
Camden Ave TN2 ....9 C6
Camden Ct Pembury TN2 ....9 D6
2 Royal Tunbridge Wells TN1 ....8 B4
Camden Hill TN2 ....8 B3
Camden Pk TN2 ....8 C2
Camden Rd
5 Eastbourne BN21 ......184 F2
Royal Tunbridge Wells TN1 ....8 B4
Camden St BN41 ....162 C6
Camden Terr BN1 ....189 A3
Camelford St BN2 ......189 C1
Cameron Cl BN27 ....152 A8
Campbell Cl TN22 ....55 C1
Campbell Cres RH19 ....1 B1
Campbell Ct TN38 ....159 A8
Campbell Mews 2 BN23 ....175 A1
Campbell Rd
Brighton BN1 ....189 A5
Royal Tunbridge Wells TN4 ....8 A6
Camperdown St TN39 ...157 B7
Canada Cl BN10 ....167 B1
Canada Way TN39 ....157 B7
Canadia Rd TN33 ....112 D8
Canal Bank TN35 ....139 B7
Canary Quay 15 BN23 ...185 F8
Canfield Cl BN2 ....143 D1
Canfield Rd BN2 ....143 D1
Canning St BN2 ....164 D5
Cannon Cvn & Camp Site BN24 ....175 B3
Cannon Pl BN1 ....189 A2
Cansiron La
Ashurst Wood RH19 ....11 F6
Holtye TN7,TN8 ....3 E2
Cantelupe Mews 5 RH19 ..1 E1
Cantelupe Rd
Bexhill TN40 ....157 D3
East Grinstead RH19 ....1 F1
Canterbury Cl BN22 .....173 C2
Canterbury Dr 5 BN2 ...189 C4
Canterbury Rd TN2 ....9 E6
Canterbury Rise TN34 ...136 E3
Cantercrow Hill BN9 ....168 F2
Canton 3 RH16 ....50 D6
Cants Cl RH15 ....73 C3
Cants La RH15 ....73 C3
Canute Cl BN23 ....185 F8
Canute Rd TN35 ....160 D7
Capel Ave BN10 ....178 D7
Capella Path BN27 ......152 D7
Capenors RH15 ....72 F1
Caple Ct TN38 ....159 B8
Caple Gdns TN38 ....159 B7
Card Hill RH18 ....11 F1
Carden Ave BN1 ....143 B6
Carden Cl BN1 ....143 A6
Carden Cres BN1 ....143 A6
Carden Hill BN1 ....143 B5
Carden Prim Sch BN1 ...143 B6
Cardiff Rd TN38 ....159 C7
Cardinal Newman RC Sch BN3 ....163 D8
Cardinals Cl TN40 ....157 F6
Carew Ct
7 Eastbourne BN21 ......185 A4
Hailsham BN27 ....129 C3
Carew Lodge 1 BN21 ...184 F4
Carew Rd BN21 ....184 F4
Carew Views 2 BN21 ...184 F4
Carey Down BN10 ......167 B1
Carfax Cl TN39 ....157 B8
Carinus Gdns TN37 .....136 A6
Carisbrooke Cl BN23 ...174 B4
Carisbrooke Rd
Brighton BN2 ....164 D7
St Leonards TN38 ....159 C7
Carlisle Bldngs 2 BN21 .185 A1
Carlisle Par TN34 ....159 F7
Carlisle Rd
Eastbourne BN20,BN21 ...184 F1
Hove BN3 ....162 F6
Carlton Cl BN25 ....180 E4
Carlton Cres TN1 ....8 C4
Carlton Ct
1 Bexhill TN40 ....157 D3
Portslade-by-S BN41 .....162 C8
Carlton Hill BN2 ....189 C2
Carlton Hill Prim Sch BN2 ....189 C2
Carlton Ho 6 BN1 ......142 E2
Carlton Pl 5 BN2 ....189 C2
Carlton Rd
Eastbourne BN22 ....185 C4
Royal Tunbridge Wells TN1 ....8 C4
Seaford BN25 ....180 D4

Carlton Terr
  3 Crowborough TN6 .....37 F8
  Portslade-by-S BN3,BN41 ..162 C8
Carlyle Ave BN2 .....143 D1
Carlyle St BN2 .....164 C7
Carmel Ct TN39 .....156 D3
Carmel Ho BN3 .....163 A7
Carmelstead Cl RH16 .....51 A3
Carmen Ct BN20 .....173 B3
Carn Ct 7 BN2 .....164 C6
Carnoustie Ct TN38 .....158 F7
Carnoustie Ct 18 RH16 .....50 E4
Carol Cl BN1 .....142 F6
Caroline Cl BN1 .....180 D5
Caroline Way BN3 .....175 B1
Carpenter Dr TN38 .....135 F4
Carpenters Croft BN8 .....105 A5
Carpenters Way BN27 .....152 A6
Carr Taylor Vineyard*
  TN35 .....114 C4
Carrier's Path BN27 .....152 B8
Carriers Pl TN13 .....8 A2
Carroll Wlk BN23 .....174 E2
Carvel Ct TN37 .....135 E7
Cashman Lodge BN1 .....143 A5
Caspian Ct 8 BN1 .....189 A4
Caspian Sq BN2 .....165 F1
Castle Banks BN7 .....190 A2
Castle Bolton BN2 .....174 C4
Castle Ct BN7 .....190 B3
Castle Ditch La BN7 .....190 A2
Castle Dr BN2 .....175 C4
Castle Farm Cotts TN7 .....13 E4
Castle Gate BN7 .....190 A2
Castle Gdns 2 TN34 .....159 F7
Castle Hill TN6 .....39 A5
Castle Hill Pas TN34 .....159 F8
Castle Hill Rd TN34 .....159 F7
Castle Hurst TN32 .....65 B8
Castle La BN7 .....190 A2
Castle Mount BN20 .....184 D1
Castle Prec BN7 .....190 A2
Castle Rd Pevensey BN24 .....175 A6
  Royal Tunbridge Wells TN4 .....8 A3
Castle Rise Lewes BN7 .....190 A2
  Uckfield TN22 .....78 D4
Castle Sq BN1 .....189 B2
Castle St Brighton BN1 .....163 E5
  8 Hastings TN34 .....159 C5
  1 Royal Tunbridge Wells
  TN1 .....8 A2
  Winchelsea TN36 .....117 F7
Castle Terr BN24 .....175 B6
Castle View Cvn & Camp Site
  BN24 .....175 B3
Castle View Gdns BN24 .....174 E6
Castle Way TN22 .....78 D4
Castle Wlk TN5 .....29 E4
Castledean BN1 .....143 C2
Castledown Ave TN34 .....160 A4
Castledown Com Prim Sch
  TN34 .....160 A5
Castledown Terr 7
  TN34 .....160 A4
Castlefields TN7 .....13 E4
Castleham Ind Est TN38 .....135 F5
Castleham Rd TN38 .....135 E5
Castleross Rd BN24 .....175 C4
Castleview Mews TN34 .....160 A4
Cat St TN7 .....12 F1
Cathedral Wlk BN27 .....127 B3
Catherine Pl 7 TN1 .....8 B4
Catherine Vale BN8 .....165 E8
Catkin Way RH16 .....51 B4
Catley Ct 4 TN39 .....157 A4
Catsfield CE Prim Sch
  TN33 .....133 F8
Catsfield Cl
  Eastbourne BN23 .....173 F4
  St Leonards TN38 .....135 D2
Catsfield Rd TN33 .....111 E2
Catt's Corner Cotts TN6 .....27 D1
Catt's Hill TN6 .....27 E1
Cattswood La RH16 .....50 C2
Causeway Sch The
  BN23 .....174 A3
Causeway The
  Brighton BN2 .....164 D6
  16 Seaford BN25 .....180 E2
Cavalry Way RH19 .....10 F7
Cavalry Cres BN20 .....184 B5
Cavendish Mews 12
  BN1 .....163 D5
Cavell Ave BN10 .....178 B7
Cavell Ave N BN10 .....178 C8
Cavell Cl BN10 .....178 B7
Cavendish Ave
  Eastbourne BN23 .....185 B4
  St Leonards TN38 .....159 A7
Cavendish Cl BN10 .....167 B1
Cavendish Ct 10 TN40 .....157 D3
Cavendish Dr TN2 .....8 B1
Cavendish Ho
  8 Brighton BN1 .....163 E5
  Haywards Heath RH16 .....50 F2
  6 St Leonards TN37 .....159 C7
Cavendish Pl
  Brighton BN1 .....163 E5
  Eastbourne BN21 .....185 B3
  4 Hastings TN34 .....160 A4
Cavendish Sch The
  BN21 .....184 C5
Cavendish St 11 BN2 .....189 C2
Caveridge La BN8 .....100 E8
Caves Rd TN38 .....159 A6
Cavix Field TN31 .....67 B7
Caxton Way 13 RH16 .....50 E4

Cecil Ct 2 BN21 .....184 F2
Cedar Cl Burgess Hill RH15 .....73 B5
  Eastbourne BN22 .....173 D2
  St Leonards TN37 .....136 D5
Cedar Ct TN4 .....8 A5
Cedar Ho TN4 .....4 A5
Cedar Lodge TN4 .....7 F3
Cedar Ridge TN2 .....8 D5
Cedar Way RH16 .....51 B4
Cedars Cl TN22 .....78 C8
Cedars Gdns BN1 .....142 E3
Cedars The
  1 Brighton BN2 .....189 C5
  Brighton,Withdean BN1 .....142 E3
  Hailsham BN27 .....129 B1
  Haywards Heath RH16 .....50 D7
  Peacehaven BN10 .....167 C1
  Uckfield TN22 .....78 D8
Cedarwell Cl BN1 .....168 B2
Cedarwood 4 BN1 .....142 E3
Celandine Dr TN34 .....136 A1
Cello Cl BN2 .....164 C5
Centenary Ho 4 BN1 .....142 E2
Centenary Ind Est 6
  BN2 .....164 B8
Central Ave
  Eastbourne BN20 .....184 B5
  Polegate BN26 .....173 B7
  Telscombe Cliffs BN10 .....178 A8
Central Par TN5 .....29 F4
Centurion Rd BN1 .....189 A3
Centurion Rise TN34 .....160 A8
Ceylon Pl BN21,BN22 .....185 B3
Ceylon Wlk TN39 .....156 E3
Chadborn Cl BN1 .....164 D5
Chaffinch Cl RH15 .....72 D4
Chaffinch Rd BN23 .....174 E2
Chaffinch Wlk TN22 .....78 D5
Chailey Ave BN2 .....164 D6
Chailey Cl
  Eastbourne BN23 .....174 E1
  Hastings TN34 .....136 F5
Chailey Common Nature
  Reserve* BN8 .....75 C7
Chailey Cres BN2 .....177 E5
Chailey Ct Brighton BN1 .....142 C5
  2 Haywards Heath RH16 .....50 F2
Chailey Heritage Sch
  BN8 .....75 C7
Chailey Heritage Sch & Hospl
  (New Heritage) BN8 .....52 E1
Chailey La BN8 .....76 B5
Chailey Rd BN1 .....143 E4
Chailey St Peter's CE Prim
  Sch BN8 .....52 E1
Chailey Windmill Rural Life
  Mus* BN8 .....75 D7
Chain La TN31 .....112 C5
Chain Pier Ho BN2 .....189 C1
Chalden Pl TN2 .....156 C6
Chalex Ind Est BN42 .....162 A7
Chalfont Dr BN3 .....142 C3
Chalk Farm La BN20 .....173 B1
Chalkers La BN6 .....97 B8
Chalket La TN2 .....9 C5
Chalkland Rise BN2 .....165 E8
Chalky Rd BN41 .....141 A3
Challoners RH17 .....33 C4
Challoners Cl BN2 .....177 A6
Challoners Mews BN2 .....165 F2
Challow Cl BN6 .....97 E4
Chaloner Cl RH16 .....51 B7
Chaloner Rd RH16 .....51 B7
Chalvington Cl
  Brighton BN1 .....143 E6
  Seaford BN25 .....180 E6
Chalvington Dr TN37 .....136 C6
Chalvington Ho 10
  BN21 .....184 D4
Chalvington Rd BN21 .....184 C4
Chamberlain Rd BN21 .....184 C4
Chamberlanes La BN8 .....124 F6
Chambers Cres TN38 .....135 F3
Chambers Rd TN38 .....135 F3
Champions Row BN1 .....163 C8
Chancellor Ho TN4 .....7 F3
Chancellors Pk BN6 .....97 F4
Chancellory Dr TN34 .....136 E5
Chanctonbury Rd
  Burgess Hill RH15 .....73 A1
  Hove BN3 .....163 E7
Chandler Rd TN39 .....157 A4
Chandler's Mead BN8 .....123 A7
Chandos Cl 1 TN40 .....157 C3
Chandos Rd TN1 .....8 C5
Channel Grange BN10 .....178 A7
Channel View
  8 Bexhill TN40 .....157 E2
  15 Southwick BN42 .....161 E7
Channel View E TN40 .....157 C3
Channel View Rd
  Eastbourne BN20 .....185 D5
  Pevensey Bay BN24 .....175 E5
  Woodingdean BN2 .....165 F1
Channel View W 5
  TN40 .....157 C3
Channel Way TN35 .....138 E3
Channers La BN8 .....126 E1
Chant La TN6 .....27 C1
Chantlers Cl RH19 .....1 C2
Chantlers Mead TN8 .....4 A3
Chantry Ave TN40 .....157 D6
Chantry Com Prim Sch
  TN40 .....157 C5

Chantry La TN40 .....157 C5
Chantry The 12 BN21 .....184 E4
Chapel Barn Cl BN27 .....152 C7
Chapel Cl
  Burgess Hill RH15 .....72 F4
  Seaford BN25 .....180 E4
Chapel Cotts TN33 .....112 E3
Chapel Field TN31 .....67 A7
Chapel Gn TN6 .....25 F2
Chapel Hill
  Alfriston BN26 .....171 B3
  Crowhurst TN33 .....134 F4
  Lewes BN7 .....190 C2
  Sedlescombe TN33 .....113 E7
Chapel Ho BN2 .....189 C2
Chapel La
  Ashurst Wood RH19 .....11 D6
  Blackboys TN22 .....80 B7
  East Chiltington BN7 .....100 A3
  Forest Row RH18 .....11 F7
  Guestling Green TN35 .....138 A8
  Horsted Keynes RH17 .....33 C5
  Westfield TN35 .....114 A1
Chapel Mews 8 BN3 .....163 D5
Chapel Park Rd TN37 .....159 C8
Chapel Pl
  Portslade-by-S BN41 .....162 B7
  14 Royal Tunbridge Wells
  TN1 .....8 A2
Chapel Rd
  Plumpton Green BN7 .....99 E7
  Portslade-by-S BN41 .....162 A7
Chapel St Brighton BN2 .....189 C2
  Newhaven BN9 .....179 D7
Chapel Terr 2 BN2 .....164 D4
Chapel Terrace Mews 21
  BN2 .....164 D4
Chapman Way TN2 .....8 C8
Chapman's La
  East Grinstead RH19 .....1 B1
Chapman's Town Rd
  TN22 .....83 B2
Charis Ct 18 BN3 .....163 C7
Charity Farm Way TN6 .....26 A3
Charles Ave RH15 .....72 D2
Charles Bennett Ct RH16 .....51 A4
Charles Cl Hove BN3 .....142 A3
  Seaford BN25 .....180 D5
Charles Ct TN4 .....8 C4
Charles Kingston Gdns
  BN1 .....142 E4
Charles Moore Ct BN26 .....173 A7
Charles Rd TN38 .....159 D8
Charles Rd W TN38 .....159 B8
Charles St Brighton BN2 .....189 B1
  Royal Tunbridge Wells TN4 .....8 A8
Charleston Farmhouse*
  BN8 .....149 A2
Charleston Manor Gdns*
  BN25 .....182 A6
Charleston Rd BN1 .....184 D4
Charlesworth Pk RH16 .....51 C4
Charlotte St BN2 .....189 C1
Charlston Ave BN9 .....179 A5
Charlton Gdns BN6 .....98 D3
Charlton's Way TN4 .....7 E1
Charltons The BN1 .....143 D6
Charlwood Gdns RH15 .....73 D5
Charlwood Rd RH15 .....73 D6
Charlwoods Bsns Ctr
  RH19 .....1 D2
Charlwoods Pl RH19 .....1 E3
Charlwoods Rd RH19 .....1 E3
Charter Gate RH19 .....50 D5
Charters Ancaster Coll
  TN40 .....157 F5
Charters Ancaster Sch
  TN40 .....157 F5
Chartfield BN3 .....142 A2
Chartfield Way BN3 .....142 B2
Chartres TN40 .....157 D6
Chartres Cl TN40 .....157 D6
Chartwell Cl BN25 .....180 E6
Chartwell Ct BN1 .....189 B1
Chates Farm Ct BN2 .....189 C3
Chatfield Cl TN38 .....135 F4
Chatfield Cres TN33 .....173 C1
Chatfield Rd RH17 .....50 A4
Chatham Pl
  Brighton BN1 .....189 A4
  Seaford BN25 .....180 E2
Chatsworth Ave BN10 .....167 A1
Chatsworth Cl BN10 .....178 A8
Chatsworth Ct BN1 .....163 E8
Chatsworth Gdns BN10 .....188 F8
Chatsworth Pk BN10 .....167 B2
Chatsworth Rd BN1 .....163 E8
Chatsworth Sq BN1 .....163 D2
Chaucer Ave 4 RH19 .....1 C1
Chaucer Ct TN39 .....156 E1
Chaucer Ind Est BN26 .....173 D6
Chaucer Wlk BN23 .....174 E3
Chawbrook Mews BN22 .....185 A4
Chawbrook Rd BN22 .....185 A4
Cheal Cl BN43 .....161 A6
Cheapside BN1 .....189 B3
Cheeleys RH17 .....33 C8
Chedgates TN39 .....156 C3
Chelmsford Ct 4 BN20 .....184 F1
Chelsea Arc TN40 .....157 D4
Chelsea Mews 17 TN38 .....159 C7
Chelston Ave BN3 .....162 D7
Cheltenham Pl BN1 .....189 B4
Chelwood Cl BN1 .....143 A5

Chelwood Ct RH15 .....73 A4
Chelwood Gate Rd RH17,
  TN22 .....34 F7
Chelworth Rd BN22 .....173 D2
Chene Rd BN10 .....178 F6
Chenies Cl TN2 .....17 A8
Chepbourne Rd TN40 .....157 C4
Chepstow Ct BN1 .....143 F5
Chequer Grange RH18 .....11 E1
Chequer Mead Arts Ctr
  RH19 .....1 F1
Chequer Rd RH19 .....1 F1
Chequers Cl TN6 .....26 A2
Chequers Way TN6 .....26 A2
Cherington Cl BN6 .....97 B5
Cherith Cotts 3 TN21 .....82 A6
Cheriton Ct BN2 .....184 C4
Cherry Cl RH15 .....72 E3
Cherry Clack TN21 .....83 D6
Cherry Cotts
  Fletching TN22 .....54 A4
  Hastings TN35 .....160 C2
Cherry Garden Rd BN20 .....184 B3
Cherry Gdns
  Heathfield TN21 .....82 B5
  High Hurstwood TN22 .....56 B8
Cherry Side BN27 .....152 A7
Cherry Tree Cl TN37 .....159 D8
Cherry Tree Ct TN21 .....106 F7
Cherry Tree Gdns TN40 .....157 F6
Cherry Tree Rd TN2 .....7 E1
Cherrywood 2 BN1 .....142 E3
Cherwell Cl BN24 .....173 F5
Cherwell Ct BN21 .....82 A8
Cherwell Lo TN21 .....82 A8
Cherwell Rd TN21 .....82 A8
Chesham Pl BN2 .....164 D4
Chesham Rd BN2 .....164 D4
Cheshire Cl 3 BN2 .....185 B4
Chester Ave TN2 .....8 D2
Chester Cl 12 BN3 .....163 E7
Chester Terr BN1 .....143 A1
Chesterfield Gdns BN20 .....188 E8
Chesterfield Rd BN20 .....188 E8
Chesterton Ave BN25 .....181 B3
Chesterton Cl RH19 .....10 F7
Chesterton Dr BN25 .....181 B3
Chestnut Ave
  Golden Cross BN27 .....127 B4
  Royal Tunbridge Wells TN4 .....8 B8
Chestnut Cl
  Broad Oak TN31 .....90 B5
  Burgess Hill RH15 .....73 B5
  East Grinstead RH19 .....2 A1
  Eastbourne BN22 .....173 C2
  Hailsham BN27 .....129 A1
  Herstmonceux BN27 .....130 E6
  Royal Tunbridge Wells TN4 .....8 B8
Chestnut Cotts
  Fletching TN22 .....53 F3
  1 Heathfield TN21 .....82 A7
Chestnut Ct TN2 .....17 A8
Chestnut Dr BN26 .....173 A6
Chestnut Pr TN11 .....4 A6
Chestnut Way BN27 .....179 B7
Chestnut Wlk
  Bexhill TN39 .....156 C5
  Felcourt RH19 .....2 D3
Chestnuts Cl RH16 .....51 A7
Chestnuts The
  Haywards Heath RH16 .....50 F7
  The Moor TN18 .....45 F8
Chetnole RH19 .....1 D2
Cheviot Cl BN23 .....174 C3
Cheviots The TN34 .....160 C8
Cheyne Ct BN43 .....161 C7
Chichester Cl
  Bexhill TN39 .....157 B6
  3 Brighton BN2 .....164 D4
  Eastbourne BN22 .....173 D2
  Hove BN3 .....141 E4
  Peacehaven BN10 .....178 F7
  Saltdean BN2 .....177 C5
  Seaford BN25 .....180 E3
Chichester Ct
  Bexhill TN39 .....157 B6
  Seaford BN25 .....180 E2
Chichester Dr E BN2 .....177 C5
Chichester Dr W BN2 .....177 B5
Chichester Ho TN40 .....157 D4
Chichester Lodge BN25 .....180 E3
Chichester Pl BN2 .....164 D4
Chichester Rd
  Seaford BN25 .....180 E3
Chichester Terr 18 BN2 .....164 D4
Chichester Way TN35 .....73 C5
Chick Hill TN35 .....139 B8
Chicks La TN17 .....20 F2
Chiddingly Cl BN2 .....164 F5
Chiddingly Ho 11 BN3 .....163 D7
Chiddingly Prim Sch
  BN8 .....127 C7
Chieveley Cotts TN38 .....136 B1
Chieveley Dr TN2 .....8 D1
Chilcomb RH15 .....73 C1
Chilham Cl BN23 .....174 D2
Chillies La TN22,TN6 .....37 B3
Chilling St RH19 .....21 D3
Chillis Wood Rd RH16 .....50 C5
Chilston Cl TN4 .....8 A5
Chilston Rd TN4 .....8 A5
Chiltern Cl
  Eastbourne BN23 .....174 D3
  Shoreham-by-S BN43 .....161 C8
Chiltern Ct BN26 .....173 A7

Chiltern Dr TN34 .....160 B7
Chiltern Wlk TN2 .....8 D4
Chiltington Cl
  Burgess Hill RH15 .....72 F5
  Saltdean BN2 .....177 C6
Chiltington La BN7 .....100 D3
Chiltington Way BN2 .....177 C6
Chiswick Pl BN21 .....185 A2
Chitcombe Rd TN31 .....89 E5
Chitcombe Wlk TN34 .....137 A5
Chorley Ave BN2 .....177 B6
Chown's Hill TN35 .....137 A6
Chownes Mead La RH16 .....50 B4
Chrisdory Rd BN41 .....140 F3
Christ Church CE Prim Sch
  TN37 .....136 C1
Christchurch Ct BN9 .....179 D7
Christie Ave BN8 .....124 D6
Christie Rd BN2 .....123 A4
Christies RH19 .....10 D8
Christine Cl TN40 .....158 A7
Christopher Rd RH19 .....1 E1
Church App TN22 .....79 B5
Church Ave
  Haywards Heath RH16 .....50 E6
  Westham BN24 .....175 A6
Church Bailey TN21 .....175 A5
Church Bailey Ct BN24 .....175 A5
Church Cl Brighton BN1 .....142 F5
  Eastbourne BN20 .....173 A4
Church Ct
  3 Haywards Heath RH16 .....50 E4
  Hove BN3 .....141 F1
Church Farm Cl TN19 .....44 C1
Church Gn BN43 .....161 C7
Church Hill Bexhill TN39 .....156 D4
  Brighton BN1 .....142 E7
  Etchingham TN19 .....44 B2
  Newhaven BN9 .....179 C7
  Pyecombe BN45 .....119 C6
  Ringmer BN8 .....124 D6
Church Hill Ave TN39 .....156 D4
Church House Cl TN34 .....137 F3
Church in the Wood La
  TN38 .....135 F1
Church La
  Burgess Hill RH17 .....73 F6
  Buxted TN22 .....56 C5
  Catsfield TN33 .....133 E8
  Clayhill TN21 .....67 E4
  Danehill RH17 .....34 A3
  Ditchling BN6 .....98 D3
  East Grinstead RH19 .....1 F1
  8 Eastbourne BN21 .....184 D3
  Etchingham TN19 .....44 C2
  Frant TN3 .....17 A4
  Guestling Green TN35 .....116 B1
  Hellingly BN27 .....129 A6
  Hooe TN33 .....155 C7
  Horsted Keynes RH17 .....33 C5
  Iden TN31 .....70 D4
  Jevington BN26 .....183 C7
  Kingston near Lewes BN7 .....145 D5
  Laughton BN8 .....126 C5
  Lewes,South Malling BN7 .....190 E6
  Lewes,St Anne's BN7 .....146 B8
  Ninfield TN33 .....133 B6
  Northbridge Street TN32 .....64 C5
  Nutbourne TN31 .....67 C6
  Pevensey BN24 .....175 C6
  Pyecombe BN45 .....119 C6
  Ripe BN27,BN8 .....149 E8
  Rye Foreign TN31 .....92 B8
  Seaford BN25 .....180 A2
  Southwick BN42 .....161 D7
  Westfield TN35 .....114 A3
Church Marks La BN8 .....105 F1
Church Mead BN6 .....98 B3
Church Mews TN34 .....173 B1
Church Pas TN34 .....160 A4
Church Path
  Hellingly BN27 .....129 A5
  Ninfield TN33 .....133 A5
  Pett TN36 .....114 E4
Church Rd
  Barcombe BN8 .....101 C4
  Burgess Hill RH15 .....73 A3
  Buxted TN22 .....56 B4
  Catsfield TN33 .....133 F7
  Crowborough TN6 .....25 F2
  Flowers Green BN27 .....131 A1
  Haywards Heath RH16 .....50 E4
  Hove BN3 .....163 B6
  Kilndown TN17 .....20 F3
  Lamberhurst TN3 .....20 C6
  Mountfield TN32 .....87 B5
  Newick BN8 .....76 E6
  Pembury TN2 .....9 D8
  Polegate BN26 .....173 A6
  Portslade-by-S BN41 .....162 B7
  Rotherfield TN6 .....39 A8
  Royal Tunbridge Wells TN1 .....8 A2
  Sandhurst Cross TN18 .....46 F4
  Scaynes Hill RH17 .....51 F3
  St Leonards TN37 .....159 D7
Church Row
  Brighton BN1 .....190 A2
Church Sq TN31 .....93 C5
Church St Bexhill TN40 .....157 D5
  Brighton BN1 .....189 B2
  Cowden TN8 .....4 B5
  Eastbourne BN20,BN22 ...173 C2
  Eastbourne,Old Town
  BN20,BN21 .....184 D3

Church St continued
Hartfield TN7 ....13 D4
Hastings TN35 ....160 C7
Old Heathfield TN21 ....82 D5
Portslade-by-S BN41 ..162 B7
Seaford BN25 ....180 C2
Ticehurst TN5 ....31 D1
Uckfield TN22 ....78 C7
Wadhurst TN5 ....30 A4
Church Twitten TN7 ...190 B2
Church Vale Rd TN40 .157 B7
Church Walk Mews RH15 .73 A3
Church Way [3] BN2 ...189 C3
Church Wlk RH15 ......73 A3
Church Wood Dr TN38 .135 E4
Church Wood Way
  TN38 ....135 F2
Churchdale Ave BN22 .185 C6
Churchdale Pl BN22 ..185 B6
Churchdale Rd BN22 ..185 C6
Churchfield
  East Dean BN20 ....187 B8
  Westfield TN35 .....114 D3
Churchfield Rd [3] BN23 .184 F4
Churchfields TN22 ....35 C4
Churchfields Ind Est
  TN38 ....135 E4
Churchill Ave TN35 ..137 D5
Churchill Cl BN20 ...184 D3
Churchill Ct TN38 ...136 B2
Churchill Ho Hove BN3 .141 E2
  Seaford BN25 ......181 C4
Churchill Rd
  Heathfield TN21 ....82 B6
  Lewes BN7 ....123 B3
  Seaford BN25 ......180 D5
Churchill Sq BN1 ....189 A2
Churchill Square Sh Ctr
  BN1 ....189 A2
Churchill Way RH15 ..73 C2
Churchland La TN33 ..88 E3
Churchsettle La TN5 ..42 B7
Churchwood Com Prim Sch
  TN38 ....135 F3
Churchyard Cotts TN3 .7 A8
Chyngton Ave BN25 ..181 B4
Chyngton Cl BN23 ...174 A4
Chyngton Gdns BN25 .181 C2
Chyngton La BN25 ...181 C2
Chyngton La N BN25 .181 C3
Chyngton Pl BN25 ...181 B2
Chyngton Rd BN25 ..181 A2
Chyngton Sch BN25 .181 B4
Chyngton Way BN25 .181 C3
Cider Hollow BN27 ..131 B5
Cider House Wlk BN8 .105 A5
Cinder Hill Chailey BN8 .75 F3
  Cinder Hill RH19 ...21 B1
Cinderford La BN27 .129 F8
Cinque Ports St TN31 .93 B5
Cinque Ports Way
  Seaford BN25 ......181 C4
  St Leonards TN38 ..158 E6
Cinquefoil BN10 ....178 C8
Circus Par BN1 .....189 B4
Circus St BN2 ......189 B2
Circus The BN23 ....185 D8
Cissbury Ave BN10 ..178 E2
Cissbury Cres BN2 ..177 E5
Cissbury Rd
  Burgess Hill RH15 ..72 E4
  Hove BN3 ....163 E7
City Coll Brighton & Hove
  Brighton BN1 ......189 A5
  Brighton BN1 ......189 B3
  Brighton BN2 ......189 C4
  Hove BN3 ....163 A6
Civic App TN2 ......78 C7
Civic Way
  Burgess Hill RH15 ..73 A3
  Royal Tunbridge Wells TN1 ..8 A3
CJ Gallards Almshouses
  N6 ....8 A8
Clackhams La TN6 ...38 D7
Clair Ct RH16 ......50 E5
Clair Rd RH16 ......50 E5
Clanricarde Gdns [1] TN1 ..8 A3
Clanricarde Rd [2] TN1 ..8 A3
Clapham La BN26 ...182 A8
Claphatch La TN5 ...31 A5
Clappers The TN32 ..64 B4
Clare Rd BN7 ......123 A2
Clare Wlk BN2 .....164 D5
Claremont [3] TN34 ..159 E7
Claremont Ct
  [4] Royal Tunbridge Wells
  TN2 ....8 C7
  Seaford BN25 ......180 D3
Claremont Gdns TN2 ..8 B2
Claremont Pl TN22 ..55 C1
Claremont Prim Sch TN2 ..8 B2
Claremont Rd
  Bexhill TN39 ....157 B7
  Newhaven BN9 .....168 F1
  Royal Tunbridge Wells TN1 ..8 B2
  Seaford BN25 ......180 D3
Claremont Rise TN22 .55 C1
Clarence [1] TN37 ...114 B1
Clarence Ct BN24 ...175 C3
Clarence Dr [2] RH19 ..10 F7
Clarence Gdns BN1 ..189 A2
Clarence Rd
  Eastbourne BN22 ..185 B4
  Royal Tunbridge Wells TN1 ..8 A3

Clarence Rd continued
  St Leonards TN37 ..136 C1
Clarence Row TN1 ...8 A3
Clarence Sq BN1 ...189 A2
Clarendon Cl TN37 .136 B4
Clarendon Gdns TN2 .8 A1
Clarendon Ho [2] BN2 .163 B7
Clarendon Pl
  [5] Brighton BN2 ..164 C4
  Portslade-by-S BN41 .162 C6
Clarendon Rd Hove BN3 .163 B7
  Shoreham-by-S BN42,
  BN43 ....161 D8
Clarendon Terr [10] BN2 .164 D4
Clarendon Villas BN3 .163 B7
Clarendon Way TN2 ..8 A1
Claridge TN1 ......8 B6
Clark's Yd TN5 ....32 A3
Clarke Ave BN3 ...141 F3
Clarke Ct BN3 ....162 F6
Clarks Ind Est BN3 .163 B8
Claverham Cl TN33 .112 B4
Claverham Com Coll
  TN33 ....112 A4
Claverham Way TN33 .112 B4
Clavering Wlk BN3 ..156 B2
Claxton Cl BN21 ...184 D5
Claxton Rd TN40 ..158 A5
Clay Cnr BN8 .....101 F6
Clay Hill Rd TN3 ..19 D6
Clayfields BN10 ...178 B7
Clays Cl RH19 ....10 E8
Clayton Ave BN6 ..97 F3
Clayton Dr RH15 ..72 F1
Clayton Hill BN6,BN45 .119 D7
Clayton Mill Rd BN24 .174 B5
Clayton Pk BN6 ...97 E4
Clayton Rd Brighton BN2 .164 D7
  Ditchling BN6 .....98 C3
Clayton Way BN3 ..141 F3
Clayton Windmills*
  BN6 ....119 E7
Clayton's La TN5 ..5 E2
Clearwater La RH17 .52 A3
Clearwaters La RH16 .73 D8
Cleeve Ave TN2 ...8 D2
Cleevelands BN22 .173 E2
Clement Hill Rd TN34 .160 B7
Clement La BN26 ..173 A5
Clementine Ave BN25 .180 D5
Clerks Acre BN6 ..98 A4
Clermont Cl BN1 ..142 E2
Clermont Rd BN1 .142 E2
Clermont Terr BN1 .142 E2
Cleve Terr BN7 ...146 B8
Clevedon Rd TN39 .157 A6
Clevedown BN7 ...146 A8
Cleveland TN2 ....8 D4
Cleveland Cl BN23 .174 C3
Cleveland Gdns BN25 .73 B2
Cleveland Rd BN1 .143 A1
Clevelands RH16 ..50 E6
Cliff App BN2 ....164 F4
Cliff Ave BN10 ...178 E5
Cliff Cl BN25 .....180 F1
Cliff Ct TN38 .....158 D6
Cliff End La TN35 .139 B7
Cliff Gdns Seaford BN25 .180 F1
Cliff Park Cl BN10 .178 F7
Cliff Rd Brighton BN2 .164 E4
  Eastbourne BN20 ..188 E7
  Seaford BN25 .....180 F1
Cliff The BN2 ....164 F4
Cliff Way TN35 ...138 F5
Cliffe High St BN7 .190 B2
Cliffe Ind Est BN8 .146 F8
Cliffe Leas BN7 ...190 C2
Cliffe Rd BN21 ...184 C6
Clifford Ct
  [6] Bexhill TN40 ..157 C4
  Crowborough TN6 ..25 F2
Clifford Rd [10] TN40 .157 C4
Clifton Cl BN22 ...184 D8
Clifton Cotts TN2 ..8 D8
Clifton Ct TN34 ...159 E8
Clifton Hill BN1 ..189 A3
Clifton Ho BN22 ..184 D8
Clifton Mews BN1 .189 A3
Clifton Pl Brighton BN1 .163 E6
  Royal Tunbridge Wells TN1 .8 B2
Clifton Rd Brighton BN1 .189 A3
  Burgess Hill RH15 ..72 D5
  Hastings TN35 .....160 C7
  Newhaven BN9 ....179 D7
  Royal Tunbridge Wells TN2 .8 D7
Clifton Rise TN40 .157 F5
Clifton St BN1 ....189 A3
Clifton Terr BN1 ..189 A3
Clifton Way BN10 .178 B7
Cliftonlea Ct [6] BN3 .163 B7
Cliftonville Cl TN38 .135 D6
Cliftonville Way TN38 .158 D6
Climping Cl RH16 .50 D3
Clinch Green Ave TN39 .156 F7
Clinton Ct TN38 ..136 B1
Clinton Hill RH7 ..2 A8
Clinton La [4] BN21 .180 E3
Clinton Pl BN21 ..180 E3
Clinton Way TN35 .138 F5
Clive Ave TN35 ...160 C6
Clive Ct RH16 ....50 E6
Clive Villas TN33 .112 E3
Cliveden BN25 ....180 D3
Clock House La TN22 .35 C4
Clock Tower Ct [5] TN39 .157 B3
Clockhouse TN2 ..8 F6

Cloister [16] TN40 ..157 D3
Cloisters BN9 ....179 C7
Cloisters The
  Battle TN33 ......112 C6
  Eastbourne BN22 .173 C2
  St Leonards TN37 .159 D7
Close Eight BN23 .174 E3
Close Eighteen BN23 .174 E3
Close Eleven BN23 .174 E3
Close Fifteen [6] BN23 .174 E3
Close Five BN23 .174 E3
Close Four BN23 .174 E2
Close Fourteen BN23 .174 E3
Close Nine BN23 .174 E2
Close Nineteen BN23 .174 E3
Close One BN23 .174 D2
Close Seven BN23 .174 E3
Close Seventeen BN23 .174 E3
Close Six BN23 ..174 E3
Close Sixteen BN23 .174 E2
Close Ten BN23 ..174 E3
Close The Blackboys TN22 .80 B6
  Brighton BN1 .....142 E5
  Burgess Hill RH15 .73 C4
  Crowborough TN6 ..25 E3
  East Grinstead RH19 .10 D8
  Eastbourne BN20 ..184 B8
  Eastbourne BN22 .173 C3
  Fairlight TN35 ....138 C4
  Friston BN20 .....183 A1
  Groombridge TN3 ..15 C6
  Hassocks BN6 .....97 F4
  Newhaven BN9 ....168 F2
  Royal Tunbridge Wells TN1 .8 C8
  Rye TN31 ....93 A6
  Seaford BN25 .....180 F2
Close Three BN23 .174 D2
Close Twelve BN23 .174 E2
Close Twenty BN23 .174 E3
Close Twentyfour BN23 .174 E3
Close Twentyfive [4]
  ....174 E3
Close Two BN23 ..174 E2
Cloudesley Rd TN37 .159 C8
Clovelly Ho BN26 .173 A7
Clover Ct [2] TN40 .50 E4
Clover Way BN41 .141 B2
Cloverlea TN34 ..136 E5
Clovers End BN1 .143 B7
Cluny St BN2 ....190 A1
Clyde Pk BN27 ...152 C7
Clyde Rd Brighton BN1 .189 B5
  St Leonards TN37,TN38 .159 C7
Coach & Horses La RH17 .34 C6
Coach & Horses Pas [4]
  BN2 ....190 A2
Coach House Cotts TN31 .94 F2
Coach La RH17 ...34 C6
Coach Rd TN4 ....7 C3
Coalbrook Rd BN2 .164 C5
Coast Rd BN24 ...176 B7
Coastal Counties Ho [19]
  BN2 ....189 C3
Coastguard Ct BN24 .176 D8
Coastguard Cotts
  Camber TN31 .....94 D2
  Normans' Bay BN24 .176 D8
Coastguard La TN35 .138 C4
Coastguard Sq
  [3] Eastbourne BN22 .185 C4
  Rye Harbour TN31 .94 A3
Coastguards TN35 .139 C8
Coates Ct [3] BN41 .161 E7
Cobald Rd BN24 ..175 E5
Cobbett's Ride TN2 .7 A7
Cobbetts Mead RH14 .51 B3
Cobblers Field TN19 .61 A3
Cobbold Ave BN21 .184 C5
Cobden Pl [5] BN27 .164 C7
Cobden Rd BN2 ..164 C7
Cobdown La TN22 .55 C5
Cobham Twrs [2] BN2 .157 F4
Cobhams TN3 ....7 A8
Cobourg Pl [6] TN34 .160 A4
Cobton Dr BN3 ..142 A3
Coburn Ct BN7 ...190 B2
Cochrane Cl BN23 .174 C3
Cockcrow Wood TN37 .136 D5
Cockhaise Cotts RH16 .52 A8
Cockmount La TN5 .29 F5
Cockshut Rd BN7 .190 A1
Cogger's Cross TN21 .106 F3
Cogger's La TN21 .106 F4
Coggins Mill La TN20 .40 D4
Coghurst Hall Holiday Village
  TN35 ....137 C8
Coghurst Rd TN35 .160 C8
Colbourne Ave BN2 .143 D2
Colbourne Rd BN3 .163 E7
Colchester Vale RH18 .11 E2
Colchins RH15 ...72 F1
Coldean La BN1 ..143 E6
Coldean Prim Sch BN1 .143 D6
Coldene Rd BN21 .143 C8
Coldharbour Cl TN6 .26 A1
Coldharbour La
  Iden TN31 ....70 A4
  Newick BN8 ......76 A7
  Peasmarsh TN31 ..69 E3
Coldharbour Rd
  Lower Dicker BN27 .128 B2
  White Post TN8,TN11 .5 E8
Coldthorn La BN26,BN27 .152 A4
Coldwaltham La RH15 .73 D2
Colebrook Rd
  Brighton BN1 .....142 D4
  Royal Tunbridge Wells TN4 .7 E6
  Southwick BN42 ..161 F7

Colebrooke Rd TN39 .157 A4
Coleman Ave BN3 .162 E7
Coleman St BN2 ..164 C5
Colemans Hatch Rd
  RH18,TN7 ....23 C6
Coleridge Cl BN3 .163 A8
Coleridge Wlk [7] BN23 .174 C2
Coles Ct TN2 ....8 C3
Colgate Cl BN2 ..164 F6
College Cl
  East Grinstead RH19 .1 F1
  Portslade-by-S BN41 .140 F3
College Ct [22] BN21 .185 A2
College Dr TN2 ..8 D4
College Gdns BN2 .164 C4
College La BN21 ..184 E4
College La
  East Grinstead RH19 .1 F1
  Hurst Wickham BN6 .97 C6
College Pl Brighton BN2 .164 C4
College Rd Bexhill TN40 .157 C5
  Brighton BN1 .....143 A1
  Eastbourne BN21 ..184 F2
  Haywards Heath RH16 .50 E7
  Seaford BN25 .....180 F2
College St [11] BN2 .164 C4
College Terr BN21 .164 D5
Collett Cl TN38 ..135 F5
Colley Cnr TN39 .156 F4
Collier Rd Hastings TN34 .160 A5
  Pevensey Bay BN24 .175 D4
Collier's Gn TN21 .83 F3
Collingford La RH17 .34 B4
Collington Ave TN39 .156 F3
Collington Cl BN20 .184 E1
Collington Gr TN39 .156 E4
Collington La E TN39 .156 F4
Collington La W TN39 .156 D3
Collington Man TN39 .157 B3
Collington Park Cres
  TN39 ....156 F4
Collington Rise
  Bexhill TN39 ......156 E4
  Bexhill TN39 ......156 E5
Collington Sta TN39 .157 A3
Collingwood Ave TN21 .82 B7
Collingwood Cl
  [4] East Grinstead RH19 .10 F7
  Eastbourne BN23 ..185 E6
  Peacehaven BN10 .167 D1
Collingwood Ct BN2 .165 A3
Collinstone Rd TN38 .159 A7
Collinswood Dr TN38 .159 A7
Colmer Ct RH15 ..72 E3
Colmer Pl RH15 ..72 E3
Colonnade Gdns [18]
  BN21 ....185 B3
Colonnade Rd [14] BN21 .185 B3
Colonnades The BN1 .189 B2
Colstocks Rd BN20 .188 D8
Columbus Dr BN23 .185 G7
Colville Ct [1] BN2 .184 E4
Colwell Cl RH16 ..50 F3
Colwell Gdns
  Haywards Heath RH17 .50 F1
  Haywards Heath RH17 .51 B3
Colwell Rd RH16 .50 F2
Colwood Cres BN20 .184 B6
Colwood Hospl RH17 .51 A3
Combe End TN6 ..37 E8
Combe La
  Eastbourne BN20 ..188 D7
  Standard Hill TN33 .132 F6
Combe Rise BN20 .173 A2
Combe The BN20 .173 A2
Combermere Rd TN38 .136 B1
Command Rd BN20 .184 B5
Commanders Wlk TN35 .138 E4
Commercial Mews N [6]
  BN21 ....185 A4
Commercial Rd
  Burgess Hill RH15 .72 F3
  Eastbourne BN21 ..185 A3
  Royal Tunbridge Wells TN1 .8 B5
Commercial Sq RH16 .50 E6
Common La Ditchling BN6 .98 D6
  Laughton BN8 ....126 A8
  Selmeston BN26 ..149 E1
Common View TN4 .7 C4
Common Wood Rise TN6 .25 D4
Compass Ct BN41 .140 E2
Compasses La BN27 .88 C6
Comphurst La BN27 .131 B4
Compton Ave BN1 .189 A4
Compton Cl [11] TN40 .157 C4
Compton Dr BN20 .184 C2
Compton Grange BN20 .184 E1
Compton Lodge BN21 .184 E2
Compton Place Rd
  BN20,BN21 ......184 C2
Compton Rd
  Brighton BN1 .....142 D1
  Lindfield RH16 ...51 B8
Compton St BN21 .185 A1
Compton Terr BN27 .152 C6
Compts The BN10 .167 B1
Conan Doyle Ct TN6 .25 E2
Concord Cl TN2 ..8 C4
Concorde Cl TN39 .156 F6
Condor Way TN35 .72 E3
Conduit Hill [3] TN31 .93 C6
Coney Furlong BN10 .167 D1
Coneyburrow Gdns
  TN38 ....135 E4

Coneyburrow La TN39 .155 F5
Coneyburrow Rd TN2 .8 E5
Conghurst La TN18 .46 B6
Conifer Cl TN34 ..136 F3
Conifers The [8] BN21 .184 F4
Coniston Ave TN35 .7 E5
Coniston Cl BN3 ..163 D7
Coniston Rd BN23 .174 C4
Connaught Rd
  [1] Eastbourne BN21 .185 A2
  Hove BN3 ....163 A6
  Seaford BN25 .....163 B7
Connaught Terr BN3 .163 B7
Connaught Way TN4 .7 F5
Connell Dr BN2 ..165 E7
Conqueror Ind Est TN38 .135 F6
Conqueror Rd TN38 .158 E7
Conqueror Terr TN33 .88 F1
Conquest Hospl TN37 .136 D6
Consort Way RH15 .72 E2
Constable Rd BN23 .174 D1
Constable Way TN40 .157 C4
Conway [8] Cl [9] Hove BN3 .163 B7
  [9] St Leonards TN38 .159 B6
Conway Ct BN3 ..163 A8
Conway St BN3 ..163 B8
Cooden Beach Sta
  TN39 ....156 B2
Cooden Cl TN39 .156 C3
Cooden Dr TN39 .156 B2
Cooden Ledge TN37 .135 E2
Cooden Sea Rd
  Bexhill TN39 ......156 C3
  Bexhill TN39 ......156 C3
Cook Ave BN23 ..185 C6
Cookham Dene TN40 .157 E6
Cooksbridge Rd BN2 .164 E6
Cooksbridge Sta BN8 .123 A7
Cookson Gdns TN35 .160 C7
Cookstown Cl TN33 .132 F6
Coolham Dr BN2 .164 E7
Coombe Cl BN27 .131 B5
Coombe Cotts RH19 .21 A6
Coombe Hill Rd RH19 .10 D6
Coombe La TN5 ..41 C7
Coombe Lea [5] BN3 .163 C6
Coombe Lodge BN25 .180 C3
Coombe Mdw BN2 .177 E7
Coombe Rd
  Brighton BN2 .....143 D1
  Eastbourne BN20 ..184 C4
  Lewes BN7 ....190 B3
Coombe Rise [8] BN2 .177 E7
Coombe Road Prim Sch
  BN2 ....143 D1
Coombe Shaw TN33 .133 A6
Coombe Terr BN2 .143 C1
Coombe Vale BN2 .177 D7
Coombers La RH16 .51 B5
Coombs Cl TN31 ..68 C5
Coombs Cotts TN31 .68 C5
Cooper Dr TN39 .157 B8
Cooper Rd TN37 ..93 A5
Cooper Rise TN37 .136 A5
Coopers Cl TN35 .73 B5
Coopers Hill BN20 .173 B2
Coopers La
  Crowborough TN6 .25 D4
  Poundsbridge TN11,TN3 .6 C7
Coopers Row TN22 .9 D7
Coopers Way BN27 .152 A6
Coopers Wood TN6 .25 D4
Copenhagen Dr BN1 .165 A3
Copestake Dr RH15 .73 D3
Coplands Plat TN31 .67 B7
Coplands Rise TN31 .67 B7
Coppards Cl RH17 .74 C4
Coppards La TN31 .67 C8
Copper Beeches
  Brighton BN1 .....142 E1
  St Leonards TN38 .136 C4
Copper Cl RH15 ..72 C4
Copper's Hill TN19 .61 E4
Coppers Ct TN4 ..8 A8
Coppice Ave BN20 .173 A4
Coppice Cl BN20 .173 A3
Coppice The Battle TN33 .136 E1
  Hastings TN34 ....136 E1
  Pembury TN2 .....9 D7
  Scaynes Hill RH17 .51 F3
Coppice View TN35 .82 B6
Coppice Way RH16 .50 D3
Copse Cl
  East Grinstead RH19 .2 A3
  St Leonards TN38 .135 D3
Copse Hill BN1 ..142 D5
Copse La TN39 ..156 E4
Copse The RH16 .51 B5
Copt Hall TN18 ..48 D3
Copthorne Ct [1] BN3 .163 C6
Copthorne Ho [19] BN21 .184 E4
Copthorne Rd RH19 .1 A4
Copwood Ave TN22 .78 B7
Copwood Rdbt TN22 .78 A6
Copyhold La RH17 .50 A4
Copythorne Ho [1] RH16 .50 E6
Coral Reef Cl BN43 .145 A1
Corbyn Cres BN43 .161 A7
Cordons BN7 ....147 A1
Cormorant Cl BN23 .174 C2
Cornelius Ave BN9 .179 A5
Corner Gn BN8 ..122 D5
Cornfield Cl BN25 .180 F3
Cornfield La [2] BN21 .185 A2
Cornfield Rd
  Eastbourne BN21 ..185 A2

Cornfield Rd continued
Seaford BN25 ....180 F3
Cornfield Terr
11 Eastbourne BN21 ....185 A2
St Leonards TN37 ......136 C1
Cornford Cl
Burgess Hill RH15 .....72 E5
Crowborough TN6 ......26 A1
Pembury TN2 ....9 B6
Portslade-by-S BN41 ...141 B2
Cornford La TN2 ....9 B5
Cornford Pk TN2 ....9 C6
Cornish Cl BN23 ....174 B4
Cornmill Gdns BN26 ...172 C4
Cornwall Ave BN10 ....178 E6
Cornwall Cl
Eastbourne BN20 ......184 C5
2 Hove BN3 ....163 C7
Cornwall Gdns
Brighton BN1 ....142 E2
6 East Grinstead RH19 ...10 F8
Cornwall Ho BN1 ......142 E2
Cornwall Rd TN39 .....157 B3
Cornwallis Cl BN23 ...185 C7
Cornwallis Gdns TN34 .159 E8
Cornwallis St 5 TN34 .159 E8
Cornwallis Terr TN34 .159 E8
Coronation Bldgs BN9 .179 D7
Coronation Cotts
Burwash TN19 ....62 A6
Northbridge Street TN32 ...64 C5
Ticehurst TN5 ....31 F2
Coronation Gdns
Battle TN33 ....112 F5
Hurst Green TN19 .....44 F3
Coronation Rd RH19 ...10 E7
Coronation St 8 BN2 ..164 C7
Corseley Rd TN3 ......15 B5
Corsica Cl BN25 ......180 F2
Corsica Rd BN25 ......180 F1
Costells Edge RH17 ...51 F3
Costume Mus* TN40 ...157 D4
Cotchford Hill TN7 ....13 D1
Cotchford La TN7 .....13 C1
Cotswold Cl
Eastbourne BN23 .....174 C4
Hastings TN34 ....160 B8
Cotswold Pl 7 BN2 ...164 F5
Cotswolds The BN42 ..161 E7
Cottage Cl BN9 ....168 D2
Cottage Homes BN6 ...98 E6
Cottage La
Hailsham BN24 ....152 E1
Westfield TN33,TN35 ..114 D7
Cottages The TN2 ....129 C3
Cottenden Rd TN5 ....43 A6
Cottesmore St Mary's RC
  Prim Sch BN3 ....163 D8
Coulstock Rd RH15 ....72 C3
Council Cotts
Cross-in-H TN21 ....81 C8
Crowborough TN6 .....38 A8
Robertsbridge TN32 ...63 F3
Uckfield TN22 ....78 D3
Council Hos
Ginger's Green BN27 ..130 C6
Rushlake Green TN21 ..83 D1
Countess of Thanet's
Almshouses TN8 ....3 F3
County Oak Ave BN1 ..143 B6
Courcels BN2 ....164 E3
Course The BN7 ......146 B8
Court Cl Brighton BN1 .142 E7
East Grinstead RH19 ...1 F1
Court Cres RH19 ......1 F1
Court Farm Cl BN9 ...168 A2
Court Farm Rd
Hove BN3 ....142 A2
Newhaven BN9 ....179 C5
Rottingdean BN2 .....165 F3
Court House Mus*
  BN24 ....175 B6
Court La TN2 ....55 D4
Court Leet 8 BN25 ...180 F2
Court Mdw TN6 ....39 B8
Court Meadow Sch TN6 ...39 B7
Court Meadow Sch RH17 ...50 A8
Court Ord Cotts BN2 ..165 F3
Court Ord Rd BN2 .....165 F3
Court Rd
Eastbourne BN22 .....173 F2
Lewes BN7 ....190 B2
Royal Tunbridge Wells TN1 ...7 A2
Court Royal TN2 ......16 E8
Court The BN20 ....173 B1
Courtenay Gate BN3 ..163 B5
Courtenay Terr 7 BN3 .163 B5
Courtenwell TN1 ......6 F4
Courthope Ave TN5 ...29 F4
Courthope Dr TN39 ...156 F5
Courthouse St TN34 ..160 B4
Courtland Rd BN26 ...173 A5
Courtlands
16 Brighton BN2 ......189 C3
Dodd's Hill TN22 .....35 D2
Haywards Heath RH16 ..50 E3
Newhaven BN9 ....179 C7
Courtlands Pl TN6 ....159 B6
Courtlands Rd BN22 ..145 C1
Courtney King Ho 1
  BN2 ....164 D4
Courtyard The
East Grinstead RH19 ...2 B1
12 Eastbourne BN21 ..184 F3
Falmer BN1 ....146 C6
Hastings TN34 ....136 E1
Haywards Heath RH16 ..50 F4

Courtyard The continued
8 Hove BN3 ....163 D6
Sheffield Green TN22 ..53 C5
Cousley Wood Rd TN5 ...30 C7
Coventry Ct BN2 ......185 D6
Coventry Rd TN38 ....136 B3
Coventry St BN1 .....163 E8
Coverdale Ave TN39 ..156 C3
Coverdale Ct RH19 ...1 C3
Covers The BN25 .....180 F2
Covert The TN39 .....156 C2
Cow La BN6 ....181 F8
Cowden Cl TN18 .....45 E8
Cowden Cross TN8 ...4 C7
Cowden Hall La TN21 .107 D5
Cowden La TN18 .....45 E7
Cowden Mews TN8 ...4 A5
Cowden Rd BN2 .....177 D4
Cowden Sta TN8 .....4 D8
Cowden Wlk TN38 ...136 A2
Cowdens Cl BN3 .....141 D4
Cowdray Cl TN39 ....156 C6
Cowdray Dr TN39 ....156 C6
Cowdray Ct 1 BN3 ...163 D7
Cowdray Park Rd TN39 ...156 C6
Cowfold Rd BN2 .....164 E5
Cowley Dr BN2 ......165 F7
Cownny Ct BN3 .....165 F1
Cowper St BN3 .....163 A7
Cox Gr RH15 ....72 E5
Cox's Cotts BN7 ....146 B7
Coxheath Cl TN38 ...135 E7
Crabtree Ave BN1 ...143 B5
Crabtree Ho 1 TN8 ..159 B6
Crackendale Field BN8 .124 E6
Cradle Hill Com Prim Sch
  BN25 ....181 A5
Cradle Hill Ind Est BN25 ..181 B5
Cradle Hill Rd BN25 ..181 B5
Craig Cl TN33 ....135 A6
Craigmore Hall TN6 ..26 A1
Craignair Ave BN1 ...142 F7
Cranborne Ave BN20 .188 C8
Cranbourne St BN1 ..189 A2
Cranbrook 14 BN2 ...189 C3
Cranbrook Rd TN37 ..136 C1
Cranedown BN7 .....146 B7
Cranfield Rd TN40 ...157 C4
Crangon Cotts BN20 .187 A4
Cranleigh Ave BN2 ...177 B5
Cranleigh Cl TN39 ...157 A4
Cranley Ct 2 BN2 ...162 D7
Cranmer Ave BN3 ...141 F1
Cranmer Cl BN7 .....190 B3
Cranston Ave TN39 ..157 A4
Cranston Cl TN39 ...156 F4
Cranston Rd RH19 ...1 F2
Cranston Rise TN39 ..156 F4
Cranwell Rd TN4 ....7 C4
Crates Yd TN4 ......8 A5
Craven Rd BN2 .....164 D6
Crawfurd Way RH19 ..1 F3
Crawley Cres BN22 ..173 E2
Crawley Rd BN1 .....143 D6
Crayford Rd BN2 ....143 D1
Crazy La TN33 ......113 E7
Crecy Cl TN37 ......135 F7
Creek The 11 TN34 ..160 B4
Crendon Pk TN4 ....8 A8
Crescent Cl
Burgess Hill RH15 ...73 B3
Woodingdean BN2 ...165 E8
Crescent Dr N BN2 ..165 E8
Crescent Dr S BN2 ..165 E7
Crescent Mans BN2 ..189 C5
Crescent Pl BN2 ....164 C4
Crescent Rd
Brighton BN2 ....164 B8
Burgess Hill RH15 ...73 A3
East Grinstead RH19 ...1 D1
Royal Tunbridge Wells TN1 ..8 B3
Crescent The
Brighton BN2 ....143 E2
Eastbourne BN20 ....173 A4
Eastbourne,Downside
Felcourt RH19 ....1 C8
Groombridge TN3 ....13 C7
Hastings TN34 ......136 C3
Keymer BN6 ....98 B3
Newhaven BN9 .....168 F1
Southwick BN42 ....161 F8
Crescent Way RH15 ..73 A3
Crespin Way BN1 ...143 C2
Crest Rd BN9 ......179 C7
Crest Way BN41 ....141 B3
Cresta Cl BN26 ....173 A7
Cresta Ct BN10 ....179 A6
Cresta Rd BN9 .....179 A6
Crestway Par BN1 ..143 C2
Crestway The BN1 ..143 C2
Cricket Ct RH19 ....1 E3
Cricketers Cl TN19 ..18 A5
Cricketers Field TN32 .65 E1
Cricketfield BN8 ....76 D8
Cricketfield CT 6 BN25 .180 F2
Cricketfield Rd BN25 .180 F2
Cricketing La TN22 ..130 C4
Criers La TN20,TN22 ..57 F7
Crink Hill BN8 .....101 F3
Cripland Cl RH16 ...51 B6
Cripps Ave BN10 ...167 D1
Crisp Rd BN7 ......123 A3
Crispin Ct 5 TN40 ..157 E4
Crittle's Ct TN5 ....29 F4
Crockers Hatch Cnr TN3 ...6 D2
Crockers La TN31 ...67 B8
Crocks Dean BN10 ..167 F2
Croft Ave BN42 ....161 F7

Croft Cl BN26 ......173 A4
Croft Ct
2 Eastbourne BN21 ..185 B3
7 Seaford BN25 .....180 E3
Croft Dr BN41 ......141 A3
Croft La BN25 ......180 E3
Croft Rd Brighton BN1 ..142 D4
Crowborough TN6 ...42 C5
Hastings TN34 .....160 B4
Croft Terr 2 TN34 ..160 A4
Croft The Bexhill TN39 .157 A4
14 Eastbourne BN21 ..184 F4
Eastbourne,Willingdon
Hassocks BN6 ......97 F5
Hastings TN34 .....160 A4
Lower Dicker BN27 ..128 B4
Southwick BN42 ....161 E8
Croft Works BN27 ...152 B7
Crofton Park Ave TN39 .156 E3
Croham Rd 11 TN6 ..25 F3
Cromarty Wlk 17 BN23 .185 F8
Cromer Way BN27 ..129 A1
Cromer Wlk BN23 ...185 F8
Cromleigh Way BN42 .140 E2
Cromwell Ct 3 BN3 ..163 D7
Cromwell Mews RH15 .72 F4
Cromwell Pl 1 RH19 .10 F7
Cromwell Rd
Burgess Hill RH15 ...72 F3
Hove BN3 ....163 C7
Royal Tunbridge Wells TN1 ..8 C3
Cromwell St BN2 ...164 C7
Crooked La BN21 ...180 F2
Cross La TN5 ......31 D2
Cross Lane Gdns TN5 ..31 D1
Cross Levels Way BN21,
  BN22 ....184 E7
Cross Rd BN20 .....161 D8
Cross St Brighton BN1 .189 B4
14 Hove BN3,BN3 ...163 D5
Polegate BN26 .....173 A6
St Leonards TN37 ..159 C7
Cross Way BN7 ....123 A2
Cross-in-Hand CE Prim Sch
  TN21 ....81 F7
Crossbush Rd BN2 ..164 E6
Crossroad Cl BN24 ..161 D8
Crossway The
Brighton BN1 ....143 B2
Portslade-by-S BN41 .141 A2
Royal Tunbridge Wells TN4 ..7 D2
Crossways BN8 ....148 B4
Crossways Ave
East Grinstead RH19 ..1 C1
East Grinstead RH19 ..1 D1
Crossways The
Broad Oak TN31 ....90 B4
Hassocks BN6 .....97 C4
Stone Cross BN24 ..174 A6
Crouch Cl BN20 ....173 B1
Crouch La Linkhill TN18 ..47 D6
Lower Street TN33 ..133 B3
Seaford BN25
Crouch The BN25 ..180 E2
Crouchfield Cl 2 BN25 .180 F2
Crowborough Ct 4 TN6 ..25 F3
Crowborough Hill TN6 .26 B1
Crowborough Mews TN6 .25 C2
Crowborough Rd
Hastings TN35 ......160 E8
Marlpits TN22 ......35 E6
Saltdean BN2 ......177 D4
Crowborough Sta TN6 ...38 C8
Crowders La
Crowhurst CE Prim Sch
  TN33 ....134 F5
Crowhurst La BN20 ..173 A4
Crowhurst La TN39 ..157 C7
Crowhurst Rd
Brighton BN1 ....143 C7
St Leonards TN38 ..135 B3
Crowhurst Sta TN35 ..135 A6
Crowlink Cotts BN2 ..186 E7
Crowlink La BN20 ..183 A1
Crowmere Ave TN40 .157 C5
Crowmere Terr TN40 .157 C5
Crown Cl Hailsham BN27 .152 A7
11 Hove BN3 ....163 D6
Uckfield TN22 ......78 C8
Crown Ct 25 TN34 ..160 B4
Crown Gdns BN1 ...189 A2
Crown Hill
4 Brighton BN2 ....164 C6
Seaford BN25 .....180 E7
Crown Ho TN3 .....20 D5
Crown La TN34 ....160 B4
Crown Point Ho BN2 .97 F4
Crown Rd
Portslade-by-S BN41 .162 A8
Shoreham-by-S BN43 .161 B8
4 St Brighton BN1 ..189 A2
Eastbourne BN21 ..184 D4
Crowne Ho 8 BN2 ..184 E4
Croxden Way BN20 ..173 D3
Croxton La RH16 ...51 B6
Crump's Cnr TN22 ..103 D6
Crunden Rd BN20 ..184 B4
Cubitt Way TN38 ..135 E4
Cuckfield Cl TN40 ..158 A5
Cuckfield Rd
Burgess Hill RH15 ...72 E7
Goddards' Green BN6,
  RH17 ....72 A4
Cuckmere Ct
Alfriston BN26 ......170 F3

Cuckmere Ct continued
5 Seaford BN25 ....180 E3
Cuckmere Dr BN24 ..174 A5
Cuckmere Ho BN24 ..175 E5
Cuckmere House Sch
  BN25 ....181 C3
Cuckmere Path TN22 .55 E1
Cuckmere Rd
Newhaven BN9 .....179 A5
Seaford BN25 .....181 B2
Cuckmere Rise TN21 ..82 B8
Cuckmere Way BN1 ..143 C5
Cuckmere Wlk BN22 .173 D1
Cuckoo Dr TN21 ...82 A6
Culpepper RH15 ...72 E4
Culpeper Cl BN2 ...143 D2
Culross Ave RH16 ..50 D5
Culver Cl BN23 .....174 B4
Culverden Ave TN4 ..8 A6
Culverden Down TN4 ..7 F5
Culverden Park Rd TN4 ..7 F5
Culverden Pk TN4 ..7 F5
Culverden Sq TN4 ..8 A5
Culverden St TN1 ..8 A4
Cumballa Cl BN20 ..188 F8
Cumberland Ct
3 Bexhill TN40 .....157 D4
Eastbourne BN20 ..184 B6
Cumberland Dr BN1 .142 E2
Cumberland Gdns
Royal Tunbridge Wells
  TN1 ....8 A2
St Leonards TN38 ..159 B8
Cumberland Lodge 3
  BN1 ....142 E2
Cumberland Mews 12 TN1 .8 A2
Cumberland Rd
Bexhill TN39 ....157 B7
Brighton BN1 ......142 E2
Cumberland Wlk TN1 .8 A2
Cumberland Yd 6 TN1 ..8 A2
Cunnor House Sch RH17 ..34 B5
Cunningham Cl TN4 ..8 A7
Cunningham Ct 10
  BN25 ....180 E2
Cunningham Dr BN23 .185 E7
Cunningham Ho 6
  TN39 ....157 B3
Cunningham Rd TN4 ..8 B7
Curfew Ct
Hailsham BN27 ....152 D7
St Leonards TN38 ..135 E3
Curlews The BN24 ..161 A8
Currie Rd TN4 .....8 A5
Curwen Pl BN1 ....142 E3
Curzon Ho BN2 ....177 C4
Cuthbert Cl TN39 ..157 A7
Cuthbert Rd BN2 ..164 C5
Cutter La 7 TN34 ..160 B4
Cypress Cl
Shoreham-by-S BN43 .140 A1
St Leonards TN38 ..159 A7
Cypress Gr TN2 ....17 C8
Cyprus Mews TN31 ..73 B3
Cyprus Pl TN31 ....93 B5
Cyprus Rd RH15 ...72 E5
Cyril Richings Bsns Ctr
  BN43 ....161 B7

D

D'aubigny Rd BN2 ..164 B8
Dacre Pk BN27 ....152 D7
Dacre Rd
Eastbourne BN21 ..184 C4
Herstmonceux BN27 ..130 E6
Newhaven BN9 ....179 D7
Dads Hill TN21 ....81 B8
Dagg La TN22 .....65 F5
Dairy Gn TN6 .....38 D8
Dakins The RH19 ..10 E8
Dale Ave Brighton BN2 .142 F5
Keymer BN6 ......98 A3
Dale Cres BN1 ....142 F6
Dale Dr BN1 ....143 A6
Dale Hill BN45 ....119 A6
Dale Rd Forest Row RH18 .11 F1
Lewes BN7 ....146 A8
Dale St TN1 ......8 B4
Dale View BN3 ....141 D2
Dale View Gdns BN3 .141 D2
Dalehurst TN6 ....38 C7
Dalehurst Rd TN39 .157 B7
Dales Ct BN27 ....131 B5
Dalewood Gdns RH15 .73 C2
Dalton Rd BN20 ..188 E8
Damian Way BN1 ..98 B4
Damon Cl BN10 ..178 C7
Dana Lodge BN10 ..178 A7
Dane Cl BN25 .....180 D2
Dane Court Cl TN40 .158 A6
Dane Hts 8 BN25 ..180 E2
Dane Rd Seaford BN25 .180 E3
St Leonards TN38 ..159 B8
Danehill CE Prim Sch
  RH17 ....34 B4

Danehill La RH17 ...33 E5
Danehill Rd BN2 ...164 F5
Daniel Way TN31 ..94 F2
Dannfields Ho BN25 .180 E3
Danny* BN6 ......97 A2
Danny Sheldon Ho 14
  ....164 C4
Danum Cl BN27 ...129 C3
Danworth Farm BN6 .72 A1
Danworth La BN6 ..72 B2
Darby's La TN5 ...30 B2
Darcey Dr BN1 ....143 A6
Darent Cl BN24 ...173 F5
Daresbury Cl TN39 .157 B6
Darley Rd BN20 ..188 D7
Darrick Ct 6 BN21 ..185 A1
Dart Ct RH19 .....2 A3
Dartmouth Cl BN2 .143 F1
Dartmouth Cres BN2 .143 F1
Darvel Down TN33 ..86 B2
Darwall Dr BN25 ..181 A3
Darwell Cl
Robertsbridge TN32 ..64 B3
St Leonards TN38 ..135 C1
Darwell Dr BN24 ..174 A5
Davey Cl BN1 ....143 B1
Davey's La BN7 ...190 C3
David Lloyd Club The
  BN22 ....184 F8
David Saloman's Ho*
  TN3 ....7 D8
Davids Hts BN21 ..184 E5
Davigdor Inf Sch BN3 .163 D6
Davigdor Rd BN3 ..163 E7
Davis Cl TN39 ....157 A7
Dawber Bldgs BN27 .152 B7
Dawes Ho TN19 ...62 A6
Dawlish Cl BN2 ...143 F1
Dawson Terr BN2 ..164 C6
Daynes Way RH15 ..72 E1
Daytona Quay 18 BN23 .185 F8
De Cham Ave TN37 .159 B8
De Cham Rd TN37 ..159 C8
De Chardin Dr TN34 .137 A5
De Courcel Rd BN2 ..164 E3
De Grey Cl BN2 ...190 B3
De La Warr Gn BN7 .123 B3
De La Warr Par TN40 .157 E4
De La Warr Rd TN40 .157 C3
De La Warr Rd
  Bexhill TN40 ......157 E5
  East Grinstead RH19 ..1 F1
De Moleyns Cl 1 TN40 .157 D4
De Montfort Rd
  Brighton BN2 .....164 C7
  Lewes BN7 ....123 B1
De Montfort Terr 4
  ....123 B1
De Roos Ct BN21 ..184 E5
De Roos Rd BN21 ..184 E4
De Walden Mews BN20 .188 E8
De Warrenne Rd BN7 .123 B1
Deacon Cl BN2 ...141 C2
Deadman's Cross TN21 .93 C6
Deadmantree Hill BN8 .101 B3
Deal Ave BN25 ...181 C5
Deals The 7 TN31 ..93 B5
Dean Cl
  Portslade-by-S BN41 .141 C2
  Woodingdean BN2 ..177 A6
Dean Court Rd BN2 .177 A6
Dean Gdns BN41 ..141 C2
Dean Rd BN25 ....180 F2
Dean St BN1 .....163 E5
Dean Wood Cl BN23 .174 A4
Deanery Cl BN1 ...190 B4
Deanland Rd BN27 .127 B4
Deans Cl 8 Bexhill TN39 .157 B6
  Woodingdean BN2 ..177 A6
Deans Dr TN39 ...157 A6
Deans Mdw BN26 ..101 E5
Deans Rd BN26 ...170 F3
Deanway BN3 ....141 E6
Decimus Burton Way 10
  TN37 ....159 C7
Decimus Pl TN1 ...8 B4
Deco Bldg The BN2 .143 C1
Decoy Dr BN22 ...173 D1
Deepdene TN5 ....30 A6
Deepdene Gdns TN35 .160 C7
Deepdeen Sch BN2 .162 D7
Deer Haven BN27 ..127 C4
Deer Paddock La 7
  BN27 ....152 C7
Deerswood La TN39 .156 E5
Deeside The BN1 ..143 A7
Deilsfoot Cotts TN6 .28 A3
Delamere Ct 3 BN21 .184 F2
Delavall Wlk BN23 .185 F6
Delaware Dr TN37 .135 F6
Delaware Rd BN7 ..146 A8
Delfryn BN41 ....140 F3
Dell Cl TN38 .....136 A1
Dell Dr TN2 ......8 D4
Dell The
  East Grinstead RH19 ..2 B1
  Haywards Heath RH16 .50 C5
Dellney Ave RH16 ..50 F3
Delmonden Rd TN18 .45 C8
Delves Cl BN8 ....124 D6
Delves Ho 8 BN8 ..124 D6
Delves Way BN8 ..124 D6
Den Hill BN20 ....184 A4

Denbigh Cl TN39 ....156 E4
Denbigh Ct TN39 ....156 E5
Denbigh Rd TN4 ....8 C7
Dencher Rd BN7 ....145 E3
Dene Cl BN20 ....183 B1
Dene Dr BN22 ....173 C1
Dene Path TN22 ....55 D1
Dene Rd BN20 ....183 B1
Dene The
  Eastbourne BN20 ....173 A3
  Hastings TN35 ......137 A5
  Hove BN3 ....141 D3
  Uckfield TN22 ......55 D1
Dene Vale BN1 ....142 D5
Dene Way TN3 ....7 A7
Denecroft BN1 ......142 D5
Denehurst Gdns TN35 ..137 A5
Deneside BN1 ....142 D5
Deneway The BN1 ...142 D4
Denham Cl TN38 ...135 F4
Denham Rd RH15 ...72 D3
Denham Way TN1 ...94 E2
Denman's Cl RH16 ...51 A8
Denman's La RH16 ...51 A7
Denmark Mews BN3 ..163 E7
Denmark Pl TN34 ...159 F7
Denmark Rd BN41 ...162 C7
Denmark Terr BN1 ...163 E6
Denmark Villas BN3 ..163 B7
Dennis Hobden Cl BN2 ..143 E1
Denton Cl TN31 ....93 A6
Denton Comm Prim Sch
  BN9 ....168 E1
Denton Dr Brighton BN1 ..143 A6
  Newhaven BN9 ...168 E1
Denton Rd
  Eastbourne BN20 ..188 D8
  Newhaven BN9 ...168 E1
Denton Rise BN9 ...168 E2
Dentons The BN20 ..188 D8
Derby Ct **7** BN3 ...163 E7
Derby Pl **6** BN2 ...189 C2
Derek Ave BN3 ....162 D6
Derek Ho BN3 .....162 F6
Den La TN21 ......106 B7
Dervia Ho BN3 ....163 C7
Derwent Cl BN27 ..129 A1
Derwent Ct BN1 ...189 A3
Derwent Dr TN4 ...7 E5
Derwent Rd BN20 ..188 E8
Desmond Rd BN22 ..185 D5
Desmond Way BN4 ..164 F6
Devil's Dyke Rd BN1 ..54 F4
Devon Villas RH16 ..50 F4
Devonian Ct BN2 ..189 C4
Devonport Ho **1** TN31 ..93 C6
Devonshire Cl TN2 ..16 F8
Devonshire Ct **1** BN3 ..163 C7
Devonshire Lodge **1**
  BN22 ....185 C5
Devonshire Pl
  Brighton BN2 .....189 C2
  Eastbourne BN21 ..185 A2
Devonshire Rd
  Bexhill TN40 ......157 C3
  Hastings TN34 ....159 F8
Devonshire Sq TN40 ..157 C3
Dew La TN31 ....92 A8
Dewe Rd BN2 ......143 C1
Dewhurst Cotts TN5 ..29 A7
Dewhurst La TN5 ...29 B8
Dewlands Hill TN20 ..38 F2
Dewpond The BN10 ..167 B1
Dexter Dr RH19 ...10 E8
Diamond Cotts RH17 ..74 A5
Diana Cl TN40 ....158 A6
Dickens Cl RH19 ..1 C1
Dickens Way BN23 ..174 E3
Dicklands The BN7 ..167 D8
Diggers The BN1 ...143 B3
Dillingburgh Rd BN20 ..184 C4
Dillon Way TN2 ...8 D7
Dinapore Ho **1** BN2 ..189 C3
Diplock Cl BN26 ..172 F6
Diplocks Bldgs BN27 ..152 A2
Diplocks The BN27 ..152 A8
Diplocks Way BN27 ..152 A2
Diplocks Wlk BN27 ..152 A8
Dirty La RH19 .....11 E7
Ditchling Beacon Nature
  Reserve* BN6 ....120 D7
Ditchling Bostall BN6 ..120 D7
Ditchling Cl BN23 ..173 F4
Ditchling Common Ctry Plk*
  BN6 ....73 F1
Ditchling Cres BN1 ..143 C5
Ditchling Ct **4** BN1 ..164 B8
Ditchling Dr TN35 ..160 E8
Ditchling Gdns BN1 ..143 C4
Ditchling Mus* BN6 ..98 C3
Ditchling Pl **1** BN1 ..143 A1
Ditchling Rd
  Brighton BN1,BN2 ..143 B4
  Westmeston BN1,BN6 ..120 D4
Ditchling Rise BN1 ..164 A8
Ditchling St Margaret's CE
  Prim Sch BN6 ....98 D3
Ditchling Way BN27 ..152 B6
Ditton's Cnr BN26 ..173 C6
Ditton's Rd BN26 ..173 C6
Dittons BN26 ......173 C6
Dittons Mews TN38 ..135 E2
Dittons Rd BN21 ..184 E3
Divall's Cotts RH19 ..11 D6

Dixter La TN31 ....67 B8
Dixter Rd TN31 ...67 A6
Dock The BN8 .....148 C3
Dodshill TN6 ......26 A1
Dog Cotts RH19 ..3 B1
Dog Kennel La TN22 ..57 F6
Dogs Hill Rd TN36 ..118 B5
Doleham Cotts TN35 ..115 D5
Doleham Halt TN35 ..115 D5
Doleham Hill TN35 ..115 D5
Doleham La TN35 ..115 B6
Dolphin Ct
  Eastbourne BN20 ..188 E7
  5 Hove BN3 ....163 A6
Dolphin Ind Est BN43 ..161 B7
Dolphin L Ctr The RH16 ..50 D6
Dolphin Mews
  Brighton BN2 .....189 B1
  Shoreham-by-S BN43 ..161 A7
Dolphin Rd
  Haywards Heath RH16 ..50 D4
  Shoreham-by-S BN43 ..161 B7
Dolphin Way BN43 ..161 B7
Dome The* BN1 ...189 B2
Dominica Ct BN23 ..185 G2
Donald Hall Rd BN2 ..164 D5
Donald Way TN36 ..118 A5
Donkey Mews BN4 ..163 D5
Donnington Rd BN2 ..165 E6
Dorchester TN1 ...8 B6
Dorchester Ct
  2 Brighton BN1 ..163 E5
  3 Eastbourne BN21 ..184 E4
Dordrecht Way TN34 ..136 E1
Dorin Ct TN2 .....8 C3
Dorita Ct BN10 ...178 C6
Dorking Rd TN1 ...8 C3
Dorman's Cl RH7 ..2 A8
Dormans High St RH7 ..2 A8
Dormans Park Rd
  Dormans Park RH19 ..1 E6
  East Grinstead RH19 ..1 D3
Dormans Sta Rd* RH7 ..1 F7
Dormans Station Rd RH7 ..1 F7
Dormansland Prim Sch
  RH7 ....2 A8
Dornden Dr TN3 ..7 A4
Dorothy Ave BN10 ..178 C7
Dorothy Ave N BN10 ..178 C8
Dorothy Rd BN1 ...162 D8
Dorothy Stringer High Sch
  BN1 ....142 F3
Dorset Ave RH19 ..1 C3
Dorset Cotts TN7 ..14 B4
Dorset Ct
  6 Eastbourne BN21 ..185 B3
  Hove BN3 ....162 F6
Dorset Gdns
  Brighton BN2 .....189 C2
  East Grinstead RH19 ..1 C3
Dorset Mews BN2 ..189 B2
Dorset Pl Brighton BN2 ..189 C2
  Hastings TN34 ....159 F7
Dorset Rd Bexhill TN40 ..157 D4
  Bexhill TN40 ......157 C6
  Lewes BN7 ....190 B1
  Royal Tunbridge Wells TN2 ..8 D2
Dorset Rd S TN40 ..157 D4
Dorset St BN2 ....189 B2
Doubledays RH15 ..73 B2
Doucegrove TN38 ..136 A1
Douglas Cl BN27 ..129 B2
Douglas Rd TN6 ..27 D1
Douro Stables TN4 ..8 A4
Dove Ct TN22 .....78 C8
Dovedale Gdns BN22 ..173 F2
Dover Cl BN25 ....181 C5
Dover Rd Brighton BN1 ..143 A2
  Polegate BN26 ....173 B7
Dowding Way **1** TN40 ..8 D8
Dower Cl BN2 .....165 D3
Down Ave TN3 ....20 A6
Down La TN3 ......28 C8
Down Rd TN39 ....157 A5
Down St TN22 .....54 C5
Down Terr BN2 ....164 C6
Down The BN3 ....141 D4
Down's Rd BN4 ...136 F3
Downash Cl BN21 ..164 E6
Downash Ct TN5 ..32 A3
Downash Ho TN5 ..32 A3
Downes Ct **9** BN43 ..161 C8
Downey Cl TN37 ..136 B6
Downford **15** BN2 ..164 F5
Downhill View BN2 ..165 E7
Downland Ave
  Peacehaven BN10 ..178 E6
  Southwick BN42 ..140 E1
Downland Cl
  Eastbourne BN20 ..174 C4
  Southwick BN42 ..140 D1
  Woodingdean BN2 ..165 C6
Downland Copse TN22 ..78 C8
Downland Cres BN3 ..141 F3
Downland Ct BN41 ..141 A2
Downland Dr BN41 ..141 F3
Downland Rd BN2 ..164 C6
Downlands Ave TN39 ..157 B4
Downlands Cl TN39 ..157 A4
Downlands Com Sch
  BN6 ....97 F3
Downlands Way BN30 ..183 B1
Downland Cl TN21 ..106 F7
Downs Ave BN20 ..184 B6
Downs Cl BN7 .....123 A2
Downs Inf Sch BN1 ..164 B8
Downs Jun Sch BN1 ..143 A1

Downs Park Sch BN41 ..141 B2
Downs Rd
  Burgess Hill RH15 ..72 E4
  Eastbourne BN22 ..173 B2
  Seaford BN25 .....181 A3
Downs The BN25 ..181 A3
Downs Valley Rd BN2 ..165 E8
Downs View
  Ninfield TN33 .....133 B5
  North Chailey BN8 ..75 E7
  Peacehaven BN10 ..167 D2
Downs View Cl
  East Dean BN20 ...183 C1
  North Chailey BN8 ..75 E7
Downs View La BN20 ..183 C1
Downs View Rd BN6 ..97 F3
Downs View Rd BN2 ..165 C8
Downs Villas BN9 ..168 E3
Downs Wlk
  Peacehaven BN10 ..167 B1
  Peacehaven BN10 ..167 C2
Downscroft RH15 ..73 D6
Downside Brighton BN1 ..142 D5
  Hove BN3 ....142 B3
  Lewes BN7 ....146 A8
  Shoreham-by-S BN43 ..140 A1
Downside Cl
  Eastbourne BN20 ..184 C3
  Shoreham-by-S BN43 ..140 A1
Downsmead BN2 ...184 E3
Downsvalley Rd BN20 ..173 A4
Downsview BN1 ...142 E1
  Eastbourne BN20 ..173 A3
  Heathfield TN21 ...132 B8
  Hove BN3 ....141 D3
  Hurstpierpoint BN6 ..97 A5
Downsview Cotts BN8 ..123 A7
Downsview Cres TN22 ..78 D8
Downsview Dr RH17 ..74 C4
Downsview Rd
  Brighton BN2 .....173 A3
  Golden Cross BN27 ..127 B3
  Portslade-by-S BN41 ..141 A2
  Seaford BN25 .....181 A3
Downsview Way BN27 ..152 B7
Downsway
  Arlington BN26 ....150 B3
  Southwick BN42 ..140 F1
  Woodingdean BN2 ..165 D7
Downton Cotts TN18 ..46 F4
Draffin La TN31 ...94 D3
Drake Ave BN23 ...185 E7
Drake Ct BN25 ....180 E2
Drake Ho TN39 ...156 E4
Drapers Way TN38 ..136 B2
Draxmont Way BN1 ..142 F3
Drayton Rise TN39 ..156 D4
Drive Lodge **10** BN3 ..163 C7
Drive The
  Burgess Hill RH15 ..73 B4
  Crowborough TN6 ..25 D2
  Hailsham BN27 ....152 B6
  Hellingly BN27 ....129 C5
  Hove BN3 ....163 C7
  Maresfield TN22 ...55 A1
  Maresfield Park TN22 ..55 A7
  Newhaven BN9 ...179 C5
  Royal Tunbridge Wells TN2 ..8 A1
  Southwick BN42 ..140 E1
  St Leonards TN38 ..158 F8
  Uckfield TN22 .....78 C8
  Walter's Green TN3 ..15 C6
Drockmill Cl BN26 ..173 C6
Drove Ave BN2 ....140 D2
Drove Cres BN41 ..141 A2
Drove Rd Newhaven BN9 ..179 D8
  Portslade-by-S BN41 ..141 A1
  Woodingdean BN2 ..165 B8
Drove The Brighton BN1 ..142 D1
  Falmer BN1 ....144 C5
  Newhaven BN9 ...179 B8
  Offham BN7,BN8 ..123 A5
Drovers Cl BN41 ..141 C2
Drovers Way RH15 ..73 C1
Droveway The
  Haywards Heath RH16 ..50 C6
  Hove BN3 ....142 B1
  Hove BN3 ....142 C1
  Lewes BN7 ....146 A5
Drummond Cl RH16 ..50 D4
Drummond Ct RH16 ..50 D4
Drury La TN38 ....136 A2
Drusilla's Park Zoo*
  BN26 ....171 B6
Dryden Wlk BN23 ..174 E3
Duchess Dr BN25 ..180 E6
Dudeney Lodge BN1 ..143 B1
Dudley Inf Sch TN35 ..160 C5
Dudley Lodge TN2 ..8 C4
Dudley Mews **10** BN3 ..163 D5
Dudley Rd Brighton BN1 ..143 B1
  Eastbourne BN21 ..185 B4
  Hastings TN35 ....160 C5
  Royal Tunbridge Wells TN1 ..8 A4
Dudwell Rd BN2 ...165 E7
Duke Bernard Ct **8**
  BN22 ....185 C5
Duke Mews **2** TN37 ..136 B2
Duke Rd TN37 ....136 B2
Duke St Bexhill TN39 ..156 F5
  Brighton BN1 .....189 A2
  Hastings TN37 ...136 B2
Duke Terr TN37 ...136 B2
Duke's Cl BN1 ....189 A2
Duke's Dr BN20 ...188 E7
Duke's Mound BN2 ..164 D4

Dukes Barn Ct RH16 ..51 B7
Dukes Cl BN25 ....180 D5
Dukes Hill TN33 ...112 D6
Dukes Rd Lindfield RH16 ..51 B8
  Royal Tunbridge Wells TN1 ..8 C5
Dukesbury Ho BN21 ..184 E3
Dulwich Cl BN25 ..181 B4
Dumb Woman's La TN31 ..92 D3
Dumbrell Ct BN7 ..146 B8
Dumbrells Court Rd BN6 ..98 D4
Dumbrells Ct BN6 ..98 D4
Dumbrills Cl RH15 ..73 A5
Dumfries Ct **4** TN38 ..136 B1
Dunbar Dr BN27 ..129 A1
Duncan Ho BN10 ..167 D1
Dunclutha Rd TN34 ..136 F4
Duncton Cl RH16 ..50 D4
Duncton Ho BN6 ..97 E4
Dundale Rd TN3 ..9 E1
Dundas Ave TN31 ..94 F2
Dunning's Rd RH19 ..10 E7
Dunorlan Farm Cotts TN2 ..8 E4
Dunstall Ave BN15 ..72 E4
Dunstall Farm Rd RH15 ..72 F4
Dunstan Ave TN4 ..8 B6
Dunstan Rd TN4 ..8 B6
Dunstans Croft TN20 ..40 C3
Dunster Cl BN21 ..143 B1
Dunvan Cl BN7 ...190 A4
Durham Cl BN1 ...144 A1
Durham Ct
  Eastbourne BN20 ..184 B6
  4 Hove BN3 ....163 B6
Durkins Rd RH19 ..1 D3
Durrell Cl BN23 ..174 F2
Durrington Ct BN1 ..142 D5
Dursley Rd BN22 ..185 A4
Dutchells Way BN22 ..173 E4
Dyall Cl RH15 ....72 E4
Dyke Cl BN3 .....142 B4
Dyke Road Ave BN1,BN2 ..142 C3
Dyke Road Dr BN1 ..163 F8
Dyke Road Mews BN1 ..189 A4
Dyke Road Pl BN1 ..142 C3
Dymchurch Cl
  Polegate BN26 ....173 C7
  Seaford BN25 .....181 C5
Dymock Cl BN25 ..181 B4
Dymock's The BN6 ..98 D3
Dymond Rd TN38 ..136 A3
Dynevor Rd TN4 ..8 C7

E

Eagle Cl TN22 ....78 E5
Eagle Ct **15** BN2 ..164 C8
Eagle Rd TN11 ...93 C6
Earl St TN34 .....159 F8
Earl's Rd TN4 ....7 F4
Earls Cl BN25 ....180 C5
Earls Gdn BN7 ...190 B2
Earwig Cnr BN8 ..190 C4
Earl Albany Rd BN25 ..180 C5
Earl Ascent TN38 ..159 C6
East Beach St TN34 ..160 B3
East Beeches Rd TN6 ..26 B2
East Bourne St **22** TN34 ..160 B4
East Brighton College of
  Media Arts (Sch) BN2 ..164 F5
East Cl BN26 .....173 B6
East Dean Rd BN20 ..184 B2
East Dean Rise BN25 ..181 A4
East Dr BN2 ......164 C5
East End La BN6 ..98 D3
East Gdns BN6 ...98 D3
East Grinstead Sta BN19 ..1 D1
East Grinstead Town Mus*
  RH19 ....1 F2
East Hill Cliff Rly*
  TN34 ....160 B4
East Hill Pas **7** TN34 ..160 B4
East Hoathly CE Prim Sch
  BN8 ....104 F5
East Lockside BN2 ..165 A3
East Mascalls La RH16 ..51 E6
East Meadway BN43 ..161 A6
East Par TN34 ....160 A3
East Point **6** BN43 ..161 A6
East St Brighton BN1 ..189 B1
  Coggins Mill TN20 ..40 D3
  Falmer BN1 ....144 C6
  Lewes BN7 ....190 B2
  Portslade-by-S BN41 ..162 C7
  Rye TN31 ....93 C5
  Seaford BN25 .....181 A4
East Sussex F HQ BN7 ..123 B2
East Sussex Music Sch
  BN7 ....190 A1
East Sussex Music Sch
  (Annexe) BN2 ....190 B2
East View BN21 ...82 B6
East View Fields BN7 ..99 E5
East View TN33 ...88 F1
East Way BN7 ....122 F2
East Wick RH16 ..51 C7
Eastbank BN42 ...140 F1
Eastbourne Butterfly Ctr*
  BN22 ....185 D4
Eastbourne Coll BN21 ..184 F1

Eastbourne District General
  Hospl BN21 ......184 E7
Eastbourne La BN26 ..183 C7
Eastbourne Miniature Steam
  Rly Pk* BN23 ....185 A7
Eastbourne Rd
  Brighton BN2 .....143 D1
  East Dean BN20 ..187 B8
  Eastbourne BN20 ..173 B4
  Felbridge RH19 ...1 A5
  Halland BN8 ....104 C6
  Pevensey Bay BN24 ..175 C4
  Seaford BN25 .....181 C3
  Uckfield TN22 .....78 F3
  Westham BN23,BN24 ..174 F4
Eastbourne Sta BN21 ..184 F3
Eastbourne Tech Coll
  BN21 ....173 E2
Eastbourne Terr **4**
  BN25 ....181 A3
Eastbridge Rd BN9 ..179 E7
Eastbrook Rd BN41 ..162 B7
Eastbrook Way BN42 ..162 A2
Eastdale Rd RH15 ..73 D4
Eastergate TN39 ..156 D6
Eastergate Rd BN2 ..143 F4
Eastern Ave
  Polegate BN26 ....173 B7
  Shoreham-by-S BN43 ..161 A7
Eastern Cl BN21 ..143 A2
Eastern Concourse BN2 ..165 A2
Eastern Cotts RH16 ..51 B7
Eastern Pl BN2 ...164 E4
Eastern Rd Brighton BN2 ..164 D4
  Haywards Heath RH16 ..50 F3
  Lindfield RH16 ....51 C7
  Wivelsfield RH17 ..74 B4
Eastern Ring Rd BN1 ..144 C2
Eastern St **21** BN2 ..164 D4
Eastern Terr **10** BN2 ..164 D4
Eastern Terrace Mews **9**
  BN2 ....164 D4
Eastfield Cres BN1 ..143 A4
Eastgate St BN7 ..190 B2
Eastgate Wharf BN7 ..190 B2
Easthill Dr BN41 ..141 B1
Easthill Way BN41 ..141 B1
Eastlands Cl TN4 ..16 E8
Eastlands Rd TN4 ..7 E1
Eastport La BN7 ..190 A1
Eastriver Cotts BN8 ..124 E5
Eastway TN39 ....156 D4
Eastwell Pl BN27 ..152 B8
Eastwick Cl BN1 ..143 B7
Eastwood Rd TN39 ..157 A3
Eatenden La TN32,TN33 ..87 B3
Eaton Ct **3** BN1 ..163 C7
Eaton Gardens Mans **20**
  BN3 ....163 C7
Eaton Gate **17** BN3 ..163 C7
Eaton Gdns BN3 ..163 C7
Eaton Gr BN3 ....163 C7
Eaton Hall **19** BN3 ..163 C7
Eaton Manor **11** BN3 ..163 C7
Eaton Pl BN2 .....164 D4
Eaton Rd BN3 ....163 C7
Eaton Villas BN3 ..163 B7
Eaton Wlk TN33 ..88 D1
Ebbisham Ct RH19 ..1 A4
Ebden's Hill TN37 ..136 B8
Ebenezer Rd TN34 ..160 B4
Ecclesden **7** BN2 ..189 C3
Ecmod Rd BN22 ..185 C6
Eddington Ave BN1 ..143 A1
Eden Cl BN24 ....174 A5
Eden Dr TN39 ....156 F4
Eden Rd TN1 .....8 A2
Eden Vale
  Dormans Park RH19 ..1 F5
  East Grinstead RH19 ..1 D4
Eden Wlk **9** TN1 ..8 A2
Edenbridge Rd TN7 ..13 E7
Edensor Rd BN20 ..184 C4
Edgar Rd TN35 ...160 C6
Edgehill BN41 ....140 F2
Edgehill Cl TN21 ..81 F7
Edgeland Terr BN27 ..173 F1
Edinburgh Ct
  Eastbourne BN20 ..184 C5
  Seaford BN25 .....180 D3
Edinburgh Rd
  Bexhill TN40 ......157 C5
  8 Brighton BN2 ..164 B8
  Seaford BN25 .....180 D3
  St Leonards TN38 ..158 E7
Edinburgh Way RH19 ..10 F7
Edison Rd BN23 ..174 A1
Edith Ave BN10 ..178 E7
Edith Ave N BN10 ..178 C8
Edith Rd TN35 ...160 D7
Edmond Cl BN23 ..173 E8
Edmonton Rd TN39 ..157 B7
Edmund Rd TN35 ..160 D6
Edster Ct BN41 ..140 F3
Edward Ave Hove BN3 ..142 A3
  Saltdean BN2 .....177 D7
Edward Ct BN41 ..142 A3
  Seaford BN25 .....180 A6
Edward Ho BN3 ..162 F6
Edward Rd
  Haywards Heath RH16 ..50 E2
  St Leonards TN37 ..159 D7
Edward St Brighton BN2 ..189 C2
  Lewes BN7 ....190 B2
  Royal Tunbridge Wells TN4 ..7 F8
  Rusthall TN4 ......7 C4
Edward Terr TN38 ..136 A4
Edward Way RH15 ..72 D2

Edwin Rd TN35 ....160 C6
Effingham Cl BN2 ....177 C6
Effingham Dr TN39 .....156 D3
Egbert Cl BN21 ....185 E8
Egerton Ho BN20 ....188 E8
Egerton Rd TN39 ....157 B3
Egginton Cl BN1 ....144 A5
Egginton Rd BN2 ....144 A5
Egles Gr TN22 ....78 B8
Egmont Rd BN3 ....141 D1
Egremont Pl
   Brighton BN2 ....189 C2
   Hastings TN34 ....160 B6
Eight Acre La TN35 .....115 D1
Eight Bells Cl TN22 ......56 A4
Eileen Ave BN2 ....177 B5
Eisenhower Dr TN37 ...135 F6
Elder Cl BN41 ....141 B2
Elder Pl BN1 ....189 B4
Elderwood Cl
   Bexhill TN39 ....157 C7
   Eastbourne BN22 ......173 D2
Eldon Rd BN21 ....184 C5
Eldred Ave BN1 ....142 D5
Eldridge Way TN37 ....136 C6
Eleanor Cl Lewes BN7 ..123 B2
   Seaford BN25 ....180 D5
Eleanor Terr TN35 .....160 D8
Eley Cres BN2 ....165 A3
Ely Dr BN2 ....165 E3
Elford St ③ TN34 ....159 F8
Elgar Ave BN23 ....174 E3
Elgin Gdns BN25 ....181 C3
Elim Court Gdns TN6 ....25 E4
Elim Wlk TN34 ....136 F2
Eliot Ho ⑤ RH16 ....50 E3
Elizabeth Ave BN3 .....142 A3
Elizabeth Cl Hove BN3 ..142 A3
   Seaford BN25 ....180 A6
Elizabeth Cres RH19 .....1 F3
Elizabeth Ct
   ④ Bexhill TN40 ....157 C5
   Eastbourne BN20 .....184 C5
   ② Hailsham BN27 .....152 C7
   ⑦ Hove BN3 ....163 C7
   Polegate BN26 ....184 B2
Elizabeth Garlick Ct ①
   TN1 ....8 B4
Elizabeth Rd
   Shoreham-by-S BN43 ..161 C8
   St Leonards TN38 .....136 A2
Elizabethan Cl TN33 ...132 F2
Ellen Ho ⑧ BN2 ....189 B7
Ellen St Hove BN3 ......163 B7
   Portslade-by-S BN41 ..162 C7
Ellenslea Rd TN37 ......159 C7
Ellenwhorne La TN32 ....89 A7
Ellerslie La TN33 ....156 F6
Elliots Way TN21 ....82 A8
Ellis Cl TN34 ....159 E7
Ellis Gordon Ct BN9 ...179 F7
Ellis Way TN22 ....78 A7
Ellison Cl TN6 ....25 E4
Elm Ave BN27 ....127 C3
Elm Cl Hove BN3 ....142 C2
   Laughton BN8 ....126 C7
   Seaford BN25 ....181 C3
Elm Cots Laughton BN8 .126 C7
   Upper Dicker BN27 ....151 A8
Elm Ct Brighton BN1 ...163 E8
   ④ East Grinstead RH19 ..1 D2
   Newhaven BN9 ....179 B7
   Polegate BN26 ....173 A6
   Portslade-by-S BN41 ..162 B8
Elm Dr East Grinstead RH19 ..1
   Hove BN3 ....143 A4
Elm Gn ④ BN21 ....129 B1
Elm Gr Brighton BN2 ...164 C7
   Eastbourne BN22 .....173 F1
   Lewes BN7 ....190 A1
Elm Grove Prim Sch
   BN2 ....164 C7
Elm Rd BN41 ....162 B8
Elm Way TN21 ....82 B6
Elmhurst Ave BN2 .....164 C7
Elmore Cl BN2 ....9 D8
Elmore Rd BN2 ....189 C3
Elms Ave BN21 ....185 B2
Elms La TN35 ....116 F1
Elms Lea Ave BN1 ......142 E3
Elms Rd BN2 ....185 B2
Elms The BN8 ....124 C5
Elmsdown Pl BN27 .....152 C7
Elmsmead TN31 ....70 B4
Elmstead ④ RH19 ......10 E8
Elmstead Rd TN40 .....157 E5
Elmwood ⑫ BN21 .....184 F4
Elmwood Cl BN23 ......174 C4
Elmwood Gdns BN23 ..174 C4
Elphick Pl TN6 ....25 F3
Elphick Rd
   Broyle Side BN8 ......124 F7
   Newhaven BN9 ....179 C8
Elphick's Pl TN7 ....17 B8
Elphinstone Ave TN34 .136 F2
Elphinstone Com Sch
   TN34 ....160 A6
Elphinstone Rd TN34 ..136 F3
Elphinstone Rd TN34 ..136 F2
Elrington Rd BN3 ......142 C1
Elsted Cl BN22 ....174 A1
Elsted Cres BN1 ....143 C6
Elsted Rd TN39 ....156 C2
Elven Cl BN20 ....183 C1
Elven La BN20 ....183 C1
Elven Cres BN2 ....165 E4
Elwood Cl RH15 ....72 F1
Elwyn Jones Ct BN1 ...152 E4

Ely Ct TN1 ....8 B4
Embassy Ct
   ⑩ Brighton BN1 ....163 D5
   ④ Haywards Heath RH16 ..50 E6
Emerald Quay BN43 ....161 A6
Emerson Coll RH18 .....12 B3
Emmanuel Rd TN34 ...160 A5
Encore Ho TN21 ....81 F8
Endcliffe Ct BN20 .....188 E8
Endwell Rd TN40 ......157 C3
Engalee RH19 ....1 C2
English Bsns Pk BN3 ..162 E8
English Cl BN3 ....162 E8
English's Pas BN1 .....190 B2
Enholms La RH14 ......34 A4
Ensenada Reef BN23 ..175 B1
Enterprise Ctr The
   BN21 ....184 F3
Enterprise Est BN1 ....143 C7
Enys Rd BN21 ....184 F4
Epsom Cl TN38 ....159 A8
Epsom Ct ⑥ TN40 .....157 E4
Erica Cl BN23 ....73 B2
Ericsson Way RH15 .....72 D2
Eridge Cl BN3 ....157 A4
Eridge Ct TN2 ....7 F1
Eridge Dr TN6 ....26 A3
Eridge Gdns TN6 ....26 A3
Eridge Gn BN7 ....123 B2
Eridge La TN3,TN6 ......27 B2
Eridge Rd
   Crowborough TN6 .....26 C6
   Eastbourne BN21 .....184 D7
   Groombridge TN3 ......15 D5
   Hove BN3 ....157 A4
   Royal Tunbridge Wells TN2,
   TN6 ....7 E1
   Eridge Sta TN3 ....15 E2
Erin Way RH15 ....72 E3
Erroll Mans ⑥ BN3 ....162 D7
Erroll Rd BN3 ....162 C6
Ersham Rd BN27 ......152 B5
Ersham Way BN27 .....152 B6
Erskine Park Rd TN4 ....7 C4
Esher Cl BN25 ....180 F4
Eshton Rd BN22 ....173 E3
Eskbank Ave BN1 ......143 A7
Eskdale Cl BN23 ....174 C4
Esmonde Pl BN25 .....180 E2
Esplanade Mews ⑲
   BN25 ....180 E2
Esplanade The BN10 ..177 F3
Essenden Rd TN38 ....159 A7
Essex Cl TN2 ....16 F8
Essex Cl BN20 ....184 B6
Essex Pl ③ Brighton BN2 .164 C4
   Newhaven BN9 ....179 C7
Essex St BN2 ....164 C4
Estate Rd BN9 ....179 E7
Estcots Dr RH19 ....2 A1
Estcots Prim Sch RH19 ..2 A1
Etchingham CE Prim Sch
   TN19 ....44 D2
Etchingham Rd BN23 ..174 E1
Etchingham Sta TN19 ..44 C1
Ethel St BN3 ....163 B7
Etherelred Cl BN23 ....185 E8
Etherington Hill TN3 ....8 C8
Etherton Way BN25 ...181 A4
Ethnam La TN18 ....47 E4
Eton Cl BN25 ....181 A4
Eton Mews ③ BN21 ...185 A3
Eugene Way BN23 .....175 B1
Euro Bsns Pk BN9 .....168 D1
Eurythmy Sch RH19 ....10 E6
Evelyn Ave BN9 ....179 C7
Evelyn Ct BN41 ....162 C7
Evelyn Glennie Ct ⑦
   BN2 ....164 C5
Evelyn Rd BN7 ....123 B2
Evelyn Terr BN2 ....164 C5
Everest Ho ② BN1 ....162 F7
Eversfield Cl TN37 ....159 D7
Eversfield Hospl TN38 .159 A6
Eversfield Mews N ⑤
   TN37 ....159 C7
Eversfield Mews S ⑩
   TN37 ....159 C7
Eversfield Pl TN37 .....159 D7
Eversfield Rd BN21 ....184 F4
Evershed Way BN43 ...161 B7
Eversley Cl TN37 ......136 C2
Eversley Cres TN37 ...136 C2
Eversley Ct BN21 ......184 F4
Eversley Rd Bexhill TN40 .157 C2
   St Leonards TN37 .....136 C2
Everton Cots TN19 .....62 B6
Evesham Cl TN38 .....136 A3
Ewart St BN2 ....189 C3
Ewbank Ho BN3 ....163 D7
Ewehurst La TN3 ....6 F6
Ewell Ct ⑤ TN40 .....157 E4
Ewhurst Cl TN34 ......136 F4
Ewhurst La TN31 ....66 F4
Ewhurst Rd BN2 ......143 C1
Exceat Cl Brighton BN2 .164 E6
   Eastbourne BN23 .....174 B4
Excelsior The BN1 .....142 D4
Exeter Cl BN23 ....174 F2
Exeter St BN1 ....163 E8
Exmouth Pl TN34 .....160 A4

F

Factory La BN27 ....152 A6
Fair Isle Cl BN23 ......185 E8

Fair La Robertsbridge TN32 .64 B4
   Robertsbridge TN32 ...64 C4
Fair Mdw TN31 ....93 C7
Fair Oak Cl TN21 ....82 A7
Fair View Cotts TN5 ....30 A6
Fairbanks RH16 ....50 E4
Fairbridge Way RH15 ..72 F5
Faircrouch La TN5 .....29 B5
Fairdene BN42 ....140 F1
Fairfax Ave TN37 ......135 F7
Fairfield
   Herstmonceux BN27 ..130 E6
   Peacehaven BN10 ....178 B7
Fairfield Chase TN39 ..156 F4
Fairfield Cl
   Burgess Hill RH15 .....72 F4
   Shoreham-by-S BN43 .140 C1
Fairfield Cotts BN26 ..149 D2
Fairfield Cres BN6 ......97 A6
Fairfield Gdns
   Burgess Hill RH15 .....72 F4
   Portslade-by-S BN41 ..141 B1
Fairfield Rd
   Burgess Hill RH15 .....72 F4
   East Grinstead RH19 ..10 F8
   Eastbourne BN20 .....184 E1
   St Leonards TN37 .....136 C6
Fairholme Rd TN36 ....50 D8
Fairford Cl RH16 ....50 E8
Fairglen Cotts TN5 .....29 B3
Fairglen Rd TN5 ....29 B4
Fairhaven BN7 ....99 E1
Fairholme Ct TN35 .....25 F1
Fairholme Rd BN9 ....168 F1
Fairhurst BN10 ....177 F3
Fairisle Cl BN27 ....129 A2
Fairlawn ① RH16 ....50 E4
Fairlawn Cres RH19 ....1 B2
Fairlawn Dr RH19 ......1 B2
Fairlawns ⑨ Hove BN3 .163 A6
   Shoreham-by-S BN43 .161 A8
Fairlawns Rd TN36 ....130 E6
Fairlie Cl RH15 ....72 F4
Fairlie Gdns BN1 ......142 E3
Fairlight TN22 ....55 E1
Fairlight Ave
   Hastings TN35 ....160 D4
   Telscombe Cliffs BN10 .177 F3
Fairlight Cl Bexhill TN40 .158 A5
   Polegate BN26 ....173 A6
Fairlight Field BN8 ....124 D5
Fairlight Gdns TN35 ..138 F4
Fairlight Pl ⑧ BN2 ....164 C5
Fairlight Prim Sch BN2 .164 C5
Fairlight Rd
   Eastbourne BN25 .....185 C5
   Fairlight TN35 ....138 A4
   Hastings TN35 ....138 A4
Fairlight Wood Cvn Site
   TN35 ....116 D1
Fairmile Rd TN2 ....8 E5
Fairmount Rd TN40 ...157 D6
Fairoak BN20 ....173 C6
Fairplace RH17 ....74 C4
Fairstone Cl TN35 .....160 E8
Fairview Cotts TN35 ...25 E4
Fairview Rise BN1 .....142 D5
Fairway Bsns Ctr BN22 .143 E4
Fairway Cl BN20 ......184 B7
Fairway Cres BN41 ...141 C2
Fairway The Bexhill TN39 .156 F6
   Newhaven BN9 ....179 A7
   St Leonards TN38 .....158 F8
Fairway Trad Est BN22 .143 E4
Fairways BN1 ....163 E8
Fairways Cl BN25 .....181 C2
Fairways Rd BN25 ....181 B2
Fairways The TN4 ......8 A7
Falaise Rd
   Hastings TN34 ....159 D8
   Newhaven TN34 ......168 F1
Falcon Cl BN43 ....161 C6
Falcon Way BN27 .....129 B3
Falconbury Dr TN39 ..156 D3
Falconer Dr TN33 .....112 F4
Fallowfield Cl BN23 ...141 F2
Fallowfield Cres BN41 .141 F2
Falmer Ave BN2 ......177 B6
Falmer Gdns BN2 .....165 D8
Falmer High Sch BN1 ..144 A5
Falmer Hill BN1 ....144 A5
Falmer House Rd BN1 .144 B6
Falmer Rd BN2 ....165 C5
Falmer Sta BN1 ....144 B5
Falmouth Cl BN23 ....174 B2
Faraday Ave RH19 .....10 F1
Faraday Cl BN22 ......173 E2
Faraday Lodge TN2 .....8 E5
Farlaine Rd BN21 .....184 C6
Farley Bank TN35 ....114 D2
Farley Way TN35 .....138 C5
Farleys Way TN31 .....50 F5
Farlington Ave BN6 ....50 F5
Farm Cl
   East Grinstead RH19 ..11 B8
   Hassocks BN6 ....97 E4
   Portslade-by-S BN41 ..141 A2
   Seaford BN25 ....181 B4
Farm Cotts RH16 ......50 C5
Farm Gdns TN31 ......69 C2
Farm Hill BN2 ....165 C8

Farm La Camber TN31 ...94 D3
   Ditchling BN6 ....98 E3
Farm Mews BN3 ......163 D6
Farm Rd BN3 ....163 D6
Farm Way
   Burgess Hill RH15 .....73 D1
   Southwick BN42 .....162 A7
Farm World, Great Knelle
Farm (Childrens Farm)*
   TN31 ....68 A8
Farman St ⑱ BN3 ....163 D5
Farmcombe Cl TN2 ....8 B2
Farmcombe La TN2 ....8 B2
Farmcombe Rd TN2 ....8 C2
Farmet Ct RH19 ....1 C3
Farmland Way BN27 ..129 C1
Farmlands Ave BN26 ..172 F4
Farmlands Cl
   Polegate BN26 ....173 A4
   St Leonards TN37 .....136 C5
Farmlands Ct TN38 ...136 A4
Farmlands Way BN26 .172 F5
Farmway Cl BN1 ......141 D2
Farmcombe Cl RH17 ..74 D4
Farmcombe Rd BN7 ..190 C2
Farne Cl BN22 ....129 A2
Farnham Ave BN6 ....96 A5
Farnham Beeches TN3 ..7 A3
Farnham Cl TN3 ....7 A3
Farnham La TN3 ....7 A3
Farnham Pl TN3 ....7 A3
Farnlea BN15 ....73 D5
Farnol Ho ⑥ BN21 ...184 D4
Farrance Ct TN1 ....29 E4
Farriers Pl BN8 ....124 D5
Farriers Way TN22 ....78 C6
Farthing Hill TN5 ......31 E1
Farthing La BN27,TN33 .109 E4
Farthings The TN6 .....26 A3
Fastnet Cl BN23 ......185 E8
Faulkners Way TN5 ....73 A5
Faversham Rd BN23 ..174 D2
Faygate Cl TN39 ......157 B8
Faygate Rd BN22 .....164 E6
Faygate Rd BN22 .....173 E2
Fayre Mdw TN32 ......64 C4
Fearon Rd TN34 ......136 F2
Felbridge Cl RH19 ......1 C3
Felbridge Ct RH19 ......1 A4
Felbridge Ctr The RH19 ..1 A3
Felbridge Pl RH19 .....1 A4
Felcourt Cotts RH19 ...1 C8
Felcourt La RH19 ......1 C8
Felcourt Rd RH19 .....1 C7
Feld The RH19 ....1 A4
Fellows Rd TN34 ......160 B7
Felwater Ct RH19 ......1 A4
Fen Ct TN38 ....135 E1
Fennel Wlk BN43 .....140 B1
Fennell's Ct BN21 .....184 E5
Ferbies TN3 ....7 A7
Ferbies Cl TN3 ....7 A7
Ferdinand Terr TN3 ...15 C7
Ferguson Rd TN36 .....96 D2
Fermor Rd TN6 ....38 A7
Fermor Row ② TN6 ...38 A7
Fermor Way TN6 ......38 A8
Fern Cl BN23 ....174 C3
Fern Ho ① BN27 ......129 B1
Fern Rd TN38 ....158 F8
Fernbank Sch CP TN6 ..25 F3
Ferndale TN2 ....8 D5
Ferndale Cl TN35 .....160 D8
Ferndale Point TN2 .....8 D5
Ferndale Rd
   Burgess Hill RH15 .....73 C2
   Hove BN3 ....163 D7
Fernhurst Cl BN1 .....143 A6
Fernhurst Cres BN1 ..143 B5
Fernlea Ct TN35 ......114 E4
Ferns The TN1 ....8 C5
Fernside ⑤ TN34 .....159 D8
Fernside Ave TN38 ...135 F1
Fernwood Rise BN1 ..142 D5
Ferrers Rd BN7 ....123 B1
Ferring Cl TN31 ....93 A6
Ferring Ct BN1 ....143 F5
Ferringham TN4 ....7 A4
Ferry Hill TN36 ....117 E8
Ferry Rd TN31 ....93 B5
Festival Gdns TN39 ...157 C7
Feversham Cl BN43 ...161 B6
Field End Broad Oak TN31 .90 C5
   Seaford BN25 ....181 A4
Field End TN22 ....53 A4
Field View TN20 ....64 B3
Field Way TN38 ....158 E8
Fielden La TN5 ....25 D7
Fielden Rd TN6 ....25 D2
Fieldfare Ct BN27 .....152 D7
Fields End Cl RH16 ....50 F4
Fieldway Broad Oak TN31 .90 C5
   Ditchling BN6 ....98 D3
   Haywards Heath RH16 ..50 F8
Fiennes Rd BN27 ......130 E6
Figg La TN6 ....37 F8
Filching Cl BN20 ......172 C3
Filching Ct BN20 .....184 B5
Filching Manor Motor Mus*
   BN26 ....172 D2
Filder Cl BN20 ....184 B5
Filsham Dr TN40 .....158 A6
Filsham Rd TN38 .....159 A5
Filsham Valley TN38 ..158 F7

Filsham Valley Sch
   TN38 ....158 F7
Finch Ct BN10 ....178 A7
Finches Gdns RH16 ....51 A8
Finches La RH16 ....51 A8
Finches Park Rd RH16 .51 A8
Finches The Bexhill TN40 .157 F4
   Shoreham-by-S BN43 .161 A8
   ② St Leonards TN38 ..136 A5
Findon Ave BN2 ......177 E6
Findon Cl Bexhill TN39 .156 F3
   Hove BN3 ....141 F3
   Seaford BN25 ....181 C3
Findon Rd BN2 ....164 F5
Finistere Ave BN21 ...185 E8
Finley Cl TN38 ....158 E8
Finmere Cl BN22 .....185 C6
Finmere Ct BN22 .....185 C6
Finmere Rd BN22 ....185 C6
Finsbury Lodge ① BN2 .164 C6
Finsbury Rd BN2 .....164 C6
Fir Cl BN2 ....165 F7
Fir Grove Rd TN21 .....81 B6
Fir Toll Cl TN22 ....39 F2
Fir Toll Rd
   Woolbridge TN20 ......39 C2
   Woolbridge TN20 ......39 C3
Fir Tree Cl Bexhill TN39 .156 C3
   Hailsham BN27 ....77 E5
Fir Tree Rd TN4 ....7 F3
Fir Tree Way TN6 ......98 A4
Fircroft Cl BN1 ....142 E3
Firehills Cotts TN35 ..138 C3
Firlands RH16 ....50 A8
Firle Bostal BN8 ......148 A2
Firle CE Prim Sch BN8 .148 A7
Firle Cl Hastings TN35 .160 E8
   Seaford BN25 ....180 E5
Firle Cres BN7 ....122 F2
Firle Dr BN25 ....180 E5
Firle Gn BN22 ....55 E1
Firle Grange BN25 ....180 E5
Firle Pl* BN8 ....148 C3
Firle Rd Brighton BN2 .164 D6
   Eastbourne BN22 .....185 B4
   Peacehaven BN10 ....178 C8
   Ripe BN8 ....149 B7
   Seaford BN25 ....180 E5
Firle Terr BN9 ....168 D2
First Ave TN4 ....7 F6
Firs The TN35 ....160 C5
First Ave Bexhill TN40 .157 F5
   Camber TN31 ....94 F2
   Hove BN3 ....163 C6
   Newhaven BN9 ....179 C7
First St TN6 ....6 F3
Firstone Ho TN20 ......39 F2
Firtoft Cl RH15 ....73 B3
Firtree Rd TN34 ......160 A6
Firwood Cl
   Eastbourne BN22 .....173 C4
   Heathfield TN21 ....82 A8
Firwood Rise TN21 ....82 A8
Fisher Cl BN23 ....185 F7
Fisher St BN1 ....190 B2
Fisher's Gate Cotts TN7 .14 A1
Fishermen's Mus*
   TN34 ....160 B3
Fishersgate Cl BN41 ..162 A7
Fishersgate Fst Sch
   BN41 ....162 A7
Fishersgate Sta BN41 .162 A7
Fishersgate Terr BN41 .162 A7
Fishmarket Rd TN31 ..93 C6
Fishponds La TN35 ...114 E3
Fitch Dr BN2 ....143 F1
Fitzalan Ct BN10 .....178 B7
Fitzgerald Ave BN23 ..184 F4
Fitzgerald Ave BN25 ..180 A6
Fitzgerald Cl BN20 ...184 F1
Fitzgerald Ho ⑧ BN25 .180 E3
Fitzgerald Pk BN25 ..180 F2
Fitzgerald Rd BN21 ..190 B4
Fitzherbert Dr BN2 ..164 D8
Fitzherbert Dr BN2 ..164 D8
Fitzjohn C BN6 ....97 F3
Fitzjohns Rd BN7 ....123 B1
Fitzmaurice Ave BN22 .185 B5
Fitzroy Rd BN7 ......123 B2
Five Acre Wlk TN34 ..136 E1
Five Ashes CE Prim Sch
   TN20 ....58 B6
Five Ashes Rd TN6 ....39 A3
Five Chys La TN22 .....53 D2
Five Hos The TN36 ...117 E8
Five Villages Ho TN36 .116 F6
Five Ways TN1 ....8 B4
Flag Cl BN3 ....163 B5
Flamingo Family Fun Pk*
   TN34 ....160 A3
Flamsteed Rd BN27 ..131 A1
Fleetway Cl TN31 ......93 A6
Fleming Cl BN23 ......174 F2
Fleming Wlk RH16 .....10 F6
Fletcher Ave TN37 ...135 F7
Fletcher Cl TN22 .....152 C7
Fletching CE Prim Sch
   TN22 ....53 F3
Fletching Cl TN35 ....164 F6
Fletching Rd BN22 ...174 B2
Fletching Rd TN6 ......40 E3
Flimwell Cl Brighton BN2 .164 E5
   Eastbourne BN23 .....174 A4
Flimwell TN5 ....32 D4

Flimwell Cl continued
St Leonards TN38 ......135 D3
Flint Cl
Portslade-by-S BN41 ...141 B2
Seaford BN25 ....180 E6
Flint Halls 5 BN21 .....184 D3
Flints The BN7 ....145 E5
Flitterbrook La TN21 ...8 D4
Florance La TN3 ....15 B6
Florence Ave BN3 ......162 D8
Florence Ct BN1 ....142 F2
Florence Pl BN1 ....143 B1
Florence Rd BN1 ....164 A8
Florida Ct TN38 ....158 F6
Floyd Cl TN4 ....8 A7
Fold Sch The BN3 ....162 D7
Folders Cl RH15 ....73 D1
Folders Grange RH15 ...73 C1
Folders La RH15 ....73 D1
Foley Cl BN23 ....185 E7
Folkestone Cl BN25 ...181 C5
Folkestone Rd TN31 ....93 F8
Folkington Rd BN26 ...172 D5
Follett Holt Ho BN8 ...100 E7
Folly Field BN9 ....179 C7
Fonthill Lodge Sch RH19 .10 C6
Fonthill Rd BN3 ....163 B8
Fontridge La TN19 ......62 E3
Fontwell Ave TN39 ....156 C5
Foords La BN24 ....174 C7
Foot's La TN19 ....61 B3
Ford Rd TN38 ....135 F2
Fordbrook Hill TN6 .....37 F2
Fordcombe CE Prim Sch
TN3 ....6 B5
Fordcombe Rd TN3 ......6 C4
Foredown Cl
Brighton BN2 ....184 C2
Portslade-by-S BN41 ...141 B2
Foredown Dr BN41 .....141 C1
Foredown Rd
Portslade Village BN41 .141 B4
Portslade-by-S BN41 ...141 B2
Foredown Tower Countryside
Ctr* BN41 ....141 B3
Forest Dene
Crowborough TN6 ....26 D1
Royal Tunbridge Wells TN2 ..8 C1
Forest Fold Cotts TN6 ..25 D5
Forest La TN21 ....83 D6
Forest Lodge
Crowborough TN6 ....37 D8
2 East Grinstead RH19 ..10 F8
Forest Pk
Crowborough TN6 ....25 D2
Maresfield TN22 ....54 F5
Forest Pl TN21 ....80 F6
Forest Rd Brighton BN1 .143 E6
Forest Row RH18 ....12 B2
Royal Tunbridge Wells TN2 ..8 C1
Forest Ridge RH19 .....21 A6
Forest Rise TN6 ....26 D1
Forest Row Bsns Pk
RH18 ....11 F3
Forest Row CE Prim Sch
RH18 ....11 F2
Forest View
Hailsham BN27 ....152 A8
Nutley TN22 ....35 C3
Forest View Rd RH19 ...10 E6
Forest Way
Golden Cross BN27 .....127 C3
Hastings TN34 ....136 E1
Pembury TN2 ....9 D8
Royal Tunbridge Wells TN2 ..8 D1
Foresters Rd BN26 .....173 A6
Forewood La TN33 .....135 A7
Forewood Rise TN33 ...134 F6
Forge Cl
Portslade-by-S BN41 ...141 B2
Staplecross TN32 ....65 E1
Uckfield TN22 ....78 C6
Forge Field TN5 ....42 F6
Forge La TN32 ....65 E1
Forge Lane Cotts TN22 ..55 A8
Forge Rise TN22 ....15 C2
Forge Rise TN22 ....78 C6
Forge The BN3 ....162 F8
Forge Way
Burgess Hill RH15 ....73 A4
St Leonards TN37 ......136 C5
Forgefield Cotts TN18 ...47 A4
Forstal The Cobbarn TN3 .15 F3
Pembury TN2 ....9 A4
Forstall TN3 ....7 A4
Fort Gate BN9 ....179 E5
Fort Haven BN43 ....161 C6
Fort La BN22 ....185 D6
Fort Rd Eastbourne BN22 .185 D6
Newhaven BN9 ....179 D6
Fort Rise BN9 ....179 D5
Forward Cl BN9 ....168 E2
Fosse The BN7 ....190 B2
Foster Cl BN25 ....180 E4
Foster Ct BN3 ....163 E6
Foundry Ct RH15 ....73 B3
Foundry La BN7 ....190 C2
Foundry St BN1 ....189 B3
Fountains Cl
Brighton BN1 ....143 B2
Eastbourne BN22 ....173 E3
Founthill Ave BN2 .....177 B5
Founthill Rd BN2 ......177 B5
Fourteen Acre La TN35 .115 C4

Fourth Ave BN3 ....163 B6
Fowey Cl BN43 ....161 B6
Fowlers Cl TN39 ......156 E5
Fowly La TN22 ....56 C7
Fox Cl RH15 ....72 F1
Fox Hill RH16 ....50 E1
Fox Hill Cl RH16 ....50 F1
Fox Hill Village RH16 ...50 F1
Fox Hollow BN27 ......127 B3
Fox in the Wood TN5 ...29 C6
Fox Way BN41 ....141 B2
Foxcote TN37 ....136 D5
Foxdown Rd BN2 ......165 F7
Foxglove Cl
Broyle Side BN8 ....125 A7
Burgess Hill RH15 ......72 D4
Foxglove Rd BN23 .....174 B3
Foxhill Bexhill TN39 ...156 E5
Peacehaven BN10 ......167 B1
Foxhill Ct 8 RH16 ......50 E3
Foxhole La
Four Throws TN18 ....46 D8
Wadhurst TN5 ....30 B4
Foxhunters Rd BN41 ...140 F3
Foxwarren RH16 ....50 C5
Framelle Mount TN22 ...79 B6
Framfield 1 BN2 ....64 F5
Framfield CE Prim Sch
TN22 ....79 B6
Framfield Cl BN1 ......143 E6
Framfield Rd Buxted TN22 .56 B3
Uckfield TN22 ....78 D6
Framfield Way BN21 ...184 D3
Framrose Ct BN1 ......143 B2
Francis Bird Pl TN37 ...136 C6
Francis Rd RH16 ....51 B8
Francis St BN1 ....189 B4
Francislea RH16 ....50 E2
Frankfield Rise TN2 .....8 A1
Franklands Cl RH15 .....73 B1
Franklands Gdns RH15 ..98 A8
Franklands Way RH15 ...98 A8
Franklin Rd
Brighton BN2 ....164 C2
Portslade-by-S BN41 ...162 C7
Shoreham-by-S BN43 ...140 D1
Franklin St BN2 ....164 C8
Franklynn Ct RH16 ......50 F3
Franklynn Rd RH16 .....50 F3
Frankton Ave RH16 .....51 A3
Frant Ave TN39 ....156 C5
Frant CE Prim Sch TN3 ...17 B4
Frant Cl TN39 ....156 C5
Frant Ct TN3 ....17 B3
Frant Green Rd TN3 .....17 B3
Frant Rd Hove BN3 ....142 A2
Royal Tunbridge Wells TN2,
TN3 ....17 A5
Frant Sta TN3 ....17 F5
Frary Wlk TN21 ....82 A3
Fraser Ave BN23 ......185 E7
Fraser Ct 3 BN43 .....161 C8
Freckley Hollow TN33 ...111 C1
Fred Emery Ct 16 BN1 .163 E5
Freda Gardham Com Sch
TN31 ....93 D6
Frederic Ho BN2 ......177 B5
Frederick Cotts RH16 ...51 B7
Frederick Gdns BN1 ...189 B3
Frederick Pl BN1 ......189 B3
Frederick Rd TN35 .....160 C7
Frederick St BN1 ......189 B3
Frederick Thatcher Pl
TN33 ....112 A5
Free Heath Rd TN3,TN5 ...19 C3
Freehold Terr 1 BN2 ...164 C8
Freek's La RH15 ....73 A5
Freeland Cl BN25 ......180 A6
Freeland Rd BN20 .....184 F1
Freeman Ave BN22 ....173 E1
Freemans Rd BN41 .....162 A8
Freezeland La TN39 ....134 A2
Fremlin Cl TN4 ....7 C6
French Gdns RH16 ......51 A6
French's Ct 9 BN25 ....180 E2
Frenches Farm Dr TN21 ..82 A5
Frenchgate Cl BN22 ...173 F2
Frenchgate Rd BN22 ...173 F2
Freshfield Bank RH18 ...11 E2
Freshfield Cl BN27 .....152 B6
Freshfield Crossway
RH17 ....52 C8
Freshfield La RH17 ......33 E2
Freshfield Pl BN2 ......164 C5
Freshfield Rd BN2 ......164 D6
Freshfield St BN2 ......164 C6
Freshfield Way BN2 ....164 C5
Freshfield Rd BN2 ......174 D2
Freshwater Ave TN34 ..136 E2
Freshwater Sq BN22 ...173 B3
Freshway BN22 ....173 C3
Frewen Cl TN31 ....67 B7
Frewen Coll TN31 ....67 C5
Frewyn Cl TN38 ....135 F4
Friar Cl BN1 ....143 A4
Friar Cres BN1 ....143 A3
Friar Rd BN1 ....143 A3
Friar Wlk BN1 ....142 F4
Friar's Cres TN35 ......138 B7
Friar's Hill Terr TN35 ..138 A7
Friar's Way TN34 ......136 F4
Friars Bank TN35 ......138 B7
Friars Cl BN6 ....97 F7
Friars Hill TN35 ....137 F7
Friars Mews BN7 ......190 B1
Friars Oak Rd BN6 ......97 E5
Friars Rd TN36 ....118 C6
Friars Vale TN6 ....25 C5

Friars Way TN2 ....8 D6
Friars' Ave BN10 ......178 E6
Friars' Wlk BN7 ....190 B2
Friday St BN23 ....174 C3
Fridays The BN20 ......187 B7
Friezland Rd TN4 ....7 D1
Frimley Cl BN2 ....165 F7
Friston Ave BN22 ......173 C1
Friston Cl Brighton BN2 .143 F4
Friston BN20 ....183 A1
Seaford BN25 ....180 C4
Friston Downs BN20 ...183 B2
Friston Rd BN20 ......183 A1
Frith Pk RH19 ....1 E3
Frith Rd BN3 ....163 A8
Frobisher Cl BN23 .....185 E7
Frobisher Ho BN10 ....167 C1
Frog Hole La TN20,TN21 ..58 C5
Frog La TN1 ....8 A2
Front Cotts TN5 ....31 E1
Fruitfields TN5 ....32 C3
Fry Cres RH15 ....72 E5
Fryatts Way TN39 .....156 F6
Fryman's La TN31 ......89 D2
Fulbourne Ho BN20 ...184 E1
Fulford Cl TN38 ....159 A8
Fuller Cl TN5 ....29 E5
Fuller Rd BN7 ....123 A3
Fuller's Pas BN7 ......190 B2
Fullers La TN31 ....67 B6
Fullwood Ave BN9 ....179 B7
Fulmar Cl BN3 ....142 D1
Fulmar Dr RH19 ....2 D3
Fulmar Pl 3 TN40 .....157 C4
Furlongs The BN20 ....170 F3
Furnace Ave TN3 ....20 A3
Furnace La
Beckley Furnace TN31 ...90 D7
Hook Green TN3 ....19 E4
Horam TN21 ....94 E8
Warbleton TN21 ....82 E2
Furnace Way TN2 ......78 E7
Furness Rd BN20,BN21 .184 F2
Furnival Ct TN2 ....16 F8
Furze Croft Hove BN3 ..163 D6
St Leonards TN38 ......159 A8
Furze Hill BN3 ....163 D6
Furze Hill Ct BN3 ......163 E6
Furze Hill Ho BN3 .....163 E6
Furze La RH19 ....1 B4
Furzedene BN3 ....163 D6
Furzefield Ave TN3 .....7 A8
Furzefield Chase RH19 ...1 D4
Furzefield Rd RH19 .....1 D4
Fyning Pl TN39 ....156 C5
Fyrsway TN35 ....138 E4
Fyrsway TN19 ....44 D3

G

Gables Ct 2 BN21 .....185 A3
Gables The TN34 ......136 E3
Gabriel Ho BN1 ....142 B4
Gage Ridge RH18 ....11 E2
Gages The BN27 ....152 D7
Gainsborough Cres
BN23 ....174 D1
Gainsborough Ho 10
BN3 ....163 C7
Gainsborough La BN26 .172 E6
Gainsborough Rd TN40 .157 E6
Galley Hill View TN40 ...157 E4
Galliers Cl BN1 ....143 B6
Gallipot Hill TN7 ....13 C3
Gallops The BN7 ......123 A1
Gallows Cl BN24 ......174 E6
Gallows La BN24 ......174 E6
Galveston Cl BN23 ....185 F7
Gammons Way TN33 ....88 E1
Gander Cl RH15 ....73 A5
Gander Gn RH16 ....50 F7
Gander Hill RH16 ......50 F7
Gannet Ho
5 Eastbourne BN21 ...185 A2
Hove BN3 ....142 B1
Ganton Pl TN38 ....158 F8
Garden Cl
4 Bexhill TN40 ......157 D4
East Grinstead RH19 ....10 F7
Portslade-by-S BN41 ...162 C8
Shoreham-by-S BN43 ...140 B1
Garden Cotts
Goatham Green TN31 ....89 D8
14 Hastings TN34 ....160 B4
Garden Ct Bexhill TN40 .157 D5
10 Eastbourne BN21 ...185 A3
Shoreham-by-S BN43 ...140 B1
Garden Ho The BN1 ....189 B3
Garden House La RH19 ..10 F7
Garden Mews BN20 ....188 D8
Garden Rd TN1 ....8 B4
Garden St Lewes BN7 ..190 B1
Royal Tunbridge Wells TN1 ..8 B4
Garden Wood Rd RH19 ..10 C8
Gardener St BN1 ......189 A3
Gardens The BN42 ....161 F7
Gardner Centre Rd BN1 .144 B6
Gardner Cl BN23 ......185 E7
Gardner Rd BN41 .....162 A7
Gardner St Brighton BN1 .189 B2
Herstmonceux BN27 ....130 F6
Gardner's Hill TN31 ....86 B6
Gardner's Hill TN31 .....70 B6
Garfield Rd BN27 ......152 C7
Garland Rd RH19 ....1 D2
Garnet Dr BN20 ....184 C2
Garnet Ho 16 BN2 .....164 C4

Garston Pk TN19 ....62 B6
Garth Cl TN39 ....157 A5
Gatehouse Cl TN39 ....156 C2
Gatehouse La
Framefield TN22 ....79 C7
Goddards' Green BN6,
RH15 ....72 C4
Gatelands Dr TN39 ....157 B6
Gatesmead RH16 ....50 F8
Gattons Inf Sch The
RH15 ....72 E3
Gattons The RH15 ......72 E3
Gatwick Farm Cotts RH19 .3 A4
Gaudick Cl BN20 ......184 E1
Gaudick Rd BN20 ......184 E1
Gavin Astor Cl TN40 ...158 A6
Geary Pl TN35 ....114 E3
Geering Pk BN27 ......152 D7
Geering Rd BN24 ......174 B5
Geers Wood TN21 ......81 F6
Geerswood Cotts 2
TN21 ....82 A6
Gemini Bsns Ctr BN3 ...163 B8
Gemma Cl BN27 ....152 E7
Geneva Rd BN9 ....179 D6
Genistos The BN6 ......97 E4
Gensing Rd TN38 ......159 C7
George Hill TN32 ....64 B3
George St Brighton BN2 .189 B2
Hailsham BN27 ....152 D7
Hastings TN34 ....160 A3
Hove BN3 ....163 B6
Portslade-by-S BN41 ...162 C7
Royal Tunbridge Wells TN2 ..8 C3
Sparrow's Green TN5 ....29 F5
Georgia Pl TN2 ....8 C4
Georgian Cl TN40 ......157 E5
Georgian Wlk TN38 ....158 F8
Gerald Cl RH15 ....73 D3
Gerald Rd BN25 ....180 F1
Gerard St BN1 ....189 B5
German St TN36 ....117 E7
Ghyll Ind Est TN21 ....82 A5
Ghyll Rd Crowborough TN6 .25 E4
Heathfield TN21 ....82 A6
Ghyll Side Rd TN31 .....67 B7
Ghyllside BN2 ....143 E1
Ghyllside Ave TN34 ...136 D4
Ghyllside Dr TN34 .....136 D4
Ghyllside Way TN34 ...136 D4
Gibb Cl TN40 ....158 A5
Gibbetts TN3 ....6 F3
Gibbon Rd BN9 ....179 C6
Gibraltar Rise TN21 .....82 A7
Gibson Cl BN7 ....190 B3
Giffards Cl RH19 ....1 F1
Gilbert Rd
Eastbourne BN22 ......185 B4
St Leonards TN37,TN38 ..159 B8
Gilbert Way BN27 .....152 B5
Gilberts Dr BN20 ......187 B8
Gilda Cres BN26 ......173 A6
Gildredge Rd
Eastbourne BN21 ......184 F2
Seaford BN25 ....180 F3
Gilham La RH18 ....11 E2
Gill The TN2 ....9 E8
Gillham Wood Ave
TN39 ....156 D3
Gillham Wood Rd TN39 .156 D3
Gilligans The RH15 .....72 F5
Gilridge Gn TN6 ....25 F4
Gilsman's Dr TN38 .....135 F1
Gilsman's Hill TN38 ....136 A1
Gilsman's Pk TN38 .....135 F1
Gimble Way TN2 ....9 D8
Gingerbread La TN18 ...32 F2
Gipps Cross La TN3 ......6 F3
Girton Ho BN3 ....162 F6
Girha Rd TN35 ....160 C6
Glade The
Hailsham BN27 ....151 F6
Mayfield TN20 ....40 A3
Uckfield TN22 ....78 D7
Gladepoint RH16 ....50 E5
Glades The Bexhill TN40 .157 E6
East Grinstead RH19 .....2 B1
Gladstone Bldgs BN8 ...101 E4
Gladstone Cl BN22 ....173 F1
Gladstone Pl BN2 ......164 C8
Gladstone Rd
Burgess Hill RH15 ......73 C4
Crowborough TN6 ....25 F1
Portslade-by-S BN41 ...162 B7
Rusthall TN4 ....7 B4
Gladstone Terr
Brighton BN2 ....189 C4
Hastings TN34 ....160 A5
Gladys Ave BN10 ......178 D6
Gladys Rd BN3 ....162 D8
Glanfield Ct TN1 ....8 C6
Glassenbury Dr TN40 ...157 F5
Glassenbury Rd BN3 ...162 D6
Gleave Cl RH19 ....2 A2
Glebe Cl Bexhill TN40 ...156 D3
Eastbourne BN20 ......184 D3
Lewes BN7 ....146 A8
Southwick BN42 ....161 F7
Glebe Com Mid Sch
TN40 ....161 D8
Glebe Cotts TN33 .....134 A7
Glebe Dr BN25 ....180 E3
Glebe The Felbridge RH19 ..1 A4
Hastings TN35 ....160 B5
Hurstpierpoint BN6 .....97 A6
Lindfield RH16 ....51 A8

Glebe The continued
Pembury TN2 ....9 D8
Pett TN35 ....116 F1
Southwick BN42 ....161 F8
Glebe Villas BN3 ......162 D7
Glebelands Cl BN43 ...161 B8
Glebelands The TN6 ....25 F2
Glen Cl BN26 ....172 F4
Glen Cotts BN26 ....172 F3
Glen Gordon Rd RH16 ...50 E6
Glen Rise BN1 ....142 B5
Glen Rise Cl BN1 ......142 B5
Glen The TN22 ....55 D1
Glen Vue RH19 ....1 F1
Glenburn Cl TN39 .....157 C7
Glencoe TN6 ....25 F2
Glendale Ave BN21 ...184 C5
Glendale Ct TN2 ....8 B8
Glendale Rd
Burgess Hill RH15 ......73 B2
Hove BN3 ....163 D7
Glendor Rd BN3 ....162 E6
Glendyne Cl RH19 ......11 A8
Glendyne Way RH19 ...11 A8
Gleneagles Cl
Bexhill TN40 ....157 E5
Seaford BN25 ....180 A6
Gleneagles Ct 15 RH16 ..50 E4
Gleneagles Dr
Hailsham BN27 ....152 A8
St Leonards TN38 ......158 F7
Glenfergus Ct RH16 .....50 E6
Glengorse TN33 ....112 F3
Glengorse Ct TN33 ....112 F3
Glenham Pl RH19 ......21 A5
Glenleigh Ave TN39 ...156 F6
Glenleigh Park Rd TN39 .157 A6
Glenleigh Wlk TN33 ....63 A4
Glenmore Mews 4
BN21 ....185 A3
Glenmore Pk TN2 ....16 F8
Glenmore Rd TN6 ......25 C3
Glenmore Rd E TN6 ....25 D3
Glenside 1 TN2 ....1 E1
Glenthorn Rd TN39 ....157 B6
Glenthorne Ho 17 BN21 .184 F4
Glenview Cl TN35 ......160 D5
Glessing Rd BN24 ......174 B6
Gleton Ave BN3 ....162 D8
Glottenham Farm Cotts
TN32 ....63 F1
Gloucester Ave TN40 ..158 A5
Gloucester Cl
East Grinstead RH19 ....11 A8
Eastbourne BN22 ......173 C2
Gloucester Cotts 3
TN34 ....160 A4
Gloucester Mews 2
BN1 ....189 B3
Gloucester Pas 4 BN1 .189 B3
Gloucester Rd
Brighton BN1 ....189 B3
Burgess Hill RH15 ......72 F3
Turner's Green TN5 .....29 F6
Gloucester St BN1 .....189 B3
Gloucester Yd 3 BN1 ..189 B3
Glovers La TN39 ....157 C7
Glynde Ave
Eastbourne BN22 ......173 C1
Saltdean BN2 ....177 D6
Glynde Cl BN9 ....168 D2
Glynde Ct Bexhill TN39 .156 C3
Polegate BN26 ....173 A6
Glynde Ho BN3 ....163 D6
Glynde Pl* BN8 ....147 F7
Glynde Rd BN2 ....164 D6
Glyndebourne Ave BN2 .177 C6
Glyndebourne Gdns
TN37 ....136 C6
Glyndebourne Opera Ho*
BN8 ....124 E2
Glyndley Manor Cottage Est
BN24 ....152 F2
Glyne Ascent TN40 ....157 F5
Glyne Barn Cl TN40 ...158 A5
Glyne Dr TN40 ....158 A5
Glyne Gap Sch TN40 ...158 A5
Glyne Hall TN40 ....157 D3
Glynleigh 18 BN26 ....189 D3
Glynleigh Dr BN26 ....173 A1
Glynleigh Rd BN24 ....153 A1
Glynn Rd BN10 ....167 C1
Glynn Rd W BN10 .....167 C1
Glynn Rise BN10 ......167 B1
Goatham La TN31 ......89 E5
Gochers Ct BN2 ....164 C7
Godden Cl TN31 ....66 B7
Godden Rd BN8 ....76 C7
Goddens Gill TN31 ......67 B7
Goddes The RH19 ......10 E7
Godfrey Cl BN7 ....190 A4
Godwin Rd
Hastings TN35 ....160 C5
Hove BN3 ....141 D1
Goffs The BN21 ....184 E3
Golby Ct BN10 ....178 A7
Gold La BN10 ....167 C2
Goldcrest Cl TN22 ......78 E5
Goldcrest Dr TN22 .....78 D5
Golden Cross Inn Cvn Pk The
BN8 ....127 C3
Golden Gate Way BN23 .175 B5
Golden Hill RH15 ....73 D5

Golden Jubilee Way
BN23,BN24 . . . . 173 F4
Golden La 11 BN1 . . . . 163 D5
Golden Miller La BN26 . . 172 F6
Goldhurst Gn TN36 . . . . . 116 E5
Golding Rd BN23 . . . . 174 F2
Goldsmid Mews 10 BN3 .163 D6
Goldsmid Rd BN3 . . . . 163 E7
Goldsmith Cl BN23 . . . . . . 174 E3
Goldsmiths Ave TN6 . . . . . 25 D3
Goldstone Cl BN3 . . . . 142 A2
Goldstone Cres BN3 . . . . . 142 B2
Goldstone Ct BN3 . . . . 142 A3
Goldstone Ho 4 BN3 . . . . 163 B7
Goldstone La BN3 . . . . 163 B8
Goldstone Prim Sch
BN3 . . . . 141 E1
Goldstone Rd BN3 . . . . . . 163 B7
Goldstone Ret Pk BN3 .163 B8
Goldstone St BN3 . . . . 163 B7
Goldstone Villas BN3 . . . . 163 B7
Goldstone Way BN3 . . . . . 142 A2
Golf Dr BN1 . . . . 143 B3
Goodensfield TN5 . . . . 29 E5
Goods Station Rd TN1 . . . 8 B4
Goodtrees La TN8 . . . . 4 B2
Goodwin Cl BN27 . . . . 129 A2
Goodwins Cl RH19 . . . . 1 D3
Goodwins The TN2 . . . . 7 F1
Goodwood Cl
Bexhill TN40 . . . . 157 D6
Eastbourne BN20 . . . . 173 B2
Goodwood Ct 2 BN3 . . . 163 D7
Goodwood Way BN2 . . . . 143 F3
Gooseberry La TN31 . . . . . 67 A3
Gordon Ave BN3 . . . . 161 A7
Gordon Cl RH16 . . . . 50 E6
Gordon Ho RH16 . . . . 73 C4
Gordon Pl TN39 . . . . 157 B6
Gordon Rd Brighton BN1 .142 F2
Burgess Hill RH15 . . . . 72 A4
Buxted TN22 . . . . 56 C3
Crowborough TN6 . . . . 25 F4
Hailsham BN27 . . . . 152 B7
Hastings TN34 . . . . 160 A4
Haywards Heath RH16 . . . 50 E6
Portslade-by-S,Fishersgate
BN41 . . . . 162 A7
Royal Tunbridge Wells TN4 . .8 C7
Shoreham-by-S BN43 . . . . 161 A7
Gore Park Ave BN21 . . . . 184 D4
Gore Park Rd BN21 . . . . . 184 D4
Gorham Ave BN2 . . . . 177 A6
Gorham Ct BN2 . . . . 177 A6
Gorham Ct BN10 . . . . 177 E4
Gorham Way BN10 . . . . . . 177 E4
Goring Cl BN1 . . . . 143 F5
Gorringe Cl
Eastbourne BN20 . . . . 173 A3
Shoreham-by-S BN43 . . . . 161 D7
Gorringe Dr BN20 . . . . . . 173 A3
Gorringe Rd BN22 . . . . . . 185 A4
Gorringe Valley Rd
BN20 . . . . 173 A3
Gorse Cl
Eastbourne BN20 . . . . 184 B5
Portslade-by-S BN41 . . . . 140 F4
Gorse Dr BN25 . . . . 180 F6
Gorse Hill TN21 . . . . 59 F1
Gorse Rd TN2 . . . . 8 E5
Gorselands TN33 . . . . 88 E1
Gorses The TN35 . . . . 156 C2
Gorsethorn Way TN35 . . . 138 E4
Gorseway The TN39 . . . . . 156 C5
Gosford Way BN26 . . . . . 172 F6
Gote La BN8 . . . . 124 D4
Goudhurst Cl BN23 . . . . . 174 D1
Gower Rd RH16 . . . . 50 E3
Gows Croft BN7 . . . . 145 E5
Grace Ct BN6 . . . . 97 E5
Gradwell End BN8 . . . . . . 100 D7
Graffham Cl BN2 . . . . 164 E6
Grafton St BN2 . . . . 189 C1
Graham Ave
Brighton BN1 . . . . 142 F5
Portslade-by-S BN41 . . . . 140 F4
Graham Cl BN41 . . . . 140 F4
Graham Cres BN41 . . . . . 140 F4
Grammer Ct BN8 . . . . 75 D7
Grampian Cl
Eastbourne BN23 . . . . 174 C3
Royal Tunbridge Wells TN2 . .8 B7
Granary Cotts TN33 . . . . . 112 E4
Granary Rural Bsns Ctr The
BN27 . . . . 128 F6
Grand Ave Bexhill TN40 .158 A5
Hassocks BN6 . . . . 97 F4
Seaford BN25 . . . . 180 D6
Grand Avenue Mans 4
BN3 . . . . 163 C6
Grand Cres BN2 . . . . 177 A5
Grand Ct
3 Eastbourne BN21 . . . . 185 A1
15 St Leonards TN37 . . . . 159 C6
Grand Hotel Bldgs 8
BN21 . . . . 185 A1
Grand Junction Rd BN1 .189 B1
Grand Mans 10 BN3 . . . . 185 A1
Grand Par Brighton BN2 .189 B2
Eastbourne BN21 . . . . 185 B2
Polegate BN26 . . . . 172 F6
St Leonards TN37,TN38 . 159 C6
Grand Parade Mews
BN2 . . . . 189 B2
Grange Ave TN34 . . . . . . 136 D4
Grange Cl Brighton BN1 .142 E1

Grange Cl continued
Burgess Hill RH15 . . . . 73 C5
Crowborough TN6 . . . . 25 D1
Horam TN21 . . . . 106 F6
Grange Court Dr TN39 . .157 B6
Grange Ct
Eastbourne BN21 . . . . 184 F2
Hove BN3 . . . . 162 F8
Lewes BN7 . . . . 190 A1
9 Southwick BN42 . . . . . . 161 E7
Grange End BN20 . . . . . . 184 F1
Grange Gdns
Eastbourne BN20 . . . . 184 F2
Rusthall TN4 . . . . .7 D4
Grange Ind Est The
BN42 . . . . 161 D7
Grange Mus & Art Gallery*
BN2 . . . . 165 F2
Grange Rd
Barcombe Cross BN8 . . . . 101 D4
Eastbourne BN21 . . . . 184 F1
Hastings TN34 . . . . 136 E5
Hove BN3 . . . . 162 E8
Lewes BN7 . . . . 190 A1
Rusthall TN4 . . . . .7 D4
Southwick BN42 . . . . 161 E7
Uckfield TN22 . . . . 78 C7
Grange The
Barcombe Cross BN8 . . . . 101 D4
2 Eastbourne BN21 . . . . 185 A2
Saltdean BN2 . . . . 177 D4
Grangeways BN1 . . . . 142 E5
Grant St BN2 . . . . 189 C4
Grantham Bank BN8 . . . . 101 E4
Grantham Rd BN1 . . . . . . 100 E7
Grantham Rd BN1 . . . . . . 143 A1
Grants Hill Ho TN22 . . . . . 78 C7
Granville Ct
2 Eastbourne BN21 . . . . 184 F1
10 Hove BN3 . . . . 163 B7
11 Seaford BN25 . . . . . . 180 E2
Granville Rd
Eastbourne BN21 . . . . 184 F1
Hove BN3 . . . . 163 E7
Royal Tunbridge Wells TN1 . .7 F6
Graperies The 3 BN2 . . . 164 C5
Grasmere Cl BN23 . . . . . . 174 B4
Grassington Rd BN20 . . . 184 F1
Grassmere Ave BN10 . . . 177 F4
Grassmere Ct BN10 . . . . . 178 A8
Gratton Ct TN39 . . . . 157 A3
Gravelye Cl RH16 . . . . 51 B5
Graveye La
Haywards Heath RH16 . . . 51 B6
Haywards
Heath,Franklands Village
RH16 . . . . 51 A4
Gravett Ct RH15 . . . . 72 F2
Graycoats Dr TN6 . . . . 25 F2
Grays Cotts TN33 . . . . . . 112 F3
Grays Inf Sch BN9 . . . . . . 179 D6
Graystone La TN35 . . . . . 160 D7
Graywood La BN8 . . . . . . 105 D6
Graywood Rd BN8 . . . . . . 105 C6
Grazebrook Ct TN39 . . . . 156 C3
Great Brooms Rd TN4 . . . . .8 C8
Great Cliffe Rd BN23 . . . . 174 E1
Great College St BN2 . . . 164 C4
Great Courtlands TN3 . . . . .7 F3
Great Dixter House & Gdns*
TN31 . . . . 66 F7
Great Dixter Nurseries*
TN31 . . . . 66 F7
Great Footway TN3 . . . . . . .6 F3
Great Hall Arc 3 TN1 . . . . 8 B3
Great Heathmead RH16 . . 50 D6
Great House Ct 4 BN41 .161 E7
Great Oak TN19 . . . . 45 A3
Great Rough BN8 . . . . 76 A6
Great Sanders Ho TN33 . . 88 D4
Great Walstead Sch
RH16 . . . . 51 F6
Great Wilkins BN1 . . . . 141 A6
Great Wood Woodland
Walks* TN33 . . . . 113 B5
Greater Paddock BN8 . . . 124 E6
Greatham Ct BN1 . . . . 142 E6
Grecian Rd TN1 . . . . .8 B2
Greeba Ct 8 TN38 . . . . . . 159 B6
Green Cl Ringmer BN8 . . . 124 C4
4 Southwick BN42 . . . . . . 161 E7
Green Ct 3 BN42 . . . . 161 E7
Green Field Cl BN42 . . . . 161 E8
Green Gate BN10 . . . . 167 C1
Green Gr BN27 . . . . 152 B8
Green Hedges TN32 . . . . . .63 E4
Green Hedges Ave RH19 . . 1 D2
Green Hedges Rd RH19 . . . 1 D2
Green La Bexhill TN39 . . . 156 D5
Boyle Side BN8 . . . . 103 B1
Crowborough TN6 . . . . 25 D5
Heathfield TN21 . . . . 82 B6
Jevington BN26 . . . . 172 C1
Lewes BN7 . . . . 190 A1
Seaford BN25 . . . . 180 E2
South Chailey BN8 . . . . . . 100 F2
South Street BN7 . . . . 75 E1
Wivelsfield RH17 . . . . 74 B4
Woodingdean BN2 . . . . . . 165 E6
Green Mdws RH16 . . . . 51 B8
Green Park Cnr RH17 . . . . 74 B4
Green Rd RH17 . . . . 74 B4
Green Ridge BN1 . . . . 141 E5
Green Sq TN5 . . . . 29 F5
Green St BN21 . . . . 184 C4
Green The Blackboys TN22 .80 A6
Bodiam TN32 . . . . 65 E7
Catsfield TN33 . . . . 133 E8

Green The continued
East Dean BN20 . . . . 187 B8
Ewhurst Green TN32 . . . . . 66 B5
Frant TN3 . . . . 17 B3
Hailsham BN27 . . . . 129 C2
Horsted Keynes RH17 . . . . 33 C5
Hove BN3 . . . . 142 C2
Langton Green TN3 . . . . 6 E3
Newick BN8 . . . . 76 D7
Ninfield TN33 . . . . 133 B5
Ringmer BN8 . . . . 124 D5
Rottingdean BN2 . . . . 165 F2
Sedlescombe TN33 . . . . . . 113 E8
St Leonards TN37 . . . . 161 E7
St Leonards TN38 . . . . 159 B8
Green View RH15 . . . . 72 E3
Green Wall BN7 . . . . 190 B2
Green Way TN2 . . . . 9 E8
Green Wlk
Hailsham BN27 . . . . 129 C1
Seaford BN25 . . . . 181 B2
Green Wlk The BN22 . . . . 173 B3
Greenacres Brighton BN1 .142 F1
Peacehaven BN10 . . . . . . 167 D2
Peacehaven BN10 . . . . . . 178 A7
Westfield TN35 . . . . 114 E3
Greenacres Dr
Hailsham BN27 . . . . 152 C7
Ringmer BN8 . . . . 124 D4
Greenacres Way BN27 . . 152 C8
Greenbank Ave BN2 . . . . 177 D6
Greene Ct BN7 . . . . 146 B8
Greenfield Ct
Brighton BN1 . . . . 143 A5
Rusthall TN4 . . . . .7 C5
Greenfield Cres BN1 . . . . 142 F5
Greenfield Dr TN22 . . . . . . 78 D4
Greenfield Rd
Burwash TN19 . . . . 62 C7
Eastbourne BN21 . . . . 184 D4
Greenfields BN27 . . . . 129 A1
Greenfields Sch TN37 . . . 136 B6
Greenfields Sch RH18 . . . . 11 C1
Greenhill Pk RH17 . . . . 51 A2
Greenhill Way
Haywards Heath RH17 . . . 51 A2
Peacehaven BN10 . . . . . . 167 C2
Greenlands Cl RH15 . . . . . 98 B8
Greenlands Dr RH15 . . . . . 98 B8
Greenleaf Gdns BN26 . . . 173 A8
Greenleas Hove BN3 . . . . 141 D2
Pembury TN2 . . . . 9 C6
Greenstede Ave RH19 . . . . 1 F2
Greenway BN20 . . . . 184 B6
Greenway Ct BN2 . . . . . . 177 A5
Greenways Bexhill TN39 . 156 F7
Haywards Heath RH16 . . . 50 F6
Ovingdean BN2 . . . . 165 D3
Portslade-by-S BN41 . . . . 141 B1
Southwick BN42 . . . . 140 F1
Greenways Cnr BN2 . . . . 165 D4
Greenways Cres 1 BN41 .140 A1
Greenwell Cl BN25 . . . . . . 181 B4
Greenwich Rd BN27 . . . . 152 D7
Greenwich Way RH17 . . . . 30 C3
Greenwoods La TN21 . . . . 83 D7
Greggs Wood Rd TN2 . . . . .8 E7
Gregory Ct 2 RH19 . . . . . . 1 E1
Gregory La TN39 . . . . 174 F5
Gregory Wlk TN33 . . . . . . 113 E8
Grenada 2 RH19 . . . . 157 A2
Grenada Ct Bexhill TN39 . 156 D4
Eastbourne BN23 . . . . 185 G7
Grenham Ct TN35 . . . . . . 160 D7
Grenville Rd Bexhill TN39 .156 F7
Grenville Rd BN1 . . . . 175 C4
Grenville St BN1 . . . . 189 A4
Gresham BN27 . . . . 175 B6
Gresham Cl BN21 . . . . 184 C6
Gresham Way TN38 . . . . . 159 A8
Gresley Rd TN35 . . . . 160 D8
Greville Rd TN35 . . . . 160 C7
Grey Alders RH16 . . . . 51 B6
Grey Tower Bglws
BN26 . . . . 173 A8
Grey Twr Cvn Site BN24 . 175 C3
Greyfriars BN3 . . . . 163 D8
Greyfriars Pl TN36 . . . . . . 118 B6
Greyhorses TN39 . . . . 156 B4
Greys Rd BN20 . . . . 184 D3
Greystones Ct TN6 . . . . . . 25 D4
Grinley Ct 8 TN40 . . . . . . 157 C4
Grinstead La RH19 . . . . . . 21 C7
Grinstead Mount 4
BN2 . . . . 165 F8
Gromenfield TN3 . . . . 15 C7
Groombridge Hill TN3 . . . . .6 D1
Groombridge Pl* TN3 . . . 15 C8
Groombridge Place Gdns*
TN3 . . . . 15 C8
Groombridge St Thomas' CE
Prim Sch TN3 . . . . 15 C6
Groombridge Sta TN3 . . . 15 C7
Grosvenor Bridge TN1 . . . .8 B5
Grosvenor Cres TN38 . . . 159 A6
Grosvenor Ct
Brighton BN1 . . . . 142 A3
Seaford BN25 . . . . 180 F1
Grosvenor Gdns TN38 . . . 158 F6
Grosvenor Ho RH19 . . . . . . 1 D3
Grosvenor Mans 1 BN3 . .163 B6
Grosvenor Rd
East Grinstead RH19 . . . . . 1 D1
Royal Tunbridge Wells TN1 .180 E4

Grosvenor St BN2 . . . . . . 189 C2
Grosvenor Wlk TN1 . . . . . . 8 A4
Grove Ave TN1 . . . . 8 A2
Grove Bank 9 BN2 . . . . . 189 C3
Grove Ct 12 BN3 . . . . 163 C6
Grove Hill Brighton BN2 . 189 C3
Grove Hill BN27 . . . . 129 D7
Grove Hill Gdns TN1 . . . . . 8 B3
Grove Hill Rd TN1 . . . . 8 B3
Grove La TN31 . . . . 70 C4
Grove Park Sch TN6 . . . . . 25 E1
Grove Rd
Burgess Hill RH15 . . . . 73 B3
Eastbourne BN21 . . . . 184 F2
Hastings TN35 . . . . 160 D8
Seaford BN25 . . . . 180 E2
Grove Sch The TN38 . . . . 135 F1
Grove St BN2 . . . . 189 C3
Grove The Battle TN33 . . 112 F1
Bexhill TN39 . . . . 156 E5
Crowborough TN6 . . . . 25 C1
Eastbourne BN20 . . . . 184 B7
Eastbourne,Wannock
BN20 . . . . 172 F3
Hailsham BN27 . . . . 152 B6
Haywards Heath RH16 . . . 51 A8
Mayfield TN20 . . . . 40 A2
Newhaven BN9 . . . . 179 C4
Pembury TN2 . . . . 9 D8
Rye TN31 . . . . 93 C6
Grove Villa 3 BN1 . . . . . . 189 A4
Grovebury BN27 . . . . 152 C7
Grovelands Cl RH15 . . . . . 72 F1
Grovelands Com Sch
BN27 . . . . 129 A1
Grovelands Rd BN27 . . . . 129 A1
Grovely La TN21 . . . . 84 B1
Grover St 3 TN1 . . . . 8 B4
Grovers End BN8 . . . . 76 D7
Guardian Ct BN26 . . . . . . 172 F7
Guardswell Pl BN25 . . . . . 180 F3
Guestling Bradshaw CE Prim
Sch TN35 . . . . 138 A8
Guestling Rd BN22 . . . . . 185 D5
Guildford Rd
Brighton BN1 . . . . 189 A3
7 Royal Tunbridge Wells
TN1 .8 B3
Guildford St BN1 . . . . 189 A3
Guinness Ct BN9 . . . . 168 E1
Guinness Trust Bglws
BN9 . . . . 168 E2
Guldeford Ct 1 TN31 . . . . 71 F3
Guldeford Lane Cnr
BN9 . . . . 168 E2
Guldeford Rd TN31 . . . . . . 93 E7
Gun Hill Gun Hill TN21 . . 106 D3
Lower Dicker BN27,TN21 . 128 B8
Gun Rd TN22 . . . . 80 A6
Gundreda Rd BN7 . . . . . . 123 B2
Gunter's La TN39 . . . . 157 A6
Gurth Rd TN35 . . . . 160 D6
Gwent Ct 7 BN22 . . . . . . 185 C4
Gwydyr Mans 3 BN3 . . . . 163 B6
Gwyneth Gr TN40 . . . . . . 157 F7
Gwynne Gdns RH19 . . . . . . 1 C2

H

Hackenden Cl RH19 . . . . . . 1 E3
Hackenden Cotts RH19 . . . 1 E3
Hackenden La RH19 . . . . . . 1 E3
Hackhurst La BN27 . . . . . 128 B4
Hackhurst Lane Ind Est
BN27 . . . . 128 B4
Hackwood RH19 . . . . 1 E4
Haddington Cl BN3 . . . . . 163 C8
Haddington St 11 BN3 . . 163 B7
Hadley Ct Polegate BN26 .173 A8
Royal Tunbridge Wells TN4 . .7 F6
Hadley Ho 7 BN2 . . . . . . 184 F3
Hadlow Ave BN23 . . . . . . 174 E3
Hadlow Cl BN2 . . . . 164 D6
Hadlow Down Rd TN6 . . 38 B4
Hadrian Ave BN42 . . . . . . 162 A8
Hadrian Gdns TN37 . . . . . 136 A6
Haig Ave BN1 . . . . 143 D6
Hailsham Ave BN2 . . . . . . 177 D7
Hailsham Com Coll
BN27 . . . . 152 B8
Hailsham Ct 2 TN40 . . . . 157 C3
Hailsham Rd
Heathfield TN21 . . . . 82 A6
Herstmonceux BN27 . . . . 130 E5
Polegate BN26 . . . . 172 F7
Stone Cross BN24,BN26 . 173 F8
Hairpin Croft BN10 . . . . . 167 C1
Hale Gn BN8 . . . . 106 A2
Half Mile Dro BN8 . . . . . . 125 B7
Halfway Sta* BN2 . . . . . . 164 C4
Hall La TN22 . . . . 57 C5
Hall's Hole Rd TN2 . . . . 8 E4
Halland Cl BN27 . . . . 173 D1
Halland Rd BN2 . . . . 164 D6
Hallett Rd BN15 . . . . 73 C4
Hallett Rd BN2 . . . . 164 D7
Halley Rd BN27 . . . . 152 D7
Halley Rd
Cade Street BN27 . . . . 82 E8
Wartling BN27 . . . . 131 B1
Halls Cotts TN5 . . . . 29 F5
Hallyburton Rd BN3 . . . . 162 D8
Halsford Croft RH19 . . . . . 1 B3
Halsford Gn RH19 . . . . 1 B3
Halsford La RH19 . . . . 1 C3
Halsford Park Prim Sch
RH19 . . . . 1 C2

Gol – Har 203

Halsford Park Rd RH19 . . . 1 C2
Halton Cres TN34 . . . . . . 160 B6
Halton Hts TN34 . . . . 160 B6
Halton Pl TN34 . . . . 160 B6
Halton Rd BN22 . . . . 185 C4
Halton Shaws BN6 . . . . . . 97 B5
Halton Terr TN34 . . . . . . 160 B6
Ham Bsns Ctr BN43 . . . . . 161 A7
Ham La Burwash TN19 . . . 62 B6
Lewes BN7 . . . . 190 B1
Ringmer BN8 . . . . 124 C6
Scaynes Hill RH17 . . . . 51 E3
Ham Rd BN43 . . . . 161 A7
Hamble Rd BN24 . . . . 173 F5
Hambleton Cl BN23 . . . . . 174 D3
Hambrook RH15 . . . . 73 C1
Hamelsham Ct BN27 . . . . 152 A8
Hamilton Cl BN41 . . . . . . 141 A3
Hamilton Ct
Brighton BN2 . . . . 165 A3
Royal Tunbridge Wells TN4 . 8 A5
Seaford BN25 . . . . 180 C4
Hamilton Ho
6 Eastbourne BN21 . . . . 184 E4
Royal Tunbridge Wells TN4 . . 8 A5
Seaford BN25 . . . . 180 E4
Hamilton Lodge Sch
BN2 . . . . 164 D5
Hamilton Mans 8 BN3 . . 163 B5
Hamilton Rd BN1 . . . . 189 A4
Hamilton Terr TN39 . . . . . 157 A4
Hamlands La BN22 . . . . . 173 B3
Hamlin's Cnr BN6 . . . . 72 A6
Hammer La BN27,TN21 . . 107 F5
Hammerham Pk* RH19 . . . 3 C2
Hammerwood Rd RH19 . . 11 E6
Hammonds Dr BN23 . . . . 185 C7
Hammonds Ridge RH15 . . 72 F1
Hammonds Ridge RH17 . . 72 F1
Hammy Cl BN43 . . . . 161 C8
Hammy La BN43 . . . . 161 B8
Hammy Way BN43 . . . . . . 161 B8
Hampden Ave BN22 . . . . 173 F1
Hampden Ct TN33 . . . . . . 112 B4
Hampden Gdns BN9 . . . . 168 D2
Hampden Park Dr BN22 . 184 E8
Hampden Park Inf Sch
BN22 . . . . 173 E2
Hampden Park Sta
BN22 . . . . 173 F1
Hampden Rd BN22 . . . . . 164 C7
Hampden Terr 8 BN22 . . 185 C4
Hampshire Ct
Brighton BN2 . . . . 189 C3
Eastbourne BN23 . . . . 174 E1
Hampstead Rd BN1 . . . . . 142 D1
Hampton Pl BN1 . . . . 163 E5
Hampton St 24 BN1 . . . . 163 E5
Hampton Terr 7 BN1 . . . 163 E5
Hampton Way RH19 . . . . . 10 F7
Hamsey Cl Brighton BN2 .164 F5
Eastbourne BN24 . . . . 184 B6
Hamsey Com Prim Sch
BN8 . . . . 123 A8
Hamsey Cres BN7 . . . . . . 123 B2
Hamsey La
Cooksbridge BN8 . . . . 123 B7
Seaford BN25 . . . . 181 C2
Hamsey Rd Saltdean BN2 .177 D4
Saltdean BN2 . . . . 177 D5
Sharpthorne RH19 . . . . 21 A6
Hamshaw Ct BN22 . . . . . 184 F8
Hamsland RH17 . . . . 33 C4
Hanbury La RH16 . . . . 51 A5
Hangdown Mead Bsns Pk
RH19 . . . . 21 B5
Hanging Birch La TN21 . . 81 D1
Hangleton Cl BN3 . . . . . . 141 D2
Hangleton Gdns BN3 . . . 141 C1
Hangleton Jun & Inf Sch
BN3 . . . . 141 B2
Hangleton La BN3 . . . . . . 141 D3
Hangleton Manor Cl
BN3 . . . . 141 D4
Hangleton Rd BN3 . . . . . . 141 D2
Hangleton Valley Dr
BN3 . . . . 141 D4
Hankham Hall Rd BN24 . 174 D7
Hankham Prim Sch
BN24 . . . . 174 B8
Hankham Rd BN24 . . . . . 174 B8
Hankham St BN24 . . . . . . 174 B8
Hanlye La RH17 . . . . 50 B8
Hannington Pl BN6 . . . . . . 97 F7
Hanover Cl Bexhill TN40 .157 C5
Seaford BN25 . . . . 180 B6
Hanover Cres BN2 . . . . . . 189 C4
Hanover Ct Brighton BN2 .189 C4
Eastbourne BN21 . . . . 184 D5
Haywards Heath RH16 . . . 50 D4
Hanover Lofts BN2 . . . . . 189 C3
Hanover Mans BN2 . . . . . 189 C4
Hanover Rd
Eastbourne BN22 . . . . 185 C4
Royal Tunbridge Wells TN4 . 8 A4
Hanover St BN2 . . . . 189 C4
Hanover Terr BN2 . . . . . . 189 C4
Hanson Rd BN9 . . . . 179 C6
Harbour Barn TN36 . . . . . 118 B6
Harbour Ct BN43 . . . . 161 A5
Harbour Ho RH43 . . . . . . 161 A7
Harbour Quay BN23 . . . . 175 A1
Harbour Rd TN31 . . . . 93 D4
Harbour View Cl BN25 . . 180 B6

Harbour View Rd BN9 ....179 B5
Harbour Way
  Shoreham-by-S BN43 ....161 B6
  St Leonards TN38 ......135 E7
Harbour's Yd TN33 ......112 E4
Harcourt Cl TN22 ....78 C6
Harcourt Rd TN22 ....185 B6
Harding Ave BN22 ......185 B6
Hardrada Rise TN34 ....136 E3
Hardwick Rd
  Eastbourne BN21 ......185 A2
  Hove BN3 ....141 E3
Hardwick Way BN3 ......141 E3
Hardwicke Rd TN34 ....160 B6
Hardy Dr BN23 ....185 F6
Hare Way TN37 ....136 C5
Harebeating Cl BN27 ...129 C2
Harebeating Cres BN27 .129 C2
Harebeating Dr BN27 ...129 C2
Harebeating Gdns BN27 .129 C2
Harebeating La BN27 ...129 D1
Harebell Cl BN23 ....174 C3
Harebell Dr BN41 ....141 A3
Harecombe Rd TN6 ....37 F8
Harecombe Rise TN6 .....37 F8
Haremere Hall Gdns*
  TN19 ....44 E2
Haremere Hill TN19 .....44 D2
Harescroft TN2 ....16 F7
Harewood Cl TN39 ......157 A3
Harewood Ct BN3 ......163 C6
Harfield Cl BN9 ....168 F2
Hargate Cl TN2 ....16 F8
Hargreaves Rd BN23 ...174 A1
Harison Rd BN25 ....181 A4
Harkness Dr TN34 ......137 B5
Harlands Cl RH16 ....50 C6
Harlands Ho RH16 ....50 C6
Harlands Mews TN22 ....78 D5
Harlands Prim Sch
  Haywards Heath RH16 ...50 D7
  Uckfield TN22 ....78 D5
Harlands Rd RH16 ....50 D7
Harlequin Gdns TN37 ...136 A6
Harlequin La TN6 ....37 E8
Harlequin Pl TN6 ....37 E8
Harley La TN21 ....132 A6
Harley Shute Rd TN38 ..158 E7
Harley Way TN38 ......158 E6
Harmans Dr RH19 ....2 B1
Harmans Mead RH19 .....2 B1
Harmers Hay Rd BN27 ..129 B1
Harmers Hill BN8 ....76 C7
Harmony St TN4 ....7 D4
Harmony Wood TN34 ...136 F5
Harmsworth Cres BN41 .141 E3
Harold Cl BN24 ....175 F7
Harold Dr BN23 ....185 F8
Harold Ho 2 TN2 ....8 C7
Harold Mews 2 TN38 ...159 C4
Harold Pl TN34 ....159 F7
Harold Rd TN35 ....160 C5
Harold Terr TN33 ....112 F3
Harpers Rd BN9 ....179 C7
Harrier La TN33 ....112 F4
Harriers Ct BN27 ....152 D7
Harries Rd TN2 ....8 E7
Harrington Ct BN1 .....142 E2
Harrington Mans BN1 ..142 E2
Harrington Pl BN1 .....142 E2
Harrington Rd BN1 ....142 E2
Harrington Villas BN1 ..142 E2
Harris Ct BN21 ....185 A3
Harrisons La BN8 ......124 E5
Harrow Cl BN25 ....181 A4
Harrow La TN37 ....136 B5
Hart Cl TN22 ....78 A7
Hartfield Ave BN1 ......143 A5
Hartfield Ho TN22 ......78 C6
Hartfield La BN21 ......184 F4
Hartfield Mdw TN38 ...135 D3
Hartfield Rd Bexhill TN39 .156 E2
  Cowden TN8 ....4 C6
  Eastbourne BN21 ....184 F3
  Forest Row RH18 ......12 B2
  Saltdean BN25 ....181 A3
  Seaford BN25 ....181 A3
Harting Combe TN38 ...159 B8
Hartington Mans 7
  BN21 ....185 A2
Hartington Pl
  Brighton BN2 ....164 C8
  Eastbourne BN21 ....185 A2
Hartington Rd BN2 ....164 C8
Hartington Terr BN2 ...164 C8
Hartington Villas BN3 ..163 B8
Hartley Ct 10 BN1 .....189 A4
Hartwood Lodge 6
  TN40 ....157 C4
Harvard Cl BN7 ....190 A4
Harvard Rd BN8 ....124 D5
Harvest Cl Lindfield RH16 .50 C6
  Telscombe Cliffs BN10 .167 B2
Harvest Hill RH19 ....10 E8
Harvest Way TN37 .....134 D6
Harvesters RH16 ....50 D2
Harvey Cl TN38 ....159 B8
Harvey's La BN8,TN22 ..103 D4
Harveys Way BN7 ......190 C2
Hartington Bsns Pk
  BN22 ....184 F8
Harwood Cl BN23 .....185 E7
Harwoods Cl 3 RH19 ...10 F7
Harwoods La RH19 ......10 F7
Haslam Cres TN40 .....157 F6

Hasletts Cl TN1 ....8 B6
Hassocks Cl BN23 .....173 F4
Hassocks Inf Sch BN6 ...97 F3
Hassocks Lodge BN6 ....97 F3
Hassocks Rd BN6 ....97 B5
Hassocks Sta BN6 ....97 E4
Hastings Ave BN25 ....181 C5
Hastings Castle & 1066
  Story* TN34 ....160 A4
Hastings Cl BN26 ......173 B7
Hastings Coll of Arts & Tech
  TN38 ....159 B6
Hastings Ct TN40 ......157 E5
Hastings Ctry Pk*
  TN35 ....160 E5
Hastings Ctry Pk Visitor Ctr*
  TN35 ....138 C4
Hastings Mus & Art Gall*
  TN34 ....159 E8
Hastings Rd Battle TN33 .113 B2
  Bexhill TN40 ....157 E5
  Bexhill TN40 ....157 F5
  Brighton BN2 ....164 C8
  Newenden TN17,TN18 ...48 C6
  Pembury TN2 ....9 D6
  The Moor TN18 ....45 F6
Hastings Sta TN34 .....159 E8
Hatch End RH18 ....11 F2
Hatchgate Cl TN41 ......50 A6
Hatchgate La RH17 .....50 A6
Hatfield Ct 18 BN3 ....163 C6
Hatherley Rd TN37 ....159 C7
Havana Ct 8 BN23 ....185 F8
Havelock Rd
  Bexhill TN40 ....157 C6
  Brighton BN1 ....142 F1
  Eastbourne BN22 ....185 B4
  Hastings TN34 ....159 F7
Haven Brow BN25 .....181 A4
Haven CE/Methodist Prim
  Sch The BN23 ....185 F7
Haven Cl
  Beachlands BN24 ....175 E6
  Eastbourne BN22 ....173 B3
Haven Rd BN23 ....158 D6
Haven The BN27 ......152 C6
Haven Way BN9 ....179 B6
Havering Cl TN2 ....8 F6
Hawkenbury Cl TN2 .....8 D2
Hawkenbury Mead TN2 ...8 D1
Hawkenbury Rd TN2,TN3 ..8 E1
Hawkenbury Way TN2 ...8 D1
Hawkes Farm Prim Sch
  BN27 ....129 B3
Hawkhurst CE Prim Sch
  TN18 ....45 F8
Hawkhurst Cl BN23 ....174 D2
Hawkhurst Pl BN1 .....143 D6
Hawkhurst Rd
  Brighton BN1 ....143 D6
  Flimwell TN5,TN18 .....32 E2
Hawkhurst Way TN39 ..156 E3
Hawkins Cl BN43 .....140 D1
Hawkins Cres BN43 ...140 D2
Hawkins Rd BN43 .....140 D1
Hawkins Way BN27 ...152 B8
Hawks Farm Cl BN27 ..129 B2
Hawks Rd BN27 ....129 B2
Hawks Town Cres BN27 .129 C2
Hawksbridge Cl BN27 ..173 C3
Hawkstown Cl BN27 ...129 B2
Hawkstown Gdns BN27 .129 B3
Hawkstown View BN27 .129 B3
Hawkswood Dr BN27 ..129 C3
Hawkswood Rd BN27 ..129 C3
Hawth Cl BN25 ....180 C4
Hawth Cres BN25 .....180 C4
Hawth Gr BN25 ....180 C4
Hawth Hill BN25 ......180 C5
Hawth Park Rd BN25 ..180 C4
Hawth Pl BN25 ....180 C4
Hawth Rise BN25 .....180 C5
Hawth Valley Ct 1
  BN25 ....180 C4
Hawth Way BN25 .....180 D4
Hawthorn Ave TN39 ...156 D3
Hawthorn Bank BN2 ..143 F4
Hawthorn Cl
  Burgess Hill RH15 .....73 D5
  Saltdean BN2 ....177 C6
Hawthorn Cres BN26 ..173 B6
Hawthorn Pl RH16 ......50 C2
Hawthorn Rd
  Eastbourne BN23 ....185 C2
  Hastings TN35 ....160 D6
Hawthorn Rise TN39 ..179 B7
Hawthorn Way BN41 ..141 A3
Hawthorn Wlk TN2 .....8 E8
Hawthorne Cl TN21 .....82 B6
Hawthornes The TN31 ..90 B4
Hawthorns The
  Burgess Hill RH15 .....73 A5
  Hailsham BN27 ......152 A7
  The Moor TN18 ....45 F8
Hawthylands Cres BN27 .129 B2
Hawthylands Dr BN27 ..129 B2
Hawthylands Rd BN27 ..129 B2
Haybourne Cl 2 BN2 ..164 E2
Haybourne Rd BN2 ....164 E2
Hayes Cl
  Portslade-by-S BN41 ..162 C8
  Ringmer BN8 ....124 D5
Hayes La TN31 ....91 C5
Hayes Plat TN5 ....67 C5
Hayland Gn BN27 .....129 C1
Hayland Ind Units TN38 .135 F5
Haylink Rd RH16 ......51 B5

Hayreed La BN26 .....151 A1
Haystoun Cl BN22 ....173 C2
Haystoun Ho BN22 ....173 C2
Haystoun Pk BN22 ....173 C2
Hayward Rd BN7 .....123 A3
Haywards Heath Coll
  RH16 ....50 D6
Haywards Heath Sta
  RH16 ....50 E6
Haywards Rd
  Brighton BN1 ....143 A6
  Haywards Heath RH16 ..50 E3
Haywards Villas RH16 ..50 F3
Haywood Way TN35 ...160 C8
Hazel Bank 3 BN2 ....189 C4
Hazel Cl Hove BN41 ...141 C3
  Newhaven BN9 ....179 B7
Hazel Court Sec Sch
  BN23 ....174 A3
Hazel Ct TN35 ....136 F6
Hazel Gr Burgess Hill RH15 .73 B1
  Eastbourne BN23 ....173 A3
Hazelbank TN3 ....6 F3
Hazeldene BN25 ......181 B3
Hazeldene Meads BN1 .142 D3
Hazelgrove 5 BN26 .....148 F7
Hazelgrove Gdns 8
  RH16 ....50 E4
Hazelholt BN41 ....140 F3
Hazelwood BN41 .....142 D3
Hazelwood Ave BN22 .173 D4
Hazelwood Cl
  Bexhill TN39 ....156 C3
  Royal Tunbridge Wells TN2 ..8 F8
Hazelwood Cotts TN5 ...31 D1
Hazelwood Gdns TN37 .136 D5
Hazleden Cross RH19 ...10 B6
Headland Ave BN25 ...181 A3
Headland Cl BN10 ....178 E7
Headway Ct TN4 ....7 B4
Heansill La TN18 ....45 E8
Heasewood RH16 ......50 C3
Heath Cl 9 RH16 ......50 C4
Heath Ct RH16 ....50 C5
Heath Hill Ave BN2 ...144 A2
Heath Rd RH16 ....50 C5
Heath Sq RH16 ....50 D5
Heath Stables BN27 ...123 A1
Heathcote Dr RH19 ....1 C2
Heathdown Cl BN10 ...167 D2
Heather Bank BN25 ....50 C5
Heather Cl BN23 ......174 B3
Heather Ct 8 BN1 ....163 E6
Heather Way TN35 ....138 F4
Heather Wlk TN6 ....26 D1
Heatherdune Rd TN39 .157 A5
Heathfield Ave BN2 ...177 D6
Heathfield Cl TN34 ....136 F5
Heathfield Com Coll
  TN21 ....82 E7
Heathfield Cres BN41 ..140 F3
Heathfield Dr BN41 ...140 F4
Heathfield Gdns TN32 ..64 B3
Heathfield L Ctr TN21 ..82 E7
Heathfield Rd BN25 ...180 F3
Heathfields TN2 ....8 D4
Heathlands TN35 .....114 E3
Heathy Brow BN10 ....167 B1
Heavegate Rd TN6 .....37 C8
Heaven Farm* RH17 ...34 B1
Hebrides Wlk BN13 ...185 E7
Hectors La RH19 ....11 C5
Hedge Barton Trailer Pk
  TN3 ....5 F5
Heighton Cl TN36 ....156 D3
Heighton Cres BN9 ...168 D2
Heighton Rd BN9 ....168 E2
Heights The
  Brighton BN1 ....142 B5
  Hastings TN35 ....160 E8
  8 Haywards Heath RH16 ..50 E4
Helena Cl BN41 ....141 C2
Helena Ct TN38 ......159 B7
Helena Rd BN2 ....144 C1
Helensdene Wlk TN37 .159 D8
Helenswood Sch
  Hastings TN34 ....160 B8
  Hastings TN37 ....136 D6
Helingly Cl BN2 ......164 F5
Hellingly Com Prim Sch
  BN27 ....128 F5
Helvellyn Dr BN23 ....174 C4
Hempstead Gdns TN22 ..78 D7
Hempstead La
  Hailsham BN27 ......128 F1
  Uckfield TN22 ....78 D7
  Uckfield TN22 ....78 E8
Hempstead Rd
  Saltdean BN2 ....177 D7
  Uckfield TN22 ....78 C7
Hempstead Rise TN22 ..78 C7
Hemsley Ho TN1 ....81 F8
Henderson Cl TN34 ...136 F3
Hendon St BN2 ....164 D5
Henfield Cl BN2 ......164 F5
Henfield Rd BN2 ......173 E2
Henfield Way BN3 ....141 F1
Henge Way BN41 .....141 B2
Hengist Cl BN27 .....185 F8
Henleaze BN21 ....164 A1
Henley Cl
  Royal Tunbridge Wells TN2 ..8 C1
  Rye TN31 ....93 A6
Henley Ct TN34 ......164 F4
Henley Rd BN27 .....164 F4
Henley's Hill BN27 ...131 F7

Henry Burt Way RH15 ..72 E1
Henry Terr 3 TN34 ...160 B4
Henwood Green Rd TN2 ..9 B6
Henwoods Cres TN2 ....9 D6
Henwoods Mount TN2 ...9 E6
Herbert Rd BN2 ......142 F2
Herbrand Wlk TN39 ...156 A1
Hereford Ct
  3 Brighton BN2 .....189 C2
  4 Eastbourne BN23 ..174 E1
  5 Hove BN3 ....163 C7
Hereford St BN2 .....164 C5
Hereward Rd BN23 ...185 F8
Hereward Way BN7 ...190 B4
Hermitage La RH19 ....10 F8
Hermitage Rd RH19 ....1 D3
Hermitage The TN34 ..159 E8
Herne Down TN6 ......38 A7
Herne Jun Sch TN6 ....37 F8
Herne Rd TN6 ....37 F8
Heron Cl
  Eastbourne BN23 ....174 C2
  St Leonards TN38 ...158 E8
Heron Ct RH16 ....78 D5
Heron Ct BN27 ....152 D7
Heron Pl RH19 ....10 F8
Heron Ridge BN26 ....173 B6
Heron's Tye BN6 ....97 F3
Herons Dale Sch BN43 .140 C1
Herons The BN43 .....161 A8
Herons Way
  Golden Cross BN27 ..127 C4
  Pembury TN2 ....9 E8
Heronsdale Rd BN2 ...165 F8
Heronyte Dr RH19 .....11 A8
Heronytye Ho RH19 ...10 F7
Herring's Rd TN21,TN33 .109 F8
Herstmonceux Castle Gdns*
  BN27 ....131 A1
Herstmonceux CE Prim Sch
  BN27 ....130 E6
Hertford Ct TN38 ....136 A4
Hertford Int Sch BN1 ..143 B2
Hertford Jun Sch BN1 .143 C2
Hertford Rd BN1 .....143 B2
Heskett Pk TN2 ....9 E6
Hestings Plat 2 TN34 .160 B4
Heston Ave BN1 ......142 F7
Hever Cl BN43 ....174 D2
Hever Cres TN39 .....156 F5
Heyworth Cl BN2 ....165 F8
Heyworth Prim Sch RH16 .50 F4
Heyworth Ride RH16 ...50 C4
Hickling Cl BN23 .....174 B4
Hickman Way TN34 ...136 D4
Hickman's Cl RH16 ....51 B8
Hickman's La RH16 ....51 A8
Hidden Spring Vineyard &
  Orch* TN21 ....107 B8
Hide Hollow BN23 ....174 D3
Higglers Cl TN22 ......56 C3
High Bank TN35 ......160 C7
High Bank Cl TN35 ...160 C6
High Beach Ho BN25 ..180 C3
High Beech Ct TN37 ..135 F6
High Beech Country Club
  (Chalet Pk) The TN37 .135 F6
High Beech La RH16 ...50 F8
High Beeches TN38 ....50 B6
High Branches TN39 ..156 E4
High Broom La TN6 ....37 E7
High Broom Rd TN6 ...37 F7
High Brooms Ind Pk TN2 ..8 C8
High Brooms Rd TN4 ...8 C7
High Brooms Sta TN4 ...8 C7
High Cl East Dean BN20 .183 C2
  Portslade-by-S BN41 ..141 A1
High Cross Fields TN6 ..25 F3
High Fords TN36 ......116 E5
High Fords Cl TN36 ...116 E5
High Hatch La BN6 .....72 B4
High Hurst Cl BN8 .....76 D7
High Hurstwood CE Prim Sch
  TN22 ....37 A1
High Mdw TN31 ....67 B7
High Park Ave TN3 ....141 E3
High Park Cl TN31 .....67 A7
High Point RH16 ....51 A3
High Rocks* TN3 ....7 B1
High Rocks La TN3,TN4 ..7 C1
High Rocks Sta* TN3 ...7 B1
High St Alfriston BN26 .171 A2
  Barcombe Cross BN8 .101 E4
  Battle TN33 ....135 D5
  Bexhill TN40 ....157 D5
  Blackboys TN22 ....80 A6
  Brighton BN2 ....189 C2
  Burwash TN19 ....62 A6
  Buxted TN22 ....56 C3
  Cowden TN8 ....4 B5
  Crowborough TN6 .....25 F3
  Ditchling BN6 ....98 D3
  East Grinstead RH19 ..10 F8
  East Hoathly BN8 ....105 A5
  Eastbourne BN21 ....184 E3
  Etchingham TN19 .....44 C1
  Flimwell TN5 ....33 C2
  Frant TN3 ....17 C4
  Hailsham BN27 ......152 C8
  Hartfield TN7 ....14 B2
  Hastings TN34 ....160 B4
  Heathfield TN21 ......82 A8
  Horam TN21 ....106 F8
  Hurstpierpoint BN6 ....97 A5
  Lamberhurst TN3 ......20 B5
  Lewes BN7 ....190 A2

High St continued
  Lindfield RH16 ....51 B8
  Maresfield TN22 ......55 B4
  Mayfield TN20 ....40 B2
  Newhaven BN9 ....179 C7
  Newick BN8 ....76 D7
  Ninfield TN33 ....133 A6
  Nutley TN22 ....35 C3
  Pembury TN2 ....9 C6
  Pevensey BN24 ......175 B6
  Polegate BN26 ....173 A6
  Portslade-by-S BN41 ..141 A1
  Robertsbridge TN32 ...64 B4
  Rotherfield TN6 ....39 B8
  Rottingdean BN2 .....165 F1
  Royal Tunbridge Wells TN1 ..8 A2
  Rye TN31 ....93 C5
  Seaford BN25 ....180 E2
  Ticehurst TN5 ....31 C1
  Uckfield TN22 ....78 C6
  Wadhurst TN5 ....29 F4
  Westham BN24 ....175 A6
  Winchelsea TN36 ....117 F7
High St (School Hill)
  TN22 ....55 B4
High Trees
  Eastbourne BN21 ....184 E5
  Heathfield TN21 ......82 B8
High Wickham TN35 ..160 B5
High Woods La TN3 ....9 B3
Higham Gdns TN35 ...138 A8
Higham La TN31 ......67 A7
Highbank BN1 ....142 E7
Highbridge La BN7 ...100 B4
Highbrook Cl TN34 ...143 D3
Highcliff Ct BN27 ....177 A5
Highcliffe BN20 ......188 D7
Highcroft Cres TN21 ...82 A7
Highcroft Lodge BN1 ..163 E8
Highcroft Mews BN1 ..142 D1
Highcroft Rd RH19 ....21 A6
Highcroft Villas BN1 ..163 E8
Highden 2 BN2 ......164 C6
Highden Cl BN42 .....140 D1
Highdown Cl BN42 ...140 F1
Highdown Cotts TN17 ..20 F3
Highdown Ct 3 BN1 ..142 E3
Highdown Rd
  Hove BN1,BN3 ....163 E7
  Lewes BN7 ....123 A2
Highfield Cl TN2 ....9 D6
Highfield Cres BN1 ...143 A5
Highfield Ct 7 RH16 ...50 E4
Highfield Dr
  Hurstpierpoint BN6 ....97 C5
  St Leonards TN38 ....135 D3
Highfield Gdns TN39 ..157 C2
Highfield Ind Est N
  BN23 ....174 A1
Highfield Ind Est S
  BN23 ....174 A1
Highfield Jun Sch BN23 .174 A1
Highfield Rd
  East Grinstead RH19 ...1 D3
  Horam TN21 ....106 F7
  Royal Tunbridge Wells TN4 ..8 C7
Highfields Brighton BN1 .143 E5
  Burwash TN19 ....60 A6
  Forest Row RH18 ......11 F2
  Horsted Keynes RH17 ..33 C4
  Rye TN31 ....93 B7
Highgate Flats TN6 ....27 B1
Highgate Rd RH18 ....11 F1
Highgate Works RH18 ..11 E1
Highgrove Battle TN33 .112 B4
  Royal Tunbridge Wells TN2 ..17 A8
Highland Ave TN6 .....50 E4
Highland Grange TN6 ..25 E3
Highland Lodge BN21 .184 F4
Highland Rd RH16 .....50 F3
Highlands TN2 ....8 D2
Highlands Ave TN22 ...78 D4
Highlands Cl
  Bexhill TN39 ....156 F7
  Crowborough TN6 .....25 E3
  Keymer BN6 ....98 A3
Highlands Ct TN6 .....25 E3
Highlands Dr
  Burgess Hill RH15 .....73 A4
  St Leonards TN38 ...159 B7
Highlands Gdns TN38 .159 B7
Highlands Mews 2
  TN38 ....159 B6
Highlands Rd
  Portslade-by-S BN41 ..141 B1
  Seaford BN25 ....180 F3
Highlands The
  Bexhill TN39 ....156 F7
  Cuckfield RH17 ....50 A8
Highleigh 3 BN2 TN17 .136 C5
Highleigh BN2 ....189 C3
Highsted Pk RH10 ....162 E2
Highview Ave N BN1 ..142 E6
Highview Ave S BN1 ..142 E6
Highview Cl
  St Leonards TN38 ...135 D5
  Windmill Hill BN27 ...131 B5
Highview Ct BN22 .....78 C6
Highview La TN22 .....78 D4
Highview Rd
  Brighton BN1 ....142 E6
  Broad Oak TN21 ......59 E1
  Telscombe Cliffs BN10 .177 F4
Highview Way BN1 ...142 E6

Highwater View TN37 ...135 F7
Highway CI BN2 ....143 D2
Highway The
  Brighton BN2 ....143 D3
  Newhaven BN10,BN9 ...179 A6
Highways BN41 ....141 B2
Highwoods Ave TN39 ...156 C6
Highwoods Ct TN39 ....156 E5
Hiham Bglws TN36 .....117 E7
Hiham Gn TN36 ....117 E7
Hilary CI BN26 ....172 F5
Hilary Lodge ③ BN2 ...164 C5
Hilbert CI TN2 ....8 C5
Hilbert Rd TN2 ....8 C5
Hilders Farm CI TN6 ....26 B1
Hilgrove Rd BN2 ....177 D7
Hill Brow BN3 ....142 B3
Hill CI TN6 ....25 E1
Hill Crest
  Dormans Park RH19 ......1 E6
  Royal Tunbridge Wells TN4 ..8 B8
Hill Crest Rd BN9 .....179 C6
Hill Crest Rd BN9 .....179 D6
Hill Dr BN3 ....142 B3
Hill Mead TN22 ....35 C4
Hill Rd Eastbourne BN20 184 B5
  Fairlight TN35 ....138 C4
  Lewes BN2 ....123 B2
  Newhaven BN9 ....168 F2
  Saltdean BN2 ....177 B5
Hill Rise Newhaven BN9 168 F2
  Seaford BN25 ....180 C5
Hill Side BN9 ....179 D7
Hill St Hastings TN34 ...160 A4
  Royal Tunbridge Wells TN1 ..8 B5
Hill Top BN1 ....142 B5
Hill Top Way BN1 ......179 B6
Hill View RH18 ....11 F1
Hill View Rd TN4 ....7 C4
Hillary CI RH19 ....2 A3
Hillbank CI BN41 ......140 F3
Hillborough CI TN39 ...156 D4
Hillbrow (Brighton Univ)
  BN20 ....184 E1
Hillbrow Rd BN1 ....142 D4
Hillbrow Gdns TN5 ......31 D1
Hillcrest Brighton BN1 ..142 C5
  Horsted Keynes RH17 ...33 C5
  Rye TN31 ....93 B7
Hillcrest Ave TN39 ....157 A6
Hillcrest CI RH17 ....51 F3
Hillcrest Ct BN1 ....142 C5
Hillcrest Dr TN2 ....8 D7
Hillcrest La TN31 ....51 F3
Hillcrest Sch TN35 ....137 E5
Hillcroft BN41 ....140 F2
Hillgarth TN4 ....8 A8
Hillman CI BN7 ....190 C2
Hillrise TN6 ....26 B2
Hillside Brighton BN2 ..143 E2
  ⑥ Crowborough TN6 ....37 F8
  Forest Row RH18 ....11 E3
  Friston BN20 ....183 B1
  Mayfield TN20 ....78 D1
  Shoreham-by-S BN41 ...141 C1
  Southwick BN42 ....140 F1
Hillside Ave BN25 .....181 C5
Hillside CI RH19 ....1 E3
Hillside Cotts TN5 ......30 B8
Hillside Dr TN21 ......106 F7
Hillside Rd Bexhill TN40 .157 C5
  Hastings TN34 ....136 E3
Hillside Sch BN41 .....141 B2
Hillside Way
  Brighton BN2 ....143 E2
  Brighton,Westdene BN1 ..142 C4
Hilltop Dr TN31 ....93 B7
Hillview Ho BN9 ....179 D6
Hillview Rd BN2 ....165 B8
Hillyfield BN7 ....146 B8
Hillyglen CI TN34 .....159 E8
Hilton Ct ⑪ RH16 ......50 E4
Hindleap Warren Outdoor
  Education Ctr RH18 ....22 D5
Hindover Cres BN25 ...181 A4
Hindover Rd BN25 .....181 A4
Hinton CI BN1 ....143 C2
Hippodrome BN1 ....189 A2
Hither Chantlers TN3 ...7 A2
Hoad Rd BN22 ....185 B4
Hoad's Wood Rd TN34 .160 A7
Hoadleys La TN6 ....25 D5
Hoadswood Cross TN21 ..84 B2
Hoath Hill TN32 ....87 C5
Hoathdown Ave BN9 ...179 A7
Hobart Quay BN23 .....175 A2
Hobbs CI TN31 ....68 C5
Hobbs La TN31 ....68 D6
Hoblands RH16 ....51 B4
Hobney Rise BN24 .....174 F5
Hockington La BN20 ...173 B1
Hodcombe CI BN23 ....174 B4
Hoddern Ave BN10 ....178 B8
Hoddern Jun Sch BN10 178 B8
Hodshrove La BN2 .....143 E3
Hodshrove PI BN2 .....143 E3
Hodshrove Rd BN2 ....143 E3
Hoe The TN37 ....136 B6
Hog Hole La TN3 ....19 F2
Hogarth Ho TN38 ......159 A8
Hogarth Rd
  Eastbourne BN23 ......174 D1
  Hove BN3 ....162 F7
Hogs Edge BN2 ....144 A2
Hogtrough La TN36 ....117 E7

Holbrook ⑱ BN2 ....164 F5
Holbrook CI BN20 .....188 E8
Holden Park Rd TN4 ......8 A8
Holdings The
  Kingston near Lewes BN7 145 F5
  Upper Wellingham BN8 ..124 B7
Hole Farm CI TN34 ....136 E2
Hollamby Pk BN27 .....152 D7
Holland Ave TN39 .....156 C4
Holland Mews BN3 ....163 D5
Holland Rd BN3 ....163 D6
Holland St BN2 ....189 C3
Hollands Way RH19 ......2 A4
Hollier's Hill TN40 .....157 C6
Hollies The TN20 ....40 A2
Hollin CI TN4 ....7 F4
Hollingbourne Ct ⑧
  BN2 ....164 E4
Hollingbury Copse BN1 143 B2
Hollingbury Cres BN1 .143 B2
Hollingbury Ind Est
  BN1 ....143 C7
Hollingbury Park Ave
  BN1 ....143 A2
Hollingbury PI BN1 ....143 B2
Hollingbury Rd BN1 ...143 B1
Hollingbury Rise BN1 .143 B2
Hollingbury Rise W
  BN1 ....143 A3
Hollingbury Terr BN1 ..143 A2
Hollingdean La BN1 ...164 B8
Hollingdean Rd BN2 ...164 B8
Hollingdean St BN1 ...143 B1
Hollingdean Terr BN1 .143 B2
Hollinghurst CI TN37 ..136 B5
Hollinghurst Rd TN37 .136 B4
Hollington Ct TN38 ...159 A8
Hollington Old La TN38 136 A4
Hollington Park CI
  TN38 ....136 A1
Hollington Park Rd
  TN38 ....136 A1
Hollington Prim Sch
  TN38 ....136 A1
Hollow La Blackboys TN22 .80 B4
  Dormansland RH19,RH7 ...2 D6
  East Hoathly BN8 ......105 B6
  Rushlake Green TN21 ...82 A1
Holly Bank ③ BN2 ....189 C5
Holly Bank Ct TN6 .....26 B2
Holly CI Bexhill TN39 ..156 C6
  Brighton BN1 ....142 E3
  Hailsham BN27 ....152 B6
  Heathfield TN21 ....82 A6
Holly Ct TN6 ....25 E2
Holly Dr TN31 ....82 A6
Holly PI BN22 ....173 E3
Holly Rd RH16 ....50 E5
Hollybank Gdns TN38 .136 B1
Hollycroft BN7 ....100 A3
Hollydene Rd TN5 ......29 F6
Hollyshaw TN2 ....8 C2
Hollyshaw CI TN2 ....8 C2
Hollywood Ct RH16 .....50 E5
Holm Ho RH15 ....72 F3
Holm Oak CI TN39 ....156 C6
Holmbush CI
  Haywards Heath RH16 ..50 E2
  Shoreham-by-S BN43 ..140 D2
Holmbush Ct ⑧ BN43 .161 C8
Holmbush Rd BN43 ...140 C1
Holmbush Fst Sch
  TN39 ....156 A8
Holmes Hill BN8 ....127 C6
Holmesdale CI TN5 .....29 E5
Holmesdale Ct TN6 ...159 E8
Holmesdale Gdns TN5 ..159 E7
Holmesdale Rd
  Bexhill TN39 ....157 A4
  Burgess Hill RH15 ......73 C3
Holmewood House Sch
  TN3 ....7 A2
Holmewood Rd TN4 .....8 C7
Holmewood Ridge TN3 ..6 F3
Holmhurst CI TN4 ....7 F4
Holmhurst TN37 ....136 B5
Holmhurst St Mary
  TN37 ....136 C6
Holms CI TN21 ....81 F6
Holmstead TN3 ....189 C4
Homwood Ct BN46 .....9 F7
Holt Lodge BN42 ......189 C4
Holt The Burgess Hill RH15 .73 C2
  Hailsham BN27 ....152 A6
  Seaford BN25 ....180 F5
Holters Way BN25 .....180 F5
Holton Hill BN2 ....165 E7
Holton Rd BN2 ....165 B8
Holtye Ave RH19 ....2 A3
Holtye PI RH19 ....2 B3
Holtye Rd RH19 ....2 B3
Holy Cross CE Prim Sch
  TN2 ....8 C2
Holyhead CI BN27 .....129 A1
Holyrood RH19 ....11 A8
Holywell CI BN20 .....188 E7
Holywell Rd BN20 .....188 E7
Holywell Way BN27 ...152 B7
Home Farm Bsns Ctr
  BN1 ....143 D3
Home Farm Ct Frant TN3 .17 C4

Home Farm Ct continued
  Horsted Keynes RH17 ...33 C5
Home Farm La TN7 ......3 B8
Home Farm Rd BN1,BN2 .143 D3
Home Platt RH19 ....21 A6
Home Rd BN1 ....142 E1
Homebush Ave
  Saltdean BN2 ....177 D5
  Saltdean BN7 ....177 F7
Homecoast Ho RH17 ...178 B7
Homedane Ho ④ TN34 .159 F7
Homedrive Ho BN3 ....163 C8
Homefield CI BN25 ....180 F4
Homefield Rd BN25 ...180 F4
Homegate Rd BN3 .....184 F3
Homeglade Ho BN20 ..188 E8
Homehill Ho ⑦ TN40 .157 C4
Homeladch Ho BN21 ...185 A3
Homelawn BN3 ....157 E4
Homeleigh BN1 ....142 E5
Homeridge BN2 ....177 D5
Homeshore Ho BN25 ..181 A3
Homestall Rd RH19 .....11 E8
Homestead La RH15 ....73 C6
Homestead The TN13 ...2 C8
Homesmye Ho BN25 ...180 C3
Homewarr Ho ④ TN40 .157 E4
Homewood CI BN22 ...185 B6
Homewood Rd TN3 ......6 F3
Homoeopathic Hospl TN1 .8 A3
Honey Croft BN3 ......141 D4
Honey La BN8 ....149 D7
Honeycrag CI BN26 ...173 A7
Honeysuckle CI
  Eastbourne BN23 ......174 B3
  Hailsham BN27 ....152 B5
  St Leonards TN38 ......136 D5
Honeysuckle La BN27 ..127 B3
Honeyway CI BN26 ....172 F3
Honies Ct TN39 ....156 C6
Hoo Gdns BN20 ....173 B1
Hoo The BN20 ....173 B1
Hood CI BN23 ....185 E7
Hook Hill TN5 ....31 A6
Hookswood CI TN6 .....26 A3
Hoopers CI BN7 ....190 A4
Hoover CI TN37 ....135 F7
Hope CI BN2 ....36 C2
Hope Cotts BN42 ......161 E8
Hopehouse La TN17,TN18 .47 E7
Hopfield Gdns TN12 ...78 E8
Hopgarden CI TN34 ...159 E8
Hoppers Croft La TN19 ..62 B6
Hopwood Gdns TN4 .....8 A6
Horam Manor Caravan Site
  TN21 ....106 F7
Horam Park CI TN21 ...106 F7
Horebeech La TN21 ....107 A6
Horizon CI
  Portslade-by-S BN41 ..162 B8
  Royal Tunbridge Wells TN4 ..8 B8
Horleigh Green Rd TN20 .39 C1
Horley PI BN2 ....164 E6
Hornbeam TN19 ....62 B7
Hornbeam Ave TN39 ..157 A7
Hornbeams The RH15 ...72 D4
Hornblower Cotts TN19 .44 C1
Hornbuckles CI BN8 ..100 E7
Hornby PI BN2 ....144 A1
Hornby Rd BN2 ....144 A1
Horning CI BN23 ....174 B4
Horns Rd TN18 ....45 D8
Horntye Pk TN37,TN38 .159 D8
Horntye Rd TN37 ......136 C1
Horsa CI BN23 ....185 E8
Horsegrove Ave TN5 ....31 F1
Horsegrove La TN6 .....39 B8
Horseshoe CI TN38 ...136 B2
Horseshoe La TN31 .....68 A1
Horsewalk BN27,TN33 ..134 F7
Horsfield Rd BN7 ......123 B3
Horsgate Ho BN1 ......50 A8
Horsgate Rd TN38 ......50 A6
Horsham Ave BN10 ...178 C7
Horsham Ave N BN10 .178 C8
Horsham CI BN2 ....164 F6
Horsted Ho ⑤ RH16 ...50 D7
Horsted Keynes Ind Pk
  RH17 ....33 B7
Horsted Keynes Sta
  RH17 ....33 A7
Horsted La Danehill RH17 .34 A4
  Isfield TN22 ....102 F7
  Sharpthorne RH19 ......21 B3
Horsted Pond La TN22 ..78 A3
Horsted Square Ind Est
  TN22 ....78 A6
Horsye Rd BN2 ....185 B7
Horton Rd BN1 ....143 B1
Hoskins PI RH19 ....2 A4
Hosmers Field TN6 .....39 D8
Houghton Green La
  TN31 ....70 C2
Houghton La TN31 ......70 C3
Houndean CI BN7 .....146 A8
Houndean Rise BN7 ..145 F8
Hova Villas BN3 ....163 B6
Hove Bsns Ctr BN3 ...163 B6
Hove Ent Ctr BN41 ...162 C6
Hove General Hospl
  BN3 ....163 A7
Hove Mus & Art Gall*
  BN3 ....163 A6
Hove Nuffield Hospl
  BN3 ....162 F7

Hove Park Gdns
  Hove BN3 ....142 B1
  Hove BN3 ....163 B8
Hove Park Rd BN3 ....142 C1
Hove Park Sch & Sixth Form
  Ctr (Upper) BN3 ......142 A1
Hove Park Sch (Lower)
  BN3 ....141 D2
Hove Park Villas BN3 .142 C1
Hove Park Way BN3 ..142 C1
Hove St BN3 ....163 A6
Hove Sta BN3 ....163 B8
Hove Tech Ctr ⑪ BN3 .163 A8
Hovedene BN3 ....163 C7
How's CI TN31 ....90 B5
Howard Ave RH15 ......72 E4
Howard CI BN27 ....152 D6
Howard Ct Hove BN3 ..163 C7
  Peacehaven BN10 ......178 B7
Howard Gdns TN2 ....8 A1
Howard Ho Bexhill TN39 .156 E4
  ⑪ Eastbourne BN21 ....185 A3
  Peacehaven BN10 ......167 D1
Howard PI BN1 ....189 A4
Howard Rd BN2 ....164 C2
Howard Sg BN21 ......185 A2
Howard Terr BN1 ......189 A4
Howards Cres TN39 ...156 C4
Howbourne La TN22 ....56 E5
Howes Cotts TN18 .....45 F8
Howey CI BN9 ....168 F1
Howland CI ④ BN23 ..175 A1
Howlett CI TN38 ....135 F4
Howlett Dr BN27 ......129 B2
Howletts CI BN22 .....173 F1
Hoyle Rd BN31 ....178 C7
Hudson CI BN23 ......185 G7
Hudson Ct BN22 ....173 F1
Huggett's La BN22 ....173 B3
Hughenden Ct ② TN34 .136 F2
Hughenden PI ⑪ TN34 .136 F2
Hughenden Rd TN34 ..160 A6
Hughes Rd BN2 ....164 B8
Hughes Way TN38 ......78 C8
Huglets La TN31 ....83 A7
Humboldt Ct TN2 ....8 D5
Humphrey Lodge RH15 .73 D3
Humphrey's Gap BN43 .161 A7
Hundred Acre La BN6,
  RH17 ....74 B2
Hundredhouse La TN31 .90 F4
Hungershall Park TN4 ...7 E1
Hungershall Pk TN4 ....7 E2
Hunloke Ave BN22 ....185 B6
Hunston CI BN2 ....165 F7
Hunt's Gate TN7 ....52 E3
Hunters Way
  Royal Tunbridge Wells TN2 ..7 F1
  Uckfield TN22 ....102 B3
Hunting CI TN40 ......157 C5
Huntingdon Ho TN6 .....25 F1
Huntingdon Way RH15 .73 D5
Huntington Ct BN7 .....89 D8
Huntington Dr BN7 ...190 C2
Huntley Mill Rd TN5 ...31 E3
Huntleys Pk TN4 ....7 E2
Hurdis Rd BN25 ....180 A6
Hurrell Rd TN34 ....160 B6
Hurst Cres BN41 ......162 B8
Hurst Ct BN21 ....142 D1
Hurst Farm Ho RH19 ...10 D7
Hurst Green CE Sch
  TN19 ....45 A3
Hurst Hill BN1 ....143 C5
Hurst La
  Eastbourne BN2 ....184 D4
  Sedlescombe TN33 ......88 F3
  Windmill Hill BN27 .....131 B5
Hurst Rd
  Eastbourne BN22 ......184 D5
  Hassocks BN6 ....97 D4
Hurst Shaw TN21 .....107 C8
Hurst The TN2 ....8 E7
Hurst Way TN35 ......137 A6
Hurst Wickham CI BN6 .97 C5
Hurstfield CI RH17 ....51 A2
Hurstpierpoint Coll BN6 .97 B8
Hurstwood ② BN2 ....164 F5
Hurstwood CI BN10 ...158 B5
Hurstwood La
  Haywards Heath RH17 ..51 A2
  Royal Tunbridge Wells TN4 ..7 F3
  Sharpthorne RH17,RH19 ..21 D1
Hurstwood Pk TN4 ......7 F3
Hurstwood Rd TN22 ....56 A6
Hurtis Hill TN6 ....37 E7
Hutton Rd BN1 ....143 B3
Hyde CI The BN2 ......164 F8
Hyde CI BN25 ....145 E5
Hyde Gdns BN21 ......185 B2
Hyde Rd BN21 ....185 B2
Hyde Tynings CI BN20 188 D8
Hydehurst CI TN6 ......25 F1
Hydney St BN22 ....185 C5
Hydneye The BN22 ....173 F1
Hylands Yd ⑫ TN31 ....93 B5
Hythe Ave BN25 ......188 E8
Hyperion Ave BN26 ...172 E6
Hythe Ave TN38 ......158 B5
Hythe CI Polegate BN26 .172 F3
  Seaford BN25 ....181 C5
Hythe Cres BN25 .....181 C5
Hythe Rd BN1 ....143 A2
Hythe View BN25 .....181 C4

I

Ian CI TN40 ....157 F7
Icklesham CE Prim Sch
  TN36 ....116 E6
Icklesham Dr TN38 ....135 D3
Iden CI BN2 ....164 C5
Iden Ct TN34 ....136 D3
Iden Hurst BN6 ....97 A7
Iden Rd TN31 ....70 B3
Iden St BN22 ....174 A2
Iden's La TN21 ....82 D8
Ifield CI BN24 ....177 E6
Ifield Mill CI BN24 ...174 B5
Iford & Kingston CE Prim Sch
  BN7 ....145 F5
Iford CI BN9 ....168 D1
Ilex Ct BN42 ....141 A1
Ilex Gn ⑥ BN27 ......129 B1
Image Cross Flats RH19 .21 A5
Imberhorne Bsns Ctr
  ....1 B3
Imberhorne La RH19 .....1 B3
Imberhorne Lower Sch
  RH19 ....1 D3
Imberhorne Sch RH19 ...1 B3
Imberhorne Way RH19 ...1 B3
Impala Gdns TN4 ....8 B6
Imperial Arc BN1 .....189 A2
Independent Bsns Pk The
  RH19 ....1 B3
Ingham Dr BN1 ....143 D6
Ingleside TN38 ....135 E4
Ingleside Dr TN6 .....25 E3
Inglewood Gdns TN38 .135 E4
Ingram Cres E BN2 ...162 E8
Ingram Cres W BN3 ...162 E8
Ingram Ho ④ RH16 ....50 E3
Ingrams Ave TN39 ....157 C7
Ingrams Ho ④ RH16 ...50 E3
Ingrams Way BN27 ...152 A6
Inholmes CI RH15 ......73 C3
Inholmes Park Rd RH15 .73 B3
Inkerman Terr TN31 ....94 A3
Inkpen La RH18 ....11 F1
Innham's Wood TN6 ...25 E4
Innings Dr BN24 .....175 C4
Innovation Dr RH15 ...72 D2
Insley Ct TN39 ....156 F3
Institute Wlk ④ RH19 ..1 E1
Inverness Rd ④ BN2 ..164 C8
Inwood Cres BN1 .....142 E1
Iona CI BN27 ....129 A3
Iona Way ⑪ RH16 ......50 E4
Irelands La ② TN7 ....123 B1
Ironlatch Ave TN38 ...135 E2
Ironlatch CI TN38 ....135 F2
Ironstone Way TN22 ...78 E7
Ironstones TN3 ....7 B3
Irving Ho TN31 ....93 A7
Isaac's La RH16,RH15 ..50 A2
Isabel Gdns ⑤ BN25 ..180 E5
Isabel Cres BN3 ......162 E8
Isfield Rd Brighton BN1 .143 C2
Isfield Sta* TN22 ....102 C5
Isherwood TN33 ......112 B5
Islingworth PI BN2 ...164 C6
Islingworth Rd BN2 ..164 C7
Ismay Lodge TN39 ...156 D3
Ive Grange TN33 ......132 F5
Iveagh Cres BN9 ......168 D2
Ivor CI BN22 ....144 C1
Ivors La BN8 ....123 B5
Ivory PI BN2 ....189 C3
Ivy Cotts BN8 ....104 C6
Ivy Dene La RH19 .....11 C6
Ivy La TN3 ....18 A5
Ivy Mews ⑧ BN3 .....163 D5
Ivy PI BN1,BN3 ......163 D5
Ivy Terr BN21 ....185 A2
Ivydene Ind Est RH19 ..11 D7
Ivyhouse Employment Area
  TN35 ....160 B8
Ivyhouse La TN35 ....137 B6

J

Jack O'Dandy CI BN21 .184 C7
Jackdaws The TN22 .....78 E4
Jackies La BN8 ....76 B7
Jacklin CI TN7 ....13 D2
Jackson Mews BN9 ....179 C7
Jackson St BN2 ....189 C4
Jacobs Acre TN40 ....157 C5
Jacqueline Du Pre Ct ⑥
  BN2 ....164 C5
Jamaica Way BN23 ...185 F8
James Ave BN27 ......130 E6
James Bradford Almhouses
  RH16 ....50 C8
Jameson Cres TN33 ...136 A3
Jameson Mews ⑨
  TN40 ....157 A4
Jameson Rd TN40 ....157 A4
Jane Murray Way BN6,
  ....72 C3
Janes CI RH15 ....73 C5
Janes La RH15 ....73 D4
Janeston Ct ④ BN3 ...163 C7
Japonica CI BN43 ....140 B1

Jardine Ct TN6 . . . . .25 F2
Jarretts Cl ■ TN31 . . . . . .93 B5
Jarvis Brook Ctry Pk TN6 .38 B8
Jarvis Brook Prim Sch
TN6 .38 C7
Jarvisbrook Cl TN39 . . . .156 D3
Jasmine Cotts TN3 . . . . . . .15 C7
Jasmine Ct Brighton BN1 .142 F5
Hove BN3 . . . . .163 D7
Jasmine Gn ■ BN2 . . . . .129 B1
Jasmine Way TN39 . . . . . .156 F3
Jason Cl BN10 . . . . .178 C2
Jay Cl BN23 . . . . .174 C2
Jay Rd BN10 . . . . .178 E6
Jays The Burgess Hill RH15 .72 E4
Uckfield TN22 . . . . .78 D4
Jefferies RH17 . . . . .33 C4
Jefferies Way TN6 . . . . . . .25 F4
Jefferson Way TN37 . . . . .135 F6
Jeffreys Way TN22 . . . . . . .55 D1
Jellicoe Cl BN23 . . . . .185 F7
Jenner's La TN35 . . . . .137 E6
Jephson Cl BN20 . . . . .188 F8
Jerome Cl BN23 . . . . .174 E2
Jersey St BN2 . . . . .189 C3
Jervis Ave BN23 . . . . .185 E6
Jesmond Cl BN3 . . . . .162 E7
Jesmond Rd BN3 . . . . .162 E7
Jesters RH16 . . . . .73 C7
Jevington Cl TN39 . . . . . .156 D2
Jevington Ct BN43 . . . . . .161 D6
Jevington Dr
Brighton BN2 . . . . .143 D1
Seaford BN25 . . . . .180 D2
Jevington Gdns BN21 . . . .185 A1
Jevington Ho ■ BN21 . . . .185 A1
Jevington Rd BN26 . . . . . .172 D2
Jew St BN1 . . . . .189 B2
Jikack Ind Est BN6 . . . . . . .72 B4
Jireh Ct RH16 . . . . .50 E5
Joan Hughes Ct BN46 . . . .173 A6
Joan Nightingale Ho
RH16 . . . . .50 C4
Jobs La BN6 . . . . .72 A6
Joe's La BN27 . . . . .131 B5
John Dann Cl TN22 . . . . . . .80 A6
John Macadam Way
TN37 . . . . .136 A6
John Spare Ct TN4 . . . . . . .8 A6
John St Brighton BN2 . . . .189 C3
Royal Tunbridge Wells TN4 . . . .8 A5
John Whittle Lodge
BN2 . . . . .143 C1
John's Cross Rd TN32 . . . .87 C8
Johns Cl BN10 . . . . .167 C2
Johnson Bank ■ BN21 . . .164 C7
Johnson Cl TN37 . . . . .135 F6
Johnson Dr RH15 . . . . .73 D3
Johnston Pl ■ BN23 . . . . . .175 A1
Jonas Dr TN5 . . . . .29 E5
Jonas La TN5 . . . . .29 E5
Jordan Cl BN3 . . . . .162 E8
Jordans La BN22 . . . . .173 D3
Jordans La E BN22 . . . . . .173 D3
Jordans La W BN22 . . . . . .173 C3
Jordans The RH15 . . . . .10 E8
Joyce Villas TN21 . . . . . . .106 E5
Jubilee Cl RH16 . . . . .51 A4
Jubilee Cotts ■ TN6 . . . . .37 F8
Jubilee Ct Brighton BN2 . .143 E2
Peacehaven BN10 . . . . .178 B7
Jubilee Gdns BN25 . . . . . .181 A5
Jubilee Ho
Eastbourne BN22 . . . . .185 B4
Newhaven BN9 . . . . .179 C7
Jubilee Rd Bexhill TN39 . .157 A2
Burgess Hill RH15 . . . . .72 E2
Portslade-by-S BN41 . . . . .162 A8
Judge's Terr ■ RH19 . . . . .10 E8
Judges Cl ■ RH19 . . . . . . .10 E8
Juggs Cl BN7 . . . . .146 A5
Juggs Ct BN7 . . . . .146 B8
Juggs Rd BN7 . . . . .146 A7
Julian Ct ■ BN43 . . . . . . .161 C8
Julian Rd BN3 . . . . .163 E7
Junction Cl RH15 . . . . .73 C4
Junction Rd
Bodiam TN18,TN32 . . . . . . .46 A3
Brighton BN1 . . . . .189 A3
Burgess Hill RH15 . . . . .73 B3
Cripp's Corner TN32,TN33 . .88 D5
Eastbourne BN21 . . . . .185 A3
St Leonards TN37 . . . . .136 B7
Staplecross TN32 . . . . .65 C5
Junction St BN21 . . . . .173 B6
Juniper Cl
Portslade-by-S BN41 . . . . .141 B3
Seaford BN25 . . . . .181 C3
St Leonards TN38 . . . . .135 E3
Juniper Ct RH16 . . . . .50 C2
Juniper Wlk BN43 . . . . . . .140 C1
Jury's Gap Coastguard Cotts
TN31 . . . . .95 E1
Jury's Gap Rd TN29 . . . . . .96 F5

K

Kammond Ave BN25 . . . . .181 B5
Kane Hythe Rd TN33 . . . .111 D6
Karenza Ct BN1 . . . . .164 A8
Katherine Way BN25 . . . . .180 D5
Keaton Ho ■ RH16 . . . . . . .50 E6
Keats Cl TN38 . . . . .158 F6
Keats Pl RH19 . . . . .10 E7

Keats Wlk BN23 . . . . .174 E3
Kebbell Lodge ■ BN2 . . . .189 C2
Kedale Rd BN25 . . . . .180 E4
Keel Gdns TN4 . . . . .7 E8
Keere St BN7 . . . . .190 A1
Keith Wlk BN23 . . . . .185 F6
Keld Ave TN22 . . . . .78 D6
Keld Cl TN22 . . . . .78 D6
Keld Dr TN22 . . . . .78 D6
Kelly Rd BN3 . . . . .142 D1
Kelsey Cotts BN8 . . . . .124 E6
Kelsey Cl RH15 . . . . .73 D3
Kemble Ct TN2 . . . . .8 E7
Kemp Ct BN2 . . . . .164 E4
Kemp St BN1 . . . . .189 B3
Kemp Town Pl ■ BN2 . . . .164 D4
Kemps Farm Rd TN6 . . . . .26 B1
Kemps Way TN32 . . . . .64 C5
Kemptown Mews ■
BN2 . . . . .164 E4
Kendal Ct BN9 . . . . .179 E7
Kendal Pk TN4 . . . . .7 E5
Kendal Rd BN3 . . . . .162 F8
Kendall Ct RH16 . . . . .50 F2
Kenilworth Cl BN2 . . . . . .144 A2
Kenilworth Rd TN38 . . . . .159 B7
Kenmure Ave BN1 . . . . . . .143 A7
Kennard Ct RH18 . . . . .11 E3
Kennedy Ave RH19 . . . . . . .1 D3
Kennedy Cl TN21 . . . . .82 B6
Kennedy Ct TN38 . . . . . . .136 B3
Kennedy Rd TN40 . . . . . . .157 E4
Kennedy Way BN9 . . . . . .179 B8
Kennel Cnr BN8 . . . . .124 F6
Kennett Cl BN44 . . . . .156 C4
Kennett Ct BN24 . . . . .174 D4
Kenrith Ct TN34 . . . . .136 E2
Kensington ■ BN23 . . . . . .175 A1
Kensington Cl TN38 . . . . .135 D3
Kensington Gdns BN1 . . . .189 B3
Kensington Pl BN1 . . . . . .189 B3
Kensington St BN1 . . . . . .189 B3
Kent & East Sussex Steam
Rly* TN17 . . . . .49 C5
Kent & Sussex Hospl TN4 . .8 A4
Kent Cl Bexhill TN40 . . . . .158 A5
Shoreham-by-S BN43 . . . . .161 C7
Winchelsea TN36 . . . . .117 E7
Kent Ct BN20 . . . . .184 B6
Kent Fields BN7 . . . . .145 E5
Kent Ho TN1 . . . . .8 C6
Kent La TN32 . . . . .85 F6
Kent Rd
Royal Tunbridge Wells TN4 . .8 A6
St Leonards TN38 . . . . .135 F4
Kent St TN33 . . . . .114 A3
Kent's La BN6 . . . . .99 C7
Kentish Gdns TN2 . . . . .16 E8
Kentish Mans TN1 . . . . . . .8 A2
Kenton Cl TN39 . . . . .157 A5
Kenton Ct ■ TN21 . . . . . .185 A1
Kenton Rd BN3 . . . . .162 D7
Kents Rd RH16 . . . . .50 F3
Kenwards BN1 . . . . .143 D7
Kenwood Cl TN34 . . . . . . .160 B8
Kenya Ct ■ BN1 . . . . .163 E6
Keppel Rd TN34 . . . . .136 C3
Kepplestone BN20 . . . . . . .188 E8
Kerrara Terr BN22 . . . . . . .185 B6
Kerrison Mews ■ BN3 . . .163 D5
Kestrel Cl Bexhill TN40 . . .157 E4
Hove BN3 . . . . .163 D8
Kestrel Ct BN27 . . . . .152 D7
Kestrels The
Shoreham-by-S BN43 . . . . .161 A8
St Leonards TN38 . . . . .135 F5
Ketcham Cnr BN24 . . . . . .174 E6
Ketche's La RH17,TN22 . . .52 E7
Kevin Gdns TN2 . . . . .16 E8
Kew St BN1 . . . . .189 A3
Kewhurst Ave TN39 . . . . .156 D3
Kewhurst Ho TN39 . . . . . .156 E4
Key W BN23 . . . . .185 G8
Keymer Ave BN10 . . . . . . .178 D7
Keymer Cl
Eastbourne BN23 . . . . .174 E1
St Leonards TN38 . . . . .158 E6
Keymer End RH16 . . . . .50 D3
Keymer Gdns RH15 . . . . . .73 B1
Keymer Par ■ BN1 . . . . . .184 E4
Keymer Par RH15 . . . . .73 B2
Keymer Pk BN6 . . . . .98 B3
Keymer Rd Brighton BN1 . .143 A6
Burgess Hill RH15 . . . . .98 B8
Hassocks BN6 . . . . .97 F3
Keysford La RH17 . . . . .33 A4
Kibbles La TN4 . . . . .7 E6
Kidbrook RH16 . . . . .51 B6
Kidbrooke Rise RH18 . . . . .11 E2
Kidd's Hill TN7 . . . . .28 E3
Kilburn Terr ■ BN21 . . . . .185 A3
Kilda St ■ BN21 . . . . .185 A3
Kildare Cl TN34 . . . . .160 B8
Kildare Ct BN20 . . . . .184 D6
Kiln Cl TN22 . . . . .78 D4
Kiln Dr TN31 . . . . .93 B8
Kiln La
Haywards Heath RH16 . . . . .51 B5
Hooe TN33 . . . . .155 B7
Isfield TN22 . . . . .102 E5
Kiln Rd RH16 . . . . .73 C3
Kiln The RH15 . . . . .73 C3
Kilnbank TN2 . . . . .8 B8
Kilnbarn Cl RH16 . . . . .50 D2
Kilnbarn Way RH16 . . . . . .50 D2
Kilnwood La BN8 . . . . .100 E7
Kilpatrick Cl BN23 . . . . . .174 D3

Kimberley Ct TN39 . . . . . .157 C6
Kimberley Rd
Brighton BN2 . . . . .143 D1
Seaford BN25 . . . . .180 C4
Kindersley Ct RH19 . . . . . . .2 B3
Kinfauns Ave BN22 . . . . . .185 B6
King Alfred (Swimming Pool
& Sports Ctr) BN3 . . . . . .163 A5
King Charles Pl ■
BN43 . . . . .161 A6
King Edward Ave TN34 . . .136 C3
King Edward Cl TN34 . . . . .136 C3
King Edward's Par BN20 . .188 F8
King George Ave RH19 . . . .1 C3
King George Rd BN43 . . . .161 D8
King George V Hill TN1 . . . .8 C5
King George VI Ave
BN3 . . . . .142 A3
King George VI Dr BN3 . . .142 A4
King George VI Mans
BN3 . . . . .141 F2
King Henry's Rd BN7 . . . .123 B2
King John Ct ■ TN34 . . . .161 A6
King Offa Prim Sch
TN39 . . . . .157 B5
King Offa Way TN40 . . . . .157 C5
King St Brighton BN1 . . . . .189 B2
East Grinstead RH19 . . . . . .1 E1
King Wood Hill TN31 . . . . .90 A3
King's Ave
Eastbourne BN21 . . . . .184 E5
Newhaven BN9 . . . . .168 E1
Rye TN31 . . . . .93 D6
King's Bank La TN31 . . . . . .68 A3
King's Cl BN21 . . . . .184 E5
King's Dr BN21 . . . . .184 D7
King's Espl BN3 . . . . .163 A5
King's Gdns BN3 . . . . .163 B5
King's Hill Rd TN19 . . . . . .62 B3
King's Manor Com Coll
BN43 . . . . .161 D8
King's Mead La BN25 . . . .180 D4
King's Rd
Brighton BN1,BN3 . . . . . . .163 C5
Haywards Heath RH16 . . . . .50 F3
St Leonards TN37 . . . . .159 C7
Kingfisher Cl TN22 . . . . . . .78 E5
Kingfisher Ct
Hailsham BN27 . . . . .152 D7
Uckfield TN22 . . . . .78 B6
Kingfisher Dr BN23 . . . . . .174 C2
Kingfisher Rise RH19 . . . . .10 F8
Kings Chase TN6 . . . . .25 D3
Kings Cl Bexhill TN40 . . . .157 C4
Eastbourne BN21 . . . . .184 F5
Peacehaven BN10 . . . . .167 B1
Kings Copse ■ RH19 . . . . .10 F8
Kings Ct Brighton BN1 . . . .189 B2
Crowborough TN6 . . . . .25 E2
Kings Ct E ■ BN23 . . . . . .185 F8
Kings Ct S ■ BN23 . . . . . .185 F8
Kings Ct W ■ BN23 . . . . .185 F8
Kings Dr BN6 . . . . .97 F4
Kings Gate
Haywards Heath RH16 . . . . .50 E6
Hove BN3 . . . . .163 C8
Kings Mead Ct BN20 . . . . .188 D7
Kings Mews BN3 . . . . .163 B6
Kings Par BN1 . . . . .143 A2
Kings Pk TN2 . . . . .8 D3
Kings Rd BN42 . . . . .140 E1
Kings Ride
Alfriston BN26 . . . . .170 F3
Burgess Hill RH15 . . . . .73 D1
Seaford BN25 . . . . .180 D4
Kings Toll Rd TN2 . . . . .9 F6
Kings Way RH15 . . . . .73 D2
Kings Well Ct ■ BN25 . . . .180 E2
Kings Wlk ■ TN34 . . . . . .159 F8
Kingsbury Rd BN1 . . . . . . .189 B4
Kingscliff Ave TN39 . . . . .156 D4
Kingscote Lodge BN1 . . . .143 F3
Kingscott Cl TN39 . . . . . . .157 B8
Kingsdale Cl Battle TN33 . .112 F3
St Leonards TN38 . . . . .136 C6
Kingsfield Cl BN42 . . . . . .161 E8
Kingsfield Cotts BN8 . . . . .149 E8
Kingsfold ■ BN2 . . . . .164 F5
Kingsford Cl ■ BN25 . . . . .180 F2
Kingsgate BN27 . . . . .152 D7
Kingsland Rd BN3 . . . . . . .184 F1
Kingsland Cl BN43 . . . . . .161 C7
Kingsley Cl TN37 . . . . .136 A5
Kingsley Rd
Brighton BN1 . . . . .142 D1
Lewes BN7 . . . . .123 B2
Kingsmarsh Cotts TN20 . . .58 B6
Kingsmead BN25 . . . . .180 E5
Kingsmead Cl BN25 . . . . . .180 E4
Kingsmead Way BN25 . . . .180 E4
Kingsmead Wlk BN25 . . . .180 E4
Kingsmere BN1 . . . . .142 E2
Kingsmere Cl ■ BN1 . . . .184 D4
Kingsmere Way BN23 . . . .185 F8
Kingsthorpe Rd BN3 . . . . .162 F8
Kingston Ave BN25 . . . . . .181 A6
Kingston Bay Rd BN43 . . .161 C6
Kingston Broadway
BN43 . . . . .140 D1
Kingston Buci Fst Sch
BN43 . . . . .161 D7
Kingston Cl Brighton BN1 .143 E6
Hove BN3 . . . . .141 D2
Seaford BN25 . . . . .181 B3

Kingston Cl continued
Shoreham-by-S BN43 . . . . .161 C8
Kingston Gn BN43 . . . . . . .161 C8
Kingston Gn BN25 . . . . . . .181 B3
Kingston Ho ■ BN21 . . . .184 F4
Kingston La BN42,BN43 . .161 D7
Kingston Quay ■ BN23 . . .185 F8
Kingston Rd
Eastbourne BN21 . . . . .173 F2
Lewes BN7 . . . . .146 B7
Kingston Ridge BN7 . . . . . .145 D6
Kingston Villas TN21 . . . . .106 E5
Kingston Way
Seaford BN25 . . . . .181 B3
Shoreham-by-S BN43 . . . . .140 D1
Kingsway Hove BN3,BN41 .163 B5
Seaford BN25 . . . . .180 D4
Kingsway Ct Hove BN3 . . .163 C5
Kingsway Ct BN25 . . . . . . .180 D4
Kingswood BN1 . . . . .189 B2
Kingswood Ave TN39 . . . .156 F6
Kingswood Cl TN2 . . . . .8 C3
Kingswood Flats BN2 . . . .189 C2
Kingswood Rd TN2 . . . . . . .8 C3
Kingswood St BN2 . . . . . .189 B2
Kinross Ct ■ BN21 . . . . . .185 A4
Kinsale Ct ■ BN21 . . . . . .185 A4
Kinver La TN40 . . . . .158 A6
Kipling Ave BN2 . . . . .165 E7
Kipling Ct Bexhill TN40 . . .157 C6
■ Hayward's Heath RH16 . .50 D5
Rottingdean BN2 . . . . .177 A5
Kipling Way RH19 . . . . .1 C1
Kipling Wlk ■ BN23 . . . . .174 E2
Kirby Dr BN10 . . . . .167 B8
Kirdford Cl RH15 . . . . .73 C1
Kirk Way BN20 . . . . .184 B5
Kirkdale Rd TN1 . . . . .8 B4
Kirkstall Cl BN22 . . . . .173 E3
Kitchenour La TN31 . . . . . .68 E5
Kite Cl TN38 . . . . .158 E8
Kites Nest Wlk TN39 . . . . .156 B4
Kitilear Ct BN3 . . . . .163 A6
Knelworth Rd TN39 . . . . . .156 F5
Knelle Rd TN32 . . . . .64 A4
Knelle View TN33 . . . . .67 B7
Knepp Cl BN2 . . . . .143 F2
Knight's Ridge TN2 . . . . . . .9 D7
Knights Cl TN2 . . . . .9 D7
Knights Gate Rd BN1 . . . .144 C7
Knights Gdn BN27 . . . . . . .152 B6
Knights Mdw
Battle TN33 . . . . .112 F4
Uckfield TN22 . . . . .78 E8
Knights Pk TN2 . . . . .8 F8
Knights Way TN2 . . . . .8 F8
Knightsbridge Cl TN4 . . . . .7 F5
Knightsbridge Ct TN4 . . . . .7 F5
Knockhatch Adventure Pk*
BN27 . . . . .151 E2
Knole Cl ■ TN40 . . . . .157 D3
Knole Gr RH19 . . . . .1 C3
Knole Rd Bexhill TN40 . . . .157 D3
Rottingdean BN2 . . . . .177 A5
Knoll Bsns Ctr The BN3 . .162 D8
Knoll Cl BN3 . . . . .141 D1
Knoll Cres BN22 . . . . .174 A4
Knoll Pl RH16 . . . . .51 B5
Knoll Rd BN22 . . . . .174 A2
Knoll Rise TN38 . . . . .159 A7
Knowle Cl
Crowborough TN6 . . . . .38 C8
Langton Green TN3 . . . . .6 F3
Knowle Cotts TN3 . . . . .17 E1
Knowle Ct TN38 . . . . .136 B1
Knowle Hill Bodiam TN32 . .65 D8
Mayfield TN20 . . . . .40 A1
Knowle La BN6 . . . . .104 D8
Knowle Pk
Crowborough TN6 . . . . .25 D2
Mayfield TN20 . . . . .40 A1
Knowle Rd TN35 . . . . .138 E5
Knoyle Rd BN1 . . . . .142 D4
Knyveton Ct RH15 . . . . .73 B3
Kylemore BN24 . . . . .175 B6
Kymer Gdns BN6 . . . . .98 A3

L

La Marne Ct TN34 . . . . . . .136 E2
La Senera Pl BN23 . . . . . .175 B1
Laburnum Ave BN3 . . . . . .141 E1
Laburnum Cl TN2 . . . . .8 C7
Laburnum Gn ■ BN27 . . . .129 B1
Laburnum Rd BN1 . . . . . . .143 B3
Laburnum Way RH16 . . . . .51 B4
Laburnum Wlk BN22 . . . . .173 D3
Labyrinth The ■ BN21 . . .185 A2
Lacys Hill BN8 . . . . .147 F8
Ladies Mile Brighton BN1 .143 B7
Withyham TN6,TN7 . . . . . . .14 D4
Ladies Mile Cl BN1 . . . . . .142 F6
Ladies' Mile Ct BN1 . . . . . .142 E6
Ladies' Mile Rd BN1 . . . . .142 F6
Lady Bee Ind Est BN42 . . .161 E6
Lady Oak La TN17,TN18 . . .32 C7
Lady's Gift Rd TN4 . . . . .7 E4
Ladycross Cl BN25 . . . . . . .181 C3
Ladyfern Ct TN2 . . . . .9 D7
Ladymead RH15 . . . . .73 C5
Ladysmith Rd BN2 . . . . . . .164 D8
Lagwood Cl BN6 . . . . .97 F3
Laine Cl BN1 . . . . .142 E4
Laines The TN21 . . . . .170 F3
Lake Dr BN10 . . . . .178 B8
Lake Ho TN39 . . . . .156 E4
Lake House Ct TN39 . . . . .156 D4

Lake Rd TN4 . . . . .7 E4
Lake St TN20,TN6 . . . . .40 D7
Lake View Rd RH19 . . . . . . .1 F5
Lakehurst La TN33 . . . . . . .110 B8
Lakelands Cl BN22 . . . . . .174 A1
Lakelands Dr TN39 . . . . . .156 D4
Lakeman Way TN4 . . . . .8 B7
Lakeside TN2 . . . . .8 E6
Lakeside Ct BN22 . . . . .174 A1
Lakeview ■ BN2 . . . . .164 C5
Laleham Cl
Eastbourne BN21 . . . . .184 E4
St Leonards TN37 . . . . .136 C5
Lamberhurst Rd TN3,
TN12 . . . . .20 C8
Lamberhurst St Mary's CE
Prim Sch TN3 . . . . .20 B6
Lamberhurst Vineyard*
TN3 . . . . .20 A4
Lambert Pl BN2 . . . . .190 B4
Lambert Rd BN23 . . . . .174 E1
Lamberts Cotts TN33 . . . .112 E3
Lamberts Rd TN2 . . . . .8 D8
Lambourn Ave BN24 . . . . .174 A5
Lambourn Cl RH19 . . . . .1 E2
Lambourn Way TN2 . . . . . . .8 D1
Lambourne Cl BN1 . . . . . . .143 C2
Lambourne Rd BN1 . . . . . .143 C2
Lampington Row TN3 . . . . .6 E3
Lampool Cnr TN22 . . . . . . .55 A7
Lampool Rdbt TN22 . . . . . .55 A7
Lanark Ct BN20 . . . . .184 B6
Lancaster Ct
■ Eastbourne BN22 . . . . . .185 B3
■ Hove BN3 . . . . .163 A6
Lancaster Dr RH19 . . . . . . .2 A3
Lancaster House Rd
BN1 . . . . .144 B7
Lancaster Rd
Brighton BN1 . . . . .189 A4
St Leonards TN38 . . . . .135 F5
Lancaster St BN7 . . . . .190 B2
Lancing Cl TN34 . . . . .136 D3
Lancing Ct ■ BN2 . . . . . . .164 C5
Lancing Way BN26 . . . . . .172 F4
Landgate TN31 . . . . .93 C6
Landport Farm Rd BN7 . . .123 A3
Landport Rd Lewes BN7 . .123 B3
Hove BN3 . . . . .141 E1
Landsdown Rd BN25 . . . . .181 C5
Landsdowne Way TN40 . . .157 C4
Landseer Rd BN3 . . . . .163 A8
Lane The Fordcombe TN3 . . .6 C5
Foxhole BN25 . . . . .182 A4
Langdale Cl BN23 . . . . . . .174 C4
Langdale Ct BN3 . . . . .162 F6
Langdale Gdns BN3 . . . . . .162 F6
Langdale Rd BN3 . . . . .162 F6
Langham Cl
Hastings TN34 . . . . .136 F4
Ringmer BN8 . . . . .124 D5
Langham Dr
Hastings TN34 . . . . .136 F4
Robertsbridge TN32 . . . . . .63 F4
Langholm Rd TN3 . . . . .6 F3
Langhurst ■ BN21 . . . . . .164 E4
Langley Cl TN39 . . . . .157 B8
Langley Cres BN2 . . . . . . .144 E1
Langney Gn BN23 . . . . . . .185 E6
Langney Prim Sch BN23 .174 E1
Langney Rd BN21,BN22 . .185 B3
Langney Rise BN23 . . . . . .174 C2
Langney Sh Ctr BN23 . . . .174 C2
Langney Village TN6 . . . . . .37 D8
Langridge Dr
East Grinstead RH19 . . . . . .10 E8
Portslade-by-S BN41 . . . . .141 B3
Langridge La RH16 . . . . . . .51 A5
Langridge Way RH15 . . . . .72 E5
Langridges Cl BN8 . . . . . . .76 C7
Langton Cl TN33 . . . . .112 E4
Langton Green Prim Sch
TN3 . . . . .6 E4
Langton Rd
Rusthall TN3,TN4 . . . . .7 C3
Speldhurst TN3 . . . . .7 A7
Langton Ridge TN3 . . . . . . .7 B3
Langtye La BN26,BN8 . . . .149 E6
Lansdown Pl BN2 . . . . .190 B1
Lansdown Terr ■ TN21 . . .82 A1
Lansdowne Cres BN27 . . . .129 B2
Lansdowne Ct
■ Eastbourne BN21 . . . . . .185 A1
■ Hove BN3 . . . . .163 C6
Lansdowne Dr BN27 . . . . . .129 B2
Lansdowne Gdns BN27 . . .129 B2
Lansdowne Mans ■
BN3 . . . . .163 D6
Lansdowne Mews ■
BN3 . . . . .163 D6
Lansdowne Pl BN3 . . . . . . .163 D6
Lansdowne Rd
Hailsham BN27 . . . . .129 B2
Hove BN1,BN3 . . . . .163 D6
Royal Tunbridge Wells TN1 . .8 B4
Lansdowne Sq ■
■ Hove BN3 . . . . .163 D6
■ Royal Tunbridge Wells
TN1 . . . . .8 B4
Lansdowne St BN3 . . . . . . .163 D6
Lansdowne Way TN7 . . . . .129 B3
Lanthorne Mews
Wells,Calverley Park TN1 . .8 B3
Lapierre Rd BN9 . . . . .179 B7
Lapwing Cl BN23 . . . . .174 C2

Lapwing Ct BN27 ......152 D7
Larch Cl Heathfield TN21 ...82 B5
  St Leonards TN38 .....136 A1
  Woodingdean BN2 ....165 F7
Larch Gdns BN22 .....173 D3
Larch Way RH16 ....51 B4
Larches Ho RH19 ....2 B4
Larches The RH19 ......2 B4
Lark Hill BN3 ....141 E3
Larke Cl BN43 ....161 C7
Larkfield Cl TN38 .....136 A3
Larkfield Way BN1 ....143 A4
Larkhill TN40 ....157 C4
Larkspur Dr BN23 .....174 B3
Larnach Cl TN22 ....78 D8
Lascelles Terr BN21 ...185 A1
Lashbrooks Rd
  Uckfield TN22 ....78 B7
  Uckfield TN22 ....78 B7
Latimer Rd BN22 ......185 C4
Laton Rd TN34 ....136 F2
Laughton Cl BN23 .....174 A4
Laughton Com Prim Sch
  BN8 ....126 C6
Laughton Lodge BN8 ..126 A8
Laughton Rd
  Ringmer BN8 ....125 D6
  Woodingdean BN2 ....165 F8
Laundry La RH17 ....22 D1
Laurel 2 RH16 ....50 D6
Laurel Bank Bexhill TN40 .137 F3
  Royal Tunbridge Wells TN4 ..8 B8
  Wadhurst TN5 ....30 A4
Laurel Cl RH15 ....73 D5
Laurel Dene RH19 ......1 F1
Laurel La TN36 ....116 F5
Laurel Rd TN2 ....8 D7
Laurel Way TN2 ....8 D7
Laurel Wlk TN38 ......135 E3
Laurels The
  1 Brighton BN2 ......189 C5
  11 Crowborough TN6 ..25 F3
  Uckfield TN22 ....78 E8
Lauren Ct TN38 ....158 F7
Lauriston Rd BN1 .....142 E2
Lavant Cl TN39 ....156 C6
Lavant Rd BN24 ....174 B5
Lavender Cl
  Eastbourne BN23 .....174 B3
  Hailsham BN27 ....128 F1
Lavender Gdns TN5 .....31 E1
Lavender Hill BN43 ...140 B1
Lavender Ho BN2 .....189 C1
Lavender Line* TN22 ..102 E8
Lavender St BN2 ......189 C3
Lawes Ave BN9 ....179 C7
Lawn The TN38 ....159 C7
Lawns Ave BN21 ......184 D4
Lawns The
  Eastbourne BN20 .....173 B1
  Eastbourne BN22 .....173 B2
  Eastbourne,Roselands
  BN22 ....185 C5
Lawrence Ct BN22 ....152 C6
Lawrence Ct BN23 ....174 D1
Lawrence Ho TN22 .....78 C7
Lawrence Rd BN3 .....162 F7
Lawrie La RH16 ....51 B5
Laylands Ct BN41 ....162 A7
Laylands Rd BN41 ....162 A7
Lazamby Ct TN38 ....159 B8
Le Brun Rd BN21 .....184 F5
Lea Ave TN31 ....93 A6
Lea Ct BN9 ....179 C8
Lea Rd BN10 ....178 B8
Leach Ct Brighton BN2 .164 C5
  Brighton BN2 ....189 C2
Leacroft RH19 ....1 D2
Leaf Hall Rd 11 BN22 ..185 B3
Leaf Hospl (Univ of Brighton)
  BN21 ....184 F4
Leaf Rd BN21 ....185 A3
Leahurst Court Rd BN1 ..142 E3
Leahurst Ct 1 BN1 ...142 E3
Lealands Cl TN3 ....15 C6
Lealands Dr TN22 ....55 C1
Leamland Wlk BN22 ..185 C4
Lea Cross Small Bsns Ctr
  BN27 ....129 A1
Leas The Burgess Hill RH15 .72 A4
  Peacehaven BN10 ....178 F6
  St Leonards TN38 ....159 A6
  Turner's Green TN5 ...30 A6
Leasam La TN31 ....93 B8
Leasingham Gdns TN39 .157 A5
Ledsham Ave TN37 ...136 B5
Ledsham Cl TN37 .....136 B5
Ledsham Ct TN37 .....136 B5
Ledsham Pk TN37 ....136 B5
Ledsham Way TN37 ...136 B5
Lee Bank BN2 ....189 C3
Lee Rd BN7 ....123 B2
Lee Way BN9 ....179 C8
Lee Ave BN23 ....185 D7
Leeds Cl TN35 ....160 D8
Leeds La TN40 ....58 D6
Leeford Cotts TN33 ...88 A1
Leeves Ct TN21 ....82 A6
Leeves Way TN2 ......82 A6
Leeward Quay 11 BN23 .185 F8
Leggs' La TN3 ....6 F5
Legsheath La RH18,RH19 .21 F8
Leicester Cl 3 BN22 .185 B4
Leicester Dr TN2 ......16 F8
Leicester Rd BN21 ...123 B1
Leicester St BN2 .....189 C1
Leicester Villas BN3 ..162 D7
Leighton Cl TN4 ......8 A7

Leighton Rd
  Horsted Keynes RH17 ..33 C5
  Hove BN3 ....163 A8
Leighton Villas RH17 ..33 B7
Leneda Dr TN2 ....16 E8
Lenham Ave BN2 .....177 B5
Lenham Rd E BN2 ....177 B5
Lenham Rd W BN2 ...177 A5
Lennox Cl BN22 ......184 B5
Lennox Ct TN21 ......82 B8
Lennox Rd Hove BN3 ..162 F8
  Shoreham-by-S BN43 .161 B8
Lennox St BN2 ....189 C2
Leopald Flats TN39 ..157 B4
Leopold Rd Bexhill TN39 .157 B4
  Brighton BN1 ....189 A3
Lepeland BN2 ....129 A1
Lesley Cl TN40 ....157 F7
Leslie Best Ho BN1 ...189 B4
Leslie St BN22 ....185 B4
Letheren Pl BN21 ....184 D3
Leveller End BN8 .....76 D7
Leveller Rd BN8 ......76 D7
Levett Ave BN26 .....173 C6
Levett Cl BN26 ....173 C6
Levett Rd BN26 ......173 C6
Levett Way BN26 .....173 C6
Levetts La TN3 ....46 D1
Lewes Castle* BN7 ..190 A2
Lewes Cl Bexhill TN39 ..157 A6
  Saltdean BN2 ....177 E5
Lewes Cres BN2 ......164 E4
Lewes Ct
  5 Eastbourne BN21 ..184 F4
  Falmer BN1 ....144 A8
  Southwick BN42 .....162 A7
Lewes Heights Sch BN7 .123 B1
Lewes Ho 7 BN21 ....184 F4
Lewes Mews Cl BN7 ..123 B1
Lewes New Sch The
  BN7 ....190 A2
Lewes Rd
  Brighton BN1,BN2 ...143 E3
  Chelwood Gate RH17 ..22 C1
  Danehill RH17 ....34 B3
  Ditchling BN6 ....98 E2
  Eastbourne BN21 ....184 F5
  Forest Row RH18 ....1 E2
  Horsted Keynes RH17 .33 C5
  Isfield TN22 ....102 E6
  Laughton BN8 ....126 A7
  Lindfield RH16 ....51 B7
  Newhaven BN9 ....179 C8
  Polegate BN26 ....172 C6
  Ringmer BN8 ....124 D6
  Scaynes Hill RH17 ...51 D4
  Selmeston BN26 .....149 D2
  Uckfield TN22 ....78 D4
Lewes St BN2 ....189 C3
Lewes Sta BN7 ....190 B1
Lewinscourt TN33 ....112 D5
Lewis Ave TN40 ......158 A5
Lewis Cl BN9 ....168 F2
Lewis Ct 6 BN2 ......164 B7
Lewis Rd TN36 ....136 A3
Lewry Cl BN7 ....179 B7
Lexden Cl BN25 ......181 A4
Lexden Dr BN25 ......181 A5
Lexden Lodge Ind Est
  TN6 ....38 D8
Lexden Rd BN25 .....180 F6
Leybourne Cl BN2 ...144 A1
Leybourne Gdns TN37 .136 C4
Leybourne Par BN2 ..144 A1
Leybourne Rd BN2 ...144 A1
Leyland Rd BN24 ....175 D4
Leylands Pk RH15 ....73 B4
Leylands Rd RH15 ...73 B4
Library Way TN22 ....78 C7
Lichfield Ct 10 BN2 ..164 F5
Lilac Cl BN22 ....173 D3
Lillesden Cotts TN18 .45 E7
Lillywhite Cl RH15 ...72 F5
Limden Cl TN5 ....42 F6
Lime Cl Frant TN3 ...17 B3
  St Leonards TN38 ....136 B1
  Uckfield TN22 ....78 D8
Lime Cross BN27 .....130 F5
Lime Hill Rd TN1 ....8 A4
Lime Tree Ave TN22 ..78 D7
Lime Tree Gr RH16 ...51 C7
Lime Tree Terr TN19 ..62 A6
Lime Way TN21 ......82 B6
Limekiln Ct TN6 .....26 C3
Limes La TN22 ....56 D3
Limes The
  13 Eastbourne BN21 .184 E4
  Felbridge RH19 ....1 A5
Limetree Ave BN22 ..173 D3
Limney Rd BN2 ......164 E7
Limousin Ho BN23 ...185 F8
Linchmere BN2 ......164 F7
Linchmere Ave BN2 ..177 C5
Lincoln Ave BN10 ...178 A3
Lincoln Ave B BN10 .178 A4
Lincoln Cl
  Eastbourne BN20 ....188 C3
  2 St Leonards TN38 .136 A4
Lincoln Cotts BN23 ..189 C3
Lincoln Ct
  Eastbourne BN20 ....188 C3
  Hove BN3 ....163 C8
  Peacehaven BN10 ....178 A3
Lincoln Rd BN41 .....162 B7
Lincoln St BN2 ....189 C1
Lincoln Way TN6 ....38 A8
Lincoln Wood RH16 ..50 C5
Linden Ave RH19 .....1 C2

Linden Chase TN32 ...78 D7
Linden Cl
  Eastbourne BN22 ....173 E2
  Royal Tunbridge Wells TN4 ..8 A2
Linden Ct TN22 ....78 C7
Linden Gdns
  Heathfield TN21 ......81 F6
  Royal Tunbridge Wells TN4 ..7 F1
Linden Gr Hailsham BN27 .129 C3
  Lindfield RH16 ....51 B7
Linden Park Rd TN2 ..8 A2
Linden Rd BN2 ....157 C3
Lindens The 4 BN2 ..189 C4
Lindfield BN41 ....141 A1
Lindfield Ave BN25 ..181 C2
Lindfield Cl BN2 .....177 B6
Lindfield Ct BN1 .....143 C2
Lindfield Dr BN27 ...152 B7
Lindfield Ent Pk RH16 .51 C5
Lindfield Prim Sch RH16 .51 A7
Lindfield Rd BN27 ...152 B7
Lindfield Sch The BN22 .173 D2
Lindon Cl BN20 ......183 B1
Lindsay Cl BN20 .....184 C2
Lingfield Rd RH19 ...1 D3
Link Ho 2 TN6 ....25 F3
Link Rd BN20 ....184 D1
Link The East Dean BN20 .183 C2
  Rye TN31 ....93 A5
Link Way TN2 ....8 A3
Linkden Cotts TN18 ..45 B9
Linkway Eastbourne BN20 .184 B7
  Westham BN24 ......174 E6
Linkway The TN4 ....181 B1
Linley Cl Bexhill TN40 .157 D4
  Hastings TN34 ......160 A7
Linley Dr TN34 ......160 A7
Linnet Cl BN23 ....174 C2
Linnet Gn TN22 ......78 D5
Linosa Ct 17 BN22 ...185 B3
Linthouse Cl BN10 ..167 D2
Linton Cres TN34 ...159 E8
Linton Ct BN23 ......174 C2
Linton Rd Hastings TN34 .159 E8
  Hove BN3 ....163 C8
Lion Hill BN23,BN24 .174 B5
Lion Hill Cotts BN24 .174 A5
Lion La BN21 ....185 B3
Lion Mews 4 Hove BN3 .162 F7
  Uckfield TN22 ....78 D6
Lions Cl BN2 ....164 E5
Lions Dene BN1 .....142 D4
Lions Gdns BN1 .....142 D2
Lions Pl BN25 ....180 F2
Liphook Cl BN1 .....143 C1
Lipscombe Rd TN2 ..8 D6
Liptraps La TN2 ......8 D7
Lismore Rd BN21 ...185 A2
Lister Ave RH19 .....10 A1
Lister Rd BN23 ......174 A1
Litlington Ct 4 BN25 .181 A4
Little Bayham Cotts TN3 .18 F4
Little Bentswood RH16 .50 F5
Little Bentswood Cl
  RH16 ....50 F5
Little Black Hill RH16 .51 B7
Little Common Rd TN39 .156 E5
Little Common Sch
  TN39 ....156 D4
Little Copse Rd TN6 ..97 E4
Little Cranfield Ct RH19 ..1 D1
Little Cres BN2 ......177 B5
Little East St
  Brighton BN1 ....189 B1
  Lewes BN7 ....190 B2
Little Footway TN3 ..6 F3
Little George St BN1 .189 B1
Little Horsted CE Prim Sch
  TN19 ....45 C1
Little Iridge Farm Cotts
  TN19 ....45 C1
Little King St RH19 ..1 E1
Little London Rd 106 F8
Little Mallett TN3 ....6 F3
Little Mount Sion TN1 ..8 A2
Little Paddock
  Crowborough TN6 ...25 E1
  Heathfield TN21 .....82 A6
  Ringmer BN8 ....124 D6
Little Park Cotts TN33 .112 E5
Little Pk TN5 ....29 E5
Little Preston St BN1 .163 E5
Little Ridge Ave TN37 .136 C5
Little Ridge Com Prim Sch
  TN36 ....116 D5
Little Sunnyside TN6 ..25 E1
Little Trogers La TN20 .40 B4
Little Twitten TN3 ...156 C3
Little Western St 1
  BN1 ....163 E5

Littlemead
  Cooksbridge BN8 ....123 A7
Littley TN22 ....35 C3
Littlewood La TN22 ..56 C4
Littleworth Cl BN2 ..165 F7
Living World The*
  BN25 ....181 F4
Livingstone Ho 5 BN3 .163 B7
Livingstone Rd
  Burgess Hill RH15 ...72 F3
  Hove BN3 ....163 B7
Livingstone St BN2 ..164 D5
Lloyd Cl BN2 ....163 C8
Lloyd Rd BN3 ....163 C8
Lockhart Ct RH16 ....50 F2
Locks Cres BN41 ....141 B1
Locks Crs BN41 .....141 B1
Locks Ct BN2 ....161 E7
Locks Hill BN41 .....141 B1
Lockwood Cl BN2 ....165 E7
Lockwood Cres BN2 ..165 E7
Loder Pl BN2 ....142 F2
Loder Rd BN1 ....142 F2
Lodge Ave BN22 ....173 C1
Lodge Cl
  East Grinstead RH19 .1 D1
  Lewes BN7 ....146 A8
  Portslade-by-S BN41 .140 F2
Lodge Hill La BN6 ..98 C4
Lodge La Keymer BN6 .98 A2
  Royal Tunbridge Wells TN4 ..16 A8
Lodge The Brighton BN2 .189 C5
  14 Eastbourne BN21 .185 A2
Lodsworth BN2 .....164 F7
Lodsworth Cl BN2 ..164 F7
Lomaria Ct TN2 .....8 C4
Lomas La TN18 ......47 F5
Lomond Ave BN1 ...143 B7
London Meed Com Prim Sch
  RH15 ....73 A1
London Rd Bexhill TN39 .157 B5
  Brighton BN1 ....189 B4
  Brighton,Withdean BN1 .142 D4
  Burgess Hill RH15 ...72 F3
  Crowborough TN6 ...25 E4
  Danehill RH17 ....34 A4
  East Grinstead RH19 .1 C3
  East Hoathly BN8 ...105 A5
  Flimwell TN5 ....32 D3
  Forest Row RH18 ....11 E4
  Hailsham BN27 ......129 A2
  Hassocks BN6,RH15 ..97 E6
  Hurst Green TN19 ...45 A3
  John's Cross TN33 ..87 D3
  Maresfield TN22 ....56 E4
  Pyecombe BN1,BN45 .119 C4
  Royal Tunbridge Wells,Mount Sion
  TN1 ....80 F8
  St Leonards TN37,TN38 .159 C8
  Uckfield TN22 ....55 D2
London Road (Brighton) Sta
  BN1 ....189 B4
London Terr BN1 ....189 B4
Loney Ct 1 BN43 ...161 C8
Long Acre CC BN21 ..184 D5
Long Ave TN40 .....158 A6
Long Barn Motor Mus*
  TN21 ....80 F8
Long Beach Cl BN23 .175 B1
Long Beach Mews BN23 .175 B1
Long Beach View BN23 .175 B1
Long Hos TN33 ......85 D5
Long La TN33 ....88 E1
Long Man of Wilmington
  The* BN26 ....171 E3
Long Meads TN3 ....7 B4
Long Park Cnr BN6 ..98 D2
Long Slip TN3 ....7 A3
Long Wlk BN26 .....174 C6
Longacre Cl TN37 ..136 C6
Longacre Cl TN37 ..136 C6
Longbury TN22 .....78 C5
Longfield Rd TN2 ...8 D8
Longhill Cl BN2 .....165 E4
Longhill High Sch BN2 .165 E4
Longhill Rd BN2 ....165 E4
Longhurst RH15 .....73 D2
Longinhurst Cotts BN8 ..75 D7
Longlands Rd BN20 ..184 C4
Longley Ind Est BN1 .189 B4
Longmeads BN27 ....177 D5
Longstone Rd BN21 .185 A3
Longview TN21 ......82 A5
Longview Way TN2 ..8 D7
Lonsdale Gdns TN1 ..8 A3
Looes Barn Cl BN2 ..177 D7
Lookout The BN10 ..167 D3
Loose Farm Barns TN3 .113 A2
Loose Farm Cotts TN3 .113 A2
Lordine La TN32 ....66 A4
Lords La TN35 ......160 D7
Lords The BN25 ....180 E6
Loriners Cl BN26 ...182 D8
Loriners Ct BN23 ...162 D8
Lorna Rd BN3 ......163 D7
Lorne Rd BN1 ......189 B5
Lorraine Ct 2 Hove BN3 .163 B6
  11 Hove BN3 ....163 E7
Lorraine Rd BN9 ...179 D7
Lortonbidge TN18 ..48 D3
Lottbridge Dro TN22 .173 F1
Lottbridge Dro
  Eastbourne BN23 ...185 B7
  Eastbourne BN23 ...185 D7
Lottbridge Rdbt BN23 .185 A8
Lovat Mead TN38 ...158 E6

Love La Eastbourne BN20 .184 D3
  Mayfield TN20 ....39 F2
  Rye TN31 ....93 B6
Lovegrove Ct BN3 ...162 E8
Lovell Ct 8 BN21 ...184 D4
Lover's Wlk BN1 ...163 F8
Lover's Wlk Cotts BN1 .163 F8
Lowdells Cl RH19 ...1 C4
Lowdells Dr RH19 ...1 C4
Lowdells La RH19 ..1 C3
Lower Bevendean Ave
  BN2 ....143 E1
Lower Chalvington Pl
  BN2 ....164 E5
Lower Church Rd RH15 .72 F3
Lower Cross Cotts TN1 .91 E2
Lower Dene RH16 ...2 A1
Lower Dr Seaford BN25 .180 F5
Lower Glen Rd TN37 .136 B4
Lower Green Rd
  Pembury TN2 ....9 D7
  Rusthall TN3,TN4 ....7 C6
Lower Hazelhurst TN5 .31 A4
Lower High St TN5 ..30 A4
Lower Lake TN33 ...112 E4
Lower Market St 6
  BN3 ....163 D5
Lower Mere RH19 ..10 F8
Lower Park Rd TN34 .136 E1
Lower Pl BN9 ....179 C7
Lower Platts TN5 ...31 F1
Lower Rd
  Eastbourne BN21 ...184 D4
  Forest Row RH18 ...11 F3
  Herstmonceux BN27 .130 E3
Lower Rock Gdns BN2 .189 C1
Lower Roedale Cotts
  BN1 ....143 B3
Lower Saxonbury TN6 .25 F2
Lower South Rd TN37 .136 C1
Lower Sq RH18 .....11 E3
Lower St East Dean BN20 .187 B8
Lower Street TN33 ..133 B5
Lower Station Rd BN8 .76 A6
Lower Village RH16 .50 C2
Lower Waites La TN35 .138 F4
Lowfield Rd RH16 ...50 F3
Lowlands Rd RH15 ..73 B5
Lowlands The BN27 .129 A1
Lowther Cl BN23 ...174 D3
Lowther Rd BN1 ....143 A2
Loxdale (The Swedish Folk
  High Sch) BN41 ....141 B1
Loxfield Cl TN20 ...40 A2
Loxfield Gdns TN6 ..26 B1
Loxwood Cl Bexhill TN39 .156 D5
  Eastbourne BN23 ...173 C1
Loyal Par BN1 ......142 C5
Lucas RH17 ....33 D5
Lucas Ave RH19 ....2 A1
Lucas Grange RH16 .50 D5
Lucas Shadwell Way
  TN31 ....93 F2
Lucas Way RH16 ...50 C5
Lucastes Ave RH16 .50 C6
Lucastes La RH16 ..50 C6
Lucastes Rd RH16 ..50 C6
Lucerne Cl BN41 ...141 B1
Lucerne Rd BN1 ....143 A1
Lucinda Way BN25 .180 F6
Lucraft Rd BN1,BN2 .144 A5
Lucy Way TN39 ....157 B6
Ludley Hill TN31 ...91 A6
Ludlow Rise BN2 ...144 A1
Ludpit La TN19,TN32 .63 C6
Luke Lade Ct BN27 .152 C7
Lulham Cl BN10 ....167 B2
Lullington Ave BN3 .162 F8
Lullington Cl
  Bexhill TN40 ....158 A6
  Eastbourne BN23 ...184 C7
  Seaford BN25 ....181 B2
Lullington Gdns TN37 .136 C5
Lullington Ho 6 BN2 .164 C7
Lullington Rd BN26 .173 A3
Lunce's Hill RH16,RH17 .73 F8
Lundy Wlk
  7 Eastbourne BN23 .185 F8
  Hailsham BN27 ......129 A2
Lureland Ct BN10 ..178 C6
Lurgashall RH15 ....73 C1
Lushington La TN18 .48 D3
Lushington Rd BN21 .185 A2
Lustrells Cl BN2 ....177 B6
Lustrells Cres BN2 ..177 C6
Lustrells Vale BN2 ..177 C6
Luther St BN2 ......164 C7
Luton Cl BN21 .....184 C6
Luxford Cl TN22 ...78 B8
Luxford Ct TN6 ....38 A8
Luxford Dr TN6 ....38 A8
Luxford La TN6 ....38 A8
Luxford Rd
  Crowborough TN6 ...38 A8
  Lindfield RH16 ......51 B7
Luxford's La RH19 ..11 D5
Lychgates Cl TN40 .157 F5
Lydd Cl BN23 ....174 D2
Lydd Rd TN31 ......94 F2
Lymden La TN5 ....43 A7
Lyminster Ave BN1 .143 A5
Lynch Cl BN1 ......143 C3
Lynchet Cl BN1 ....143 C3
Lynchet Down BN1 .143 C2

Lynchet Wlk BN1 ....143 C2
Lynchets Cres BN1 ....141 D3
Lynchets The BN7 .....190 C4
Lynden Ct **1** BN1 ....142 E2
Lyndhurst Ave TN34 ...160 A8
Lyndhurst Ct BN3 .....163 D7
Lyndhurst Rd BN3 .....163 D7
Lynholm Rd BN26 .....173 C6
Lynton Cl
 East Grinstead RH19 ....2 A2
 Hurstpierpoint BN6 ....97 B5
Lynton Park Ave RH19 ...2 A2
Lynton St BN2 ....164 C7
Lynwood TN3 ....15 C6
Lynwood Cl TN37 .....136 D5
Lynwood Rd BN2 .....177 C4
Lyon Cl BN3 ....163 D7
Lyoth La RH16 ....51 C4
Lyoth Villas RH16 ....51 C4
Lytham Cl TN38 ......158 F8

M

Mabb's Hill TN5 ......42 F7
Maberley Rd TN40 ....157 C6
Mackenzie Ho RH19 ....1 A4
Mackerel Hill TN31 ...68 F4
Mackerel's Rocks BN8 ..76 F3
Mackie Ave BN1 .....143 A7
 Keymer BN6 ....98 C5
Macmillan Dr BN2 ...184 C5
Macquarie Quay BN23 ..185 G8
Madehurst Cl BN2 ...164 D5
Madeira Dr Brighton BN2 ..164 C5
 Hastings TN34 ......136 C3
Madeira Pk TN2 ......8 B2
Madeira Pl BN2 ......189 C1
Madeira Way BN23 ...185 F8
Mafeking Rd BN2 ....143 D1
Magdalen Cl BN23 ...174 C3
Magdalen Ct **6** TN40 ..157 D4
Magdalen Rd
 Bexhill TN40 ....157 D4
 St Leonards TN37 ...159 D7
Magellan Way BN5 ...185 G2
Magna Ct TN40 ......157 B4
Magnolia Cl TN21 ....82 B5
Magnolia Dr BN22 ...173 D2
Magnolia Wlk BN2 ...173 D2
Magpie Cl Bexhill TN39 ..156 C6
 St Leonards TN38 ...158 E8
Magpie Rd BN23 .....174 C3
Magreed La TN21 .....59 E2
Maidstone Rd TN2 ....9 E8
Main Rd
 Icklesham TN35,TN36 ..116 D5
 Westfield TN35 .....114 E4
Main St Iden TN31 ...70 B4
 Northiam TN31 .....67 B5
 Peasmarsh TN31 ....69 B2
Mainstone Rd **1** BN3 ..162 F7
Maitland Cl TN34 ....136 C6
Major Cl BN1 ....143 B1
Major York's Rd TN4 ...7 F2
Malcolm Ct **6** BN2 ..184 F4
Malcolm Gdns BN26 ..173 A7
Malden Reach **6** BN23 ..175 A1
Maldon Rd BN1 ......142 D2
Malines Ave BN10 ...178 B8
Malines Ave S BN10 ..178 A4
Mallard Cl BN2 ......184 F8
Mallard Dr TN22 .....78 E5
Mallard Pl RH19 .....10 F8
Mallett Cl **12** BN25 ..180 E2
Malling Cl BN7 ......190 B4
Malling Down BN7,BN8 ..190 C4
Malling Hill BN7 ....190 C3
Malling House (Sussex Pol
 HQ) BN7 ....190 B4
Malling Ind Est BN7 ..190 C3
Malling St Lewes BN7 ..190 C2
 Lewes BN7 ....190 C3
Mallory Rd BN3 .....142 C2
Malt House Trad Est
 BN43 ....161 B7
Malthouse Bsns Pk The
 TN31 ....69 C2
Malthouse Ct **14** BN2 ..189 C2
Malthouse La
 Brighton BN2 ......189 C3
 Burgess Hill BN6,RH15 ..72 C2
 Burgess Hill RH15 ...72 D4
 Peasmarsh TN31 ....69 B2
Maltings The
 Burgess Hill RH15 ...72 D4
 Peasmarsh TN31 ....69 B2
Malton Way TN2 .....8 F7
Malvern Cl BN2 .....173 E4
Malvern Ho **1** TN39 ..157 B3
Malvern St **2** BN3 ..163 B7
Malvern Way TN34 ...160 B8
Manaton Cl RH16 ....50 F4
Manchester Rd TN33 ..133 A6
Manchester St BN1 ...189 B1
Mandalay Cl BN1 ....142 D3
Manhattan Ct BN1 ...142 D3
Manhattan Gdns TN35 ..160 D8
Manifold Rd BN22 ...185 B4
Mann St TN34 ......159 F8
Manning Cl RH19 .....1 D2
Manor Ave BN6 ......98 A5

Manor Cl Brighton BN2 ..164 E5
 Broyle Side BN8 ....124 F7
 Burgess Hill RH15 ...73 D4
 Eastbourne BN20 ...173 B2
 Horam TN21 ....106 F7
 Icklesham TN36 ....116 F5
 Royal Tunbridge Wells TN4 ...7 E3
 Seaford BN25 ......181 B3
 Southwick BN42 ....162 A8
 Uckfield TN22 ......78 C8
Manor Cotts
 Lamberhurst TN3 ....20 B5
 Sedlescombe TN33 ...88 E1
Manor Cres BN2 .....164 E5
Manor Ct
 North Chailey BN8 ..75 D7
 Seaford BN25 ......181 B3
 Southwick BN42 ....162 A7
Manor Dr BN10 ......167 B1
Manor End TN22 .....78 C8
Manor Field Prim Sch
 RH15 ....73 C4
Manor Gdns BN2 ....164 E5
Manor Gn BN2 ......164 E5
Manor Hall Fst Sch
 BN42 ....161 F7
Manor Hall Mid Sch
 BN42 ....161 F8
Manor Hall Rd BN42 ..161 F8
Manor Hill BN1 ......144 E6
Manor House Ct TN22 ..78 C8
Manor Paddock BN1 ..144 E6
Manor Park Cl BN27 ..129 A3
Manor Park Ct BN1 ...144 E6
Manor Park Rd BN27 ..129 A3
Manor Pk TN4 ......7 E3
Manor Pl BN2 ....164 E5
Manor Prim Sch TN22 ..78 D8
Manor Rd Bexhill TN40 ..157 D4
 Brighton BN2 ......164 E5
 Burgess Hill RH15 ...73 D3
 East Grinstead RH19 ...1 C2
 Eastbourne BN22 ...174 A2
 Hastings TN34 .....160 A5
 Horam TN21 ....106 F8
 Portslade-by-S BN41 ..141 B1
 Rusthall TN4 ....7 C4
 Seaford BN25 ......181 B3
Manor Rd N BN25 ...181 B3
Manor Terr BN1 .....190 A1
Manor The TN2 .....190 A1
Manor Way Brighton BN2 ..164 E5
 Crowborough TN6 ...37 E8
 Eastbourne BN20 ...184 B8
 Polegate BN26 .....173 B6
 Uckfield TN22 ......78 C8
Mansell Cl TN39 ....156 C4
Mansell Ct RH15 ....73 B3
Mansell Rd BN43 ...161 B8
Mansers La BN27 ...128 C3
Mansfield Rd BN3 ...162 E7
Mansion Cl RH15 ...73 D3
Manston Way TN34 ..136 E2
Mantell Cl BN1 ......123 C4
Mantell Ho **2** BN2 ..189 C2
Manton Ct BN23 ....185 D8
Manton Rd BN2 .....143 E1
Manvers Rd BN20 ...184 B3
Maple Ave TN39 ....156 C3
Maple Cl Bexhill TN39 ..156 C3
 Burgess Hill RH15 ...73 B5
 Haywards Heath RH16 ..51 B3
 Maresfield TN22 ....55 A4
 Royal Tunbridge Wells TN2 ...8 A1
 Woodingdean BN2 ..165 E7
Maple Ct
 Burgess Hill RH15 ...72 D3
 Hailsham BN27 .....152 A8
 Royal Tunbridge Wells TN4 ...7 E4
Maple Dr
 Burgess Hill RH15 ...73 A5
 East Grinstead RH19 ...2 A1
Maple Gdns BN3 ....141 F1
Maple Hts TN37 ....136 B7
Maple Leaf Cl BN9 ...179 B7
Maple Rd
 Eastbourne BN23 ...185 D7
 Peacehaven BN10 ..178 F6
Maple Wlk TN39 ....156 C3
Maplehurst Cl TN37 ..136 B7
Maplehurst Ct TN37 ..136 C8
Maplehurst Rd
 Eastbourne BN22 ...173 D2
 Portslade-by-S BN41 ..141 A1
 St Leonards TN37 ...136 B7
Maplehurst Rise TN37 ..136 B7
Mapleleaf Gdns BN26 ..173 A8
Maples Cotts TN32 ...80 A6
Maples The BN8 ....124 E6
Maplewood **6** BN1 ..142 E3
Marbles Rd BN2 .....76 D7
Marchants Cl BN6 ...97 A6
Marchants Dr TN31 ...94 E2
Marchants Rd BN6 ...97 A6
Marchants Way RH15 ..72 F5
Marcia Cl BN20 ....184 A8
Marcus Gdns TN37 ..159 B8
Mardan Ct TN38 ....159 A3
Marden Cl BN2 .....144 E1
Marden Ct TN39 ....157 A3
Marden's Hill TN6 ....25 C5
Mare Bay Cl TN38 ...135 E7
Maresfield Dr BN24 ..175 E6
Maresfield Rd BN2 ...164 E5
Margaret Ct BN10 ...178 B7
Margaret St BN2 ....189 C1
Margery Rd BN3 ....162 D8
Marianne Ho TN35 ...160 B5

Marianne Pk TN35 ...160 B5
Marina Bexhill TN40 ..157 C3
Marina Arc **7** TN40 ..157 C3
Marina Court Ave 4
 TN40 ....157 C3
Marina Way BN2 ....164 F3
Marina Wlk BN23 ...185 E8
Marine Ave
 Beachlands BN24 ...175 F6
 Hove BN3 ....162 E6
Marine Cl
 Beachlands BN24 ...175 F6
 Saltdean BN2 ......177 B5
Marine Cres BN25 ...180 F2
Marine Ct
 Newhaven BN9 .....179 D6
 Rottingdean BN2 ...177 A5
 Seaford BN25 ......180 C3
 4 St Leonards TN38 ..159 C6
 Telscombe Cliffs BN10 ..177 F3
Marine Dr
 Rottingdean BN2 ...165 C2
 Saltdean BN2 ......177 B5
 Seaford BN25 ......180 B5
Marine Gdns BN2 ...179 D6
Marine Hts TN33 ...159 A6
Marine Par Brighton BN2 ..164 C4
 Eastbourne BN21,BN22 ..185 B3
 Hastings TN34 .....160 A3
 Newhaven BN9 .....179 D6
 Pevensey Bay BN24 ..175 D5
 Seaford BN25 ......180 C3
Marine Parade Rd 15
 BN21 ....185 B3
Marine Pk TN38 ....158 F6
Marine Rd
 Eastbourne BN22 ...185 B3
 Pevensey Bay BN24 ..175 D5
Marine Sq BN2 .....164 C4
Marine Terr BN25 ...175 D5
Marine Terrace Mews 7
 BN2 ....164 C4
Marine View
 3 Brighton BN2 ..189 C2
 Newhaven BN9 .....179 B6
Mariners Quay BN2 ..164 F3
Mariteau Ho TN36 ...117 F2
Marjoram Pl BN43 ...140 B1
Mark Cl BN2 ....181 C2
Mark Cross BN6 ....181 C2
Mark Cross CE Prim Sch
 TN6 ....28 A3
Mark La BN2 ....185 A2
Market La BN7 .....190 B2
Market Pas
 6 Hastings TN34 ..160 A3
 St Leonards TN38 ...159 C6
Market Pl
 Burgess Hill RH15 ...73 A2
 Hailsham BN27 .....152 C7
 Haywards Heath RH16 ..50 C6
 18 Royal Tunbridge Wells
 ....8 A2
Market Rd Battle TN33 ..112 C5
 Rye TN31 ....93 C5
Market Sq Brighton BN1 ..189 B2
 Hailsham BN27 .....152 C7
Market St Brighton BN1 ..189 B2
 Hailsham BN27 .....152 C7
 Lewes BN7 ....190 B2
 17 Royal Tunbridge Wells
 ....8 A2
 Rye TN31 ....93 C5
 St Leonards TN38 ...159 C6
Market Terr **8** TN38 ..159 C6
Markland Way TN22 ..78 A7
Markkye La
 Heathfield TN21 ....59 B2
 Rushlake Green TN21 ..83 C3
Markstakes Cnr BN8 ..75 E1
Markstakes La BN8 ..76 C2
Markwick Terr TN38 ..159 B8
Marlborough Cl
 Eastbourne BN23 ...174 D3
 Royal Tunbridge Wells TN4 ...7 E4
 St Leonards TN38 ...136 A1
Marlborough Ct
 Burgess Hill RH15 ...72 E3
 8 Eastbourne BN21 ..184 F3
 1 Hove BN3 ......163 C6
 Newhaven BN9 .....179 C7
Marlborough Dr RH15 ..73 C2
Marlborough Ho 12
 TN37 ....159 C7
Marlborough Mews
 BN1 ....189 A2
Marlborough Pl 6 BN1,
 BN2 ....189 B3
Marlborough St BN1 ..189 B2
Marle Ave RH15 .....73 A4
Marle Green Cotts
 TN21 ....107 B6
Marley Cl TN33 .....112 F4
Marley Gdns TN33 ...112 F4
Marley La TN33 .....113 B6
Marley Rd TN31 .....93 A6
Marley Way BN2 ....164 F2
Marline Ave TN38 ...136 A4
Marline Rd TN38 ....136 A4
Marlings The TN31 ...50 C3
Marlinspike The BN43 ..161 A6
Marlow Ave BN22 ...185 B6
Marlow Ct Brighton BN2 ..189 C4
 5 Crowborough TN6 ..37 F8
Marlow Dr
 Haywards Heath RH16 ..51 C4
 St Leonards TN37 ...136 C5
Marlow Rd BN2 .....164 F4

Marlowes The TN40 ..157 E5
Marlpit Cl RH19 .....1 E4
Marlpit Gdns TN5 ...31 E1
Marlpit Rd RH19 ....21 A6
Marlpit The TN5 ....29 E5
Marlpits La TN33 ...133 A7
Marmion Rd BN3 ...162 F7
Marsden Ct BN10 ...178 A7
Marsden Rd BN23 ...174 E1
Marsh Ho **3** BN42 ..161 F2
Marsh Quarter La TN18 ..47 C3
Marshall Ct BN22 ...173 D1
Marshall La BN9 ....179 C7
Marshall Rd BN23 ...185 A8
Marshall Rdbt BN23 ..174 A1
Marshall Way BN3 ...141 F1
Marshalls Row BN1 ..189 B4
Marshfoot La BN27 ..152 D8
Marshlands La TN21 ..82 A7
Marshlands Prim Sch
 BN27 ....152 D8
Marston Ct **10** BN3 ..163 E7
Martello Beach Cvn Pk
 BN24 ....175 C3
Martello Cl TN31 ....93 B4
Martello Ct
 Hailsham BN27 .....129 A1
 Hove BN3 ....142 B3
 Portslade-by-S BN41 ..141 B3
 Southwick BN42 ....162 A8
 St Leonards TN38 ...136 A4
Martello Mews **21** BN25 ..180 E2
Martello Rd
 Eastbourne BN22 ...185 D6
 Seaford BN25 ......180 E2
Martens Field BN7 ...146 E1
Martha Gunn Rd BN2 ..143 E1
Martin Ct BN22 .....173 D1
Martin Rd BN3 .....141 D1
Martineau La TN35 ...137 F5
Martingale Cl TN37 ..136 C5
Martinique Way BN23 ..185 G2
Martins The BN10 ...167 B1
Martlet Ho Brighton BN1 ..164 A8
 Saltdean BN2 ......177 D4
Martlet The BN3 ....142 D1
Martlets Bexhill TN40 ..157 E5
 Eastbourne BN22 ...173 B3
Martlets Ct TN6 ....25 F1
Martlets The
 Broad Oak TN31 ...90 C4
 Burgess Hill RH15 ...73 A3
 Crowborough TN6 ...25 F1
 Hailsham BN27 .....152 A7
 Hastings TN34 .....136 E2
 Lewes BN7 ....190 B4
 South Chailey BN8 ..100 D7
Martletts The
 Burwash Common TN19 ..60 F3
 Ringmer BN8 ......124 E6
Martyn's Cl BN2 ....165 E4
Martyns Pl RH19 ....11 A8
Martyns Way TN40 ..158 A5
Marwick Ct TN38 ...159 B8
Mary Burfield Ct **3** TN2 ..8 A2
Mary Stanford Gn TN31 ..94 A3
Maryan Ct BN22 ....152 B8
Maryland Ct TN2 ....8 D1
Maryland Rd TN2 ....9 A2
Maskelyne Rd BN27 ..131 A1
Mason Cl RH19 ......1 C2
Mason Rd Rye TN31 ..93 A5
 Seaford BN25 ......180 F4
Matlock Rd Brighton BN1 ..142 D2
 Eastbourne BN20 ...188 E8
Matthew Ho **14** BN3 ..163 A6
Maudlin Ct TN37 ....159 C7
Maunsell Ct RH16 ...50 F3
Maunsell Rd TN38 ...135 F5
Maurice Rd BN25 ...180 F1
Maxfield Cl BN20 ...184 B5
Maxfield La TN35 ...115 D2
May Ave BN25 ......181 B3
May Rd BN2 ....164 D7
May Tree Cl BN3 ...162 D8
May Tree Gdns TN40 ..157 C6
May Tree Wlk BN3 ...141 E1
Maycroft Pl TN20 ...39 F2
Mayfair Cl BN20 ....172 F4
Mayfair Ho BN3 ....173 B1
Mayfair Mews TN40 ..157 C5
Mayfield Ave BN10 ..178 D6
Mayfield CE Prim Sch
 TN20 ....40 B3
Mayfield Cl Brighton BN1 ..143 A5
 Mayfield TN20 .....39 F2
Mayfield Cres TN40 ..142 F5
Mayfield Ct Bexhill TN38 ..156 C4
 Broad Oak TN21 ...59 E1
 Burgess Hill RH15 ...73 B3
 Saltdean BN2 ......177 D4
Mayfield Flat TN21,TN22 ..81 A8
Mayfield La Durgates TN5 ..29 D4
 St Leonards TN38 ...135 D2
Mayfield Pk TN6 ....29 E5
Mayfield Pl BN22 ...185 A4
Mayfield Rd
 Mark Cross TN6 ....28 A2
 Rotherfield TN6 ....39 A7
 Royal Tunbridge Wells TN4 ...7 F4
Mayfield Way TN40 ..157 C5
Mayflower Ct
 Haywards Heath RH16 ..51 A6
 1 Shoreham-by-S BN43 ..161 A6
Mayflower Rd RH16 ..50 F6
Mayflower Sq BN1 ...189 B4
Mayhouse Rd RH15 ..72 F1
Maynard's Green Com Prim
 Sch TN21 ....82 A2
Mayne Waye TN34 ...160 B8

Mayo Cl **5** BN2 ....164 B8
Mayo La TN39 ......157 A8
Mayo Rd BN2 ......164 B8
Mayo Rise TN39 ....157 A8
Maypole Cotts TN22 ..56 B8
Maypole Rd
 Ashurst Wood RH19 ..11 E6
 East Grinstead RH19 ...1 D2
Maytham Rd TN17 ...49 C7
Maytree Cotts BN6 ..100 C7
Mayvern Cl **5** TN6 ..25 F3
Mayview Cl TN21 ....59 E1
Maywood Ave BN22 ..173 E2
Maze Hill TN38 .....159 B7
Maze Hill Terr TN38 ..159 B7
Mcbechie Ho RH10 ...1 D3
McIndoe Rd RH19 ...1 D3
McMichaels Way TN19 ..45 A3
McNair Ct BN3 .....162 E7
McWilliam Rd BN2 ...144 C1
Meachants Ct BN20 ..173 B2
Meachants La BN20 ..173 B2
Mead Sch The TN2 ....8 A1
Mead The TN39 ....156 D4
Meadow Bank TN33 ..112 F4
Meadow Cl
 Hailsham BN27 .....129 B1
 Hove BN3 ....142 B3
 Portslade-by-S BN41 ..141 B3
 Rottingdean BN2 ...162 A8
 Southwick BN42 ....162 A8
 St Leonards TN38 ...136 A4
Meadow Cres TN39 ...157 C7
Meadow Dr RH16 ....51 B6
Meadow Hill Rd **6** TN1 ...8 B3
Meadow Ho BN8 ....100 C7
Meadow La
 Burgess Hill RH15 ...72 F1
 Lindfield RH16 .....51 B6
 Sedlescombe TN33 ...88 D1
Meadow Par BN2 ...165 F3
Meadow Pl TN22 ...78 C6
Meadow Rd
 Groombridge TN3 ...15 C7
 Hailsham BN27 .....152 A6
 Royal Tunbridge Wells TN1 ...8 A4
 Rusthall TN4 ....7 C4
Meadow Rise TN21 ..106 F7
Meadow The TN2 ....9 E8
Meadow Vale BN2 ...165 E5
Meadow View
 Hastings TN34 .....39 B7
 Union Street TN5 ...32 A3
 Westfield TN35 ....114 E4
Meadow View Cotts
 TN19 ....45 A3
Meadow Way
 Fairlight Cove TN35 ..138 E4
 Heathfield TN21 ....82 A6
 Seaford BN25 ......181 B3
Meadowcroft Cl RH19 ...1 C2
Meadowlands Ave
 BN22 ....173 D1
Meadows Rd BN6 ...97 F5
Meadows Rd BN22 ...173 B2
Meadows The
 Crowborough TN6 ...25 F2
 Hove BN3 ....141 C3
 Lewes BN7 ....190 C5
 St Leonards TN37 ...136 C5
Meadowside TN33 ...88 E1
Meadowside Cotts TN5 ..31 F1
Meadowsweet Cl TN38 ..135 L1
Meadowview
 Brighton BN2 ......143 E1
 Lower Street TN33 ..133 B5
Meads Ave Bexhill TN39 ..156 C4
 Hove BN3 ....142 B2
Meads Brow BN20 ...188 D8
Meads Cl BN3 ......141 C3
Meads Cl BN20 .....184 E1
Meads Gate BN20 ...188 E8
Meads Prim Sch The
 RH19 ....10 E7
Meads Rd Bexhill TN39 ..156 C4
 Eastbourne BN20 ...184 E1
 Seaford BN25 ......180 F3
Meads St BN20 .....188 D8
Meads The Brighton BN1 ..143 D5
 Burgess Hill RH15 ...72 F3
 East Grinstead RH19 ...8 C2
 Royal Tunbridge Wells TN2 ...8 C2
Meadsway BN20 ....188 E8
Meadway Cres BN3 ..141 C2
Meadway Ct BN42 ...161 D8
Meadway The
 Brighton BN2 ......164 F5
 Shoreham-by-S BN43 ..161 A6
Mealla Cl BN7 ......190 A4
Medina Dr BN24 ....174 B5
Medina Pl BN3 .....163 B6
Medina Terr Hove BN3 ..163 B5
 St Leonards TN38 ...159 A6
Medina Villas BN3 ...163 B6
Medmerry Hill BN2 ..143 E2
Medway Crowborough TN6 ..26 C1
Medway Cl TN38 ...135 H1
Medway Dr
 East Grinstead RH19 ...10 D6
 Forest Row RH18 ...12 A2
Medway La BN24 ...174 A5
Medway Rd TN1 ....8 B5
Medway View RH18 ..12 A2
Meeching Ct BN9 ...179 C7
Meeching Rd BN9 ...179 C7
Meeching Rise BN9 ..179 D7

Meeching Valley Prim Sch
BN9 . . . . .179 B7
Meeds Rd RH15 . . . . .73 A2
Meeting House La BN1 . .189 B7
Megrims Hill TN18 . . . . . . .47 A6
Melbourne Rd BN22 . . . .185 B4
Melbourne St BN2 . . . . .164 C8
Melfort Rd TN6 . . . . .25 D1
Melrose Ave BN41 . . . . . .141 A1
Melrose Cl Brighton BN1 .143 C2
Hailsham BN27 . . . . .152 A8
Melrose Ho TN6 . . . . .25 E1
Melvill La BN20 . . . . .173 B1
Melville Rd BN3 . . . . .163 E7
Mendip Ave BN23 . . . . . .174 D3
Mendip Gdns TN34 . . . . .160 B7
Mendip Wlk TN2 . . . . .8 D5
Menzies Rd TN38 . . . . . .136 B2
Meon Cl BN24 . . . . .174 A5
Mercatoria TN38 . . . . . . .159 C6
Mercer St TN1 . . . . .8 B5
Mercers TN3 . . . . .7 A3
Merceria Ct TN40 . . . . . .157 E4
Mercread Rd RH25 . . . . .180 F3
Meres La TN20 . . . . .58 D7
Merevale BN1 . . . . .143 B2
Merewood Ct BN21 . . . . .184 E4
Mereworth Ho TN4 . . . . . . .8 A6
Meridian Com Prim Sch
BN10 . . . . .167 C1
Meridian Ctr BN10 . . . . .178 C8
Meridian Ind Est The
BN10 . . . . .178 C7
Meridian Rd BN7 . . . . . . .123 B2
Meridian Way
East Grinstead RH19 . . . . . .1 F3
Peacehaven BN10 . . . . . . .178 C7
Merivale TN35 . . . . .137 A6
Merlin Cl BN3 . . . . .163 D8
Merlin Ct BN22 . . . . .152 E7
Merlin Way RH19 . . . . .2 A3
Merlynn BN21 . . . . .185 A2
Mermaid St TN31 . . . . . . .93 B5
Mermaid Pas [3] TN31 . . .93 B5
Merrimac Ho [1] TN40 . . .157 E4
Merrimede Cl TN38 . . . . .159 A7
Merriments Gdns* TN19 .45 B5
Merriments La TN18,
TN19 . . . . .45 D5
Merrion Cl TN4 . . . . .8 B7
Merrion Way TN4 . . . . .8 B7
Merston Ct BN2 . . . . . . .165 E6
Merton Ct
[7] Bexhill TN40 . . . . .157 E4
Brighton BN2 . . . . .165 A3
Meryon Ct TN31 . . . . .93 C5
Metcalfe Ave BN9 . . . . . .179 B8
Metropole Ct
[12] Brighton BN1 . . . . . . .163 E5
[11] Eastbourne BN22 . . .185 B3
Mewetts Ct BN20 . . . . . .173 B3
Mews Ct RH19 . . . . .10 F6
Mews Rd TN38 . . . . .19 C1
Mews The Brighton BN1 .142 E2
East Hoathly BN8 . . . . . .105 A5
Pembury TN2 . . . . .9 C6
[5] Royal Tunbridge Wells
TN1 . . . . .8 B3
Seaford BN25 . . . . .181 B4
Meyners Cl BN3 . . . . . . .141 C3
Michael Fields RH18 . . . .11 E2
Michael Hall Sch RH18 . .11 D1
Michel Cl BN20 . . . . .183 C1
Michel Dene Cl BN20 . . .183 C1
Michel Dene Rd BN20 . .183 C1
Michel Gr BN21 . . . . .184 E4
Michelbourne Cl RH15 . .72 E1
Michele Cl [5] TN38 . . . . .159 B6
Michelham Dr BN23 . . . .174 A4
Michelham Priory*
BN27 . . . . .151 B7
Michelham Rd TN22 . . . .55 E1
Michelson Cl TN38 . . . . .135 F4
Micklefield Way BN25 . .181 F1
Middle Cl TN33 . . . . .86 B2
Middle Dr TN22 . . . . .55 A6
Middle Farm Countryside
Ctr* BN8 . . . . .148 F4
Middle Field TN2 . . . . .9 E8
Middle Furlong BN25 . . .180 F3
Middle La TN21 . . . . .83 E3
Middle Rd
Bells Yew Green TN3 . . . . .18 A5
Brighton BN1 . . . . .142 E1
Hastings TN35 . . . . .160 D8
Shoreham-by-Sea BN43 . .161 B7
Middle Row [1] RH19 . . . .10 E8
Middle St Brighton BN1 .189 A2
Falmer BN1 . . . . .144 C6
[9] Hastings TN34 . . . . . .159 F8
Portslade-by-S BN41 . . . .162 B6
Middle Village RH16 . . . .50 C2
Middle Way
Burgess Hill RH15 . . . . . . .73 B3
Lewes BN7 . . . . .123 A1
Middle Wlk TN2 . . . . .8 C4
Middleham Cl BN8 . . . . .124 C4
Middleham Way BN23 . .174 C4
Middlesex Cl [4] BN22 . .174 E4
Middlesex Rd TN40 . . . . .157 D3
Middleton Ave BN3 . . . . .162 B6
Middleton Dr BN23 . . . . .185 E7
Middleton Rise BN1 . . . .143 E5
Middleway BN27 . . . . . . .131 B5
Midfields Cl RH15 . . . . . . .73 B3
Midfields Dr RH15 . . . . . .73 B3
Midfields Wlk RH15 . . . . .73 B4
Midhurst Rd BN22 . . . . .173 F2
Midhurst Rise BN1 . . . . .143 B6
Midhurst Wlk BN3 . . . . .141 F3
Midway Rd BN2 . . . . .165 C8
Midway The TN4 . . . . .7 D2
Mighell St BN2 . . . . .189 C2
Milchester Ho BN20 . . . .168 E8
Milcote Ave BN3 . . . . . . .162 F8
Mildenhall Dr TN37 . . . . .136 B3
Mildmay Cl BN8 . . . . . . .124 D6
Mildmay Rd BN7 . . . . . . .123 A1
Mile End Cotts BN1 . . . .142 E6
Mile Oak Gdns BN41 . . .140 F1
Mile Oak Gdns BN41 . . .141 A1
Mile Oak Prim Sch
BN41 . . . . .140 F3
Mile Oak Rd
Portslade-by-S BN41 . . . .140 F3
Southwick BN42 . . . . . . .140 F1
Miles Wlk BN3 . . . . .163 B6
Milestones TN21 . . . . .82 B8
Milfoil Dr BN23 . . . . .174 E4
Military Rd TN30,TN31 . . .70 F3
Mill Brooks BN8 . . . . . . .100 D7
Mill Cl East Grinstead RH19 .10 E7
Friston BN20 . . . . .183 A1
Hastings TN35 . . . . .160 E8
Heathfield TN21 . . . . .81 F7
Polegate BN26 . . . . .172 F4
Portslade-by-S BN41 . . . .141 C1
Ringmer BN8 . . . . .124 E5
South Chailey BN8 . . . . .100 D7
Staplecross TN32 . . . . . . .65 E2
Westfield TN35 . . . . .114 E5
Mill Cnr TN31 . . . . .67 A3
Mill Cres TN31 . . . . .10 E7
Mill Cres TN6 . . . . .25 F3
Mill Dr Crowborough TN6 .25 F3
Hove BN3 . . . . .162 A5
Seaford BN25 . . . . .181 A3
Mill Dro Seaford BN25 . .180 A5
Uckfield TN22 . . . . .78 C6
Mill Gap Rd BN21 . . . . . .184 F4
Mill Gdns Heathfield TN21 .82 A5
Ringmer BN8 . . . . .124 E5
Mill Green Ind Est RH16 .50 E6
Mill Green Rd RH16 . . . . .50 E6
Mill Hill Cl RH16 . . . . .50 E7
Mill Ho BN26 . . . . .173 A7
Mill La Barcombe BN8 . .101 D2
Clayton BN8,BN45 . . . . . .119 E7
Crowborough TN6 . . . . . . .25 E2
Dormans Park RH7 . . . . . . .1 F8
Flackley Ash TN31 . . . . . .68 E3
Goddards' Green BN6 . . . .72 A3
Hastings TN35 . . . . .137 E5
Hellingly BN27 . . . . .129 A6
Hooe Common TN33 . . . .132 F2
Mark Cross TN6 . . . . .28 A3
Portslade-by-S BN41 . . . .141 B1
Punnett's Town TN21 . . . .83 E6
South Chailey BN8 . . . . .100 D7
Uckfield TN22 . . . . .78 C6
Westfield TN35 . . . . .114 E5
Mill Mead BN8 . . . . .124 E5
Mill Path BN8 . . . . .124 E5
Mill Pk RH15 . . . . .73 B1
Mill Race BN6 . . . . .97 E8
Mill Rd Brighton BN1 . . .142 C6
Burgess Hill RH15 . . . . . . .73 B3
Eastbourne BN21 . . . . . .184 E5
Hailsham BN27 . . . . .152 B6
Heathfield TN21 . . . . .81 F7
Lewes BN7 . . . . .190 C4
Portslade-by-S BN41 . . . .141 B1
Ringmer BN8 . . . . .124 D5
Mill Rd Ind Est BN41 . . .162 B7
Mill Rise Brighton BN1 . .142 C5
Heathfield TN21 . . . . .82 A8
Robertsbridge TN32 . . . . .64 A3
Mill Row BN1 . . . . .189 A3
Mill St Barcombe BN8 . . . .89 E4
Mill St BN1 . . . . .144 C7
Mill Stream Mdw RH16 . .50 D7
Mill View BN8 . . . . .124 C4
Mill View Cl BN24 . . . . . .174 D6
Mill View Hospl BN1 . . . .141 E1
Mill View Rd TN9 . . . . . . .157 B7
Mill Way
East Grinstead RH19 . . . . .10 E7
Polegate BN26 . . . . .172 E4
Mill Wood RH15 . . . . .73 B3
Milland Cl TN40 . . . . .157 E6
Milland Rd BN27 . . . . . . .129 B1
Millbank RH7 . . . . .2 A8
Millberg Rd BN25 . . . . . .181 C4
Millbrook Bsns Pk TN6 . .38 D8
Millbrook Rd BN1 . . . . . .107 A7
Millbrook Gdns BN20 . . .184 B6
Millbrook Ind Est TN6 . . .38 D8
Millbrook Rd TN6 . . . . . . .26 A3
Millcroft BN1 . . . . .142 C5
Millcroft Ave BN42 . . . . .140 E5
Millcroft Gdns BN42 . . .140 E5
Millcross Rd BN41 . . . . .141 B3
Milldown Rd BN25 . . . . .180 F3
Miller's Hill TN35 . . . . . .114 E6
Miller's Rd BN1 . . . . .142 E1
Millers Rise BN27 . . . . . .152 A6
Millers Way RH15 . . . . . . .73 B4
Millfield [2] Bexhill TN40 .157 F3
Ninfield TN33 . . . . .133 A6
Millfield Cl Newick BN8 . .76 C7
Seaford BN25 . . . . .181 B4
Millfield Cotts [8] BN2 . .164 D4
Millfield Ct [3] TN40 . . . .157 C4
Millfield Rise TN40 . . . . .157 C4
Millfields BN26 . . . . .173 A7
Millfields Ct TN26 . . . . . .173 A7
Millham Cl TN39 . . . . . . .156 F5
Millington Ct TN22 . . . . . .78 C6
Millrace The BN26 . . . . . .172 F4
Millstream BN1 . . . . .5 D2
Millstream Gdns BN26 . .172 F4
Millward Rd BN24 . . . . . .175 C3
Millwood Cl TN22 . . . . . . .55 D4
Millwood La TN22 . . . . . . .55 C4
Millwood Rd TN39 . . . . . .157 A8
Milnard Cres BN21 . . . . .165 D7
Milner Flats BN2 . . . . . . .189 C2
Milner Rd BN2 . . . . .143 D1
Milnthorpe Gdns BN20 . .188 E8
Milnthorpe Rd
Brighton BN20 . . . . .188 E8
Eastbourne BN20 . . . . . .188 E8
Milton Cres
East Grinstead RH19 . . . . .10 C3
Eastbourne BN21 . . . . . .184 C4
Milton Ct [6] RH16 . . . . . .50 D5
Milton Dr
Royal Tunbridge Wells TN2 . .8 D7
Southwick BN42 . . . . . . .161 F8
Milton Rd Brighton BN2 .189 C4
Eastbourne BN21 . . . . . .184 C4
Hayward's Heath RH16 . . .50 D6
Milton St BN24 . . . . .175 B2
Milward Cres TN34 . . . . .160 A4
Milward Ct [3] BN43 . . . .161 C8
Mimosa Cl BN20 . . . . . . .173 A7
Mimosa Ct BN1 . . . . .143 B3
Mimram Rd BN24 . . . . . .174 A5
Mindelheim Ave RH19 . . .2 B2
Minnels The BN6 . . . . . . .98 E4
Minsted Sq TN39 . . . . . .156 C2
Minster Cl BN26 . . . . . . .173 A7
Mint The TN31 . . . . .93 B5
Mistley Cl TN40 . . . . .158 A6
Mitcheldean BN10 . . . . . .167 C1
Mitre Ho [28] BN1 . . . . . .163 E5
Mitre Way TN33 . . . . . . .112 D1
Mitten Rd TN40 . . . . .157 C4
Moat Croft Ct BN21 . . . .184 E3
Moat Croft Rd BN21 . . . .184 E4
Moat Farm TN21 . . . . .82 B4
Moat Ho BN21 . . . . .184 E3
Moat La Cowden TN8 . . . .4 E7
Waldron TN21 . . . . .80 D2
Monastery TN33 . . . . .114 B3
Moat Lake Cotts TN21 . . .80 F4
Moat Rd RH19 . . . . .1 E2
Mocatta Way RH15 . . . . . .72 D5
Modena Rd BN3 . . . . . . .162 F7
Moira House Sch BN20 . .188 D8
Mole Cl BN24 . . . . .174 A5
Molesey Ct TN22 . . . . . . .78 C7
Molesworth St BN3 . . . . .162 F8
Monarch Almshouses
TN4 . . . . .7 B4
Molyneux Ct TN4 . . . . .7 B4
Molyneux Park Gdns TN4 . .7 A4
Molyneux Park Rd TN4 . . .7 A4
Mona Rd BN22 . . . . .185 B5
Monarch Gdns
Eastbourne BN23 . . . . . .174 F1
Seaford BN25 . . . . .181 A5
St Leonards TN37 . . . . . .136 A5
Monarch Ho BN22 . . . . .185 E5
Monastery Gdns TN6 . . . .39 B8
Monceux Rd
Eastbourne BN21 . . . . . .184 C4
Herstmonceux BN27 . . . .130 E6
Monckton Way BN7 . . . .145 E5
Monger's Mead BN8 . . . . .76 C4
Monk Cl BN1 . . . . .143 E6
Monks La Lewes BN7 . . .190 A1
Newbury's TN5 . . . . .30 B8
Monks Way Lewes BN7 . .190 A4
Northiam TN31 . . . . .67 B8
Monks' Wlk TN36 . . . . . .117 C7
Monson Rd TN1 . . . . .8 B4
Monson Way [5] TN1 . . . .8 B4
Montacute Gdns TN2 . . . .7 F2
Montacute Rd
Lewes BN7 . . . . .146 A8
Royal Tunbridge Wells TN2 . .8 A1
Montague Cl TN22 . . . . . .78 D8
Montague Ct BN43 . . . . .161 D7
Montague Ct
[6] Brighton BN2 . . . . . . .164 E4
[2] Shoreham-by-S BN43 .161 D7
Montague Pl BN2 . . . . . .164 C4
Montague St [4] BN2 . . .164 C4
Montague Way BN24 . . .174 F5
Montana Ct TN38 . . . . . .135 C6
Montargis Way TN6 . . . . .26 A1
Montefiore Rd BN3 . . . . .163 E7
Monteith Ct TN2 . . . . .8 A1
Monterey Cl TN39 . . . . . .156 F3
Monterey Gdns BN3 . . . .142 E3
Monterey Wharf [5]
BN23 . . . . .175 A1
Montes Hill RH16 . . . . . . .51 F8
Monteswood La BN8 . . . . .77 A8
Montford Cl BN43 . . . . . .161 D8
Montfort Cl BN24 . . . . . .174 F6
Montfort Rd BN24 . . . . . .174 F6
Montgomery Rd
Hastings TN35 . . . . .137 D5
Montgomery Rd continued
Royal Tunbridge Wells TN4 . .8 B7
Montgomery St BN3 . . . .163 A7
Montgomery Terr [2]
BN3 . . . . .163 A7
Montpelier Cres BN1 . . .163 E6
Montpelier Lodge [9]
BN1 . . . . .163 E6
Montpelier Pl BN1 . . . . . .163 E6
Montpelier Rd BN1 . . . . .163 E5
Montpelier St BN1 . . . . . .163 E6
Montpelier Terr BN1 . . . .163 E6
Montpelier Villas BN1 . .163 E6
Montpellier Apartments [25]
BN21 . . . . .184 C5
Montreal Rd BN2 . . . . . .189 C3
Montserrat [3] TN39 . . . .157 A2
Monument View BN2 . . .164 D6
Moon's La BN7,TN8 . . . . . .2 E8
Moonrise Way BN27 . . . .127 C3
Moons Yd TN6 . . . . .39 B8
Moor Hall TN18 . . . . .45 F8
Moor La Ringmer BN8 . .125 B3
Westfield TN35 . . . . .114 E3
Moor Pl RH19 . . . . .1 D2
Moor The TN18 . . . . .45 F8
Moore Pk BN27 . . . . .152 D7
Moore's La TN31 . . . . .90 E8
Moorhen Cl TN38 . . . . . .158 E8
Moorhurst Rd BN24 . . . .135 F5
Moorings The
Eastbourne BN20 . . . . . .188 E8
Felbridge RH19 . . . . .1 A3
Lewes BN7 . . . . .190 C2
Shoreham-by-S BN43 . . . .161 C6
Moray Wlk BN22 . . . . . . .129 A2
Morehouse Farm Bsns Ctr
RH17 . . . . .74 A6
Morestead BN10 . . . . . . .167 D1
Moreton Cl BN41 . . . . . . .162 B8
Morgan Cl TN39 . . . . . . .157 B8
Morgay Wood La TN35 . .115 E2
Morlais Pl TN36 . . . . . . .118 B6
Morlais Ridge TN36 . . . .118 B6
Morland Dr TN3 . . . . .20 B5
Morlands Cl TN33 . . . . . .133 B5
Morley Cl BN7 . . . . .146 B8
Morley Lodge BN2 . . . . .189 C4
Morley St BN2 . . . . .189 C3
Morningside Cl BN25 . . .180 F4
Mornington Cres BN3 . . .162 D7
Mornington Mans [4]
BN3 . . . . .162 D7
Morris Rd BN7 . . . . .190 C2
Mortain Pk BN27 . . . . . .152 D7
Mortain Rd BN24 . . . . . .174 F6
Mortimer Gdns BN26 . . .172 F4
Mortimer Mews BN3 . . .163 A8
Mortimer Rd
Eastbourne BN26 . . . . . .185 A6
Hove BN3 . . . . .162 F8
Morton Rd RH19 . . . . .10 E7
Moscow Rd TN35 . . . . . .160 C7
Moss Ho BN21 . . . . .184 F2
Motcombe Cl [9] TN40 . .157 D3
Motcombe Inf Sch
BN21 . . . . .184 C5
Motcombe La BN21 . . . .184 D4
Motcombe Rd BN21 . . . .184 D4
Motte Field TN7 . . . . .13 E4
Mottins Hill TN6 . . . . .38 D8
Moulsecoomb Prim Sch
BN2 . . . . .143 E3
Moulsecoomb Sta BN2 . .143 D2
Moulsecoomb Way BN2 .143 F4
Mount Caburn Cres
BN10 . . . . .167 C2
Mount Cl BN9 . . . . .179 E8
Mount Dr BN2 . . . . .177 D6
Mount Edgcumbe Rd TN4 . .8 A4
Mount Ephraim TN4 . . . . .8 A4
Mount Ephraim Ct TN4 . . .7 F4
Mount Ephraim Rd TN1 . . .8 B4
Mount Harry Rd BN7 . . .123 B2
Mount Idol View TN39 . .157 A8
Mount Joy TN33 . . . . . . .112 D5
Mount Pl BN7 . . . . .190 A2
Mount Pleasant
Blackboys TN22 . . . . .80 A6
Brighton BN2 . . . . .189 C2
Crowborough TN6 . . . . . . .38 B7
Durgates TN5 . . . . .29 E5
Lamberhurst TN4 . . . . .9 A6
Lewes BN7 . . . . .190 A2
Spithurst BN8 . . . . .101 E6
[8] St Leonards TN38 . . . .159 C6
The Moor TN18 . . . . .45 F8
Uckfield TN22 . . . . .78 C6
Mount Pleasant Ave [2]
TN34 . . . . .8 B3
Mount Pleasant Cres [2]
TN34 . . . . .136 F1
Mount Pleasant Ct
TN34 . . . . .160 A6
Mount Pleasant Rd
Hastings TN34 . . . . .160 A6
Royal Tunbridge Wells TN1 . .8 A3
Mount Rd
Eastbourne BN20 . . . . . .188 F8
Hastings TN35 . . . . .160 C6
Newhaven BN9 . . . . .179 F8
Mount Sion TN1 . . . . .8 A2
Mount St Battle TN33 . . .112 D5
Lewes BN7 . . . . .190 A1

Mount The
Hailsham BN27 . . . . .152 C6
St Leonards TN38 . . . . . .159 B7
Mount View Terr BN27 . .152 C6
Mount Zion Pl BN1 . . . . .189 A3
Mountain Ash Cl BN27 . .152 A8
Mountbatten Cl TN35 . . .137 D5
Mountbatten Cl BN3 . . .162 E8
Mountbatten Dr BN23 . .185 F7
Mountfield & Whatlington CE
Prim Sch TN32 . . . . .87 D7
Mountfield Ct [4] TN1 . . .8 B3
Mountfield Gdns TN1 . . . .8 B3
Mountfield La TN32 . . . . .86 C8
Mountfield Rd
Eastbourne BN20 . . . . . .173 F1
Lewes BN7 . . . . .190 B1
Royal Tunbridge Wells TN1 . .8 B3
Mountfield Villas TN32 . . .87 C5
Mountfields BN1 . . . . . . .143 C2
Mountney Bridge Bsns Pk
BN24 . . . . .174 F4
Mountney Dr BN24 . . . . .175 F7
Mountney Rd BN21 . . . . .184 C4
Mountreed TN20 . . . . .58 B7
Mowden Sch BN3 . . . . . .142 F1
Moy Ave BN22 . . . . .185 B5
Moyne Cl BN3 . . . . .141 E1
Muddles Gn BN8 . . . . . . .127 F2
Muirfield Ct [10] RH16 . . .50 E4
Muirfield Rise TN38 . . . .158 C4
Mulberry Cl Bexhill TN39 .156 C4
Brighton BN1 . . . . .142 F3
Eastbourne BN22 . . . . . .173 E3
Shoreham-by-S BN43 . . . .140 D1
Mulberry La BN26 . . . . . .173 A6
Mulberry La BN3 . . . . .98 D3
Mulberry Pk TN22 . . . . . .55 B5
Mulberry Way TN21 . . . . .82 B5
Mulberry Wlk TN37 . . . .136 D5
Mullany Bsns Pk BN27 . .122 B4
Munns Dr RH15 . . . . .73 B4
Munster Cotts BN8 . . . . .101 E4
Munster Gn BN41 . . . . . .162 A3
Murray Ave BN9 . . . . . . .179 C7
Museum of Local History*
TN33 . . . . .112 D4
Museum of Rural Life*
TN32 . . . . .64 B4
Museum of Shops*
BN21 . . . . .185 A2
Musgrave Ave RH19 . . . . .10 E8
Mushroom Field BN7 . . .145 E5
Muskerry Ct TN4 . . . . .7 B4
Muster Ct RH16 . . . . .50 D4
Muster Gn N RH16 . . . . .50 D4
Muster Gn S RH16 . . . . .50 D4
Mutton Hall Hill TN21 . . .82 B8
Mutton Hall La TN21 . . . .82 B8
Mutton Hill TN7 . . . . .12 B7
Myrtle Cotts [3] TN6 . . . .25 F3
Myrtle Rd
Crowborough TN6 . . . . . . .25 F1
Eastbourne BN26 . . . . . .185 D6

N

Namrik Mews BN3 . . . . .163 A6
Nan Kemp's Grave BN7 .145 E6
Nan Tucks La TN22 . . . . .56 C2
Nanson Rd BN1 . . . . .143 C6
Naomi Cl BN20 . . . . .184 E1
Napier Ho [3] BN2 . . . . . .164 C7
Napier Rd
Royal Tunbridge Wells TN2 . .8 D2
St Leonards TN38 . . . . . .135 E4
Nash La RH17 . . . . .52 B4
Natal Rd BN2 . . . . .143 D1
Neale Cl RH19 . . . . .1 B3
Neath Rd TN31 . . . . .96 A2
Neaves La BN8 . . . . .125 A5
Neills Rd TN3 . . . . .19 D2
Neilson Ct TN34 . . . . . . .136 D1
Nellington Ct TN4 . . . . . . .7 B4
Nellington Rd TN3,TN4 . . .7 B4
Nelson Dr BN23 . . . . .185 E6
Nelson Ho TN39 . . . . . . .156 E4
Nelson Pl [17] BN2 . . . . .189 C3
Nelson Rd Hastings TN34 .160 A5
Royal Tunbridge Wells TN2 . .8 D2
Neptune Ct BN2 . . . . . . .164 F3
Nesbitt Rd BN2 . . . . .143 D1
Nestor Cl BN1 . . . . .163 E8
Nether La TN22 . . . . .55 C3
Netherfield Ave BN23 . . .174 F2
Netherfield CE Prim Sch
TN33 . . . . .86 C2
Netherfield Gn BN2 . . . .165 F8
Netherfield Hill TN33 . . .112 C7
Netherfield Rd TN33 . . . .111 F8
Netherfield Way TN35 . . .136 E5
Netherwood Ct TN34 . . .136 F5
Nettleton Ct BN1 . . . . . . .143 C6
Nevill Ave
Eastbourne BN22 . . . . . .173 E1
Hove BN3 . . . . .141 F1
Nevill Cl Crowborough TN6 .37 C8
Hove BN3 . . . . .142 A2
Nevill Cotts BN6 . . . . .98 D2

Nevill Cres BN7 ....123 A1
Nevill Ct Crowborough TN6 .37 C8
Hove BN3 ....142 A1
Nevill Gate TN2 ....8 B1
Nevill Gdns BN3 ....142 A2
Nevill Gn TN22 ....55 D1
Nevill Lodge TN2 ....8 C4
Nevill Pk BN3 ....7 E3
Nevill Pl BN3 ....142 A2
Nevill Rd Crowborough TN6 .25 F3
Hove BN3 ....142 A2
Lewes BN7 ....123 A2
Rottingdean BN2 ....165 F1
Uckfield TN22 ....55 D1
Nevill Ridge TN4 ....7 D3
Nevill St TN2 ....8 A2
Nevill Terr
⬛ Crowborough TN6 ....25 F3
⬛ Lewes BN7 ....123 B1
Royal Tunbridge Wells TN2 ..7 F2
Nevill Way BN3 ....142 A2
Neville Rd
⬛ Eastbourne BN22 ....185 B4
Peacehaven BN10 ....178 D6
New Barn Cl
Hailsham BN27 ....152 C6
Portslade-by-S BN41 .....141 B2
Shoreham-by-S BN43 .....140 B1
New Barn La TN22 ....78 C5
New Barn Rd
Rottingdean BN2 ....165 F3
Shoreham-by-S BN43 .....140 B1
New Church Rd BN3 ......162 E7
New Coastguards Cotts ⬛
BN25 ....180 C4
New College Cl BN23 ....174 F4
New Cotts
Crowborough TN6 ....38 C8
Eastbourne BN20 ....188 D8
Poundford TN20 ....58 B6
Scaynes Hill RH17 ....51 F1
The Moor TN18 ....45 B7
New Cut Mountfield TN32 .87 C5
Westfield TN35 ....114 E4
New Dorset St BN1 ....189 A3
New England Ho BN1 ....189 B4
New England La
Rye TN31 ....93 C8
Sedlescombe TN33 ......113 F6
New England Rd
Brighton BN1 ....189 A4
Haywards Heath RH16 ....50 F4
Royal Tunbridge Wells TN4 ..8 A7
New England Rise BN41 .141 A4
New England St BN1 .....189 B4
New Farthingdale RH7 ....2 A8
New Horizons Sch
TN38 ....136 A4
New Langney Ct BN23 ...174 E1
New Lydd Rd TN31 ....94 E2
New Moorsite TN35 .....114 F3
New Park Ave TN40 .....157 C4
New Pl Eastbourne BN21 .184 D3
Uckfield TN22 ....78 D3
New Pond Hill TN21 ......81 D6
New Rd Brighton BN1 ....189 B2
Crowborough TN6 ....25 F3
Eastbourne BN22 ....185 B4
Fairlight TN35 ....138 D4
Hailsham BN27 ....129 C4
Hastings TN35 ....160 D6
Keymer BN6 ....98 B2
Lewes BN7 ....190 A2
Mill Corner TN31 ....67 B3
Newhaven BN9 ....168 D1
Polegate BN26 ....173 B6
Rotherfield TN6 ....39 C8
Rye TN31 ....93 D6
Saint's Hill TN11 ....6 A8
Uckfield TN22 ....78 D3
New Steine BN2 ....189 C2
New Steine Mews BN2 ...189 C2
New Upperton Rd ⬛
BN21 ....184 E4
New Way La BN6 ....97 B2
New Winchelsea Rd
TN31,TN36 ....93 B3
Newark Pl BN2 ....189 C2
Newbury Cotts TN5 ......30 B8
Newbury La TN5 ....30 C8
Newcomen Rd TN4 ....8 A5
Newdigate Rd ⬛ TN40 .157 D3
Newells Cl BN2 ....124 E1
Newfield La BN9 ....179 C7
Newfield Rd BN9 ....179 C7
Newgate Rd TN37 ....136 C1
Newhaven Fort* BN9 ....168 C7
Newhaven Harbour Sta
BN9 ....179 D6
Newhaven Hts BN9 ......179 C5
Newhaven Local & Maritime
Mus* BN9 ....168 D1
Newhaven Rd BN25 .....180 B5
Newhaven Sq BN9 ......179 D7
Newhaven St BN2 ....189 C3
Newhaven Town Sta
BN9 ....179 D8
Newhaven Wlk TN38 ....136 A3
Newick CE Prim Sch
BN8 ....76 C6
Newick Cl BN25 ....181 C2
Newick Dr BN7 ....76 C7
Newick Hill BN8 ....76 C8
Newick House Sch RH15 .73 C1

Newick La TN20,TN21 ....59 C5
Newick Rd Brighton BN1 .143 E4
Eastbourne BN20 ....184 C6
Newington Ct TN5 ....31 E1
Newlands TN3 ....7 A3
Newlands Ave TN39 ....157 B5
Newlands Cl
Hastings TN34 ....136 E5
Keymer BN6 ....98 B3
Newlands Cres RH19 ....1 D2
Newlands Manor Sch
BN25 ....181 A4
Newlands Park Way BN8 .76 C7
Newlands Pl RH18 ....11 F3
Newlands Rd
Rottingdean BN2 ....177 A5
Royal Tunbridge Wells TN4 ..8 B7
Newlands Rise TN4 ....8 A6
Newlands Sch BN25 ....181 A4
Newlands Way BN8 ....4 B7
Newlyn Ct ⬛ TN40 .....157 D3
Newmans Way TN3 ......160 D8
Newmarket Rd BN2 .....164 C8
Newmarket Terr ⬛
BN2 ....164 C8
Newnham Rd BN21 ......82 A6
Newnham Way TN21 .....82 A7
Newport Rd RH15 ....72 F3
Newport St BN2 ....189 C4
Newstead ⬛ BN1 ......189 A4
Newtimber Dr BN41 .....141 A1
Newton Ave RH19 ....10 F6
Newton Cl RH16 ....51 B7
Newton Ct RH16 ....50 E5
Newton Pk BN27 ....152 D7
Newton Rd Lewes BN7 ..123 B2
Lindfield RH16 ....51 C7
Peacehaven BN10 ....178 C7
Newton Willows TN3 .....15 C7
Newton's Hill TN7 ....13 D3
Newtown Rd BN3 ....163 B8
Newts Way TN38 ....135 E1
Nicholson Ct BN23 .....174 E1
Nicolson Dr BN43 ......161 A8
Nightingale Cl
East Grinstead RH19 ....10 D7
Eastbourne BN23 ....174 C2
Haywards Heath RH16 ...50 F6
Nightingale Cotts TN35 .114 D4
Nightingale La RH15 .....73 C1
Nightingale Rise TN22 ...78 D4
Nightingales The
Royal Tunbridge Wells TN4 ..8 A5
Uckfield TN22 ....78 E5
Nile St BN1 ....189 B2
Ninfield CE Prim Sch
TN33 ....133 B5
Ninfield Pl BN2 ....164 E7
Ninfield Rd TN39 ....157 B7
Nizells Ave BN3 ....163 F7
Noahs Ark La RH16 ......51 C7
Noble Ct BN3 ....162 E7
Nodes La BN27 ....129 F4
Noel Gn RH15 ....73 B4
Noel Rise RH15 ....73 B4
Nolan Rd BN2 ....165 E7
Nook Cl TN35 ....160 D7
Nook The TN22 ....78 D4
Norbury Cl TN6 ....25 E4
Nook Rd BN9 ....179 B6
Norfolk Bldgs ⬛ BN1 ..163 E5
Norfolk Mews ⬛ BN1 ..163 E5
Norfolk Pl ⬛ BN1 ......163 E5
Norfolk Rd Brighton BN1 .163 E6
Royal Tunbridge Wells TN1 ..8 C4
Norfolk Sq BN1 ....163 E5
Norfolk St BN1 ....163 E5
Norfolk Terr BN1 ....163 E5
Norfolk Way TN22 ....78 C8
Norlington Ct BN8 .....124 D6
Norlington Fields BN8 ..124 D7
Norlington La BN8 ......124 D7
Norman Cl Battle TN33 ..112 F4
Seaford BN25 ....180 B6
Norman Ct ⬛ TN34 ...159 E7
Norman Rd
Eastbourne BN20,BN21 .184 C4
Hastings TN35 ....135 D2
Northam Rise TN38 .....135 D2
Northiam Sta* TN31 ....67 B5
Northlands Ave RH16 ...51 A4
Northlands Cotts TN32 ..46 C1
Northlands Wood Com Prim
Sch RH16 ....51 B4
Northridge TN31 ....67 A7

North Beeches Rd TN6 ..26 A2
North Camp La BN25 ...180 F5
North Cl Polegate BN26 .173 B7
Portslade-by-S BN41 ...141 A2
North Cnr TN21 ....107 C4
North Common Rd BN8,
RH17 ....74 E5
North Crescent Ind Est
BN27 ....152 A7
North Ct Hassocks BN6 ..97 E4
Dormans Park RH19 .....2 B6
North Dr Brighton BN2 ..98 D4
North End BN6 ....98 D4
North Farm Cotts BN41 .141 A2
North Farm Rd TN2 ......8 C8
North Gdns BN1 ....189 A3
North Heath Cl BN27 ...129 C2
North La
Portslade-by-S BN41 ...141 A3
Clive Vale TN35 ....115 E5
North Pl BN1 ....189 B2
North Point ⬛ BN43 ...161 A6
North Quay Rd BN9 .....179 D8
North Rd Alfriston BN26 .170 F3
Bexhill TN39 ....157 C7
Bodle Street Green BN27 .109 C2
Brighton BN1 ....189 A3
Brighton,Preston BN1 ..142 E1
Haywards Heath RH16 ...51 A4
Pevensey Bay BN24 ....175 D5
Portslade-by-S BN41 ...141 A2
Ringmer BN8 ....124 D6
St Leonards TN37 ......136 C1
North Road Cotts BN8 ..124 D6
North Row TN7 ....13 D5
North Salts TN31 ....93 C6
North St Alfriston BN26 .171 A3
Brighton BN1 ....189 B2
Cowden TN8 ....A6
Eastbourne BN21 ......185 B3
Hailsham BN27 ....152 B8
Hellingly BN27 ....129 A7
Lewes BN7 ....190 B3
Lower Horsebridge BN27 .107 A2
Lower Horsebridge BN27 .128 F4
Mayfield TN20 ....40 B3
Portslade-by-S BN41 ...162 C7
Punnett's Town TN21 ....83 D6
Roser's Cross TN21 .....80 F5
Rotherfield TN6 ....39 B8
Royal Tunbridge Wells TN2 ..8 C7
Winchelsea TN36 ......117 E8
North St Quadrant BN1 .189 A2
North Terr TN34 ....160 C6
North Trade Rd TN33 ...112 B4
North Way Lewes BN7 ..123 A2
Newhaven BN9 ....179 C8
Seaford BN25 ....180 F5
North-South Rd BN1 ...144 B7
Northampton Way ⬛
TN38 ....136 A4
Northbourne Rd BN22 .185 C6
Northbridge St TN32 ....64 B5
Northcliffe Cl BN25 ....180 F4
Northcote La BN21 .....167 A1
Northdown Cl BN9 .....179 C6
Northdown Rd BN9 .....179 B6
Northdown Terr RH19 ...1 D3
Northease Cl BN3 ......141 D2
Northease Dr BN3 ......141 E3
Northease Gdns BN3 ...141 E3
Northease Wall BN7 ....146 D3
Northerlea BN41 ....141 A1
Northern Ave BN26 ....173 B7
Northfield Cl BN25 .....172 F5
Northfield Cotts TN22 .102 D8
Northfield Rise
Hove BN3 ....141 D4
Rottingdean BN2 ......177 A6
Northfield Way BN1 ...143 A4
Northfields BN3 ....7 A8
Northfields Bsns Pk
BN27 ....128 A4
Northgate Cl BN2 .....165 F2
Northiam CE Prim Sch
TN31 ....67 B5
Northiam Rd
Broad Oak TN31 ....90 A6
Northlands Ave RH16 ...51 A4
Northlands Cotts TN32 ..46 C1
Northlands Wood Com Prim
Sch RH16 ....51 B4

Nuffield Hospl TN2 ....8 C3
Nunnery La TN11 ....5 F8
Nunnery Stables ⬛
.......................123 B1
Nursery Cl
Hailsham BN27 ....152 C8
Haywards Heath RH16 ...50 D5
Polegate BN26 ....173 B6
Portslade-by-S BN43 ...140 E4
Shoreham-by-S BN43 ..161 B8
Union Street TN5 ....32 B3
Nursery Ct TN34 ....159 E8
Nursery La
Maresfield Park TN22 ...55 B7
Nutley TN22 ....55 B7
Uckfield TN22 ....78 D4
Waldron Down TN21,TN22 .80 E8
Windmill Hill BN27 .....131 B5
Nursery Path BN27 ....152 B8
Nursery Rd TN4 ....8 B8
Nursery The RH15 ......73 C4
Nursery Way TN21 ......81 E7
Nutbourne Cl BN23 ....174 E2
Nuthatch Rd BN2 ......164 F6
Nuthurst Cl BN2 ....164 F6
Nuthurst Pl BN2 ....164 F5
Nutley Ave BN2 ....177 D4
Nutley CE Prim Sch
TN22 ....35 C5
Nutley Cl Hove BN3 ....141 F3
Rye TN31 ....93 A6
Nutley Mill Rd BN24 ...174 B5
Nutley Windmill* TN22 ..35 E7
Nye Cl TN6 ....25 F1
Nye La Ditchling BN6 ....96 D1
Westmeston BN6 ....120 D8
Nye Rd RH15 ....73 C3
Nyetimber Hill BN2 .....143 E2
Nym Cl BN8 ....100 E7

O

Oak Ave BN27 ....127 C3
Oak Bank RH16 ....50 F7
Oak Cl BN1 ....142 E3
Oak Croft RH15 ....11 A8
Oak Field The TN35 ....116 F1
Oak Hall RH15 ....73 B1
Oak Ho ⬛ TN2 ....8 C2
Oak Lodge TN2 ....8 D7
Oak Pas ⬛ TN34 ......160 A4
Oak Rd ⬛ Bexhill TN40 .157 C5
Royal Tunbridge Wells TN2 ..8 D7
Oak Terr TN31 ....67 B6
Oak Tree Cl
East Grinstead RH19 ....1 C3
Eastbourne BN23 ......174 C4
Royal Tunbridge Wells TN2 ..8 A1
Oak Tree Cotts
Burgess Hill RH15 ....73 B3
Danehill RH17 ....34 A4
Oak Tree La TN22 ....78 D8
Oak Tree La BN23 .....174 C4
Oak Tree Way BN27 ...129 C2
Oakapple Rd BN42 ....140 E1
Oakdale Rd
Haywards Heath RH16 ..50 F3
Royal Tunbridge Wells TN4 ..7 F4
Oakdene RH16 ....50 D5
Oakdene Ave BN41 ....140 E3
Oakdene Cl BN41 ......140 E3
Oakdene Cres BN41 ...140 E3
Oakdene Gdns BN41 ...140 E3
Oakdene Rise BN41 ...140 E4
Oakdene Way BN41 ...140 E3
Oakey Cl TN19 ....61 A4
Oakendene BN2 ....143 F4
Oakenfield RH15 ....73 A5
Oakfield Cl RH16 ....51 A7
Oakfield Court Rd TN2 ..8 C3
Oakfield Rd BN25 .....160 C7
Oakfield The TN31 ......93 B8
Oakfield Way
Bexhill TN39 ....156 C6
East Grinstead RH19 ....1 F3
Oakhill Cotts TN31 ......68 C4
Oakhill Dr TN31 ....90 B5
Oakhurst RH16 ....50 D8
Oakhurst Cl TN34 .....136 E5
Oakhurst Dr The 26 A3
Oakhurst Gdns RH19 ...1 C2
Oakhurst La RH16 ......50 D8
Oakhurst Rd TN33 ....112 D7
Oakland Dr TN32 ....63 D4
Oakland Villas TN3 ......15 B7
Oaklands
Crowborough TN6 ....26 B1
Eastbourne BN21 ......185 A4
South Chailey BN8 ....100 C7
Westham BN24 ....174 D6
Oaklands Ave BN2 .....177 D5
Oaklands Cl BN26 .....173 B6
Oaklands Rd
Groombridge TN3 ....15 B6
Haywards Heath RH16 ..50 D5
Oaklands Way BN27 ...152 D8
Oaklea Cl TN7 ....13 C4
Oaklea Ct TN34 ....136 C4
Oaklea Way TN22 ......78 C7
Oakleaf Cl BN26 ......173 A7
Oakleaf Dr BN26 ......173 A7
Oakleigh Cl BN27 .....152 B6
Oakleigh Rd TN39 ....156 C4
Oakley Cl RH19 ....11 E7
Oakley Cotts RH19 .....11 E7
Oakley Ct TN22 ....78 D6
Oakley Ho BN2 ....189 C2

Oakley Sch TN2 ....9 A5
Oakmead Rd RH15 .....72 F1
Oakmead Way BN8 ....124 D5
Oakmeeds Com Coll
RH15 ....73 A2
Oakroyd Cl RH15 ....73 D5
Oaks Cl TN19 ....63 B8
Oaks Forstal TN18 ......47 C5
Oaks The
Burgess Hill RH15 ......72 D4
East Grinstead RH19 ....11 B8
Haywards Heath RH16 ..51 A4
Haywards Heath RH16 ..51 C4
Heathfield TN21 ....82 B6
St Leonards TN37 .....136 D5
Oaktree BN8 ....101 E4
Oakwood RH16 ....50 D4
Oakwood Ave TN39 ...157 B7
Oakwood Cl
Burgess Hill RH15 ......73 B2
Hastings TN34 ....136 F3
Oakwood Dr TN22 ......78 E8
Oakwood Pk
Forest Row RH18 ....11 F2
Nutley TN22 ....35 C4
Oakwood Rd
Burgess Hill RH15 ......73 B2
Haywards Heath RH16 ..50 D4
Oakwood Rise TN2 ......2 B3
Oakwood Sch BN22 ...173 D3
Oast Cl TN12 ....9 A2
Oast House Dr TN31 ....92 F4
Oast House Field TN36 .116 F6
Oast House Rd TN36 ..116 D5
Oathall Ave RH16 ....50 F6
Oathall Com Coll RH16 .50 F6
Oathall Rd RH16 ....50 F5
Oban Rd TN37 ....136 B3
Observatory Science Ctr
The* BN27 ....131 C1
Observatory View BN27 .131 C1
Ocean Bldg The TN4 ...189 A3
Ocean Ct BN23 ....185 F7
Oceania ⬛ TN39 ......157 B3
Ochiltree Cl TN34 ......160 A8
Ochiltree Rd TN34 .....160 A8
Ocho Rios Mews ⬛
BN23 ....185 F8
Ockenden Way BN6 .....97 C3
Ockham La BN6,RH15 ..98 B4
Ockley La
Burgess Hill RH15 ......98 B7
Keymer BN6 ....98 B4
Ockley Way BN6 ....98 A5
Ockling Piece BN21 ...184 D4
Ocklynge Ave ⬛ BN21 .184 D4
Ocklynge Cl TN39 .....156 C5
Ocklynge Ct ⬛ BN21 .184 D4
Ocklynge Jun Sch BN21 .184 C6
Ocklynge Rd BN21 ....184 C6
Ockman La ⬛ TN31 ....93 C5
Octagon The BN2 ......164 F3
Offa Cl TN40 ....157 C4
Offa Rd TN35 ....160 B8
Offham Cl
Eastbourne BN23 .....173 F4
Seaford BN25 ....180 F5
Offham Ct ⬛ BN25 ...180 C4
Offham Rd BN7 ....123 B2
Okehurst Rd BN1 ......184 C3
Old Barn Cl BN20 .....173 B1
Old Barn Rd TN6 ....180 D2
Old Barn Way BN42 ...162 A7
Old Barn Homes BN25 .180 F4
Old Boat Cnr BN1 .....143 D8
Old Boat Wlk BN1 .....143 B7
Old Brickyard TN31 .....93 A5
Old Camp Rd BN20 ...184 C2
Old Church Rd TN38 ..135 A4
Old Coastguard Cotts
BN9 ....179 D6
Old Coastguards TN35 .139 C7
Old Convent The RH19 ..1 E2
Old Court Cl BN1 ......142 F4
Old Dr BN26 ....172 F6
Old Dro BN23 ....173 F4
Old Farm Cl RH17 ......51 A2
Old Farm Rd
Bexhill TN39 ....157 B6
Brighton BN1 ....142 F5
Old Fire Station The ⬛
BN22 ....185 A3
Old Foord Cl BN8 .....100 D7
Old Forest La TN6 ......38 E8
Old Forewood La TN33 .134 F7
Old Forge La TN22 ......36 A1
Old Fort Rd BN43 .....161 B6
Old Gardens Cl TN2 .....17 B8
Old Ghyll Rd TN21 ......82 A5
Old Harbour Farm La
TN36 ....118 B5
Old Harrow Rd TN37 ..136 B4
Old Heath Cl BN8 .....104 C6
Old Hop Garden The
TN3 ....69 C2
Old House Gdns TN34 .136 F4
Old House La
Langton Green TN3 ......6 D4
Uckfield TN22 ....78 E4
Old Humphrey Ave ⬛
TN34 ....160 B4
Old La
Crowborough,Poundfield
TN6 ....26 B1
Crowborough,St John's
TN6 ....25 D3

Old La *continued*
Mayfield TN20 ....40 A2

Old London Rd
Brighton BN1 ....142 E6
Hastings TN34,TN35 ......160 C6
Old Lydd Rd TN31 ....94 E2
Old Malling Way BN7 ....190 A4
Old Manor Cl TN40 ....157 D4
Old Mansion Cl BN20 ....184 A8
Old Market Cotts
17 Hove BN3 ....163 D5
8 Seaford BN25 ....180 E3
Old Mill Cl Brighton BN1 ..142 E5
Hailsham BN27 ....129 A3
Portslade-by-S BN41 ....162 A7
Old Mill Ct TN6 ....25 E2
Old Mill La BN26 ....172 F4
Old Mill Pk TN39 ....157 A6
Old Mill Wlk TN33 ....112 D5
Old Mint Ho* BN24 .....175 B6
Old Motcombe Mews 11
BN21 ....184 D4
Old Nursery Cl BN25 ....181 B5
Old Orch TN18 ....47 B5
Old Orchard Pl BN27 ....152 B7
Old Orchard Rd BN21 ...184 F2
Old Parish La BN2 ......165 C8
Old Park Cl RH17 ....50 A6
Old Patcham Mews
BN1 ....142 E6
Old Place Ct BN2 ....165 F1
Old Rd East Grinstead RH19 ..1 F1
Magham Down BN27 .....130 A4
Old Rectory Gdns BN24 .161 D8
Old Riding School The
TN3 ....15 B2
Old River Way TN36 .....118 B7
Old Roar Rd TN37 ....136 C5
Old School Cl
Polegate BN26 ....173 A7
Ringmer BN8 ....124 E6
Old School Cotts BN7 ....99 E5
Old School Ct RH16 ....51 B7
Old School Fields TN22 ...78 C5
Old School Ho BN27 .....131 B5
Old School Pl RH15 ......72 F2
Old Shoreham Rd
Portslade-by-S BN3,BN41 .162 C8
Southwick BN42 ....140 E1
Old Station Rd TN5 ....29 E6
Old Steine BN1 ....189 B2
Old Stone Link 2 RH19 ..10 E8
Old Swan La BN27 ......152 D6
Old Timbers La TN22 .....78 C6
Old Top Rd TN35 ....160 D8
Old Town Hall Mus*
TN34 ....160 A4
Old Viaduct Ct 10 BN2 ..164 C8
Old Wardsdown TN5 .....32 B3
Old Wickham La RH16 ...50 E7
Old Willingdon Rd
BN20 ....183 B2
Old Wish Rd BN21 ......184 F1
Old World Cotts TN31 ...94 D2
Oldaker Rd BN8 ....76 D7
Olde Place Mews BN2 ..165 F1
Oldfield Ave BN20 ......173 A4
Oldfield Cres
Hailsham BN27 ....129 B1
Southwick BN42 ....161 E8
Oldfield Rd BN20 ....173 A4
Oldlands Ave BN6 ....98 A4
Oldlands Hall TN22 ....36 C4
Oldlands Hill TN22 ....36 C2
Olive Rd BN3 ....162 D8
Oliver Cl Crowborough TN6 .26 A1
Hastings TN34 ....159 F7
Oliver Ho 10 BN3 ....163 B5
Olivers Mews TN33 .....112 E4
Olives Mdw TN22 ....78 D7
Olivier Cl BN2 ....164 C5
Onslow Rd BN1 ....143 C1
Open Mkt The BN1 ......189 B4
Orange Row BN1 ....189 B2
Orchard Ave BN3 ....142 A1
Orchard Bsns Ctr TN2 .....8 D8
Orchard Cl Fairwarp TN22 .36 B2
Hastings TN34 ....136 F2
Haywards Heath RH16 ....50 D8
Royal Tunbridge Wells TN2 ..8 D6
Scaynes Hill RH17 ....51 F3
Orchard Ct RH16 ....51 B5
Orchard Cotts TN6 ....39 B8
Orchard Gdns BN3 ......142 B1
Orchard Gr TN1 ....8 B5
Orchard Grange TN7 ....128 C3
Orchard La Ditchling BN6 .98 D4
Hassocks BN6 ....97 F4
Orchard Mews BN9 .....182 B3
Orchard Par BN20 ......173 A3
Orchard Rd Bexhill TN40 .157 C6
Burgess Hill RH15 ....72 E3
Hove BN3 ....142 B1
Lewes BN7 ....190 C3
Orchard Rise TN3 ....15 B7
Orchard The
Broad Oak TN31 ....90 B4
Etchingham TN19 ....44 C1
Hassocks BN6 ....97 F3
Nutley TN22 ....35 C4
Shoreham-by-S BN43 ....161 B5
Orchard View Pk BN27 .131 B6
Orchard Way
Burgess Hill RH15 ....72 F3
East Grinstead RH19 ......1 E1
Haywards Heath RH16 ....50 D8
Peasmarsh TN31 ....69 C1

Orchard Way *continued*
Sedlescombe TN33 ....88 E1
Orchards Sh Ctr RH16 .....50 E4
Orchards The BN2 ....143 E3
Orchid Cl BN23 ....174 B3
Orchid Pk RH16 ....51 C4
Orchid View BN1 ....143 C6
Orchidhurst TN2 ....8 D7
Ore Pl TN34 ....137 A5
Ore Bsns Pk TN35 ....160 B6
Ore Sta TN34 ....160 A6
Oriental Pl BN1 ....163 E5
Orion Cl BN27 ....152 D7
Orion Par BN6 ....97 F3
Orkney Ct BN20 ....184 B6
Orlando Ho BN1 ....164 A8
Ormerod Ave TN38 .....136 A4
Ormerod Ct RH16 ....50 E5
Orpen Rd BN2 ....142 D1
Orwell Cl BN24 ....174 B5
Osborn Cl TN39 ....157 A6
Osborne Cl TN34 ....136 E2
Osborne Ct
Polegate BN26 ....173 A7
7 Shoreham-by-S BN43 .161 C8
Osborne Hill TN6 ....38 C8
Osborne Rd
Brighton BN1 ....143 A2
Crowborough TN6 ....38 C8
Eastbourne BN20 ....184 B4
Osborne Villas BN3 .....163 B6
Osmers Hill TN5 ....29 F7
Osmond Gdns BN3 .....163 E7
Osmond Rd BN3 ....163 E7
Osmunda Bank RH19 .....1 E4
Osmunda Ct TN2 ....8 C4
Osprey Dr TN22 ....78 E5
Osprey Ho 18 BN1 ......163 E5
Ospringe Pl TN2 ....8 D8
Oswald Ct TN40 ....157 C4
Otham Court La BN26 ...173 B8
Otham Pk BN27 ....152 D7
Otham Rd BN22 ....174 A2
Ottafield Ct RH16 ....50 F6
Otteham Cl BN20 ....173 B6
Otterbourne Pl RH19 .....1 B1
Oulton Cl BN23 ....174 B4
**Our Lady of Lourdes RC Prim
Sch** BN2 ....165 F1
Ousedale Cl BN7 ....123 B1
Outlook Ave BN10 ......178 F6
Outlook The BN20 ......183 A1
Oval Cl BN10 ....167 C2
Over St BN1 ....189 B3
Overdown Rise BN41 ...140 F4
Overhill BN42 ....140 E1
Overhill Dr BN1 ....142 E5
Overhill Gdns BN1 ......142 E5
Overhill Way BN1 ....142 E6
Overton Shaw RH19 .....1 E4
Ovingdean Cl BN2 ......165 D5
Ovingdean Hall Sch
BN2 ....165 D4
Ovingdean Rd BN2 .....165 D4
Owen Cl RH15 ....72 F1
Owl Hous Gdns* TN3 ...19 E7
Owls Gdns TN5 ....42 F5
Owlsbury Cross TN21 ...83 B5
Ox Lea TN3 ....7 A3
Oxbottom Cl BN8 ....76 B6
Oxenbridge La TN19 .....63 B8
Oxenbridge Row TN19 ...63 B8
Oxendean Gdns BN22 ..173 B4
Oxford Cl BN1 ....189 B4
Oxford Mews BN3 ......163 C7
Oxford Pl BN1 ....189 B4
Oxford Rd
8 Eastbourne BN22 .....185 A8
St Leonards TN38 ....136 A3
Oxford St BN1 ....189 B4
Oxford Terr 9 TN34 ....160 B4
Oxshott Cl TN34 ....157 F4
Oyster Creek TN31 ....94 A3

P

Pacific Dr BN23 ....175 B2
Pacific Heights N 11
BN23 ....175 A1
Pacific Heights S 10
BN23 ....175 A1
Packer Cl RH19 ....2 A3
Packham Way RH15 ....72 F4
Paddock Cl Bexhill TN40 .157 D6
Fordcombe TN3 ....7 B8
Paddock Cotts BN24 ...175 A6
Paddock Ct BN41 ....140 F3
Paddock Field BN1 .....144 B5
Paddock Gdns
East Grinstead RH19 .....10 E7
Polegate BN26 ....172 F4
Paddock La BN7 ....190 A2
Paddock Rd Lewes BN7 .190 A2
St Leonards BN7 ....136 C5
Paddock Terr BN7 ......190 A2
Paddocks The
Eastbourne BN22 ....173 F2
Hove BN3 ....142 C1
Maresfield TN22 ....55 A4
Northiam TN31 ....67 B7
Pembury TN2 ....9 B2
Walter's Green TN3 ......5 F5
Paddockhall Rd RH16 ....50 D5
Paddocks The Cowden TN8 .4 B7
Hailsham BN27 ....129 A2
Haywards Heath RH16 ....50 C3
Plumpton Green BN7 .....99 E6

Paddocks The *continued*
Rodmell BN7 ....167 D8
Padgham Cnr TN21 .....109 E8
Padgham La TN21 ......109 D8
Padua Ho BN2 ....165 F8
Padua House Flats BN2 .165 F8
Pages Ave TN39 ....156 F2
Pages Cl TN21 ....81 E7
Pages La TN39 ....156 E3
Pagham Cl BN8 ....76 D7
Pagham Cl BN23 ....174 B8
Pain's Flat RH15,RH17 ..72 D8
Paine's Cnr TN21 ....60 C4
Paines Cotts TN31 ....94 A3
Palace Ct 11 TN34 ......159 E7
Palace Pier BN2 ....189 B1
Palace Pl BN1 ....189 B2
Palesgate La TN6 ....26 C2
Palesgate Way BN20 ...184 B5
Palliser Cl BN23 ....185 E6
Palm Ct 2 BN3 ....163 D6
Palma Cl BN3 ....173 A7
Palmeira Ave BN3 ......163 D6
Palmeira Avenue Mans 24
BN3 ....163 C6
Palmeira Ct BN3 ....163 C6
Palmeira Grande 8
BN3 ....163 D6
Palmeira Ho 6 BN3 .....163 D6
Palmeira Mans 21 BN3 ..163 C6
Palmeira Pl BN3 ....163 D6
Palmeira Sq BN3 ....163 C6
Palmer Ho BN8 ....100 E7
Palmers Row BN27 .....152 D7
Palmerston Rd BN7 .....168 F1
Palmyra BN23 ....185 G8
Panama Reach BN23 ...185 G8
Pangdean La BN6,RH15 ..72 C1
Pangdene Cl RH15 ....72 F1
Pankhurst Cl TN39 .....157 A8
Pankhurst Rise TN39 ...157 A8
Pannel La TN35,TN36 ...116 E2
Pannell Cl RH19 ....1 D1
Pannett RH15 ....72 E4
Pantiles The
20 Royal Tunbridge Wells
TN1 ....8 A2
* Royal Tunbridge Wells TN2 .8 A2
Parade The
Beachlands BN24 ....175 F6
Brighton BN1 ....142 B4
Crowborough TN6 ....25 F3
East Grinstead RH19 ......1 B1
Hove BN3 ....141 C2
Pevensey Bay BN24 .....175 E5
Paradise Cl BN20 ....184 D2
Paradise Dr BN20 ......184 D2
Paradise Family L Pk*
BN20 ....168 D1
Paragon The BN20 .....172 F3
Parham Cl BN2 ....164 D5
Parham Ho BN2 ....163 D7
Park Aparments The
BN1 ....142 D4
Park Ave Bexhill TN39 ...157 B2
Brighton BN21,BN22 ....184 D7
Hastings TN34 ....136 D3
Hove BN3 ....162 F7
Keymer BN6 ....98 A2
Shoreham-by-S BN43 ...161 A1
Park Cl Brighton BN1 ...143 C6
Burgess Hill RH15 ....72 F3
Eastbourne BN20 ....184 D3
Hailsham BN27 ....152 B6
Hastings TN34 ....136 D3
Hove BN3 ....141 B3
Hurstpierpoint BN6 ....97 A6
Portslade-by-S BN41 .....141 B1
Park Cres Brighton BN2 ..189 C4
Crowborough TN6 ....25 F3
Forest Row RH18 ....12 A2
Hastings TN34 ....136 D2
Portslade-by-S BN41 .....162 A8
Rottingdean BN2 ....165 F1
Park Crescent Pl BN2 ...189 C4
Park Crescent Terr BN2 .189 C4
Park Croft BN26 ....173 C5
Park Ct 2 Brighton BN2 ..164 C6
Brighton,Patcham BN1 ..142 E6
Burgess Hill RH15 ....72 F3
4 Haywards Heath RH16 ..50 E4
Hove BN3 ....163 D7
Peacehaven BN10 ....178 B7
Park E TN34 ....136 D3
Park Drive Cl BN9 ......168 F2
Park E RH16 ....50 F2
Park Farm Bsns Pk RH17 .74 B2
Park Farm Cl TN21 ......63 B8
Park Gate Brighton BN1 ..163 F8
Hailsham BN27 ....129 D3
Hove BN3 ....163 D6
Park Gates BN2 ....185 A2
Park Hill BN2 ....189 C2
Park La
Ashurst Wood RH19 ......11 D3
Battle TN33 ....112 D4
Bexhill TN39 ....157 A6
6 Crowborough TN6 ......25 F3
Eastbourne BN21 ....184 C8
Hove BN3 ....163 D6
Southwick BN42 ....161 A3
Whatlington TN33 ....88 A5

Park Lodge
10 Eastbourne BN21 ....185 A2
Hove BN3 ....163 D8
Park Lodge Ct TN38 ....159 B7
Park Manor BN1 ....142 D3
Park Mead Prim Sch
BN27 ....151 A7
Park Par RH16 ....50 E4
Park Rd Bexhill TN39 ...157 B3
Brighton BN1 ....143 E5
Burgess Hill RH15 ....73 A3
Crowborough TN6 ....25 F3
Dormans Park RH19 ....1 F6
East Grinstead RH19 ......1 D1
Forest Row RH18 ....12 A2
Hailsham BN27 ....129 B4
Haywards Heath RH16 ....50 E4
Heathfield TN21 ....82 B7
Heathfield TN21 ....82 C6
Lewes BN7 ....190 A2
Peacehaven BN10 ....178 F6
Rottingdean BN2 ....165 F1
Royal Tunbridge Wells TN4 .8 B5
Seaford BN25 ....180 D3
Shoreham-by-S BN43 ...161 A8
Park Rise Brighton BN1 ..141 D3
Haywards Heath RH16 ....50 E4
Park Road Terr 4 BN2 ..189 C2
Park Royal BN1 ....143 C6
Park Shaw TN33 ....88 E1
Park Sq BN2 ....164 F3
Park St Brighton BN2 ....189 C2
Falmer BN1 ....144 C6
Royal Tunbridge Wells TN2 ..8 C3
Park The Crowborough TN6 .25 F2
Rottingdean BN2 ....177 A5
Park View Brighton BN2 .164 C6
Brighton,Preston BN1 ....142 F1
Buxted TN22 ....56 C4
Hastings TN34 ....136 D2
Haywards Heath RH16 ....50 E6
Herstmonceux BN27 ....130 E5
Northiam TN31 ....67 A6
Peasmarsh TN31 ....69 B2
Park View Cl Hove BN3 ..142 B1
Park View Rd Hove BN3 .142 B1
Park View Terr BN1 .....163 E8
Park Village The BN1 ...144 A8
Park Village TN21 ....82 B6
Park W RH16 ....50 F2
Park Way Hastings TN34 .136 D3
Southwick BN42 ....161 F8
Park Way Cl BN42 ......161 F8
Park Wood Rd TN34 ....136 F6
Parker Cl BN23 ....184 E5
Parker Ct BN1 ....141 B2
Parker Rd TN34 ....160 B4
Parkfield Ave BN22 .....173 E1
Parkfield Way RH15 ......50 C3
Parkhurst Rd TN40 .....157 C3
Parkland Inf Sch BN22 .173 D1
Parkland Jun Sch BN22 .173 D1
Parklands Maresfield TN22 .55 A5
Royal Tunbridge Wells TN2 ..7 E8
Parklands Rd BN3 ......161 C8
Parklands Rd BN3 ....97 F3
Parkmere BN1 ....189 A5
Parks The BN41 ....141 B3
Parks Yd TN33 ....112 D4
Parkside Burgess Hill RH15 .72 F3
East Grinstead RH19 ......1 C1
Heathfield TN21 ....82 B6
Keymer BN6 ....98 A4
Shoreham-by-S BN43 ...161 A1
Parkside Com Prim Sch
TN21 ....82 C5
Parkside Rd BN25 ......180 E4
Parkstone Par TN34 ....136 D4
Parkstone Rd TN34 .....136 D4
Parkstone Terr TN34 ...136 D4
Parkview
Hurstpierpoint BN6 ....97 A5
Royal Tunbridge Wells TN2 ..8 D2
Parkview Rd TN22 ....55 D1
Parkway BN20 ....184 B8
Parkwood TN31 ....70 B4
Parnell Ct 3 BN3 ....163 B6
Parochial Terr BN2 .....189 B2
Parrock La TN7 ....12 E2
Parry Cl BN23 ....174 E3
Parsonage Cl TN4 ....7 B5
Parsonage La
Icklesham TN36 ....116 F6
Lamberhurst TN3 ....20 B6
Westfield TN35 ....114 C4
Parsonage Rd
Eastbourne BN24 ....184 D4
Rusthall TN4 ....7 B5
Parsons Cl TN38 ....135 F4
Partridges La TN5 ....28 E6
Parve Ct TN40 ....157 C4
Pashley Down Cty Inf Sch
BN20 ....184 B4
Pashley Manor Gdns*
TN5 ....44 B7
Pashley Rd BN20 ....184 C2
Paston Ho BN1 ....163 F8
Paston Pl BN2 ....164 D4
Pasture Hill Rd RH16 .....50 D6
Patagonia Ho RH12 ......8 C3
Patcham By-Pass BN1 ..142 E6
Patcham Grange BN1 ...142 E5
Patcham High Sch BN1 .142 F6

Old – Pen 211

Patcham House Special Sch
BN1 ....142 E6
Patcham Inf Sch BN1 ...142 F6
Patcham Jun Sch BN1 ..142 F6
Patcham Mill Rd BN24 .174 B5
Patchdean BN1 ....142 F5
Patching Lodge 5 BN2 .164 C5
Paton Rd TN39 ....157 A8
Paul Cl BN27 ....129 A3
Pavilion Bldgs BN1 .....189 B2
Pavilion Cl BN6 ....97 E5
Pavilion Ct 15 BN1 .....163 E7
Pavilion Par BN2 ....189 B2
Pavilion Rd BN1 ....144 C7
Pavilion Ret Pk BN2 ....143 C1
Pavilion Rise BN1 ......189 B2
Pavilion Way RH19 ......10 E8
Paxhill Cl TN38 ....135 E4
Paygate Rd TN33 ....113 E7
Payne Ave BN3 ....162 F8
Payne Terr BN1 ....143 B1
Paynsbridge Way TN21 .107 A7
Paynters Way BN1 ....76 C7
Paynton Rd TN37 ......136 B3
Paythorne Cl BN42 .....140 E2
Payton Pl RH15 ....72 F2
Payton Ho RH15 ....73 D3
Peace Cl BN1 ....143 C1
Peacehaven Com Sch
BN10 ....178 C8
Peacehaven Inf Sch
BN10 ....178 B7
Peacock Ind Est BN3 ...163 D7
Peakdean Cl BN20 .....183 B2
Peakdean La BN20 .....183 B2
Pearl Ct 3 BN21 ....185 A2
Pearse Pl TN3 ....20 B5
Peartree Cl RH15 ....72 E3
Peartree Field TN36 ...116 F6
Peartree Hill TN5 ....42 E4
Peartree La TN39 ......156 D6
Peasmarsh CE Prim Sch
TN31 ....69 B1
Pebble Rd BN24 ....158 A5
Pebsham Comm Prim Sch
TN40 ....158 A6
Pebsham Dr TN40 ......158 A6
Pebsham La TN38,TN40 .158 A6
Peckham Cl BN7 ....190 A4
Peel Rd BN2 ....164 F4
Peelings La BN24 ......174 D6
Peelings Manor Barns
BN24 ....174 B6
Peeps La TN6 ....39 A6
Pegasus Way RH19 ......2 B3
Pegwell Cl TN34 ....136 E2
Pelham Arc 11 TN34 ...160 B4
Pelham Cl
Peacehaven BN10 ....167 D1
Westham BN24 ....174 F5
Pelham Cres
Hailsham BN27 ....152 C6
Hastings TN34 ....160 A3
Pelham Ct 13 BN25 ....180 E3
Pelham Pl TN34 ....160 A3
Pelham Place Cotts
RH16 ....51 A7
Pelham Rd Lindfield RH16 .51 A6
Seaford BN25 ....180 E3
Pelham Rise BN10 .....167 D1
Pelham Sq BN1 ....189 B3
Pelham St Brighton BN1 .189 B3
Pelham Terr
Brighton BN1 ....143 C1
Lewes BN7 ....190 A3
Pelham Yd 7 BN25 .....180 E3
Pell Cl TN5 ....30 A6
Pellbrook Rd BN7 ......123 B3
Pellings Cl TN6 ....26 B3
Pellings Rise TN6 ....26 B3
Pells CE Prim Sch BN7 .190 A3
Pelwood Rd TN31 ....95 A2
Pembroke Ave BN3 ....163 A7
Pembroke Cl BN27 .....129 A3
Pembroke Cres BN3 ...163 A7
Pembroke Ct
2 Hove BN3 ....163 B6
St Leonards TN37 ......159 C8
Pembroke Ho 6 BN21 ..184 F3
Pembury Cl
Haywards Heath RH16 ....51 B3
Pembury TN2 ....9 D7
Pembury Gr TN39 ......157 A7
Pembury Grange TN2 ....9 A6
Pembury Hospl TN2 ......9 B7
Pembury Rd
Eastbourne BN23 ....174 D1
Royal Tunbridge Wells TN2 ..8 E4
Pembury Sta TN2 ....9 D8
Pendean RH15 ....73 C1
Pendennis Ct BN3 ......163 A8
Pendrill Pl TN5 ....29 F5
Penhale Rd BN2 ....165 A2
Penhurst Cl
Eastbourne BN22 ....174 A1
St Leonards TN37 ......159 C8
Penhurst Dr TN40 ......158 A6
Penhurst La TN33 ......110 E6
Penhurst Pl BN2 ....164 F6
Penland Cl RH15 ....50 F4
Penland Ct 9 TN34 ....157 E4
Penland Rd Bexhill TN40 .157 E5

Penland Rd continued
Haywards Heath RH16 . . . . **50** D7
Penn Cres
Haywards Heath RH16 . . . . . **51** A4
Ringmer BN8 . . . .**124** D5
Penn Yd TN2 . . . .**9** C6
Pennett Ho RH16 . . . .**50** D2
Pennine Rise TN34 . . . .**160** B8
Pennine Way BN23 . . . .**174** D3
Pennine Wlk TN2 . . . .**8** D5
Pennington Ho RH16 . . . . . .**51** A3
Penny La TN40 . . . .**158** A5
Pennybridge La TN20 . . . . . .**40** D5
Penrith Way BN23 . . . .**174** C4
Penrose Ct TN40 . . . .**157** D3
Pensford Dr BN23 . . . .**174** C3
Penshurst Rd TN11,TN3 . . . . .**6** E8
Penstock Terr TN11 . . . .**93** F3
Penstone Ct BN43 . . . .**161** C8
Pentland Cl
Eastbourne BN23 . . . .**174** E3
St Leonards TN37 . . . .**136** C5
Pentlands BN26 . . . .**183** C7
Pepper Dr RH15 . . . .**7** E7
Pepper Hall Cotts RH17 . . . .**74** B5
Peppercombe Rd BN20 . . . .**184** B4
Pepys Wlk BN3 . . . .**163** C4
Percival Cres BN22 . . . .**173** F3
Percival Mans BN2 . . . .**164** D4
Percival Rd BN22 . . . .**173** F3
Percival Terr BN2 . . . .**164** D4
Percy & Wagner Almshouses
BN2 . . . .**189** C4
Percy Rd TN35 . . . .**160** C7
Percy Terr TN4 . . . .**8** A6
Peredur Ctr for the Arts
RH19 . . . .**10** E6
Perrone Ct TN22 . . . .**78** C7
Perry Ave RH19 . . . .**1** E3
Perry Hill RH2 . . . .**177** C7
Perryfields RH15 . . . .**72** E4
Perryhill Cotts TN7 . . . .**13** E8
Perryhill La TN7 . . . .**13** E8
Perryman's La TN34 . . . .**34** D3
Perrymans La TN22 . . . .**36** F1
Perrymans's Cross TN31 . . .**67** B3
Perrymount Rd RH16 . . . . . .**50** E5
Perth Cl BN25 . . . .**181** C3
Perth Ct BN21 . . . .**185** A4
Perth Rd TN37 . . . .**136** C8
Peter Gladwin Prim Sch
BN41 . . . .**141** B2
Peter James Cl TN31 . . . .**94** E2
Peter James La TN35 . . . . .**138** C6
Peterhouse TN40 . . . .**157** D5
Petersfield TN2 . . . .**9** E7
Petland Gdns RH16 . . . .**50** F3
Petlands Rd RH16 . . . .**50** E3
Pett Cl BN22 . . . .**164** F6
Pett Level Rd TN35 . . . .**139** C7
Pett Rd TN35 . . . .**138** C8
Petworth Dr RH15 . . . .**73** A4
Petworth Ho BN3 . . . .**163** D7
Petworth Pl BN22 . . . .**173** E2
Petworth Rd BN1 . . . .**143** B6
Pevensey & Westham CE
Prim Sch BN24 . . . .**175** A6
Pevensey & Westham Sta
BN24 . . . .**174** F5
Pevensey Bay Rd BN23 . . . .**175** A4
Pevensey Bay Sta BN24 . . .**175** C6
Pevensey Castle*
BN24 . . . .**175** A6
Pevensey Cl BN25 . . . .**181** B4
Pevensey Ct
 Bexhill TN39 . . . .**157** B3
Pevensey Bay TN24 . . . . . .**175** B3
Pevensey Park Rd BN24 . . .**174** F6
Pevensey Rd
 Brighton BN2 . . . .**164** C8
Eastbourne BN21,BN22 . . .**185** B3
Newhaven BN9 . . . .**179** B5
Polegate BN26 . . . .**173** C6
St Leonards TN38 . . . .**159** B7
Peverells The BN25 . . . .**181** A5
Peyton Cl BN23 . . . .**185** F7
Philip Cole Cl TN34 . . . .**160** B4
Philip Ct BN3 . . . .**163** C7
Phoenix Brewery Halls
BN2 . . . .**189** C4
Phoenix Cl
Eastbourne BN23 . . . .**185** G8
Hailsham BN27 . . . .**152** E7
Phoenix Cres BN42 . . . .**161** D8
Phoenix Cswy BN7 . . . .**190** B2
Phoenix Ct BN22 . . . .**185** B3
Phoenix Dr BN23 . . . .**175** A1
Phoenix Ho TN6 . . . .**25** F3
Phoenix Ind Est BN7 . . . . . .**190** B2
Phoenix La RH19 . . . .**11** E6
Phoenix Pl Brighton BN2 . . .**189** C3
Lewes BN7 . . . .**190** B2
Phoenix Rise BN22 . . . .**173** E2
Phoenix Way BN41 . . . .**161** D8
Phyllis Ave BN10 . . . .**178** B8
Piazza The BN23 . . . .**185** F8
Picardy Cl TN33 . . . .**112** E4
Picardy Rd BN23 . . . .**185** E8
Piccadilly La TN20 . . . .**40** C1
Pickers La RH16 . . . .**51** A8
Picketts La TN22 . . . .**54** D8
Pickforde La TN5 . . . .**31** D1
Picton St BN2 . . . .**164** C7

Piddinghoe Ave BN10 . . . . .**178** D6
Piddinghoe Cl BN10 . . . . . .**178** D7
Piddinghoe Mead BN9 . . . .**168** B1
Pierpoint Mews
BN23 . . . .**175** A1
Pilgrim Ct RH16 . . . .**51** A5
Pilgrims Way TN34 . . . .**136** F4
Pilmer Rd TN6 . . . .**25** F4
Pilot Ho BN2 . . . .**189** C2
Pilot Rd TN34 . . . .**160** B8
Piltdown Cl Bexhill TN39 . . .**157** B4
Hastings TN34 . . . .**136** E1
Piltdown Rd BN22 . . . .**164** F6
Piltdown Rise TN22 . . . .**78** D8
Piltdown Way BN22 . . . .**174** A4
Pinders Rd TN35 . . . .**160** D6
Pine Ave TN36 . . . .**160** B8
Pine Ct BN25 . . . .**180** B3
Pine Gr Crowborough TN6 . . .**25** E2
East Grinstead RH19 . . . .**1** B3
Pine Tree Cl
Hurstpierpoint BN6 . . . .**97** B5
Newhaven BN9 . . . .**179** C7
Pine Tree Rd TN21 . . . .**82** A6
Pine Trees BN6 . . . .**97** D4
Pine Trees Ct BN6 . . . .**97** D4
Pine Way BN27 . . . .**152** A7
Pine Way Cl RH19 . . . .**10** E7
Pine Wlk TN22 . . . .**78** D8
Pineham Copse RH16 . . . . . .**50** F4
Pinehurst RH15 . . . .**73** A1
Pinehurst Wlk TN34 . . . .**160** B7
Pines The
 Brighton BN2 . . . .**189** C4
Hastings TN34 . . . .**160** B7
Haywards Heath RH16 . . . . .**51** B4
Hove BN3 . . . .**163** E6
Pinewood BN1 . . . .**142** E3
Pinewood Chase TN6 . . . . . .**25** D3
Pinewood Cl
Brighton BN1 . . . .**142** D2
Eastbourne BN22 . . . .**173** D2
Seaford BN25 . . . .**180** F4
Pinewood Ct BN16 . . . .**50** D2
Pinewood Rd TN2 . . . .**8** D5
Pinewood Way
Haywards Heath RH16 . . . . .**50** D2
St Leonards TN38 . . . .**135** E3
Pinewoods TN39 . . . .**156** E4
Pinewoods Ct TN39 . . . .**156** E4
Pinfold RH16 . . . .**50** D6
Pinfold Cl BN2 . . . .**165** E6
Pinton Hill TN5 . . . .**31** B3
Pinwell Rd BN7 . . . .**190** B1
Pipe Pas BN7 . . . .**190** A2
Piper's Gate TN22 . . . .**78** A2
Pipers Ct Bexhill TN40 . . . . .**157** C5
Hove BN3 . . . .**141** C3
Wadhurst TN5 . . . .**30** A4
Pipers Field TN22 . . . .**78** D4
Pipers Yd TN20 . . . .**40** C3
Pipit Rd BN22 . . . .**78** D5
Pippin Cl BN27 . . . .**131** B5
Pit La BN6 . . . .**97** A5
Pitcairn Ave BN23 . . . .**175** B2
Pitreavie Dr BN27 . . . .**152** A8
Pitt Dr BN25 . . . .**181** A5
Pitt Gdns BN2 . . . .**165** D7
Place La BN25 . . . .**180** E3
Plainfields Ave BN1 . . . .**143** A7
Plaistow Cl BN2 . . . .**164** F6
Plashett Park Gates
TN22 . . . .**102** F5
Plat The TN31 . . . .**67** B6
Platt The Dormansland RH7 . . .**2** A8
Frant TN3 . . . .**17** B1
Haywards Heath RH16 . . . . .**51** B5
Plaw Hatch La RH18,RH19 . . .**21** E5
Playden Cl BN2 . . . .**164** E4
Playden Gdns TN34 . . . . . .**160** B8
Playden La TN31 . . . .**70** C3
Pleasant Row TN34 . . . . .**160** B6
Pleasant View Cotts TN6 . . .**25** E4
Pleasant View Rd TN6 . . . . . .**25** F4
Plemont Gdns TN39 . . . . . .**157** A6
Pleyden Rise TN39 . . . .**155** F4
Plough La TN37 . . . .**136** B5
Plover Cl BN23 . . . .**174** C2
Plover Ct Hailsham BN27 . .**152** D7
St Leonards TN38 . . . .**135** E3
Plum Tree Cotts TN18 . . . . . .**45** E8
Plumey Feather Cotts
TN3 . . . .**14** E3
Plumpton Bostall BN6,
BN7 . . . .**121** E6
Plumpton Cl
Bexhill TN40 . . . .**157** C6
Eastbourne BN23 . . . .**174** A4
Plumpton Coll BN6 . . . . . .**121** D8
Plumpton Cross BN7 . . . .**99** F2
Plumpton Crossways
BN7,BN8 . . . .**74** F1
Plumpton La BN7 . . . .**99** F5
Plumpton Prim Sch BN7 . . . .**99** F5
Plumpton Race Course
BN7 . . . .**99** E4
Plumpton Rd BN2 . . . .**164** D6
Plumpton Sta BN7 . . . .**99** E5
Plymouth Ave BN23 . . . . . .**143** F1
Plymouth Cl BN23 . . . .**185** F8
Plynlimmon Rd TN34 . . . . . .**160** A4
Pocock's Rd RH16 . . . .**50** D7
Poels Ct RH19 . . . .**1** E2
Polegate By-Pass BN26 . . .**172** F7
Polegate Prim Sch
BN26 . . . .**173** A7
Polegate Sta BN26 . . . .**173** A6

Polegate Windmill*
BN26 . . . .**173** A5
Polesden Rd TN2 . . . .**8** D2
Polley Cl TN2 . . . .**9** D7
Pollington Pl TN6 . . . .**25** F2
Pomper La BN6 . . . .**72** A2
Pond Cl TN31 . . . .**90** B5
Pond Way RH19 . . . .**2** B1
Pondcroft Rd RH16 . . . .**51** B7
Pondside RH16 . . . .**50** C3
Pondsyde Ct BN25 . . . .**180** F6
Ponswood Rd TN38 . . . .**136** B2
Pont Cl TN21 . . . .**83** C6
Pook Reed Cl TN21 . . . .**81** F6
Pook Reed La TN21 . . . .**81** F6
Pool Pas BN1 . . . .**189** B1
Pool Valley BN1 . . . .**189** B1
Poona Rd TN1 . . . .**8** A5
Popes Ct BN22 . . . .**143** B1
Popes Row Cotts TN17 . . . . .**20** F2
Poplar Ave BN3 . . . .**141** E3
Poplar Cl Bexhill TN39 . . . . .**157** A7
Brighton BN1 . . . .**142** F2
Hove BN3 . . . .**141** E3
Poplar Mews RH16 . . . .**50** C2
Poplar Wlk BN22 . . . .**173** D3
Poplars The BN2 . . . .**98** A3
Poppinghole La TN32 . . . .**87** E8
Popps La TN39 . . . .**156** C3
Poppyfield TN31 . . . .**70** C1
Port Hall Ave BN1 . . . .**163** B6
Port Hall Mews BN1 . . . .**163** B8
Port Hall Pl BN1 . . . .**163** B6
Port Hall Rd BN1 . . . .**163** B8
Port Hall St BN1 . . . .**163** B6
Port Rd BN22 . . . .**174** A1
Port View BN9 . . . .**168** E2
Porters Way BN26 . . . .**173** B6
Portfield Ave BN1 . . . .**143** A6
Portfield Cl TN40 . . . .**157** D5
Portland Ave BN3 . . . .**162** E7
Portland Bsns Pk BN3 . . . . .**162** D8
Portland Cl BN27 . . . .**129** A1
Portland Cotts TN34 . . . .**159** F8
Portland Ho RH19 . . . .**10** F8
Portland La BN3 . . . .**162** D7
Portland Mews BN2 . . . .**164** C4
Portland Pl
 Brighton BN2 . . . .**164** C4
 Hastings TN34 . . . .**159** F8
Portland Rd
Burgess Hill RH15 . . . .**72** F3
East Grinstead RH19 . . . . . .**10** F8
Hove BN3 . . . .**162** E7
Portland Road Trad Est
BN3 . . . .**162** D8
Portland Sq TN21 . . . .**82** D7
Portland St BN1 . . . .**189** A2
Portland Terr
 Hastings TN34 . . . .**159** F8
Newhaven BN9 . . . .**168** D2
Portland Villas
 Hastings TN34 . . . .**159** F8
Hove BN3 . . . .**162** D7
Portlands The BN23 . . . .**185** G7
Portsdown Way BN20 . . . . .**173** B2
Portside BN2 . . . .**164** F3
Portslade Com Coll
Portslade-by-S BN41 . . . . .**140** F2
Portslade-by-S BN41 . . . . .**141** A1
Portslade Com Coll (Lower)
BN41 . . . .**141** A3
Portslade Inf Sch BN41 . . . .**162** B8
Portslade La RH16 . . . .**50** F8
Portsmouth Wood Cl BN41 . .**50** F8
Portsmouth Wood Dr
RH16 . . . .**50** F8
Posey Cotts BN27 . . . .**131** B5
Possingworth Cl TN21 . . . . .**80** F8
Post Horn Cl RH18 . . . .**12** B2
Post Horn La RH18 . . . .**12** B2
Post Office Pas TN34 . . .**160** A4
Post Office Sq TN1 . . . .**8** A3
Potato La BN8 . . . .**124** F5
Potman's La TN33,TN39 . . .**133** F4
Pottens Mill La TN21 . . . .**59** F4
Potter's La BN7 . . . .**190** A1
Potteries Cl BN27 . . . .**153** A6
Potteries Cotts BN27 . . . . . .**153** A6
Potteries The TN22 . . . .**78** D4
Potters Field BN8 . . . .**124** D6
Potters La RH15 . . . .**72** F1
Pottery Cl TN31 . . . .**90** A2
Pottery Cotts BN6 . . . .**74** A1
Pottery La TN31 . . . .**90** A2
Pottingfield Rd TN31 . . . .**93** A6
Potts Marsh Ind Est
BN24 . . . .**174** F4
Pouchlands Dr BN8 . . . .**100** C7
Pound Cl BN23 . . . .**185** F6
Pound Cnr BN8 . . . .**101** D4
Pound Gate BN6 . . . .**97** D3
Pound La Alfriston BN26 . . . .**171** A7
Framefield TN22 . . . .**79** E7
Laughton BN8 . . . .**126** C7
Pound The RH15 . . . .**72** F8
Poundfield Farm TN6 . . . . . .**26** B2
Poundfield Rd
Crowborough TN6 . . . .**26** B2
Sandhurst TN18 . . . .**47** B5
Poundsbridge Hill TN11,
TN3 . . . .**5** E4
Poveys Cl RH15 . . . .**72** D3
Powder Mill La TN4 . . . .**8** B8
Powdermill Cl TN4 . . . .**8** C8

Powdermill La
Battle TN33 . . . .**112** C1
Goatham Green TN31,TN33 . . .**93** E7
Powell Gdns BN9 . . . .**168** D1
Powell Rd BN2 . . . .**76** D7
Powis Gr BN1 . . . .**189** A3
Powis Rd BN1 . . . .**163** E6
Powis Sq BN1 . . . .**163** E6
Powis Villas BN1 . . . .**189** A3
Poynings Cl BN25 . . . .**181** C2
Poynings Dr BN3 . . . .**141** F3
Poynter Rd BN3 . . . .**163** A8
Pratt's Folly La TN6 . . . .**25** E1
Prescott Gdns RH15 . . . .**73** A3
Preston Cir BN1 . . . .**189** B4
Preston Dro BN1 . . . .**142** F2
Preston Gr BN22 . . . .**79** B6
Preston Grange BN1 . . . . . .**142** E1
Preston Manor Mus*
BN1 . . . .**142** E1
Preston Park Ave BN1 . . . . .**142** F1
Preston Park Sta BN1 . . . . .**142** D2
Preston Rd Bexhill TN39 . . .**157** B7
Brighton BN1 . . . .**163** F8
Preston St BN1 . . . .**163** E5
Preston Village Mews
BN1 . . . .**142** E1
Prestonville Ct
 Brighton BN1 . . . .**163** E7
 Brighton BN1 . . . .**189** A4
Prestonville Rd BN1 . . . .**189** A4
Pride View BN24 . . . .**174** B5
Prideaux Ct BN21 . . . .**184** E5
Prideaux Gdns TN34 . . . . . .**160** B7
Primrose Acre BN27 . . . . . .**127** B3
Primrose Cl
Burgess Hill RH15 . . . .**72** D4
Eastbourne BN23 . . . .**174** B3
Primrose Hill
Bexhill TN39 . . . .**156** F6
Fairlight Cove TN35 . . . . . .**138** F5
Primrose La RH18 . . . .**12** A1
Primrose Way BN27 . . . .**127** B3
Prince Albert St BN1 . . . . . .**189** B2
Prince Charles Cl BN42 . . . .**141** A1
Prince Charles Rd BN7 . . . .**190** C4
Prince Edward's Rd
BN7 . . . .**123** B1
Prince Of Wales Ct BN3 . . .**162** F6
Prince Regent's Cl BN3 . . . .**141** F3
Prince Regent's Ct
BN2 . . . .**164** E4
Prince William Par
BN23 . . . .**185** F6
Prince's Cres BN2 . . . .**189** C5
Prince's Ho BN1 . . . .**189** B2
Prince's Pl BN1 . . . .**189** B2
Prince's Rd Brighton BN2 . .**189** B2
St Leonards TN37 . . . .**159** D7
Prince's St Brighton BN2 . . .**189** B2
Royal Tunbridge Wells TN4 . . .**8** C3
Prince's Terr BN2 . . . .**164** E4
Princes Ave BN3 . . . .**163** A6
Princes Cl Seaford BN25 . . .**180** E5
Uckfield TN22 . . . .**78** A7
Princes Cres BN3 . . . .**163** A6
Princes Cres BN3 . . . .**163** A6
Princes Ct BN3 . . . .**163** A6
Princes Field BN26 . . . .**150** B3
Princes Rd BN23 . . . .**185** E7
Princes Sq BN3 . . . .**163** A6
Princes Dr BN25 . . . .**180** D5
Princess Royal Hospl The
RH16,RH17 . . . .**51** A2
Principal Cl TN19 . . . .**155** F5
Prinkle La BN27 . . . .**127** C6
Prinsep Rd BN3 . . . .**163** A8
Prior's Way TN8 . . . .**4** A6
Priory Ave TN34 . . . .**136** E1
Priory Cl Hastings TN34 . . .**136** E1
Pevensey Bay BN24 . . . . . .**175** D5
Priory Cres BN7 . . . .**190** A1
Priory Ct Bexhill TN40 . . . . .**157** C5
Brighton BN1 . . . .**163** F1
 Eastbourne BN20 . . . .**184** F1
Lewes BN7 . . . .**190** B1
Priory Flats BN7 . . . .**190** A1
Priory Ho BN7 . . . .**190** B1
Priory Hts BN20 . . . .**184** A5
Priory La BN23 . . . .**174** A1
Priory Meadow Sh Ctr
TN34 . . . .**159** F8
Priory Orch BN7 . . . .**190** C4
Priory Rd
Burgess Hill RH15 . . . .**73** A1
Eastbourne BN23 . . . .**174** E2
Forest Row RH18 . . . .**11** D2
Hassocks BN6 . . . .**97** E5
Hastings TN34 . . . .**160** B5
St Leonards TN37 . . . .**159** C7
Priory St Hastings TN34 . . . .**159** F7
Lewes BN7 . . . .**190** A1
Priory The Brighton BN1 . . .**142** D5
 Hove BN3 . . . .**163** B5
Priory View TN34 . . . .**160** A5
Priory Way RH16 . . . .**50** F4
Promenade BN10 . . . .**178** C6
Promenade The BN24 . . . . .**175** D4
Prospect Cotts
Burwash TN19 . . . .**62** B6
Crowborough TN6 . . . .**25** D4
Lamberhurst TN3 . . . .**23** A3
Prospect Gdns BN24 . . .**175** D4
Prospect Pl TN34 . . . .**159** E7
Prospect Rd
Heathfield TN21 . . . .**82** B6
Royal Tunbridge Wells TN4 . . .**8** C4
Royal Tunbridge
Wells,Camden Park TN2 . . .**8** C3

Prospect Terr TN21 . . . .**82** A7
Provence Ho BN23 . . . .**174** F1
Providence Cotts
Crowborough TN6 . . . .**25** D4
Groombridge TN3 . . . .**15** C7
Providence Pl BN1 . . . .**189** B4
Prowting Mead TN39 . . . . . .**156** C4
Pudding Cake La TN22 . . . . .**78** C7
Pulborough Ave BN22 . . . . .**173** E2
Pulborough Cl BN2 . . . .**164** F7
Pump Ho The BN3 . . . .**162** D8
Pump La TN22 . . . .**79** D4
Pump Terr TN1 . . . .**8** B4
Punnetts Town Com Prim
Sch TN21 . . . .**83** B6
Purbeck Cl BN23 . . . .**174** C4
Purbeck Ho BN2 . . . .**189** C2
Putlands Cres TN39 . . . .**157** A8
Pyecombe St BN45 . . . .**119** A6

Quadrangle The BN8 . . . . .**105** C5
Quadrant BN1 . . . .**189** A2
Quadrant The
Eastbourne BN21 . . . .**184** E4
Keymer BN6 . . . .**98** A4
Quail Ct BN27 . . . .**152** D7
Quakers La RH14 . . . .**51** A5
Quantock Cl
Eastbourne BN23 . . . .**174** D3
Royal Tunbridge Wells TN2 . . .**8** D5
Quantock Gdns TN34 . . . . .**160** B7
Quarry Bank Rd BN1 . . . . . .**143** B2
Quarry Cl RH15 . . . .**73** D3
Quarry Cotts TN5 . . . .**29** D7
Quarry Cres TN34 . . . .**160** A5
Quarry Hill
Haywards Heath RH16 . . . . .**50** C6
St Leonards TN38 . . . .**159** B7
Quarry La BN25 . . . .**181** A5
Quarry Rd Hastings TN34 . .**160** A5
Newhaven BN9 . . . .**179** D5
Royal Tunbridge Wells TN1 . . .**8** B5
Quarry Rise RH19 . . . .**2** A3
Quarry Terr TN34 . . . .**136** F1
Quarry View TN6 . . . .**37** F8
Quay Ct BN43 . . . .**161** A6
Quay The BN43 . . . .**161** A6
Quay Units BN10 . . . .**178** D7
Quebec Cl Bexhill TN39 . . . .**157** A5
Eastbourne BN23 . . . .**185** F7
Quebec Mans TN38 . . . .**159** A4
Quebec Rd TN38 . . . .**136** A4
Quebec St BN2 . . . .**189** C3
Queen Alexandra Ave
BN3 . . . .**142** A3
Queen Anne's Cl BN7 . . . . .**190** A2
Queen Caroline Cl BN3 . . . .**142** A3
Queen Elizabeth Ave
RH15 . . . .**73** A2
Queen Mary Ave BN3 . . . . .**142** A3
Queen Sq BN1 . . . .**189** A2
Queen St TN18 . . . .**47** B5
Queen Victoria Ave
BN3 . . . .**142** A3
Queen Victoria Hospl The
RH19 . . . .**1** F3
Queen's Ave TN34 . . . . . .**159** F7
Queen's Cres BN23 . . . .**185** E7
Queen's Ct RH16 . . . .**50** F6
Queen's Gdns
Brighton BN1 . . . .**189** B3
Eastbourne BN21 . . . .**185** B3
Hove BN3 . . . .**163** C5
Royal Tunbridge Wells TN4 . . .**8** B6
Queen's Par
Eastbourne BN22 . . . .**173** F1
Hove BN3 . . . .**141** E2
Queen's Park Prim Sch
BN2 . . . .**164** C6
Queen's Park Rd BN2 . . . . .**164** C6
Queen's Park Rise BN2 . . . .**164** C6
Queen's Park Terr BN2 . . . .**164** C6
Queen's Pl Brighton BN1 . . .**189** B4
Hove BN3 . . . .**163** C6
Queen's Rd Brighton BN1 . . .**189** A3
East Grinstead RH19 . . . .**1** E1
Queen's Rd BN23 . . . .**185** D7
Hastings TN34 . . . .**159** F8
Lewes BN7 . . . .**190** B4
Royal Tunbridge Wells TN4 . . .**8** B6
Queens App TN22 . . . .**55** D1
Queens Cotts TN5 . . . .**29** C6
Queens Cres RH15 . . . .**73** A2
Queens Dr Brighton TN39 . .**157** B3
Queens Dr Hassocks BN6 . . .**97** F4
Maresfield TN22 . . . .**54** F4
Queens Par TN34 . . . . . .**159** F8
Queens Park Gdns
BN25 . . . .**180** C4
Queens Park Mews
BN2 . . . .**164** C6
Queens Rd
Crowborough TN6 . . . .**25** F1
Haywards Heath RH16 . . . . .**50** E6
Herstmonceux BN27 . . . . .**130** C5
Southwick BN42 . . . .**140** E1
Queens Sq TN34 . . . .**159** F8
Queensbury Mews BN3 . . . .**163** C5
Queensdown Sch Rd
BN1,BN2 . . . .**143** D2
Queensmount TN20 . . . .**58** B7
Queensway Brighton BN2 . .**164** D6

Queensway continued
East Grinstead RH19 ....1 E1
Seaford BN25 ....181 A6
St Leonards TN37,TN38 .....135 E5
Quernby Cl BN43 ....52 D2
Quickbourne La TN31 ....67 D7
Quinnell Dr BN27 ....129 B2
Quintin Cl BN27 ....152 A5
Quintins The BN27 ....152 C8

R

Radcliffe Cl TN37 ....136 C3
Radinden Dr BN3 ....142 D1
Radinden Manor Rd
  BN3 ....163 D8
Radnor Ho RH16 ....50 D6
Radnor Mews TN38 ....135 E2
Ragged Dog La TN21 ....81 B3
Raglan Ct Brighton BN1 ....189 A2
  Pevensey Bay BN24 ....175 C3
Railway App
  East Grinstead RH19 ....1 E1
  Newhaven BN9 ....179 D7
Railway Cotts Cowden TN8 ...4 D8
  Horsted Keynes RH17 ......33 A8
  Ripe BN8 ....149 A6
  St Leonards TN38 ....158 F6
Railway La BN7 ....190 B2
Railway Rd BN9 ....179 D7
Railway St BN1 ....189 A3
Railway View TN6 ....38 C8
Rainey Ct BN21 ....185 B3
Raleigh Cl BN23 ....185 E7
Ramsay Way BN23 ....185 F7
Ramslye Rd TN4 ....16 E8
Ranalah Est BN9 ....179 D8
Randiddles Cl BN6 ....97 B4
Randolph Ho TN39 ....156 E5
Randolph La TN31 ....70 B3
Ranelagh Ct BN23 ....185 E6
Ranelagh Villas BN1 ....163 B8
Rangemore Dr BN21 ....184 D6
Rankine Rd TN2 ....8 D7
Ranmore Ct TN34 ....136 C6
Rannoch Rd TN6 ....25 D2
Rannoch Rd W TN6 ....25 D2
Ranscombe Hill BN8 ....147 A6
Ranscombe La BN8 ....147 D6
Ranworth Cl BN23 ....174 B4
Raphael Rd BN3 ....163 C7
Rapson's Rd BN20 ....173 A3
Rastrick Cl RH15 ....72 F1
Rattle Rd BN24 ....174 D6
Ratton Dr BN20 ....184 B7
Ratton Gdn BN21 ....184 B7
Ratton Rd BN21 ....184 C4
Ratton Sch BN21 ....184 E4
Raven Ct Battle TN33 .....112 F4
  St Leonards TN38 ....135 E3
Ravens Cl TN39 ....156 C3
Ravens Croft BN20 ....188 F8
Ravens Cl BN20 ....188 F8
Ravensdale Ret & L Pk
  TN40 ....158 A4
Ravenswood Dr BN2 ....165 F6
Ravenswood Ave TN2 ....8 C6
Ravenswood Rd RH15 ....73 B3
Ravine Cl TN34 ....160 A7
Rayford Cl BN10 ....178 C7
Rayford Ct
  Bexhill TN40 ....157 D4
  Seaford BN25 ....180 E2
Raymond Cl BN25 ....181 A5
Rayner Cl TN6 ....25 F3
Raystede Ctr for Animal
  Welfare* BN8 ....103 D1
Readers La TN31 ....69 F5
Reading Rd BN2 ....164 F4
Reba Ct BN2 ....177 D4
Rectory Cl Burwash TN19 ...62 B6
  East Hoathly BN8 ....105 A5
  Eastbourne BN20 ....184 D3
  Hove BN3 ....162 D7
  Newhaven BN9 ....179 C6
  Shoreham-by-S BN43 .....161 D7
  St Leonards TN38 ....136 B2
Rectory Ct BN43 ....161 C8
Rectory Field TN7 ....13 E4
Rectory La Beckley TN31 ...67 F4
  Rye TN31 ....93 C8
  Winchelsea TN36 ....117 E7
Rectory Pk TN35 ....116 E1
Rectory Rd
  Newhaven BN9 ....168 E2
  Shoreham-by-S BN43 .....161 D7
Rectory Way TN40 ....157 D5
Red Barn Mews TN3 ....112 D4
Red Dyke Cotts BN24 ......173 A5
Red Lake Com Prim Sch
  TN35 ....160 D8
Red Lake Terr TN35 ....160 D8
Red Lion Mobile Home Pk
  TN31 ....132 E2
Red Oak TN18 ....123 A5
Red Oast Cotts TN5 ....32 C3
Redbridge La TN6 ....37 D5
Redbrook La TN22 ....56 D4
Redcross St BN1 ....189 B3
Redford Cl BN23 ....174 E1
Redford Ct TN39 ....156 F4
Redgarth Ct RH19 ....1 B3
Redgeland Rise TN38 ......13 F2
Redgill La BN8 ....53 B1
Redhill Cl BN1 ....142 C5
Redhill Dr BN1 ....142 C5

Redleaf Cl TN2 ....8 D6
Redman King Ho BN20 .....184 F2
Redmayne Dr TN34 ....159 E7
Redoubt Rd BN22 ....185 C4
Redoubt The* BN22 ....185 C4
Redshank Ct BN27 ....152 D7
Redvers Rd BN2 ....143 D1
Redward Bsns Pk BN23 ....185 B7
Redwell Ave TN39 ....157 B8
Reed Ho BN6 ....100 E7
Reed Pond Wlk RH16 ....51 A4
Reedham Rd BN23 ....174 B4
Reedswood Rd
  Broad Oak TN31 ....90 B4
  St Leonards TN38 ....158 E8
Reeves Ct TN3 ....6 B5
Reeves Hill BN1 ....143 D5
Reeves Terr TN5 ....31 E1
Refectory Rd BN1 ....144 B7
Regal Dr BN1 ....10 F8
Regency Cl TN22 ....78 C8
Regency Ct Brighton BN1 ..142 D3
  Eastbourne BN20 ....185 A1
Regency Gdns TN38 ....159 A8
Regency Hall 1 TN2 ....8 A2
Regency Ho TN2 ....8 B2
Regency Mews
  1 Brighton BN1 ....163 E5
  11 Eastbourne BN20 .....185 A1
Regency Rd BN1 ....189 A2
Regency Sq BN1 ....163 E5
Regent Arc BN1 ....189 B2
Regent Bsns Pk RH15 ......72 E2
Regent Hill BN1 ....189 A2
Regent Pl Heathfield TN21 ..82 A8
  Royal Tunbridge Wells TN2 ..8 D3
  St Leonards TN37 ....135 F7
Regent Row TN31 ....189 A2
Regent Sq TN31 ....93 C6
Regent St BN1 ....189 B2
Regents Cl BN25 ....180 E5
Regina Ct TN4 ....7 F4
Reginald Rd TN39 ....157 B4
Regnum Cl BN22 ....173 E4
Reigate Rd BN1 ....142 D1
Renascent Ho 18 BN21 ....185 B3
Renfields RH15 ....50 C3
Renown Cl TN40 ....157 D6
Resting Oak Hill BN8 .....100 F3
Reynolds Dr TN21 ....157 E5
Reynolds La TN4 ....7 F7
Reynolds Rd
  Eastbourne BN23 ....174 E1
  Hove BN3 ....162 F7
Reynoldstown La BN26 ....172 F6
Ribbetts Cotts BN6 ....97 A5
Ribbetts Ho BN6 ....97 A5
Riccards La TN33 ....88 A2
Rices Hill RH19 ....1 F1
Rich Ind Est BN9 ....168 E1
Richard Allen Ct BN2 .....143 C1
Richard Beau Nash
  Apartments TN1 ....8 B4
Richardson Ct 5 BN3 .....162 F7
Richardson Rd Hove BN3 ...162 F7
  Royal Tunbridge Wells TN4 ..8 A5
Richborough Cl TN34 ......136 D4
Richington Way BN25 ......181 B5
Richland Cl TN35 ....160 D8
Richmead Gdns TN20 ....40 B2
Richmond Ave TN39 ....156 F3
Richmond Cl TN35 ....160 D8
Richmond Ct
  9 Hove BN3 ....163 E7
  Seaford BN25 ....180 E3
Richmond Gdns 2 BN1 .....189 C3
Richmond Gr TN39 ....157 A2
Richmond Hts 12 BN2 .....189 C4
Richmond Mews BN25 .....180 E2
Richmond Par BN1 ....189 C3
Richmond Pl
  Brighton BN2 ....189 B3
  Eastbourne BN21 ....184 F4
  Royal Tunbridge Wells TN2 ..8 B1
Richmond Rd
  Bexhill TN39 ....157 A3
  Brighton BN2 ....164 B8
  Pevensey Bay BN24 ......175 D5
  Seaford BN25 ....180 E3
Richmond St
  Brighton BN2 ....189 C3
  Hastings TN34 ....160 C6
Richmond Terr
  Brighton BN2 ....189 C4
  2 Seaford BN25 ....180 E3
Richmond Way TN39 ....10 F8
Riddens Cl BN7 ....99 E5
Riddens La BN7 ....99 E5
Riddens The BN7 ....99 E5
Riddlesdale Ave TN4 ....8 A6
Ride The BN1 ....142 A1
Riders Bolt TN39 ....156 E5
Ridge Cl Nutley TN22 .....35 C5
  Portslade-by-S BN41 ....141 A4
Ridge The
  Groombridge TN3 ....15 A4
  St Leonards TN34,TN37 ...160 A4
  Winchelsea Beach TN36 ...118 C6
Ridge View BN1 ....143 C5
Ridge W The TN37 ....136 A7
Ridge Way RH17 ....51 B2
Ridgelands BN20 ....184 C3
Ridgeside Ave BN1 ....142 E5

Ridgeway
  East Grinstead RH19 .....10 E7
  Hurst Green TN19 ....45 A3
  Pembury TN2 ....9 D7
  Southwick BN41,BN42 ....140 F1
  The Moor TN18 ....45 E8
Ridgeway Cl
  Heathfield TN21 ....82 A8
  Southwick BN42 ....140 F1
Ridgeway The
  Burgess Hill RH15 ....73 B4
  Friston BN20 ....183 B1
  Herstmonceux BN27 ......130 E6
  Seaford BN25 ....180 F4
Ridgeway The TN4 ....8 A8
Ridgewood Ave BN27 ......177 C7
Ridgewood Cl TN22 ....78 D4
Ridgewood Gdns
  Bexhill TN40 ....157 F4
  Hastings TN34 ....136 E5
Ridgewood Ind Pk TN22 ....78 E4
Ridgway Cl BN1 ....165 D8
Ridgway Paddock BN7 .....145 E6
Ridgway The BN7 ....165 D8
Ridings The Burgess Hill RH15 .73 C2
  Newick BN8 ....76 C7
  Ovingdean BN2 ....165 C4
Rigden Rd BN21 ....142 C1
Riley Rd BN2 ....143 C1
Rill Wlk RH19 ....2 B1
Ringle Gn TN18 ....47 C5
Ringles Cross TN22 ....55 D2
Ringmer Bsns Pk BN8 .....124 E6
Ringmer Com Coll BN8 ....124 E6
Ringmer Dr BN1 ....143 F4
Ringmer Pk Cotts BN8 ....124 B6
Ringmer Prim Sch BN8 ....124 E5
Ringmer Rd
  Brighton BN1 ....143 E4
  Newhaven BN9 ....179 B6
  Seaford BN25 ....180 E2
Ringmer Way BN23 ....174 B4
Ringwood Cl 6 BN22 ......185 B5
Ringwood Ct BN22 ....185 B5
Ringwood Rd
  Bexhill TN39 ....157 C7
  Eastbourne BN22 ....185 B5
Ripley Chase BN1 ....184 E3
Ripsley Cl BN23 ....174 E1
Risden La TN18 ....46 D7
Rise Park Gdns BN23 .....174 E2
Rise The
  East Grinstead RH19 .....10 F8
  Haywards Heath RH16 .....51 B5
  Horam TN21 ....106 F7
  Portslade-by-S BN41 ....141 A4
Riseden Rd TN5 ....29 C1
Rising The BN20 ....174 E2
Risings The BN20 ....180 F4
Rissom Ct BN1 ....142 E2
Ritz Bldg TN5 ....31 E1
River La BN8 ....171 A3
River Way TN22 ....78 C8
Riverbourne Ho 10 BN22 ..185 B4
Riverbridge Cotts TN33 ...113 E8
Riverdale BN7 ....190 A3
Riverhall Hill TN5 ....28 F8
Riverside Forest Row RH18 11 E3
  Hadlow Down TN22 ....57 D1
  Seaford BN25 ....161 E7
Riverside Bsns Ctr
  BN43 ....161 A7
Riverside Gdns TN6 ....38 C8
Riverside Ho BN9 ....179 D6
Riverside Ind Est BN7 ....190 B3
Riverside Rd BN9 ....179 D7
Riverside Sch BN9 ....179 C6
Rixons Cl RH17 ....33 C5
Rixons Orch RH17 ....33 C5
RNLI Lifeboat Mus*
  BN21 ....185 A1
Robert Lodge BN2 ....164 A4
Robert St BN1 ....189 B3
Robert Tressel Cl TN34 ...136 C1
Robert Tressell Workshops*
  TN34 ....159 F8
Roberts Hill TN34 ....117 E8
Roberts Row TN31 ....68 C5
Robertsbridge Com Coll
  TN32 ....63 F4
Robertson Pas TN34 ....64 A4
Robertson St TN34 ....159 F7
Robertson Terr 1 TN34 ...159 F7
Robertsons Hill TN34 ....160 A6
Robian Cl TN22 ....55 A4
Robin Cl
  East Grinstead RH19 ......1 F2
  Eastbourne BN23 ....174 C2
Robin Ct TN3 ....157 A3
Robin Davis Cl BN2 ......143 E1
Robin Dene BN2 ....165 C4
Robin Hill TN39 ....156 D4
Robin Post La BN26 ......151 B1
Robin Rd RH15 ....72 D2
Robin Rise RH16 ....50 E8
Robinia Lodge BN1 ....142 E2

Robins Reach BN27 ....127 B3
Robins Row BN41 ....141 A1
Robinson Rd BN9 ....179 C8
Robinsons Ct BN22 ......185 C6
Roborough Cl BN1 ....185 A4
Robsack Ave TN38 ....135 E2
Robsack Wood Com Prim Sch
  TN38 ....135 E2
Rochdale Ho TN1 ....8 C6
Rochdale Rd TN1 ....8 C6
Rochester Cl
  Eastbourne BN20 ....188 C8
  5 Hove BN3 ....163 D6
Rochester Ct 4 BN3 ......163 D6
Rochester Gdns BN3 ......163 D6
Rochester Ho TN6 ....26 C1
Rochester Rd 4 TN37 .....136 B2
Rochester St BN3 ....164 D5
Rochester Way TN6 ....26 B1
Rochford Rd BN25 ....180 B6
Rochmans Way TN6 ....38 A8
Rock Channel TN31 ....93 C5
Rock Cl Hastings TN35 ...160 D8
  5 Southwick BN42 ....161 E7
Rock Cotts TN3 ....17 B1
Rock Gr BN27 ....164 C4
Rock Hall Cotts TN22 .....78 E8
Rock La TN35 ....137 D7
Rock Rd BN21 ....189 C1
Rock St BN2 ....164 E4
Rock Villa Rd TN1 ....8 B3
Rock-a-Nore Par TN34 ....160 B4
Rock-a-Nore Rd TN34 .....160 B3
Rockall Ave BN23 ....185 F8
Rockall Dr BN27 ....129 A2
Rockhurst Dr BN20 ....184 B6
Rockington Way TN6 ....38 B8
Rocklands Cotts BN27 ....131 B5
Rocklands Holiday Pk
  TN35 ....160 D5
Rocklands La TN35 ....160 C5
Rockmead Rd TN35 ....138 F4
Rocks La TN22 ....55 F7
Rocks Park Prim Sch
  TN22 ....78 B8
Rocks Park Rd TN22 ....78 B7
Rocks The RH19 ....11 D6
Rocky La RH16 ....50 D1
Roderick Ave
  Peacehaven BN10 ....178 B7
  Peacehaven BN10 ....178 B7
Roderick Ave N BN10 .....167 C2
Roderick Cl BN10 ....178 C8
Rodmell Ave BN2 ....164 A4
Rodmell CE Prim Sch
  BN7 ....146 E1
Rodmell Cl 5 BN25 ....180 C4
Rodmell Pl BN1 ....143 A4
Rodmell Rd
  Royal Tunbridge Wells TN2 ..8 A2
Rodmill Dr BN22 ....184 D6
Rodmill Rd BN21 ....184 D5
Rodney Cl BN23 ....185 F7
Roebuck St 18 TN34 .....160 B4
Roedale Cl 1 BN1 ....143 B1
Roedale Rd BN1 ....143 B1
Roedean Cl Bexhill TN39 ..157 C8
  Seaford BN25 ....181 A4
Roedean Cres BN2 ....165 A4
Roedean Ct BN2 ....164 F4
Roedean Hts BN2 ....165 A4
Roedean Path BN2 ....165 A3
Roedean Rd
  Brighton BN2 ....164 F4
  Royal Tunbridge Wells TN2 ..8 A1
Roedean Sch BN2 ....165 C3
Roedean Terr BN2 ....165 B3
Roedean Vale BN2 ....165 B3
Roedean Way BN2 ....165 B3
Roeheath BN8 ....75 F4
Roffrey Ave BN22 ....173 D1
Rolfe Dr BN7 ....73 D3
Roman Cl TN25 ....180 B6
Roman Cres BN42 ....161 E8
Roman Croft BN21 ....184 E4
Roman Rd Hove BN3 ....162 D6
  Southwick BN42 ....161 E8
Roman Way
  Southwick BN42 ....161 E8
  Uckfield TN22 ....78 C2
Romans Way BN24 ....174 A6
Romany Cl BN41 ....162 B8
Romford Rd TN2 ....9 F7
Romney Cl BN25 ....181 C4
Romney Ct 8 TN40 ....157 D4
Romney Rd
  Polegate BN26 ....173 B7
  Southwick BN42 ....177 A5
Romney St BN2 ....185 C5
Romsey Cl BN1 ....143 C2
Rookery Cl Brighton BN1 ..142 E1
  Newhaven BN9 ....168 E2
Rookery Way
  Haywards Heath RH16 .....50 E1
  Newhaven BN9 ....168 F2
  Seaford BN25 ....180 B5
Rookhurst Rd TN40 ....157 F5
Rookley Cl TN22 ....78 C1
Rookwood Cl TN22 ....78 C1

Roopers TN3 ....7 A7
Roosevelt Ct TN38 ....136 B3
Rope Wlk Hailsham BN27 ..152 B8
  Rye TN31 ....93 C6
Rope Wlk The TN18 ....47 B5
Roper's Gate TN2 ....7 C7
Rosary Ct RH15 ....73 B2
Rose Cotts Danehill RH17 ..34 A4
  Forest Row RH18 ....11 F3
Rose Ct BN6 ....97 E4
Rose Gr BN27 ....127 B3
Rose Hill BN2 ....189 C4
Rose Hill Cl BN1 ....189 B4
Rose Hill Ct BN1 ....189 B4
Rose Hill Sch TN4 ....7 C7
Rose Hill Terr BN1 ......189 B4
Rose Walk Cl BN9 ....179 C7
Rose Wlk BN25 ....180 F4
Rose Wlk The BN9 ....179 C7
Rosebarn Ct RH15 ....73 C1
Rosebery Ave
  Eastbourne BN22 ....173 C1
  Woodingdean BN2 ....165 C8
Rosedale Pl BN22 ....173 D3
Rosedene Cl BN22 ....165 E6
Rosefield Cotts TN32 .....65 F1
Rosehill Gdns TN6 ....26 C1
Rosehill Wlk TN1 ....8 A3
Roseland Ct BN22 ....185 C5
Roselands Bexhill TN39 ...156 F6
  Sedlescombe TN33 ....88 E1
Roselands Ave
  Eastbourne BN22 ....185 C5
  Wellbrook TN20 ....39 F1
Roselands Cl BN22 ....185 C5
Roselands Inf Sch BN22 ..185 B5
Roseleigh Gdns RH17 .....51 F3
Rosemary Cl
  Haywards Heath RH16 .....50 B6
  Peacehaven BN10 ....167 C1
Rosemary Dr BN43 ....140 C1
Rosemary Gdns TN19 ......62 B7
Rosemary La
  Guestling Green TN35 ...138 D6
  Icklesham TN36 ....32 A5
Rosemount
  Lower Dicker BN8,BN27 ..128 A7
  Muddles Green BN8 .....127 F7
Rosemount Cl BN25 ....180 A6
Rosetti Rd BN24 ....175 D4
Roseveare Rd BN22 ....185 C6
Rossdale TN2 ....8 D5
Rossington Cl BN21 ......184 D5
Rosslyn Ave BN43 ....161 A7
Rosslyn Rd BN43 ....161 A7
Rotary Lodge BN1 ....143 E6
Rotary Point BN41 ....141 B1
Rothbury Rd BN3 ....162 D7
Rother Ave BN24 ....173 F5
Rother Cl Burwash TN19 ...62 B6
  East Grinstead RH19 .....10 F8
Rother Ho TN21 ....159 B6
Rother Ironworks The 5
  TN31 ....93 C5
Rother Rd BN25 ....181 C4
Rother Valley Rly* TN32 ..64 A4
Rother View
  Burwash TN19 ....62 B7
  Hastings TN34 ....44 C1
Rotherfield Ave
  Bexhill TN40 ....157 D4
  Eastbourne BN23 ....174 A4
  Hastings TN34 ....160 B5
Rotherfield Cl BN1 ......143 B6
Rotherfield Cres BN1 ....143 B5
Rotherfield La TN20 ......39 F4
Rotherfield Prim Sch
  TN6 ....39 B8
Rotherfield Rd TN6 ....38 E8
Rotherham Rd TN6 ....38 A7
Rotherhurst La TN6 ....39 B6
Rothermead TN20 ....39 F1
Rothermere TN32 ....64 C5
Rothley Chase RH16 ......50 E4
Rothsay Ct TN38 ....159 B7
Rothsay Rd TN38 ....159 B7
Rothwell Ct BN27 ....179 A7
Rotten Row Lewes BN7 ....146 B8
  Lewes BN7 ....190 A1
Rottingdean Pl BN2 ......165 F4
Rotunda BN23 ....185 D8
Rotyngs The BN2 ....165 F2
Rough Brow BN25 ....181 A4
Rough Field RH19 ....1 C4
Rough The BN8 ....76 C7
Round Hill Cres BN2 .....164 B8
Round Hill Rd BN2 ....164 B8
Round Hill St 3 BN2 .....164 B8
Roundacres Way TN40 ....157 C6
Roundel The TN27 ....156 C6
Roundhay Ave BN10 ......178 E6
Roundhill Rd TN6 ....8 D1
Roundhouse Cotts TN21 ...82 D7
Roundway BN1 ....143 E5
Roundwood La RH16 ....50 F8
Roundwood Rd TN37 ......136 E6
Rowan Ave
  Eastbourne BN22 ....173 D3
  Hove BN3 ....141 E1
Rowan Cl
  Haywards Heath RH16 .....51 B4
  Heathfield TN21 ....82 A5
  Portslade-by-S BN41 ....141 A1
  Seaford BN25 ....181 C3

Rowan Cl *continued*
St Leonards TN37 . . . .**136** D6
Rowan Ct Brighton BN1 . . . .**142** E1
Polegate BN26 . . . .**173** A6
Rowan Gdns TN40 . . . .**157** F6
Rowan Ho
6 Brighton BN2 . . . .**7** C4
Royal Tunbridge Wells TN4 . . . .**7** E4
Rowan Tree Rd TN2 . . . .**7** E1
Rowan Way BN2 . . . .**165** E4
Rowan's Ct BN7 . . . .**190** A2
Rowanden Ct BN2 . . . .**177** C4
Rowans The
Burgess Hill RH15 . . . .**72** D4
Hurstpierpoint BN6 . . . .**97** A7
Rowbarns TN33 . . . .**112** C6
Rowe Ave BN10 . . . .**178** B7
Rowe Ave N BN10 . . . .**178** B8
Rowsley Rd BN20 . . . .**188** D7
**Royal Alexandra Hospl for
Sick Children The** BN1 . .**189** A3
Royal Chase TN4 . . . .**7** F4
Royal Cres BN2 . . . .**164** C4
Royal Crescent Mans **10**
BN2 . . . .**164** C4
Royal Crescent Mews
BN2 . . . .**164** C4
Royal Ct TN34 . . . .**136** F1
Royal Dr BN25 . . . .**180** E4
Royal George Ct RH15 . . . . .**72** F3
Royal George Par BN43 . . . .**140** C1
Royal George Rd RH15 . . . . .**72** F3
Royal Mews TN38 . . . .**159** A6
Royal Military Rd TN36 . . . .**118** A8
Royal Oak La TN22 . . . .**56** B8
Royal Par
Eastbourne BN22 . . . .**185** C4
Eastbourne BN22 . . . .**185** D5
Royal Pavilion* BN1 . . . .**189** B2
Royal Sovereign View
BN23 . . . .**185** F6
Royal Sussex Cres BN4 . . . .**184** B5
Royal Sussex Ct BN7 . . . .**190** A2
Royal Sussex Cty Hospl
BN2 . . . .**164** D4
Royal Terr **4** TN37 . . . .**159** C7
Royal Victoria Place Sh Ctr
TN1 . . . .**8** B4
Royles Cl BN2 . . . .**177** A6
Royston Cl BN20 . . . .**183** A1
Royston Gdns TN40 . . . .**157** F6
Rubislaw **3** BN21 . . . .**184** F4
Rudyard Cl BN2 . . . .**165** E8
Rudyard Kipling Prim Sch
BN2 . . . .**165** C7
Rudyard Rd BN2 . . . .**165** E8
Rue De Bayeux TN33 . . . . . .**112** D5
Ruffet Ct TN4 . . . .**7** E1
Rufus Cl BN7 . . . .**190** A2
Rugby Cl BN25 . . . .**181** B4
Rugby Ct **6** BN2 . . . .**164** E4
Rugby Pl BN2 . . . .**164** E4
Rugby Rd BN1 . . . .**143** A1
Rumbolds La RH16 . . . .**50** D2
Rumsey Ct TN6 . . . .**25** F1
Rusbridge La BN7 . . . .**190** C2
Rush Ct **4** BN22 . . . .**185** B3
Rushers Cross TN20 . . . .**40** E5
Rushes The RH16 . . . .**51** C4
Rushetts TN3 . . . .**6** F4
Rushey Cl BN8 . . . .**124** E5
Rushlake Cl BN1 . . . .**143** E5
Rushlake Cres BN21 . . . .**184** D6
Rushlake Rd BN1 . . . .**143** E5
Rushlye Cl TN3 . . . .**17** F5
Rushmere Rise TN38 . . . . . .**135** E1
Rushwood Cl RH16 . . . .**51** B4
Ruskin Pl BN3 . . . .**162** F7
Ruskin Rd
Eastbourne BN20 . . . .**173** B1
Hove BN3 . . . .**162** F8
Rusper Ho **16** BN2 . . . .**184** E4
Rusper Rd Brighton BN1 . . .**143** D6
Eastbourne BN20 . . . .**184** B6
Ruspers RH15 . . . .**73** D2
Russell Cotts **5** BN21 . . . .**184** E4
Russell Cres **2** BN1 . . . . . .**189** A4
Russell Ct **5** TN34 . . . .**160** A3
Russell Mews **14** BN1 . . . .**189** A3
Russell Pl BN1 . . . .**189** A2
Russell Rd BN1 . . . .**189** A2
Russell Row BN7 . . . .**189** A2
Russell Sq BN1 . . . .**189** A2
Russell St TN4 . . . .**159** F8
Russet Cl BN26 . . . .**173** C6
Russett Way BN27 . . . .**131** B5
Rusthall Grange TN4 . . . .**7** D4
Rusthall High St TN4 . . . .**7** C4
Rusthall Pk TN4 . . . .**7** D4
Rusthall Rd TN4 . . . .**7** D4
Rustic Cl BN10 . . . .**167** B1
Rustic Pk BN10 . . . .**167** B2
Rustic Rd BN10 . . . .**167** B2
Rustington Ct BN20 . . . .**188** F8
Rustington Rd BN1 . . . .**143** A5
Rustlings Cl RH16 . . . .**51** B5
Rustwick TN4 . . . .**7** D4
Rutherfords Bsns Pk
TN39 . . . .**113** B3
Rutland Cl BN21 . . . .**184** D6
Rutland Ct
3 Eastbourne BN23 . . . . . .**174** E1
Hove BN3 . . . .**162** F7
Rutland Gdns BN3 . . . .**162** F7
Rutland Rd BN3 . . . .**163** A7

Rutley Cl TN32 . . . .**64** C5
Ruxley Ct BN23 . . . .**174** D2
Rydal Cl TN4 . . . .**7** E5
Rydal Dr TN4 . . . .**7** E5
Rydal Way BN23 . . . .**174** C4
Ryde Cl BN3 . . . .**141** D1
Ryde Rd BN2 . . . .**164** D7
Ryders TN3 . . . .**7** A3
Rye Cl Polegate BN26 . . . . . .**173** C7
Saltdean BN2 . . . .**177** F6
Seaford BN25 . . . .**181** C4
**Rye Harbour Local Nature
Reserve*** TN31 . . . .**94** B1
**Rye Harbour Nature
Reserve***
Rye TN36 . . . .**93** C2
* Winchelsea Beach TN36 . . .**118** F8
Rye Ind Pk TN31 . . . .**93** D4
Rye Rd Four Throws TN18 . . .**46** D8
Hastings TN35 . . . .**137** D5
Iden TN30 . . . .**70** A8
Peasmarsh TN31 . . . .**69** E2
Rye Sta TN31 . . . .**93** B6
Ryecroft **12** Brighton BN2 . .**164** F5
Haywards Heath RH16 . . . .**50** E3
Ryefield Cl BN21 . . . .**184** C7
Ryelands BN21 . . . .**143** D3
Rylstone Rd BN22 . . . .**185** C4
Rymers Cl TN2 . . . .**8** D7
Rymill Rd TN38 . . . .**136** A3
Ryst Wood Rd RH18 . . . .**12** B1

S

Sackville Cl
East Grinstead RH19 . . . .**1** C3
Lewes BN7 . . . .**190** A2
Sackville Coll* RH19 . . . .**1** F1
Sackville Com Coll RH19 . .**11** A8
Sackville Ct Bexhill TN40 . .**157** D5
3 East Grinstead RH19 . . . .**10** F8
Sackville Gdns
East Grinstead RH19 . . . .**1** C3
Hove BN3 . . . .**162** F6
Sackville La RH19 . . . .**1** C3
Sackville Rd Bexhill TN39 .**157** B3
Eastbourne BN22 . . . .**173** F2
Hailsham BN27 . . . .**152** C6
Hove BN3 . . . .**163** A7
Sackville Trad Est BN3 . . . .**163** B8
Sacred Heart RC Prim Sch
TN35 . . . .**160** B5
Sacred Heart Sch TN5 . . . . . .**29** D5
Saddler's Ct **6** TN38 . . . . . .**159** B6
Saddlers CI RH15 . . . .**73** D1
Sadler Way BN2 . . . .**164** F6
Sadlers Way BN8 . . . .**124** D4
Saffreys Ct TN38 . . . .**159** B7
Saffron Cl BN43 . . . .**140** C1
Saffron Gate BN3 . . . .**163** C7
Saffron Gdns BN26 . . . .**170** F3
Saffrons Ct BN21 . . . .**184** E2
Saffrons Mead **9** BN20 . . .**184** F2
Saffrons Pk BN20 . . . .**184** E1
Saffrons Rd BN21 . . . .**184** F2
Saffrons The RH15 . . . .**72** F5
Saint Hill Gn RH19 . . . .**10** C4
Saint Hill Manor* RH19 . . .**10** C4
Saint Hill Rd RH19 . . . .**10** C5
Saints Hill TN11 . . . .**4** B8
St Agnes Rd RH19 . . . .**1** E2
St Aidan's Ct **2** BN2 . . . . .**185** C5
St Andrew's CE Inf Sch
BN22 . . . .**185** D6
St Andrew's CE Prim Sch
BN3 . . . .**163** B7
St Andrew's Dr BN9 . . . .**179** B7
St Andrew's Dr BN25 . . . . . .**180** B6
St Andrew's La BN1 . . . .**190** B2
St Andrew's Rd
Bexhill TN40 . . . .**157** C5
Brighton BN1 . . . .**143** A1
Portslade-by-S BN41 . . . .**162** C7
St Andrew's Sch BN20 . . . .**188** D7
St Andrew's Sq BN3 . . . .**159** F8
St Andrew's Villas
TN34 . . . .**160** A4
St Andrews Cl BN27 . . . .**129** A1
St Andrews Rd RH15 . . . .**73** C4
St Ann's Ct BN3 . . . .**163** D7
St Ann's Ct BN24 . . . .**175** D4
St Anne's Cl TN40 . . . .**157** D3
St Anne's Cres **3** BN7 . . . .**123** B1
St Anne's Ct
1 Brighton BN1 . . . .**189** A4
2 Brighton BN1 . . . .**164** C4
St Anne's Gdns BN6 . . . .**98** A3
St Anne's Ho **7** BN1 . . . . . .**189** A4
St Anne's Rd BN21 . . . .**184** F4
St Anne's Sch BN7 . . . .**146** B8
St Anne's Terr **8** BN7 . . . .**123** B1
St Annes Gn TN19 . . . .**62** A6
St Annes Rd BN20 . . . .**173** B3
St Annes Well Ho **6**
BN3 . . . .**163** D6
St Anns Mans **5** BN1 . . . . .**189** A4
St Anthony's Ave BN23 . . . .**185** E8
St Anthonys BN8 . . . .**124** E6
St Aubyn's Gdns **13** BN3 . .**163** A6
St Aubyn's Mead BN2 . . . . .**177** A5
St Aubyn's Rd
Eastbourne BN22 . . . .**185** B3
Portslade-by-S,Fishersgate
BN41 . . . .**162** A7

St Aubyns BN3 . . . .**163** B6
St Aubyns Mans BN3 . . . . . .**163** A5
St Aubyns S BN3 . . . .**163** A5
St Aubyns Sch BN2 . . . .**165** F1
St Augustine's CE Prim Sch
RH17 . . . .**51** F3
St Augustine's Cl TN39 . . . .**156** F3
St Augustine's RC Prim Sch
TN4 . . . .**8** A7
St Augustines Cl RH17 . . . . .**51** F3
St Barnabas CE Prim Sch
TN1 . . . .**8** B5
St Barnabas' Cl TN1 . . . .**8** B5
**St Bartholomew's CE Prim
Sch** BN1 . . . .**189** B4
St Bede's Prep Sch
BN20 . . . .**188** E7
St Bede's Sch BN27 . . . .**151** A8
St Bernadette's RC Prim Sch
BN1 . . . .**142** E2
St Boswells Cl BN27 . . . .**152** A8
St Brelades BN21 . . . .**185** B2
St Catherine's Cl TN37 . . . .**159** D8
St Catherine's Ct **8**
RH19 . . . .**1** D2
St Catherine's Terr **6**
BN3 . . . .**163** B5
St Christopher's Rd BN3 . . . .**97** A6
St Christopher's Sch
BN3 . . . .**163** A6
St Clement's Caves*
TN34 . . . .**160** A4
St Clement's Ct BN21 . . . . .**184** D6
St Clements Pl **5** TN38 . . .**159** C6
St Crispians BN25 . . . .**180** D3
St Crispians BN25 . . . .**180** D3
St Cuthmans Cl BN2 . . . . . .**164** F6
St David's Ave TN40 . . . .**157** C5
St David's Ct BN10 . . . .**178** B8
St David's Rd TN4 . . . .**8** B6
St Davids Cl BN2 . . . .**173** D4
St Denys BN21 . . . .**185** B2
St Dominic Cl TN38 . . . .**159** A8
St Edmund's Rd RH16 . . . . . .**50** F3
St Edward's Cl RH19 . . . .**1** C1
St Elizabeth's BN25 . . . .**180** F4
St Francis Chase TN39 . . . .**157** A5
St Francis Cl RH16 . . . .**50** F2
St George's Ho BN6 . . . .**97** B5
St George's La BN6 . . . .**97** B5
St George's Mews BN1 . . .**189** B3
St George's Pk TN2 . . . .**16** F8
St George's Pl
Brighton BN1 . . . .**189** B3
Hurstpierpoint BN6 . . . .**97** B5
St George's Rd
Bexhill TN40 . . . .**157** C5
Brighton BN2 . . . .**164** D4
Eastbourne BN22 . . . .**185** B4
Hastings TN34 . . . .**160** A5
St George's Terr **5**
BN2 . . . .**164** C4
St Georges Ct
11 Bexhill TN40 . . . .**157** D3
East Grinstead RH19 . . . .**1** C3
Royal Tunbridge Wells TN4 . . . .**8** A5
St Georges Mount **14**
TN37 . . . .**159** C7
St Giles CE Prim Sch
RH17 . . . .**33** C6
St Giles St
Shoreham-by-S BN43 . . . . . .**161** B8
Winchelsea TN36 . . . .**117** E7
St Gregory Cl BN20 . . . .**188** E8
**St Gregory's Catholic Comp
Sch** TN4 . . . .**8** A7
St Helen's Ave TN34 . . . . . .**136** E3
St Helen's Cres
Hastings TN34 . . . .**136** E2
Hove BN3 . . . .**141** D3
St Helen's Ct TN34 . . . .**136** E2
St Helen's Down TN34 . . . .**160** A7
St Helen's Park Rd
TN34 . . . .**136** E3
St Helen's Rd
Brighton BN2 . . . .**164** D7
Hastings TN34 . . . .**136** D2
St Helena La BN7 . . . .**74** E1
St Helena's Ct **1** BN21 . . .**184** E4
St Helen's Wood Rd
TN34 . . . .**136** E5
St Heliers Ave BN3 . . . .**162** E7
St James Ct BN24 . . . .**176** D8
St James Ct RH19 . . . .**1** D1
St James La TN22 . . . .**35** C4
St James Rd BN22 . . . .**185** C4
St James's Ave BN1 . . . .**190** A1
St James's Ave TN38 . . . . . .**159** A6
St James' Ave BN20 . . . .**157** D6
St James' CE Inf Sch TN4 . . .**7** D1
St James' CE Jun Sch TN2 . .**8** C4
St James' Cl TN40 . . . .**157** C7
St James' Cres TN40 . . . . . .**157** C7
St James' Ho **15** BN2 . . . . .**189** C2
St James' Pk TN1 . . . .**8** C5
St James' Rd
Bexhill TN40 . . . .**157** C6
Royal Tunbridge Wells TN4 . . . .**7** D1
St James' Rd
East Grinstead RH19 . . . .**1** D1
Hastings TN34 . . . .**136** F1
St James's Rd BN2 . . . .**189** C2
St James's Street Mews
BN2 . . . .**189** C2

St John Bank BN8 . . . .**100** D8
St John the Baptist RC Sch
BN2 . . . .**164** D5
St John's CE Prim Sch
TN6 . . . .**25** C4
St John's CE Prim Sch
TN4 . . . .**8** B7
St John's Cl
Crowborough TN6 . . . .**25** C3
East Grinstead RH19 . . . .**1** A7
South Chailey BN8 . . . .**100** D7
St John's Dr BN24 . . . .**174** E6
St John's Hill BN7 . . . .**190** A2
St John's Ho BN20 . . . .**188** F8
St John's Meads CE Prim Sch
BN20 . . . .**188** F8
St John's Mount **8** BN2 . .**189** C2
St John's Pk TN4 . . . .**8** A8
St John's Rd
Bexhill TN40 . . . .**157** D6
Crowborough TN6 . . . .**25** D4
East Grinstead RH19 . . . .**1** A7
Eastbourne BN20 . . . .**188** F8
Haywards Heath RH16 . . . .**50** C5
Hove BN3 . . . .**162** E7
Polegate BN26 . . . .**173** A6
Seaford BN25 . . . .**180** E2
St Leonards TN37 . . . .**159** C7
St John's Res Sch BN2 . . . .**164** D5
St John's Sch BN25 . . . .**180** E6
St John's St BN7 . . . .**190** B2
St John's Terr BN7 . . . .**190** A2
St Johns Ct
Burgess Hill RH15 . . . .**73** A3
Polegate BN26 . . . .**173** A6
St Johns Rd RH15 . . . .**73** A3
St Joseph's Cl BN2 . . . .**164** D7
St Joseph's RC Prim Sch
Brighton BN2 . . . .**143** C1
Haywards Heath RH16 . . . .**50** E4
St Joseph's Trad Est **3**
BN3 . . . .**163** A8
St Josephs Bsns Pk **2**
BN3 . . . .**163** A8
St Josephs Way RH16 . . . . . .**50** E4
St Julian's La BN43 . . . .**161** D7
St Julians Ct BN43 . . . .**161** C7
St Keyna Ave BN3 . . . .**162** D6
St Kilda Mans **3** BN21 . . .**184** F3
St Kitts Cl TN39 . . . .**157** A2
St Kitts Dr BN23 . . . .**185** G7
St Laurence Cl BN10 . . . . . .**167** A1
St Lawrence CE Prim Sch
BN6 . . . .**97** A6
St Lawrence Mews
BN23 . . . .**175** A1
St Lawrence Rd BN23 . . . . .**175** A1
St Lawrence Rd TN39 . . . . .**157** B7
St Lawrence Way
Eastbourne BN23 . . . .**175** A1
Hurstpierpoint BN6 . . . .**97** A7
St Leonard's Ave BN2 . . . . .**162** C7
St Leonard's Gdns BN2 . . . .**162** D7
St Leonard's Rd
9 Brighton BN2 . . . .**164** C8
Eastbourne BN21 . . . .**185** A2
Hove BN3 . . . .**162** C7
St Leonards TN37 . . . .**159** A7
St Leonards Cl BN9 . . . .**168** F2
St Leonards Ho TN38 . . . . . .**159** A6
St Leonards Pk RH19 . . . .**1** E1
St Leonards Rd
Bexhill TN40 . . . .**157** C3
Newhaven BN9 . . . .**168** F2
St Leonards Terr BN26 . . . .**172** F7
**St Leonards Warrior Square
Sta** TN38 . . . .**159** C7
St Leonards-Mayfield Sch
TN20 . . . .**40** A3
St Louie BN42 . . . .**162** A8
St Lucia TN39 . . . .**157** A2
St Lucia Wlk **6** BN23 . . . . .**185** F8
St Luke's CE Inf Sch TN4 . . . .**8** C7
St Luke's Inf Sch BN2 . . . . .**164** C6
St Luke's Jun Sch BN2 . . . .**164** C6
St Luke's La BN9 . . . .**179** C7
St Luke's Rd
Brighton BN2 . . . .**164** C6
Royal Tunbridge Wells TN4 . . . .**8** B6
St Luke's Terr BN2 . . . .**164** C6
St Lukes Ct RH15 . . . .**73** A3
St Margaret's Ave RH19 . . . .**1** F6
St Margaret's CE Prim Sch
BN2 . . . .**177** A6
St Margaret's Pl BN1 . . . . .**189** A2
St Margaret's Rd
East Grinstead RH19 . . . .**1** F3
St Leonards TN37 . . . .**159** D7
St Margaret's Rise
BN25 . . . .**180** A6
St Margaret's Terr
TN37 . . . .**159** D7
St Margarets BN2 . . . .**177** A5
St Margarets Cres TN39 . .**156** B8
St Margarets Terr **8**
TN31 . . . .**93** B5
St Mark's CE Prim Sch
Brighton BN2 . . . .**165** F1
Hadlow Down TN22 . . . .**57** C5
Royal Tunbridge Wells TN4 . . . .**7** D1

St Mark's Mews **13**
BN2 . . . .**164** C8
St Mark's Rd TN2 . . . .**16** F7
St Mark's St BN2 . . . .**164** E4
St Marks Cl TN39 . . . .**156** D5
St Marks Field TN22 . . . .**57** B5
St Martin's Ct BN1 . . . .**189** C5
St Martin's Flats **6** BN2 . .**164** C7
St Martin's La BN1 . . . .**190** A1
St Martin's Pl BN2 . . . .**164** C7
St Martin's St BN2 . . . .**189** C5
St Martins TN33 . . . .**112** E3
St Martins CE Prim Sch
BN2 . . . .**164** C8
St Martins Cres BN9 . . . . . .**168** D1
St Martins Ho BN3 . . . .**124** E6
St Martins Rd BN2 . . . .**173** D3
**St Mary Magdalen RC Prim
Sch** BN1 . . . .**163** C6
**St Mary Magdalene RC Prim
Sch** TN40 . . . .**157** F6
St Mary Magdalene St
BN2 . . . .**189** C5
**St Mary Star of the Sea RC
Prim Sch** TN37 . . . .**159** D8
**St Mary the Virgin CE Prim
Sch** TN7 . . . .**13** D4
St Mary's CE Sch RH19 . . . . .**1** D2
St Mary's Cl
Cackle Street TN31 . . . .**90** A2
Eastbourne BN22 . . . .**173** B2
Ticehurst TN5 . . . .**31** D1
St Mary's Cnr **3** BN21 . . . .**184** D3
St Mary's Cotts
Battle TN33 . . . .**112** E3
Bexhill TN39 . . . .**156** F8
4 Eastbourne BN20 . . . . . .**184** D3
St Mary's Ct
2 Eastbourne BN21 . . . . . .**184** D3
8 St Leonards TN37 . . . . . .**159** C7
St Mary's Farmhouse
TN33 . . . .**112** E3
St Mary's Gdns TN33 . . . . . .**112** E3
St Mary's La Bexhill TN39 .**156** F8
Speldhurst TN3 . . . .**7** A8
Ticehurst TN5 . . . .**31** D1
St Mary's Pl BN2 . . . .**189** C2
St Mary's RC Prim Sch
Crowborough TN6 . . . .**26** A2
Portslade-by-S BN41 . . . .**162** B7
St Mary's Rd
Burgess Hill RH15 . . . .**72** F4
Eastbourne BN21 . . . .**184** D4
Hastings TN34 . . . .**160** A5
St Mary's Rd W RH15 . . . . . .**72** E4
St Mary's Sch
Bexhill TN40 . . . .**157** E6
Maynard's Green TN21 . . . . . .**82** A1
St Mary's Sq **17** BN2 . . . . .**164** D4
St Mary's Terr
Battle TN33 . . . .**112** E3
Hastings TN34 . . . .**160** A5
St Mary's Villas TN33 . . . . .**112** E3
St Mary's Wlk BN27 . . . .**152** C7
St Mary-in-the-Fields
TN20 . . . .**40** E7
St Marys Ave TN21 . . . .**80** E7
St Marys Ave BN27 . . . .**152** C7
St Marys Cotts **18** TN38 . .**159** C7
St Marys Garth TN22 . . . .**56** B3
St Marys Mead TN22 . . . .**56** B3
St Marys Pl **3** BN43 . . . . . .**161** B8
St Matthew's Dr TN38 . . . .**136** C1
St Matthew's Gdns
BN2 . . . .**136** B1
**St Matthew's High Brooms CE
Prim Sch** TN4 . . . .**8** B8
St Matthew's Rd TN38 . . . .**136** B1
St Matthews Ct BN2 . . . . . .**164** C5
St Mellion Cl BN27 . . . .**151** F8
St Michael's CE Prim Sch
BN1 . . . .**70** C2
St Michael's Pl
Brighton BN1 . . . .**163** E6
8 Hastings TN34 . . . .**159** F7
St Michael's Prim Sch
TN7 . . . .**14** B5
St Michaels
Crowborough TN6 . . . .**38** B8
Stone Cross BN24 . . . .**174** A6
St Michaels Rd RH19 . . . .**1** E2
St Nicholas Cl RH16 . . . .**51** A6
St Nicholas La BN1 . . . .**190** B2
St Nicholas Lodge BN1 . . .**189** A2
St Nicholas Pl **8** BN43 . . .**161** A6
St Nicholas Rd
Brighton BN1 . . . .**189** A3
Portslade-by-S BN41 . . . .**162** B7
St Nicholas' CE Jun Sch
BN41 . . . .**162** B7
**St Nicolas & St Mary CE Fst &
Mid Sch** BN43 . . . .**161** B8
St Nicolas Cl BN24 . . . .**175** B6
St Olive's Cl TN21 . . . .**81** C7
St Pancras Gdns BN7 . . . . . .**146** E8
St Pancras Gn BN7 . . . .**145** C5
St Pancras RC Prim Sch
BN7 . . . .**123** B1
St Pancras Rd BN7 . . . .**146** B8
St Patrick's Cres TN40 . . . .**157** C5
St Patrick's Rd BN3 . . . .**163** A7
St Paul's CE Prim Sch
BN1 . . . .**189** A3

St Paul's CE Prim Sch
TN37 . . . . 136 D1
St Paul's Cl RH16 . . . . 50 F5
St Paul's Ct Rusthall TN4 . . . . 7 C4
St Leonards TN37 . . . . 159 D8
St Paul's Pl TN37 . . . . 159 D8
St Paul's RC Coll RH16 . . . . 50 F5
St Paul's Rd TN37 . . . . 136 C1
St Paul's St Brighton BN2 . 189 C5
Rusthall TN4 . . . . 7 C4
St Pauls CE Inf Sch TN4 . . . 7 B4
St Pauls CE Jun Sch TN4 . . 7 B4
St Pauls Cl BN22 . . . . 173 D3
St Peter & St Paul CE Prim
Sch TN40 . . . . 157 C4
St Peter's Ave BN10 . . . . 178 A8
St Peter's CE Prim Sch
TN2 . . . . 8 C3
St Peter's Cl Hove BN3 . . . 141 F2
Seaford BN25 . . . . 180 E5
St Peter's Com Inf Sch
BN41 . . . . 162 B7
St Peter's Cres TN40 . . . . 157 D5
St Peter's Mews TN40 . . . 157 D5
St Peter's Pl BN1,BN2 . . . 189 B3
St Peter's RC Prim Sch
East Grinstead RH19 . . . . 1 C1
Shoreham-by-S BN43 . . . . 161 A8
St Peter's Rd
Portslade-by-S BN41 . . . . 162 B7
Seaford BN25 . . . . 180 E5
St Leonards TN37 . . . . 159 C8
St Peter's St
Brighton BN1 . . . . 189 B4
Royal Tunbridge Wells TN2 . . . 8 C3
St Peters Mead TN6 . . . . 39 A7
St Peters Pl BN7 . . . . 190 A2
St Peters Rd RH15 . . . . 73 A4
St Peters Row TN3 . . . . 6 A5
St Philip's Ave BN22 . . . . 185 B5
St Philip's RC Prim Sch
TN22 . . . . 78 C5
St Philips Ct TN2 . . . . 8 D6
St Philips Mews [3] BN3 . 162 F7
St Richard's Ct BN3 . . . . 141 D1
St Richard's Flats BN41 . 162 B7
St Richard's RC Coll
TN40 . . . . 157 E4
St Richard's Rd BN41 . . . 162 B7
St Richards Ho [3] TN38 . 159 C7
St Richards Rd TN6 . . . . 38 A7
St Saviour's Rd TN38 . . . . 158 F6
St Saviours TN22 . . . . 78 D6
St Saviours Ct [1] BN1 . . . 164 B8
St Stephens Ct TN1 . . . . 8 B5
St Swithun's Cl RH19 . . . . 1 F1
St Swithun's La BN7 . . . . 190 A1
St Swithun's Terr BN7 . . . 190 A1
St Thomas [5] TN39 . . . . 157 A2
St Thomas a Becket RC Inf
Sch BN21 . . . . 184 F5
St Thomas a Becket RC Jun
Sch BN21 . . . . 184 F5
St Thomas CE Prim Sch
TN36 . . . . 117 F7
St Thomas Ct BN7 . . . . 190 C2
St Thomas of Canterbury Ct
TN20 . . . . 40 A2
St Thomas's Rd TN34 . . . 160 A5
St Thomas's St TN36 . . . 117 F7
St Vincent's Ct BN2 . . . . 165 A3
St Vincents Flats TN37 . . 136 B4
St Vincents Pl BN20 . . . . 184 E1
St Vincents Rd TN38 . . . . 158 F7
St Wilfred's Ct [5] RH16 . . . 50 E4
St Wilfred's Pl BN25 . . . . 181 B3
St Wilfrid's CE Prim Sch
RH16 . . . . 50 F3
St Wilfrid's Ct BN27 . . . . 152 B8
St Wilfrid's Gn BN27 . . . . 152 C8
St Wilfrid's RC Prim Sch
RH15 . . . . 72 F2
St Wilfrid's Way RH16 . . . 50 E4
St Wilfrids Rd RH15 . . . . 73 B4
Salcey Cl TN38 . . . . 135 E2
Salehurst CE Prim Sch
TN32 . . . . 64 B4
Salehurst Gdns TN38 . . . 135 D2
Salehurst Rd BN21 . . . . 184 C4
Salisbury Cl BN22 . . . . 173 C2
Salisbury Ct BN25 . . . . 180 E4
Salisbury Rd
Bexhill TN40 . . . . 157 B5
Eastbourne BN20 . . . . 188 C8
Hove BN3 . . . . 163 C6
Langton Green TN3 . . . . 6 F3
Royal Tunbridge Wells TN4 . . . 8 C8
Seaford BN25 . . . . 180 E3
St Leonards TN37 . . . . 136 C1
Salisbury Terr TN21 . . . . 81 B8
Salisbury Yd TN37 . . . . 136 C1
Sally Ct [3] BN22 . . . . 185 B3
Salomons Rd TN4 . . . . 7 C4
Saltcote La TN31 . . . . 93 C7
Saltcote Mews TN31 . . . . 93 C7
Saltdean Cl TN39 . . . . 156 E3
Saltdean Dr BN2 . . . . 177 B5
Saltdean Park Rd BN2 . . 177 C5
Saltdean Prim Sch BN2 . 177 C6
Saltdean Vale BN2 . . . . 177 D6
Saltdean Way TN39 . . . . 156 D3
Salters La TN34 . . . . 160 B4
Saltwood Rd BN25 . . . . 181 C4
Salvador Cl BN23 . . . . 185 F7
Salvadori Ct TN2 . . . . 9 D6
Salvington Cres TN39 . . . 156 F4
Samoa Way BN23 . . . . 175 B2
San Feliu Ct RH19 . . . . 2 B2
San Jose Cl TN35 . . . . 160 C6
San Juan Ct BN23 . . . . 185 G7
Sancroft Rd BN20 . . . . 184 B3
Sanctuary The BN20 . . . . 184 B4
Sand Hill La BN8,TN22 . . 104 B8
Sand Rd TN3 . . . . 20 A4
Sandbanks Cl BN27 . . . . 152 A5
Sandbanks Gdns BN27 . . 152 B5
Sandbanks Gr BN27 . . . . 152 B6
Sandbanks Way
Hailsham BN27 . . . . 152 A6
Hailsham BN27 . . . . 152 B6
Sandbrook BN6 . . . . 97 F3
Sanders Ho BN3 . . . . 162 E8
Sanderstead [1] BN2 . . . . 164 F5
Sandfield Rd TN11 . . . . 6 A7
Sandford Mews BN23 . . 174 D3
Sandgate Cl BN25 . . . . 181 C5
Sandgate Rd BN1 . . . . 143 A2
Sandhawes Hill RH19 . . . . 2 A4
Sandhill La
Churches Green BN27 . . . 109 B6
Crowborough TN6 . . . . 26 E7
Sandhurst Ave
Pembury TN2 . . . . 9 E6
Woodingdean BN2 . . . . 144 D1
Sandhurst Cl
Royal Tunbridge Wells TN2 . . . 8 C6
Sandhurst Cross TN18 . . . . 47 A4
Sandhurst Gdns TN34 . . . 136 F6
Sandhurst Ho TN2 . . . . 8 D5
Sandhurst La TN39 . . . . 156 B6
Sandhurst Mews BN23 . . 174 E1
Sandhurst Pk TN2 . . . . 8 C6
Sandhurst Prim Sch
TN18 . . . . 47 C5
Sandhurst Rd TN2 . . . . 8 D6
Sandhurst Vineyards*
TN18 . . . . 47 E5
Sandore Cl BN25 . . . . 181 A4
Sandore Rd BN25 . . . . 181 A4
Sandown Cl
Eastbourne BN23 . . . . 174 B4
Royal Tunbridge Wells TN2 . . . 8 F6
Sandown Ct BN3 . . . . 141 D1
Sandown Gr TN2 . . . . 8 F6
Sandown Ho TN6 . . . . 25 F3
Sandown Pk TN2 . . . . 8 F6
Sandown Prim Sch
TN34 . . . . 160 C8
Sandown Rd
Brighton BN2 . . . . 164 D7
Hastings TN35 . . . . 160 C7
Southwick BN42 . . . . 161 E8
Sandown Way TN40 . . . . 157 E6
Sandpiper Wlk BN23 . . . 174 C2
Sandpit Cotts BN6 . . . . 99 C2
Sandridge TN6 . . . . 25 F1
Sandringham Cl
East Grinstead RH19 . . . . 11 A8
Hove BN3 . . . . 142 A3
Seaford BN25 . . . . 181 A6
Sandringham Dr BN3 . . . 142 A3
Sandringham Hts TN38 . 135 D3
Sandringham Lodge [17]
BN3 . . . . 163 C6
Sandringham Mews TN4 . . 8 A5
Sandrock Hall TN34 . . . . 136 F5
Sandrock Hill TN33,
TN38 . . . . 135 A4
Sandrock Ho TN2 . . . . 8 D4
Sandrock Pk TN34 . . . . 136 F5
Sandrock Rd TN2 . . . . 8 C4
Sandrocks Way RH16 . . . 50 E2
Sandwich Dr TN38 . . . . 158 F8
Sandwich St BN22 . . . . 185 C6
Sandy Cl TN37 . . . . 136 B5
Sandy Cross Cotts TN21 . 82 A5
Sandy Cross La TN21 . . . 82 B5
Sandy La
Chelwood Gate RH17 . . . . 34 C8
Coleman's Hatch TN7 . . . . 23 D6
East Grinstead RH19 . . . . 1 F1
Framefield TN22 . . . . 79 A7
Horam TN21 . . . . 81 E2
Sandy Vale RH16 . . . . 50 E2
Sanshaw Ct BN21 . . . . 184 E3
Santa Cruz Dr BN23 . . . . 185 F7
Santer Ho TN18 . . . . 45 E8
Santos Wharf [19] BN23 . . 185 F8
Sanyhils Ave BN1 . . . . 142 F7
Saunders Cl
Hastings TN34 . . . . 160 A5
Uckfield TN22 . . . . 78 A8
Saunders Hill BN1 . . . . 143 D7
Saunders Park Ho [2]
BN2 . . . . 164 C8
Saunders Park Rise
BN2 . . . . 143 C1
Saunders Park View
BN2 . . . . 143 C1
Saunders Rd TN4 . . . . 7 E1
Saunders Way TN31 . . . . 95 A2
Savill Rd RH16 . . . . 51 A8
Sawyard Cotts TN22 . . . . 53 C5
Sawyers Cl RH15 . . . . 73 D1
Saxby Cl BN23 . . . . 174 E1
Saxby Rd Bexhill TN39 . . . 157 A5
Burgess Hill RH15 . . . . 72 D4
Saxon Cl BN2 . . . . 177 C6
Saxon Ct Hove BN3 . . . . 162 D6
Pevensey Bay BN24 . . . . 175 D5
St Leonards TN37 . . . . 159 C8
Saxon Ground BN21 . . . . 184 E4
Saxon La BN25 . . . . 180 E2
Saxon Mount Sch TN38 . 158 E7
Saxon Pl BN21 . . . . 184 C6
Saxon Rd Hastings TN35 . . 160 D7
Saxon Rd *continued*
Hove BN3 . . . . 162 D6
Newhaven BN9 . . . . 179 C7
Saxon Rise TN40 . . . . 157 E4
Saxon St TN37 . . . . 159 C6
Saxonbury [16] BN2 . . . . 189 C3
Saxonbury Cl TN6 . . . . 25 F2
Saxonhurst Ct TN37 . . . . 136 B4
Saxons TN39 . . . . 156 F3
Saxonwood Rd TN33 . . . . 112 C5
Sayerland La BN26 . . . . 173 A8
Sayerland Rd BN26 . . . . 173 A8
Sayers The [5] RH19 . . . . 1 C1
Scamps Hill RH16 . . . . 51 C6
Scanlon Cl BN20 . . . . 173 A3
Scarborough Rd BN1 . . . 142 D1
Scarletts Cl TN22 . . . . 78 B7
Scaynes Hill Rd RH16 . . . 51 D6
Sceptre BN1 . . . . 142 E2
Schofield Way BN23 . . . . 185 F7
School Cl
Burgess Hill RH15 . . . . 72 F2
[1] Southwick BN42 . . . . 161 E7
School Cotts
East Chiltington BN7 . . . . 100 A3
Maresfield TN22 . . . . 55 B4
School Field BN8 . . . . 101 E5
School Hill
Barcombe Cross BN8 . . . . 101 E4
Lamberhurst TN3 . . . . 20 B6
Old Heathfield TN21 . . . . 82 D5
Winchelsea TN36 . . . . 117 E8
School La
Ashurst Wood RH19 . . . . 11 E6
Blackboys TN22 . . . . 80 A6
Crowborough TN6 . . . . 25 F1
Crowborough,St John's
TN6 . . . . 25 D4
Danehill RH17 . . . . 34 B5
Forest Row RH18 . . . . 11 F2
Hadlow Down TN22 . . . . 57 B5
Nutley TN22 . . . . 35 C5
Peasmarsh TN31 . . . . 69 B2
Polegate BN26 . . . . 173 A7
Pyecombe BN45 . . . . 119 C6
Saltdean BN2 . . . . 177 C6
School Path BN8 . . . . 101 D4
School Pl TN40 . . . . 158 A5
School Rd Hastings TN35 . 160 C7
Hove BN3 . . . . 162 F8
School Rise
Brighton BN2 . . . . 164 E6
Royal Tunbridge Wells TN2 . . . 7 F1
School Terr TN32 . . . . 64 C5
Schwerte Way [5] TN37 . . 159 E7
Science Park Rd BN1 . . . 144 B7
Science Park Sq BN1 . . . 144 B6
Scotland St BN2 . . . . 189 C3
Scotney Castle* TN3 . . . . 20 D3
Scotney Castle Gdns*
TN3 . . . . 20 D3
Scotsford Cl TN21 . . . . 59 F1
Scotsford Hill TN20 . . . . 40 E1
Scotsford Rd TN21 . . . . 59 F2
Scott Rd BN3 . . . . 162 F7
Scotts Acre TN31 . . . . 94 E2
Scotts Way TN2 . . . . 16 E8
Scrace Hill Terr RH16 . . . 73 F8
Scraper's Hill BN8 . . . . 128 A8
Scrase Lodge RH15 . . . . 73 D3
Scutes Cl TN34 . . . . 160 A7
Sea Cotts [5] BN25 . . . . 180 F2
Sea Ct BN24 . . . . 175 D4
Sea Ho [14] BN42 . . . . 161 E7
Sea Rd Bexhill TN40 . . . . 157 D3
Camber TN31 . . . . 94 F2
Fairlight Cove TN35 . . . . 139 A5
Pevensey Bay BN24 . . . . 175 D5
St Leonards TN38 . . . . 158 F6
Winchelsea Beach TN36 . . . 118 B7
Sea View Cotts BN27 . . . 129 D3
Sea-Saw Way BN2 . . . . 164 F7
Seabeach La BN22 . . . . 185 C5
Seabourne Rd TN40 . . . . 158 A6
Seacliffe BN10 . . . . 177 F3
Seafield Cl BN25 . . . . 181 B5
Seafield Rd BN3 . . . . 163 B6
Seaford Ct [1] BN25 . . . . 180 E2
Seaford Head Com Coll
Seaford BN25 . . . . 180 F2
Seaford BN25 . . . . 181 A2
Seaford Mus of Local
History* BN25 . . . . 180 E1
Seaford Prim Sch BN25 . 180 E4
Seaford Rd
Eastbourne BN22 . . . . 185 C5
Hove BN3 . . . . 162 C6
Newhaven BN9 . . . . 179 F8
Seaford Sta BN25 . . . . 180 E3
Seagrave Cl BN25 . . . . 180 A6
Seagrove Way BN25 . . . . 180 F5
Searle Ave BN10 . . . . 178 E6
Seaside BN22,BN23 . . . . 185 C5
Seaside Pas TN38 . . . . 158 F6
Seaside Rd
Eastbourne BN21 . . . . 185 B3
St Leonards TN38 . . . . 158 F6
Seaside Rdbt BN23 . . . . 185 D7
Seaside Way TN38 . . . . 158 F6
Seattle Dr BN23 . . . . 175 A1
Seaview Ave BN10 . . . . 178 E6
Seaview Cotts TN36 . . . . 116 E5
Seaview Est BN42 . . . . 161 F7
Seaview Ho BN9 . . . . 179 D6
Seaview Rd
Newhaven BN9 . . . . 168 F1
Peacehaven BN10 . . . . 178 E6
Woodingdean BN2 . . . . 165 B8
Seaview Terr
Icklesham TN36 . . . . 116 E5
[2] Rye TN31 . . . . 93 C5
Seaville Dr
Eastbourne BN23 . . . . 185 D8
Pevensey Bay BN24 . . . . 175 D5
Second Ave Bexhill TN40 . . 157 F5
Camber TN31 . . . . 94 F2
Hove BN3 . . . . 163 C6
Newhaven BN9 . . . . 179 C6
Second Rd BN10 . . . . 178 A7
Sedgebrook Gdns TN34 . 136 E2
Sedges The TN38 . . . . 135 E1
Sedgewick Rd TN40 . . . . 157 C6
Sedlescombe CE Prim Sch
TN33 . . . . 88 E1
Sedlescombe Gdns
TN38 . . . . 136 B2
Sedlescombe Organic
Vineyard* TN32 . . . . 88 D5
Sedlescombe Rd N
TN37 . . . . 136 B4
Sedlescombe Rd S
TN38 . . . . 136 B1
Sefton Chase TN6 . . . . 26 A3
Sefton Rd BN41 . . . . 140 F3
Sefton Way TN6 . . . . 26 A3
Segrave Cl BN7 . . . . 123 B2
Selba Dr BN2 . . . . 143 E3
Selborne Pl BN3 . . . . 163 C7
Selborne Rd BN3 . . . . 163 C6
Selby Cl TN22 . . . . 78 D5
Selby Ct RH16 . . . . 50 E3
Selby Gdns TN22 . . . . 78 D5
Selby Rd
Eastbourne BN21 . . . . 184 D5
Uckfield TN22 . . . . 78 D6
Selby Rise TN22 . . . . 78 D5
Selham Cl BN1 . . . . 143 D6
Selham Dr BN1 . . . . 143 D6
Selham Pl BN1 . . . . 143 D6
Selhurst Rd BN2 . . . . 165 E6
Sellbourne Pk TN3 . . . . 17 C4
Selmeston Cl TN34 . . . . 136 D1
Selmeston Ct [2] BN25 . . 180 C4
Selmeston Ho [8] BN21 . . 184 D4
Selmeston Rd BN21 . . . . 184 C7
Selmestone Pl BN2 . . . . 164 F6
Selmestone Rd BN2 . . . . 164 F5
Selsey Cl BN1 . . . . 143 E6
Selsfield Cl BN21 . . . . 184 D6
Selsfield Dr BN2 . . . . 143 D3
Selwyn Dr BN21 . . . . 184 E4
Selwyn Ho [10] BN21 . . . . 184 E4
Selwyn Park Ct [9] BN21 . 184 E4
Selwyn Rd BN21 . . . . 184 E4
Semley Lodge BN6 . . . . 97 E4
Semley Rd Brighton BN1 . . 143 A1
Hassocks BN6 . . . . 97 E4
Sempstead La TN31,TN32 . 66 C4
Senlac Gdns TN33 . . . . 112 E4
Senlac Ct TN33 . . . . 112 D5
Senlac Gn TN22 . . . . 78 E8
Senlac Pl TN3 . . . . 15 C7
Senlac Rd BN9 . . . . 179 D7
Senlac Way TN37 . . . . 136 C5
Sergison Cl RH16 . . . . 50 C5
Sergison Rd RH16 . . . . 50 D5
Setfords Field BN8 . . . . 75 E1
Sett The BN41 . . . . 141 B2
Sevelands Cl BN2 . . . . 164 F7
Seven Acre Cl TN37 . . . . 136 A5
Seven Dials BN1 . . . . 189 A4
Seven Sisters Ctry Pk*
BN25 . . . . 182 A2
Seven Sisters Rd BN22 . 173 C3
Seven Sisters Sheep Ctr*
BN20 . . . . 187 B7
Seven Sisters Visitor Ctr*
BN25 . . . . 181 F4
Sevenfields RH15 . . . . 72 D4
Sevenoaks Rd BN23 . . . . 174 D2
Seville St BN2 . . . . 164 C7
Sewell Ave TN40 . . . . 157 C5
Seymour Cotts TN6 . . . . 27 D1
Seymour Ho [5] BN2 . . . . 164 D4
Seymour Sq [3] BN2 . . . . 164 D4
Seymour St [4] BN2 . . . . 164 D4
Seymour Villas TN34 . . . 160 A7
Shaftesbury Ct TN22 . . . . 78 C8
Shaftesbury Pl BN1 . . . . 164 A8
Shaftesbury Rd
Brighton BN1 . . . . 189 B5
Royal Tunbridge Wells TN4 . . . 8 A5
Shakespeare St BN3 . . . . 163 A8
Shakespeare Wlk BN23 . 174 D2
Shalesbrook La RH18 . . . . 12 A1
Shalfleet Cl BN23 . . . . 174 B3
Shandon Cl TN2 . . . . 8 C4
Shands BN6 . . . . 97 F3
Shanklin Cl BN23 . . . . 174 B4
Shanklin Ct
[11] Brighton BN2 . . . . 164 C8
Hove BN3 . . . . 141 D1
Shanklin Rd BN2 . . . . 164 C8
Shannon Cl BN10 . . . . 167 B1
Shannon Way BN23 . . . . 185 F8
Sharp's Cnr TN21 . . . . 106 E8
Sharpthorne Cres BN41 . 141 C1
Sharrow Cl RH16 . . . . 50 E5
Shaw The TN2 . . . . 8 C2
Shawcross Ho [5] BN1 . . . 142 E2
Shawfield TN6 . . . . 26 B2
Shaws Cnr TN31 . . . . 67 B7
Shearbarn Holiday Pk
TN35 . . . . 160 E7
Shedden Ct TN21 . . . . 82 A8
Sheddingdean Bsns Ctr
RH15 . . . . 72 F5
Sheddingdean Cl RH15 . . . 73 A4
Sheddingdean Com Prim Sch
RH15 . . . . 73 A5
Sheddingdean Ct RH15 . . . 72 F4
Sheddingdean
Neighbourhood Ctr
RH15 . . . . 73 A5
Sheen Rd BN22 . . . . 185 B4
Sheep Pen La [3] BN25 . . . 181 A3
Sheep Plain TN6 . . . . 37 D8
Sheep Wlk BN2 . . . . 165 F1
Sheepbell Cl BN41 . . . . 141 B3
Sheepcote La
Chalvington BN27 . . . . 150 C8
Golden Cross BN27 . . . . 127 D3
Sheepfair BN7 . . . . 123 A2
Sheepfold The BN10 . . . . 167 C1
Sheepsetting La TN21 . . . 81 E7
Sheepstreet La TN19,TN5 . 43 E5
Sheepwash La TN22 . . . . 80 C8
Sheerwater Cres TN34 . . 136 D4
Sheerwater Terr TN34 . . 136 D4
Sheffield Mill La TN22 . . . 53 C8
Sheffield Park Gdn*
TN22 . . . . 53 D5
Sheffield Park Sta*
TN22 . . . . 53 A4
Sheffield Park Way
BN23 . . . . 174 A4
Sheiling Rd TN6 . . . . 25 E3
Shell La [9] TN34 . . . . 160 A3
Shelldale Ave BN41 . . . . 162 B7
Shelldale Cres BN41 . . . . 162 B7
Shelldale Rd BN41 . . . . 162 B8
Shelley Cl BN7 . . . . 123 B1
Shelley Ct [4] RH16 . . . . 50 D5
Shelley Pk [4] TN21 . . . . 82 A7
Shelley Rd
East Grinstead RH19 . . . . 1 D1
Hove BN3 . . . . 162 F7
Ringmer BN8 . . . . 124 D5
Shelley Wlk [3] BN23 . . . . 174 E2
Shelley Wood RH15 . . . . 72 D4
Shenfield Way BN1 . . . . 143 B3
Shenstone RH16 . . . . 51 B8
Shepham Ave BN2 . . . . 177 D6
Shepham La BN26 . . . . 173 C8
Shepherd St [3] TN38 . . . 159 C6
Shepherd's Cl TN39 . . . . 156 D4
Shepherd's Hill TN7 . . . . 23 D8
Shepherd's Way TN35 . . . 138 E4
Shepherds Cl
Eastbourne BN22 . . . . 173 F3
Piddinghoe BN9 . . . . 168 B2
Ringmer BN8 . . . . 124 E5
Shepherds Cot BN10 . . . . 167 D2
Shepherds Croft BN1 . . . 142 C4
Shepherds Ct TN35 . . . . 138 E4
Shepherds Mead RH15 . . . 72 F4
Shepherds Way
Ringmer BN8 . . . . 124 E5
South Chailey BN8 . . . . 100 C7
Uckfield TN22 . . . . 78 C5
Shepherds Wlk
Crowborough TN6 . . . . 26 C1
Hassocks BN6 . . . . 97 F5
Royal Tunbridge Wells TN2 . . . 8 D4
Shepherdsgrove La RH19 . . 3 A4
Sheppard Way BN41 . . . . 141 A3
Sheppey Wlk BN27 . . . . 129 A3
Sheppeys RH16 . . . . 50 D2
Shepway Par BN25 . . . . 180 E3
Shepway The BN25 . . . . 181 B4
Sheraton Cl BN21 . . . . 184 F2
Sherborne Ct [5] BN21 . . 184 D4
Sherbourne Cl
Hove BN3 . . . . 141 D3
Royal Tunbridge Wells TN2 . . . 8 D2
Sherbourne Rd BN3 . . . . 141 D3
Sherbourne Way BN3 . . . 141 D3
Sheridan Mans BN3 . . . . 163 A8
Sheridan Pl RH19 . . . . 1 C1
Sheridan Terr BN3 . . . . 163 A8
Sheriff's La TN6 . . . . 39 D7
Sheringham Cl TN32 . . . . 65 E2
Sherrington Rd BN2 . . . . 165 F8
Sherwood Cl TN34 . . . . 136 F1
Sherwood Dr RH16 . . . . 50 C5
Sherwood Gn BN27 . . . . 152 B6
Sherwood Park Com Prim
Sch TN2 . . . . 8 D6
Sherwood Pl TN3 . . . . 6 E3
Sherwood Rd
Royal Tunbridge Wells TN2 . . . 8 E5
Seaford BN25 . . . . 180 F4
Sherwood Rise BN25 . . . 180 F4
Sherwood Way TN2 . . . . 8 D6
Shinewater Ct BN23 . . . . 174 B3
Shinewater La BN23 . . . 174 B4
Shinewater Prim Sch
BN23 . . . . 174 B4
Shinewater Rdbt BN23 . . 174 B1
Shingle Ct TN38 . . . . 135 E7
Shingle Rd BN43 . . . . 161 A6
Shining Cliff TN34 . . . . 136 F4
Ship St Brighton BN1 . . . . 189 A2
East Grinstead RH19 . . . . 10 E8
Newhaven BN9 . . . . 179 C8
Ship Street Gdns BN1 . . . 189 A2
Shipley La TN39 . . . . 156 D3
Shipley Mill Cl BN24 . . . . 174 B5
Shipley Rd BN2 . . . . 165 E7

Shipwreck Heritage Ctr* TN34 ....160 B3
Shipyard La TN31 ....93 C5
Shirlea View TN33 ....112 E4
Shirley Ave BN3 ....142 B2
Shirley Cl BN43 ....161 D8
Shirley Dr Hove BN3 ....142 C2
St Leonards TN37 ....136 B4
Shirley Gdns TN4 ....7 C5
Shirley Gr TN4 ....7 C5
Shirley Mews BN3 ....163 B7
Shirley Rd BN3 ....163 C8
Shirley St BN3 ....163 B7
Shirleys BN6 ....98 E2
Shoreham Beach Com Fst Sch BN43 ....161 A6
Shoreham By-Pass BN41,BN43 ....140 D2
Shoreham Coll BN43 ....161 D7
Short Brow BN25 ....181 A4
Short Brow Cl BN22 ....173 B3
Shortdean Pl BN21 ....184 D4
Shortgate La Laughton BN8 ....126 B8
Shortgate BN8 ....104 B2
Shortgate Rd BN2 ....143 F4
Shortlands Cl BN22 ....173 C1
Shorts Cl RH16 ....50 E3
Shotters RH15 ....72 E1
Shovelstrode La RH19 ....11 D8
Showfields Rd TN2 ....7 F1
Shropshire Ct BN20 ....184 B7
Shrub La TN19 ....62 C7
Shrublands Ct TN2 ....8 C4
Shrublands The TN39 ....156 E3
Sicklehatch La TN21 ....82 B2
Sidcup Cl BN23 ....174 D2
Sidehill Dr BN41 ....140 F2
Sidehills BN1 ....101 D4
Sidley Com Prim Sch TN39 ....157 C7
Sidley Gn TN39 ....157 C7
Sidley Rd BN22 ....185 C5
Sidley St TN39 ....157 C7
Sidney Cl TN12 ....16 F8
Sidney Tidy Ho [5] BN2 ....164 C6
Silchester Rd TN4 ....159 C7
Sillwood Ct BN1 ....163 E5
Sillwood Hall [2] BN1 ....163 E5
Sillwood Pl [17] BN1 ....163 E5
Sillwood Rd BN1 ....163 E5
Sillwood St BN1 ....163 E5
Sillwood Terr [22] BN1 ....163 E5
Silva Cl TN40 ....158 A6
Silvan Rd TN38 ....135 E4
Silver Bank Cotts TN19 ....64 B8
Silver Birches Brighton BN1 ....142 E1
Haywards Heath RH16 ....51 A4
Silver Ct RH19 ....1 C2
Silver Hill TN19 ....45 B1
Silver Strand E [8] BN23 ....175 A1
Silver Strand W BN23 ....175 A1
Silverdale BN8 ....98 B3
Silverdale Ave BN3 ....163 D7
Silverdale Cl BN27 ....152 B8
Silverdale La Royal Tunbridge Wells TN4 ....8 B6
Sandhurst Cross TN18 ....46 F5
Silverdale Prim Sch TN38 ....136 B3
Silverdale Rd Burgess Hill RH15 ....73 B2
Eastbourne BN20 ....184 F1
Hove BN3 ....163 D7
Royal Tunbridge Wells TN4 ....8 B6
Silverden Cotts TN18 ....46 F4
Silverhill Ave TN37 ....136 C4
Silverlands Rd [1] TN37 ....136 B2
Silvester Rd TN40 ....157 C5
Silwood Cl TN2 ....8 E7
Simmonds Ct TN4 ....7 B4
Simons Cl TN6 ....26 A1
Singleton Mill Rd BN24 ....174 C5
Singleton Rd BN1 ....143 A6
Singleton Way RH15 ....73 C1
Singleton Wlk TN40 ....158 A6
Sinnock Sq [1] TN34 ....160 B4
Sion Wlk [8] TN1 ....8 A2
Sir David's Pk TN4 ....7 E8
Sir Henry Fermor CE Prim Sch TN6 ....26 A2
Six Bells Mews TN31 ....67 C5
Skinner's La TN33 ....133 D8
Skinners' Sch The TN4 ....8 A5
Skippers Hill Manor Sch TN20 ....58 B7
Skyline View BN10 ....167 D1
Slade The TN3 ....20 A3
Sleeches Cross TN3 ....17 B2
Sleepers Stile Rd TN5 ....19 B1
Slider's La Fletching TN22 ....53 A7
Furner's Green TN22 ....34 B1
Slides The TN38 ....135 F3
Slimbridge Rd RH15 ....72 F3
Slindon Ave BN10 ....178 D6
Slindon Cres BN21 ....184 E5
Slinfold Cl BN2 ....164 D5
Sliverick's La TN33 ....109 F7
Sloane Ct [4] BN2 ....164 C5
Sloe La BN26 ....173 A3
Sloe Hill Rd BN43 ....140 A1
Sloop La RH17 ....52 D5
Slugwash La RH17 ....74 B7
Small Acre BN27 ....127 B3

Smeatons La TN36 ....118 B5
Smith Cl TN33 ....133 B5
Smithlands La BN8 ....106 A3
Smithy The Best Beech Hill TN5 ....29 A3
Uckfield TN22 ....78 B6
Smithy's Cl TN37 ....136 C5
Smolletts RH19 ....10 C8
Smugglers Cl BN26 ....170 F3
Smugglers La TN6 ....25 D5
Smugglers Way TN35 ....138 F4
Snape La TN6 ....29 D1
Snape View TN5 ....29 F4
Snatt's Rd TN22 ....55 C1
Snednore BN7 ....145 F5
Snipe Cl TN2 ....8 B2
Snowdon Cl BN23 ....174 D3
Snowdrop La RH16 ....51 C4
Snowflakes La RH16 ....51 D6
Soames Ct RH15 ....72 F4
Solomon's La TN32 ....87 C4
Solomons Cl BN23 ....175 B2
Solway BN27 ....129 A2
Solway Ave BN1 ....142 F7
Somerhill Ave BN3 ....163 D7
Somerhill Ct [10] BN3 ....163 D7
Somerhill Jun Sch BN3 ....163 D6
Somerhill La BN3 ....163 D6
Somerhill Rd BN3 ....163 D6
Somerset Ct Eastbourne BN23 ....174 E1
[3] Hove BN3 ....163 C7
Somerset Point [1] BN2 ....164 C4
Somerset Rd TN4 ....8 A6
Somerset St BN2 ....164 C5
Somerset Villas TN3 ....15 C7
Somerville Ct BN23 ....185 E2
Somerville Gdns TN4 ....7 F4
Sompting Cl BN2 ....164 F7
Sompting Ct [3] BN43 ....161 B8
Sorrel Cl BN23 ....174 D3
Sorrel Dr BN23 ....174 C3
South Ave Brighton BN2 ....164 C5
Eastbourne BN20 ....184 B5
Hurstpierpoint BN6 ....97 A5
South Bank BN6 ....97 E3
South Brooks Rd TN29 ....96 F2
South Cl Beachlands BN24 ....175 F6
Burgess Hill RH15 ....72 E3
Hailsham BN27 ....152 B6
South Cliff Bexhill TN39 ....156 F2
[18] Eastbourne BN20 ....185 A1
Eastbourne BN20 ....188 F8
South Cliff Ave Bexhill TN39 ....156 E2
Eastbourne BN20 ....184 F1
South Cliff Twr BN20 ....188 F8
South Coast Rd Peacehaven BN10 ....178 D6
Telscombe Cliffs BN2, BN10 ....177 E4
South Ct Lewes BN7 ....190 C3
Royal Tunbridge Wells TN4 ....8 A6
South Downs TN7 ....99 E5
South Downs Bsns Pk BN7 ....190 C3
South Downs Rd BN7 ....190 B3
South Downs Sch Com Specl The BN20 ....184 B4
South Dr RH15 ....72 E3
South Gr TN1 ....8 A2
South La Newhaven BN9 ....179 D7
Wood's Corner TN21 ....84 E2
South Lodge [8] BN1 ....164 F5
South Lodge Cl RH15 ....72 F4
South Lynn Dr BN21 ....184 F4
South Malling CE Prim Sch BN7 ....190 C4
South Pl BN7 ....190 B2
South Point [8] BN43 ....161 A6
South Rd Brighton BN1 ....142 E1
Hailsham BN27 ....152 B6
Haywards Heath RH16 ....50 E4
Newhaven BN9 ....179 D7
Wivelsfield Green RH17 ....74 D4
South Rd Mews BN1 ....142 E1
South Rough BN8 ....76 C7
South Side TN21 ....59 E1
South St Brighton BN1 ....189 A2
Crowborough TN6 ....25 F1
Ditchling BN6 ....98 D3
East Hoathly BN8 ....104 F4
Eastbourne BN21 ....185 A2
Falmer BN1 ....144 C6
Lewes BN7 ....190 C2
Mayfield TN20 ....80 B2
Portslade-by-S BN41 ....141 A1
Rotherfield TN6 ....39 B8
Seaford BN25 ....180 E2
St Leonards TN37 ....159 C7
South Terr Broad Oak TN21 ....59 E1
Hastings TN34 ....159 F8
Westfield TN35 ....114 E3
South Undercliff TN31 ....93 C5
South View Ditchling BN6 ....98 E5
[1] Eastbourne BN21 ....184 E4
Hastings TN34 ....160 B4
Newhaven BN9 ....179 D7
South View Cl TN19 ....44 F3
South View Rd Crowborough TN6 ....25 E1
Royal Tunbridge Wells TN4 ....8 B8
Turner's Green TN5 ....29 F6
South Way Lewes BN7 ....123 A1
Newhaven BN9 ....179 D7
Seaford BN25 ....181 C1

South Woodlands BN1 ....142 E5
Southall Ave BN2 ....143 D2
Southampton St [6] BN23 ....185 F8
Southampton St [6] 189 C3
Southborough CE Prim Sch & Tunbridge Wells Language Unit TN4 ....7 F8
Southbourne Rd BN22 ....185 C6
Southcliffe BN7 ....130 C5
Southcourt Ave TN39 ....156 F2
Southdown Ave Brighton BN1 ....143 A1
Eastbourne BN20 ....173 A3
Hastings TN34 ....160 B7
Lewes BN7 ....146 A8
Peacehaven BN10 ....178 E6
Portslade-by-S BN41 ....162 C8
Southdown Cl Haywards Heath RH16 ....50 D2
Newhaven BN9 ....179 B6
Southdown Com Sch BN23 ....174 B3
Southdown Cotts BN23 ....173 B3
Southdown Ct [5] Hailsham BN27 ....152 C7
Polegate BN26 ....172 F6
Southdown Ho [7] Eastbourne BN20 ....184 F1
[9] Eastbourne BN20 ....185 A1
Southdown Jun Sch BN9 ....179 C7
Southdown Mews BN2 ....164 C5
Southdown Pl Brighton BN1 ....143 A1
Lewes BN7 ....190 C3
Southdown Rd Brighton BN1 ....143 A1
Eastbourne BN20 ....173 A3
Newhaven BN9 ....179 B6
Portslade-by-S BN41 ....141 A2
Seaford BN25 ....181 A2
Southwick BN42 ....161 E7
Southease Sta BN8 ....168 A7
Southerden Cl BN27 ....152 C7
Southern Ave BN26 ....173 B6
Southern Cross BN41 ....162 B8
Southern Rd BN22 ....173 F2
Southern Ring Rd BN1 ....144 B6
Southfield BN26 ....172 F5
Southfield Rd TN4 ....8 A6
Southfields Speldhurst TN3 ....7 A7
Southfields [9] BN21 ....184 F3
Southfields Rd BN21 ....184 F3
Southfields Way TN4 ....8 B8
Southgate TN4 ....7 F2
Southlands RH19 ....10 E7
Southlands Ave TN39 ....157 A7
Southlands Rd [1] BN3 ....161 B8
Southlands Rd TN39 ....157 A7
Southlands Gen Hospl BN43 ....140 B1
Southlands Rd TN39 ....157 A7
Southlands Cl TN20 ....40 D3
Southon Cl BN41 ....140 F3
Southover CE Prim Sch BN7 ....190 A1
Southover High St BN7 ....190 A1
Southover Manor Ho BN7 ....190 A1
Southover Pl BN2 ....189 C4
Southover Rd BN7 ....190 A1
Southover St BN2 ....189 C3
Southport Cl TN38 ....158 F7
Southridge Rd TN6 ....37 E8
Southridge Rise TN6 ....37 E8
Southview RH17 ....51 F3
Southview Rd Peacehaven BN10 ....178 C8
Southwick BN42 ....161 E8
Southwater Cl BN2 ....164 C7
Southwater Rd TN37 ....159 C8
Southway RH15 ....72 E3
Southway Jun Sch RH15 ....72 D3
Southwick Cl RH19 ....1 D2
Southwick Sq BN42 ....161 E7
Southwick Sta BN42 ....161 E7
Southwood Cl TN38 ....136 A1
Southwood Rd TN4 ....7 B5
Sovereign Bsns Pk RH15 ....72 E2
Sovereign Cl Hastings TN34 ....160 A8
Seaford BN25 ....181 A5
Sovereign Ct Hastings TN34 ....157 E5
Brighton BN2 ....165 A3
[1] Eastbourne BN21 ....185 C5
Sovereign Ctr Burgess Hill RH15 ....72 E2
Eastbourne BN21 ....185 E6
Sovereign Ho TN38 ....136 A1
Sovereign Mews TN38 ....159 A6
Spa Ct [1] BN1 ....163 B5
Spa Inf Pk TN2 ....8 B2
Spa Valley Rly* TN3 ....15 D7
Spaldings The TN38 ....135 E1
Spanish Cl RH15 ....73 B4
Sparke Gdns TN33 ....133 A6
Sparrow Way RH15 ....73 D3

Sparrows Green Rd TN5 ....29 F5
Sparrows The BN10 ....167 D1
Spatham La BN6 ....98 F4
Speckled Wood TN35 ....160 C7
Speldhurst CE Prim Sch TN3 ....7 A7
Speldhurst Hill TN3 ....7 B8
Speldhurst Rd Langton Green TN3 ....6 F4
Royal Tunbridge Wells TN3, TN4 ....7 B8
Spencer Ave BN3 ....141 D3
Spencer Mews [6] TN1 ....8 A2
Spencer Rd BN21 ....185 A2
Spences Field BN7 ....190 C3
Spences La BN7 ....190 C3
Spicers Cl RH15 ....73 A6
Spindlewood Country Holiday Pk TN35 ....160 C6
Spindlewood Dr TN39 ....156 C4
Spinnals Gr BN42 ....161 D7
Spinney Cl BN6 ....97 C5
Spinney The BN1 ....112 F3
Bexhill TN39 ....156 D3
Burgess Hill RH15 ....73 B5
Golden Cross BN27 ....127 B3
Hassocks BN6 ....97 F5
Hastings TN34 ....136 C1
Haywards Heath RH16 ....50 D8
Haywards Heath,Franklands Village RH16 ....50 F3
Hove BN3 ....142 C3
Robertsbridge TN32 ....63 F3
Spinneys The Heathfield TN21 ....82 B6
Lewes BN7 ....190 C3
Spital Rd BN7 ....123 B1
Spithurst Rd BN8 ....101 E6
Spode La TN6 ....4 A7
Sponden La TN18 ....47 A7
Sportcentre Rd BN1 ....144 A6
Spotted Cow La TN22 ....56 E5
Spout Hill TN6 ....27 D1
Spray Hill TN3 ....20 B4
Spray's La TN33,TN35 ....114 B4
Spring Cl BN20 ....173 B1
Spring Copse RH19 ....1 F4
Spring Gdns Brighton BN1 ....189 B2
Glynde BN8 ....147 F5
Lewes BN7 ....190 B2
Rusthall TN4 ....7 B4
[6] Southwick BN42 ....161 E7
Spring Hill Northiam TN31 ....67 A7
Saint's Hill TN11,TN3 ....6 A7
Spring La Bexhill TN39 ....156 C5
Burwash TN19 ....61 F6
Clayton BN6 ....96 A8
Poundford TN20 ....58 A5
Spring Lodge Cl BN23 ....174 E2
Spring Mdw RH18 ....1 F2
Spring Pk TN21 ....82 A8
Spring St Brighton BN1 ....163 E5
St Leonards TN37 ....136 C1
Spring Stps TN36 ....117 F8
Spring Way RH19 ....2 A4
Springate Rd BN21 ....161 F8
Springett Almshouses TN18 ....45 E8
Springett Ave BN8 ....124 D5
Springett Cotts BN8 ....124 D5
Springfield RH19 ....1 D4
Springfield Ave BN10 ....177 F4
Springfield Cl Crowborough TN6 ....26 B2
Westham BN24 ....173 D7
Springfield Cotts Cackle Street TN31 ....90 A2
Rotherfield TN6 ....39 B8
Springfield Rd Bexhill TN40 ....157 C6
Brighton BN1 ....164 A8
Eastbourne BN20 ....185 B4
Groombridge TN3 ....15 C7
St Leonards TN38 ....136 B1
Springfield Valley TN38 ....136 B1
Springfields TN5 ....31 A1
Springfields Farm Ind Est RH17 ....73 F5
Springhead TN6 ....8 D5
Springhead Way TN6 ....37 E8
Springside Wlk TN38 ....135 F1
Springview Apartments BN3 ....8 D6
Springwood Rd TN21 ....82 A8
Spruce Cl BN22 ....173 D2
Spruce Ho TN4 ....7 E4
Spur Rd BN26 ....173 B5
Spurway Pk BN26 ....173 B5
Squab La BN27 ....130 A5
Square The Beachlands BN24 ....175 F6
Brighton BN1 ....142 E6
Cowden TN8 ....4 B6
Hailsham BN27 ....152 A7
Wadhurst TN5 ....30 A4
Squires Farm Ind Est TN22 ....79 D1
Squirrel Cl Bexhill TN39 ....156 E5
St Leonards TN38 ....135 E8
Squirrel Way TN22 ....8 E5
Squirrel Wlk BN27 ....127 B3
Squirrels Drey BN27 ....127 B3
Stable Ctyd TN22 ....23 A1
Stable Mews TN34 ....136 C5
Stabledene Way TN2 ....9 D6
Stablefield TN35 ....114 E4
Stables La BN21 ....185 A3

Stables The Ponts Green TN33 ....110 D3
The Moor TN18 ....45 E8
Stacey's Cnr TN21 ....85 A5
Stafford Ct Brighton BN2 ....189 C2
[2] Eastbourne BN23 ....174 E1
Stafford Ho [10] Eastbourne BN21 ....184 F3
Keymer BN6 ....98 A3
Stafford Jun Sch BN22 ....185 A6
Stafford Rd Brighton BN1 ....163 E8
Royal Tunbridge Wells TN2 ....8 E3
Seaford BN25 ....180 F3
Stafford Way BN3 ....98 A3
Stag Rd TN2 ....8 D8
Stainsby St [1] TN37 ....159 C7
Stalkers La BN8 ....105 E5
Stalkhurst Camping & Cvn Pk TN35 ....137 B5
Stamford [6] RH16 ....50 D6
Stamford Bldgs BN1 ....189 B2
Stamford Ct TN35 ....160 D6
Stamford Lodge [1] BN1 ....142 E2
Stanam Rd TN2 ....9 E6
Standard Hill TN33 ....132 E4
Standard Hill Cl TN33 ....132 F6
Standean Cl BN1 ....143 D6
Standen* RH19 ....10 D4
Standen Cl RH19 ....1 A1
Standen St Royal Tunbridge Wells TN4 ....8 A5
Standen Street TN17 ....47 E8
Stanford Ave Brighton BN1 ....143 A1
Hassocks BN6 ....97 E4
Stanford Cl Hassocks BN6 ....97 E4
Hove BN3 ....142 C1
Stanford Ct BN1 ....163 F8
Stanford Inf Sch BN1 ....163 E8
Stanford Jun Sch BN1 ....163 E8
Stanford Rd BN1 ....143 A1
Stanford Terr BN6 ....97 E4
Stanhope Pl [1] TN38 ....159 C6
Stanhope Rd TN1 ....8 C5
Stanier Rd TN38 ....135 F5
Stanley Ave BN41 ....140 F3
Stanley Ave S BN41 ....140 F3
Stanley Cl [3] BN2 ....164 C8
Stanley Deason L Ctr BN2 ....164 F5
Stanley Rd Brighton BN1 ....189 B4
[2] Eastbourne BN22 ....185 B4
Hastings TN34 ....7 F4
Peacehaven BN10 ....167 B1
Portslade-by-S BN41 ....162 A8
Royal Tunbridge Wells TN1 ....8 B5
Stanley St BN2 ....189 C3
Stanmer BN1 ....143 F8
Stanmer Ave BN2 ....177 D7
Stanmer Ct BN1 ....143 A2
Stanmer Dr BN22 ....173 D1
Stanmer Ho BN1 ....143 B2
Stanmer Park Rd BN1 ....143 B2
Stanmer St BN1 ....143 B2
Stanmer Villas BN1 ....143 A2
Stansfield Rd BN7 ....123 B2
Stanstead Cres BN2 ....165 F6
Stansted Rd BN2 ....185 A4
Staplecross Methodist Prim Sch TN32 ....65 E2
Staplefield Dr BN2 ....143 F3
Stapley Cl BN3 ....162 D8
Stapley Rd BN3 ....141 D1
Star Ho TN3 ....20 B5
Star La Alfriston BN26 ....171 A3
Blackboys TN22 ....80 B6
Mayfield TN20 ....40 B2
Star Mews TN20 ....40 B2
Star Rd [8] BN21 ....184 E4
Starboard Ct BN2 ....164 F3
Starfield TN6 ....25 E1
Starling Cl RH15 ....73 C4
Star's Green La TN33 ....113 A3
Starrs Mead TN33 ....113 A3
Starvecrow La TN31 ....91 D6
Starwell Cl TN34 ....136 D3
Station App Battle TN33 ....112 E3
Eastbourne BN22 ....173 F1
Etchingham TN19 ....44 C1
Falmer BN1 ....144 B6
Hassocks BN6 ....97 F4
Hastings TN34 ....159 F8
Heathfield TN21 ....82 A7
Horsted Keynes RH17 ....33 A7
Hove BN3 ....163 B8
Mayfield TN20 ....39 F2
Rye TN31 ....93 B6
Seaford BN25 ....180 E3
St Leonards TN37 ....159 C7
Station App E BN6 ....97 E4
Station App W BN6 ....97 E4
Station Cl Plumpton Green BN7 ....99 E5
Town Row TN6 ....27 C2
Station Cotts Crowhurst TN33 ....135 A6
Hassocks BN6 ....97 F4
Winchelsea TN36 ....92 D1
Station Mews TN2 ....9 A6
Station Par [11] BN21 ....184 F3
Station Rd Arlington BN26 ....150 B2
Bexhill TN40 ....157 C4
Brighton BN1 ....142 D3
Burgess Hill RH15 ....72 F3
Crowhurst TN33 ....134 F5

Station Rd continued
East Grinstead RH19 ......1 D1
Forest Row RH18 ......11 F3
Groombridge TN3 ......15 C7
Hailsham BN27 ......152 C6
18 Hastings TN34 ......159 F8
Heathfield TN21 ......82 A7
Hellingly BN27 ......129 A5
Horsted Keynes RH17 ......33 C5
Hurst Green TN19 ......45 A3
Isfield TN22 ......102 D8
Lewes BN7 ......190 B1
Mayfield TN20 ......40 A2
Newhaven BN9 ......168 F1
North Chailey BN8 ......75 F7
Northiam TN31 ......67 B8
Plumpton Green BN7 ......99 E6
Polegate BN26 ......173 A6
Portslade-by-S BN3,BN41 ...162 C7
Robertsbridge TN22 ......64 B4
Rockrobin TN5 ......29 C6
Seaford BN25 ......180 B5
Sharpthorne RH19 ......21 A6
7 Southwick BN42 ......161 E7
Stonegate TN5 ......42 E5
Town Row TN6 ......27 C1
Winchelsea TN36 ......92 E1
Withyham TN7 ......14 A6
Station Road Ind Est
BN27 ......152 C6
Station St Brighton BN1 ...189 B3
8 Eastbourne BN21 ......185 A3
Lewes BN7 ......190 B2
Staveley Rd BN20 ......188 E8
Steelhands Rise TN5 ......31 F1
Steep Hill TN31 ......89 E2
Steep Rd TN6 ......38 D3
Steine Gdns BN1 ......189 B2
Steine Cl BN1 ......189 B2
Steine St BN1 ......189 B1
Stennings The RH19 ......1 C2
Stephen's Rd TN4 ......8 B6
Stephens Cl BN8 ......124 D5
Stephens Rd BN1 ......143 B2
Stephenson Dr RH19 ......10 F7
Stevens Cl TN39 ......157 C7
Stevens Ct BN3 ......162 E7
Stevenson Cl BN23 ......174 E3
Stevenson Rd
Brighton BN2 ......164 C5
7 St Leonard's TN37 ......136 B3
Stewards Inn La BN7 ......190 A1
Stewart Rd TN4 ......8 C7
Steyne Cl 4 BN25 ......180 F2
Steyne Ct 18 BN25 ......180 E2
Steyne Rd BN25 ......180 F2
Steyne The BN25 ......180 E2
Steyning Ave Peacehaven BN10 ...178 C7
Steyning Cl BN25 ......181 C2
Steyning Ct 7 BN3 ......163 B7
Steyning Rd
Rottingdean BN2 ......177 A5
Seaford BN25 ......181 C4
Stiles The BN27 ......152 C7
Stirling Ave BN25 ......181 C4
Stirling Cl
Burgess Hill RH15 ......73 C4
Seaford BN25 ......181 C3
Stirling Court Rd RH15 ...73 C4
Stirling Ct 5 BN3 ......163 C7
Stirling Pl BN3 ......163 A6
Stirling Rd TN38 ......135 F5
Stirling Way BN27 ......152 A8
Stock Dale TN35 ......138 F4
Stockland Green Rd TN3 ...7 B8
Stockland La TN22 ......52 B6
Stockleigh BN25 ......181 B4
Stockleigh 15 TN38 ......159 C7
Stockleigh Rd TN38 ......159 C7
Stocks Mdw TN33 ......133 B5
Stockwell Cl
Burgess Hill RH15 ......72 F3
3 Haywards Heath RH16 ...50 E3
Stockwell Rd RH19 ......10 E6
Stoddards La TN31 ......67 E7
Stoke Brunswick Sch
RH19 ......11 E7
Stoke Cl BN25 ......181 B3
Stoke Manor Cl BN25 ...181 B4
Stokes Ho 6 TN30 ......157 A4
Stone Cotts TN3 ......19 F4
Stone Court La TN2 ......9 E8
Stone Cross Mayfield TN20 ...39 F2
Stone Cross BN24 ......174 B5
Stone Cross Prim Sch
BN24 ......174 A5
Stone Cross Rd
Crowborough TN6 ......38 A7
Wadhurst TN5 ......30 A4
Stone Cross Windmill *
BN24 ......174 B5
Stone Pit La TN18 ......47 E5
Stone Quarry Rd RH17 ...34 D7
Stone Row TN3 ......6 D1
Stone St Brighton BN1 ...163 E5
12 Hastings TN34 ......159 F8
Royal Tunbridge Wells TN1 ...8 A4
Stone Works Cotts TN31 ...93 F3
Stonebeach Rise TN38 ...135 F7
Stonebridge La TN22 ......79 F5
Stonecott Cl TN6 ......37 F8
Stonecroft Cl BN3 ......141 E4
Stonecross Rd BN2 ......142 E3
Stonedene CI RH18 ......12 B2
Stonefield Pl 9 TN34 ...159 F8
Stonefield Rd TN34 ......159 F8
Stonefield Way RH15 ......72 F5

Stonegate CE Prim Sch
TN5 ......42 F5
Stonegate Rd TN5 ......42 F5
Stonegate Ct TN5 ......42 F5
Stonegate Rd TN5 ......30 C1
Stonegate Sta TN5 ......42 D3
Stonegate Way TN21 ......82 B8
Stoneham Cl BN7 ......190 A4
Stoneham Rd BN3 ......162 F7
Stonehaven St 5 TN40 ...157 D3
Stonehill BN8,TN21 ......106 C3
Stonehouse Dr
Hastings,Beauport Park
TN33,TN38 ......113 F1
St Leonards TN38 ......136 A2
Stonehurst Cl 10 BN2 ...164 C6
Stonehurst La TN20,TN22 ...57 D7
Stoneleigh Ave BN1 ......142 F6
Stoneleigh Cl
Brighton BN1 ......142 F6
East Grinstead RH19 ......1 F1
Stonelink Cl TN4 ......135 F7
Stonepark Dr RH18 ......12 A2
Stonepound Crossroads
BN6 ......97 D4
Stonepound Rd BN6 ......97 E4
Stonery Cl BN41 ......141 A2
Stonery Rd BN41 ......141 A2
Stonestile La TN35 ......136 F8
Stonewall Park Rd TN3 ...6 F3
Stonewood Cl
Royal Tunbridge Wells TN4 ...8 A8
Seaford BN25 ......181 C4
Stoney La Hailsham BN27 ...152 C7
Shoreham-by-S BN43 ...161 C8
Stoneywish Nature Reserve *
BN6 ......97 D4
Storrington Cl BN13 ......141 E2
Stour Cl BN24 ......173 F5
Straight Half Mile TN22 ...55 F8
Strand TN3 ......93 B5
Strand Ct 1 TN3 ......93 B5
Strand Hill TN36 ......117 F7
Strand Mdw TN30 ......62 B7
Strand The BN2 ......165 A3
Stratford St TN1 ......8 C5
Strathenden Ct 10 BN25 ...180 E2
Strathfield Ct RH16 ......50 F4
Strawberry Cl TN2 ......16 E7
Strawberry Fields TN3 ...67 A7
Strawberry Rd BN27 ......99 E6
Stream La
Fairlight Cove TN35 ......139 A5
Sedlescombe TN33 ......88 C2
The Moor TN18 ......46 A7
Stream Lane Cotts TN18 ...46 A7
Stream Pit La TN18 ......47 B5
Stream Pk RH19 ......1 A3
Streamside Cl TN34 ......136 E3
Streat Bostall BN6 ......121 C6
Streat La BN6 ......121 C6
Streatfield Gdns TN21 ...81 F8
Streatfield Ho TN22 ......78 C8
Streatfield Rd
Heathfield TN21 ......81 F8
Uckfield TN22 ......78 B7
Streele La TN22 ......56 D1
Streele View TN22 ......78 E8
Street End La
Broad Oak TN21 ......59 E1
Broad Oak TN21 ......59 E5
Street The
Framefield TN22 ......79 B6
Kingston near Lewes BN7 ...145 E5
Litlington BN26 ......182 A8
Muddles Green BN8 ......127 B7
Sedlescombe TN33 ......88 E1
West Firle BN8 ......148 B3
Westmeston BN26 ......120 F8
Wilmington BN26 ......171 F6
Streetlands TN33 ......88 E1
Stringer Way BN1 ......142 F3
Stringwalk The BN27 ......152 C7
Stroma Gdns BN41 ......141 B2
Strome Ho TN39 ......157 C7
Strongs Pas 5 TN34 ......160 B4
Strood Gate RH17 ......74 C5
Strood Rd TN37 ......136 C2
Stuart Ave BN21 ......184 C6
Sturart Cl TN2 ......16 E7
Sturart Way RH19 ......10 F7
Stubb La TN31 ......90 D2
Stud Cotts BN27 ......151 A8
Studdens La BN27 ......108 D1
Sturdee Cl BN23 ......185 F7
Sturdee Pl TN34 ......160 A3
Sturton Pl BN27 ......152 B7
Sudeley Pl BN2 ......164 D4
Sudeley St BN2 ......164 D4
Sudeley Terr 8 BN2 ......164 D4
Suffolk Ct 5 BN22 ......185 C4
Suffolk Ho 18 TN40 ......157 D3
Suffolk Rd TN39 ......157 C7
Suffolk St BN2 ......182 F8
Sugar La RH17 ......33 C4
Sugworth Cl BN27 ......152 C7
Sullington Cl BN2 ......143 F4
Sullington Way BN43 ...161 A8
Sumach Cl BN27 ......173 E2
Summer Cl BN41 ......162 A7
Summer Ct BN20 ......188 D7
Summer Hayes BN9 ......179 C7
Summer Hill TN38 ......159 B8
Summer Hill Rd TN38 ...159 B8
Summercourt BN27 ......152 B8
Summerdale Rd BN3 ......141 D2

Summerdown Cl BN20 ...184 D3
Summerdown La BN20 ...183 C1
Summerdown Rd BN20 ...184 D3
Summerfields Ave
BN27 ......152 A8
Summerheath Rd BN27 ...152 B8
Summerhill Cl RH16 ......50 F7
Summerhill Dr RH16 ......51 A7
Summerhill Grange RH16 ...50 F7
Summerhill La RH16 ......50 F7
Summerlands Rd BN22 ...173 C2
Summersdeane BN42 ...140 F1
Summervale Rd TN4 ......7 F1
Sun La 8 TN34 ......160 A3
Sun St BN7 ......190 A2
Sunhill Ct TN2 ......9 C6
Sunningdale Cl
10 Bexhill TN40 ......157 E4
Hailsham BN27 ......129 A1
Seaford BN25 ......181 A2
Sunningdale Dr TN38 ...158 F7
Sunninghall Ave BN1 ......143 F2
Sunninghill Cl BN3 ......141 E2
Sunnybank TN5 ......32 E3
Sunnybrooke Cl TN2 ......78 D7
Sunnycroft RH17 ......51 E2
Sunnydale Ave BN1 ......143 A6
Sunnydale Cl BN1 ......143 A6
Sunnyside Cvn Pk BN25 ...180 B4
Sunnyside Rd TN4 ......7 C4
Sunnywood Dr RH16 ......50 D3
Sunset Ave TN34 ......127 C3
Sunset Cl
Beachlands BN24 ......175 F6
Peacehaven BN10 ......167 B1
Sunstar La BN26 ......172 E6
Sunte Ave RH16 ......50 F7
Sunte Cl RH16 ......50 E7
Sunview Ave BN10 ......178 D6
Surrenden Cl BN1 ......142 F4
Surrenden Cres BN1 ......142 F4
Surrenden Holt BN1 ......142 F3
Surrenden Lodge BN1 ...142 F2
Surrenden Pk BN1 ......143 A4
Surrenden Rd BN1 ......142 F3
Surrey Cl
Royal Tunbridge Wells TN2 ...16 F8
Seaford BN25 ......180 D4
Surrey Ho 12 BN2 ......164 D4
Surrey Rd BN25 ......180 D4
Surrey St BN1 ......189 A3
Susan's Rd BN21 ......185 A3
Susans Cl BN8 ......105 A5
Sussex Amb HQ BN7 ...190 B2
Sussex Cl Bexhill TN39 ...156 F5
Hailsham BN27 ......152 B8
Royal Tunbridge Wells TN2 ...8 C1
Sussex Cotts RH19 ......21 A6
Sussex Ct
Eastbourne BN20 ......185 B5
2 Haywards Heath RH16 ...50 E3
18 Hove BN3 ......163 C6
4 Shoreham-by-S BN43 ...161 A6
Sussex Cty Cricket Gd
BN3 ......163 C7
Sussex Downs Coll
BN21 ......184 E7
Sussex Downs Coll (Cliffe
Bldg) BN7 ......190 B1
Sussex Downs Coll
(Southover Bldg) BN7 ...190 B1
Sussex Eye Hospl BN2 ...164 D4
Sussex Farm Mus & Nature
Trails * TN21 ......106 E2
Sussex Gdns
East Dean BN20 ......183 C1
Haywards Heath RH17 ......51 B3
Sussex Ho
6 Eastbourne BN21 ......185 A2
Telscombe Cliffs BN10 ...177 F3
Sussex Hts 18 BN1 ......163 E5
Sussex Mews
4 Brighton BN2 ......164 E4
19 Royal Tunbridge Wells
TN2 ......8 A2
Sussex Nuffield Hospl
BN2 ......165 C8
Sussex Pl BN2 ......189 C3
Sussex Rd
Haywards Heath RH16 ......50 E3
Hove BN3 ......163 B5
St Leonards TN38 ......159 A6
Sussex Sq Brighton BN2 ...164 E4
17 Haywards Heath RH16 ...50 E4
Sussex Terr BN2 ......189 C3
Sussex View BN3 ......163 D7
Sussex Way
Burgess Hill RH15 ......72 E5
Telscombe Cliffs BN10 ...177 F3
Sutherland Ave TN39 ...157 A4
Sutherland Cl 1 TN39 ...157 A4
Sutherland Rd
Brighton BN2 ......164 C5
Royal Tunbridge Wells TN1 ...8 B3
Sutton Ave
Peacehaven BN10 ......178 B7
Seaford BN25 ......181 A3
Sutton Ave N BN10 ......178 B8
Sutton Cl BN2 ......144 E1
Sutton Cnr BN27 ......146 B3
Sutton Croft La 6 BN25 ...180 E4
Sutton Dro BN25 ......180 F4

Sutton Mews BN25 ......181 A4
Sutton Par BN25 ......181 A4
Sutton Park Rd BN25 ...180 E3
Sutton Pl TN40 ......157 E4
Sutton Rd
Eastbourne BN21 ......185 A3
Seaford BN25 ......181 A3
Sutton Wall BN7 ......146 D4
Suttons Ind Pk TN36 ...118 A7
Suttons The Camber TN31 ...95 A1
St Leonards TN38 ......135 F2
Swaine's Pas 6 TN34 ...160 B4
Swaines Way TN21 ......82 A6
Swainham La TN38 ......135 B4
Swainsthorpe Cl RH16 ...50 F3
Swale Cl BN24 ......174 A5
Swallow Bank TN38 ......135 F2
Swallow Cl BN23 ......174 C2
Swallow Ct TN2 ......78 D5
Swallow Dr Battle TN33 ...112 F4
Royal Tunbridge Wells TN2 ...8 D5
Swallow Rest RH15 ......72 C3
Swallows The BN20 ......167 B1
Swan Ave 9 TN34 ......160 A4
Swan Barn Cvn Site
BN27 ......152 D5
Swan Bsns Ctr BN27 ...152 D6
Swan Cl BN8 ......100 E7
Swan Ct BN20 ......188 C7
Swan Rd BN27 ......152 D6
Swan Terr TN34 ......160 A4
Swanborough Cotts
BN7 ......146 A4
Swanborough Dr BN2 ...164 F7
Swanborough Dro BN7 ...145 F4
Swanborough Hollow
BN7 ......146 A4
Swanborough Pl BN2 ...164 F7
Swanley Cl BN2 ......174 D2
Swann Cl RH15 ......73 D3
Swannee Cl BN10 ......167 D1
Swans Ghyll RH18 ......11 E3
Swansbrook La TN21 ...106 E2
Swaylands Ave TN6 ......37 F7
Sweda Cl BN2 ......164 F7
Sweeps Hill Cl TN2 ......9 D7
Sweethaws La TN6 ......37 C6
Sweetings La TN3,TN5 ...19 D1
Sweetlands BN6 ......98 B5
Swife La TN21 ......60 D5
Swift Cl Burgess Hill RH15 ...72 D3
Crowborough TN6 ......25 D1
Uckfield TN22 ......78 D5
Swiftsden Cotts TN19 ...44 F6
Swinburne Ave BN22 ...173 C3
Swingate Cross BN27 ...129 C5
Swissland Hill RH19,RH17 ...1 E7
Swynford Dr 1 TN38 ...136 A5
Sybron Way TN34 ......38 D8
Sycamore Cl
Bexhill TN39 ......156 E5
Eastbourne BN22 ......173 D3
Heathfield TN21 ......82 B6
Hove BN41 ......141 C3
Seaford BN25 ......181 B3
St Leonards TN38 ......136 A1
Woodingdean BN2 ......165 E8
Sycamore Cotts 9 C6
Sycamore Dr
East Grinstead RH19 ......2 A1
Hailsham BN27 ......152 B5
Sycamores The
Peacehaven BN10 ......167 D1
St Leonards TN37 ......159 C8
Sydenham Ct TN40 ......157 D3
Sydney Cl TN38 ......136 B3
Sydney Little Rd TN38 ...135 D4
Sydney Rd
Eastbourne BN22 ......185 B4
Haywards Heath RH16 ...50 E6
Sydney St BN1 ......189 B3
Sylvan Cl RH16 ......51 B4
Sylvester Way BN2 ......141 C3
Symbister Rd BN2 ......162 C7
Syresham Gdns RH16 ...50 F4

T

Tackleway TN34 ......160 B4
Taddington Ho 2 BN21 ...152 C8
Taddington Rd 1 BN21 ...185 C4
Tainter's Brook TN22 ...78 E8
Talbot Cres BN1 ......143 D6
Talbot Pk TN2 ......8 D5
Talbot Rd TN18 ......45 F8
Talbot Terr BN7 ......190 A2
Tall Ash Dr TN2 ......9 C6
Tall Timbers BN27 ......127 B2
Talland Par 8 BN25 ......180 F2
Tamar Cl BN24 ......174 C5
Tamarack Cl BN22 ......173 D2
Tamerisk Sgns 24 TN34 ...160 B4
Tamplin Terr BN2 ......189 C3
Tamworth Rd BN3 ......162 F7
Tan Yard Cotts TN36 ...117 F8
Tandridge Rd BN23 ......174 C2
Tandridge Rd BN41 ......162 E6
Tangier La TN7 ......17 B6
Tanglewood Coppice
TN39 ......156 E3
Tangmere Ct TN39 ......156 F2
Tangmere Rd BN1 ......143 A6
Tanhouse La TN31 ......66 F8
Tanneries The BN27 ......129 F4
Tanners Cross RH16 ......50 C2
Tanners Field RH17 ......74 A5

Tanners Way TN6 ......26 A1
Tanners' Brook BN7 ...190 B1
Tanyard TN18 ......47 B5
Tanyard Ave BN27 ......11 A8
Tanyard Cotts
Battle TN33 ......112 E3
Buxted TN22 ......56 C1
Tanyard La
Chelwood Common RH17,
TN22 ......34 C4
Winchelsea TN36 ......117 F8
Tapsell's La TN5 ......29 D5
Tarland Ho TN2 ......8 D3
Tarner Rd BN2 ......189 C3
Tarragon Way BN43 ...140 C1
Tarring Cl BN9 ......168 D2
Tas Combe Way TN3 ...173 B2
Tasmania Way BN23 ...175 A2
Tate Cres RH15 ......72 F5
Taunton Gr BN2 ......144 A1
Taunton Pl BN2 ......144 A1
Taunton Rd BN2 ......143 F1
Taunton Way BN2 ......144 A1
Tavistock 8 BN21 ......185 A2
Tavistock & Summerhill Sch
RH16 ......50 F7
Tavistock Down BN1 ...143 C2
Taylor Cl TN38 ......135 F4
Taylor Ct 1 TN2 ......8 C7
Taylor St TN4 ......8 A8
Tea Garden La TN3 ......7 C2
Teal Ct Hailsham BN27 ...152 D7
St Leonards TN38 ......135 E3
Teasley Mead TN3 ......5 C4
Tedder Rd TN4 ......8 B7
Tedder Terr TN35 ......137 D5
Teg Cl BN41 ......141 C2
Teise Cl TN4 ......8 D2
Teknol Ho RH15 ......72 E2
Telegraph St 12 BN2 ...164 C4
Telford Rd TN38 ......136 A5
Telham Cl TN34 ......137 A5
Telham La TN33 ......112 E1
Telscombe Cliffs Prim Sch
BN10 ......178 A8
Telscombe Cliffs Way
BN10 ......178 A8
Telscombe Pk BN10 ...167 C2
Telscombe Rd
Eastbourne BN23 ......174 C2
Peacehaven BN10 ......167 D2
Temple Gdns BN1 ......163 E6
Temple Gr RH15 ......72 D4
Temple Grove Sch TN22 ...36 E3
Temple Hts 14 BN1 ......163 E6
Temple St BN1 ......163 E6
Tenantry Down Rd BN2 ...164 D8
Tenantry Rd BN2 ......164 D8
Tenbury Rd TN2 ......157 B7
Tennis Rd BN2 ......162 E6
Tennyson Ct 5 RH16 ...50 D5
Tennyson Rise RH19 ...10 C8
Tennyson Wlk BN23 ...174 E3
Tenterden Cl BN23 ......174 D2
Tenterden Rise TN34 ...136 E2
Tenterden Rise TN39 ...157 A3
Terminus Pl
9 Brighton BN1 ......189 A4
6 Haywards Heath BN27 ...152 C7
Terminus Rd
Bexhill TN39 ......157 B3
Blackboys TN22 ......80 A6
Brighton BN1 ......189 A4
Framefield TN22 ......79 F6
Terminus St BN1 ......189 A3
Terrace Rd TN37 ......159 C7
Terraces The BN2 ......189 C3
Tescombe Grange BN10 ...177 F3
Teynham Ho BN2 ......177 C4
Thackeray Cl BN23 ......174 E3
Thakeham Cl TN40 ......158 A6
Thalia Ho TN40 ......157 B4
Thames Cl BN2 ......189 C2
Thanet Way TN34 ......136 E2
Thatchers Cl RH15 ......73 D1
Thatchings The BN26 ...173 A5
Theaklen Dr TN38 ......159 C8
Theobald Ho 5 BN1 ......189 B3
Theobalds Rd BN1 ......82 A5
Theobalds Rd RH15 ......73 D6
Theodore Cl TN2 ......8 E7
Third Ave Bexhill TN40 ...157 F6
Hove BN3 ......163 A6
Newhaven BN9 ......179 C6
Third Rd BN10 ......177 B3
Third St TN3 ......6 F3
Thirlmere Rd TN4 ......7 E5
Thomas Brassey Cl
TN37 ......136 B3
Thomas Peacocke Com Coll
TN31 ......93 B6
Thomas St Lewes BN7 ...190 C3
Royal Tunbridge Wells TN1 ...8 A5
Thomas Turner Dr BN8 ...105 A5
Thompson Rd
Brighton BN1 ......143 C1
Newhaven BN9 ......168 F2
Thorn Cotts TN35 ......116 A4
Thornbank Cres TN39 ...156 D3
Thornbush Cres BN41 ...141 B3
Thorndean Rd BN2 ......143 D3
Thornden Ct TN17 ......49 A8
Thornden La TN17 ......49 A8
Thorne Cres TN39 ......133 E1

Thornfield Gdns TN2 .....8 F5
Thornhill Ave BN1 .....143 A7
Thornhill CI BN3 .....141 E2
Thornhill Rise BN41 .....141 A4
Thornhill Way BN41 .....141 A3
Thornhurst RH15 .....73 C1
Thorns The TN35 .....138 A8
Thornsdale 5 BN2 .....189 C3
Thornton Ct 5 BN22 .....185 D4
Thornwell Rd BN26 .....171 F7
Thornwood Ct BN22 .....173 E2
Thorny CI TN21 .....82 A7
Three Gables TN22 .....35 C4
Three Leg Cross Rd TN5 .....31 D3
Three Oaks La TN5 .....29 D7
Three Oaks Sta TN35 .....115 D2
Thunders Hill BN27 .....128 A7
Thurrock CI BN20 .....173 B4
Thyme CI BN41 .....140 C1
Thyssel La TN31 .....67 B6
Tibbs Mill La TN22 .....37 E2
Ticehurst Ave TN39 .....155 F5
Ticehurst CE Prim Sch
  TN5 .....43 D8
Ticehurst CI Bexhill TN39 .....155 F4
  Hastings TN35 .....160 C7
Ticehurst Ct TN38 .....159 B7
Ticehurst Rd BN2 .....164 F5
Tichborne Cotts RH16 .....51 C6
Tichborne St BN1 .....189 B2
Tickerage La TN22 .....79 F6
Tidebrook TN5,TN20 .....40 F7
Tidebrook Gdns BN23 .....174 F2
Tideswell Rd BN21 .....185 A3
Tideway Com Sch BN9 .....179 B6
Tidy St BN1 .....189 B3
Tilbury PI BN2 .....189 C2
Tilbury Way BN2 .....189 C3
Tile Barn CI TN22 .....102 D8
Tile Barn Rd TN38 .....135 F4
Tile Kiln BN8 .....124 C6
Tilehurst Dr RH16 .....50 E2
Tilehurst Dr BN27 .....122 A6
Tilekiln La TN31 .....160 E8
Tilers CI RH15 .....73 D3
Tilford CI 1 TN40 .....157 F4
Tilgate CI Brighton BN2 .....164 D6
  Eastbourne BN21 .....184 D7
Tilgate Dr TN39 .....156 D3
Tilling La BN27 .....131 E6
Tilling Green Inf Sch
  TN31 .....93 A5
Tillingham Ave TN31 .....93 B6
Tillingham CI BN24 .....174 A5
Tillingham Ct TN31 .....93 A5
Tillingham View TN31 .....92 A6
Tillingham Way BN24 .....174 A5
Tillington BN2 .....164 F7
Tillington Terr TN35 .....160 C6
Tilstone CI BN2 .....143 D2
Tilstone St BN2 .....189 C2
Tilsmore 17 BN2 .....164 F5
Tilsmore Cnr TN21 .....81 F7
Tilsmore Rd TN21 .....81 F7
Timber Yard Cotts BN7 .....190 C2
Timberlaine Rd BN24 .....175 C4
Timberley Gdns TN22 .....78 E4
Timberley Rd BN2 .....173 D1
Timbers Ct BN27 .....152 C8
Tindal CI RH15 .....73 D3
Tinker's La TN22 .....57 E3
Tinkers La TN5 .....31 E3
Tintagel Ct BN3 .....163 A8
Tintern CI Brighton BN1 .....143 B1
  Eastbourne BN22 .....173 E3
Tisbury Rd BN3 .....163 C6
Titchfield CI RH15 .....73 D1
Tithe Barn Field TN36 .....116 F5
Titian Rd BN3 .....162 F7
Tiverton Dr TN40 .....157 C5
Tivoli BN1 .....142 E2
Tivoli Cres BN1 .....142 D1
Tivoli Cres N BN1 .....142 D2
Tivoli PI BN1 .....142 D2
Tivoli Rd BN1 .....142 D2
Tobago 6 TN39 .....157 A2
Tobias Sch of Art RH19 .....10 E6
Tolkien Rd BN2 .....158 A7
Toll La Dodd's Hill TN22 .....35 F1
  Fairwarp TN22 .....36 A1
Toll Wood Rd TN21 .....106 F7
Tollgate Lindfield RH16 .....51 B8
  Peacehaven BN10 .....167 B1
Tollgate Com Jun Sch
  BN23 .....185 D7
Tollgate Gdns BN23 .....185 D7
Tollgate Lock TN31 .....93 B4
Tollgate The TN31 .....65 E1
Tollgates TN33 .....112 B4
Tollwood Pk TN6 .....26 B1
Tollwood Rd TN6 .....38 B8
Tompset's Bank RH18 .....11 F1
Tomtits La RH18 .....11 E1
Tonbridge Rd TN2 .....9 F4
Tonbridge Way TN31 .....94 E2
Tongdean Ave BN3 .....142 C2
Tongdean La BN1 .....142 C4
Tongdean PI BN3 .....142 C3
Tongdean Rd BN3 .....142 C3
Tongdean Rise BN1 .....142 C4
Top Cross Rd TN40 .....158 A7
Top Dr TN22 .....55 A6
Top Hill CI BN41 .....140 F2
Top Rd RH19 .....21 B5

Tor Rd BN10 .....167 C1
Tor Rd W BN10 .....167 C2
Torcross CI TN34 .....143 E1
Torfield CI TN34 .....160 B4
Torfield Ho TN34 .....160 B4
Torfield Rd BN21 .....184 C4
Torfield Sch TN34 .....160 B5
Toronto Terr
  Brighton BN2 .....164 C6
  Lewes BN7 .....190 A2
Torrance CI BN3 .....141 F1
Totland Rd BN2 .....164 D7
Tott Hill BN8 .....97 B5
Tott Yew Rd BN20 .....173 A1
Tottington Way BN43 .....140 B1
Tovey CI BN41 .....184 D6
Tower CI
  East Grinstead RH19 .....1 E2
  Uckfield TN22 .....55 D1
Tower Ho Brighton BN1 .....142 E2
  Burgess Hill RH15 .....73 B2
Tower Mill PI BN26 .....173 A5
Tower Rd Brighton BN2 .....164 C6
  St Leonards TN37 .....136 C1
Tower Rd W TN37,TN38 .....159 B8
Tower Ride Uckfield TN22 .....55 D1
  Uckfield TN22 .....55 E1
Tower St Heathfield TN21 .....82 B8
  Rye TN31 .....93 C6
Tower View TN22 .....78 D8
Towergate BN1 .....189 A3
Towerscroft Ave TN37 .....136 C5
Town Hill TN3 .....20 A4
Town Place Farm Cotts
  RH17 .....52 C7
Town Wall TN31 .....93 B5
Towner Art Gall & Mus*
  BN21 .....184 D3
Townlands Rd TN5 .....29 F4
Tozer Ct BN41 .....162 B7
Traders Pas 6 TN31 .....93 B5
Trafalgar CI
  Peacehaven BN10 .....167 C1
  St Leonards TN37 .....135 F7
Trafalgar Cotts 8 TN34 .....160 B4
Trafalgar Ct BN1 .....189 B3
Trafalgar Gate BN2 .....144 F3
Trafalgar La 8 TN40 .....157 D3
Trafalgar La BN1 .....189 B3
Trafalgar Mews 9
  BN22 .....185 C4
Trafalgar PI BN1 .....189 B3
Trafalgar Rd BN41 .....162 B8
Trafalgar St BN1 .....189 B3
Trafalgar Terr BN1 .....189 B3
Tram Rd BN1 .....189 A2
Transit Rd BN9 .....179 D7
Travellers La TN35 .....160 C8
Trebilco CI TN7 .....13 B8
Treblers Rd TN6 .....38 E6
Tredcroft Rd BN3 .....141 F1
Treemaines Rd BN23 .....174 F2
Treemans Rd (Lewes Rd)
  RH17 .....33 B2
Treetops CI BN8 .....165 E8
Tremola Ave BN2 .....177 C6
Trenches Rd TN6 .....25 F1
Trevelyan PI RH16 .....50 E5
Trevor Gdns BN8 .....147 F6
Treyford CI BN2 .....144 E1
Triangle Ho 4 RH16 .....50 E3
Triangle Rd RH16 .....50 E3
Triangle The BN20 .....173 B3
Triangle Way RH15 .....72 D5
Trickland Cotts TN22 .....53 C5
Trinity CI 1 D4
Trinity Cotts TN31 .....71 F2
Trinity CI TN6 .....97 B5
Trinity Field RH16 .....124 E6
Trinity Mews 1 TN34 .....159 E7
Trinity PI BN21 .....185 B2
Trinity Rd BN6 .....97 A6
Trinity St Brighton BN2 .....189 C4
  10 Hastings TN34 .....159 E7
Trinity Trees BN21 .....185 A2
Trinity Villas 2 TN34 .....159 E7
Tristan Gdns TN4 .....7 D4
Trojans Plat TN36 .....117 E7
Troon CI BN25 .....180 A6
Troon Ct RH16 .....50 A8
Trossachs CI BN23 .....174 D3
Troy CI TN6 .....26 A1
Trujillo Ct BN2 .....185 G8
Truleigh CI BN2 .....165 F7
Truleigh Dr BN41 .....141 A4
Truleigh Way BN43 .....140 A1
Truman Dr TN37 .....135 F6
Trumpet La BN27 .....109 C2
Tubwell La
  Crowborough TN6 .....38 D7
  Horam TN21 .....81 F2
Tudor Ave TN38 .....159 A7
Tudor CI
  East Grinstead RH19 .....10 F8
  Hove BN3 .....141 F2
  Rottingdean BN2 .....177 A6
  Seaford BN25 .....180 D4
Tudor Ct Bexhill TN39 .....156 F4
  Royal Tunbridge Wells TN2 .....7 E1
Tudor Gdns RH15 .....72 F4
Tudor Rose Pk BN10 .....178 E5
Tudor Wlk TN22 .....79 B5
Tugwell Rd BN2 .....177 C7
Tumulus Rd BN2 .....177 C7

Tunbridge Wells Gram Sch
  for Boys TN4 .....8 A7
Tunbridge Wells Gram Sch
  for Girls TN4 .....8 A6
Tunbridge Wells High Sch
  TN2 .....8 F5
Tunbridge Wells Ind Hospl
  The TN3 .....6 B3
Tunbridge Wells Mus*
  TN2 .....8 D8
Tunbridge Wells Sta TN1 .....8 D2
Tunbridge Wells Trade Pk
  TN2 .....8 D8
Tunbridge Wells West Sta*
  TN2 .....7 F1
Tunnel Rd TN1 .....8 B4
Tuppen Ho BN2 .....145 E5
Tuppenney CI TN35 .....160 C7
Turkey Cock La 2 TN31 .....93 C6
Turkey Rd TN39 .....73 B3
Turkey Rd TN39 .....156 F7
Turley Cotts TN3 .....7 A8
Turnberry CI TN38 .....158 F7
Turnberry Ct 14 RH16 .....50 E4
Turnberry Dr TN39 .....156 F7
Turner CI Bexhill TN40 .....157 E5
  Eastbourne BN23 .....174 D1
Turner Ct RH19 .....1 D3
Turner's Hill Rd RH19 .....10 B6
Turners CI TN35 .....68 C5
Turners Green La TN5 .....29 F6
Turners Green Rd TN5 .....29 F6
Turners Mill CI BN7 .....50 D7
Turners Mill Rd RH16 .....50 D6
Turners Way RH15 .....72 F4
Turnpike CI
  Broyle Side BN8 .....125 A8
  Peacehaven BN10 .....167 C1
Turnpike Piece BN1 .....144 B6
Turret Ct BN2 .....171 C3
Turton CI BN2 .....164 D5
Tuscan Ct BN10 .....177 F3
Tutts Barn Ct BN21 .....184 F5
Tutts Barn La BN22 .....185 A5
Tuxford Rd TN4 .....7 B5
Tweedsmuir CI BN23 .....174 C3
Twineham CI BN2 .....164 F7
Twineham Rd BN2 .....184 D7
Twitten CI BN43 .....140 A1
Twitten The Bexhill TN39 .....156 D4
  Burgess Hill RH15 .....73 B4
  Crowborough TN6 .....25 E1
  Ditchling BN6 .....98 D3
  Southwick BN42 .....161 E7
Twyford Cres TN37 .....136 C4
Twyford Rd BN1 .....143 E6
Twyfords TN6 .....25 E1
Twyhurst Ct RH19 .....1 D3
Twysden Cotts TN18 .....47 A4
Tye CI BN2 .....177 D4
Tye Hill Rd BN26 .....151 A4
Tye View BN10 .....167 A1
Tyedean Rd BN10 .....177 F4
Tyhurst PI TN22 .....78 C6
Tyler's Gn RH16,RH17 .....50 B4
Tylers La TN22 .....35 E1
Tyndale Ave TN39 .....156 C3
Tyson CI BN2 .....189 C2

Uplands Com Tech Coll
  TN5 .....30 A4
Uplands Dr TN22 .....55 D1
Uplands Pk TN21 .....59 E1
Uplands Rd BN1 .....143 C2
Uplands Sch BN1 .....143 C2
Uplands The TN38 .....159 B7
Upper Abbey Rd BN2 .....164 D4
Upper Ave BN21 .....185 A4
Upper Bedford St BN2 .....164 C4
Upper Belgrave Rd
  BN25 .....180 F5
Upper Bevendean Ave
  BN2 .....143 E1
Upper Broomgrove Rd
  TN34 .....160 B7
Upper Carlisle Rd BN20 .....188 D8
Upper Chalvington PI
  BN2 .....164 E5
Upper Church Rd TN37 .....136 B4
Upper Chyngton Gdns
  BN25 .....181 B4
Upper CI RH18 .....11 F2
Upper Clarence Rd
  TN37 .....136 C2
Upper Cumberland Wlk
  TN37 .....136 C2
Upper Dr The BN3 .....163 D8
Upper Duke's Dr BN20 .....188 C2
Upper Dunstan Rd TN4 .....8 B1
Upper Gardner St BN1 .....189 B3
Upper Glen Rd TN37 .....136 A5
Upper Gloucester Rd
  BN1 .....189 A3
Upper Greenwoods La
  TN21 .....83 C6
Upper Grosvenor Rd TN1,
  TN4 .....8 B1
Upper Hamilton Rd
  BN1 .....189 A5
Upper Hollingdean Rd
  BN1 .....143 B1
Upper Horsebridge Rd
  BN27 .....129 A3
Upper King's Dr BN20 .....173 B1
Upper Kingston La
  BN42,BN43 .....140 D1
Upper Lake TN33 .....112 E4
Upper Lewes Rd BN2 .....189 C4
Upper Lodges BN2 .....143 D8
Upper Market St 5
  BN3 .....163 D5
Upper Maze Hill TN38 .....159 B7
Upper Nellington TN3 .....7 B4
Upper North St BN1 .....189 A3
Upper Park PI 7 BN2 .....189 C2
Upper Park Rd TN37 .....136 C1
Upper Platts TN5 .....31 F1
Upper Profit TN3 .....7 A2
Upper Ratton Dr BN20 .....184 B8
Upper Rock Gdns BN2 .....189 C2
Upper Roedale Cotts
  BN1 .....143 B4
Upper Sea Rd TN40 .....157 D4
Upper Sherwood Rd
  BN25 .....181 A4
Upper Shoreham Rd
  Shoreham-by-S BN43 .....140 B1
  Shoreham-by-S BN43 .....140 D1
  Shoreham-by-S BN43 .....161 A8
Upper South Rd TN37 .....136 C1
Upper Sq RH18 .....11 E3
Upper St East Dean BN20 .....187 B8
  Rusthall TN4 .....7 D4
Upper St James's St
  BN2 .....189 C1
Upper St Johns Rd RH15 .....73 A4
Upper Stables RH16 .....50 C3
Upper Station Rd TN21 .....82 A7
Upper Stephens TN3 .....7 A4
Upper Sudeley St 7
  BN2 .....164 D4
Upper Valley Rd BN9 .....179 B6
Upper Wellington St 6
  BN2 .....164 C7
Upper Winfield Ave
  BN1 .....142 F6
Upper Wish Hill BN20 .....184 B8
Upperton Gdns BN21 .....184 F3
Upperton La BN21 .....184 F3
Upperton Rd BN21 .....184 F3
Upton Ave BN42 .....140 E1
Upton Quarry TN3 .....6 E3
Upwick Rd BN20 .....184 C3

U

Uckfield CI BN2 .....164 F6
Uckfield Com Coll TN22 .....78 D8
Uckfield Com Hospl
  TN22 .....78 D6
Uckfield Rd
  Poundgate TN6 .....37 B7
  Upper Wellingham BN8 .....124 B7
Uckfield Sta TN22 .....78 C6
Uckham La TN33 .....112 E6
Udiam Cotts TN32 .....65 C5
Udimore Rd TN31 .....91 C3
Under Rd BN27 .....130 B3
Undercliff
  St Leonards TN38 .....159 B6
  St Leonards TN38 .....159 B6
Undercliff Terr 7 TN38 .....159 C6
Underdown Rd BN42 .....161 C6
Underhill TN22 .....55 B5
Underhill La Clayton BN6 .....119 E8
  Westmeston BN6 .....120 C8
Underwater World*
  TN34 .....160 B3
Unicorn Ho 1 TN34 .....160 A4
Union Rd BN2 .....189 A4
Union Rd BN2 .....189 C4
Union Sq 22 TN2 .....8 A2
Union St Brighton BN2 .....189 B2
  11 St Leonards TN38 .....159 C7
Union Street TN5 .....32 B3
Univ of Brighton
  Brighton BN1 .....189 A4
  Eastbourne BN20 .....188 D8
  Falmer BN1 .....144 B6
Univ of Brighton
  (Cockcroft/Watts Annexes)
  BN2 .....164 C4
Univ of Brighton (St Peter's
  Ho) BN2 .....189 B3
Univ of Sussex BN1 .....144 A7
Updown Hill RH16 .....50 D4
Upland Rd BN20 .....184 C3
Uplands CI Bexhill TN39 .....156 F6
  Uckfield TN22 .....55 C1

V

Val Mascal TN38 .....136 A1
Val Prinseps Rd BN24 .....175 C4
Vale Ave Brighton BN1 .....142 E7
  Royal Tunbridge Wells TN1 .....8 A3
Vale CI BN25 .....181 B4
Vale Ct BN41 .....162 B7
Vale Gdns BN41 .....162 B7
Vale Rd Battle TN33 .....112 B5
  Haywards Heath RH16 .....50 E2
  Mayfield TN20 .....40 B2
  Portslade-by-S BN41 .....162 B7
  Saltdean BN25 .....177 D7
  Seaford BN25 .....181 A4
Vale The BN2 .....165 C2
Vale View Rd TN21 .....82 B6
Valebridge CI RH15 .....73 C6
Valebridge Dr RH15 .....73 C5
Valebridge Rd RH15 .....73 C6

Valence Rd BN7 .....123 B1
Valentine Ct
  2 Eastbourne BN21 .....185 A2
  7 Hove BN3 .....163 C7
Valentine Dr RH15 .....72 E4
Valerie CI BN41 .....141 C2
Vallance CI 7 BN3 .....163 A6
Vallance Ct 7 BN3 .....163 A6
Vallance Gdns BN3 .....163 A6
Vallance Rd BN3 .....163 A6
Vallensdean Cotts BN41 .....141 C2
Valley CI Brighton BN1 .....142 C4
  Newhaven BN9 .....179 B8
Valley Dene BN9 .....179 B7
Valley Dr Brighton BN1 .....142 C4
  Seaford BN25 .....181 A5
Valley Rd
  Crowborough TN6 .....25 E1
  Lewes BN7 .....146 A8
  Newhaven BN9 .....179 A7
  Newhaven BN9 .....179 B7
  Peacehaven BN10 .....167 C2
  Portslade-by-S BN41 .....141 A2
  Rusthall TN4 .....7 D4
Valley Rise BN25 .....180 F4
Valley Side Rd TN35 .....160 C7
Valley View TN22 .....53 A8
Valley View Cvn Site
  TN32 .....64 C4
Valverde Ho BN3 .....163 C7
Van Allen Bldg The
  BN2 .....189 C1
Van Allen Mews BN2 .....189 C1
Vanbrugh Ct BN3 .....163 C7
Vancouver Rd BN23 .....175 B2
Vantage Wlk 1 TN38 .....136 B1
Varndean CI BN1 .....142 E3
Varndean Coll BN1 .....142 F3
Varndean Dr BN1 .....142 E3
Varndean Gdns BN1 .....142 E3
Varndean Holt BN1 .....142 E3
Varndean Rd BN1 .....142 E3
Varndean Sch BN1 .....143 A3
Vega CI BN23 .....152 D7
Ventnor CI BN23 .....174 B4
Ventnor Villas BN3 .....163 B6
Venture CI TN40 .....157 F4
Verbania Way RH19 .....2 B1
Verdant CI TN34 .....159 D8
Vere Rd BN1 .....189 B5
Veric BN3 .....163 C7
Vermont Rd TN4 .....7 C4
Vermont Way TN37 .....135 F6
Vernon Ave
  Peacehaven BN10 .....178 D6
  Woodingdean BN2 .....165 C8
Vernon CI BN3 .....163 E6
Vernon Gdns 4 BN1 .....163 E6
Vernon Lodge 9 BN21 .....185 A2
Vernon Rd
  Royal Tunbridge Wells TN1 .....8 B6
  Uckfield TN22 .....78 D6
Vernon Terr BN1 .....163 E7
Veronns Rd BN8 .....76 D2
Veronica Way BN2 .....189 C1
Verrall's Wlk BN7 .....190 A1
Verulam PI TN37 .....159 E7
Viaduct Rd BN1 .....189 B4
Vian Ave BN23 .....185 F7
Vicarage CI
  Newhaven BN9 .....168 E2
  Ringmer BN8 .....124 D5
  Seaford BN25 .....180 F3
Vicarage Dr BN20 .....184 D3
Vicarage Field BN27 .....152 C8
Vicarage La
  Burwash Common TN19 .....61 A3
  Eastbourne BN20 .....184 D3
  Hailsham BN27 .....152 C8
  Hellingly BN27 .....165 F1
  Scaynes Hill RH17 .....51 F3
  Westfield TN35 .....114 D3
Vicarage Rd
  Burwash Common TN19 .....61 A3
  Eastbourne BN20 .....184 D3
  Hailsham BN27 .....152 C7
  Hellingly BN27 .....165 F1
Vicarage Terr BN2 .....164 C5
Vicarage Way
  Hurst Green TN19 .....45 A3
  Ringmer BN8 .....124 D5
Viceroy Lodge 10 BN3 .....163 A6
Victor CI BN25 .....180 E5
Victoria Ave
  Burgess Hill RH15 .....72 E3
  Hastings TN35 .....160 C8
  Peacehaven BN10 .....178 C7
Victoria Bsns Ctr RH15 .....72 E2
Victoria CI
  Burgess Hill RH15 .....72 F2
  Polegate BN26 .....172 F7
Victoria Cotts
  Cross TN6 .....39 C6
  4 Hove BN3 .....163 B5
  St Leonards TN37 .....136 A5
  Stone Cross BN24 .....174 B7
Victoria Ct 6 Hove BN3 .....163 C6
  Portslade-by-S BN41 .....162 C8
  St Leonards TN38 .....159 B6
Victoria Dr BN20,BN20,BN21 .....184 C5
Victoria Gdns
  Burgess Hill RH15 .....72 F2
  Eastbourne BN20 .....184 C4
Victoria General Hospl
  BN7 .....123 A1

Victoria Gr **7** BN3 ....163 C6
Victoria Ind Est RH15 ......72 E2
Victoria Mans BN2 ....185 B2
Victoria Mews BN2 ....165 F1
Victoria Pl **6** BN1 ....163 E6
Victoria Rd Bexhill TN39 .157 B4
　Brighton BN1 ....163 E6
　Burgess Hill RH15 ....72 E2
　Crowborough TN6 ....38 C8
　Eastbourne BN20 ....184 C5
　Hailsham BN27 ....152 C7
　Haywards Heath RH16 .....51 A3
　Mayfield TN20 ....40 A3
　Polegate BN26 ....172 F7
　Portslade-by-S BN41 ......162 C8
　Royal Tunbridge Wells TN1 ...8 B4
　Southwick BN42 ....161 D7
　St Leonards TN37 ....159 D7
　Windmill Hill BN27 ....131 B5
Victoria Road Trad Est
　BN41 ....162 C8
Victoria St BN1 ....163 E6
Victoria Terr
　Burwash TN19 ....62 A6
　1 Hove BN3 ....163 B5
Victoria Way
　Burgess Hill RH15 ....72 F2
　East Grinstead RH19 ....10 F7
　Winchelsea Beach TN36 ..118 A5
Victory Mews BN2 ....165 A3
View Bank TN35 ....160 D6
View Rd BN10 ....178 C8
View Terr RH7 ....2 A8
Views Path RH1 ....10 D4
Views Wood Path TN22 ...55 D1
Viking Cl BN25 ....180 B6
Viking Way BN23 ....185 F8
Villa Rd TN37 ....159 D7
Village Barn The BN1 ......142 E7
Village Cl Bexhill TN39 ...156 C4
　Portslade-by-S BN41 ......141 B2
Village Mews TN39 ....156 C4
Village The
　Alfriston BN26 ....170 F7
　Alfriston,Alciston BN26 ..170 D8
　Eastbourne BN20 ....188 D8
Village Way BN1 ....144 C6
Village Wks BN8 ....105 A5
Villiers Cl BN2 ....165 E8
Villiers Ct BN1 ....189 B3
Vincent Cl BN1 ....185 F7
Vine Cotts TN6 ....3 C4
Vine Farm Cotts BN8 .....104 A5
Vine Pl BN1 ....189 A3
Vine Sq BN22 ....185 D6
Vine St BN1 ....189 B3
Vinehall Cl TN34 ....137 A5
Vinehall Rd TN32 ....87 E5
Vinehall Sch TN32 ....87 E5
Vineries The
　Burgess Hill RH15 ....73 D3
　Eastbourne BN23 ....174 D2
　Hove BN3 ....163 E6
Vines Cross Rd
　Brighton BN2 ....164 F7
　Horam TN21 ....107 B7
Vineyard La TN5 ....31 C2
Vintry The
　Eastbourne BN21 ....184 C7
　Nutley TN22 ....35 C4
Virgin's Croft TN33 ....112 D6
Virgin's La TN33 ....112 D6
Volks Electric Rly*
　BN1,BN2 ....164 C4
Vue Gris Nez TN36 ....118 B5

W

Wade Cl BN23 ....185 F7
Wadhurst Bsns Pk TN5 ...29 B7
Wadhurst CE Prim Sch
　TN5 ....29 F5
Wadhurst Cl
　Eastbourne BN22 ....173 F2
　St Leonards TN37 ....136 B5
Wadhurst La TN33 ....111 E6
Wadhurst Rd Frant TN3 ...17 C7
　Mark Cross TN6 ....28 C3
Wadhurst Rise BN2 ....164 F5
Wadhurst Sta TN5 ....29 C6
Wadlands Brook Rd RH19 .1 D5
Wagg Cl RH19 ....2 A1
Waghorns La TN22 ....57 C6
Wainwright Cl TN30 ....135 D3
Wainwright Rd TN39 ....157 B4
Waite Cl BN7 ....190 B3
Waites La TN35 ....138 C5
Wakefield Rd BN2 ....190 C5
Wakehams Cl TN3 ....157 C7
Waldegrave Cl BN2 ....177 D7
Waldegrave Rd BN1 ....141 C4
Waldegrave St **4** TN34 .159 F8
Walden Terr TN33 ....112 E4
Waldene Cl TN34 ....136 F2
Waldron Ave BN1 ....143 D6
Waldron Cl BN22 ....184 D8
Waldron Ct TN21 ....82 B8
Waldron Pl BN1 ....143 D6
Waldron Thorns TN21 ....82 A7
Waldshut Rd BN7 ....123 A3
Wales Farm Cotts BN7 ..121 C7
Walesbeech Rd BN2 ....177 D4
Wallhatch Cl RH18 ....13 E7
Walker Cl BN23 ....185 F7
Walks The TN3 ....15 C8
Wall Hill Rd RH18,RH19 ...11 E5

Wallace Cl TN2 ....17 A8
Wallands Com Prim Sch
　BN7 ....123 A2
Wallands Cres BN7 ....190 A2
Walled Gdn The TN22 ....55 D4
Wallers TN3 ....7 A8
Wallington Twrs **4**
　TN40 ....157 F4
Wallis Ave BN23 ....185 E7
Wallis Cl TN6 ....26 A1
Wallis Field TN3 ....15 B6
Wallis Ho RH19 ....1 E1
Wallis Pl BN23 ....185 E8
Wallis Way RH15 ....72 E4
Wallsend Rd BN24 ....175 C6
Walmer Cres BN2 ....144 B1
Walmer Rd BN25 ....181 C4
Walnut Cl Brighton BN1 ..142 E3
　Peacehaven BN10 ....82 B6
Walnut Ct BN26 ....173 A6
Walnut Pk RH16 ....51 B4
Walnut Tree Wlk BN2 .....184 B8
Walnut Way TN4 ....8 D8
Walnut Wlk BN26 ....173 A6
Walpole Rd BN2 ....164 D5
Walpole Terr BN2 ....164 D5
Walpole Wlk BN23 ....174 E3
Walshes Rd TN6 ....38 B7
Walsingham Cl BN22 ......173 D3
Walsingham Rd BN3 ....162 F6
Walter May Ho **14** BN2 ..164 F5
Walters Green Rd TN11 .....5 F6
Walton Bank BN1 ....143 E5
Walton Cl
　Eastbourne BN23 ....174 E3
　St Leonards TN37 ....136 C5
Walton Pk BN2 ....156 F4
Walwers La BN7 ....190 B2
Wanderdown Cl BN2 ....165 E4
Wanderdown Dr BN2 ......165 E4
Wanderdown Rd BN2 ......165 D4
Wanderdown Way BN2 ....165 E4
Wannock Ave BN20 ....172 F3
Wannock Cl TN40 ....158 A6
Wannock Dr BN20 ....172 F5
Wannock Gdns BN26 ......172 F3
Wannock La BN20,BN26 ..172 F3
Wannock Rd
　Eastbourne BN22 ....185 D5
　Polegate BN26 ....172 F5
War Meml Hos BN20 ......184 C6
War Meml Hospl TN6 ....25 E1
Warberry Park Gdns TN4 ...2 E4
Warbleton Cl TN34 ....164 E5
Warburton Cl
　East Grinstead RH19 ....11 A8
　Eastbourne BN21 ....184 C8
　Uckfield TN22 ....78 D8
Ward Cl TN5 ....29 E5
Ward Way TN39 ....157 A4
Ward's La TN5 ....30 E4
Warden Cl RH17 ....50 A6
Warden Park Sch RH17 ...50 A5
Wardsbrook Rd TN5 ....43 D7
Ware Ct RH15 ....73 D3
Warelands RH15 ....72 F1
Warenne Rd BN3 ....141 C4
Wares Field TN22 ....79 D4
Wares Rd TN22 ....78 D4
Warleigh Rd BN1 ....189 B5
Warmdene Ave BN1 ....142 F4
Warmdene Cl BN1 ....142 F5
Warmdene Rd BN1 ....142 E5
Warmdene Way BN1 ....142 F6
Warminster Rd BN24 ......175 D5
Warner Cl RH15 ....73 C3
Warnham Ct BN3 ....163 C5
Warnham Gdns TN39 ......156 E2
Warnham Rise BN1 ....143 A5
Warren Ave BN1 ....165 C8
Warren Cl
　Crowborough TN6 ....25 C2
　Eastbourne BN22 ....185 B2
　Friston BN20 ....183 B1
　Lewes BN7 ....146 B8
　Roser's Cross TN21 ....81 A6
　St Leonards TN38 ....158 E8
　Woodingdean BN2 ....165 B8
Warren Cnr TN21 ....81 A8
Warren Cotts
　Mayfield TN20 ....40 C3
　North Chailey BN8 ....75 F7
Warren Ct
　9 Crowborough TN6 ......25 F3
　Southwick BN42 ....140 E1
Warren Dr BN7 ....146 A8
Warren Farm La TN3 ....16 B4
Warren Gdn TN6 ....25 E2
Warren Hill BN20 ....183 B1
Warren La Friston BN20 ..183 B1
　North Chailey BN8 ....75 E8
　Roser's Cross TN21 ....81 A7
Warren Lodge BN10 ....167 A1
Warren Rd
　Crowborough TN6 ....25 C1
　Friston TN35 ....138 C4
　Woodingdean BN2 ....165 B8
Warren Ridge
　Crowborough TN6 ....25 D2
　Frant TN3 ....17 C3
Warren Rise TN6 ....165 B8
Warren The
　Burgess Hill RH15 ....73 C1
　Mayfield TN20 ....40 C2
Warren Way
　North Chailey BN8 ....75 F8
　Telscombe Cliffs BN10 ...167 A1

Warren Way continued
　Woodingdean BN2 ....165 D8
Warren Wood TN6 ....25 D1
Warrenwood Rd BN8 ....53 A1
Warrior Cl TN37 ....159 D7
Warrior Ct TN37 ....159 D7
Warrior Gdns TN37 ....159 C7
Warrior Ho BN20 ....188 E8
Warrior Sq
　3 Eastbourne BN20 ......184 C5
　St Leonards TN37 ....159 D7
Wartling Cl BN8 ....75 E8
Wartling Cl TN38 ....135 F3
Wartling Dr TN38 ....155 F5
Wartling Rd
　Eastbourne BN20 ....185 D6
　Wartling BN27 ....131 C2
Warwick Cl BN27 ....129 C3
Warwick Ct
　4 Eastbourne BN23 ......174 E1
　2 Hove BN3 ....163 E7
Warwick Mount **2** BN2 ..164 C4
Warwick Pk TN2 ....8 B1
Warwick Rd Bexhill TN39 .156 F5
　Eastbourne BN22 ....185 A4
　Seaford BN25 ....180 E3
Washington Ave TN37 .....159 C8
Washington Rd RH16 ....51 A5
Washington St BN2 ....189 C4
Washwell La TN5 ....29 F3
Wassall La TN17 ....48 E7
Watchbell La **3** TN31 .....93 C5
Watchbell St TN31 ....93 C5
Water Mint Cl TN38 ....135 E1
Waterbury Hill RH17 ....33 B5
Waterdown Rd TN4 ....7 E1
Waterdyke Ave BN42 ......161 E7
Waterfield TN2 ....17 A7
Waterford Cl BN10 ....167 C2
Waterfrets Cotts TN5 ....6 F5
Waterfront TN2 ....164 F3
Waterfront The BN23 ......185 G8
Watergate BN7 ....147 A6
Watergate La BN7 ....190 A1
Waterhall Rd BN1 ....142 C6
Waterloo Cl TN37 ....135 F7
Waterloo Ho **9** BN3 ....163 D5
Waterloo Pas **18** TN34 .160 B4
Waterloo Pl
　1 Brighton BN1 ....189 C3
　15 Hastings TN34 ....160 B4
　Lewes BN7 ....190 B2
Waterloo Sq BN26 ....171 A3
Waterloo St BN3 ....163 D5
Watermen's Cl TN34 ....136 F3
Watermill Cl
　Bexhill TN39 ....157 B7
　Polegate BN26 ....173 A5
Watermill Dr TN38 ....135 D3
Watermill La
　Bexhill TN39 ....134 B2
　Clayhill TN31 ....67 D2
　Icklesham TN35,TN36 ....116 C3
Watermill Lane Cotts
　TN35 ....138 C8
Waters Cotts TN5 ....30 A4
Waters Edge **18** BN43 ...161 A6
Waterside
　Crowborough TN6 ....25 F2
　East Grinstead RH19 ....2 B1
Waterside Cl TN35 ....160 C7
Waterside Ctr BN7 ....190 A3
Waterworks CI RH18 ....11 F3
Waterworks Cotts
　Friston BN20 ....183 A1
　1 Hastings TN34 ....159 F8
　Hove BN3 ....142 A2
Waterworks Rd
　Eastbourne BN22 ....185 A4
　1 Hastings TN34 ....136 F1
Watling Cl **5** BN42 ....161 E7
Watling Ct **8** BN42 ....161 E7
Watling Rd BN42 ....161 E7
Wattle's Wish TN33 ....112 C6
Watts Cl TN5 ....29 F4
Watts La BN21 ....184 E4
Watts Lodge RH15 ....73 D3
Watts' Palace La TN31 .....89 D7
Waverley Cres BN1 ....143 C1
Waverley Ct
　8 Hastings TN34 ....159 E7
　7 Seaford BN25 ....180 F2
Waverley Dr TN4 ....8 C6
Waverley Gdns BN24 ......175 D5
Wayfaring Down BN26 .....39 C2
Wayfield Ave BN3 ....141 F1
Wayfield Cl BN3 ....141 F1
Wayford Cl BN24 ....174 D2
Wayland Ave BN1 ....142 C3
Wayland Hts BN1 ....142 C2
Wayside Brighton BN1 .....142 D6
　Friston BN20 ....183 B1
Wayside Wlk TN31 ....81 F6
Weald Ave BN3 ....162 F8
Weald Cl
　Barcombe Cross BN8 ....101 E4
　Lewes BN7 ....190 A3
Weald Rd RH15 ....72 E3
Weald Rise RH16 ....50 E1
Weald The RH19 ....11 A4
Weald View
　Barcombe Cross BN8 ....101 E4
　Staplecross TN32 ....65 E2
　Turner's Green TN5 ....29 F6
Wealden Cl TN6 ....25 F2
Wealden Cotts TN19 ....61 C3
Wealden Ho TN19 ....82 A8

Wealden Ind Est TN6 ....38 C8
Wealden Pk BN22 ....173 C1
Wealden View TN19 ....62 B7
Wealden Way
　Bexhill TN39 ....156 C6
　Haywards Heath RH16 .....50 D4
Wealdview Rd TN21 ....81 F7
Weare Rd TN4 ....8 C8
Weatherby Cl BN21 ....184 C8
Weavers Cl RH15 ....73 D1
Weavers La BN26 ....170 F3
Weavers Rock La TN21 .....82 C5
Wedderburn Rd BN20 ......173 B1
Week La BN6 ....106 E4
Weir Wood Cotts RH18 ....11 C3
Weir Wood Resr (Nature
　Reserve)* RH19 ....10 D1
Welbeck Ave Hove BN3 ...162 D1
　Royal Tunbridge Wells TN4 ...8 C8
　St Leonards TN38 ....159 A7
Welbeck Cl
　Burgess Hill RH15 ....73 D5
　Eastbourne BN22 ....173 D3
Welbeck Ct Hove BN3 .....162 E6
　9 Seaford BN25 ....180 E3
Welbeck Mans BN3 ....162 E6
Welesmere Rd BN2 ....177 A7
Welkin (Brighton Univ)
　BN20 ....184 E1
Welkin The RH16 ....51 B8
Welland Cl TN6 ....38 A8
Wellcombe Cres BN20 ....188 D7
Weller Rd TN4 ....7 C4
Wellesley Cl
　Bexhill TN39 ....156 D3
　Crowborough TN6 ....25 D1
Wellesley Ct **12** TN34 ....160 B4
Wellesley Rd **7** BN21 ....185 A3
Wellfield RH19 ....11 C7
Wellgreen La BN7 ....145 F5
Wellhouse La RH15 ....98 C7
Wellhouse Pl BN7 ....190 A2
Wellington Cl **3** BN23 ....175 A1
Wellington Ct
　Brighton BN2 ....189 C4
　4 Eastbourne BN22 ......185 C5
Wellington Gdns TN34 ....159 F8
Wellington Ho **7** TN34 ...159 F8
Wellington Lodge BN27 ..152 B8
Wellington Mews TN34 ...159 F8
Wellington Pk **1** BN25 ..181 A3
Wellington Pl
　6 Hastings TN34 ....159 F7
　Sparrow's Green TN5 ......29 F7
Wellington Quay BN23 ....175 A1
Wellington Rd
　Brighton BN2 ....189 C4
　Hastings TN34 ....160 A4
　Newhaven BN9 ....66 E2
　Peacehaven BN10 ....178 E6
　Portslade-by-S BN41 ......162 B8
　Wellington Sq TN34 ....159 F8
Wellington St
　Brighton BN2 ....164 C7
　Lewes BN7 ....190 B2
Wellington Terr **4**
　TN34 ....159 F8
Wellington Town Rd RH19 ...1 D2
Wellingtonia Ct **8** BN1 ..142 E3
Wellis Ct TN38 ....159 A8
Wellis Gdns TN38 ....159 A8
Wellplace Cotts TN36 .....116 F5
Wells Chase BN7 ....99 E6
Wells Cl
　Eastbourne BN20 ....188 C8
　Plumpton Green BN7 ......75 A5
　Royal Tunbridge Wells TN1 ...8 A3
Wells Ho TN7 ....7 F4
Wells Lea RH19 ....1 D3
Wells Mdw RH19 ....1 D4
Wellsbourne **8** BN2 ....164 F5
Wellsbourne Rd BN24 .....174 A5
Wellsmead Pk BN20 ....188 C8
Welsley Mews TN6 ....25 F2
Wendale Dr BN10 ....167 D2
Wendover Grange **3**
　BN3 ....163 A6
Wenham Gdns BN8 ....104 C5
Went Hill Gdns BN22 ......173 B3
Went Hill Pk BN25 ....181 A5
Went La BN20 ....183 C1
West Way BN20 ....183 B1
Wenthill Cl BN20 ....187 B8
Wentworth Cl
　Bexhill TN40 ....157 F5
　Hailsham BN27 ....129 A4
Wentworth Ct BN23 ....159 A8
Wentworth St BN2 ....164 C4
Wentworth Way TN38 .....158 F8
Wessex Pl BN27 ....129 A4
West Ascent TN38 ....159 B6
West Beach Ct BN25 ......159 A8
West Beeches Rd TN6 .....26 B2
West Blatchington Inf Sch
　BN3 ....141 E4
West Blatchington Jun Sch
　BN3 ....141 E4
West Blatchington Windmill
　(dis)* BN3 ....141 F4
West Cl Alfriston BN26 ....170 F3
　Polegate BN26 ....173 A6
West Comm RH16 ....50 F6
West Common Dr RH16 ....50 F5
West Dean Rise BN25 .....181 A4
West Dean Rd TN39 ....157 A1
West Dr BN2 ....164 C6

West End BN27 ....130 E6
West Furlong Ct BN6 ....97 A5
West Furlong La BN6 ....97 A5
West Gate BN7 ....190 A3
West Gdns BN27 ....99 E6
West Hill
　Dormans Park RH19 ....1 E6
　East Grinstead RH19 ....10 A3
West Hill Arc **3** TN34 ....160 A3
West Hill Cliff Rly*
　.......................................160 A4
West Hill Ct
　Eastbourne BN21 ....184 E4
　4 St Leonards TN38 .....159 B6
West Hill Mews TN38 .....158 F6
West Hill Pl BN1 ....189 A3
West Hill Rd
　Brighton BN1 ....189 A3
　St Leonards TN38 ....159 A6
West Hill St BN1 ....189 A4
West Ho BN21 ....185 A2
West Hoathly Rd RH19 ....10 D4
West Hove Inf & Jun Schs
　BN3 ....162 F7
West La RH19 ....10 D8
West Leigh RH19 ....10 F7
West Mallion RH16 ....50 F7
West Par TN39 ....157 B2
West Park Cres RH15 ....72 D4
West Point **8** BN43 ....161 A6
West Quay BN9 ....179 D6
West Rd Kildown TN17 ....20 F3
　Portslade-by-S BN41 ......162 A7
　Pyecombe BN45 ....119 A6
West Rise Com Inf Sch
　BN23 ....174 C2
West Rise Jun Sch
　BN23 ....174 C2
West St Alfriston BN26 ...170 F3
　Brighton BN1 ....189 A2
　Burgess Hill RH15 ....72 E4
　Ditchling BN6 ....98 D3
　Dormansland RH7 ....2 A8
　East Grinstead RH19 ......10 E8
　Eastbourne BN21 ....184 F2
　Hastings TN34 ....160 A3
　Lewes BN7 ....190 B2
　Mayfield TN20 ....40 A2
　Portslade-by-S BN41 ......162 C7
　Rottingdean BN2 ....165 F1
　Rye TN31 ....93 C5
　Seaford BN25 ....180 E3
West St Leonards Prim Sch
　TN38 ....158 F6
West St Leonards Sta
　TN38 ....158 F7
West Street La BN1 ....81 F2
West Terr
　Eastbourne BN21 ....184 F2
　Herstmonceux BN27 ......130 E6
West Undercliff TN31 ....93 A5
West View Hastings TN34 ...5 B7
　Hove BN3 ....163 C8
　Lindfield RH16 ....51 B6
　Seaford BN25 ....180 E2
　Uckfield TN22 ....55 D1
West View Cots RH16 ....51 B6
West View Ct **3** BN25 ....180 E2
West View Gdns RH19 .....10 E8
West View Terr BN9 ....168 D2
West Way BN3 ....141 D2
Westaway Dr TN39 ....157 A4
Westbourne Ct TN39 ....156 C2
Westbourne Gdns BN3 ...163 A7
Westbourne La BN3 ....163 A7
Westbourne Pl BN3 ....163 A6
Westbourne St BN3 ....163 A7
Westbourne Villas BN3 ...162 F6
Westbrook
　Forest Row RH18 ....11 B3
　Saltdean BN2 ....177 C6
Westbrook La TN35 ....114 E5
Westbrook Way BN42 ......161 F7
Westcliff Man BN20 ....188 F8
Westcombe **1** BN1 ....163 E7
Westcourt BN27 ....152 B7
Westcourt Dr TN39 ....156 C2
Westdean Ave BN9 ....179 A5
Westdene Cl TN37 ....136 C6
Westdene Dr BN1 ....142 C5
Westdene Prim Sch
　BN1 ....142 C5
Westdown La TN5 ....29 A6
Westdown La TN5 ....185 A2
Westdown Ho **4** BN21 ..185 A2
Westdown Pk TN19 ....61 A3
Westdown Rd BN25 ....180 D4
Westergate Rd BN2 ....143 E4
Westerings The **4** TN21 ..32 A6
Westerleigh Cl TN38 ....159 A8
Western Ave Battle TN33 .112 C5
　Polegate BN26 ....173 B7
Western Concourse
　.......................................164 F3
Western Esp BN3 ....179 C6
Western Espl BN41 ....162 D6
Western Gdns TN6 ....25 D8
Western Rd Bexhill TN40 .157 F5
　Burgess Hill RH15 ....72 E3
　Crowborough TN6 ....38 C7
　Eastbourne BN22 ....185 B4
　Hailsham BN27 ....152 A8
　Haywards Heath RH16 .....50 F4
　Hove BN3 ....163 E5
　Hurstpierpoint BN6 ....97 A7

Western Rd continued
Lewes BN7 ....123 B1
Newhaven BN9 ....179 C6
Newick BN8 ....76 C7
Pevensey Bay BN24 ....175 D4
Royal Tunbridge Wells TN1 ..8 C5
St Leonards TN37 ......159 C7
Turner's Green TN5 .....29 F6
Western Road Prim Sch
BN7 ....190 A1
Western St BN1 ....163 D5
Western Terr 21 BN1 ..163 E5
Westfield Ave BN42 ...177 D7
Westfield Ave N BN2 ..177 D7
Westfield Ave S BN2 ..177 D7
Westfield Cl
Brighton BN1 ....143 A4
Polegate BN26 ....58 B6
Westfield Cres BN1 ...143 A5
Westfield Ct BN26 .....173 A7
Westfield La TN35,TN37 ..136 C8
Westfield Prim Sch
TN35 ....114 E4
Westfield Rd BN21 ....184 D6
Westfield Rise BN2 ....177 E7
Westgate St BN7 ......190 E2
Westham 15 BN2 ......164 F5
Westham Ct TN39 .....156 E3
Westham Dr BN24 .....175 F6
Westhill Dr RH15 ....72 E3
Westland Cl BN41 .....162 A7
Westlands Rd RH16 ....51 B5
Westlands BN21 ......184 C8
Westmeston Ave BN2 ..177 D6
Westminster Cl BN22 ..173 D4
Westminster Cres TN40 ..160 A8
Westmoreland Cl TN38 ..135 F3
Westmoreland Ct TN22 ..78 C5
Westmorland Ct
15 Brighton BN1 ....163 E7
Eastbourne BN20 ......184 B7
Westmount 9 BN2 ....164 C6
Westmount Cl BN42 ....161 D8
Westpoint BN8 ....76 C7
Westville Rd TN39 .....157 A4
Westway TN2 ....9 D7
Westway Cl BN41 ......140 E4
Westway Gdns BN41 ...140 E4
Westwood Rd TN4 ....7 C5
Wharf Rd
Eastbourne BN21 ......184 F3
Hove BN3 ....162 D6
Whatlington Rd TN33 ...112 E7
Whatlington Way TN38 ..135 D2
Wheatfield Cl TN37 .....136 C5
Wheatfield Way BN2 ...143 F3
Wheatland Cl BN10 ....167 B2
Wheatsheaf Cl RH15 ...72 E5
Wheatsheaf Gdns BN1 ..190 C3
Wheatsheaf La RH17 ...50 A6
Wheel Farm Bsns Pk
TN35 ....114 D4
Wheel La TN35 ....114 D3
Wheeler Ct RH16 ......50 F2
Wheelers Lane Cotts
TN22 ....57 D5
Wheelwright Cl BN22 ...173 D4
Wheelwright La RH15 ...73 D1
Whichelo Pl BN2 ......164 C6
Whiffens Cl BN27 ......152 A6
Whincroft Pk TN6 ......37 D8
Whipping Post La BN2 ..165 F1
Whippingham Rd BN2 ..164 C7
Whippingham St BN2 ...164 C8
Whistler Ct BN1 ....142 F1
Whitbread Cl BN23 ....174 B4
White Bear Pas 3 TN1 ..8 C2
White Chys TN6 ....26 A1
White Ct BN26 ....170 F2
White Hill Ave TN39 ...156 E4
White Hill Dr TN39 .....156 E4
White House Prim Sch
BN27 ....152 B8
White Lodge Hove BN3 ..163 C8
Royal Tunbridge Wells TN1 ..8 C4
White Rock Gdns 7
TN34 ....159 E7
White Rock Pleasure
Grounds* TN34 ....159 E7
White Rock Rd TN34,
TN38 ....159 E7
White St BN2 ....189 C2
White Way
Alfriston BN26 ....170 F1
Lewes BN7 ....146 B1
White's Cl BN41 ....97 A7
Whitebread La TN31 ...67 E8
Whitecross St BN1 ....189 B3
Whitefield Rd TN4 ......8 A6
Whitefriars Rd TN34 ...160 A5
Whitegate Cl TN4 .....8 A8
Whitegates Cl BN8 ....100 E7
Whitegates La TN5 .....29 F6
Whitegates Ph TN35 ...114 D2
Whitehall Par 3 RH19 ..1 E1
Whitehawk Cl BN2 .....164 E5
Whitehawk Cres BN2 ...164 E5
Whitehawk Hill Rd BN2 ..164 D5
Whitehawk Prim Sch
BN2 ....164 E6

Whitehawk Rd
Brighton BN2 ....164 E6
Brighton BN2 ....164 F5
Whitehawk Way BN2 ...164 F6
Whitehill Cl
Crowborough TN6 ......25 F1
Eastbourne BN20 ......184 B5
Whitehill Ct TN39 ......156 E5
Whitehill Inf Sch TN6 ...26 A1
Whitehill Rd TN37 .....37 F8
Whitehouse Ave TN39 ..157 B7
Whitehouse La TN21 ...81 B4
Whitelot Cl BN42 ......140 E2
Whitelot Way BN42 ....140 E2
Whiterock Pl BN42 .....161 E7
Whitesmith BN1 ....105 B1
Whitesmith La BN1 ....105 B1
Whitethorn Dr BN1 ....142 B4
Whiteway Cl BN25 .....180 E6
Whiteway La BN2 ......177 A6
Whiteways Cotts BN7 ..146 C2
Whitfeld La BN8 ....123 C6
Whitley Rd BN22 ......185 B5
Whittinghame Gdns
BN1 ....142 F3
Whittington Coll RH19 ..1 A4
Whittington's Way TN34 ..160 B8
Whittle Dr BN23 ....174 A1
Whittlewood Cl TN38 ...135 E2
Whitworth Rd TN37 ....136 B7
Whybourne Crest TN2 ..8 D1
Whydown Hill TN33 ....113 E6
Whydown Rd TN39 ....156 B7
Wick Hall BN3 ....163 D6
Wick Hurst Rd BN41 ...141 A2
Wickets The RH15 .....72 F5
Wickham Ave TN39 ....157 B3
Wickham La RH16 .....50 E7
Wickham Dr BN6 ......97 C5
Wickham Gdns TN4 ....7 D5
Wickham Hill BN6 ......97 C4
Wickham La BN7,BN8 ..100 C1
Wickham Rock La TN36 ..117 C5
Wickham Way RH16 ...50 E7
Wickhurst Cl BN41 .....140 F2
Wickhurst Rise BN41 ...140 F3
Wicklands Ave BN2 ....177 D5
Widbury TN3 ....6 F3
Widdicombe Way BN2 ..143 E2
Wigmore Cl BN1 ....143 B1
Wilbury Ave BN3 ....163 C8
Wilbury Cres BN3 ......163 D7
Wilbury Gdns BN3 .....163 C8
Wilbury Gr BN3 ....163 C6
Wilbury Grange 9 BN3 ..163 C6
Wilbury Lodge 12 BN3 ..163 C6
Wilbury Rd BN3 ....163 C6
Wilbury Villas BN3 ......163 C7
Wilby Ave BN42 ....140 E1
Wild Park Cl BN2 ....143 D5
Wild Park Nature Trail* BN2 ..143 D5
Wilderness Gdns TN31 ..67 B7
Wilderness La TN22 ....57 C3
Wilderness Pk TN6 .....25 E2
Wilderness Rd BN6 ....97 A6
Wilderness Rise RH19 ..2 A6
Wilderness The RH16 ...51 B8
Wilderness Wood Visitor
Ctr* TN22 ....57 D4
Wilderwick Rd RH19,RH7 ..2 A1
Wildwood BN23 ....174 C4
Wilfrid Rd BN3 ....141 D1
Wiliamson Cott Homes
BN3 ....163 A7
Wilkins Way TN40 .....157 F6
Wilkinson Cl BN2 ......164 E5
Wilkinson Way BN25 ..180 E4
Willard Cl BN22 ....185 A6
Wille Cotts BN7 ....190 C2
Willetts Cotts TN3 .....5 C4
Willetts Field BN8 ......127 E8
Willetts La TN3 ....5 A8
William Allen La RH16 ..51 B6
William Parker Sch
TN34 ....136 D4
William Rd TN38 ....158 E7
William St Brighton BN2 ..189 B2
Portslade-by-S BN41 ...162 B7
William Street Trad Est
BN41 ....162 B7
William Sutton Ho BN1 ..189 B2
Williams Ct 7 BN23 ...174 F1
Williams Rd BN1 ....161 C8
Willicombe Ho TN2 ....8 D4
Willicombe Pk TN2 ....8 D4
Willingdon Ave
Bexhill TN39 ....157 A4
St Leonards TN38 ....136 A5
Willingdon Cl
Eastbourne BN20 ......173 B1
St Leonards TN38 .....136 A5
Willingdon Com Sch
BN20 ....172 F4
Willingdon Dro BN23 ...174 B2
Willingdon La BN26 ....183 C7
Willingdon Park Dr
BN22 ....173 D2
Willingdon Prim Sch
BN20 ....173 A3
Willingdon Rd
Brighton BN2 ....143 E1
Eastbourne BN20,BN21 ..184 C6
Willingdon Way
Eastbourne BN22 ......173 B2
St Leonards TN38 .....136 A5

Willingford La TN19 ....61 C2
Willoughby Cres BN22 ..185 C6
Willow Ave BN27 ......129 B1
Willow Bank TN32 .....64 B3
Willow Cl
East Grinstead RH19 ...1 D3
Etchingham TN19 .....63 B8
Heathfield TN21 ......82 B8
Hurstpierpoint BN6 ....97 A7
Woodingdean BN2 ....165 E8
Willow Ct 4 Hove BN3 ..163 D7
Polegate BN26 ....173 A6
Willow Dr Bexhill TN39 ..156 C5
Polegate BN26 ....173 A5
Seaford BN25 ....181 C3
Willow End TN34 ......136 F4
Willow Est The BN9 ....179 E8
Willow Gdns BN6 ......97 A7
Willow Ho BN6 ....97 E5
Willow La TN36 ....118 B6
Willow Lodge TN4 .....7 E4
Willow Mead 8 RH19 ..10 F8
Willow Mews
16 Eastbourne BN22 ....185 B3
Robertsbridge TN32 ...64 B3
Willow Pk RH16 ....51 B4
Willow Stream Cl TN35 ..115 C3
Willow Tree Rd TN2 ....7 F1
Willow Way BN6 ......97 A8
Willow Wlk
Eastbourne BN2 ....173 D2
Newhaven BN9 ....179 C8
Royal Tunbridge Wells TN1 ..8 E8
Willowbed Wlk TN34 ...136 E5
Willowbrook Way BN6 ..98 A3
Willowdene Cl BN26 ...173 A5
Willowfield Rd BN22 ...185 B4
Willowfield Sq 9 BN22 ..185 B3
Willowmead TN6 ....37 E8
Willows Cl TN22 ......78 A8
Willows Mobile Home Pk The
BN27 ....129 A3
Willows Rise TN22 ......79 B5
Willows The
Barcombe Cross BN8 ..101 E5
2 Brighton BN2 ......189 C5
Burgess Hill RH15 .....73 B5
Hassocks BN6 ....97 E4
St Leonards TN37 ....136 A6
Wilman Rd TN4 ....8 B7
Wilmington Cl
Brighton BN1 ....143 A5
Hassocks BN6 ....97 F4
Wilmington Gdns BN21 ..185 A1
Wilmington Par BN1 ....142 F5
Wilmington Rd
Hastings TN34 ....160 A7
Newhaven BN9 ....179 B6
Seaford BN25 ....180 D4
Wilmington Sq BN21 ...185 A1
Wilmington Way
Brighton BN1 ....143 A5
Hayward's Heath RH16 ..51 A5
Wilmot Ct 6 BN43 ....161 C8
Wilmot Rd BN43 ......161 C8
Wilson Ave BN2 ....164 F6
Wilson Gr TN22 ......78 A7
Wilson's Cross BN27 ...131 F7
Wilton 1 RH16 ....50 D6
Wilton Ho TN38 ....158 F6
Wilton Rd TN40 ....157 C3
Wiltshire Cl BN23 .....174 E1
Wiltshire Ho 18 BN2 ...189 C2
Wiltshire Way TN2 .....8 D7
Winceby Cl TN39 ......156 E2
Winchcombe Rd BN22 ..185 A4
Winchelsea Beach Holiday
Village TN36 ....118 A4
Winchelsea Cl BN25 ...181 C5
Winchelsea La
Cock Marling TN31,TN36 ..92 C1
Hastings TN35 ....137 E5
Winchelsea Mus* TN36 ..117 E7
Winchelsea Rd
Eastbourne BN22 .....185 D6
Guestling Green TN35 ..137 F7
Hastings TN38 ....160 D8
Rye TN31 ....93 B5
Winchelsea Sta TN36 ..92 D1
Winchester Ho BN22 ...173 E3
Winchester St BN1 ....189 B5
Winchester Way BN21 ..173 C2
Windermere Cl
Eastbourne BN23 ......173 A2
Windermere Cres BN22 ..185 C5
Windermere Ct 9 BN2 ..164 C6
Windermere Rd RH16 ..50 F4
Windgrove Cotts TN33 ..112 D6
Windgrove Ho TN33 ...112 D6
Winding St 21 TN34 ...160 B4
Windlesham Ave BN1 ...163 E6
Windlesham Cl
Crowborough TN6 .....25 F1
Portslade-by-S BN41 ...141 A1
Windlesham Ct 14 BN1 ..163 E7
Windlesham Gdns BN1,
BN3 ....163 E7
Windlesham Ho 15 BN1 ..163 E7
Windlesham Mans 17
BN3 ....163 E7
Windlesham Rd BN1 ....163 E6
Windlesham Sch BN1 ...163 E6
Windmill Ave BN6 ......97 F3
Windmill Cl
Eastbourne BN21 ......184 D6
Heathfield TN21 ......82 B8
Hove BN3 ....141 F2

Windmill Ct
Royal Tunbridge Wells TN2 ..8 C3
Winchelsea Beach TN36 ..118 B6
Windmill Dr Bexhill TN39 ..157 B6
Brighton BN1 ....142 C6
Burgess Hill RH15 ....73 A4
Cousley Wood TN5 ...140 C5
Durgates TN5 ....29 E4
East Grinstead RH19 ..1 D3
Friston BN20 ....183 A1
Windmill Par BN42 ....140 C1
Windmill Park Cvn Pk
TN36 ....118 B6
Windmill Pl BN26 ......173 A5
Windmill Rd
Polegate BN26 ....173 A6
Southwick BN42 ......140 E1
St Leonards TN38 ....136 B2
Windmill St
Brighton BN2 ....189 C3
Royal Tunbridge Wells TN2 ..8 C3
Windmill Terr 20 BN2 ...189 C3
Windmill View BN1 ....143 B7
Windmill Way TN36 ...118 B7
Windmills Jun Sch The
BN6 ....98 A3
Windover Cres BN7 ....123 A2
Windover Way BN22 ...173 B3
Windsor Bsns Units TN6 ..38 C8
Windsor Cl
Eastbourne BN23 ......174 C3
Hayward's Heath RH16 ..50 E2
Hove BN3 ....142 A3
Seaford BN25 ....180 B6
Windsor Ct Brighton BN1 ..189 A2
Brighton,Withdean BN1 ..142 D4
Crowborough TN6 .....38 C8
3 Eastbourne BN22 ...185 B3
Polegate BN26 ....173 A7
Windsor Lodge 5 BN3 ..163 B6
Windsor Pl
Crowborough TN6 .....38 C8
East Grinstead RH19 ..1 E1
Hastings TN34 ....136 E2
Windsor Rd Bexhill TN39 ..157 B4
Crowborough TN6 .....38 C8
Hailsham BN27 ....152 B6
St Leonards TN37 ....136 B3
Windsor St BN1 ....189 A2
Windsor Way
Polegate BN26 ....173 A7
Winchelsea Beach TN36 ..118 A5
Windward Quay 10
BN23 ....185 F8
Wineham Way TN40 ...157 F4
Winfield Ave BN1 ......142 F4
Winfield Cl Brighton BN1 ..142 F5
Portslade-by-S BN41 ...141 A3
Wingate Cl TN38 ......136 A1
Wingle Tye Rd RH15 ...98 A8
Wingrove BN26 ....173 A3
Winkfield Ct TN6 ......50 D5
Winkhurst Way RH15 ...73 D1
Winkney Rd BN22 .....173 D3
Winnals Pk RH16 ......50 D5
Winscote Cl TN6 ......25 D1
Winston Cres BN27 ....152 B7
Winston Cres BN23 ...185 D7
Winston Dr TN39 .....156 F4
Winstone Scott Ave TN3 ..6 E4
Winterbourne Cl
Hastings TN34 ....159 D8
Lewes BN7 ....146 A8
Winterbourne Hollow
BN7 ....146 B8
Winterbourne La BN7 ..146 A8
Winterbourne Mews
BN7 ....146 A8
Winterton Way BN43 ..161 B6
Winton Ave BN2 ......177 C7
Winton St BN26 ......171 A4
Wisden Ave RH15 .....97 E5
Wiseacre TN3 ....20 A3
Wish Ct BN3 ....162 E8
Wish Hill BN20 ....173 B1
Wish Rd
Eastbourne BN21 ......185 A2
Hove BN3 ....162 E6
Wish St TN31 ....93 B5
Wish Tower Puppet Mus*
BN21 ....185 A1
Wisham Ward TN31 ...93 B5
Wishing Tree Cl TN38 ..135 B8
Wishing Tree La TN38 ..135 F2
Wishing Tree Rd TN38 ..135 F2
Wishing Tree Rd N
TN38 ....136 A4
Wiston Cl 12 BN43 ....161 C8
Wiston Rd BN2 ....164 F6
Wiston Way BN2 ......164 F7
Withdean Ave BN1 ....142 D2
Withdean Cl BN1 ......142 D3
Withdean Court Ave
BN1 ....142 D3
Withdean Cres BN1 ...142 E3
Withdean Ct 7 BN1 ....142 E3
Withdean Hall 8 BN1 ..142 E3
Withdean Rd BN1 .....142 C3
Withdean Rise BN1 ...142 D3
Withdean Stad (Brighton &
Hove Albion FC) BN1 ..142 D3
Witherenden Rd TN20 ..41 A1
Withy Bush RH15 ......72 F5
Withyham Ave BN2 ...177 C5
Withyham Cl BN22 ....173 F1

Withyham Rd
Bexhill TN39 ....156 C2
Groombridge TN3 .....10 B5
Wittersham La TN31 ...70 B5
Wittersham Rd Iden TN31 ..70 B7
Potman's Heath TN17,
TN30 ....49 D8
Wittersham Road Sta*
TN17 ....49 D6
Wivelsfield Prim Sch
RH17 ....73 F6
Wivelsfield Rd
Hayward's Heath RH16 ..50 E2
Saltdean BN2 ....177 C7
Wivelsfield Sta RH15 ...73 C4
Woburn Cl BN27 ......129 A1
Woburn Pl BN1 ....143 F5
Woburn Way BN22 ...173 D3
Wode Rd TN33 ....133 A3
Wolfe Cl TN6 ....38 A8
Wolseley Rd
Brighton BN1 ....143 D6
Portslade-by-S BN41 ...162 A8
Winchelsea Beach TN36 ..8 C7
Wolstead Lodge 3 RH16 ..50 F3
Wolstonbury Cl BN1 ...97 B4
Wolstonbury Ct RH15 ..73 B2
Wolstonbury Rd BN3 ...163 E7
Wolstonbury Way RH15 ..73 B2
Wolverstone Dr BN1 ...143 C2
Wood Gdns BN27 .....131 D2
Wood Ride RH16 ......50 D3
Wood St
East Grinstead RH19 ...1 D1
Royal Tunbridge Wells TN1 ..8 B4
Wood's Pas 4 TN34 ...160 B4
Woodbourne Ave BN1 ..143 A4
Woodbrook Rd TN34 ...136 F2
Woodbury Ave RH19 ...2 B1
Woodbury Cl
East Grinstead RH19 ...11 B8
Royal Tunbridge Wells TN4 ..8 A5
Woodbury Park Gdns TN4 ..8 A5
Woodbury Rd TN4 ....8 B5
Woodcombe TN34 .....136 F4
Woodcote Rd RH18 ....11 F2
Woodcrest Rd RH15 ...72 F1
Woodcroft RH15 ......72 F5
Woodcroft Dr BN21 ....184 C7
Woodcutters RH17 ....51 F3
Woodgate Mdw BN7 ...99 E7
Woodgate Rd BN22 ...185 C5
Woodhams Cl TN33 ...112 D5
Woodhill Pk TN2 ......9 C6
Woodhouse Cl BN3 ....162 E7
Woodhouse Rd BN3 ...162 E7
Woodingdean Prim Sch
BN2 ....165 C8
Woodland Ave
Burgess Hill RH15 .....73 C4
Eastbourne BN22 .....173 C1
Hove BN3 ....142 B3
Woodland Cl
Burgess Hill RH15 .....73 C4
Hove BN3 ....142 B2
Royal Tunbridge Wells TN4 ..8 A5
Woodland Cres RH15 ...73 C4
Woodland Ct BN3 .....142 B4
Woodland Dr BN3 .....142 B4
Woodland Mews TN21 ..82 B6
Woodland Par BN3 ....142 B3
Woodland Rd TN4 .....8 A5
Woodland Rise TN40 ..157 C6
Woodland Vale Rd
TN37,TN38 ....159 C8
Woodland Way
Brighton BN1 ....142 F4
Crowborough TN6 .....37 F8
Crowhurst TN33 ......134 F4
Fairlight Cove TN35 ...82 B6
Heathfield TN21 ......82 B6
Woodland Wlk BN2 ....165 D4
Woodlands Hove BN3 ..142 C2
Pembury TN2 ....9 F7
Woodlands Cl
Hailsham BN27 ....129 C2
Heathfield TN21 ......82 B5
Peacehaven BN10 ....167 B1
Peasmarsh TN31 .....69 C2
Uckfield TN22 ....78 D8
Woodlands Rd
East Grinstead RH19 ...2 A4
Hayward's Heath RH16 ..50 F4
Woodlands The
Brighton BN1 ....142 E5
Hastings TN34 ....136 E5
Woodlands Way TN34 ..136 E5
Woodleigh Rd RH15 ...73 C4
Woodmans Oak TN33 ..112 D5
Woodpecker Cres RH15 ..72 D3
Woodpecker Dr BN27 ..152 A8
Woodpecker La BN27 ..127 B3
Woodpecker Rd BN23 ..173 A2
Woodpecker Way
Golden Cross BN27 ....127 B3
Uckfield TN22 ....78 D5
Woodridge Cl RH16 ...51 A3
Woodruff Ave BN3 ....142 C2
Woods Green Cotts TN5 ..29 F7
Woods Ground RH17 ..74 B4
Woods Hill Cl RH19 ....11 D6
Woods Hill La RH19 ...11 C6
Woods Ho BN3 ....163 A8
Woodsgate Ave TN40 ..157 C6
Woodsgate Pk TN39 ...157 B6
Woodsgate Way TN39 ..157 B7
Woodside Broad Oak TN31 ..90 B5
Crowborough TN6 .....25 E2

Woodside *continued*
Kilndown TN17 . . . . .20 F2
Woodside Ave BN1 . . . . .142 D2
Woodside Cl TN2 . . . . .9 E6
Woodside Lodge BN1 . . .142 D2
Woodside Rd Pembury TN2 . .9 E6
Rusthall TN4 . . . . .7 D4
Woodside Terr BN27 . . . .151 F4
Woodside Way BN27 . . . .152 A4
Woodsland Cl BN6 . . . . . .97 F4
Woodslands Rd BN6 . . . . . .97 F4
Woodspring Cl TN37 . . . .136 B5
Woodstock RH19 . . . . .1 C2
Woodstock Rd TN39 . . . .156 C6
Woodview Cl BN1 . . . . . .143 D6
Woodville Ct 9 TN39 . . .157 B3
Woodville Rd TN39 . . . .157 B3
Woodward BN23 . . . . . . .185 E7
Woodwards Cl RH15 . . . . .73 B1
Woolven Cl RH15 . . . . . . .72 E1
Worcester Ct
5 Eastbourne BN23 . . . . . .174 E1
1 Hove BN3 . . . . .163 E6
Worcester Villas BN3 . . .162 C7
Worcester Way BN27 . . .131 B5

Wordsworth Dr BN23 . . .174 E2
Wordsworth Rise 6 RH19 . .1 C1
Wordsworth St BN3 . . . . .163 A7
Workhouse La
Icklesham TN36 . . . . .116 F5
Westfield TN35 . . . . .114 E3
Worsham Ct TN39 . . . . . .156 C4
Worsham La TN40 . . . . . .157 F7
Worsted La RH19 . . . . .11 B8
Wray Cl RH19 . . . . .11 D6
Wren Cl Burgess Hill RH15 . .72 D3
Heathfield TN21 . . . . .82 A7
Wren Ct Battle TN33 . . . .112 F4
St Leonards TN38 . . . . .135 E3
Wrentham Ho RH15 . . . . . .73 B3
Wrestwood Ave BN22 . . .173 C1
Wrestwood Cl TN40 . . . .157 D6
Wrestwood Rd TN40 . . . .157 D6
Wrotham Cl
Eastbourne BN23 . . . . . . .174 D1
Hastings TN34 . . . . .136 E5
Wroxham Rd BN23 . . . . .174 B4
Wyatts La RH17 . . . . .33 D5
Wyberlye Rd RH15 . . . . . . .73 A4
Wybourne Rise TN2 . . . . .17 B8

Wychperry Rd RH16 . . . . .50 D5
Wychurst Gdns TN40 . . .157 D6
Wyck Ct BN41 . . . . .162 A7
Wykeham Ct TN34 . . . . .159 E8
Wykeham Rd TN34 . . . .159 E8
Wykeham Terr BN1 . . . .189 A2
Wykeham Way RH15 . . . .73 C2
Wynberg Cotts TN6 . . . . .39 C6
Wyndham St BN2 . . . . . .189 C1
Wynnes Mews BN3 . . . .163 A7
Wynnstay RH15 . . . . .73 B2
Wyshe The BN45 . . . . . . .119 C6
Wythwood RH16 . . . . .50 E1

Y

Yardley St BN1 . . . . .189 B5
Yarrow Rd BN7 . . . . .123 B2
Yates Cl TN31 . . . . .95 A2
Yeomans BN8 . . . . .125 A7
Yesterdays World Mus*
TN33 . . . . .112 D4
Yew Ct 1 RH19 . . . . .1 D2
Yew La RH19 . . . . .1 B3

Yew Tree Cl
Broyle Side BN8 . . . . .124 F7
Hastings TN34 . . . . .136 E6
Heathfield TN21 . . . . .82 A6
Yew Tree Cotts
Burgess Hill RH15 . . . . . . .73 B3
Groombridge TN3 . . . . .15 F8
Yew Tree Rd TN4 . . . . .8 B8
Yewtree La TN6 . . . . .39 E8
Yielding's Cl BN21 . . . .184 D5
York Ave
East Grinstead RH19 . . . . . .11 A8
Hove BN3 . . . . .163 E6
York Bldgs 5 TN34 . . . .159 F7
York Ct 18 BN3 . . . . .163 E7
York Gdns 4 TN34 . . . . .159 F7
York Gr BN1 . . . . .189 A4
York Hill BN1 . . . . .189 B4
York Ho BN41 . . . . .162 B8
York Mansions E 18
BN3 . . . . .163 E6
York Mansions W 12
BN3 . . . . .163 E6
York Pl Brighton BN1 . . . .189 B3
Hove BN3 . . . . .163 E6

York Rd Bexhill TN40 . . . .158 A5
Burgess Hill RH15 . . . . .72 D2
Eastbourne BN21 . . . . . . .184 F2
Hove BN1,BN3 . . . . .163 E6
Peacehaven BN10 . . . . . . .178 E6
Royal Tunbridge Wells TN1 . . .8 A4
St Leonards TN37 . . . . . . .136 C2
York Villas BN1 . . . . . . .189 A4
Yorklands BN3 . . . . .142 B4
Yorkshire Ct BN20 . . . . .184 B7
Youl Grange BN20 . . . . .184 D1
Youngsmere Cl BN1 . . . .143 B6
Ypres Tower Mus* TN31 . . .93 C5
Yvonne Robertson Ho
TN40 . . . . .157 D5
Zion Gdns BN1 . . . . .189 A2

Addresses

Name and Address	Telephone	Page	Grid reference
CHARLESTON MANOR		182	A6

NH	NJ	NK	
NN	NO	NP	
NS	NT	NU	
NX	NY	NZ	
SC	SD	SE	TA
SH	SJ	SK	TF	TG
SN	SO	SP	TL	TM
SS	ST	SU	TQ	TR
SX	SY	SZ	TV	

Using the Ordnance Survey National Grid

Any feature in this atlas can be given a unique reference to help you find the same feature on other Ordnance Survey maps of the area, or to help someone else locate you if they do not have a Street Atlas.

The grid squares in this atlas match the Ordnance Survey National Grid and are at 500 metre intervals. The small figures at the bottom and sides of every other grid line are the National Grid kilometre values (**00** to **99** km) and are repeated across the country every 100 km (see left).

To give a unique National Grid reference you need to locate where in the country you are. The country is divided into 100 km squares with each square given a unique two-letter reference. Use the administrative map to determine in which 100 km square a particular page of this atlas falls.

The bold letters and numbers between each grid line (**A** to **F**, **1** to **8**) are for use within a specific Street Atlas only, and when used with the page number, are a convenient way of referencing these grid squares.

Example   The railway bridge over DARLEY GREEN RD in grid square B1

Step 1: Identify the two-letter reference, in this example the page is in **SP**

Step 2: Identify the 1 km square in which the railway bridge falls. Use the figures in the southwest corner of this square: Eastings **17**, Northings **74**. This gives a unique reference: **SP 17 74**, accurate to 1 km.

Step 3: To give a more precise reference accurate to 100 m you need to estimate how many tenths along and how many tenths up this 1 km square the feature is (to help with this the 1 km square is divided into four 500 m squares). This makes the bridge about **8** tenths along and about **1** tenth up from the southwest corner.

This gives a unique reference: **SP 178 741**, accurate to 100 m.

Eastings (read from left to right along the bottom) come before Northings (read from bottom to top). If you have trouble remembering say to yourself "Along the hall, THEN up the stairs"!

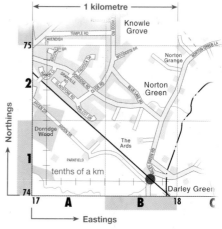

PHILIP'S MAPS
the Gold Standard for drivers

◆ **Philip's street atlases cover every county in England, Wales and much of Scotland**

◆ Every named street is shown, including alleys, lanes and walkways

◆ Thousands of additional features marked: stations, public buildings, car parks, places of interest

◆ Route-planning maps to get you close to your destination

◆ Postcodes on the maps and in the index

◆ Widely used by the emergency services, transport companies and local authorities

For national mapping, choose **Philip's Navigator Britain** the most detailed road atlas available of England, Wales and Scotland. Hailed by Auto Express as 'the ultimate road atlas', this is the only one-volume atlas to show every road and lane in Britain.

Street atlases currently available

England
Bedfordshire
Berkshire
Birmingham and West Midlands
Bristol and Bath
Buckinghamshire
Cambridgeshire
Cheshire
Cornwall
Cumbria
Derbyshire
Devon
Dorset
County Durham and Teesside
Essex
North Essex
South Essex
Gloucestershire
Hampshire
North Hampshire
South Hampshire
Herefordshire Monmouthshire
Hertfordshire
Isle of Wight
Kent
East Kent
West Kent
Lancashire
Leicestershire and Rutland
Lincolnshire
London
Greater Manchester
Merseyside
Norfolk
Northamptonshire
Northumberland
Nottinghamshire
Oxfordshire
Shropshire
Somerset
Staffordshire
Suffolk
Surrey

East Sussex
West Sussex
Tyne and Wear
Warwickshire
Birmingham and West Midlands
Wiltshire and Swindon
Worcestershire
East Yorkshire Northern Lincolnshire
North Yorkshire
South Yorkshire
West Yorkshire

Wales
Anglesey, Conwy and Gwynedd
Cardiff, Swansea and The Valleys
Carmarthenshire, Pembrokeshire and Swansea
Ceredigion and South Gwynedd
Denbighshire, Flintshire, Wrexham
Herefordshire Monmouthshire
Powys

Scotland
Aberdeenshire
Ayrshire
Dumfries and Gallow
Edinburgh and East Central Scotland
Fife and Tayside
Glasgow and West Central Scotland
Inverness and Mora
Lanarkshire
Scottish Borders

Northern Irelan
County Armagh and County Down
Belfast
County Londonderry and County Antrim
County Tyrone and County Fermanagh

*Publishing autumn 2006

How to order Philip's maps and atlases are availc from bookshops, motorway services and petrol station You can order direct from the publisher by phoning **O 828503** or online at **www.philips-maps.co.** For bulk orders only, phone 020 7644 6940